AF819955

QUE Bee

From Doubts to **Distinction**
Your ICSE 2026 Exams Partner

GIST OF THE TEXTBOOK
Crisp & Complete Theory - No need to go back to textbooks!

ALL TYPES OF LATEST PATTERN QUESTIONS
MCQs | Case-based | Assertion-Reason | Statements; All in one place!

KEY WORDS HIGHLIGHTED
Important points and formulae neatly highlighted never miss what matters

COUNCIL-STYLE ANSWERS
Write responses like an examiner expects

SAMPLE PAPER
Practice in real-exam mode. Perfect your timing, strategy and confidence.

ARIHANT PRAKASHAN
(School Division Series)

ADMINISTRATIVE & PRODUCTION OFFICES

Regd. Office
'Ramchhaya' 4577/15, Agarwal Road, Darya Ganj, New Delhi -110002
Tele: 011- 47630600, 43518550; Fax: 011- 23280316

Head Office
Kalindi, TP Nagar, Meerut (UP) - 250002, Tel: 0121-7156203, 7156204

SALES & SUPPORT OFFICES
Agra, Ahmedabad, Bengaluru, Bareilly, Chennai, Delhi, Guwahati, Hyderabad, Jaipur, Jhansi, Kolkata, Lucknow, Nagpur & Pune.

PO No : TXT-XX-XXXXXXX-X-XX

Published By Arihant Publications (India) Ltd.

For further information about the books published by Arihant, log on to www.arihantbooks.com or e-mail at info@arihantbooks.com

Follow us on

PRICE ₹350.00

PRODUCTION TEAM

Publishing Manager
Keshav Mohan

Project Head
Ashwani

Cover Designer
Bilal Hashmi

Inner Designer
Ankit Tyagi

Page Layouting
Shivam Prajapati

Proof Reader
Mukul Kaushik, Ankur Kumar

QUE Bee

ICSE
MATHS
Class 9

Types of Questions & their Respective Number

Types of Questions	Total Number
Multiple Choice Questions (MCQs)	173
Assertion-Reason (A-R)	75
Statement I & II Type Questions	69
Short Answer Type Questions (SA)	328
Long Answer Type Questions (LA)	185
Case Based Questions	30
TOTAL NO. OF QUESTIONS	**860**

Created by

Rita Anand

BSc, B.Ed,
30 Yrs. Experienced
TGT (Retired), St Thomas English Medium School, Meerut

From Learner to Leader

Step-Into the Spotlight

QUE Bee is more than just a book - it's a platform for young achievers like you to guide future toppers. If you've cracked the code to smart study or have insights that can make learning easier for others, this is your moment to shine!

What Can You Share?

- Your study techniques, time management tips, or motivation hacks
- Feedback or suggestions to make QUE Bee even better
- Real experiences that can guide other students through the exam maze

What's in It for You?

- Your name will be featured in our exclusive Student Panel in the next edition
- Win exciting & surprise rewards for impactful suggestions
- **Get published** - your photo, Ideas-or even interviews can be featured in the book
- **Become a student icon** - recognized and followed by peers across schools

Let your learning become someone else's ladder.
Be remembered. Be featured. Be the guide.

SCAN TO SHARE YOUR IDEA

Index

Latest
Course Structure

There will be **one** paper of **three** hours duration carrying 80 Marks and Internal Assessment of 20 Marks.
Certain questions may require the use of mathematical tables (Logarithms and Trigonometric Tables).

The solution of a question may require the knowledge of more than one branch of the syllabus.

Pure Arithmetic

Rational and Irrational Numbers

Rational, irrational numbers as real numbers, their place in the number system. Surds and rationalization of surds.
Simplifying an expression by rationalizing the denominator.
Representation of rational and irrational numbers on the number line. Proofs of irrationality
$\sqrt{2}$, $\sqrt{3}$, $\sqrt{5}$.

Commercial Mathematics

Compound Interest

(a) Compound interest as a repeated Simple Interest computation with a growing Principal. Use of this in computing Amount over a period of 2 or 3 years.

(b) Use of formula $A = P\left(1 + \frac{r}{100}\right)^n$. Finding CI from the relation CI = $A - P$.

- Interest compounded half-yearly included.
- Using the formula to find one quantity given different combinations of *A, P, r, n,* CI and SI; difference between CI and SI type included. Rate of growth and depreciation.

Note Paying back in equal installments, being given rate of interest and installment amount, **not included.**

Algebra

(i) Expansions

Recall of concepts learned in earlier classes.

$(a \pm b)^2$

$(a \pm b)^3$

$(x \pm a)(x \pm b)$

$(a \pm b \pm c)^2$

(ii) Factorisation

$a^2 - b^2$

$a^3 \pm b^3$

$ax^2 + bx + c$, by splitting the middle term.

(iii) Simultaneous Linear Equations in two variables. (With numerical coefficients only)

- Solving algebraically by
  - Elimination
  - Substitution and
  - Cross-multiplication method
- Solving simple problems by framing appropriate equations.

(iv) Indices/ Exponents

Handling positive, fractional, negative and "zero" indices.

Simplification of expressions involving various exponents

$a^m \times a^n = a^{m+n}$, $a^m \div a^n = a^{m-n}$, $(a^m)^n = a^{mn}$

etc. Use of laws of exponents.

(v) Logarithms

(a) Logarithmic form vis-à-vis exponential form: interchanging.

(b) Laws of Logarithms and their uses.

Expansion of expression with the help of laws of logarithms

e.g. $y = \frac{a^4 \times b^2}{c^3}$

$\log y = 4 \log a + 2 \log b - 3 \log c$ etc.

Geometry

(i) Triangles

(a) Congruency : four cases : SSS, SAS, AAS and RHS. Illustration through cutouts. Simple applications.

(b) Problems based on

- Angles opposite equal sides are equal and converse.
- If two sides of a triangle are unequal, then the greater angle is opposite the greater side and converse.
- Sum of any two sides of a triangle is greater than the third side.
- Of all straight lines that can be drawn to a given line from a point outside it, the perpendicular is the shortest.

Proofs not required.

(c) Mid-Point Theorem and its converse, equal intercept theorem
   (i) Proof and simple applications of mid-point theorem and its converse.
   (ii) Equal intercept theorem: proof and simple application.

(d) Pythagoras Theorem
   Area based proof and simple applications of Pythagoras Theorem and its converse.

(ii) Rectilinear Figures

(a) Proof and use of theorems on parallelogram.
   - Both pairs of opposite sides equal (without proof).
   - Both pairs of opposite angles equal.
   - One pair of opposite sides equal and parallel (without proof).
   - Diagonals bisect each other and bisect the parallelogram.
   - Rhombus as a special parallelogram whose diagonals meet at right angles.
   - In a rectangle, diagonals are equal, in a square they are equal and meet at right angles.

(b) Constructions of Polygons
   Construction of quadrilaterals (including parallelograms and rhombus) and regular hexagon using ruler and compasses only.

(c) Proof and use of Area theorems on parallelograms:
   - Parallelograms on the same base and between the same parallels are equal in area.
   - The area of a triangle is half that of a parallelogram on the same base and between the same parallels.
   - Triangles between the same base and between the same parallels are equal in area (without proof).
   - Triangles with equal areas on the same bases have equal corresponding altitudes.

(iii) Circle

(a) Chord properties
   - A straight line drawn from the centre of a circle to bisect a chord which is not a diameter is at right angles to the chord.
   - The perpendicular to a chord from the centre bisects the chord (without proof).
   - Equal chords are equidistant from the centre.
   - Chords equidistant from the centre are equal (without proof).
   - There is one and only one circle that passes through three given points not in a straight line.

(b) Arc and chord properties
   - If two arcs subtend equal angles at the centre, they are equal and its converse.
   - If two chords are equal, they cut off equal arcs and its converse (without proof).

Note **Proofs of the theorems given above are to be taught unless specified otherwise.**

Statistics

Introduction, collection of data, presentation of data, Graphical representation of data, Mean, Median of ungrouped data.

(i) Understanding and recognition of raw, arrayed and grouped data.
(ii) Tabulation of raw data using tally-marks.
(iii) Understanding and recognition of discrete and continuous variables.
(iv) Mean, median of ungrouped data.
(v) Class intervals, class boundaries and limits, frequency, frequency table, class size for grouped data.
(vi) Grouped frequency distributions: the need to and how to convert discontinuous intervals to continuous intervals.
(vii) Drawing a frequency polygon.

Mensuration

Area and perimeter of a triangle and a quadrilateral. Area and circumference of circle. Surface area and volume of Cube and Cuboids. .

(a) Area and perimeter of triangle (including Heron's formula), all types of Quadrilaterals.
(b) Circle: Area and Circumference. Direct application problems including Inner and Outer area.
   Areas of sectors of circles other than quarter-circle and semi-circle are not included.

(c) Surface area and volume of 3D solids : cube and cuboid including problems of type involving:
- Different internal and external dimensions of the solid.
- Cost.
- Concept of volume being equal to area of cross-section x height.
- Open/closed cubes/cuboids.

Trigonometry

(a) Trigonometric Ratios: sine, cosine, tangent of an angle and their reciprocals.

(b) Trigonometric ratios of standard angles– 0°, 30°, 45°, 60°, 90°. Evaluation of an expression involving these ratios.

(c) Simple 2D problems involving one right-angled triangle.

(d) Concept of trigonometric ratios of complementary angles and their direct application

$\sin A = \cos (90° - A)$, $\cos A = \sin (90° - A)$

$\tan A = \cot (90° - A)$, $\cot A = \tan (90° - A)$

$\sec A = \operatorname{cosec} (90° - A)$, $\operatorname{cosec} A = \sec (90° - A)$

Coordinate Geometry

Cartesian System, Plotting of points in the plane for given coordinates, solving simultaneous linear equations in 2 variables graphically and finding the distance between two points using distance formula.

(a) Dependent and independent variables.

(b) Ordered pairs, coordinates of points and plotting them in the Cartesian plane.

(c) Solution of Simultaneous Linear Equations graphically.

(d) Distance formula.

INTERNAL ASSESSMENT

A minimum of two assignments are to be done during the year as prescribed by the teacher.

Suggested Assignments

- Conduct a survey of a group of students and represent it graphically - height, weight, number of family members, pocket money, etc.
- Planning delivery routes for a postman/milkman.
- Running a tuck shop/canteen.
- Study ways of raising a loan to buy a car or house, e.g. Bank loan or purchase a refrigerator or a television set through hire purchase.
- Cutting a circle into equal sections of a small central angle to find the area of a circle by using the formula $A = \pi r^2$.
- To use flat cutouts to form cube, cuboids and pyramids to obtain formulae for volume and total surface area.
- Draw a circle of radius r on a $\frac{1}{2}$ cm graph paper and then on a 2 mm graph paper. Estimate the area enclosed in each case by actually counting the squares. Now try out with circles of different radii. Establish the pattern, if any, between the two observed values and the theoretical value (area = πr^2). Any modifications?

01

RATIONAL AND IRRATIONAL NUMBERS

Rational Numbers

The numbers, which can be expressed in the form of $\frac{p}{q}$, where p and q both are integers and $q \neq 0$, are known as rational numbers and they are denoted by Q.

e.g. $\frac{-1}{2}, \frac{3}{2}, \frac{1}{3}, \frac{7}{5}$ etc.

Every natural number, whole number and integer is a rational number.

e.g. $1 = \frac{1}{1}$ or $5 = \frac{5}{1}$.

Properties of Rational Numbers

(i) The sum of two or more rational numbers is always a rational number.

e.g. If $\frac{2}{3}, \frac{5}{2} \in Q$, then $\frac{2}{3} + \frac{5}{2} = \frac{19}{6} \in Q$

(ii) The difference of two rational numbers is always a rational number.

e.g. If $\frac{1}{2}, \frac{1}{3} \in Q$, then $\frac{1}{2} - \frac{1}{3} = \frac{1}{6} \in Q$

(iii) The product of two or more rational numbers is always a rational number.

e.g. If $\frac{1}{2}, \frac{2}{3} \in Q$, then $\frac{1}{2} \times \frac{2}{3} = \frac{1}{3} \in Q$

(iv) The division of rational number by a non-zero rational number is always a rational number.

e.g. If $\frac{2}{3}, \frac{4}{3} \in Q$, then $\frac{2}{3} \div \frac{4}{3} = \frac{1}{2} \in Q$.

(v) For every rational number $\frac{a}{b}$, there is another rational number $\frac{-a}{b}$ such that $\frac{a}{b} + \left(\frac{-a}{b}\right) = 0$.

Then, $\left(\frac{-a}{b}\right)$ is called **additive inverse** of $\frac{a}{b}$.

If $\frac{a}{b} + 0 = \frac{a}{b}$, then 0 is called **additive identity** for rational numbers.

(vi) For every rational number $\frac{a}{b}$, there is another rational number $\frac{b}{a}$ such that $\frac{a}{b} \times \frac{b}{a} = 1$.

Then, $\frac{b}{a}$ is called **multiplicative inverse** of $\frac{a}{b}$.

If $\frac{a}{b} \times 1 = \frac{a}{b}$, then 1 is called **multiplicative identity**.

(vii) The set of rational numbers is ordered i.e. if $a, b \in Q$, then either $a < b$ or $a > b$ or $a = b$.

e.g. Let $-\frac{1}{2}, \frac{3}{2}, \frac{1}{3}, \frac{7}{5} \in Q$

Then, order of rational numbers is either $-\frac{1}{2} < \frac{1}{3} < \frac{7}{5} < \frac{3}{2}$ or $\frac{3}{2} > \frac{7}{5} > \frac{1}{3} > -\frac{1}{2}$.

Methods to Determine Rational Numbers Between Two Numbers

(i) When One Rational Number is Determined

Let x and y be any two rational numbers, $\frac{x+y}{2}$ is a rational number lying between x and y.

(a) if $x > y \Rightarrow x > \frac{x+y}{2} > y$ (b) if $x < y \Rightarrow x < \frac{x+y}{2} < y$

e.g. A rational number between 3 and $\frac{4}{7}$ is $\frac{3+\frac{4}{7}}{2} = \frac{25}{14}$.

(ii) When More than One Rational Numbers are Determined

Let x and y be any two rational numbers and we have to find n rational numbers between x and y $(x < y)$. Equating the denominators can be done either by finding their LCM or by multiplying the denominators of one to both the numerator and denominator of the other and make given rational numbers with same denominator, then multiplying the numerator and denominator by $n + 1$.

Since, the denominators are the same for the two rational numbers, therefore we can write the rational numbers between the two rationals, in the increasing order of numerator of x.

e.g. Find three rational numbers between $\frac{1}{2}$ and $\frac{2}{3}$.

First change the denominators of $\frac{1}{2}$ and $\frac{2}{3}$ to 6 i.e. LCM of 2 and 3.

$\therefore \quad \frac{1}{2} \times \frac{3}{3}$ and $\frac{2}{3} \times \frac{2}{2}$ i.e. $\frac{3}{6}$ and $\frac{4}{6}$

Now, for three rationals, we multiply both the numerator and denominator by $3 + 1 = 4$.

$\frac{3}{6} \times \frac{4}{4}$ and $\frac{4}{6} \times \frac{4}{4}$ i.e $\frac{12}{24}$ and $\frac{16}{24}$

Therefore, $\frac{13}{24}, \frac{14}{24}, \frac{15}{24}$ are three rational numbers between $\frac{1}{2}$ and $\frac{2}{3}$.

Representation of a Rational Number on a Number Line

Let us represent $\frac{1}{2}, \frac{-3}{2}, \frac{-1}{2}$ etc., on a number line XY. So, we take one half of the unit and mark all these points as follows

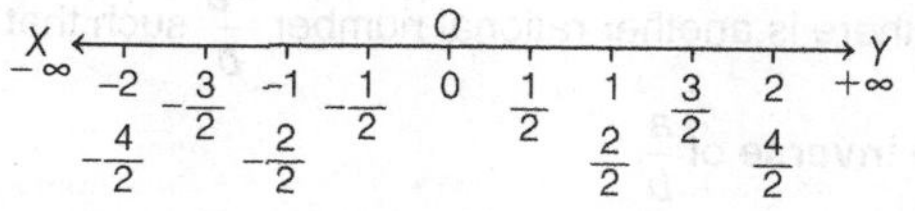

Similarly, represent $\frac{1}{3}, \frac{2}{3}, \frac{3}{3}, \frac{4}{3}, \ldots$ and $\frac{-1}{3}, \frac{-2}{3}, \frac{-3}{3}, \frac{-4}{3}, \ldots$ and so on, then we take one-third of the unit and mark as follows

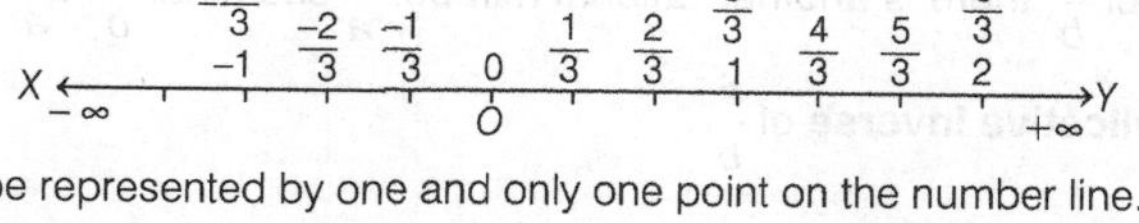

Note Each rational number can be represented by one and only one point on the number line.

Irrational Numbers

The numbers, which cannot be expressed in the form of $\frac{p}{q}$ and where p, q both are integers and $q \neq 0$, are called irrational numbers.

In other words, the square roots, cube roots and nth roots etc., of natural number are irrational numbers if their exact value cannot be obtained.

e.g. $\sqrt{2}, \sqrt{3}, \frac{1}{\sqrt{3}}, 5+\sqrt{7}, \sqrt{2}-\sqrt{5}$ etc., are irrational numbers.

Properties of Irrational Numbers

(i) The sum of a rational and an irrational number is always an irrational number.

e.g. $4+\sqrt{3}$.

(ii) The sum of two irrational numbers may or may not be an irrational number.

e.g. (a) $(2+\sqrt{7})+(3-\sqrt{7})=5$; 5 is a rational number.

(b) $(\sqrt{5}+8)+(\sqrt{3}-8)=\sqrt{5}+\sqrt{3}$; $\sqrt{5}+\sqrt{3}$ is an irrational number.

(iii) The difference of a rational and an irrational number is always an irrational number.

e.g. $5-\sqrt{2}$

(iv) The difference of two irrational numbers may or may not be an irrational number.

e.g. (a) $(4-\sqrt{11})-(2-\sqrt{11})=2$; 2 is a rational number.

(b) $(\sqrt{5}+8)-(-\sqrt{5}-7)=2\sqrt{5}+15$; $2\sqrt{5}+15$ is an irrational number.

(v) The product of a non-zero rational and an irrational number is always an irrational number.

e.g. $4\times\sqrt{5}=4\sqrt{5}$

(vi) The product of two irrational numbers may or may not be an irrational number.

e.g. (a) $(7-\sqrt{7})\times(7+\sqrt{7})=42$; 42 is a rational number.

(b) $(5+\sqrt{3})\times(7-\sqrt{5})=35-5\sqrt{5}+7\sqrt{3}-\sqrt{15}$; which is an irrational number.

(vii) The division of a non-zero rational and an irrational number is always an irrational number.

e.g. $\frac{4}{\sqrt{2}}$

(viii) If $p+q\sqrt{x}=r+s\sqrt{x}$, then on comparing the corresponding terms, we get

$$p=r \text{ and } q=s$$

e.g. If $p+5\sqrt{2}=6+q\sqrt{2}$, then $p=6$ and $q=5$

Methods to Determine Irrational Numbers

(i) Irrational Number between Two Rational Numbers

Let a and b be two positive irrational numbers and ab is not a perfect square. Then, $\sqrt{ab}$ is an irrational number lying between a and b.

Now, we insert another irrational number between a and $\sqrt{ab}$ is $\sqrt{a\times\sqrt{ab}}$.

Similarly, we can insert another irrational number.

(ii) Irrational Number between Two Irrational Numbers

$\sqrt{a}$ and $\sqrt{b}$ are two irrational numbers. Then, irrational number between two irrational numbers $\sqrt{a}$ and $\sqrt{b}$ is $(\sqrt{ab})^{1/2}$.

To Locate an Irrational Number on the Number Line

To locate irrational numbers of the form $\sqrt{n}$, where n is a positive integer, on the number line can be understood with the help of following example.

e.g. Locate $\sqrt{2}$ and $\sqrt{3}$ on the number line.

Here, $2=1+1=1^2+1^2$ [sum of square of two natural numbers]

Draw a number line and mark a point O, representing zero on it. Suppose, point A represents one unit distance from O i.e. $OA=1$.

REVISION NOTES

Now, draw a right ΔOAB such that $AB = OA = 1$.

By Pythagoras theorem, we have

$$OB^2 = OA^2 + AB^2$$
$$\Rightarrow \quad OB^2 = 1^2 + 1^2$$
$$\Rightarrow \quad OB^2 = 1 + 1 = 2$$
$$\Rightarrow \quad OB = \sqrt{2}$$

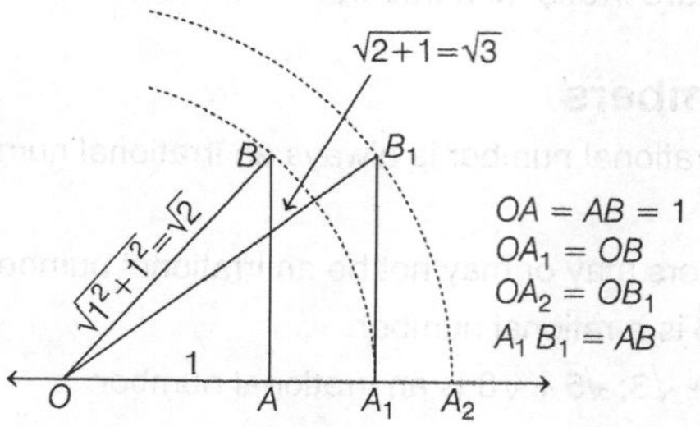

Now, draw a circle with centre O and radius OB. We find that the circle cuts the number line at A_1.

Clearly, $OA_1 = OB =$ Radius of the circle $= \sqrt{2}$. Thus, A_1 represents $\sqrt{2}$ on the number line.

Now, we draw again right ΔOA_1B_1 such that $A_1B_1 = AB = 1$.

Again, by using Pythagoras theorem, we have

$$OB_1^2 = OA_1^2 + A_1B_1^2$$
$$\Rightarrow \quad OB_1^2 = (\sqrt{2})^2 + 1^2$$
$$\Rightarrow \quad OB_1^2 = 3$$
$$\Rightarrow \quad OB_1 = \sqrt{3}$$

Now, again draw a circle with centre O and radius $OB_1 = \sqrt{3}$.

This circle cuts the number line at A_2 as shown in the figure.

$$OA_2 = OB_1 = \sqrt{3}$$

Hence, A_2 represents $\sqrt{3}$ on the number line.

Decimal Expansion of Rational Numbers

Case I When remainder becomes zero.

On dividing p by q, if remainder becomes zero after some steps, then decimal expansion terminates or ends after a finite number of steps. Such decimal expansion is called **terminating decimal expansion.**

e.g. $\frac{639}{250} = 2.556$

On dividing 639 by 250, we get the exact value 2.556, i.e. remainder is zero, so $\frac{639}{250}$ has the terminating decimal expansion.

Case II When remainder never becomes zero.

On dividing p by q, if remainder never becomes zero and set of digits repeats periodically (or in same interval), then the decimal expansion is called **non-terminating repeating decimal.** It is also known as **non-terminating recurring decimal expansion.** The block of repeated digit is denoted by the bar over it.

e.g. $\frac{1}{7} = 0.1428571428571\ldots = 0.\overline{142857}$

On dividing 1 by 7, we get the block of repeated number 142857 again and again i.e. remainder never becomes zero, so $\frac{1}{7}$ has the non-terminating repeating decimal expansion.

Decimal Expansion of Irrational Numbers

The decimal expansion of an irrational number is non-terminating non-recurring. In other words, a number whose decimal expansion is non-terminating non-recurring is an irrational number.

e.g. Let $\sqrt{2}$ and π be irrational numbers. Then, their decimal expansions are

$\sqrt{2} = 1.41421356237309504880168872420 96...$

and $\pi = 3.14159265358979323846264338327950...$

Generally, $\frac{22}{7}$ is an approximate value of π but $\pi \neq \frac{22}{7}$.

Important Concepts Related to Decimal Expansion of Rational Numbers

(i) Let $x = p/q$ be a rational number such that the prime factorisation of q is of the form $2^n 5^m$, where n and m are non-negative integers. Then, x has a decimal expansion, which terminates.

e.g. $\frac{33}{500} = \frac{33}{2^2 \times 5^3}$

Here, denominator is of the form $2^n \times 5^m$. Therefore, the decimal expansion of $\frac{33}{500}$ is terminating.

(ii) Let $x = p/q$ be a rational number such that the prime factorisation of q is not of the form $2^n 5^m$, where n and m are non-negative integers. Then, x has a decimal expansion, which is non-terminating repeating (recurring).

e.g. $\frac{35}{108} = \frac{35}{2^2 \times 3^3}$

Here, the denominator is not of the form $2^n \times 5^m$. Therefore, the decimal expansion of $\frac{35}{108}$ is non terminating recurring.

Method to Convert Non-terminating Recurring Decimal Expansion into Rational Number

Suppose, the number of the form $x = a \cdot b\bar{c}$, where a, b and c are the digits of the number. i.e. $a, b, c \in \{0, 1, 2, 3, \ldots, 9\}$, we have to transform the given number in the form of $\frac{p}{q}$, where p and q are coprime integers and $q \neq 0$.

Example. To convert $5.2\bar{7}$ into rational number.

Sol. Let $x = 5.2\bar{7}$

First, to shift the decimal point just before the recurring term, we multiply by 10.

$\therefore \quad 10x = 52.\bar{7} \quad \ldots(i)$

Thus, one digit is repeating.

So, on multiplying Eq. (i) by 10, we get

$$100x = 527.\bar{7} \quad \ldots(ii)$$

On subtracting Eq. (i) from Eq. (ii), we get

$$100x - 10x = 527.\bar{7} - 52.\bar{7}$$

$$\Rightarrow \quad 90x = 475 \Rightarrow x = \frac{475}{90} \Rightarrow x = \frac{95}{18}$$

Hence, $\frac{95}{18}$ is a rational representation of $5.2\bar{7}$.

Surds

Let $a > 0$ be a positive rational number and n be a positive integer such that $a^{1/n} = \sqrt[n]{a}$ is an irrational number. Then, n is called **exponent**, a is called **radicand** and $\sqrt{\ }$ is called surd.

e.g. $\sqrt{3}, \sqrt[5]{16}, \sqrt[3]{20}$ are surds as 3, 16, 20 are positive real numbers.

But $\sqrt{16}, \sqrt[4]{81}, \sqrt[3]{27}$ etc are not surds because $\sqrt{16} = 4, \sqrt[4]{81} = 3, \sqrt[3]{27} = 3$ i.e. $\sqrt{16}, \sqrt[4]{81}, \sqrt[3]{27}$ are not irrational numbers.

Every surd is an irrational number but every irrational number is not a surd.

e.g. π is an irrational number but not a surd.

Types of Surds

(i) **Pure surds** A surd is a pure surd, if it does not have any other rational coefficient except unity.
e.g. $\sqrt{3}, \sqrt{2}, \sqrt[3]{7}$, etc.

(ii) **Mixed surds** A surd is a mixed surd, if it has some rational coefficient other than unity.
e.g. $3\sqrt{7}, 2\sqrt{11}, 54\sqrt[3]{7}$, etc.

(iii) **Similar surds** Two or more surds are said to be similar or like, if they have the same surd factor and same radical sign i.e. the surds which have same irrational factor are called similar surds.
e.g. $3\sqrt{13}, \sqrt{13}, \sqrt{52}$ etc.

Laws of Surds

Let a are b positive rational numbers, then

(i) $(\sqrt[n]{a})^n = a \ (n > 1)$

(ii) $\sqrt[n]{ab} = \sqrt[n]{a} \cdot \sqrt[n]{b}$

(iii) $\sqrt[n]{\dfrac{a}{b}} = \dfrac{\sqrt[n]{a}}{\sqrt[n]{b}}$

(iv) $(\sqrt{a} + \sqrt{b})(\sqrt{a} - \sqrt{b}) = a - b$

(v) $(\sqrt{a} + \sqrt{b})^2 = a + 2\sqrt{ab} + b$

(vi) $(\sqrt{a} - \sqrt{b})^2 = a - 2\sqrt{ab} + b$

(vii) $(\sqrt{a} + \sqrt{b})(\sqrt{c} + \sqrt{d}) = \sqrt{ac} + \sqrt{ad} + \sqrt{bc} + \sqrt{bd}$

(viii) If $\sqrt{a}$ and $\sqrt{b}$ are two positive irrational numbers, then (a) $\sqrt{a} < \sqrt{b}$, if $a < b$ (b) $\sqrt{a} > \sqrt{b}$, if $a > b$

(ix) If a is a positive rational number and $\sqrt{b}$ is an irrational number, then (a) $a < \sqrt{b}$, if $a^2 < b$ (b) $a > \sqrt{b}$, if $a^2 > b$

(x) $\sqrt{a} + \sqrt{b} \neq \sqrt{a + b};\ a \neq b$

Rationalisation of Surds

When we multiply a surd by another surd and get a rational number, then this process is known as rationalisation of surds or simple rationalisation. In this result, each surd is known as rationalising factor of the other surd.

e.g. $(\sqrt{2} + 3)(\sqrt{2} - 3) = (\sqrt{2})^2 - 3^2 = 2 - 9 = -7$ $\quad [\because (a + b)(a - b) = a^2 - b^2]$

$\therefore (\sqrt{2} + 3)$ and $(\sqrt{2} - 3)$ are rational factors of each other.

Rationalising the Denominator

If the denominator of an expression contains a term with a square root (or a number under a radical sign), then we multiply and divide the numerator and denominator of the given expression by the conjugate of its denominator and simplify.

Conjugate of $\sqrt{a} + \sqrt{b}$ is $\sqrt{a} - \sqrt{b}$ and $\sqrt{a} - \sqrt{b}$ is $\sqrt{a} + \sqrt{b}$.

e.g. Let $Y = \dfrac{\sqrt{2}}{3 - \sqrt{5}}$ ...(i)

Here, denominator is $3 - \sqrt{5}$. Now, the conjugate of denominator $3 - \sqrt{5}$ is $3 + \sqrt{5}$.

On multiplying by $3 + \sqrt{5}$ in numerator and denominator of Eq. (i), we get

$$Y = \frac{\sqrt{2}}{3 - \sqrt{5}} \times \frac{3 + \sqrt{5}}{3 + \sqrt{5}}$$

$$\Rightarrow \quad Y = \frac{\sqrt{2}(3 + \sqrt{5})}{9 - 5} \quad [\because (a + b)(a - b) = a^2 - b^2]$$

$$\Rightarrow \quad Y = \frac{3\sqrt{2} + \sqrt{10}}{4}$$

EXAM ORIENTED QUESTIONS

TYPE - 1 01 Mark

Multiple Choice Questions

Q.1 Which of the following is rational?

(a) $\frac{5}{0}$ (b) π

(c) $\sqrt{2}$ (d) $\frac{0}{5}$

Q.2 Which one is the greatest rational number?

$$\frac{4}{5}, \frac{9}{7}, \frac{5}{7} \text{ and } \frac{8}{7}$$

(a) $\frac{5}{7}$ (b) $\frac{4}{5}$ (c) $\frac{9}{7}$ (d) $\frac{8}{7}$

Q.3 Additive inverse of $\frac{85}{289}$ is

(a) $\frac{289}{85}$ (b) $\frac{-5}{17}$ (c) $\frac{5}{17}$ (d) 0

Q.4 Which of the following is irrational?

(a) 0.015 (b) 0.1527

(c) $0.1516\overline{3}$ (d) 0.1528763910...

Q.5 The rational number between $\sqrt{5}$ and $\sqrt{6}$ is

(a) 2.58 (b) 2.373

(c) 2.207 (d) 2.46

Q.6 Which of the following is the lowest irrational number?

$$5\sqrt{3}, 4\sqrt{5}, \sqrt{50} \text{ and } 2\sqrt{7}$$

(a) $5\sqrt{3}$ (b) $4\sqrt{5}$

(c) $\sqrt{50}$ (d) $2\sqrt{7}$

Q.7 The number $x = 1.242424...$ can be expressed in the form $x = \frac{p}{q}$, where p and q are positive integers having no common factors. Then, $p + q$ is equal to

(a) 53 (b) 41 (c) 72 (d) 74

Q.8 $2\sqrt{5} \times 4\sqrt{5}$ is equal to

(a) 40 (b) $50\sqrt{5}$ (c) 50 (d) 55

Q.9 The smallest among $\sqrt{5}$, $\sqrt[3]{2}$ and $\sqrt[4]{3}$ is

(a) $\sqrt{5}$ (b) $\sqrt[3]{2}$

(c) $\sqrt[4]{3}$ (d) None of these

Q.10 If $\sqrt{2} = 1.4142$, then the value of $\sqrt{\frac{\sqrt{2}-1}{\sqrt{2}+1}}$ is

(a) 2

(b) 0.4142

(c) 3.56

(d) 2.4142

Answers

1. (d)	**2.** (c)	**3.** (b)	**4.** (d)	**5.** (b)
6. (d)	**7.** (d)	**8.** (a)	**9.** (b)	**10.** (b)

TYPE - 2 01 Mark

Assertion-Reason Type Questions

Q.1 Assertion (A) Zero is a rational number.

Reason (R) The number, which can be expressed in the form of $\frac{p}{q}$, where p, q are integers and $q \neq 0$, is known as rational number.

(a) A is true, R is false.

(b) A is false, R is true.

(c) Both A and R are true and R is the correct reason for A.

(d) Both A and R are true and R is incorrect reason for A.

Q.2 Assertion (A) The irrational number $4\sqrt{2}$ lies between 5 and 6 on number line.

Reason (R) The numbers which cannot be expressed in the form of $\frac{p}{q}$ and p, q both are integers and $q \neq 0$, are called irrational numbers.

(a) A is true, R is false.

(b) A is false, R is true.

(c) Both A and R are true and R is the correct reason for A.

(d) Both A and R are true and R is incorrect reason for A.

Q.3 Assertion (A) The decimal value of $\frac{437}{999}$ is 0.437437..., which is rational.

Reason (R) A non-terminating repeating decimal number is a rational number.

(a) A is true, R is false.
(b) A is false, R is true.
(c) Both A and R are true and R is the correct reason for A.
(d) Both A and R are true and R is incorrect reason for A.

Q.4 Assertion (A) If $5 - 2\sqrt{6} = a - b\sqrt{c}$, then the values of a, b and c are 0, 2 and 3, respectively.

Reason (R) If $p + q\sqrt{x} = r + s\sqrt{x}$, then $p = r$ and $q = s$.

(a) A is true, R is false.
(b) A is false, R is true.
(c) Both A and R are true and R is the correct reason for A.
(d) Both A and R are true and R is incorrect reason for A.

Q.5 Assertion (A) If simplified value of $\frac{2-\sqrt{3}}{\sqrt{3}}$ upto three decimal place is 0.154. [take, $\sqrt{3} = 1.732$]

Reason (R) A non terminating and non recurring decimal number is a rational number.

(a) A is true, R is false.
(b) A is false, R is true.
(c) Both A and R are true and R is the correct reason for A.
(d) Both A and R are true and R is incorrect reason for A.

Answers

1. (c) 2. (d) 3. (c) 4. (b) 5. (a)

TYPE - 3 — 01 Mark

Statement Based Questions

Q.1 Statement I Additive inverse of $\frac{-35}{17}$ is $\frac{17}{35}$

Statement II Those numbers which have no common factor other than 1, are known as coprime numbers.

Which of the following is valid?

(a) Both the Statements are true.
(b) Both the Statements are false.
(c) Statement I is true and Statement II is false.
(d) Statement I is false and Statement II is true.

Q.2 Statement I $\sqrt{7}$ is an irrational number but not a real number.

Statement II There are finitely many rational numbers between two rational numbers.

Which of the following is valid?

(a) Both the Statements are true.
(b) Both the Statements are false.
(c) Statement I is true and Statement II is false.
(d) Statement I is false and Statement II is true.

Q.3 Statement I If a and b are natural numbers, then $(\sqrt{a} + \sqrt{b})(\sqrt{a} - \sqrt{b})$ is rational number.

Statement II If $a = 4\sqrt{21}$ and $b = 2\sqrt{3}$, then $\frac{a}{b}$ is a rational number.

Which of the following is valid?

(a) Both the Statements are true.
(b) Both the Statements are false.
(c) Statement I is true and Statement II is false.
(d) Statement I is false and Statement II is true.

Q.4 Statement I The decimal expansion of an irrational number is non terminating and non recurring.

Statement II Rationalising factor of $(13 - 5\sqrt{7})$ is $(-13 - 5\sqrt{7})$.

Which of the following is valid?

(a) Both the Statements are true.
(b) Both the Statements are false.
(c) Statement I is true and Statement II is false.
(d) Statement I is false and Statement II is true.

Answers

1. (d) 2. (b) 3. (c) 4. (c)

TYPE - 4 — 03 Marks

Short Answer Type Questions

Q.1 Find five rational numbers between $\frac{8}{5}$ and $\frac{7}{2}$. Also, arrange in ascending order.

Q.2 Represent the rational number $\frac{-3}{5}$ on the number line.

Q.3 Find four irrational numbers between $4\sqrt{2}$ and $3\sqrt{3}$.

Q.4 Show how $\sqrt{5}$ can be represented on the number line?

Q.5 Locate $2\sqrt{2}$ on the number line.

Q.6 Represent $\sqrt{9.3}$ on the number line.

Q.7 Show that $0.0\overline{72}$ is rational number.

Q.8 Without actually performing the long division method, state $\frac{14588}{625}$ has a terminating decimal expansion or not. Also, write decimal expansion.

Q.9 State that $\frac{\sqrt[6]{256}}{\sqrt[6]{4}}$ is a surd or not.

Q.10 Prove that $\frac{1}{2+\sqrt{3}} + \frac{2}{\sqrt{5}-\sqrt{3}} + \frac{1}{2-\sqrt{5}} = 0.$

Q.11 Rationalise $\frac{4\sqrt{3}+5\sqrt{2}}{\sqrt{48}+\sqrt{18}}$.

Q.12 Simplify $\sqrt{7+2\sqrt{10}} + \sqrt{12-2\sqrt{35}}$.

Q.13 Write the lowest rationalising factor of $(5\sqrt{3}+3\sqrt{5})$.

Q.14 Rationalise the denominator of $\frac{2}{\sqrt{5}+\sqrt{3}+2}$.

Q.15 Simplify $\frac{(\sqrt{3}-\sqrt{5})(\sqrt{5}+\sqrt{3})}{7-2\sqrt{5}}$.

Q.16 If $\frac{3+\sqrt{7}}{3-\sqrt{7}} = a + b\sqrt{7}$, then find the values of a and b.

Q.17 Find the value of $\frac{8}{\sqrt{3}+\sqrt{5}}$, where it is given that $\sqrt{3} = 1.732$ and $\sqrt{5} = 2.236$.

Q.18 If $x = 2-\sqrt{3}$, then find the value of $\left(x - \frac{1}{x}\right)^3$.

Answers

1. $\frac{17}{10}, \frac{18}{10}, \frac{19}{10}, \frac{20}{10}$ and $\frac{21}{10}$

   In ascending order, $\frac{8}{5} < \frac{17}{10} < \frac{9}{5} < \frac{19}{10} < 2 < \frac{21}{10} < \frac{7}{2}$

3. $\sqrt{3^{-}}, \sqrt{30}, \sqrt{29}, \sqrt{28}$ 8. Yes, 23.3408

9. No   11. $\frac{9+4\sqrt{6}}{15}$ 12. $\sqrt{2}+\sqrt{7}$ 13. $3\sqrt{5}-5\sqrt{3}$

14. $\frac{\sqrt{5}+3\sqrt{3}-2\sqrt{15}+4}{11}$ 15. $\frac{-14-4\sqrt{5}}{29}$ 16. $a = 8, b = 3$

17. 2.016   18. $-24\sqrt{3}$

TYPE - 5   4/5 Marks

Long Answer Type Questions

Q.1 Find four rational numbers between 0 and 0.3 and arrange in ascending order. Also, find the difference between the largest and the smallest of these rational numbers. Express this difference as a decimal fraction correct upto two decimal places.

Q.2 Find the sum of 0.0333 ... and 0.444... .

Q.3 If $x = \sqrt{3} + \frac{1}{\sqrt{3}}$, then calculate the value of

$$\left(x - \frac{\sqrt{126}}{\sqrt{42}}\right)\left(x - \frac{1}{x - \frac{2\sqrt{3}}{3}}\right)$$

Q.4 Show that $\frac{1}{(3-\sqrt{8})} - \frac{1}{(\sqrt{8}-\sqrt{7})} + \frac{1}{(\sqrt{7}-\sqrt{6})} - \frac{1}{(\sqrt{6}-\sqrt{5})} + \frac{1}{(\sqrt{5}-2)} = 5.$

Q.5 If $x = (5+2\sqrt{6})$, then show that $\sqrt{x} + \frac{1}{\sqrt{x}} = 2\sqrt{3}$.

Q.6 Simplify $\frac{x-\sqrt{x^2-1}}{x+\sqrt{x^2-1}} - \frac{x+\sqrt{x^2-1}}{x-\sqrt{x^2-1}}$

Q.7 If $x = 3+\sqrt{8}$, then find

(i) $\frac{1}{x}$

(ii) $x + \frac{1}{x}$

(iii) $x^2 + \frac{1}{x^2}$

Q.8 Show that $\frac{15}{\sqrt{10}+\sqrt{20}+\sqrt{40}-\sqrt{5}-\sqrt{80}} = \sqrt{10}+\sqrt{5}.$

Q.9 If $x = \frac{\sqrt{5}-2}{\sqrt{5}+2}$ and $y = \frac{\sqrt{5}+2}{\sqrt{5}-2}$, then find the value of $x^2 + y^2 + xy$.

Q.10 Prove that $\sqrt{2}$ is an irrational number.

Q.11 Prove that $\sqrt{3}$ is an irrational number.

Q.12 Prove that $\sqrt{5}$ is an irrational number.

Q.13 Show that $\sqrt{7}-\sqrt{5}$ is an irrational number.

Answers

1. Rational numbers are $\frac{1}{50}, \frac{2}{50}, \frac{3}{50}, \frac{4}{50}$

   In ascending order,

   $\frac{1}{50} < \frac{2}{50} < \frac{3}{50} < \frac{4}{50}$,

   Largest $= \frac{4}{50}$ and smallest $= \frac{1}{50}$, difference = 0.06

2. $\frac{43}{90}$ 3. 0.83   6. $-4x\sqrt{x^2-1}$

7. (i) $3-\sqrt{8}$ (ii) 6   (iii) 34

9. 323

TYPE - 6

Case Based Questions

Q.1 Vasu represents $\sqrt{4.5}$ on the number line PW. The length of TS = 1unit. His representation is shown below.

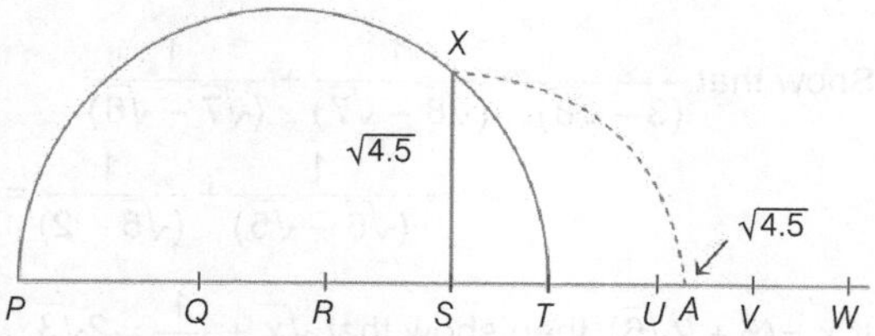

Based on the above information, answer the following questions.

(i) Which letter represents 0 on the number line?

(ii) Between which two points does $\sqrt{5.2}$ lie on this number line? **(4 M)**

Q.2 To support helpless people and orphans is the collective responsibility of the whole society.

To measure this spirit a survey was conducted in a city. It was found that 7 out of every 13 households are donating some amounts of their income to an orphanage or old age home or institutions for physically handicapped.

On the basis of above information, answer the following questions.

(i) Write the fraction of households, which are donating their income?

(ii) Write the fraction of households, which are not donating their income?

(iii) Write the decimal form of the fraction of households, which are donating their income?

Or Write the decimal form of the fraction of households, which are not donating? **(4 M)**

Answers

1. (i) Letter S (ii) U and V
2. (i) $\frac{7}{13}$ (ii) $\frac{6}{13}$ (iii) $0.\overline{538461}$ or $0.\overline{461538}$

EXPLANATIONS

MUltiple Choice Questions

1. (d) Rational number can be expressed in the form of $\frac{p}{q}$, where p and q both are integers and $q \neq 0$.

Then, $\frac{5}{0}$, π and $\sqrt{2}$ are not rational numbers.

Hence, $\frac{0}{5}$ is a rational number.

2. (c) Here, $\frac{4}{5}, \frac{9}{7}, \frac{5}{7}$ and $\frac{8}{7}$

$\Rightarrow \frac{4\times7}{5\times7} = \frac{28}{35}, \frac{9\times5}{7\times5} = \frac{45}{35}, \frac{5\times5}{7\times5} = \frac{25}{35}$ and $\frac{8\times5}{7\times5} = \frac{40}{35}$

[$\because$ LCM of 7 and 5 = 35]

Since, $25 < 28 < 40 < 45$

$\Rightarrow \frac{25}{35} < \frac{28}{35} < \frac{40}{35} < \frac{45}{35}$

$\therefore \frac{9}{7}$ is greater.

3. (b) Given, $\frac{85}{289} = \frac{5}{17}$

$\therefore$ Additive inverse of $\frac{85}{289}$ is $\frac{-5}{17}$.

4. (d) As we know that the decimal expansion of an irrational number is non terminating and non recurring.

$\therefore$ 0.1528763910 ...... is an irrational number.

5. (b) The decimal expansions of $\sqrt{5}$ and $\sqrt{6}$ are

$\sqrt{5} = 2.236067977499$ ....

and $\sqrt{6} = 2.4494897427$ ....

Now, $2.207 < \sqrt{5} < 2.373 < \sqrt{6} < 2.46 < 2.58$

Therefore, the rational number between $\sqrt{5}$ and $\sqrt{6}$ is 2.373.

6. (d) Here, $5\sqrt{3}$, $4\sqrt{5}$, $\sqrt{50}$ and $2\sqrt{7}$

Now, $5\sqrt{3} = \sqrt{75}$, $4\sqrt{5} = \sqrt{80}$

and $2\sqrt{7} = \sqrt{28}$

$\because \sqrt{28} < \sqrt{50} < \sqrt{75} < \sqrt{80}$

$\therefore 2\sqrt{7}$ is lowest.

7. (d) Given, $x = 1.2424...$ ...(i)

On multiplying 100 both sides, we get

$100x = 124.24...$ ...(ii)

On subtracting Eq. (i) from Eq. (ii), we get

$100x - x = 124.24 - 1.2424$

$\Rightarrow 99x = 123 \Rightarrow x = \frac{123}{99} = \frac{41}{33}$

Here, $p = 41, q = 33$

Hence, $p + q = 41 + 33 = 74$

8. (a) We have, $2\sqrt{5} \times 4\sqrt{5} = 2 \times 4\sqrt{5\times5}$

$= 8 \times 5 = 40$

9. (b) First, we take LCM of 2, 3 and 4 which is 12.

Here, $\sqrt{5} = 5^{\frac{1}{2}} = (5^6)^{\frac{1}{12}} = (15625)^{\frac{1}{12}}$,

$\sqrt[3]{2} = 2^{\frac{1}{3}} = (2^4)^{\frac{1}{12}} = (16)^{\frac{1}{12}}$

and $\sqrt[4]{3} = (3)^{\frac{1}{4}} = (3^3)^{\frac{1}{12}} = (27)^{\frac{1}{12}}$

Thus, $15625 > 27 > 16$

$\Rightarrow (15625)^{\frac{1}{12}} > (27)^{\frac{1}{12}} > (16)^{\frac{1}{12}}$

$\Rightarrow \sqrt{5} > \sqrt[4]{3} > \sqrt[3]{2}$

Hence, $\sqrt[3]{2}$ is smallest.

10. (b) Given, $\sqrt{2} = 1.4142$

We have, $\sqrt{\frac{\sqrt{2}-1}{\sqrt{2}+1}} = \sqrt{\frac{(\sqrt{2}-1)}{(\sqrt{2}+1)} \times \frac{(\sqrt{2}-1)}{(\sqrt{2}-1)}}$

[by rationalising the denominator]

$= \sqrt{\frac{(\sqrt{2}-1)^2}{2-1}} = \frac{\sqrt{(\sqrt{2}-1)^2}}{1}$

$= \sqrt{2} - 1 = 1.4142 - 1$

$= 0.4142$ $[\because \sqrt{2} = 1.4142]$

Assertion-Reason Type Questions

1. (c) Zero is a rational number, since we can write

$$0 = \frac{0}{1} = \frac{0}{2} = \frac{0}{-5} = \frac{0}{11} \dots$$

Hence, both A and R are true and R is the correct reason for A.

2. (d) We have to represent $4\sqrt{2}$ on the number line.

Here, $2 = 1^2 + 1^2$

Firstly, we draw $OA = 1$ unit on number line and then draw $AB = 1$ unit such that $AB \perp AO$.

$OB = \sqrt{OA^2 + AB^2}$ [by Pythagoras theorem]

$= \sqrt{2}$ units

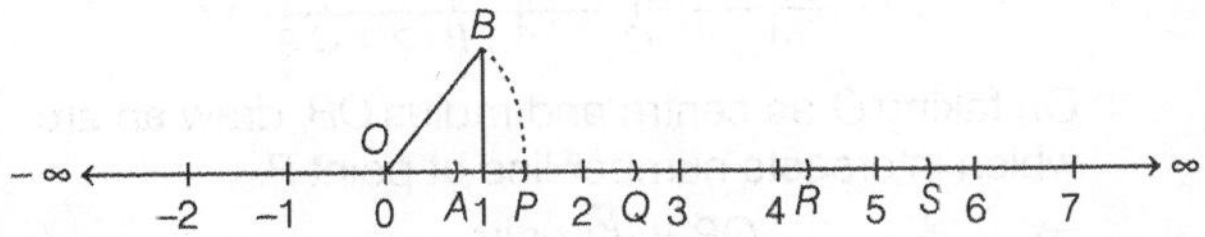

On taking O as centre and radius OB, draw an arc which intersects number line at P. Again, taking P as centre and radius OB, draw an arc which intersects number line at Q and so on, we get points R and S.

The length $OS = 4\sqrt{2}$ units

Hence, S represents $4\sqrt{2}$ on number line which lies between 5 and 6.

So, both A and R are true and R is incorrect reason for A.

3. (c) **Assertion** When we divide 437 by 999, we get 0.4374374374374...

Here, we see that decimal number is a non-terminating but it is repeated, so it is a rational number. Hence, A is true.

Reason It is true that a non-terminating repeating decimal number is a rational number. And it is a correct reason for of A.

4. (b) We have, $a - b\sqrt{c} = 5 - 2\sqrt{6}$

On comparing both sides, we get

$a = 5, b = 2$ and $c = 6$

Hence, A is false, R is true.

5. (a) We have, $\frac{2-\sqrt{3}}{\sqrt{3}} = \frac{(2-\sqrt{3})\sqrt{3}}{3}$ [by rationalising]

$= \frac{2\sqrt{3}-3}{3} = \frac{2\sqrt{3}}{3} - 1$

$= \frac{3.464}{3} - 1$ [given, $\sqrt{3} = 1.732$]

$= 1.154666 - 1 = 0.154666 = 0.154$

Hence, A is true.

As we know that a non terminating and non recurring decimal number is an irrational number.

$\therefore$ R is false.

Statement Based Questions

1. (d) We know that additive inverse of rational number $\frac{a}{b}$ is $\frac{-a}{b}$.

$\therefore$ Additive inverse of $\frac{-35}{17}$ is $\frac{35}{17}$.

Hence, Statement I is false and Statement II is true.

2. (b) **Statement I** $\sqrt{7}$ is also a real number because irrational number is a part of a real number.

Hence, Statement I is false.

Statement II There are infinitely many rational numbers between two rational numbers.

Hence, Statement II is false.

3. (c) **Statement I** We have,

$(\sqrt{a} + \sqrt{b})(\sqrt{a} - \sqrt{b})$

$= (\sqrt{a})^2 - (\sqrt{b})^2$ $[\because (x+y)(x-y) = x^2 - y^2]$

$= a - b$

$\because a$ and b are natural numbers and difference of two natural numbers is also a natural number and all natural numbers are rational numbers.

Hence, $(\sqrt{a} + \sqrt{b})(\sqrt{a} - \sqrt{b})$ is rational number.

Statement I is true.

Statement II Given, $a = 4\sqrt{21}$ and $b = 2\sqrt{3}$

Now, $\frac{a}{b} = \frac{4\sqrt{21}}{2\sqrt{3}} = \frac{4 \times \sqrt{7 \times 3}}{2\sqrt{3}}$

$= \frac{4 \times \sqrt{7} \times \sqrt{3}}{2\sqrt{3}} = 2\sqrt{7}$

So, $2\sqrt{7}$ is not a rational number.

Hence, Statement II is false.

4. (c) **Statement I** We know that the decimal expansion of an irrational number is non terminating and non repeating.

Hence, Statement I is true.

Statement II We know that rationalising factor of any surd is conjugate of its number.

$\therefore$ Rationalising factor of $(13 - 5\sqrt{7})$ is $(13 + 5\sqrt{7})$.

Hence, Statement II is false.

Short Answer Type Questions

1. We have, $\frac{8}{5}$ and $\frac{7}{2}$

LCM of 2 and 5 = 10

$\therefore$ Write the given rational numbers with the same denominator, we get

$$\frac{8}{5} \times \frac{2}{2} = \frac{16}{10} \text{ and } \frac{7}{2} \times \frac{5}{5} = \frac{35}{10}$$

$\therefore$ Rational numbers lying between $\frac{8}{5}$ and $\frac{7}{2}$ are $\frac{17}{10}, \frac{18}{10}, \frac{19}{10}, \frac{20}{10}$ and $\frac{21}{10}$.

In ascending order,

$$\frac{8}{5} < \frac{17}{10} < \frac{18}{10} < \frac{19}{10} < \frac{20}{10} < \frac{21}{10} < \frac{7}{2}$$

$$\Rightarrow \quad \frac{8}{5} < \frac{17}{10} < \frac{9}{5} < \frac{19}{10} < 2 < \frac{21}{10} < \frac{7}{2}$$

2. Here, – 3/5 lies between – 1 and 0.

$\therefore$ We take one-fifth of unit length and mark points on the number line XY on both sides of 0 (zero), then we represent – 3/5 as point A.

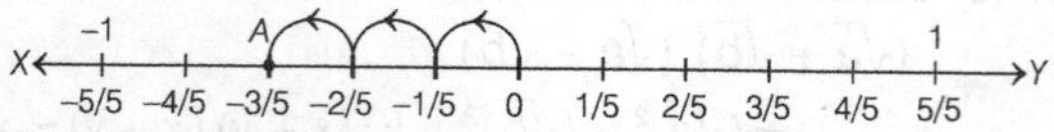

3. On taking squares of $4\sqrt{2}$ and $3\sqrt{3}$, we get

$$(4\sqrt{2})^2 = 32 \text{ and } (3\sqrt{3})^2 = 27$$

Here, 32 > 27

Four numbers between 32 and 27 are

$$32 > 31 > 30 > 29 > 28 > 27$$

On taking square root, we get

$$\sqrt{32} > \sqrt{31} > \sqrt{30} > \sqrt{29} > \sqrt{28} > \sqrt{27}$$

Thus, $\sqrt{31}, \sqrt{30}, \sqrt{29}$ and $\sqrt{28}$ lie between $4\sqrt{2}$ and $3\sqrt{3}$.

4. We have, $\sqrt{5}$

Now, 5 can be written as $5 = 4 + 1 = (2)^2 + (1)^2$

So, we take $OQ = 2$ units and $PQ = 1$ unit

Draw $OQ = 2$ units on the number line and then draw $PQ = 1$ unit, such that $PQ \perp OQ$. Join OP.

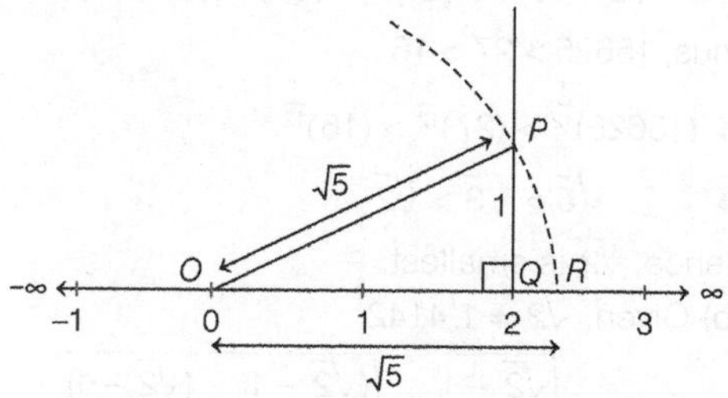

Now, using Pythagoras theorem in right ΔOQP, we get

$$OP^2 = OQ^2 + PQ^2$$

On taking positive square root, we get

$$OP = \sqrt{OQ^2 + PQ^2}$$

$$= \sqrt{2^2 + 1^2}$$

$$= \sqrt{4 + 1}$$

$$= \sqrt{5} \text{ units}$$

On taking O as centre and $OP = \sqrt{5}$ as radius, draw an arc, which intersects the number line at point R.

Hence, R represents $\sqrt{5}$ on the number line.

5. Here, $2 = 1^2 + 1^2$

Firstly, we draw $OA = 1$ unit on number line and then draw $AB = 1$ unit such that $AB \perp AO$.

$OB = \sqrt{OA^2 + AB^2}$ [by Pythagoras theorem]

$= \sqrt{2}$ units

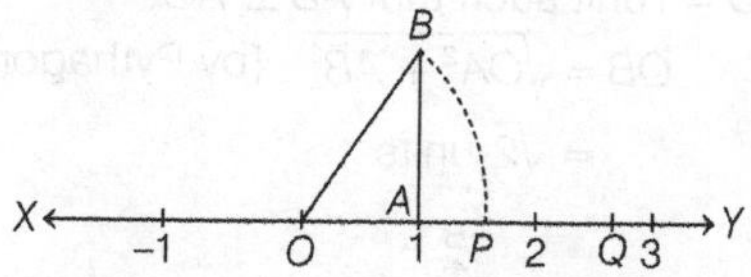

On taking O as centre and radius OB, draw an arc which intersects number line at point P.

$\Rightarrow \quad OP = \sqrt{2}$ units

Again, draw an arc with centre P and radius OP, which meets the number line at Q.

$\Rightarrow \quad OQ = 2 \times OP = 2\sqrt{2}$

Hence, Q represents $2\sqrt{2}$ on the number line.

6. I. Firstly, we draw $AB = 9.3$ units left side of 0 on number line.

II. Now, from B, mark a distance of 1 unit. Let this point be C.

III. Let O be the mid-point of AC. Now, draw a semi-circle with centre O and radius OA.

IV. Let us draw a line perpendicular to AC passing through point B and intersecting the semi-circle at point D.

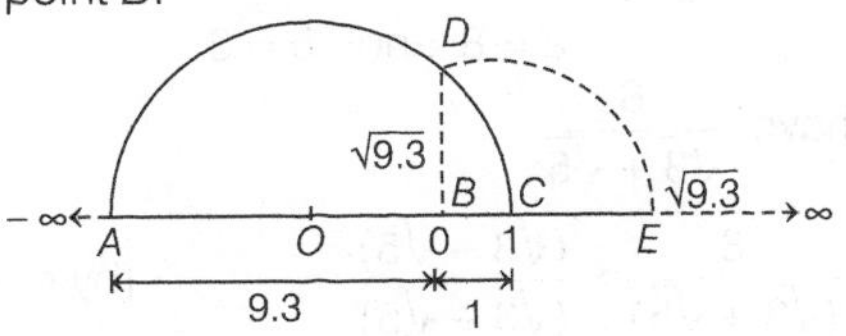

Thus, $BD = \sqrt{9.3}$ units

V. Draw an arc with centre B and radius BD, which intersects the number line at point E. So, point E represents $\sqrt{9.3}$.

7. Let $x = 0.0\overline{72}$

First, to shift the decimal point just before the recurring term, we multiply by 10, we get

$$10x = 0.\overline{72} \quad \ldots\text{(i)}$$

Thus two digits are repeating.

So, on multiplying Eq. (i) by 100, we get

$1000x = 72.\overline{72}$

It can be written as

$$1000x = 72 + 0.\overline{72} = 72 + 10x \quad \text{[using Eq. (i)]}$$

$$\Rightarrow \quad 990x = 72$$

$$\Rightarrow \quad x = \frac{72}{990}$$

$$\Rightarrow \quad x = \frac{4}{55}$$

Here, $\frac{4}{55}$ is a rational representation of $0.0\overline{72}$.

Therefore, $0.0\overline{72}$ is a rational number.

8. We have, $\frac{14588}{625}$

The factors of the denominator 625 are $5^4 \times 2^0$.

So, it has a terminating decimal expansion.

$$\text{Now, } \frac{14588}{625} = \frac{14588}{5^4} \times \frac{2^4}{2^4}$$

$$= \frac{233408}{10^4}$$

$$= 23.3408$$

which is the required decimal expansion.

9. We have, $\frac{\sqrt[6]{256}}{\sqrt[6]{4}} = \sqrt[6]{\frac{256}{4}} = \sqrt[6]{64}$ $\left[\because \frac{\sqrt[n]{a}}{\sqrt[n]{b}} = \sqrt[n]{\frac{a}{b}}\right]$

$= \sqrt[6]{2^6} = (2^6)^{\frac{1}{6}}$ $\left[\because \sqrt[n]{a} = (a)^{\frac{1}{n}}\right]$

$= 2$, which is not a surd.

Hence, $\frac{\sqrt[6]{256}}{\sqrt[6]{4}}$ is not a surd.

10. $$\text{LHS} = \frac{1}{2+\sqrt{3}} + \frac{2}{\sqrt{5}-\sqrt{3}} + \frac{1}{2-\sqrt{5}}$$

$$= \frac{1}{2+\sqrt{3}} \times \frac{2-\sqrt{3}}{2-\sqrt{3}} + \frac{2}{\sqrt{5}-\sqrt{3}} \times \frac{\sqrt{5}+\sqrt{3}}{\sqrt{5}+\sqrt{3}} + \frac{1}{2-\sqrt{5}} \times \frac{2+\sqrt{5}}{2+\sqrt{5}}$$

[by rationalising]

$$= \frac{(2-\sqrt{3})}{4-3} + \frac{2(\sqrt{5}+\sqrt{3})}{5-3} + \frac{2+\sqrt{5}}{4-5}$$

$$= \frac{2-\sqrt{3}}{1} + \frac{2(\sqrt{5}+\sqrt{3})}{2} - \frac{2+\sqrt{5}}{1}$$

$$= 2 - \sqrt{3} + \sqrt{5} + \sqrt{3} - 2 - \sqrt{5}$$

$= 0 = \text{RHS}$ **Hence proved.**

11. We have, $\frac{4\sqrt{3}+5\sqrt{2}}{\sqrt{48}+\sqrt{18}} = \frac{4\sqrt{3}+5\sqrt{2}}{4\sqrt{3}+3\sqrt{2}}$

$$= \frac{4\sqrt{3}+5\sqrt{2}}{4\sqrt{3}+3\sqrt{2}} \times \frac{4\sqrt{3}-3\sqrt{2}}{4\sqrt{3}-3\sqrt{2}}$$

[by rationalising]

$$= \frac{(4\sqrt{3}+5\sqrt{2})(4\sqrt{3}-3\sqrt{2})}{(4\sqrt{3})^2-(3\sqrt{2})^2}$$

$[\because (a-b)(a+b) = a^2 - b^2]$

$$= \frac{48 - 12\sqrt{6} + 20\sqrt{6} - 30}{48-18}$$

$$= \frac{18+8\sqrt{6}}{30} = \frac{9+4\sqrt{6}}{15}$$

12. Here, $\sqrt{7+2\sqrt{10}} = \sqrt{5+2+2\sqrt{10}}$

$$= \sqrt{(\sqrt{5}+\sqrt{2})^2} = \sqrt{5}+\sqrt{2}$$

and $\sqrt{12-2\sqrt{35}} = \sqrt{7+5-2\sqrt{35}}$

$$= \sqrt{(\sqrt{7}-\sqrt{5})^2} = \sqrt{7}-\sqrt{5}$$

$$\therefore \sqrt{7+2\sqrt{10}} + \sqrt{12-2\sqrt{35}} = \sqrt{5}+\sqrt{2}+(\sqrt{7}-\sqrt{5})$$

$$= \sqrt{2}+\sqrt{7}$$

13. We have, $5\sqrt{3}+3\sqrt{5}$

Now, conjugate of $(5\sqrt{3}+3\sqrt{5})$ is $(5\sqrt{3}-3\sqrt{5})$ or $(3\sqrt{5}-5\sqrt{3})$.

$\therefore$ Rationalising factor of $(5\sqrt{3}+3\sqrt{5})$ is $(5\sqrt{3}-3\sqrt{5})$ or $(3\sqrt{5}-5\sqrt{3})$.

$\because$ $5\sqrt{3} = \sqrt{75}$ and $3\sqrt{5} = \sqrt{45}$

and $\sqrt{45} < \sqrt{75} \Rightarrow 3\sqrt{5} < 5\sqrt{3}$

$\therefore$ $3\sqrt{5}-5\sqrt{3} < 5\sqrt{3}-3\sqrt{5}$

Therefore, lowest rationalising factor of $(5\sqrt{3}+3\sqrt{5})$ is $(3\sqrt{5}-5\sqrt{3})$.

14. We have, $\dfrac{2}{\sqrt{5}+\sqrt{3}+2}$

$$= \frac{2}{(\sqrt{5}+\sqrt{3})+2} \times \frac{(\sqrt{5}+\sqrt{3})-2}{(\sqrt{5}+\sqrt{3})-2}$$

[by rationalising]

$$= \frac{2(\sqrt{5}+\sqrt{3}-2)}{(\sqrt{5}+\sqrt{3})^2-2^2}$$

$[\because (a+b)(a-b)=a^2-b^2]$

$$= \frac{2(\sqrt{5}+\sqrt{3}-2)}{5+3+2\sqrt{5}\sqrt{3}-4} = \frac{2(\sqrt{5}+\sqrt{3}-2)}{4+2\sqrt{15}}$$

$$= \frac{\sqrt{5}+\sqrt{3}-2}{2+\sqrt{15}} = \frac{\sqrt{5}+\sqrt{3}-2}{2+\sqrt{15}} \times \frac{2-\sqrt{15}}{2-\sqrt{15}}$$

[by rationalising]

$$= \frac{2\sqrt{5}+2\sqrt{3}-4-\sqrt{5}\sqrt{15}-\sqrt{3}\sqrt{15}+2\sqrt{15}}{2^2-(\sqrt{15})^2}$$

$[\because (a+b)(a-b)=a^2-b^2]$

$$= \frac{2\sqrt{5}+2\sqrt{3}-4-5\sqrt{3}-3\sqrt{5}+2\sqrt{15}}{4-15}$$

$$= \frac{-\sqrt{5}-3\sqrt{3}-4+2\sqrt{15}}{-11}$$

$$= \frac{\sqrt{5}+3\sqrt{3}-2\sqrt{15}+4}{11}$$

15. We have, $\dfrac{(\sqrt{3}-\sqrt{5})(\sqrt{3}+\sqrt{5})}{7-2\sqrt{5}}$

$$= \frac{(\sqrt{3})^2-(\sqrt{5})^2}{7-2\sqrt{5}} = \frac{3-5}{7-2\sqrt{5}}$$

$[\because (a-b)(a+b)=a^2-b^2]$

$$= \frac{-2}{7-2\sqrt{5}} \times \frac{7+2\sqrt{5}}{7+2\sqrt{5}}$$ [by rationalising]

$$= \frac{-2(7+2\sqrt{5})}{(7)^2-(2\sqrt{5})^2}$$ $[\because (a-b)(a+b)=a^2-b^2]$

$$= \frac{-2(7+2\sqrt{5})}{49-20} = \frac{-2(7+2\sqrt{5})}{29} = \frac{-14-4\sqrt{5}}{29}$$

16. Given, $a+b\sqrt{7} = \dfrac{3+\sqrt{7}}{3-\sqrt{7}}$

$$\Rightarrow \quad a+b\sqrt{7} = \frac{3+\sqrt{7}}{3-\sqrt{7}} \times \frac{3+\sqrt{7}}{3+\sqrt{7}}$$ [by rationalising]

$$\Rightarrow \quad a+b\sqrt{7} = \frac{(3+\sqrt{7})^2}{(3)^2-(\sqrt{7})^2}$$

$[\because (a-b)(a+b)=a^2-b^2]$

$$= \frac{9+7+6\sqrt{7}}{9-7}$$

$[\because (a+b)^2=a^2+b^2+2ab]$

$$\Rightarrow \quad a+b\sqrt{7} = \frac{16+6\sqrt{7}}{2} = 8+3\sqrt{7}$$

On comparing the coefficients of a and b both sides, we get

$$a=8 \text{ and } b=3$$

17. We have, $\dfrac{8}{\sqrt{3}+\sqrt{5}}$

$$= \frac{8}{(\sqrt{3}+\sqrt{5})} \times \frac{(\sqrt{3}-\sqrt{5})}{(\sqrt{3}-\sqrt{5})}$$ [by rationalising]

$$= \frac{8(\sqrt{3}-\sqrt{5})}{(\sqrt{3})^2-(\sqrt{5})^2}$$ $[\because (a+b)(a-b)=a^2-b^2]$

$$= \frac{8(\sqrt{3}-\sqrt{5})}{3-5} = \frac{8}{-2}(\sqrt{3}-\sqrt{5})$$

$$= -4(\sqrt{3}-\sqrt{5})$$

On putting the values of $\sqrt{3}$ and $\sqrt{5}$, we get

$$-4(1.732-2.236) = (-4)\times(-0.504) = 2.016$$

18. Given, $x = 2-\sqrt{3}$

$$\Rightarrow \quad \frac{1}{x} = \frac{1}{2-\sqrt{3}} = \frac{1}{2-\sqrt{3}} \times \frac{2+\sqrt{3}}{2+\sqrt{3}}$$ [by rationalising]

$$= \frac{2+\sqrt{3}}{2^2-(\sqrt{3})^2}$$ $[\because (a+b)(a-b)=a^2-b^2]$

$$= \frac{2+\sqrt{3}}{4-3} = \frac{2+\sqrt{3}}{1} = 2+\sqrt{3}$$

$$\therefore \; x-\frac{1}{x} = (2-\sqrt{3})-(2+\sqrt{3}) = -2\sqrt{3}$$

Thus, $\left(x-\dfrac{1}{x}\right)^3 = (-2\sqrt{3})^3$

$$= (-2)^3(\sqrt{3})^3 = -8\times 3\sqrt{3}$$

$$= -24\sqrt{3}$$

Long Answer Type Questions

1. We have, 0 and 0.3 i.e. $\dfrac{0}{1}$ and $\dfrac{3}{10}$

LCM of 1 and 10 = 10

$\therefore$ Write the given rational numbers with the same denominator, we get

$$\frac{0}{1}\times\frac{10}{10} = \frac{0}{10} \text{ and } \frac{3}{10}\times\frac{1}{1} = \frac{3}{10}$$

On multiplying the numerator and denominator by $4+1=5$, we get

$$\frac{0}{10}\times\frac{5}{5} = \frac{0}{50} \text{ and } \frac{3}{10}\times\frac{5}{5} = \frac{15}{50}$$

Thus, rational numbers are $\dfrac{1}{50}, \dfrac{2}{50}, \dfrac{3}{50}$ and $\dfrac{4}{50}$.

Thus, the numbers in ascending order are

$$\frac{1}{50} < \frac{2}{50} < \frac{3}{50} < \frac{4}{50}.$$

Here, the largest rational number $= \frac{4}{50}$

and the smallest rational number $= \frac{1}{50}$

Now, the difference between the largest and smallest rational number $= \frac{4}{50} - \frac{1}{50} = \frac{3}{50}$

and the decimal expansion of the difference $= \frac{3}{50} = 0.06$

2. First add the two numbers.

Sum = 0.0333 ......
+ 0.4444 ......
0.4777 ......

Sum of given two numbers = 0.4777 ......

Now,

let $x = 0.4777......$ ... (i)

Here, to shift the decimal point just before the recurring term, we multiply by 10, we get

$10x = 4.777......$ ... (ii)

Thus, one digit is repeating. So, on multiplying Eq. (ii) by 10, we get

$100x = 47.777......$ ... (iii)

On subtracting Eq. (ii) from Eq. (iii), we get

$90x = 43$

$\Rightarrow \quad x = \frac{43}{90}$

3. Given, $x = \sqrt{3} + \frac{1}{\sqrt{3}}$

Now, $\left(x - \frac{\sqrt{126}}{\sqrt{42}}\right)\left(x - \frac{1}{x - \frac{2\sqrt{3}}{3}}\right)$

On putting the value of x, we get

$$= \left(\sqrt{3} + \frac{1}{\sqrt{3}} - \sqrt{3}\right)\left(\sqrt{3} + \frac{1}{\sqrt{3}} - \frac{1}{\sqrt{3} - \frac{1}{\sqrt{3}} - \frac{2\sqrt{3}}{3}}\right)$$

$$= \left(\frac{1}{\sqrt{3}}\right)\left(\sqrt{3} + \frac{1}{\sqrt{3}} - \frac{1}{\frac{9+3-6}{3\sqrt{3}}}\right)$$

$$= \frac{1}{\sqrt{3}}\left(\sqrt{3} + \frac{1}{\sqrt{3}} - \frac{3\sqrt{3}}{6}\right) = \frac{1}{\sqrt{3}}\left(\sqrt{3} + \frac{1}{\sqrt{3}} - \frac{\sqrt{3}}{2}\right)$$

$$= \frac{\sqrt{3}}{\sqrt{3}} + \frac{1}{\sqrt{3}} \times \frac{1}{\sqrt{3}} - \frac{\sqrt{3}}{2} \times \frac{1}{\sqrt{3}}$$

$$= 1 + \frac{1}{3} - \frac{1}{2} = \frac{6+2-3}{6} = \frac{5}{6} = 0.83$$

4. LHS $= \frac{1}{(3 - \sqrt{8})} - \frac{1}{(\sqrt{8} - \sqrt{7})} + \frac{1}{(\sqrt{7} - \sqrt{6})} - \frac{1}{(\sqrt{6} - \sqrt{5})} + \frac{1}{(\sqrt{5} - 2)}$

$$= \frac{1}{(3-\sqrt{8})} \times \frac{3+\sqrt{8}}{3+\sqrt{8}} - \frac{1}{(\sqrt{8}-\sqrt{7})} \times \frac{\sqrt{8}+\sqrt{7}}{\sqrt{8}+\sqrt{7}} + \frac{1}{(\sqrt{7}-\sqrt{6})} \times \frac{\sqrt{7}+\sqrt{6}}{\sqrt{7}+\sqrt{6}} - \frac{1}{(\sqrt{6}-\sqrt{5})} \times \frac{\sqrt{6}+\sqrt{5}}{\sqrt{6}+\sqrt{5}} + \frac{1}{\sqrt{5}-2} \times \frac{\sqrt{5}+2}{\sqrt{5}+2}$$ [by rationalising]

$$= \frac{3+\sqrt{8}}{(3)^2 - (\sqrt{8})^2} - \frac{(\sqrt{8}+\sqrt{7})}{(\sqrt{8})^2 - (\sqrt{7})^2} + \frac{(\sqrt{7}+\sqrt{6})}{(\sqrt{7})^2 - (\sqrt{6})^2} - \frac{(\sqrt{6}+\sqrt{5})}{(\sqrt{6})^2 - (\sqrt{5})^2} + \frac{(\sqrt{5}+2)}{(\sqrt{5})^2 - (2)^2}$$

$[\because (a-b)(a+b) = a^2 - b^2]$

$$= \frac{3+\sqrt{8}}{9-8} - \frac{(\sqrt{8}+\sqrt{7})}{8-7} + \frac{(\sqrt{7}+\sqrt{6})}{7-6} - \frac{(\sqrt{6}+\sqrt{5})}{6-5} + \frac{(\sqrt{5}+2)}{5-4}$$

$$= 3 + \sqrt{8} - \sqrt{8} - \sqrt{7} + \sqrt{7} + \sqrt{6} - \sqrt{6} - \sqrt{5} + \sqrt{5} + 2$$

$= 3 + 2 = 5 =$ RHS **Hence proved.**

5. We have, $x = 5 + 2\sqrt{6}$ ...(i)

$\therefore \quad \frac{1}{x} = \frac{1}{(5+2\sqrt{6})} \times \frac{(5-2\sqrt{6})}{(5-2\sqrt{6})}$ [by rationalising]

$\Rightarrow \quad \frac{1}{x} = \frac{5-2\sqrt{6}}{(5)^2 - (2\sqrt{6})^2}$

$[\because (a+b)(a-b) = a^2 - b^2]$

$\Rightarrow \quad \frac{1}{x} = \frac{5-2\sqrt{6}}{25-24}$

$\Rightarrow \quad \frac{1}{x} = 5 - 2\sqrt{6}$ ...(ii)

Now, $x + \frac{1}{x} = 5 + 2\sqrt{6} + 5 - 2\sqrt{6}$ [from Eqs. (i) and (ii)]

$\Rightarrow \quad x + \frac{1}{x} = 10 \Rightarrow (\sqrt{x})^2 + \left(\frac{1}{\sqrt{x}}\right)^2 = 10$

On adding 2 both sides, we get

$(\sqrt{x})^2 + \left(\frac{1}{\sqrt{x}}\right)^2 + 2 = 10 + 2$

$\Rightarrow \quad \left(\sqrt{x} + \frac{1}{\sqrt{x}}\right)^2 = 12$ $[\because a^2 + b^2 + 2ab = (a+b)^2]$

$\Rightarrow \quad \sqrt{x} + \frac{1}{\sqrt{x}} = \sqrt{12} = 2\sqrt{3}$ **Hence proved.**

6. We have, $\dfrac{x-\sqrt{x^2-1}}{x+\sqrt{x^2-1}}-\dfrac{x+\sqrt{x^2-1}}{x-\sqrt{x^2-1}}$

On rationalising the denominator, we get

$$\frac{x-\sqrt{x^2-1}}{x+\sqrt{x^2-1}}\times\frac{x-\sqrt{x^2-1}}{x-\sqrt{x^2-1}}-\frac{x+\sqrt{x^2-1}}{x-\sqrt{x^2-1}}\times\frac{x+\sqrt{x^2-1}}{x+\sqrt{x^2-1}}$$

$$=\frac{(x-\sqrt{x^2-1})^2}{x^2-(\sqrt{x^2-1})^2}-\frac{(x+\sqrt{x^2-1})^2}{x^2-(\sqrt{x^2-1})^2}$$

$$=\frac{x^2+(\sqrt{x^2-1})^2-2x\sqrt{x^2-1}}{x^2-(x^2-1)}-\frac{x^2+(\sqrt{x^2-1})^2+2x\sqrt{x^2-1}}{x^2-(x^2-1)}$$

$[\because (a+b)^2=a^2+b^2+2ab$ and $(a-b)^2=a^2+b^2-2ab]$

$$=\frac{x^2+(x^2-1)-2x\sqrt{x^2-1}}{x^2-x^2+1}-\frac{x^2+x^2-1+2x\sqrt{x^2-1}}{x^2-x^2+1}$$

$$=2x^2-2x\sqrt{x^2-1}-1-(2x^2+2x\sqrt{x^2-1}-1)$$

$$=2x^2-2x\sqrt{x^2-1}-1-2x^2-2x\sqrt{x^2-1}+1$$

$$=-4x\sqrt{x^2-1}$$

7. Given, $x=3+\sqrt{8}$ ...(a)

(i) $\dfrac{1}{x}=\dfrac{1}{3+\sqrt{8}}\times\dfrac{3-\sqrt{8}}{3-\sqrt{8}}$ [by rationalising]

$\Rightarrow \dfrac{1}{x}=\dfrac{3-\sqrt{8}}{(3)^2-(\sqrt{8})^2}$ $[\because (a+b)(a-b)=a^2-b^2]$

$\Rightarrow \dfrac{1}{x}=\dfrac{3-\sqrt{8}}{9-8}$

$\Rightarrow \dfrac{1}{x}=3-\sqrt{8}$ ...(b)

(ii) $x+\dfrac{1}{x}=3+\sqrt{8}+3-\sqrt{8}$ [from Eqs. (a) and (b)]

$\Rightarrow x+\dfrac{1}{x}=6$

(iii) We have, $x+\dfrac{1}{x}=6$ ...(c)

On squaring both sides, we get

$\left(x+\dfrac{1}{x}\right)^2=(6)^2$ [from Eq. (c)]

$\Rightarrow x^2+\dfrac{1}{x^2}+2\times x\times\dfrac{1}{x}=36$

$\Rightarrow x^2+\dfrac{1}{x^2}=36-2=34$

8. LHS $=\dfrac{15}{\sqrt{10}+\sqrt{20}+\sqrt{40}-\sqrt{5}-\sqrt{80}}$

$$=\frac{15}{\sqrt{10}+2\sqrt{5}+2\sqrt{10}-\sqrt{5}-4\sqrt{5}}$$

$$=\frac{15}{3\sqrt{10}-3\sqrt{5}}$$

$$=\frac{5}{\sqrt{10}-\sqrt{5}}$$

$=\dfrac{5}{\sqrt{10}-\sqrt{5}}\times\dfrac{\sqrt{10}+\sqrt{5}}{\sqrt{10}+\sqrt{5}}$ [by rationalising]

$=\dfrac{5(\sqrt{10}+\sqrt{5})}{(\sqrt{10})^2-(\sqrt{5})^2}$ $[\because (a+b)(a-b)=a^2-b^2]$

$$=\frac{5(\sqrt{10}+\sqrt{5})}{10-5}=\frac{5(\sqrt{10}+\sqrt{5})}{5}$$

$=\sqrt{10}+\sqrt{5}=$ RHS **Hence proved.**

9. Given, $x=\dfrac{\sqrt{5}-2}{\sqrt{5}+2}$ and $y=\dfrac{\sqrt{5}+2}{\sqrt{5}-2}$

Now, $x=\dfrac{\sqrt{5}-2}{\sqrt{5}+2}$

On rationalising the RHS, we get

$$x=\frac{\sqrt{5}-2}{\sqrt{5}+2}\times\frac{\sqrt{5}-2}{\sqrt{5}-2}$$

$$=\frac{(\sqrt{5}-2)^2}{(\sqrt{5}+2)(\sqrt{5}-2)}$$

$$=\frac{(\sqrt{5})^2+(2)^2-2\times\sqrt{5}\times 2}{(\sqrt{5})^2-(2)^2}$$

$\left[\because (a-b)^2=a^2+b^2-2ab \text{ and } (a+b)(a-b)=a^2-b^2\right]$

$=\dfrac{5+4-4\sqrt{5}}{5-4}=9-4\sqrt{5}$ ...(i)

On squaring both sides, we get

$$x^2=(9-4\sqrt{5})^2$$

$$=9^2+(4\sqrt{5})^2-2\times 9\times(4\sqrt{5})$$

$$=81+80-72\sqrt{5}$$

$=161-72\sqrt{5}$ ...(ii)

and $y=\dfrac{\sqrt{5}+2}{\sqrt{5}-2}$

$=\dfrac{\sqrt{5}+2}{\sqrt{5}-2}\times\dfrac{\sqrt{5}+2}{\sqrt{5}+2}$ [by rationalising]

$$=\frac{(\sqrt{5}+2)^2}{(\sqrt{5})^2-2^2}=\frac{5+4+4\sqrt{5}}{5-4}$$

$=9+4\sqrt{5}$ ...(iii)

On squaring both sides, we get

$$y^2 = (9 + 4\sqrt{5})^2 = 81 + 80 + 72\sqrt{5}$$

$$\Rightarrow \quad y^2 = 161 + 72\sqrt{5} \quad \text{...(iv)}$$

Now, $xy = (9 - 4\sqrt{5})(9 + 4\sqrt{5})$ [from Eqs. (i) and (iii)]

$$\Rightarrow \quad xy = 9^2 - (4\sqrt{5})^2$$

$$\Rightarrow \quad xy = 81 - 80 \Rightarrow xy = 1 \quad \text{...(v)}$$

$$\therefore x^2 + y^2 + xy = 161 - 72\sqrt{5} + 161 + 72\sqrt{5} + 1 = 323$$

[from Eqs. (ii), (iv) and (v)]

10. Let us assume $\sqrt{2}$ be a rational number.

Then, it will be of the form $\frac{a}{b}$, where a, b are integers and $b \neq 0$.

Again, let a and b have no common factor other than 1.

$$\therefore \sqrt{2} = \frac{a}{b}$$

On squaring both sides, we get

$$2 = \frac{a^2}{b^2} \Rightarrow 2b^2 = a^2 \quad \text{...(i)}$$

$\Rightarrow 2$ divides $a^2 \Rightarrow$ 2 divides a

Then, a can be written as $2m$, where m is an integer.

On putting $a = 2m$ in Eq. (i), we get

$$2b^2 = (2m)^2 \Rightarrow 2b^2 = 4m^2$$

$$\Rightarrow \quad b^2 = 2m^2$$

So, 2 divides $b^2 \Rightarrow$ 2 divides b

Thus, 2 is a common factor of a and b.

But this contradicts the fact that a and b have no common factor other than 1.

The contradiction arises by assuming that $\sqrt{2}$ is a rational number.

So, our assumption is wrong.

Hence, $\sqrt{2}$ is an irrational number. **Hence proved.**

11. Let us assume $\sqrt{3}$ be a rational number.

Then, it will be of the form $\frac{a}{b}$, where a, b are integers and $b \neq 0$.

Again, let a and b have no common factor other than 1.

$$\therefore \sqrt{3} = \frac{a}{b}$$

On squaring both sides, we get

$$3 = \frac{a^2}{b^2} \Rightarrow 3b^2 = a^2 \quad \text{...(i)}$$

If a^2 is divisible by 3, then a is also divisible by 3.

Then, a can be written as $3m$, where m is an integer.

On putting $a = 3m$ in Eq. (i), we get

$$3b^2 = (3m)^2 \Rightarrow 3b^2 = 9m^2 \Rightarrow b^2 = 3m^2$$

So, 3 divides $b^2 \Rightarrow$ 3 divides b

Thus, 3 is a common factor of a and b.

But this contradicts the fact that a and b have no common factor other than 1.

The contradiction arises by assuming that $\sqrt{3}$ is a rational number.

So, our assumption is wrong.

Hence, $\sqrt{3}$ is an irrational number. **Hence proved.**

12. Let us assume $\sqrt{5}$ be a rational number.

Then, it will be of the form $\frac{a}{b}$, where a, b are integers and $b \neq 0$.

Again, let a and b have no common factor other than 1.

$$\therefore \sqrt{5} = \frac{a}{b}$$

On squaring both sides, we get

$$5 = \frac{a^2}{b^2} \Rightarrow 5b^2 = a^2 \quad \text{...(i)}$$

If a^2 is divisible by 5, then a is also divisible by 5.

Then, a can be written as $5m$, where m is an integer.

On putting $a = 5m$ in Eq. (i), we get

$$5b^2 = (5m)^2 \Rightarrow 5b^2 = 25m^2 \Rightarrow b^2 = 5m^2$$

So, 5 divides $b^2 \Rightarrow$ 5 divides b

Thus, 5 is a common factor of a and b.

But this contradicts the fact that a and b have no common factor other than 1.

The contradiction arises by assuming that $\sqrt{5}$ is a rational number.

So, our assumption is wrong.

Hence, $\sqrt{5}$ is an irrational number. **Hence proved.**

13. Assume that $\sqrt{7} - \sqrt{5}$ is a rational number.

Let $\sqrt{7} - \sqrt{5} = x$, a rational number.

On squaring both sides, we get

$$(\sqrt{7} - \sqrt{5})^2 = x^2$$

$$\Rightarrow \quad 7 + 5 - 2\sqrt{35} = x^2 \quad [\because (a - b)^2 = a^2 + b^2 - 2ab]$$

$$\Rightarrow \quad 12 - 2\sqrt{35} = x^2$$

$$\Rightarrow \quad \sqrt{35} = \frac{12 - x^2}{2} \quad \text{...(i)}$$

Here, x is rational.

$\therefore \frac{12 - x^2}{2}$ is rational.

So, $\sqrt{35}$ is also rational.

But we know that $\sqrt{35}$ is irrational number.

$\therefore \frac{12 - x^2}{2}$ is irrational, [from Eq. (i)]

which is a contradiction.

$\therefore$ Our assumption is wrong.

Thus, $\sqrt{7} - \sqrt{5}$ is an irrational number.

Case Based Questions

1. (i) Here, $XS = \sqrt{4.5}$

$\therefore$ To draw the position of $\sqrt{4.5}$ on the number line, we take S as centre and make an arc of radius $XS = \sqrt{4.5}$ units, which cuts the number line at A.

$\therefore$ $SA = \sqrt{4.5}$ units

$\therefore$ Letter S represents 0 on the number line.

(ii) $\because$ $\sqrt{4.5}$ lies between U and V on number line and $\sqrt{5.2} > \sqrt{4.5}$

but $\sqrt{5.2} < 3$.

$\therefore \sqrt{5.2}$ lies between points U and V on the number line.

2. (i) Total households = 13

Number of households which are donating their income = 7

$\therefore$ Fraction of household which are donating $= \frac{7}{13}$

(ii) Total households = 13

Number of houses which are not donating their income = 13 − 7 = 6

$\therefore$ Fraction of households which are not donating $= \frac{6}{13}$

(iii) We have, $\frac{7}{13} = 0.53846153\ldots$

$\therefore \quad \frac{7}{13} = 0.\overline{538461}$

Or We have, $\frac{6}{13} = 0.46153846\ldots$

$\therefore \quad \frac{6}{13} = 0.\overline{461538}$

02

COMPOUND INTEREST

Interest

When a person borrows some amount of money (principal) from another person or an organisation (bank), then the person borrowing money (borrower) pays some extra money during repayment and that extra money during repayment is called interest.

$$\text{Simple Interest (SI)} = \frac{\text{Principal } (P) \times \text{Rate } (R) \times \text{Time } (T)}{100}$$

and $$\text{Amount } (A) = \text{Principal } (P) + \text{Simple Interest (SI)}$$

Compound Interest (CI)

Compound interest refers to the process where interest is computed on the principal amount and the accrued interest of previous tenures.

In other words, the difference between the original principal and the final amount is called the compound interest.

$$\text{Compound interest (CI)} = \text{Final amount } (A) - \text{Original principal } (P)$$

Example 1. ₹ 10000 is lent at 5% compound interest per year for 2 yr. Find the final amount and the compound interest.

Sol. **For the first year,** $P = ₹\,10000$, $R = 5\%$ and $T = 1\text{yr}$

$$\therefore \quad \text{Interest} = \frac{P \times R \times T}{100} = \frac{10000 \times 5 \times 1}{100} = ₹\,500$$

Amount after first year = ₹ (10000 + 500) = ₹ 10500

Now, principal for the second year = ₹ 10500

Now, for the second year, $P = ₹\,10500$, $R = 5\%$ and $T = 1$ yr

$$\therefore \quad \text{Interest} = \frac{P \times R \times T}{100} = \frac{10500 \times 5 \times 1}{100} = ₹\,525$$

Amount after second year = ₹ (10500 + 525) = ₹ 11025

∴ Compound interest = Final amount − Original amount = ₹ (11025 − 10000) = ₹ 1025

Compound Interest, when Interest is Compounded Yearly

When the interest is compounded yearly, the formula for finding the amount is

$$A = P\left(1 + \frac{R}{100}\right)^n,$$

where P = Principal, R = Rate of interest per annum and n = Time (number of years).

$$\therefore \quad \text{Compound Interest, CI} = A - P \Rightarrow \text{CI} = P\left(1 + \frac{R}{100}\right)^n - P = P\left[\left(1 + \frac{R}{100}\right)^n - 1\right]$$

If the rate of interest for the successive years are $R_1\%$, $R_2\%$ and $R_3\%$, then compound interest is given by

$$\text{CI} = P\left[\left(1 + \frac{R_1}{100}\right)\left(1 + \frac{R_2}{100}\right)\left(1 + \frac{R_3}{100}\right)\ldots - 1\right]$$

REVISION NOTES

Example 2. Solve Example - 1 by compound interest formula.

Sol. $P = ₹\,10000$

$R = 5\%$

$T = 2$ yr

$$\text{CI} = P\left[\left(1+\frac{R}{100}\right)^n - 1\right] = 10000\left[\left(1+\frac{5}{100}\right)^2 - 1\right]$$

$$= 10000\left[\frac{21}{20}\times\frac{21}{20} - 1\right] = 10000\left[\frac{441}{400} - 1\right]$$

$$= 10000 \times \frac{41}{400} = ₹\,1025$$

Example 3. Find the compound interest on ₹ 10000 for 3 yr, if the rate of interest is 4% for the first year, 5% for the second year and 6% for the third year.

Sol. Here, $P = 10000$, $R_1 = 4\%$, $R_2 = 5\%$ and $R_3 = 6\%$.

$$\therefore \text{ Compound interest, CI} = P\left[\left(1+\frac{R_1}{100}\right)\left(1+\frac{R_2}{100}\right)\left(1+\frac{R_3}{100}\right) - 1\right]$$

$$= 10000\left[\left(1+\frac{4}{100}\right)\left(1+\frac{5}{100}\right)\left(1+\frac{6}{100}\right) - 1\right]$$

$$= 10000\left[\left(1+\frac{1}{25}\right)\left(1+\frac{1}{20}\right)\left(1+\frac{3}{50}\right) - 1\right]$$

$$= 10000\left[\left(\frac{26}{25}\right)\left(\frac{21}{20}\right)\left(\frac{53}{50}\right) - 1\right]$$

$$= 10000[1.15752 - 1] = 10000\,(0.15752)$$

$$= ₹\,1575.2$$

Compound Interest When Interest is Compounded Half–Yearly (6 months)

In this case, the rate of interest R becomes $\frac{R}{2}$ and time n becomes $2T$, where T is the number of years.

$$\therefore \quad A = P\left(1+\frac{R}{2\times 100}\right)^{2T}$$

and

$$\text{CI} = A - P = P\left[\left(1+\frac{R}{2\times 100}\right)^{2T} - 1\right]$$

Example 4. Find the compound interest on ₹ 20000 for 2 yr at 20% per annum interest being compounded semi-annually.

Sol. Here, $P = ₹\,20000$, $R = 20\%$ and $T = 2$ yr.

Since, the interest is compounded semi-annually.

$$\therefore \quad A = P\left(1+\frac{R}{2\times 100}\right)^{2T} = 20000\left(1+\frac{20}{2\times 100}\right)^4$$

$$= 20000\left(1+\frac{1}{10}\right)^4 = 20000\left(\frac{11}{10}\right)^4 = 20000\times\frac{11}{10}\times\frac{11}{10}\times\frac{11}{10}\times\frac{11}{10}$$

$$= ₹\,29282$$

Hence, $\text{CI} = A - P = ₹\,(29282 - 20000) = ₹\,9282$

Important Facts

(i) **Computation of Compound Interest as a Repeated Simple Interest** Simple interest for the first period, add it to the original amount and then calculate the simple interest on the accumulated amount for the next period and so on, until the amount for the last period has been found.

(ii) When the interest is compounded yearly, the principal changes (increases) every year.

(iii) When the interest is compounded half yearly, the principal increases every six months.

(iv) The period (time), after which the principal changes, is called the conversion period.

(v) Simple Interest and Compound Interest are equal for the first conversion period on the same sum and at the same rate.

(vi) CI of second conversion period is more than the CI of first conversion period.

(vii) CI for the kth conversion period = Amount after k conversion periods – Amount after $(k-1)$ conversion periods

(viii) When the total time is not a complete number of conversion periods, then we consider simple interest for the last partial period.

(ix) CI of second conversion period – CI of first conversion period = SI on the interest of the first conversion period.

(x) Rate of interest (when CI of any two consecutive conversion periods are given)

$$\text{Rate of interest} = \frac{\text{Difference in the interest of two consecutive conversion periods}}{\text{CI of preceding period} \times \text{Time}} \times 100\%$$

Rate of Growth

The relative increase in a quantity is called its growth and the growth per year (or unit of time) is the rate of growth.

(i) If P is the population of a city at the beginning of a certain year and r% per annum be the constant rate of growth of population, then

$$\text{Population after } n \text{ yr} = P\left(1+\frac{r}{100}\right)^n$$

Example 5. The population of a city in the year 2016 was 424000. What will be the population in 2018, if it increases 5% per year.

Sol. Here, $P = 424000$, $r = 5\%$ per annum and $n = 2$ yr.

$$\therefore \text{Population after 2 yr} = 424000\left(1+\frac{5}{100}\right)^2 = 424000\left(\frac{21}{20}\right)^2 = 424000 \times \frac{21}{20} \times \frac{21}{20} = 467460$$

(ii) If P is the population at the beginning of a certain year. If the rate of growth be r_1% during first year, r_2% during second year and r_3% during third year, then

$$\text{Population after 1 yr} = P\left(1+\frac{r_1}{100}\right)$$

$$\text{Population after 2 yr} = P\left(1+\frac{r_1}{100}\right)\left(1+\frac{r_2}{100}\right)$$

and

$$\text{Population after 3 yr} = P\left(1+\frac{r_1}{100}\right)\left(1+\frac{r_2}{100}\right)\left(1+\frac{r_3}{100}\right)$$

Example 6. The population of a particular area A of a city is 5000. It increases by 10% in 1st yr. It decreases by 20% in the 2nd yr because of some reason. In the 3rd yr, the population increases by 30%. What will be the population of area A at the end of 3 yr?

Sol. Given that, $P = 5000$, $R_1 = 10\%$, $R_2 = -20\%$ (decrease) and $R_3 = 30\%$

$$\therefore \text{Population at the end of 3rd year} = P\left(1+\frac{R_1}{100}\right)\left(1+\frac{R_2}{100}\right)\left(1+\frac{R_3}{100}\right) = 5000\left(1+\frac{10}{100}\right)\left(1-\frac{20}{100}\right)\left(1+\frac{30}{100}\right)$$

$$= 5000 \times \frac{11}{10} \times \frac{4}{5} \times \frac{13}{10} = 10 \times 11 \times 4 \times 13 = 5720$$

(iii) If n yr ago, P_0 is the population of city and the rate of growth is r% per annum, then present value of population (P) is calculated by $P = P_0\left(1+\frac{r}{100}\right)^n$

Example 7. The population of a place increased to 54000 in 2003 at a rate of 5% per annum. Find the population in 2001.

Sol. Here, population in 2003 = 54000, rate of increase = 5% and time period (n) = 2 yr

Let the population in 2001 be P.

$$\therefore \text{ Present population} = P\left(1+\frac{R}{100}\right)^n = P\left(1+\frac{5}{100}\right)^2 = P\left(1+\frac{1}{20}\right)^2$$

$$\Rightarrow \quad 54000 = P\times\left(\frac{21}{20}\right)^2$$

$$\Rightarrow \quad 54000 = P\times\frac{21}{20}\times\frac{21}{20}$$

$$\therefore \quad P = \frac{54000\times 20\times 20}{21\times 21}$$

$$= \frac{21600000}{21\times 21} = 48979.59 = 48980 \text{ (approx.)}$$

Hence, the population in 2001 is 48980.

Depreciation

The number of years, a machine or an article can be effectively used is called its **life span**. After that it is sold as waste or scrap.

The relative decrease in the value of a machine or an article is called its depreciation and the decrease in the value per year (or unit of time) is called rate of depreciation.

(i) If V is the value of a machine at a certain time and r% per annum is the rate of depreciation, then V_n the depreciated value of machine after n yr, $V_n = V\left(1-\frac{r}{100}\right)^n$

(ii) If n yr ago, V_0 is the value of a machine and the rate of depreciation is r% per annum, then present value (V) is calculated by

$$V = V_0\left(1-\frac{r}{100}\right)^n$$

Example 8. The value of a residential flat constructed at a cost of ₹ 112000 is depreciating at the rate 15% per annum. What will be its value 3 yr after construction.

Sol. Here, present value = ₹ 112000, rate of depreciation = 15% per annum and n = 3 yr.

$$\therefore \quad \text{Value after 3 yr} = 112000\left(1-\frac{15}{100}\right)^3$$

$$= \left[112000\times\left(\frac{85}{100}\right)^3\right]$$

$$= \left(112000\times\frac{17}{20}\times\frac{17}{20}\times\frac{17}{20}\right)$$

$$= (14\times 17\times 17\times 17)$$

$$= ₹\, 68782$$

EXAM ORIENTED QUESTIONS

TYPE - 1 01 Mark

Multiple Choice Questions

Q.1 The compound interest on ₹ 100 at 10% per annum compounded annually for 2 yr is
(a) ₹ 21 (b) ₹ 20
(c) ₹ 24 (d) ₹ 19

Q.2 The sum of money that will amount to ₹ 15972 in 3 yr at 10% per annum compounded yearly is
(a) ₹ 11000
(b) ₹ 5000
(c) ₹ 15000
(d) ₹ 12000

Q.3 In how many years will ₹ 1000 amount to ₹ 1331 at 10% per annum compounded yearly?
(a) 3 yr (b) 2 yr
(c) 5 yr (d) 1 yr

Q.4 The time when ₹ 1200 will yield ₹ 252 as compound interest at 10% per year compounded annually is
(a) 3 yr (b) 2 yr
(c) 3.5 yr (d) 1 yr

Q.5 The compound interest on ₹ 10000 for 3 yr, if the rate of interest is 4% for the first year, 5% for the second year and 6% for the third year is
(a) ₹ 1575.2 (b) ₹ 1750
(c) ₹ 829 (d) ₹ 800

Q.6 A sum ₹ 25000 invested at 8% per annum compounded semi-annually amounts to ₹ 28121.60. Then, the time period of investment is
(a) 3 yr (b) 1.5 yr (c) 2 yr (d) 2.5 yr

Q.7 The population of a city in the year 2016 was 424000. If it increases 5% per year, then the population in 2018 is
(a) 467460 (b) 37540
(c) 55750 (d) 47600

Q.8 The population of a city is 20000. If the annual birth rate is 4% and annual death rate is 2%, then the population after 2 yr will be
(a) 21500
(b) 20808
(c) 27400
(d) 26551

Q.9 The population of a particular area A of a city is 5000. It increases by 10% in 1st year. It decreases by 20% in the 2nd year because of some reason. In the 3rd year, the population increases by 30%, then the population of area A at the end of 3 yr is
(a) 5545 (b) 4550
(c) 5720 (d) 6770

Q.10 The value of a residential flat constructed at a cost of ₹ 112000 is depreciating at the rate 15% per annum. Then, its value after 3 yr construction is
(a) ₹ 78522 (b) ₹ 97560
(c) ₹ 55270 (d) ₹ 68782

Answers

1. (a)	2. (d)	3. (a)	4. (b)	5. (a)
6. (b)	7. (a)	8. (b)	9. (c)	10. (d)

TYPE - 2 01 Mark

Assertion-Reason Type Questions

Q.1 Assertion (A) The compound interest on ₹ 2500 for 2 yr at 11% per annum is ₹ 580.25.
Reason (R) Compound interest varies with each year for the same principal amount and increases for successive years.
(a) A is true, R is false.
(b) A is false, R is true.
(c) Both A and R are true and R is the correct reason for A.
(d) Both A and R are true and R is incorrect reason for A.

Q.2 Assertion (A) The compound interest on ₹ 160000 for 2 yr at 10% per annum, compounded half yearly is ₹ 34481.
Reason (R) The compound interest compounded half yearly is $CI = P\left[\left(1+\frac{R}{200}\right)^{2n}-1\right]$.
(a) A is true, R is false.
(b) A is false, R is true.
(c) Both A and R are true and R is the correct reason for A.
(d) Both A and R are true and R is incorrect reason for A.

Q.3 **Assertion** (A) CI of two consecutive years are ₹ 530 and ₹ 556.50. If interest is compounded annually, then the rate of interest is 6%.

Reason (R) $A = P\left(1+\frac{R}{100}\right)^n$.

(a) A is true, R is false.
(b) A is false, R is true.
(c) Both A and R are true and R is the correct reason for A.
(d) Both A and R are true and R is incorrect reason for A.

Q.4 **Assertion** (A) The population of a city is 20000. If the annual growth rate is 2%, then the population of city after 5 yr is 22000.

Reason (R) If P is the present population of a city and r% per annum is the growth rate, then population after n yr $= P\left(1+\frac{r}{100}\right)^n$.

(a) A is true, R is false.
(b) A is false, R is true.
(c) Both A and R are true and R is the correct reason for A.
(d) Both A and R are true and R is incorrect reason for A.

Answers

1. (d) **2.** (c) **3.** (b) **4.** (b)

TYPE - 3 01 Mark

Statement Based Questions

Q.1 **Statement I** A certain sum of money is borrowed at 5% at compound interest. After three years, it amounts to ₹ 10000. The sum borrowed is ₹ 8500.

Statement II Simple interest and compound interest are equal for the first conversion period on the same sum and at the same rate.

Which of the following is valid?

(a) Both the Statements are true.
(b) Both the Statements are false.
(c) Statement I is true and Statement II is false.
(d) Statement I is false and Statement II is true.

Q.2 **Statement I** If the number of conversion periods ≥ 2, then the compound interest is greater than the simple interest.

Statement II A sum is invested at compound interest compounded yearly. If the interests for successive years are ₹ 4500 and ₹ 4950, then rate of interest is 10%.

(a) Both the Statements are true.
(b) Both the Statements are false.
(c) Statement I is true and Statement II is false.
(d) Statement I is false and Statement II is true.

Q.3 **Statement I** The present population of a town is 140000. If it increases 5% annually, then the population after 2 yr will be 154350.

Statement II The value of a car (V_0) depreciates by 12.5% every year, then the value of the car after 3 yr will be $V_0\left(\frac{8}{7}\right)^3$.

(a) Both the Statements are true.
(b) Both the Statements are false.
(c) Statement I is true and Statement II is false.
(d) Statement I is false and Statement II is true.

Q.4 **Statement I** If the present population of a city is 1.331 times the population of that city, 3 yr ago. Then, the rate of growth is 10%.

Statement II The difference of CI of two consecutive years is equal to simple interest of preceding years interest.

Which of the following is valid?

(a) Both the Statements are true.
(b) Both the Statements are false.
(c) Statement I is true and Statement II is false.
(d) Statement I is false and Statement II is true.

Answers

1. (d) **2.** (a) **3.** (c) **4.** (a)

TYPE - 4 03 Marks

Short Answer Type Questions

Q.1 ₹ 15000 is lent at 6% compound interest per year for 2 yr. Find the final amount and the compound interest.

Q.2 Calculate the interest on ₹ 6000 in 3 yr at 5% per annum compounded annually.

Q.3 Find the amount when ₹ 10000 is invested for $2\frac{1}{2}$ yr at 10% interest compounded yearly.

Q.4 At what rate per annum compound interest, will ₹ 5000 amount to ₹ 5832 in 2 yr?

Q.5 Calculate the compound interest and amount for 2 yr at 10% per annum on ₹ 4700.

Q.6 The difference between simple interest and compound interest for 2 yr at 5% per annum is ₹ 20. Find the principal amount.

Q.7 Compound interest on a certain sum of money at 5% per annum for 2 yr is ₹ 246. Calculate the simple interest on the same sum for 3 yr at 6% per annum.

Q.8 The difference between CI and SI on ₹ 6000 for 2 yr is ₹ 15 at the same rate of interest per year. Find the rate of interest.

Q.9 Determine the amount and the compound interest on ₹ 20000 in 2 yr when the rate of interest for the successive years is 7% and 8% per annum, respectively.

Q.10 On a certain sum, the compound interest for 2 yr is ₹ 2172. If the rates of interest for successive years are 6% and 8% per annum, then find the sum.

Q.11 Prabsimran won a lottery of ₹ 50000, 30% was paid as income tax. She deposited the balance in a bank paying 10% per annum, interest compounded bi-annually. What sum will she get after 3 yr?

Q.12 Find the compound interest on ₹ 25000 for 2 yr at 10% per annum interest being compounded semi-annually.

Q.13 In a laboratory, the count of bacteria in a certain experiment was increasing at the rate of 2.5% per hour. Find the bacteria at the end of 2 h, if the count was initially 506000.

Q.14 The population of a town increases 4% annually but it decreases by emigration annually to the extent of 1%. Find the increase percent in 3 yr.

Q.15 Carbon decays at a constant rate in such a way that it reduces to 50% in 5568 yr. Find the age of an old wooden piece in which the carbon is only 12.5% of the original.

Answers

1. ₹ 1854 2. ₹ 945.75 3. ₹ 12705 4. 8%
5. ₹ 987 6. ₹ 8000 7. ₹ 432 8. 5%
9. amount = ₹ 23112, compound interest = ₹ 3112
10. ₹ 15000 11. ₹ 46903.35 12. ₹ 5387.65 13. 531616
14. 9.2727% 15. 16704 yr

TYPE - 5 4/5 Marks

Long Answer Type Questions

Q.1 Find the compound interest to the nearest rupee on ₹ 7500 for 2 yr 4 months at 12% per annum compounded annually.

Q.2 Calculate the amount and the compound interest on ₹ 16000 for 3 yr when the rate of interest on successive years are 10%, 14% and 15%, respectively.

Q.3 Kriti invests ₹ 50000 for 2 yr at certain rate of interest, compound annually. At the end of one year, this sum amounts to ₹ 54500. Find

(i) the rate of interest per annum.
(ii) the amount due to the end of second year.
(iii) the compound interest earned in 2 yr.

Q.4 Calculate the amount and the compound interest on ₹ 6000 at 20% per annum for $1\frac{1}{2}$ yr, when interest is compounded half-yearly.

Q.5 A man borrows ₹ 5000 at 12% compound interest payable every six months. He pays ₹ 1800 at the end of every six months. Calculate the third payment, he has to make at the end of 18 months in order to clear the entire loan.

Q.6 A sum of money is lent at 10% per annum compound interest. If the interest for the second year exceeds that for the first year by ₹ 104, then find the sum of money.

Q.7 Mohan borrowed ₹ 15000 at some rate of interest compounded annually. After one year, he paid back ₹ 5000. If compound interest for the second year is ₹ 1150, then find the rate of interest charged and also find the amount of debt at the end of the second year.

Q.8 A man borrowed a sum of money and agrees to pay it off by paying ₹ 43200 at the end of the first year and ₹ 34992 at the end of the second year. If the rate of compound interest is 8% per annum, then find the sum borrowed.

Q.9 A sum of money at compound interest amounts in two years to ₹ 2809 and in three years to ₹ 2977.54. Find the rate of interest and the original sum.

Q.10 ₹ 39527 is divided between Seeta and Geeta, both aged 28 yr and 26 yr, respectively. Their money is invested at 5% per annum compound interest in such a way that both receive equal money at the age of 30 yr. Find the share of each.

Q.11 The ages of Ram and Ashok are 20 yr and 22 yr, respectively. In what ratio must they invest money at 10% per annum compounded yearly so that both get the same sum on attaining the age of 30 yr?

Q.12 On a certain sum of money, the difference between the compound interest for a year, payable half-yearly, and the simple interest for a year is ₹ 180. Find the sum lent out, if the rate of interest in both the cases is 10%.

Q.13 Calculate the compound interest on ₹ 3500. For first 2 yr at 8% per annum, interest paid half yearly, 12% per annum for the third year interest compounded annually and 15% per annum for the fourth year interest compounded annually. Find the earning at the end of 4 yr.

Q.14 A certain sum of amounts is lent at CI. Interest for first, second and third years are ₹ 1750, ₹ 2275 and ₹ 2550, respectively. Find the rate of interest for the
(i) second year (ii) third year.

Answers

1. ₹ 2284 (to nearest ruppee) 2. amount = ₹ 23073.6, compound interest = ₹ 7073.6 3. (i) 9% (ii) ₹ 59405 (iii) ₹ 9405
4. amount = ₹ 7986, compound interest = ₹ 1986 5. ₹ 2024.60 6. ₹ 10400 7. 10%, 12650 8. ₹ 70000 9. 6%, ₹ 2500
10. Seeta's share = ₹ 20727, Geeta' share = ₹ 18800 11. 100 : 121 12. ₹ 72000 13. ₹ 1773.72 14. (i) 30% (ii) 12.09%

TYPE - 6

Case Based Questions

Q.1 A sum of ₹ 9800 is invested for 3 yr at 10% per annum at compound interest.
(i) What is the sum due at the end of first year?
(ii) What is the sum due at the end of second year?
(iii) Find the difference between the answers in (ii) and (i) and find the interest on this sum (difference) for one year.
(iv) Write down the compound interest for the third year. **(4 M)**

Q.2 The population of a place increased to 54000 in 2003 at a rate of 5% per annum.
(i) Find the population in 2001.
(ii) What would be its population in 2005? **(4 M)**

Q.3 The cost of a washing machine depreciates by ₹ 720 during the second year and by ₹ 648 during the third year. Calculate
(i) the rate of depreciation per annum.
(ii) the original cost of the machine.
(iii) the value of the machine at the end of third year. **(3 M)**

Answers

1. (i) ₹ 10780 (ii) ₹ 11858 (iii) ₹ 107.80 (iv) ₹ 1185.80
2. (i) 48980 (ii) 59535
3. (i) 10% (ii) ₹ 8000 (iii) ₹ 5832

EXPLANATIONS

Multiple Choice Questions

1. (a) We have, $P = 100$, $R = 10\%$ and $n = 2$ yr

Now, $$A = P\left(1+\frac{R}{100}\right)^n$$

$$\Rightarrow A = 100\left(1+\frac{10}{100}\right)^2$$

$$\Rightarrow A = 100\left(\frac{110}{100}\right)^2$$

$$\Rightarrow A = 100 \times \frac{110}{100} \times \frac{110}{100}$$

$$\Rightarrow A = ₹ 121$$

Now, $\text{CI} = A - P = 121 - 100 = ₹ 21$

Hence, the compound interest is ₹ 21.

2. (d) Let P (principal) be the required money.

Given, amount $(A) = ₹ 15972$, rate of interest $(R) = 10\%$ and time $(n) = 3$ yr

$$\because A = P\left(1+\frac{R}{100}\right)^n$$

$$\therefore 15972 = P\left(1+\frac{10}{100}\right)^3$$

$$\Rightarrow 15972 = P\left(\frac{11}{10}\right)^3$$

$$\Rightarrow 15972 = P \times \frac{11}{10} \times \frac{11}{10} \times \frac{11}{10}$$

$$\therefore P = \frac{15972 \times 10 \times 10 \times 10}{11 \times 11 \times 11}$$

$$= ₹ (12 \times 1000)$$

$$= ₹ 12000$$

3. (a) We have, $A = 1331$, $P = 1000$ and $R = 10\%$

Now, we know that

$$A = P\left(1+\frac{R}{100}\right)^n$$

On substituting the values, we get

$$1331 = 1000\left(1+\frac{10}{100}\right)^n$$

$$\Rightarrow \quad \frac{1331}{1000} = \left(\frac{110}{100}\right)^n \Rightarrow \left(\frac{11}{10}\right)^3 = \left(\frac{11}{10}\right)^n$$

On equating the powers of both sides, we get

$$n = 3$$

Hence, the required time is 3 yr.

4. (b) Let n yr be the required time period.

Given, principal (P) = ₹ 1200, CI = ₹ 252 and $R = 10\%$

$$\because \quad CI = P\left[\left(1+\frac{R}{100}\right)^n - 1\right]$$

$$\Rightarrow \quad 252 = 1200\left[\left(1+\frac{10}{100}\right)^n - 1\right]$$

$$\Rightarrow \quad \frac{252}{1200} = \left(\frac{11}{10}\right)^n - 1$$

$$\Rightarrow \quad \left(\frac{11}{10}\right)^n = \frac{252}{1200} + 1 = \frac{1452}{1200}$$

$$\Rightarrow \quad \left(\frac{11}{10}\right)^n = \frac{121}{100} = \left(\frac{11}{10}\right)^2 \Rightarrow n = 2 \text{ yr}$$

Hence, the required time is 2 yr.

5. (a) Here, $P = 10000$, $R_1 = 4\%$, $R_2 = 5\%$ and $R_3 = 6\%$.

$\therefore$ Compound interest,

$$CI = P\left[\left(1+\frac{R_1}{100}\right)\left(1+\frac{R_2}{100}\right)\left(1+\frac{R_3}{100}\right) - 1\right]$$

$$= 10000\left[\left(1+\frac{4}{100}\right)\left(1+\frac{5}{100}\right)\left(1+\frac{6}{100}\right) - 1\right]$$

$$= 10000\left[\left(1+\frac{1}{25}\right)\left(1+\frac{1}{20}\right)\left(1+\frac{3}{50}\right) - 1\right]$$

$$= 10000\left[\left(\frac{26}{25}\right)\left(\frac{21}{20}\right)\left(\frac{53}{50}\right) - 1\right]$$

$$= 10000\,[1.15752 - 1]$$

$$= 10000\,(0.15752) = ₹\ 1575.2$$

6. (b) Let the number of conversion periods be n.

We know that when compound interest is compounded semi-annually, then

$$A = P\left(1+\frac{R}{200}\right)^{2n}$$

$$\Rightarrow \quad 28121.60 = 25000\left(1+\frac{8}{200}\right)^{2n}$$

$$\Rightarrow \quad \frac{28121.60}{25000} = \left(1+\frac{1}{25}\right)^{2n}$$

$$\Rightarrow \quad \frac{2812160}{100 \times 25000} = \left(\frac{26}{25}\right)^{2n}$$

$$\Rightarrow \quad \left(\frac{17576}{15625}\right) = \left(\frac{26}{25}\right)^{2n}$$

$$\Rightarrow \quad \left(\frac{26}{25}\right)^3 = \left(\frac{26}{25}\right)^{2n} \Rightarrow 2n = 3$$

$$\Rightarrow \quad n = \frac{3}{2} = 1.5 \text{ yr}$$

Hence, the time period of investment is 1.5 yr.

7. (a) Here, $P_0 = 424000$,

$r = 5\%$ per annum

and $n = 2$ yr

$\therefore$ Population after 2 yr

$$= 424000\left(1+\frac{5}{100}\right)^2$$

$$= 424000\left(\frac{21}{20}\right)^2$$

$$\left[\because \text{ population after } n \text{ yr} = P_0\left(1+\frac{r}{100}\right)^n\right]$$

$$= 424000 \times \frac{21}{20} \times \frac{21}{20} = 467460$$

8. (b) We have, $P_0 = 20000$, $r = (4-2)\% = 2\%$ and $n = 2$ yr

Then, population after two years $= P_0\left(1+\frac{r}{100}\right)^n$

$$= 20000\left(1+\frac{2}{100}\right)^2$$

$$= 20000\left(\frac{102}{100}\right)^2$$

$$= 20000 \times \frac{102}{100} \times \frac{102}{100}$$

$$= 2 \times 102 \times 102$$

$$= 20808$$

Hence, the population after 2 yr will be 20808.

9. (c) Given that $P = 5000$, $R_1 = 10\%$,

$R_2 = -20\%$ (decrease) and $R_3 = 30\%$

$\therefore$ Population at the end of 3rd year

$$= P\left(1+\frac{R_1}{100}\right)\left(1+\frac{R_2}{100}\right)\left(1+\frac{R_3}{100}\right)$$

$$= 5000\left(1+\frac{10}{100}\right)\left(1-\frac{20}{100}\right)\left(1+\frac{30}{100}\right)$$

$$= 5000 \times \frac{11}{10} \times \frac{4}{5} \times \frac{13}{10}$$

$$= 10 \times 11 \times 4 \times 13 = 5720$$

10. (d) Here, present value = ₹ 112000,
rate of depreciation = 15% per annum and $n = 3$ yr.

$\therefore$ Value after 3 yr $= 112000\left(1-\dfrac{15}{100}\right)^3$

$$\left[\because V = V_0\left(1-\frac{r}{100}\right)^n\right]$$

$$= \left[112000 \times \left(\frac{85}{100}\right)^3\right]$$

$$= \left(112000 \times \frac{17}{20} \times \frac{17}{20} \times \frac{17}{20}\right)$$

$$= (14 \times 17 \times 17 \times 17) = ₹\,68782$$

Assertion-Reason Type Questions

1. (d) **Assertion** Given, $P = ₹\,2500$, $R = 11\%$, $T = 2$ yr

Then, amount $= P\left(1+\dfrac{R}{100}\right)^n = 2500\left(1+\dfrac{11}{100}\right)^2$

$$= 2500\left(\frac{111}{100}\right)^2 = \frac{111 \times 111 \times 25}{100}$$

$$= ₹\,3080.25$$

$\therefore$ Compound interest = Final amount – Original amount

$$= ₹\,(3080.25 - 2500)$$

$$= ₹\,580.25$$

Hence, A and R are true and R is incorrect reason for A.

2. (c) **Assertion** We have, $P = ₹\,160000$, $n = 2$ yr and $R = 10\%$

Then, $\text{CI} = P\left[\left(1+\dfrac{R}{200}\right)^{2n} - 1\right]$

$$= 160000\left[\left(1+\frac{10}{200}\right)^{2\times 2} - 1\right]$$

$$= 160000\left[\left(\frac{210}{200}\right)^4 - 1\right]$$

$$= 160000\left[\left(\frac{21}{20}\right)^4 - 1\right]$$

$$= 160000\left[\frac{194481}{160000} - 1\right]$$

$$= 160000\left[\frac{194481 - 160000}{160000}\right]$$

$$= 160000 \times \frac{34481}{160000} = ₹\,34481$$

Hence, the compound interest is ₹ 34481.

So, both A and R are true and R is the correct reason for A.

3. (b) Given, compound interest of two consecutive years are ₹ 530 and ₹ 556.5.

We know that

Rate of interest

$$= \frac{\text{Difference in interest of two consecutive period} \times 100\%}{\text{CI of preceding period} \times \text{Time}}$$

$$= \frac{556.5 - 530}{530} \times 100\% = \frac{26.5}{530} \times 100 = 5\%$$

Hence, A is false, R is true.

4. (b) Given, $P = 20000$, $r = 2\%$ and $n = 5$ yr

Population after 5 yr $= P\left(1+\dfrac{r}{100}\right)^n = 20000 \times \left(1+\dfrac{2}{100}\right)^5$

$$= 20000 \times \left(\frac{51}{50}\right)^5$$

$$= 22081$$

Hence, A is false, R is true.

Statement Based Questions

1. (d) Let the sum be P.

Given, $R = 5\%$, $T = 3$ yr and $A = ₹\,10000$

$\therefore \quad A = P\left(1+\dfrac{R}{100}\right)^T$

$\Rightarrow \quad 10000 = P\left(1+\dfrac{5}{100}\right)^3$

$\Rightarrow \quad 10000 = P\left(\dfrac{21}{20}\right)^3$

$\Rightarrow \quad P = \dfrac{10000 \times 8000}{9261} \Rightarrow P = ₹\,8638.37$

Hence, Statement I is false and Statement II is true.

2. (a) **Statement I** In compound interest, the interest is always calculated on the compounded principal whereas in simple interest, the interest is calculated on the initial principal, so for conversion periods ≥ 2, compound interest will be greater than simple interest.

Hence, Statement I is true.

Statement II We know that

Rate of interest

$$= \left[\frac{\text{Difference in the interest of two successive years}}{\text{CI of preceding year} \times \text{Time}}\right] \times 100\%$$

$$= \frac{4950 - 4500}{4500 \times 1} \times 100\%$$

$$= \frac{450}{4500} \times 100\% = 10\%$$

Hence, Statement II is true.

3. (c) **Statement I** We have,

$P = 140000$, $r = 5\%$ and $n = 2$ yr

As we know, population after n years $= P\left(1+\frac{r}{100}\right)^n$

$$= 140000\left(1+\frac{5}{100}\right)^2 = 140000\left(\frac{105}{100}\right)^2$$

$$= 140000 \times \frac{105}{100} \times \frac{105}{100}$$

$$= 14 \times 105 \times 105 = 154350$$

Hence, Statement I is true.

Statement II Given, the present value of the car is V_0.

Now, value of the car after 3 yr

$$= V_0\left(1-\frac{12.5}{100}\right)^3 \quad \left[\because V = V_0\left(1-\frac{r}{100}\right)^n\right]$$

$$= V_0 \times \left(1-\frac{1}{8}\right)^3 = V_0 \times \left(\frac{7}{8}\right)^3$$

Hence, Statement II is false.

4. (a) Let 3 yr ago population of city be P and rate of growth be $R\%$.

$\therefore$ Present population of city $= 1.331P$

Time = 3 yr

Present population of city $= P\left(1+\frac{R}{100}\right)^T$

$$\Rightarrow \quad 1.331P = P\left(1+\frac{R}{100}\right)^3$$

$$\Rightarrow \quad (1.331)^{\frac{1}{3}} = \left(1+\frac{R}{100}\right)$$

$$\Rightarrow \quad \frac{R}{100} = 1.1 - 1 = 0.1$$

$$\Rightarrow \quad R = 10\%$$

Hence, both the Statements are true.

Short Answer Type Questions

1. For the first year,

$P = ₹\,15000$, $R = 6\,\%$ and $T = 1$ yr

$$\therefore \text{Simple interest} = \frac{P \times R \times T}{100} = \frac{15000 \times 6 \times 1}{100} = ₹\,900$$

Amount after first year = ₹ (15000 + 900) = ₹ 15900

Now, principal for the second year = ₹ 15900

Now, for the second year,

$P = ₹\,15900$, $R = 6\,\%$ and $T = 1$ yr

$$\therefore \text{Simple interest} = \frac{P \times R \times T}{100} = \frac{15900 \times 6 \times 1}{100} = ₹\,954$$

Amount after second year = ₹ (15900 + 954)

= ₹ 16854

$\therefore$ Compound interest = Final amount − Original amount

= ₹ (16854 − 15000) = ₹ 1854

2. For the first year, $P = ₹\,6000$, $R = 5\%$ and $T = 1$ yr

$$\therefore \quad \text{Simple interest} = \frac{P \times R \times T}{100} = \frac{6000 \times 5 \times 1}{100} = ₹\,300$$

Amount after first year = ₹ (6000 + 300) = ₹ 6300

Now, for the second year,

$P = ₹\,6300$, $R = 5\%$ and $T = 1$ yr

$$\therefore \quad \text{Simple interest} = \frac{P \times R \times T}{100} = \frac{6300 \times 5 \times 1}{100} = ₹\,315$$

Amount after second year = ₹ (6300 + 315) = ₹ 6615

Now, for the third year,

$P = ₹\,6615$, $R = 5\%$ and $T = 1$ yr

$$\therefore \quad \text{Simple interest} = \frac{P \times R \times T}{100} = \frac{6615 \times 5 \times 1}{100}$$

$$= ₹\,330.75$$

Hence, total interest is ₹ (300 + 315 + 330.75)

= ₹ 945.75

3. First find the amount in 2 yr.

$$\text{Amount in 2 yr} = ₹\,10000\left(1+\frac{10}{100}\right)^2 = ₹\,12100$$

$$\left[\because A = P\left(1+\frac{R}{100}\right)^n\right]$$

After 2 yr, ₹ 12100 is the principal for the remaining half-year.

So, interest for next half-year

$$= \frac{P \times R \times T}{100} = ₹\left(\frac{12100 \times 10 \times 1/2}{100}\right) = ₹\,605$$

Hence, the amount in $2\frac{1}{2}$ yr = ₹ (12100 + 605)

= ₹ 12705

4. Let the rate of interest be $R\%$ per annum.

Given, principal (P) = ₹ 5000, amount (A) = ₹ 5832 and time (n) = 2 yr.

Now, $A = P\left(1+\frac{R}{100}\right)^n$

$$\therefore \quad 5832 = 5000\left(1+\frac{R}{100}\right)^2$$

$$\Rightarrow \quad \frac{5832}{5000} = \left(1+\frac{R}{100}\right)^2 \Rightarrow \frac{729}{625} = \left(1+\frac{R}{100}\right)^2$$

$$\Rightarrow \quad \left(\frac{27}{25}\right)^2 = \left(1+\frac{R}{100}\right)^2$$

$$\Rightarrow \quad \frac{27}{25} = 1 + \frac{R}{100} \quad \text{[taking square root]}$$

$$\Rightarrow \quad \frac{R}{100} = \frac{27}{25} - 1 \Rightarrow \frac{R}{100} = \frac{27-25}{25}$$

$$\Rightarrow \quad \frac{R}{100} = \frac{2}{25} \Rightarrow R = 8$$

Hence, the rate of interest is 8%.

5. Given, rate of interest, $R = 10\%$, $P = ₹\ 4700$ and number of years, $n = 2$ yr.

Now, amount $(A) = P\left(1+\frac{R}{100}\right)^n$

$$= 4700\left(1+\frac{10}{100}\right)^2$$

$$= 4700\left(1+\frac{1}{10}\right)^2$$

$$= 4700\left(\frac{11}{10}\right)^2$$

$$= \frac{4700 \times 121}{100} = 47 \times 121 = ₹\ 5687$$

$\therefore$ Compound interest, CI $= A - P = ₹\ (5687 - 4700)$
$= ₹\ 987$

6. Given, CI $-$ SI $= ₹\ 20$, $n = 2$ yr and $R = 5\%$.

Clearly, $\text{CI} = P\left[\left(1+\frac{R}{100}\right)^n - 1\right] = P\left[\left(1+\frac{5}{100}\right)^2 - 1\right]$

$$= P\left[\left(\frac{21}{20}\right)^2 - 1\right] = P\left(\frac{441}{400} - 1\right)$$

$$\text{CI} = P \times \frac{41}{400} \quad \ldots\text{(i)}$$

and $\text{SI} = \frac{P \times R \times T}{100} = \frac{P \times 5 \times 2}{100} = \frac{P}{10} \quad \ldots\text{(ii)}$

Now, CI $-$ SI $= 20 \Rightarrow \frac{41P}{400} - \frac{P}{10} = 20$

[from Eqs. (i) and (ii)]

$\Rightarrow \frac{P}{400} = 20$

$\Rightarrow P = ₹\ 8000$

Hence, the principal amount is ₹ 8000.

7. We have, $R = 5\%$, $n = 2$ yr, CI $= ₹\ 246$

We know that

$$\text{CI} = P\left[\left(1+\frac{R}{100}\right)^n - 1\right]$$

$\Rightarrow 246 = P\left[\left(1+\frac{5}{100}\right)^2 - 1\right]$

$\Rightarrow 246 = P\left[\left(\frac{105}{100}\right)^2 - 1\right]$

$\Rightarrow 246 = P\left[\frac{11025}{10000} - 1\right] \Rightarrow 246 = P\left[\frac{1025}{10000}\right]$

$\Rightarrow 246 = P \times \frac{41}{400}$

$\Rightarrow P = \frac{246 \times 400}{41} = ₹\ 2400$

Now, Simple interest (SI) $= \frac{P \times R \times T}{100}$

Here, $P = 2400$, $R = 6\%$, $T = 3$ yr

$\therefore \text{SI} = \frac{2400 \times 6 \times 3}{100} = ₹\ 432$

Hence, the simple interest is ₹ 432.

8. Let the rate of interest be $R\%$ per annum.
Given, principal $(P) = ₹\,6000$, time $(n) = 2$ yr and CI $-$ SI $= ₹15$

Clearly, $\text{CI} = P\left[\left(1+\frac{R}{100}\right)^n - 1\right] = 6000\left[\left(1+\frac{R}{100}\right)^2 - 1\right]$

$$= 6000\left(1+\frac{R}{100}\right)^2 - 6000 \quad \ldots\text{(i)}$$

and $\text{SI} = \frac{P \times R \times T}{100} = \frac{6000 \times R \times 2}{100} \quad \ldots\text{(ii)}$

$\because$ CI $-$ SI $= 15$

$\therefore 6000\left(1+\frac{R}{100}\right)^2 - 6000 - \frac{6000 \times R \times 2}{100} = 15$

[from Eqs. (i) and (ii)]

$\Rightarrow 6000\left[1+\frac{R^2}{10000}+\frac{2R}{100} - 1 - \frac{2R}{100}\right] = 15$

$[\because (a+b)^2 = a^2 + b^2 + 2ab]$

$\Rightarrow 6000\left[\frac{R^2}{10000}\right] = 15$

$\Rightarrow \frac{R^2}{10} = \frac{15}{6}$

$\Rightarrow R^2 = \frac{15 \times 10}{6} = 25$

$\Rightarrow R = 5$

Hence, the rate of interest is 5%.

9. We have, $P = ₹\ 20000$, $R_1 = 7\%$, $R_2 = 8\%$ and $n = 2$ yr

Now, we know that

$A = P\left(1+\frac{R_1}{100}\right)\left(1+\frac{R_2}{100}\right)$, where A is amount

On substituting the values, we get

$$A = 20000\left(1+\frac{7}{100}\right)\left(1+\frac{8}{100}\right)$$

$$= 20000\left(\frac{107}{100}\right)\left(\frac{108}{100}\right)$$

$$= 2 \times 107 \times 108$$

$$= ₹\ 23112$$

Now, compound interest (CI) $= A - P$

$\Rightarrow$ CI $= 23112 - 20000 = ₹\ 3112$

Hence, the amount is ₹ 23112 and the compound interest is ₹ 3112.

10. Let the sum be P.

We have, $R_1 = 6\%$, $R_2 = 8\%$ and CI = ₹ 2172

Now, we know that

$$A = P\left(1+\frac{R_1}{100}\right)\left(1+\frac{R_2}{100}\right)$$

$$= P\left(1+\frac{6}{100}\right)\left(1+\frac{8}{100}\right) = P\left(\frac{106}{100}\right)\left(\frac{108}{100}\right)$$

$$= P\left(\frac{53}{50}\right)\left(\frac{27}{25}\right) = \frac{1431}{1250}P$$

$\because$ CI $= A - P$

$\therefore$ $2172 = \frac{1431}{1250}P - P$

$\Rightarrow$ $2172 = \frac{181P}{1250}$

$\Rightarrow$ $P = \frac{1250 \times 2172}{181} \Rightarrow P = ₹\ 15000$

Hence, the sum is ₹ 15000.

11. Income tax paid $= ₹\left(\frac{30}{100} \times 50000\right) = ₹\ 15000$

Now, the remaining amount = 50000 – 15000

= ₹ 35000

$\because$ She deposited remaining amount in the bank.

$\therefore$ $P = ₹\ 35000$

Now, $A = 35000\left(1+\frac{10}{200}\right)^{2\times 3}$ $\left[\because A = P\left(1+\frac{R}{2\times 100}\right)^{2T}\right]$

$$= 35000\left(\frac{21}{20}\right)^6$$

$$= 35000 \times \frac{21}{20} \times \frac{21}{20} \times \frac{21}{20} \times \frac{21}{20} \times \frac{21}{20} \times \frac{21}{20}$$

$$= \frac{35 \times 9261 \times 9261}{64000} = ₹\ 46903.35$$

Hence, she will get ₹ 46903.35 after 3 yr.

12. Here, $P = ₹\ 25000$, $R = 10\%$ and $T = 2$ yr

Since, the interest is compounded semi-annually.

$\therefore$ $$A = P\left(1+\frac{R}{2\times 100}\right)^{2T}$$

$$= 25000\left(1+\frac{10}{2\times 100}\right)^4$$

$$= 25000\left(1+\frac{1}{20}\right)^4 = 25000\left(\frac{21}{20}\right)^4$$

$$= 25000 \times \frac{21}{20} \times \frac{21}{20} \times \frac{21}{20} \times \frac{21}{20}$$

$$= ₹\ 30387.65$$

Hence, CI $= A - P = ₹\ (30387.65 - 25000)$

$= ₹5387.65$

13. Here, initial count of bacteria, $P = 506000$

and time, $n = 2$ h

Rate of increasing bacteria, $R = 2.5\%$ per hour

$= \frac{5}{2}\%$ per hour

Bacteria count after 2 h, $A = P\left(1+\frac{R}{100}\right)^n$

$$= 506000\left(1+\frac{5}{2\times 100}\right)^2$$

$$= 506000\left(1+\frac{1}{40}\right)^2 = 506000\left(\frac{41}{40}\right)^2$$

$$= 506000 \times \frac{41}{40} \times \frac{41}{40} = \frac{5060 \times 41 \times 41}{4 \times 4}$$

$$= \frac{1265 \times 41 \times 41}{4} = \frac{2126465}{4}$$

$= 531616.25 = 531616$ (approx.)

Hence, the number of bacteria count at the end of 2 h is 531616.

14. According to the question,

Net annual growth rate

= Rate of increases – Rate of decreases

= (4 – 1)% = 3%

Let the population of town be $P_0 = 100$.

Now, the population after 3 yr $= P_0\left(1+\frac{R}{100}\right)^n$

$$= 100\left(1+\frac{3}{100}\right)^3 \quad [\because P_0 = 100, R = 3 \text{ and } n = 3]$$

$$= 100\left(\frac{103}{100}\right)^3 = 100 \times \frac{103}{100} \times \frac{103}{100} \times \frac{103}{100}$$

$$= \frac{1092727}{10000} = 109.2727$$

Now, % increase = 109.2727 – 100 = 9.2727%

Hence, the increase percent in 3 yr is 9.2727%.

15. Let rate of decay be R % per annum and the age of wooden piece be n years.

$\therefore$ $\left(1-\frac{R}{100}\right)^{5568} = 50\% = \frac{50}{100} = \frac{1}{2}$ $\left[\because A = P\left(1+\frac{R}{100}\right)^n\right]$

$\Rightarrow$ $1-\frac{R}{100} = \left(\frac{1}{2}\right)^{\frac{1}{5568}}$ ...(i)

and $\left(1-\frac{R}{100}\right)^n = \frac{12.5}{100} = \frac{1}{8}$

$\Rightarrow$ $1-\frac{R}{100} = \left(\frac{1}{2}\right)^{\frac{3}{n}}$ ...(ii)

On comparing Eqs. (i) and (ii), we get

$$\frac{1}{5568} = \frac{3}{n}$$

$\Rightarrow \quad n = 3 \times 5568$

$\Rightarrow \quad n = 16704$ yr

Hence, the age of wooden piece is 16704 yr.

Long Answer Type Questions

1. For the first year,

$P = ₹\,7500,\ R = 12\%$ and $T = 1$ yr

$\therefore$ Simple interest $= \dfrac{P \times R \times T}{100}$

$= ₹\left(\dfrac{7500 \times 12 \times 1}{100}\right) = ₹\,900$

Amount after first year = ₹ (7500 + 900) = ₹ 8400

Now, for the second year,

$P = ₹\,8400,\ R = 12\%$ and $T = 1$ yr

$\therefore$ Simple interest $= \dfrac{P \times R \times T}{100}$

$= ₹\left(\dfrac{8400 \times 12 \times 1}{100}\right) = ₹\,1008$

Amount after second year = ₹ (8400 + 1008) = ₹ 9408

Now, for the next 4 months,

$P = ₹\,9408,\ R = 12\%$ and $T = \dfrac{4}{12} = \dfrac{1}{3}$ yr

$\therefore$ Simple interest $= \dfrac{P \times R \times T}{100} = ₹\left(\dfrac{9408 \times 12 \times 1/3}{100}\right)$

$= ₹\,376.32$

Hence, the compound interest for 2 yr 4 months

= ₹ (900 + 1008 + 376.32) = ₹ 2284.32

= ₹ 2284 (to nearest rupee)

2. For the first year,

$P = ₹\,16000,\ R = 10\%$ and $T = 1$ yr

$\therefore$ Simple interest $= \dfrac{P \times R \times T}{100}$

$= ₹\left(\dfrac{16000 \times 10 \times 1}{100}\right)$

$= ₹1600$

Amount after first year = ₹ (16000 + 1600)

= ₹ 17600

Now, for the second year,

$P = ₹\,17600,\ R = 14\%$ and $T = 1$ yr

$\therefore$ Simple interest $= \dfrac{P \times R \times T}{100}$

$= ₹\left(\dfrac{17600 \times 14 \times 1}{100}\right)$

$= ₹\,2464$

Amount after second year = ₹ (17600 + 2464)

= ₹ 20064

Now, for the third year,

$P = ₹\,20064,\ R = 15\%$ and $T = 1$ yr

$\therefore$ Simple interest $= \dfrac{P \times R \times T}{100}$

$= ₹\left(\dfrac{20064 \times 15 \times 1}{100}\right)$

$= ₹3009.6$

Amount after third year = ₹ (20064 + 3009.6)

= ₹ 23073.6

Hence, compound interest is ₹ (23073.6 − 16000)

= ₹ 7073.6

3. Let the rate of interest be $R\%$ per annum.

(i) For the first year,

principal (P) = ₹ 50000, rate = $R\%$, $T = 1$ yr

and amount (A) = ₹ 54500

$\because$ Interest for the first year = Final amount − Original amount

= ₹ (54500 − 50000)

= ₹ 4500

$\therefore$ Simple interest $= \dfrac{P \times R \times T}{100} = ₹\left(\dfrac{50000 \times R \times 1}{100}\right)$

$= ₹(500R)$

$\Rightarrow \quad 4500 = 500R$

$\Rightarrow \quad R = 9$

$\therefore$ Rate of interest is 9% per annum.

(ii) Now, for the second year,

$P = ₹\,54500,\ R = 9\%$ and $T = 1$ yr

$\therefore$ Simple interest $= \dfrac{P \times R \times T}{100} = ₹\left(\dfrac{54500 \times 9 \times 1}{100}\right)$

= ₹ 4905

Amount after second year = ₹(54500 + 4905)

= ₹ 59405

(iii) Compound interest earned in 2 yr

= ₹ (59405 − 50000)

= ₹ 9405

4. For the first half-year,

$P = ₹\,6000,\ R = 20\%$ and $T = 1/2$ yr

$\therefore$ Simple interest $= \dfrac{P \times R \times T}{100}$

$= ₹\left(\dfrac{6000 \times 20 \times \frac{1}{2}}{100}\right) = ₹600$

Amount after first half-year = ₹(6000 + 600) = ₹ 6600

Now, for the second half-year,

$P = ₹\,6600$, $R = 20\%$ and $T = 1/2$ yr

$\therefore$ Simple interest $= \dfrac{P \times R \times T}{100} = ₹\left(\dfrac{6600 \times 20 \times \frac{1}{2}}{100}\right)$

$= ₹660$

Amount after second half-year $= ₹(6600 + 660) = ₹\,7260$

For the third half-year,

$P = ₹\,7260$, $R = 20\%$ and $T = 1/2$ yr

$\therefore$ Simple interest $= \dfrac{P \times R \times T}{100} = ₹\left(\dfrac{7260 \times 20 \times \frac{1}{2}}{100}\right)$

$= ₹\,726$

Amount after third half-year $= ₹(7260 + 726) = ₹\,7986$

Hence, compound interest $= ₹(7986 - 6000) = ₹\,1986$

5. We have, $P = ₹\,5000$, $R = 12\%$,

$T = 6$ months $\Rightarrow T = \dfrac{1}{2}$ yr

Now, simple interest for the first six months

$= ₹\,\dfrac{P \times R \times T}{100} = ₹\left(\dfrac{5000 \times 12 \times 1/2}{100}\right)$

$= ₹\,300$

Now, amount after first six months,

$A = ₹\,(5000 + 300)$ $\quad [\because A = P + \text{SI}]$

$= ₹\,5300$

Principal for the second six months $= ₹\,(5300 - 1800)$

$= ₹\,3500$

$\therefore$ Simple interest for the second six months

$= ₹\left(\dfrac{3500 \times 12 \times 1/2}{100}\right) \quad \left[\because \text{SI} = \dfrac{P \times R \times T}{100}\right]$

$= ₹\,210$

Now, amount after second six months,

$A = ₹\,(3500 + 210) = ₹\,3710$

Principal for the third six months $= ₹\,(3710 - 1800)$

$= ₹\,1910$

Simple interest for the third six months

$= ₹\left(\dfrac{1910 \times 12 \times 1/2}{100}\right)$

$= ₹\,114.60$

Now, the payment to be made at the end of 18 months to clear the entire loan $= ₹\,(1910 + 114.60) = ₹\,2024.60$

6. Let the sum of money be x.

For the first year,

$P = ₹\,x$, $R = 10\%$, $T = 1$yr

$\because$ Simple interest for the first year $= \dfrac{P \times R \times T}{100}$

$= \dfrac{x \times 10 \times 1}{100} = \dfrac{x}{10}$

$\therefore$ Amount = Principal + Interest

$= x + \dfrac{x}{10} = ₹\,\dfrac{11x}{10}$

For the second year,

$P = ₹\,\dfrac{11x}{10}$, $R = 10\%$ and $T = 1$ yr

$\therefore$ Simple interest $= \dfrac{P \times R \times T}{100} = \dfrac{11x \times 10 \times 1}{10 \times 100} = \dfrac{11x}{100}$

Now, difference between the interest for the second year and the first year $= \dfrac{11x}{100} - \dfrac{x}{10} = \dfrac{x}{100}$

Now, according to the question,

$\dfrac{x}{100} = 104$

$\Rightarrow \quad x = 104 \times 100 \Rightarrow x = ₹\,10400$

Hence, the sum of money is ₹ 10400.

7. Let the rate of interest charged be $x\%$.

For the first year,

$P = ₹\,15000$, $R = x\%$ and $T = 1$ yr

Now, simple interest $= \dfrac{P \times R \times T}{100} = \dfrac{15000 \times x \times 1}{100}$

$= ₹\,150x$

Amount $= P + I = ₹\,15000 + ₹\,150x$

Now, according to the question,

after one year, Mohan paid back ₹ 5000.

$\therefore$ Principal for the second year $= 15000 + 150x - 5000$

$= ₹\,(10000 + 150x)$

For the second year,

$P = ₹\,(10000 + 150x)$, $R = x\%$, $T = 1$ yr

According to the question,

$\dfrac{(10000 + 150x)x \times 1}{100} = 1150$

$\left[\because \text{simple interest} = \dfrac{P \times R \times T}{100}\right]$

$\Rightarrow \quad 10000x + 150x^2 = 115000$

$\Rightarrow \quad 150x^2 + 10000x - 115000 = 0$

$\Rightarrow \quad 3x^2 + 200x - 2300 = 0$

$\Rightarrow \quad 3x^2 + (230 - 30)x - 2300 = 0$

$\Rightarrow \quad 3x^2 + 230x - 30x - 2300 = 0$

$\Rightarrow \quad x(3x + 230) - 10(3x + 230) = 0$

$\Rightarrow \quad (3x + 230)(x - 10) = 0 \Rightarrow x = 10, \dfrac{-230}{3}$

As we know, the rate of interest cannot be negative.

$\therefore \quad x = 10\%$

Now, the principal for the second year

$= 10000 + 150x$

$= 10000 + 150 \times 10 = ₹\,11500$

And amount at the end of the second year

$= 11500 + 1150 = ₹\,12650$

8. Let the money borrowed be ₹ x. Then, amount to be paid after first year

$$= x\left(1+\frac{8}{100}\right) = ₹\, x\left(\frac{27}{25}\right) \left[\because A = P\left(1+\frac{R}{100}\right)^n\right]$$

Money refunded at the end of first year = ₹ 43200

$\therefore$ Principal for the second year = ₹ $\left(\frac{27}{25}x - 43200\right)$

Amount at the end of second year

$$= \left(\frac{27}{25}x - 43200\right)\left(1+\frac{8}{100}\right)$$

$$= \left(\frac{27}{25}x - 43200\right)\left(\frac{27}{25}\right)$$

But the money paid at the end of the second year = ₹ 34992

$$\therefore \quad \left(\frac{27x}{25} - 43200\right)\left(\frac{27}{25}\right) = 34992$$

$$\Rightarrow \frac{27}{25} \times \frac{27x}{25} - 43200 \times \frac{27}{25} = 34992$$

$$\Rightarrow \frac{27}{25} \times \frac{27x}{25} = 34992 + 43200 \times \frac{27}{25}$$

$$\Rightarrow \frac{729}{625}x = 34992 + 46656$$

$$\Rightarrow \frac{729}{625}x = 81648$$

$$\Rightarrow x = \frac{81648 \times 625}{729} = 70000$$

Hence, the borrowed sum is ₹ 70000.

9. We have, amounts in 2 yr = ₹ 2809

and amounts in 3 yr = ₹ 2977.54

Let P be the original sum and R% be the rate of interest.

Now, according to the question,

$$P\left(1+\frac{R}{100}\right)^2 = 2809 \quad \ldots\text{(i)}$$

$$\text{and} \quad P\left(1+\frac{R}{100}\right)^3 = 2977.54 \quad \ldots\text{(ii)} \quad \left[\because A = P\left(1+\frac{R}{100}\right)^n\right]$$

On dividing Eq. (i) by Eq. (ii), we get

$$\frac{P\left(1+\frac{R}{100}\right)^2}{P\left(1+\frac{R}{100}\right)^3} = \frac{2809}{2977.54}$$

$$\Rightarrow \frac{1}{\left(1+\frac{R}{100}\right)} = \frac{280900}{297754}$$

$$\Rightarrow \frac{297754}{280900} = \left(1+\frac{R}{100}\right) \Rightarrow \frac{R}{100} = \frac{297754}{280900} - 1$$

$$\Rightarrow \frac{R}{100} = \frac{16854}{280900} \Rightarrow R = 6\%$$

Now, on putting the value of R in Eq. (i), we get

$$P\left(1+\frac{6}{100}\right)^2 = 2809$$

$$\Rightarrow P\left(\frac{106}{100}\right)^2 = 2809$$

$$\Rightarrow P \times \frac{53}{50} \times \frac{53}{50} = 2809$$

$$\Rightarrow P \times \frac{2809}{2500} = 2809$$

$$\Rightarrow P = \frac{2809}{2809} \times 2500$$

$$\Rightarrow P = ₹\, 2500$$

Hence, the value of rate of interest is 6% and the original sum is ₹ 2500.

10. Let Seeta's share = ₹ x

Then, Geeta's share = ₹ $(39527 - x)$

Now, amount received by Seeta at the age of 30

$$= x\left(1+\frac{5}{100}\right)^2$$

$$\left[\because A = P\left(1+\frac{R}{100}\right)^n; \text{ here } P = x,\ R = 5\% \text{ and } n = 2 \text{ yr}\right]$$

and amount received by Geeta at the age of 30

$$= (39527 - x)\left(1+\frac{5}{100}\right)^4$$

$$[\because P = 39527 - x,\ R = 5\% \text{ and } n = 4 \text{ yr}]$$

Now, according to the question,

$$x\left(1+\frac{5}{100}\right)^2 = (39527 - x)\left(1+\frac{5}{100}\right)^4$$

$$\Rightarrow x\left(\frac{105}{100}\right)^2 = (39527 - x)\left(\frac{105}{100}\right)^4$$

$$\Rightarrow x = (39527 - x)\left(\frac{105}{100}\right)^2$$

$$\Rightarrow x = (39527 - x)\left(\frac{21}{20} \times \frac{21}{20}\right)$$

$$\Rightarrow x = (39527 - x) \times \frac{441}{400}$$

$$\Rightarrow \frac{400x}{441} = 39527 - x$$

$$\Rightarrow \frac{400x}{441} + x = 39527$$

$$\Rightarrow \frac{841x}{441} = 39527$$

$$\Rightarrow x = \frac{39527 \times 441}{841}$$

$$\Rightarrow x = 20727$$

Hence, Seeta's share = ₹ 20727

and Geeta's share = ₹ (39527 − 20727) = ₹ 18800

11. Let Ram invest the money be ₹ x and Ashok invest the money be ₹ y.

For Ram,

$$P_1 = ₹\, x,\ r_1 = 10\%,\ n_1 = (30 - 20) = 10 \text{ yr}$$

$$\therefore \quad A_1 = P_1\left(1+\frac{r_1}{100}\right)^{n_1} \quad \left[\because A = P\left(1+\frac{r}{100}\right)^n\right]$$

$$\Rightarrow \quad A_1 = x\left(1+\frac{10}{100}\right)^{10} \quad \ldots\text{(i)}$$

For Ashok,

$$P_2 = ₹\, y,\ r_2 = 10\%,\ n_2 = (30 - 22) = 8 \text{ yr}$$

$$\therefore \quad A_2 = P_2\left(1+\frac{r_2}{100}\right)^{n_2} \Rightarrow A_2 = y\left(1+\frac{10}{100}\right)^8 \quad \ldots\text{(ii)}$$

Now, according to the question,

$$A_1 = A_2$$

$$x\left(1+\frac{10}{100}\right)^{10} = y\left(1+\frac{10}{100}\right)^8 \quad \text{[from Eqs. (i) and (ii)]}$$

$$\Rightarrow \quad x\left(1+\frac{10}{100}\right)^2 = y \Rightarrow x\left(\frac{11}{10}\right)^2 = y$$

$$\Rightarrow \quad \left(\frac{11}{10}\right)^2 = \frac{y}{x} \Rightarrow \frac{y}{x} = \frac{121}{100}$$

$$\therefore \quad \frac{x}{y} = \frac{100}{121}$$

$$\Rightarrow \quad x : y = 100 : 121$$

Hence, Ram and Ashok should invest the money in the ratio 100 : 121.

12. Let sum be x.

Now, simple interest (SI) for 1 yr when $R = 10\%$

$$= \frac{x \times 10 \times 1}{100} \quad \left[\because \text{SI} = \frac{P \times R \times T}{100}\right]$$

$$= \frac{x}{10} \quad \ldots\text{(i)}$$

Now, rate of interest per conversion period (half year)

$$= \frac{1}{2} \text{ of } 10\%$$

$$= 5\%$$

and the number of conversion periods = 2

$$\therefore \quad \text{CI} = P\left[\left(1+\frac{R}{100}\right)^n - 1\right]$$

$$\Rightarrow \quad \text{CI} = x\left[\left(1+\frac{5}{100}\right)^2 - 1\right] \quad [\because P = x, R = 5\%, n = 2]$$

$$= x\left[\left(\frac{105}{100}\right)^2 - 1\right]$$

$$\Rightarrow \quad CI = x\left[\frac{441}{400} - 1\right] = \frac{41x}{400} \quad \ldots\text{(ii)}$$

Now, according to question,

$$\text{CI} - \text{SI} = 180$$

$$\Rightarrow \quad \frac{41x}{400} - \frac{x}{10} = 180 \quad \text{[from Eqs. (i) and (ii)]}$$

$$\Rightarrow \quad \frac{41x - 40x}{400} = 180 \Rightarrow \frac{x}{400} = 180$$

$$\Rightarrow \quad x = 72000$$

Hence, the sum is ₹ 72000.

13. We have, $P = ₹\, 3500$, $R_1 = 8\%$ per annum and $T_1 = 2$ yr

$$\therefore \quad R_1 = \frac{8}{2}\% = 4\% \text{ and } n_1 = 4 \text{ (half years)}$$

$$R_2 = 12\% \text{ per annum and } n_2 = 1 \text{ yr}$$

$$R_3 = 15\% \text{ per annum and } n_3 = 1 \text{ yr}$$

We know that

$$A = P\left(1+\frac{R_1}{100}\right)^{n_1}\left(1+\frac{R_2}{100}\right)^{n_2}\left(1+\frac{R_2}{100}\right)^{n_3}$$

$$= 3500\left(1+\frac{4}{100}\right)^4\left(1+\frac{12}{100}\right)^1\left(1+\frac{15}{100}\right)^1$$

$$= 3500\left(\frac{26}{25}\right)^4\left(\frac{28}{25}\right)\left(\frac{23}{20}\right)$$

$$= \frac{3500 \times 26 \times 26 \times 26 \times 26 \times 28 \times 23}{25 \times 25 \times 25 \times 25 \times 25 \times 20}$$

$$A = ₹\, 5273.72$$

Now, $\text{CI} = A - P$

$$\text{CI} = 5273.72 - 3500$$

$$\text{CI} = ₹\, 1773.72$$

Hence, the earning is ₹ 1773.72 .

14. We know that

$$\text{Rate of interest} = \frac{\text{Difference in the interest of two consecutive conversion period}}{\text{CI of preceding period} \times \text{Time}} \times 100\% \quad \ldots\text{(a)}$$

(i) Interest for first year = ₹ 1750
and interest for second year = ₹ 2275

Then, rate of interest for second year

$$= \frac{2275 - 1750}{1750 \times 1} \times 100\% \quad \text{[from Eq. (a)]}$$

$$= \frac{525}{1750} \times 100\% = 30\%$$

(ii) Interest for second year = ₹ 2275
and interest for third year = ₹ 2550
Then, rate of interest for third year

$$= \frac{2550 - 2275}{2275 \times 1} \times 100\% \quad \text{[from Eq. (a)]}$$

$$= \frac{275}{2275} \times 100\%$$

$$= 12.09\%$$

Case Based Questions

1. We have, $P = ₹\ 9800$, $T = 3$ yr, $R = 10\%$

Then, we know that

$$SI = \frac{P \times R \times T}{100}$$

(i) Interest for the 1st year $= ₹\left(\frac{9800 \times 10 \times 1}{100}\right) = ₹\ 980$

The sum due at the end of the 1st year

$$= ₹\ (9800 + 980) = ₹\ 10780$$

(ii) Interest for the 2nd year

$$= ₹\left(\frac{10780 \times 10 \times 1}{100}\right) = ₹\ 1078$$

$[\because P = ₹\ 10780, R = 10\%, T = 1\text{yr}]$

The sum due at the end of the 2nd year

$$= ₹\ (10780 + 1078) = ₹\ 11858$$

(iii) Required difference $= ₹\ (11858 - 10780) = ₹\ 1078$

Interest for one year on this difference

$$= ₹\left(\frac{1078 \times 10 \times 1}{100}\right) = ₹\ 107.80$$

(iv) Compound interest for the 3rd year

$$= ₹\ (1078 + 107.80)$$
$$= ₹\ 1185.80$$

2. (i) Here, population in 2003 = 54000,

rate of increase = 5% and time period $(n) = 2$ yr

Let the population in 2001 be P.

$\therefore$ Present population $= P\left(1 + \frac{R}{100}\right)^n$

$$= P\left(1 + \frac{5}{100}\right)^2 = P\left(1 + \frac{1}{20}\right)^2$$

$$\Rightarrow \quad 54000 = P \times \left(\frac{21}{20}\right)^2$$

$$\Rightarrow \quad 54000 = P \times \frac{21}{20} \times \frac{21}{20}$$

$$\therefore P = \frac{54000 \times 20 \times 20}{21 \times 21} = \frac{21600000}{21 \times 21}$$

$$= 48979.59 = 48980 \text{ (approx.)}$$

Hence, the population in 2001 is 48980.

(ii) For population in 2005 i.e. 2 yr after 2003,

initial population = 54000 i.e. in the year 2003,

time $(n) = 2$ yr and rate of increase, $R = 5\%$

Let population in 2005 be A.

$$\therefore \quad A = P\left(1 + \frac{R}{100}\right)^n = 54000\left(1 + \frac{5}{100}\right)^2$$

$$= 54000\left(1 + \frac{1}{20}\right)^2 = 54000\left(\frac{21}{20}\right)^2$$

$$= 54000 \times \frac{21}{20} \times \frac{21}{20}$$

$$= 135 \times 21 \times 21 = 59535$$

Hence, the population in 2005 is 59535.

3. (i) Given, $V\left(1 - \frac{r}{100}\right) - V\left(1 - \frac{r}{100}\right)^2 = 720$ ...(a)

and $V\left(1 - \frac{r}{100}\right)^2 - V\left(1 - \frac{r}{100}\right)^3 = 648$ ...(b)

$$\left[\because V_n = V\left(1 - \frac{r}{100}\right)^n\right]$$

On dividing Eq. (b) by Eq. (a), we get

$$\frac{V\left(1 - \frac{r}{100}\right)^2 - V\left(1 - \frac{r}{100}\right)^3}{V\left(1 - \frac{r}{100}\right) - V\left(1 - \frac{r}{100}\right)^2} = \frac{648}{720}$$

$$\Rightarrow \quad \frac{V\left(1 - \frac{r}{100}\right)^2\left[1 - 1 + \frac{r}{100}\right]}{V\left(1 - \frac{r}{100}\right)\left[1 - 1 + \frac{r}{100}\right]} = \frac{648}{720} \Rightarrow 1 - \frac{r}{100} = \frac{648}{720}$$

$$\Rightarrow \quad 1 - \frac{648}{720} = \frac{r}{100} \Rightarrow \frac{72}{720} = \frac{r}{100}$$

$$\Rightarrow \quad r = \frac{72 \times 100}{720}$$

$$\Rightarrow \quad r = 10\%$$

Hence, the rate of depreciation per annum is 10%.

(ii) We know that

$V_n = V\left(1 - \frac{r}{100}\right)^n$, where V is the original value of machine.

Let value of machine after 1st year,

$$V_1 = V\left(1 - \frac{10}{100}\right) = \frac{9}{10}V$$

and value of machine after 2nd year,

$$V_2 = V\left(1 - \frac{10}{100}\right)^2 = \frac{81V}{100}$$

Value depreciated during 2nd year = 720

$$\Rightarrow \quad \frac{9V}{10} - \frac{81V}{100} = 720$$

$$\Rightarrow \quad \frac{9V}{100} = 720$$

$$\Rightarrow \quad V = ₹\ 8000$$

(iii) The value of the machine at the end of third year

$$= 8000\left(1 - \frac{10}{100}\right)^3$$

$$= 8000 \times \frac{729}{1000} = ₹\ 5832$$

03

EXPANSIONS

Expansion means the expanded form of an algebraic expression i.e. conversion of product form to addition or subtraction form. e.g. $a^2 + 2ab + b^2$ is an expanded form of $(a+b)^2$.

Expansion of the form $(a \pm b)^2$

(a) $(a+b)^2 = a^2 + 2ab + b^2$

(b) $(a-b)^2 = a^2 - 2ab + b^2$

e.g. $(4x^2y + 6z)^2 = (4x^2y)^2 + 2 \times 4x^2y \times 6z + (6z)^2$

$= 16x^4y^2 + 48x^2yz + 36z^2$

Expansion of difference of two squares

$a^2 - b^2 = (a+b)(a-b)$

e.g. $16x^2 - 25y^2 = (4x)^2 - (5y)^2 = (4x+5y)(4x-5y)$

Expansion of the form $(x \pm a)(x \pm b)$

(a) $(x+a)(x+b) = x^2 + (a+b)x + ab$

(b) $(x-a)(x-b) = x^2 - (a+b)x + ab$

(c) $(x-a)(x+b) = x^2 - (a-b)x - ab$

(d) $(x+a)(x-b) = x^2 + (a-b)x - ab$

e.g. $(x-4)(x+6) = [x + (-4)](x+6)$

$= x^2 + (-4+6)x + (-4) \times 6 = x^2 + 2x - 24$

Expansion of the form $(a \pm b \pm c)^2$

(a) $(a+b+c)^2 = a^2 + b^2 + c^2 + 2ab + 2bc + 2ca$

(b) $(a-b-c)^2 = a^2 + b^2 + c^2 - 2ab + 2bc - 2ca$

(c) $(a+b-c)^2 = a^2 + b^2 + c^2 + 2(ab - bc - ca)$

(d) $(a-b+c)^2 = a^2 + b^2 + c^2 + 2(ca - ab - bc)$

e.g. $(4x - 2y - 3z)^2 = (4x)^2 + (-2y)^2 + (-3z)^2 + 2 \times 4x \times (-2y) + 2 \times (-2y) \times (-3z) + 2 \times (-3z) \times (4x)$

$= 16x^2 + 4y^2 + 9z^2 - 16xy + 12yz - 24xz$

Expansion of the form $(a \pm b)^3$

(a) $(a+b)^3 = a^3 + b^3 + 3ab(a+b)$

(b) $(a-b)^3 = a^3 - b^3 - 3ab(a-b)$

e.g. $(2x+3y)^3 = (2x)^3 + (3y)^3 + 3 \times 2x \times 3y(2x+3y)$

$= 8x^3 + 27y^3 + 18xy(2x+3y) = 8x^3 + 27y^3 + 36x^2y + 54xy^2$

Expansion of $a^3 \pm b^3$

(a) $(a^3 + b^3) = (a+b)(a^2 - ab + b^2)$

(b) $(a^3 - b^3) = (a-b)(a^2 + ab + b^2)$

e.g. $x^6 - 512y^6 = (x^2)^3 - (8y^2)^3 = (x^2 - 8y^2)(x^4 + 8x^2y^2 + 64y^4)$

Expansion of the form

(a) $(a+b+c)(a^2 + b^2 + c^2 - ab - bc - ca) = a^3 + b^3 + c^3 - 3abc$

(b) $(x+a)(x+b)(x+c) = x^3 + (a+b+c)x^2 + (ab+bc+ca)x + abc$

(c) If $a+b+c = 0$, then $a^3 + b^3 + c^3 = 3abc$

e.g. $(2x+y+3z)(4x^2 + y^2 + 9z^2 - 2xy - 3yz - 6xz) = (2x+y+3z)(4x^2 + y^2 + (3z)^2 - 2x \times y - y \times 3z - 6z \times x)$

$= [8x^3 + y^3 + (3z)^3 - 3 \times 2xy \times 3z]$

$= 8x^3 + y^3 + 27z^3 - 18xyz$

EXAM ORIENTED QUESTIONS

TYPE - 1   01 Mark

Multiple Choice Questions

Q.1 If $(x+2)^2 = 49$, then the value of x is

(a) 9   (b) 7   (c) 2   (d) 5

Q.2 If $(x+2)^2 - 4 = (3x-5) + x^2$, then the value of x is

(a) 5   (b) $\frac{-5}{7}$ (c) -5 (d) $\frac{5}{7}$

Q.3 If $x - \frac{1}{x} = 4$, then the value of $x^2 + \frac{1}{x^2}$ is

(a) 16   (b) 20

(c) 18   (d) 14

Q.4 If $a^{1/2} + b^{1/2} - c^{1/2} = 0$, then the value of $(a+b-c)^2$ is

(a) $5ab$ (b) $4ab$ (c) $6ab$ (d) $7ab$

Q.5 $(3a+2b-c+d)^2 - 12a(2b-c+d)$ is

(a) a perfect square   (b) not a perfect square

(c) a cube root   (d) None of these

Q.6 If $\frac{x}{y} + \frac{y}{x} = 1$, then $x^3 + y^3$ is equal to

(a) 1   (b) -1 (c) $\frac{1}{2}$ (d) 0

Q.7 If $x^3 + y^3 + z^3 = 3xyz$ and $x + y + z \neq 0$ then the relation between x, y and z is

(a) $x = y = z$ (b) $x > y > z$

(c) $x < y = z$ (d) $x < y > z$

Answers

1. (d)   2. (c)   3. (c)   4. (b)   5. (a)
6. (d)   7. (a)

TYPE - 2   01 Mark

Assertion-Reason Type Questions

Q.1 Assertion (A) If $x^2 + \frac{1}{x^2} = 20$, then the value of $\left(x + \frac{1}{x}\right)$ is 22.

Reason (R) $(a+b)^2 = a^2 + b^2 + 2ab$.

(a) A is true, R is false.
(b) A is false, R is true.
(c) Both A and R are true and R is the correct reason for A.
(d) Both A and R are true and R is incorrect reason for A.

Q.2 Assertion (A) The expansion of $\left(a + \frac{1}{a}\right)^2 - 4$ is $\left(a - \frac{1}{a}\right)^2$.

Reason (R) $(a+b)(a-b) = a^2 - b^2$.

(a) A is true, R is false.
(b) A is false, R is true.
(c) Both A and R are true and R is the correct reason for A.
(d) Both A and R are true and R is incorrect reason for A.

Q.3 Assertion (A) The coefficient of y^2 in the expansion of $(4x - 2y - 3z)^2$ is 4.

Reason (R) $a^2 - b^2 = (a+b)(a-b)$.

(a) A is true, R is false.
(b) A is false, R is true.
(c) Both A and R are true and R is the correct reason for A.
(d) Both A and R are true and R is incorrect reason for A.

Q.4 Assertion (A) The value of $(9.98)^2$ is 99.6003.

Reason (R) $(a-b)^3 = a^3 - b^3 - 3ab(a-b)$.

(a) A is true, R is false.
(b) A is false, R is true.
(c) Both A and R are true and R is the correct reason for A.
(d) Both A and R are true and R is incorrect reason for A.

Q.5 Assertion (A) If $x + 2y + 3z = 0$, then value of $x^3 + 8y^3 + 27z^3$ is $18xyz$.

Reason (R) If $a + b + c = 0$, then $a^3 + b^3 + c^3 = 3abc$.

(a) A is true, R is false.
(b) A is false, R is true.
(c) Both A and R are true and R is the correct reason for A.
(d) Both A and R are true and R is incorrect reason for A.

Answers

1. (c)   2. (d)   3. (d)   4. (b)   5. (c)

TYPE - 3 01 Mark

Statement Based Questions

Q.1 **Statement I** If $x - y = 6$ and $xy = 24$, then the value of $x + y$ is 132.

Statement II $(a \pm b)^2 = a^2 + b^2 \mp 2ab$

Which of the following is valid?
(a) Both the Statements are true.
(b) Both the Statements are false.
(c) Statement I is true and Statement II is false.
(d) Statement I is false and Statement II is true.

Q.2 **Statement I** $(a + b)^2 - (a - b)^2 = 4ab$

Statement II $(a + b)^2 + (a - b)^2 = 2(a^2 + b^2)$

Which of the following is valid?
(a) Both the Statements are true.
(b) Both the Statements are false.
(c) Statement I is true and Statement II is false.
(d) Statement I is false and Statement II is true.

Q.3 **Statement I** The value of $(x + 5y)(x - 8y)$ is $x^2 - 3xy - 40y^2$.

Statement II The value of $(x + 7)(x + 9)$ is $x^2 - 16x + 63$.

Which of the following is valid?
(a) Both the Statements are true.
(b) Both the Statements are false.
(c) Statement I is true and Statement II is false.
(d) Statement I is false and Statement II is true.

Q.4 **Statement I** The expansion of $\left(\frac{3a}{2} - \frac{2}{3b}\right)^2$ is $\frac{9}{4}a^2 - \frac{2a}{b} + \frac{4}{9b^2}$.

Statement II The expansion of $(x + y)^3 - (x - y)^3$ is $3(y^3 + 3x^2y)$.

Which of the following is valid?
(a) Both the Statements are true.
(b) Both the Statements are false.
(c) Statement I is true and Statement II is false.
(d) Statement I is false and Statement II is true.

Answers

1. (b) 2. (a) 3. (a) 4. (c)

TYPE - 4 03 Marks

Short Answer Type Questions

Q.1 Evaluate $(4a + 3b)^2 - (4a - 3b)^2 + 48ab$.

Q.2 In the expansion of $(5x - 3)(x + 2)^2$, find
(i) coefficients of x^3, x^2 and x. (ii) constant term.

Q.3 Prove that $\left(2x - \frac{1}{2x}\right)^2 - \left(2x + \frac{1}{2x}\right)\left(2x - \frac{1}{2x}\right) = \frac{1}{2x^2} - 2$.

Q.4 Evaluate 105×106 without multiplying directly.

Q.5 Simplify $(x + y + z)^2 + (x - y - z)^2$.

Q.6 If $x + y - z = 4$ and $x^2 + y^2 + z^2 = 38$, then find the value of $xy - yz - zx$.

Q.7 Evaluate $(999)^3$ using identity.

Q.8 If $a - \frac{1}{a} = \frac{1}{5}$, then evaluate $a^3 - \frac{1}{a^3}$.

Q.9 If $a + b = 1 + ab$, then prove that $a^3 + b^3 = 1 + a^3b^3$.

Q.10 Find the cube of $x - \frac{1}{x} + y$, where $x \neq 0$.

Q.11 Find the coefficients of x^2 and x in the expansion of $(x - 5)(x + 3)(x + 7)$.

Q.12 Use property to evaluate $(21)^3 + (-17)^3 + (-4)^3$.

Q.13 If $x = y + 5$, then find the value of $x^3 - y^3 - 15xy - 125$.

Answers

1. $96ab$ 2. (i) 5, 17, 8 (ii) -12 4. 11130
5. $2(x^2 + y^2 + z^2 + 2yz)$ 6. -11 7. 997002999
8. $\frac{76}{125}$ 10. $x^3 - 3x + \frac{3}{x} - \frac{1}{x^3} + 3x^2y + \frac{3y}{x^2} - 6y + 3xy^2 - \frac{3y^2}{x} + y^3$
11. 5 and -29 12. 4284 13. 0

TYPE - 5 4/5 Marks

Long Answer Type Questions

Q.1 Simplify $\left(\frac{a}{2b} + \frac{2b}{a}\right)^2 - \left(\frac{2b}{a} - \frac{a}{2b}\right)^2$

Q.2 If $a^2 - 4a - 1 = 0$ and $a \neq 0$, then find the values of

(i) $a - \frac{1}{a}$ (ii) $a + \frac{1}{a}$ (iii) $a^2 - \frac{1}{a^2}$

Q.3 If $x - 2 = \frac{1}{4x}$, then find the values of

(i) $x^2 + \frac{1}{16x^2}$ (ii) $x^4 + \frac{1}{256x^4}$

Q.4 If the number p is 7 more than the number q and the sum of the squares of p and q is 85, then find the product of p and q.

Q.5 If $x \neq 0$, $x + \frac{1}{2x} = p$ and $x - \frac{1}{2x} = q$, then find a relation between p and q.

Q.6 If $\dfrac{a}{b}=\dfrac{b}{c}$, then prove that
$(a+b+c)(a-b+c)=a^2+b^2+c^2$.

Q.7 If $x \neq 0$ and $x+\dfrac{1}{x}=2$, then show that

$$x^2+\frac{1}{x^2}=x^3+\frac{1}{x^3}=x^4+\frac{1}{x^4}.$$

Q.8 If $x=7+4\sqrt{3}$, then find the value of
(i) $\sqrt{x}+\dfrac{1}{\sqrt{x}}$ (ii) $x^3-\dfrac{1}{x^3}$

Q.9 Simplify $\dfrac{(x^2-y^2)^3+(y^2-z^2)^3+(z^2-x^2)^3}{(x-y)^3+(y-z)^3+(z-x)^3}$.

Q.10 If $a+3b+5c=0$ and $a^3+9b^3+25c^3=36abc$, then evaluate $\dfrac{(a+3b)^2}{ab}+\dfrac{(3b+5c)^2}{bc}+\dfrac{(5c+a)^2}{ca}$.

Q.11 If the difference between two positive numbers is 5 and the difference between their cubes is 650, then find
(i) their product.
(ii) the sum of their squares.

Answers

1. 4 **2.** (i) 4 (ii) $\pm 2\sqrt{5}$ (iii) $\pm 8\sqrt{5}$ **3.** (i) $\dfrac{9}{2}$ (ii) $\dfrac{161}{8}$
4. 18 **5.** $p^2-q^2=2$ **8.** (i) ± 4 (ii) $1560\sqrt{3}$
9. $(x+y)(y+z)(z+x)$ **10.** 36 **11.** (i) 35 (ii) 95

EXPLANATIONS

Multiple Choice Questions

1. (d) Given, $(x+2)^2=49$

$\Rightarrow x^2+(2)^2+2\times x\times 2=49$ $[\because (a+b)^2=a^2+b^2+2ab]$
$\Rightarrow \quad x^2+4+4x=49$
$\Rightarrow \quad x^2+4x=49-4 \Rightarrow x^2+4x=45$
$\Rightarrow \quad x^2+4x-45=0$
$\Rightarrow \quad x^2+9x-5x-45=0$ [by splitting the middle term]
$\Rightarrow \quad x(x+9)-5(x+9)=0$
$\Rightarrow \quad (x+9)(x-5)=0$
$\therefore \quad x=-9, 5$

2. (c) Given, $(x+2)^2-4=(3x-5)+x^2$

$\Rightarrow \quad x^2+4+4x-4=3x-5+x^2$
$[\because (a+b)^2=a^2+b^2+2ab]$
$\Rightarrow \quad 4x-3x=-5 \Rightarrow x=-5$

3. (c) Given, $x-\dfrac{1}{x}=4$

On squaring both sides, we get

$$\left(x-\frac{1}{x}\right)^2=(4)^2$$

$\Rightarrow x^2+\left(\dfrac{1}{x}\right)^2-2\times x\times\dfrac{1}{x}=16$
$[\because (a-b)^2=a^2+b^2-2ab]$

$\Rightarrow \quad x^2+\dfrac{1}{x^2}-2=16$

$\Rightarrow \quad x^2+\dfrac{1}{x^2}=16+2$

$\therefore \quad x^2+\dfrac{1}{x^2}=18$

4. (b) Given, $a^{1/2}+b^{1/2}-c^{1/2}=0$

$\Rightarrow \quad a^{1/2}+b^{1/2}=c^{1/2}$

On squaring both sides, we get

$$(a^{1/2}+b^{1/2})^2=(c^{1/2})^2$$

$\Rightarrow (a^{1/2})^2+(b^{1/2})^2+2\times a^{1/2}\times b^{1/2}=c$
$[\because (x+y)^2=x^2+y^2+2xy]$
$\Rightarrow \quad a+b+2\sqrt{ab}=c$
$\Rightarrow \quad a+b-c=2\sqrt{ab}$

Again, on squaring both sides, we get

$$(a+b-c)^2=(-2\sqrt{ab})^2$$

$\therefore \quad (a+b-c)^2=4ab$

5. (a) We have, $(3a+2b-c+d)^2-12a(2b-c+d)$

$=(3a)^2+(2b-c+d)^2+2\times 3a\times(2b-c+d)$
$-12a(2b-c+d)$
$[\because (A+B)^2=A^2+B^2+2AB]$
$=(3a)^2+(2b-c+d)^2+6a(2b-c+d)-12a(2b-c+d)$
$=(3a)^2+(2b-c+d)^2-6a(2b-c+d)$
$=(3a)^2+(2b-c+d)^2-2\times 3a\times(2b-c+d)$
$=[3a-(2b-c+d)]^2$ $[\because A^2+B^2-2AB=(A-B)^2]$

Hence, the given expression is a perfect square.

6. (d) Given, $\dfrac{x}{y}+\dfrac{y}{x}=1$

$\Rightarrow \quad \dfrac{x^2+y^2}{yx}=1$

$\Rightarrow \quad x^2+y^2=xy$

$\Rightarrow \quad x^2+y^2-xy=0$ ...(i)

As we know, $x^3 + y^3 = (x + y)(x^2 + y^2 - xy)$

$\Rightarrow \quad x^3 + y^3 = (x + y) \times 0$ [from Eq. (i)]

$\therefore \quad x^3 + y^3 = 0$

7. (a) Given, $x^3 + y^3 + z^3 = 3xyz$

$\Rightarrow x^3 + y^3 + z^3 - 3xyz = 0$

$\Rightarrow (x + y + z)(x^2 + y^2 + z^2 - xy - yz - zx) = 0$

$[\because (a + b + c)(a^2 + b^2 + c^2 - ab - bc - ca) = a^3 + b^3 + c^3 - 3abc]$

Here, $x^2 + y^2 + z^2 - xy - yz - zx = 0$

$[\because x + y + z \neq 0]$

On multiplying 2 both sides, we get

$2(x^2 + y^2 + z^2 - xy - yz - zx) = 0$

$\Rightarrow \quad 2x^2 + 2y^2 + 2z^2 - 2xy - 2yz - 2zx = 0$

$\Rightarrow x^2 + y^2 - 2xy + y^2 + z^2 - 2yz + z^2 + x^2 - 2zx = 0$

$\Rightarrow \quad (x - y)^2 + (y - z)^2 + (z - x)^2 = 0$

$[\because a^2 + b^2 - 2ab = (a - b)^2]$

This equation can only be true, if $x = y = z$

Assertion-Reason Type Questions

1. (c) Given, $x^2 + \dfrac{1}{x^2} = 20$ ...(i)

We know that $(a + b)^2 = a^2 + b^2 + 2ab$

$\therefore \quad \left(x + \dfrac{1}{x}\right)^2 = x^2 + \dfrac{1}{x^2} + 2 \times x \times \dfrac{1}{x}$

$\Rightarrow \quad \left(x + \dfrac{1}{x}\right)^2 = 20 + 2$ [from Eq. (i)]

$\Rightarrow \quad \left(x + \dfrac{1}{x}\right)^2 = 22$

Hence, both A and R are true and R is the correct reason for A.

2. (d) **Assertion** (A) We have,

$\left(a + \dfrac{1}{a}\right)^2 - 4 = a^2 + \dfrac{1}{a^2} + 2 \times a \times \dfrac{1}{a} - 4$

$[\because (a + b)^2 = a^2 + 2ab + b^2]$

$= a^2 + \dfrac{1}{a^2} + 2 - 4$

$= a^2 + \dfrac{1}{a^2} - 2 = \left(a - \dfrac{1}{a}\right)^2$

Hence, both A and R are true and R is incorrect reason for A.

3. (d) We have, $(4x - 2y - 3z)^2$

Using identity $(a + b + c)^2 = a^2 + b^2 + c^2 + 2ab + 2bc + 2ac$, we get

$(4x)^2 + (-2y)^2 + (-3z)^2 + 2 \times 4x \times (-2y) + 2 \times (-2y) \times (-3z) + 2 \times (-3z) \times (4x)$

$= 16x^2 + 4y^2 + 9z^2 - 16xy + 12yz - 24xz$

So, the coefficient of y^2 is 4.

Hence, both A and R are true and R is incorrect reason for A.

4. (b) **Assertion** We have,

$(9.98)^2 = (10 - 0.02)^2$

$= (10)^2 + (0.02)^2 - 2 \times 10 \times 0.02$

$[\because (a - b)^2 = a^2 + b^2 - 2ab]$

$= 100 + 0.0004 - 0.4 = 99.6004$

Hence, A is false, R is true.

5. (c) **Assertion** Given, $x + 2y + 3z = 0$

$\therefore \; x^3 + 8y^3 + 27z^3 = x^3 + (2y)^3 + (3z)^3$

$= 3 \times x \times 2y \times 3z$

[$\because$ if $a + b + c = 0$, then $a^3 + b^3 + c^3 = 3abc$]

$= 18xyz$

Hence, both A and R are true and R is the correct reason for A.

Statement Based Questions

1. (b) **Statement I** Given, $x - y = 6$ ...(i)

and $xy = 24$ ...(ii)

Now, $(x + y)^2 = (x - y)^2 + 4xy$

$\left[\begin{array}{l}\because (a + b)^2 = a^2 + b^2 + 2ab \\ (a - b)^2 = a^2 + b^2 - 2ab\end{array}\right]$

$\Rightarrow \quad (x + y)^2 = 6^2 + 4 \times 24$ [from Eqs. (i) and (ii)]

$\Rightarrow \quad (x + y)^2 = 36 + 96$

$\Rightarrow \quad (x + y)^2 = 132 \Rightarrow x + y = \pm\sqrt{132}$

Hence, Statement I is false.

Statement II We know that

$(a + b)^2 = a^2 + b^2 + 2ab$ and

$(a - b)^2 = a^2 + b^2 - 2ab$

Hence, Statement II is false.

2. (a) **Statement I** Given, $(a + b)^2 - (a - b)^2 = 4ab$

$\Rightarrow a^2 + b^2 + 2ab - (a^2 + b^2 - 2ab) = 4ab$

$\left[\begin{array}{l}\because (x + y)^2 = x^2 + y^2 + 2xy \\ \text{and } (x - y)^2 = x^2 + y^2 - 2xy\end{array}\right]$

$\Rightarrow \quad a^2 + b^2 + 2ab - a^2 - b^2 + 2ab = 4ab \Rightarrow 4ab = 4ab$

$\Rightarrow \quad$ LHS = RHS

Hence, Statement I is true.

Statement II Given,

$(a + b)^2 + (a - b)^2 = 2(a^2 + b^2)$

$\Rightarrow \quad a^2 + b^2 + 2ab + a^2 + b^2 - 2ab = 2(a^2 + b^2)$

$\Rightarrow \quad a^2 + b^2 + a^2 + b^2 = 2(a^2 + b^2)$

$\Rightarrow \quad 2a^2 + 2b^2 = 2(a^2 + b^2)$

$\Rightarrow \quad 2(a^2 + b^2) = 2(a^2 + b^2)$

$\Rightarrow \quad$ LHS = RHS

Hence, Statement II is true.

3. (a) **Statement I** We have,

$$(x+5y)(x-8y) = x^2 + (5y-8y)x - 5y \times 8y$$
$$[\because (x+a)(x-b) = x^2 + (a-b)x - ab]$$
$$= x^2 - 3xy - 40y^2$$

Statement II We have,

$$(x+7)(x+9) = x^2 + (7+9)x + 7 \times 9$$
$$[\because (x+a)(x+b) = x^2 + (a+b)x + ab]$$
$$= x^2 + 16x + 63$$

Hence, both the Statements are true.

4. (c) **Statement I** We have,

$$\left(\frac{3a}{2} - \frac{2}{3b}\right)^2 = \left(\frac{3a}{2}\right)^2 - 2 \times \frac{3a}{2} \times \frac{2}{3b} + \left(\frac{2}{3b}\right)^2$$
$$[\because (a-b)^2 = a^2 - 2ab + b^2]$$
$$= \frac{9a^2}{4} - \frac{2a}{b} + \frac{4}{9b^2}$$

Statement II We have, $(x+y)^3 - (x-y)^3$

$$= x^3 + y^3 + 3xy(x+y) - [x^3 - y^3 - 3xy(x-y)]$$
$$= x^3 + y^3 + 3x^2y + 3xy^2 - x^3 + y^3 + 3x^2y - 3xy^2$$
$$= 2y^3 + 6x^2y = 2(y^3 + 3x^2y)$$

Hence, Statement I is true and Statement II is false.

Short Answer Type Questions

1. We have, $(4a+3b)^2 - (4a-3b)^2 + 48ab$

$$= (4a)^2 + (3b)^2 + 2(4a)(3b) - [(4a)^2 + (3b)^2 - 2(4a)(3b)] + 48ab$$
$$[\because (A+B)^2 = A^2 + B^2 + 2AB \text{ and } (A-B)^2 = A^2 + B^2 - 2AB]$$
$$= 16a^2 + 9b^2 + 24ab - [16a^2 + 9b^2 - 24ab] + 48ab$$
$$= 24ab + 24ab + 48ab = 96ab$$

2. We have, $(5x-3)(x+2)^2 = (5x-3)(x^2+4+4x)$

$$[\because (a+b)^2 = a^2 + b^2 + 2ab]$$
$$= 5x^3 + 17x^2 + 8x - 12$$

(i) Coefficient of $x^3 = 5$, coefficient of $x^2 = 17$ and coefficient of $x = 8$

(ii) Constant term $= -12$

3. Consider, LHS

$$= \left(2x - \frac{1}{2x}\right)^2 - \left(2x + \frac{1}{2x}\right)\left(2x - \frac{1}{2x}\right)$$
$$= (2x)^2 + \left(\frac{1}{2x}\right)^2 - 2 - \left[(2x)^2 - \left(\frac{1}{2x}\right)^2\right]$$
$$\left[\because \left(a - \frac{1}{a}\right)^2 = a^2 + \frac{1}{a^2} - 2 \text{ and } (a+b)(a-b) = a^2 - b^2\right]$$
$$= 4x^2 + \frac{1}{4x^2} - 2 - 4x^2 + \frac{1}{4x^2}$$
$$= 2 \times \frac{1}{4x^2} - 2 = \frac{1}{2x^2} - 2 = \text{RHS}$$ **Hence proved.**

4. First, write 105 as 100 + 5 and 106 as 100 + 6.

Then, $105 \times 106 = (100+5)(100+6)$

$$= (100)^2 + (5+6)(100) + (5 \times 6)$$
$$[\because (x+a)(x+b) = x^2 + (a+b)x + ab]$$
$$= 10000 + 11 \times 100 + 30$$
$$= 10000 + 1100 + 30 = 11130$$

5. We have, $(x+y+z)^2 + (x-y-z)^2$

$$= x^2 + y^2 + z^2 + 2xy + 2yz + 2zx + x^2 + y^2 + z^2 - 2xy + 2yz - 2zx$$
$$\left[\because (a+b+c)^2 = a^2 + b^2 + c^2 + 2ab + 2bc + 2ca \text{ and } (a-b-c)^2 = a^2 + b^2 + c^2 - 2ab + 2bc - 2ca\right]$$
$$= 2x^2 + 2y^2 + 2z^2 + 4yz$$
$$= 2(x^2 + y^2 + z^2 + 2yz)$$

6. Given, $(x+y-z) = 4$ ...(i)

and $x^2 + y^2 + z^2 = 38$ ...(ii)

We know that

$(x+y-z)^2 = x^2 + y^2 + z^2 + 2xy - 2yz - 2zx$

$\Rightarrow \quad 4^2 = 38 + 2(xy - yz - zx)$ [from Eqs. (i) and (ii)]

$\Rightarrow \quad 16 = 38 + 2(xy - yz - zx)$

$\Rightarrow 16 - 38 = 2(xy - yz - zx)$

$\Rightarrow \quad -22 = 2(xy - yz - zx)$

$\Rightarrow \quad \frac{-22}{2} = xy - yz - zx$

$\Rightarrow xy - yz - zx = -11$

Hence, the value of $xy - yz - zx$ is -11.

7. We have, $(999)^3 = (1000-1)^3$

$$= (1000)^3 - (1)^3 - 3(1000)^2(1) + 3(1000)(1)^2$$
$$[\because (a-b)^3 = a^3 - b^3 - 3a^2b + 3ab^2]$$
$$= 1000000000 - 1 - 3000000 + 3000$$
$$= 1000000000 - 1 - 2997000$$
$$= 997002999$$

8. Given, $a - \frac{1}{a} = \frac{1}{5}$ ...(i)

On taking cube both sides, we get

$$\left(a - \frac{1}{a}\right)^3 = \left(\frac{1}{5}\right)^3$$

$\Rightarrow \quad a^3 - \frac{1}{a^3} - 3 \times a \times \frac{1}{a}\left(a - \frac{1}{a}\right) = \frac{1}{125}$

$$[\because (A-B)^3 = A^3 - B^3 - 3AB(A-B)]$$

$\Rightarrow \quad a^3 - \frac{1}{a^3} - 3 \times \frac{1}{5} = \frac{1}{125}$ [from Eq. (i)]

$\Rightarrow \quad a^3 - \frac{1}{a^3} = \frac{1}{125} + \frac{3}{5}$

$\Rightarrow \quad a^3 - \frac{1}{a^3} = \frac{76}{125}$

Hence, the value of $a^3 - \frac{1}{a^3}$ is $\frac{76}{125}$.

9. Given, $a + b = 1 + ab$ ...(i)

On cubing both sides in Eq. (i), we get

$$(a+b)^3 = (1+ab)^3$$

$\Rightarrow a^3 + b^3 + 3ab(a+b) = 1^3 + (ab)^3 + 3 \times 1 \times ab(1+ab)$

[$\because (A+B)^3 = A^3 + B^3 + 3AB(A+B)$]

$\Rightarrow a^3 + b^3 + 3ab(1+ab) = 1 + a^3b^3 + 3ab(1+ab)$ [from Eq. (i)]

$\Rightarrow a^3 + b^3 = 1 + a^3b^3 + 3ab(1+ab) - 3ab(1+ab)$

$\therefore a^3 + b^3 = 1 + a^3b^3$ **Hence proved.**

10. Consider, $\left(x - \frac{1}{x} + y\right)^3 = \left[\left(x - \frac{1}{x}\right) + y\right]^3$

$= \left(x - \frac{1}{x}\right)^3 + y^3 + 3\left(x - \frac{1}{x}\right)^2 y + 3\left(x - \frac{1}{x}\right)y^2$

[$\because (a+b)^3 = a^3 + b^3 + 3a^2b + 3ab^2$]

$= \left[x^3 - \frac{1}{x^3} - 3x^2\left(\frac{1}{x}\right) + 3x\left(\frac{1}{x}\right)^2\right] + y^3$

$+ 3\left(x^2 + \frac{1}{x^2} - 2 \times x \times \frac{1}{x}\right)y + 3\left(x - \frac{1}{x}\right)y^2$

[$\because (a-b)^3 = a^3 - b^3 - 3a^2b + 3ab^2$ and $(a-b)^2 = a^2 + b^2 - 2ab$]

$= \left(x^3 - \frac{1}{x^3} - 3x + \frac{3}{x}\right) + y^3 + 3\left(x^2 + \frac{1}{x^2} - 2\right)y + 3\left(x - \frac{1}{x}\right)y^2$

$= x^3 - \frac{1}{x^3} - 3x + \frac{3}{x} + y^3 + 3x^2y + \frac{3y}{x^2} - 6y - 3xy^2 - \frac{3y^2}{x}$

$= x^3 - 3x + \frac{3}{x} - \frac{1}{x^3} + 3x^2y + \frac{3y}{x^2} - 6y + 3xy^2 - \frac{3y^2}{x} + y^3$

11. We have, $(x-5)(x+3)(x+7)$

$= x^3 + (-5+3+7)x^2 + ((-5) \times 3 + 3 \times 7 + 7 \times (-5))x + (-5) \times 3 \times 7$

[$\because (x+a)(x+b)(x+c) = x^3 + (a+b+c)x^2 + (ab+bc+ca)x + abc$]

$= x^3 + 5x^2 - 29x - 105$

Hence, the coefficients of x^2 and x are 5 and -29, respectively.

12. We have, $(21)^3 + (-17)^3 + (-4)^3$

Let $a = 21, b = -17, c = -4$

Then, $(a+b+c) = 21 + (-17) + (-4) = 0$

We know that, if $a + b + c = 0$, then $a^3 + b^3 + c^3 = 3abc$.

$\therefore (21)^3 + (-17)^3 + (-4)^3 = 3 \times 21 \times (-17) \times (-4) = 4284$

13. Given, $x = y + 5 \Rightarrow x - y - 5 = 0$

$\Rightarrow x + (-y) + (-5) = 0$

Now, $(x)^3 + (-y)^3 + (-5)^3 = 3(x)(-y)(-5)$

[$\because (a+b+c) = 0$, then $a^3 + b^3 + c^3 = 3abc$]

$\Rightarrow x^3 - y^3 - 125 = 15xy$

$\therefore x^3 - y^3 - 15xy - 125 = 0$

Long Answer Type Questions

1. We have, $\left(\frac{a}{2b} + \frac{2b}{a}\right)^2 - \left(\frac{2b}{a} - \frac{a}{2b}\right)^2$

$= \left(\frac{a}{2b}\right)^2 + \left(\frac{2b}{a}\right)^2 + 2 \times \frac{a}{2b} \times \frac{2b}{a} - \left[\left(\frac{2b}{a}\right)^2 + \left(\frac{a}{2b}\right)^2 - 2 \times \frac{2b}{a} \times \frac{a}{2b}\right]$

[$\because (A+B)^2 = A^2 + B^2 + 2AB$ and $(A-B)^2 = A^2 + B^2 - 2AB$]

$= \frac{a^2}{4b^2} + \frac{4b^2}{a^2} + 2 - \left[\frac{4b^2}{a^2} + \frac{a^2}{4b^2} - 2\right]$

$= \frac{a^2}{4b^2} + \frac{4b^2}{a^2} + 2 - \frac{4b^2}{a^2} - \frac{a^2}{4b^2} + 2 = 4$

2. (i) We have, $a^2 - 4a - 1 = 0 \Rightarrow a^2 - 1 = 4a$

$\Rightarrow \frac{a^2 - 1}{a} = 4$

$\Rightarrow a - \frac{1}{a} = 4$ ...(a)

(ii) Consider, $\left(a + \frac{1}{a}\right)^2 = a^2 + \frac{1}{a^2} + 2$

[$\because (A+B)^2 = A^2 + B^2 + 2AB$]

$= a^2 + \frac{1}{a^2} - 2 + 2 + 2$ [adding and subtracting 2]

$= a^2 + \frac{1}{a^2} - 2 \times a \times \frac{1}{a} + 4$ [multiplying and dividing by a]

$= \left(a - \frac{1}{a}\right)^2 + 4$ [$\because A^2 + B^2 - 2AB = (A-B)^2$]

$= 4^2 + 4 = 16 + 4 = 20$ [from Eq. (a)]

$\Rightarrow a + \frac{1}{a} = \pm\sqrt{20} = \pm 2\sqrt{5}$

[taking square root both sides] ...(b)

(iii) We have, $a^2 - \frac{1}{a^2} = \left(a - \frac{1}{a}\right)\left(a + \frac{1}{a}\right)$

[$\because (x-y)(x+y) = x^2 - y^2$]

$= 4 \times (\pm 2\sqrt{5}) = \pm 8\sqrt{5}$

[from Eqs. (a) and (b)]

3. (i) We have, $x - 2 = \frac{1}{4x}$

$\Rightarrow x - \frac{1}{4x} = 2$

On squaring both sides, we get

$$\left(x - \frac{1}{4x}\right)^2 = 2^2$$

$$\Rightarrow (x)^2 + \left(\frac{1}{4x}\right)^2 - 2 \times x \times \frac{1}{4x} = 4$$

$[\because (a-b)^2 = a^2 + b^2 - 2ab]$

$$\Rightarrow \quad x^2 + \frac{1}{16x^2} - \frac{1}{2} = 4$$

$$\Rightarrow \quad x^2 + \frac{1}{16x^2} = 4 + \frac{1}{2} = \frac{9}{2}$$

(ii) Now, consider $x^2 + \frac{1}{16x^2} = \frac{9}{2}$

On squaring both sides, we get

$$\left(x^2 + \frac{1}{16x^2}\right)^2 = \left(\frac{9}{2}\right)^2$$

$$\Rightarrow x^4 + \frac{1}{256x^4} + 2 \times x^2 \times \frac{1}{16x^2} = \frac{81}{4}$$

$[\because (a+b)^2 = a^2 + b^2 + 2ab]$

$$\Rightarrow \quad x^4 + \frac{1}{256x^4} + \frac{1}{8} = \frac{81}{4}$$

$$\Rightarrow \quad x^4 + \frac{1}{256x^4} = \frac{81}{4} - \frac{1}{8}$$

$$\Rightarrow \quad x^4 + \frac{1}{256x^4} = \frac{162-1}{8} = \frac{161}{8}$$

4. Given, $p = 7 + q$ ...(i)

and $p^2 + q^2 = 85$ ...(ii)

Now, $p - q = 7$ [from Eq. (i)]

On squaring both sides, we get

$$(p-q)^2 = (7)^2$$

$\Rightarrow p^2 + q^2 - 2pq = 49$ $[\because (a-b)^2 = a^2 + b^2 - 2ab]$

$\Rightarrow \quad 85 - 2pq = 49$ [using Eq. (ii)]

$\Rightarrow \quad -2pq = 49 - 85$

$\Rightarrow \quad -2pq = -36$

$\Rightarrow \quad 2pq = 36$

$\therefore \quad pq = 18$

5. We have, $x + \frac{1}{2x} = p$ ...(i)

and $\quad x - \frac{1}{2x} = q$ ...(ii)

On squaring both sides of Eq. (i), we get

$$\left(x + \frac{1}{2x}\right)^2 = p^2 \Rightarrow x^2 + \frac{1}{4x^2} + 2 \times x \times \frac{1}{2x} = p^2$$

$[\because (a+b)^2 = a^2 + b^2 + 2ab]$

$$\Rightarrow x^2 + \frac{1}{4x^2} + 1 = p^2$$

$$\Rightarrow \quad x^2 + \frac{1}{4x^2} = p^2 - 1 \quad \text{...(iii)}$$

Now, on squaring both sides of Eq. (ii), we get

$$\left(x - \frac{1}{2x}\right)^2 = q^2$$

$$\Rightarrow \quad x^2 + \frac{1}{4x^2} - 2 \times x \times \frac{1}{2x} = q^2$$

$[\because (a-b)^2 = a^2 + b^2 - 2ab]$

$$\Rightarrow \quad x^2 + \frac{1}{4x^2} - 1 = q^2$$

$$\Rightarrow \quad x^2 + \frac{1}{4x^2} = q^2 + 1 \quad \text{...(iv)}$$

From Eqs. (iii) and (iv), we get

$$p^2 - 1 = q^2 + 1$$

$$\Rightarrow \quad p^2 - q^2 = 2$$

6. We have, $\frac{a}{b} = \frac{b}{c} = k$ (say)

$\Rightarrow \quad a = bk$ and $b = ck$

$\therefore \quad a = ck^2$

Consider, LHS $= (a + b + c)(a - b + c)$

$= (ck^2 + ck + c)(ck^2 - ck + c)$

$[\because a = ck^2$ and $b = ck]$

$= c^2 (k^2 + k + 1)(k^2 - k + 1)$

$= c^2 [\{(k^2 + 1) + k\} \{(k^2 + 1) - k\}]$

$= c^2 \{(k^2 + 1)^2 - k^2\}$

$[\because (a+b)(a-b) = a^2 - b^2]$

$= c^2 \{k^4 + 1 + 2k^2 - k^2\}$

$[\because (a+b)^2 = a^2 + b^2 + 2ab]$

$= c^2 \{k^4 + k^2 + 1\}$ ...(i)

Now, consider RHS $= a^2 + b^2 + c^2 = (ck^2)^2 + (ck)^2 + c^2$

$[\because a = ck^2$ and $b = ck]$

$= c^2k^4 + c^2k^2 + c^2$

$= c^2 (k^4 + k^2 + 1)$ ...(ii)

From Eqs. (i) and (ii), we get

LHS = RHS **Hence proved.**

7. Given, $x + \frac{1}{x} = 2$ ...(i)

On squaring both sides, we get

$$\left(x + \frac{1}{x}\right)^2 = (2)^2$$

$\Rightarrow \quad x^2 + \frac{1}{x^2} + 2 = 4$ $[\because (a+b)^2 = a^2 + b^2 + 2ab]$

$\Rightarrow \quad x^2 + \frac{1}{x^2} = 2$ ...(ii)

On cubing both sides of Eq. (i), we get

$$\left(x + \frac{1}{x}\right)^3 = 2^3$$

$$\Rightarrow x^3 + \frac{1}{x^3} + 3 \times x \times \frac{1}{x}\left(x + \frac{1}{x}\right) = 8$$

$[\because (a+b)^3 = a^3 + b^3 + 3ab(a+b)]$

$$\Rightarrow x^3 + \frac{1}{x^3} + 3 \times 2 = 8 \quad \text{[from Eq. (i)]}$$

$$\Rightarrow x^3 + \frac{1}{x^3} = 8 - 6$$

$$\Rightarrow x^3 + \frac{1}{x^3} = 2 \quad \text{...(iii)}$$

On squaring both sides of Eq. (ii), we get

$$\left(x^2 + \frac{1}{x^2}\right)^2 = 2^2$$

$$\Rightarrow (x^2)^2 + \left(\frac{1}{x^2}\right)^2 + 2 \times x^2 \times \frac{1}{x^2} = 4$$

$$\Rightarrow x^4 + \frac{1}{x^4} + 2 = 4$$

$$\Rightarrow x^4 + \frac{1}{x^4} = 2 \quad \text{...(iv)}$$

From Eqs. (ii), (iii) and (iv), we get

$$x^2 + \frac{1}{x^2} = x^3 + \frac{1}{x^3} = x^4 + \frac{1}{x^4}$$

Hence proved.

8. (i) Given, $x = 7 + 4\sqrt{3}$ ...(a)

$$\therefore \frac{1}{x} = \frac{1}{7 + 4\sqrt{3}}$$

$$\Rightarrow \frac{1}{x} = \frac{7 - 4\sqrt{3}}{(7 + 4\sqrt{3})(7 - 4\sqrt{3})}$$

[rationalising RHS]

$$\Rightarrow \frac{1}{x} = \frac{7 - 4\sqrt{3}}{(7)^2 - (4\sqrt{3})^2} \quad [\because (a+b)(a-b) = a^2 - b^2]$$

$$\Rightarrow \frac{1}{x} = \frac{7 - 4\sqrt{3}}{49 - 48}$$

$$\Rightarrow \frac{1}{x} = 7 - 4\sqrt{3} \quad \text{...(b)}$$

Now, $x + \frac{1}{x} = 7 + 4\sqrt{3} + 7 - 4\sqrt{3}$

[from Eqs. (a) and (b)]

$$\Rightarrow x + \frac{1}{x} = 14$$

$$\Rightarrow (\sqrt{x})^2 + \left(\frac{1}{\sqrt{x}}\right)^2 = 14$$

On adding 2 both sides, we get

$$(\sqrt{x})^2 + \left(\frac{1}{\sqrt{x}}\right)^2 + 2 = 14 + 2$$

$$\Rightarrow \left(\sqrt{x} + \frac{1}{\sqrt{x}}\right)^2 = 16$$

$[\because (a^2 + b^2 + 2ab) = (a + b)^2]$

$$\therefore \sqrt{x} + \frac{1}{\sqrt{x}} = \pm 4$$

(ii) $x - \frac{1}{x} = 7 + 4\sqrt{3} - (7 - 4\sqrt{3})$

$$\Rightarrow x - \frac{1}{x} = 7 + 4\sqrt{3} - 7 + 4\sqrt{3}$$

$$\Rightarrow x - \frac{1}{x} = 8\sqrt{3} \quad \text{...(c)}$$

On cubing both sides, we get

$$\left(x - \frac{1}{x}\right)^3 = (8\sqrt{3})^3$$

$$\Rightarrow x^3 - \frac{1}{x^3} - 3 \times x \times \frac{1}{x}\left(x - \frac{1}{x}\right) = 1536\sqrt{3}$$

$[\because (a - b)^3 = a^3 - b^3 - 3ab(a - b)]$

$$\Rightarrow x^3 - \frac{1}{x^3} - 3 \times 8\sqrt{3} = 1536\sqrt{3} \quad \text{[from Eq. (c)]}$$

$$\Rightarrow x^3 - \frac{1}{x^3} = 1536\sqrt{3} + 24\sqrt{3}$$

$$\therefore x^3 - \frac{1}{x^3} = 1560\sqrt{3}$$

9. We have, $\dfrac{(x^2 - y^2)^3 + (y^2 - z^2)^3 + (z^2 - x^2)^3}{(x - y)^3 + (y - z)^3 + (z - x)^3}$ ...(i)

Let $a = (x^2 - y^2)$, $b = (y^2 - z^2)$ and $c = (z^2 - x^2)$

Here, $a + b + c = x^2 - y^2 + y^2 - z^2 + z^2 - x^2 = 0$

We know that

If $(a + b + c) = 0$, then $a^3 + b^3 + c^3 = 3abc$

$\therefore (x^2 - y^2)^3 + (y^2 - z^2)^3 + (z^2 - x^2)^3 = 3(x^2 - y^2)(y^2 - z^2)(z^2 - x^2)$ ...(ii)

Again, let $A = (x - y)$, $B = (y - z)$, $C = (z - x)$

Here, $A + B + C = x - y + y - z + z - x = 0.$

If $(A + B + C) = 0$, then $A^3 + B^3 + C^3 = 3ABC$

$\therefore (x - y)^3 + (y - z)^3 + (z - x)^3 = 3(x - y)(y - z)(z - x)$ ...(iii)

On putting the value of Eqs. (ii) and (iii) in Eq. (i), we get

$$= \frac{3(x^2 - y^2)(y^2 - z^2)(z^2 - x^2)}{3(x - y)(y - z)(z - x)}$$

$$= \frac{(x + y)(x - y)(y + z)(y - z)(z + x)(z - x)}{(x - y)(y - z)(z - x)}$$

$[\because a^2 - b^2 = (a + b)(a - b)]$

$$= (x + y)(y + z)(z + x)$$

10. Given, $a + 3b + 5c = 0$ ...(i)

and $a^3 + 9b^3 + 25c^3 = 36abc$ ...(ii)

$\therefore$ $a + 3b = -5c$ ...(iii)

or $a + 5c = -3b$ ...(iv)

or $3b + 5c = -a$ ...(v) [from Eq. (i)]

Now, $\frac{(a+3b)^2}{ab}+\frac{(3b+5c)^2}{bc}+\frac{(5c+a)^2}{ca}$

$=\frac{(-5c)^2}{ab}+\frac{(-a)^2}{bc}+\frac{(-3b)^2}{ca}$ [from Eqs. (iii), (iv) and (v)]

$=\frac{25c^2}{ab}+\frac{a^2}{bc}+\frac{9b^2}{ca}$

$=\frac{25c^3+a^3+9b^3}{abc}$

$=\frac{36abc}{abc}$ [from Eq. (ii)]

$=36$

11. Let two positive numbers be x and y, where $x > y$.

According to the question, we have

$x-y=5$ and $x^3-y^3=650$

(i) Consider, $x-y=5$

On cubing both sides, we get $(x-y)^3=5^3$

$\Rightarrow x^3-y^3-3xy(x-y)=125$

$[\because (a-b)^3=a^3-b^3-3ab(a-b)]$

$\Rightarrow 650-3xy(5)=125$

$[\because x-y=5 \text{ and } x^3-y^3=650]$

$\Rightarrow 650-125=15xy$

$\Rightarrow 15xy=525$

$\Rightarrow xy=\frac{525}{15}=35$

$\therefore xy=35$ ...(a)

(ii) Again, consider $x-y=5$

On squaring both sides, we get $(x-y)^2=(5)^2$

$[\because (a-b)^2=a^2+b^2-2ab]$

$\Rightarrow x^2+y^2-2xy=25$

$\Rightarrow x^2+y^2-2\times 35=25$ [from Eq. (a)]

$\Rightarrow x^2+y^2-70=25$

$\Rightarrow x^2+y^2=95$

04

FACTORISATION

The process of expressing an algebraic expression as the product of two or more algebraic expressions is called **factorisation** and these expressions are called **factors** of given algebraic expression.

Factorisation by Taking Out Common Factors

If various terms of an expression have common factors, then the given expression can be factorised by dividing the each term of expression by common factor and enclose the quotient within brackets.

e.g. $20\,l^2m + 30\,alm = 10\,lm\left[\dfrac{20\,l^2m}{10\,lm} + \dfrac{30\,alm}{10\,lm}\right] = 10\,lm\,[2l + 3a]$

Factorisation of Grouping of Terms

An expression of even number of terms can be factorised into factors, if the terms are arranged in such a way that each group has a common factor.

e.g. $a^3 - 4a^2 + 3a - 12 = a^2(a-4) + 3(a-4)$

$= (a-4)(a^2+3)$

Factorisation by Making the Perfect Squares

Sometimes a given expression can be written as the perfect square of combination of two or more terms. In this case, the given expression can be expressed as the product of terms involved in perfect squares.

- $(a+b)^2 = a^2 + b^2 + 2ab$
- $(a-b)^2 = a^2 + b^2 - 2ab$

e.g. $9x^2 + 12xy + 4y^2 = (3x)^2 + 2 \times 3x \times 2y + (2y)^2$

$= (3x+2y)^2 = (3x+2y)(3x+2y)$

Factorisation of Difference of Two Squares

If the given expression is expressible as the difference of two squares, then we use the following identity $a^2 - b^2 = (a+b)(a-b)$ to factorise it.

e.g. $4x^2 - 169y^2 = (2x)^2 - (13y)^2 = (2x+13y)(2x-13y)$

Factorisation of Sum and Difference of Two Cubes

The sum and difference of two cubes can be factorised by using the following formulae.

- $a^3 + b^3 = (a+b)(a^2 - ab + b^2)$
- $(a^3 - b^3) = (a-b)(a^2 + ab + b^2)$

e.g. $a^6 + 512b^6 = (a^2)^3 + (8b^2)^3 = (a^2 + 8b^2)(a^4 - 8a^2b^2 + 64b^4)$

Factorisation of Trinomial by Splitting the Middle Term

A trinomial of the form $ax^2 + bx + c$, where $a \neq 0$ and a, b, c are constants. To factorise $ax^2 + bx + c$, b can be written as the sum of two numbers, whose product is equal to ac.

e.g. $6x^2 + 17x + 12 = 6x^2 + (9+8)x + 12 = 6x^2 + 9x + 8x + 12$

$= 3x(2x+3) + 4(2x+3) = (2x+3)(3x+4)$

EXAM ORIENTED QUESTIONS

TYPE - 1 — 01 Mark

Multiple Choice Questions

Q.1 Which one is the common factor of $4(a-b)^3 + 7(a-b)$?

(a) $(a+b)$ (b) $(a-b)$
(c) $(a-b)^2$ (d) $(a-b)^3$

Q.2 Factorise the expression $a(x-7y)^2 + b(7y-x) + 3x - 21y$.

(a) $(x-7y)[ax+7ay+b+3]$
(b) $(x+7y)[ax-7ay-b+3]$
(c) $(x-7y)[ax-7ay-b+3]$
(d) $(x+7y)[ax+7ay+b+3]$

Q.3 Factorise $18x^3y - 45x^2yz + 63x^3yz^2$.

(a) $9x^2y(2x-5z+7xz^2)$ (b) $9x^2y(2x+5z-7xz^2)$
(c) $9x^2y(2x+5z+7xz^2)$ (d) $9x^2y(2x-5z-7xz^2)$

Q.4 Factorise $pq^2 - 4pq + 4q - 16$.

(a) $(pq-4)(q+4)$ (b) $(pq+4)(pq+4)$
(c) $(pq-4)(q-4)$ (d) $(pq+4)(q-4)$

Q.5 Factorise $3ax - 6ay - 8by + 4bx + 9az + 12bz$.

(a) $(3a-4b)(x-2y+3z)$
(b) $(3a-4b)(x-2y-3z)$
(c) $(3a+4b)(x-2y+3z)$
(d) $(3a+4b)(x-2y-3z)$

Q.6 Find the factors of $121b^2 - 88bc + 16c^2$.

(a) $(11b-4c)(11b+4c)$
(b) $(11c-4b)(11c+4b)$
(c) $(11b-4c)(11b-4c)$
(d) $(11b+4c)(11b-4c)$

Q.7 Factorise $\left(x-\frac{1}{x}\right)^2 + 6\left(x-\frac{1}{x}\right) + 9$.

(a) $\left(x-\frac{1}{x}-3\right)\left(x-\frac{1}{x}-3\right)$

(b) $\left(x+\frac{1}{x}-3\right)\left(x+\frac{1}{x}-3\right)$

(c) $\left(x-\frac{1}{x}+3\right)\left(x-\frac{1}{x}+3\right)$

(d) $\left(x+\frac{1}{x}+3\right)\left(x+\frac{1}{x}+3\right)$

Q.8 Factorise $1-(p+q)^2$.

(a) $(1-p-q)(1+p+q)$
(b) $(1-p+q)(1-p-q)$
(c) $(1+p+q)(1+p-q)$
(d) $(1+p-q)(1-p-q)$

Q.9 Factorise $x^4 - 625$.

(a) $(x^2+25)(x+5)(x-5)$
(b) $(x^2-25)(x+5)$
(c) $(x^2+25)(x+5)^2$
(d) $(x^2+5)(x+25)(x-25)$

Q.10 Factorise the expression $\frac{x^3}{27} - \frac{y^3}{125}$

(a) $\left(\frac{x}{3}-\frac{y}{5}\right)\left(\frac{x^2}{9}-\frac{xy}{15}+\frac{y^2}{25}\right)$

(b) $\left(\frac{x}{3}+\frac{y}{5}\right)\left(\frac{x^2}{9}-\frac{xy}{15}+\frac{y^2}{25}\right)$

(c) $\left(\frac{x}{3}-\frac{y}{5}\right)\left(\frac{x^2}{9}+\frac{xy}{15}+\frac{y^2}{25}\right)$

(d) $\left(\frac{x}{3}+\frac{y}{5}\right)\left(\frac{x^2}{9}+\frac{xy}{15}+\frac{y^2}{25}\right)$

Q.11 Factorise $\frac{x^6}{343} + \frac{343}{x^6}$.

(a) $\left(\frac{x^2}{7}+\frac{7}{x^2}\right)\left(\frac{x^4}{49}-1+\frac{49}{x^4}\right)$

(b) $\left(\frac{x^2}{7}-\frac{7}{x^2}\right)\left(\frac{x^4}{49}+1-\frac{49}{x^4}\right)$

(c) $\left(\frac{x^2}{7}-\frac{7}{x^2}\right)\left(\frac{x^4}{49}-1-\frac{49}{x^4}\right)$

(d) $\left(\frac{x^2}{7}+\frac{7}{x^2}\right)\left(\frac{x^4}{49}+1+\frac{49}{x^4}\right)$

Q.12 Simplify the expression $a^3 - 0.064$.

(a) $(a-0.4)(a^2-0.16-0.4a)$
(b) $(a+0.4)(a^2+0.16-0.4a)$
(c) $(a+0.4)(a^2-0.16+0.4a)$
(d) $(a-0.4)(a^2+0.16+0.4a)$

Q.13 Factorise the polynomial $4x^2 + 7x + 3$.

(a) $(x + 1)(4x + 3)$ (b) $(4x + 1)(x + 3)$
(c) $(4x + 3)(x + 2)$ (d) $(x + 3)(4x + 1)$

Q.14 Factorise $(3x^2 - 2x - 5)(3x^2 - 2x - 1)$.

(a) $(3x + 5)(x + 1)(x - 1)(3x + 1)$
(b) $(3x + 5)(3x - 1)(x + 1)(x - 1)$
(c) $(3x - 5)(x + 1)(x - 1)(3x + 1)$
(d) $(3x - 5)(x - 1)(x + 1)(x - 1)$

Answers

1. (b)	**2.** (c)	**3.** (a)	**4.** (d)	**5.** (c)
6. (c)	**7.** (c)	**8.** (a)	**9.** (a)	**10.** (c)
11. (a)	**12.** (d)	**13.** (a)	**14.** (c)	

TYPE - 2 01 Mark

Assertion-Reason Type Questions

Q.1 Assertion (A) Factors of $5x^3 - 125x$ are $5x$, $(x - 5)$ and $(x + 5)$.

Reason (R) $a^3 - b^3 = (a - b)(a^2 + b^2 + ab)$.

(a) A is true, R is false.
(b) A is false, R is true.
(c) Both A and R are true and R is the correct reason for A.
(d) Both A and R are true and R is incorrect reason for A.

Q.2 Assertion (A) Factors of $x^3 - 5x^2 - x + 5$ are $(x - 5), (x + 1)$ and $(x - 1)$.

Reason (R) $a^2 - b^2 = (a + b)(a - b)$

(a) A is true, R is false.
(b) A is false, R is true.
(c) Both A and R are true and R is the correct reason for A.
(d) Both A and R are true and R is incorrect reason for A.

Q.3 Assertion (A) $35^3 + 27^3$ is divisible by 62.

Reason (R) $a^3 + b^3 = (a + b)(a^2 + b^2 + ab)$.

(a) A is true, R is false.
(b) A is false, R is true.
(c) Both A and R are true and R is the correct reason for A.
(d) Both A and R are true and R is incorrect reason for A.

Answers

1. (d) **2.** (c) **3.** (a)

TYPE - 3 01 Mark

Statement Based Questions

Q.1 Statement I The common factor of this expression $10x(x + 2y)^3 - 15y(x + 2y)^2 + 35(x + 2y)$ is $5(x + 2y)$.

Statement II $(x + 3y)$ is a factor of the expression $(x^4 - 81y^4)$.

Which of the following is valid?
(a) Both the Statements are true.
(b) Both the Statements are false.
(c) Statement I is true and Statement II is false.
(d) Statement I is false and Statement II is true.

Q.2 Statement I $(a - \sqrt{5}b)$ and $(a^2 + 5b^2 + \sqrt{5}ab)$ are the factors of $a^3 - 5\sqrt{5}b^3$.

Statement II $(5x - 2)$ is not the factor of the expression, $5x^2 - 32x + 12$.

Which of the following is valid?
(a) Both the Statements are true.
(b) Both the Statements are false.
(c) Statement I is true and Statement II is false.
(d) Statement I is false and Statement II is true.

Q.3 Statement I Factors of $x^2 - 21$ are $(x + 21)$ and $(x - 21)$.

Statement II Factors of $x^8 - y^8$ are $(x^4 + y^4)$, $(x^2 + y^2)$, $(x + y)$, $(x - y)$ and $(x + y)$.

Which of the following is valid?
(a) Both the Statements are true.
(b) Both the Statements are false.
(c) Statement I is true and Statement II is false.
(d) Statement I is false and Statement II is true.

Q.4 Statement I If $\frac{x}{y} + \frac{y}{x} = 1$, then the value of $x^3 + y^3$ is 10.

Statement II $(a - 1)$ is a factor of the expression $a - 1 - (a - 1)^2 + ax - x$.

Which of the following is valid?
(a) Both the Statements are true.
(b) Both the Statements are false.
(c) Statement I is true and Statement II is false.
(d) Statement I is false and Statement II is true.

Answers

1. (a) **2.** (c) **3.** (b) **4.** (d)

TYPE - 4 — 03 Marks

Short Answer Type Questions

Q.1 Find the factors of $6xy^2 + 9x^2y - 21xy$.

Q.2 Find the factors of $x^2 - \left(\frac{a+b}{a} + \frac{a}{a+b}\right)x + 1$.

Q.3 Factorise $x^4 + y^4 - 18x^2y^2$.

Q.4 Factorise $\left(x^2 + \frac{1}{x^2}\right) - 4\left(x + \frac{1}{x}\right) + 6$.

Q.5 Find the factors of this expression $36(x-y)^2 - 25(2x+y)^2$.

Q.6 If $a^2 + 6a + x = (a+3)^2$, then find the value of x.

Q.7 If $x - \frac{1}{x} = \sqrt{2}$, then find $x^2 + \frac{1}{x^2}$.

Q.8 Find the factors of $9(x+y)^2 - 24(x^2 - y^2) + 16(x-y)^2$.

Q.9 Find the factors of $x^4 + 36x^2 - 12x^3 - 49$.

Q.10 Simplify $\frac{0.87 \times 0.87 \times 0.87 + 0.13 \times 0.13 \times 0.13}{0.87 \times 0.87 - 0.87 \times 0.13 + 0.13 \times 0.13}$.

Q.11 Find the factors of $5\sqrt{5}x^2 + 20x + 3\sqrt{5}$.

Q.12 Factorise $x^{12} - y^{12}$.

Q.13 Factorise $\frac{-12}{2} + \frac{5x}{2} + x^2$.

Q.14 A rectangle whose area is $2x^2 + 14x - 16$, find its length and breadth.

Q.15 Factorise $5 - (3x^2 - 2x)(6 - 3x^2 + 2x)$.

Answers

1. $3xy(2y + 3x - 7)$
2. $\left(x - \frac{a}{a+b}\right)\left(x - \frac{a+b}{a}\right)$
3. $(x^2 - y^2 + 4xy)(x^2 - y^2 - 4xy)$
4. $\left[\left(x + \frac{1}{x}\right) - 2\right]\left[\left(x + \frac{1}{x}\right) - 2\right]$
5. $-[(4x + 11y)(16x - y)]$
6. 9
7. 4
8. $(7y - x)(7y - x)$
9. $(x^2 - 6x + 7)(x - 7)(x + 1)$
10. 1
11. $(\sqrt{5}x + 3)(5x + \sqrt{5})$
12. $(x - y)(x^2 + xy + y^2)(x + y)(x^2 - xy + y^2) \times (x^2 + y^2)(x^4 - x^2y^2 + y^4)$
13. $\frac{1}{2}[(x+4)(2x-3)]$
14. length = $(x + 8)$, breadth = $(2x - 2)$
15. $(3x - 5)(x + 1)(3x + 1)(x - 1)$

TYPE - 5 — 4/5 Marks

Long Answer Type Questions

Q.1 Find the factors of $(a^2 - b^2)(c^2 - d^2) - 4abcd$.

Q.2 If $xya^2 = (x-y)^2(a+1)$ then find the value of $1 + \frac{4}{a} + \frac{4}{a^2}$

Q.3 Find the factors of $\left(2x - \frac{1}{2x}\right)^2 - 4x^2 + \frac{1}{4x^2}$.

Q.4 If $a > 1$ and $a + \frac{1}{a} = \frac{9}{2}$ then find the values of

(i) $a^2 + \frac{1}{a^2}$ (ii) $a - \frac{1}{a}$ (iii) $a^4 - \frac{1}{a^4}$ (iv) $a^3 - \frac{1}{a^3}$

Q.5 Factorise the given expression

$$27a^3 + \frac{1}{64b^3} + \frac{27a^2}{4b} + \frac{9a}{16b^2}$$

Answers

1. $(ac - bd + ad + bc)(ac - bd - ad - bc)$
2. $\left(\frac{x+y}{x-y}\right)^2$
3. $\frac{1}{2}\left(\frac{1}{x} - 2\right)\left(\frac{1}{x} + 2\right)$
4. (i) $\frac{73}{4}$ (ii) $\frac{\sqrt{65}}{2}$ (iii) $\frac{657\sqrt{65}}{16}$ (iv) $\frac{77\sqrt{65}}{8}$
5. $\left(3a + \frac{1}{4b}\right)\left(3a + \frac{1}{4b}\right)\left(3a + \frac{1}{4b}\right)$

EXPLANATIONS

Multiple Choice Questions

1. (b) We have, $4(a-b)^3+7(a-b)$

$$=(a-b)[4(a-b)^2+7]$$

Hence, the common factor is $(a-b)$.

2. (c) We have, $a(x-7y)^2+b(7y-x)+3x-21y$

$$=a(x-7y)^2+b(7y-x)+3(x-7y)$$
$$=a(x-7y)^2-b(x-7y)+3(x-7y)$$
$$=(x-7y)[a(x-7y)-b+3]$$
$$=(x-7y)[ax-7ay-b+3]$$

3. (a) We have, $18x^3y-45x^2yz+63x^3yz^2$.

$$=9x^2y\left[\frac{18x^3y}{9x^2y}-\frac{45x^2yz}{9x^2y}+\frac{63x^3yz^2}{9x^2y}\right]$$
$$=9x^2y[2x-5z+7xz^2]$$

4. (d) We have, $pq^2-4pq+4q-16$

$$=pq(q-4)+4(q-4)$$

Now, $(q-4)$ is common factor in both groups.

So, $(q-4)(pq+4)$.

5. (c) We have, $3ax-6ay-8by+4bx+9az+12bz$

Now, arranging the given expression into groups

$$=(3ax+4bx)-6ay-8by+9az+12bz$$
$$=(3ax+4bx)-(6ay+8by)+(9az+12bz)$$
$$=x(3a+4b)-2y(3a+4b)+3z(3a+4b)$$

Now, $(3a+4b)$ is common factor for each group.

So, $(3a+4b)(x-2y+3z)$, which is the required factorisation of given expression.

6. (c) We have, $121b^2-88bc+16c^2$

$$=(11b)^2-2\times 11b\times 4c+(4c)^2$$
$$=(11b-4c)^2 \quad [\because a^2-2ab+b^2=(a-b)^2]$$
$$=(11b-4c)(11b-4c)$$

7. (c) We have, $\left(x-\dfrac{1}{x}\right)^2+6\left(x-\dfrac{1}{x}\right)+9$

Let $\left(x-\dfrac{1}{x}\right)=y$ ...(i)

Then, y^2+6y+9

$$=(y)^2+2\times y\times 3+(3)^2$$
$$=(y+3)^2 \quad [\because a^2+2ab+b^2=(a+b)^2]$$
$$=\left(x-\frac{1}{x}+3\right)^2 \quad \text{[from Eq. (i)]}$$
$$=\left(x-\frac{1}{x}+3\right)\left(x-\frac{1}{x}+3\right)$$

8. (a) We have, $1-(p+q)^2$

$$=1^2-(p+q)^2$$
$$=[1-(p+q)][1+(p+q)] \quad [\because a^2-b^2=(a-b)(a+b)]$$
$$=(1+p+q)(1-p-q)$$

9. (a) We have, x^4-625

$$=(x^2)^2-(25)^2$$
$$=(x^2+25)(x^2-25) \quad [\because a^2-b^2=(a+b)(a-b)]$$
$$=(x^2+25)(x^2-5^2)$$
$$=(x^2+25)(x+5)(x-5)$$

10. (c) We have, $\dfrac{x^3}{27}-\dfrac{y^3}{125}=\dfrac{x^3}{3^3}-\dfrac{y^3}{5^3}=\left(\dfrac{x}{3}\right)^3-\left(\dfrac{y}{5}\right)^3$

$$=\left(\frac{x}{3}-\frac{y}{5}\right)\left(\frac{x^2}{9}+\frac{xy}{15}+\frac{y^2}{25}\right)$$
$$[\because (a^3-b^3)=(a-b)(a^2+ab+b^2)]$$

11. (a) We have, $\dfrac{x^6}{343}+\dfrac{343}{x^6}=\dfrac{(x^2)^3}{7^3}+\dfrac{7^3}{(x^2)^3}$

$$=\left(\frac{x^2}{7}\right)^3+\left(\frac{7}{x^2}\right)^3$$
$$=\left(\frac{x^2}{7}+\frac{7}{x^2}\right)\left[\left(\frac{x^2}{7}\right)^2-\frac{x^2}{7}\times\frac{7}{x^2}+\left(\frac{7}{x^2}\right)^2\right]$$
$$[\because a^3+b^3=(a+b)(a^2-ab+b^2)]$$
$$=\left(\frac{x^2}{7}+\frac{7}{x^2}\right)\left(\frac{x^4}{49}-1+\frac{49}{x^4}\right)$$

12. (d) We have, $a^3-0.064=a^3-(0.4)^3$

$$=(a-0.4)(a^2+0.16+0.4a)$$
$$[\because a^3-b^3=(a-b)(a^2+b^2+ab)]$$

13. (a) We have, $4x^2+7x+3$

$$=4x^2+(4+3)x+3 \quad \text{[by splitting the middle term]}$$
$$=4x^2+4x+3x+3$$
$$=4x(x+1)+3(x+1)=(x+1)(4x+3)$$

14. (c) We have, $(3x^2-2x-5)(3x^2-2x-1)$

On splitting the middle term, we get

$$[3x^2-(5-3)x-5][3x^2-(3-1)x-1]$$
$$=[3x^2-5x+3x-5][3x^2-3x+x-1]$$
$$=[x(3x-5)+1(3x-5)][3x(x-1)+1(x-1)]$$
$$=(3x-5)(x+1)(x-1)(3x+1)$$

Assertion-Reason Type Questions

1. (d) We have, $5x^3 - 125x$

$$= 5x(x^2 - 25) = 5x(x^2 - 5^2)$$
$$= 5x(x-5)(x+5)$$
$$[\because a^2 - b^2 = (a-b)(a+b)]$$

Hence, both A and R are true and R is incorrect reason for A.

2. (c) We have, $x^3 - 5x^2 - x + 5$

$$= x^2(x-5) - 1(x-5) = (x-5)(x^2-1)$$
$$= (x-5)(x^2-1^2)$$
$$= (x-5)(x+1)(x-1)$$
$$[\because a^2 - b^2 = (a+b)(a-b)]$$

Hence, both A and R are true and R is the correct reason for A.

3. (a) **Assertion** We have,

$$35^3 + 27^3 = (35+27)(35^2 + 27^2 - 35 \times 27)$$
$$[\because a^3 + b^3 = (a+b)(a^2 + b^2 - ab)]$$
$$= 62\,(35^2 + 27^2 - 35 \times 27)$$

So, $35^3 + 27^3$ is divisible by 62.

Hence, A is true, R is false.

Statement Based Questions

1. (a) **Statement I** We have,

$10x(x+2y)^3 - 15y(x+2y)^2 + 35(x+2y)$

In this expression, we see that each term can be divided by $5(x+2y)$.

$$5(x+2y)[2x(x+2y)^2 - 3y(x+2y) + 7]$$

So, $5(x+2y)$ is the common factor of the given expression.

Hence, Statement I is true.

Statement II We have,

$$(x^4 - 81y^4) = (x^2)^2 - (9y^2)^2 = (x^2 + 9y^2)(x^2 - 9y^2)$$
$$[\because a^2 - b^2 = (a+b)(a-b)]$$

We see that $x^2 - 9y^2$ is again expressed as a difference of two squares.

$$\therefore\ (x^2 + 9y^2)[x^2 - (3y)^2] = (x^2 + 9y^2)(x+3y)(x-3y)$$

So, $(x + 3y)$ is a factor of the given expression.

Hence, Statement II is true.

2. (c) **Statement I** We have,

$$a^3 - 5\sqrt{5}b^3 = a^3 - (\sqrt{5}b)^3$$
$$= (a - \sqrt{5}b)(a^2 + 5b^2 + \sqrt{5}ab)$$
$$[\because a^3 - b^3 = (a-b)(a^2 + b^2 + ab)]$$

Hence, Statement I is true.

Statement II We have,

$$5x^2 - 32x + 12 = 5x^2 - (30+2)x + 12$$
[by splitting the middle term]
$$= 5x^2 - 30x - 2x + 12$$
$$= 5x(x-6) - 2(x-6)$$
$$= (5x-2)(x-6)$$

Here, we can see that $(5x - 2)$ is a factor of the given expression. So, Statement II is false.

3. (b) **Statement I** We have,

$$x^2 - 21 = x^2 - (\sqrt{21})^2$$
$$= (x + \sqrt{21})(x - \sqrt{21})$$
$$[\because A^2 - B^2 = (A+B)(A-B)]$$

Statement II We have,

$$x^8 - y^8 = (x^4)^2 - (y^4)^2$$
$$= (x^4 + y^4)(x^4 - y^4)$$
$$[\because A^2 - B^2 = (A+B)(A-B)]$$
$$= (x^4 + y^4)((x^2)^2 - (y^2)^2)$$
$$= (x^4 + y^4)(x^2 + y^2)(x^2 - y^2)$$
$$= (x^4 + y^4)(x^2 + y^2)(x+y)(x-y)$$

Hence, both the Statements are false.

4. (d) **Statement I** If $\frac{x}{y} + \frac{y}{x} = 1$

$$\Rightarrow \quad \frac{x^2 + y^2}{xy} = 1$$
$$\Rightarrow \quad x^2 + y^2 = xy \qquad \ldots(i)$$

We have, $x^3 + y^3 = (x+y)(x^2 + y^2 - xy)$

$$[\because A^3 + B^3 = (A+B)(A^2 + B^2 - AB)]$$
$$= (x+y)(xy - xy) \text{ [from Eq. (i)]}$$
$$= (x+y) \times 0 = 0$$

Statement II We have,

$$a - 1 - (a-1)^2 + ax - x = (a-1)(1 - (a-1) + x)$$

Hence, Statement I is false and Statement II is true.

Short Answer Type Questions

1. We have, $6xy^2 + 9x^2y - 21xy$

In this expression, we can see that each term can be divided by $3xy$.

So, $3xy$ is common term.

Here, $3xy\left[\frac{6xy^2}{3xy} + \frac{9x^2y}{3xy} - \frac{21xy}{3xy}\right] = 3xy(2y + 3x - 7)$,

which is the required factorisation of the given expression.

2. We have, $x^2 - \left(\frac{a+b}{a} + \frac{a}{a+b}\right)x + 1$

$$= x^2 - \left(\frac{a+b}{a}\right)x - \left(\frac{a}{a+b}\right)x + 1$$

Here, first two terms have x as common factor and in last two terms, we take $-\frac{a}{a+b}$ as common factor.

So, $x\left(x - \frac{a+b}{a}\right) - \frac{a}{a+b}\left(x - \frac{a+b}{a}\right)$

$$= \left(x - \frac{a}{a+b}\right)\left(x - \frac{a+b}{a}\right),$$

which is the required factorisation of given expression.

3. We have, $x^4 + y^4 - 18x^2y^2$

$$= (x^2)^2 + (y^2)^2 - 2x^2y^2 - 16x^2y^2$$

$$= (x^2 - y^2)^2 - 16x^2y^2 \quad [\because a^2 + b^2 - 2ab = (a-b)^2]$$

$$= (x^2 - y^2)^2 - (4xy)^2$$

$$= (x^2 - y^2 + 4xy)(x^2 - y^2 - 4xy)$$

$$[\because a^2 - b^2 = (a+b)(a-b)]$$

4. We have, $\left(x^2 + \frac{1}{x^2}\right) - 4\left(x + \frac{1}{x}\right) + 6$

On adding and subtracting 2, we get

$$x^2 + \frac{1}{x^2} + 2 - 2 - 4\left(x + \frac{1}{x}\right) + 6$$

$$= \left(x + \frac{1}{x}\right)^2 - 2 - 4\left(x + \frac{1}{x}\right) + 6$$

$$[\because (a+b)^2 = a^2 + b^2 + 2ab]$$

$$= \left(x + \frac{1}{x}\right)^2 - 4\left(x + \frac{1}{x}\right) + 4$$

$$= \left(x + \frac{1}{x}\right)^2 - 2 \times \left(x + \frac{1}{x}\right) \times 2 + (2)^2$$

$$= \left[\left(x + \frac{1}{x}\right) - 2\right]^2 = \left[\left(x + \frac{1}{x}\right) - 2\right]\left[\left(x + \frac{1}{x}\right) - 2\right]$$

5. We have, $36(x-y)^2 - 25(2x+y)^2$

$$= 36(x^2 + y^2 - 2xy) - 25(4x^2 + y^2 + 4xy)$$

$$\left[\begin{array}{ll}\because & (a-b)^2 = a^2 + b^2 - 2ab \\ \text{and} & (a+b)^2 = a^2 + b^2 + 2ab\end{array}\right]$$

$$= 36x^2 + 36y^2 - 72xy - 100x^2 - 25y^2 - 100xy$$

$$= -64x^2 + 11y^2 - 172xy$$

$$= -[64x^2 + 172xy - 11y^2]$$

$$= -[64x^2 + 176xy - 4xy - 11y^2]$$

[by splitting the middle term]

$$= -[16x(4x + 11y) - y(4x + 11y)]$$

$$= -[(4x + 11y)(16x - y)]$$

6. Given, $a^2 + 6a + x = (a+3)^2$

$$a^2 + 6a + x = a^2 + 6a + 9$$

$$[\because (A+B)^2 = A^2 + B^2 + 2AB]$$

On comparing both sides, we get

$$x = 9$$

7. Given, $x - \frac{1}{x} = \sqrt{2}$

On squaring both sides, we get

$$\left(x - \frac{1}{x}\right)^2 = (\sqrt{2})^2$$

$$\Rightarrow x^2 + \frac{1}{x^2} - 2 \times x \times \frac{1}{x} = 2 \quad [\because (a-b)^2 = a^2 + b^2 - 2ab]$$

$$\Rightarrow \quad x^2 + \frac{1}{x^2} - 2 = 2 \Rightarrow x^2 + \frac{1}{x^2} = 4$$

Hence, the value of $\left(x^2 + \frac{1}{x^2}\right)$ is 4.

8. We have, $9(x+y)^2 - 24(x^2 - y^2) + 16(x-y)^2$

$$= [3(x+y)]^2 - 2 \times 3(x+y) \times 4(x-y) + [4(x-y)]^2$$

$$= [3(x+y) - 4(x-y)]^2 \quad [\because a^2 - 2ab + b^2 = (a-b)^2]$$

$$= [3x + 3y - 4x + 4y]^2$$

$$= [-x + 7y]^2$$

$$= [7y - x]^2 = (7y - x)(7y - x)$$

9. We have, $x^4 + 36x^2 - 12x^3 - 49$

$$= (x^2)^2 + (6x)^2 - 2 \times x^2 \times 6x - 7^2$$

$$= (x^2 - 6x)^2 - 7^2 \quad [\because a^2 + b^2 - 2ab = (a-b)^2]$$

$$= [(x^2 - 6x) + 7][(x^2 - 6x) - 7]$$

$$= (x^2 - 6x + 7)(x^2 - 7x + x - 7)$$

[by splitting middle term]

$$= (x^2 - 6x + 7)(x - 7)(x + 1)$$

10. We have, $\frac{0.87 \times 0.87 \times 0.87 + 0.13 \times 0.13 \times 0.13}{0.87 \times 0.87 - 0.87 \times 0.13 + 0.13 \times 0.13}$

$$= \frac{(0.87)^3 + (0.13)^3}{[(0.87)^2 - (0.87 \times 0.13) + (0.13)^2]}$$

$$= \frac{(0.87 + 0.13)[(0.87)^2 - (0.87 \times 0.13) + (0.13)^2]}{[(0.87)^2 - (0.87 \times 0.13) + (0.13)^2]}$$

$$[\because a^3 + b^3 = (a+b)(a^2 + b^2 - ab)]$$

$$= 0.87 + 0.13 = 1$$

11. We have, $5\sqrt{5}x^2 + 20x + 3\sqrt{5}$

$$= 5\sqrt{5}x^2 + (15 + 5)x + 3\sqrt{5}$$

[by splitting the middle term]

$$= 5\sqrt{5}x^2 + 15x + 5x + 3\sqrt{5}$$

$$= 5x(\sqrt{5}x + 3) + \sqrt{5}(\sqrt{5}x + 3)$$

$$= (\sqrt{5}x + 3)(5x + \sqrt{5})$$

12. We have, $x^{12} - y^{12}$

$= (x^6)^2 - (y^6)^2 = (x^6 - y^6)(x^6 + y^6)$

$[\because a^2 - b^2 = (a+b)(a-b)]$

$= [(x^3)^2 - (y^3)^2][(x^2)^3 + (y^2)^3]$

$= [(x^3 - y^3)(x^3 + y^3)][(x^2 + y^2)(x^4 - x^2y^2 + y^4)]$

$= (x-y)(x^2 + xy + y^2)(x+y)(x^2 - xy + y^2) \times (x^2 + y^2)(x^4 - x^2y^2 + y^4)$

$[\because a^3 + b^3 = (a+b)(a^2 + b^2 - ab)$ and $a^3 - b^3 = (a-b)(a^2 + b^2 + ab)]$

13. We have, $\frac{-12}{2} + \frac{5x}{2} + x^2 = \frac{-12 + 5x + 2x^2}{2}$

$= \frac{1}{2}[2x^2 + 5x - 12] = \frac{1}{2}[2x^2 + (8-3)x - 12]$

[by splitting middle term]

$= \frac{1}{2}[2x^2 + 8x - 3x - 12]$

$= \frac{1}{2}[2x(x+4) - 3(x+4)]$

$= \frac{1}{2}[(x+4)(2x-3)]$

14. Given, area of the rectangle $= 2x^2 + 14x - 16$

$= 2x^2 + (16-2)x - 16$ [by splitting the middle term]

$= 2x^2 + 16x - 2x - 16 = 2x(x+8) - 2(x+8)$

Area of rectangle $= (x+8)(2x-2)$ ...(i)

As we know,

Area of rectangle = Length × Breadth ...(ii)

If length $= (x+8)$,

then breadth $= (2x-2)$

15. We have, $5 - (3x^2 - 2x)(6 - 3x^2 + 2x)$

Let $3x^2 - 2x = y$ ...(i)

Then, $5 - y(6-y) = 5 - 6y + y^2 = y^2 - 6y + 5$

$= y^2 - (5+1)y + 5$

[by splitting the middle term]

$= y^2 - 5y - y + 5 = y(y-5) - 1(y-5)$

$= (y-5)(y-1)$

$= (3x^2 - 2x - 5)(3x^2 - 2x - 1)$

[from Eq. (i)]

Now, again splitting the middle term, we get

$= [3x^2 - 5x + 3x - 5][3x^2 - 3x + x - 1]$

$= [x(3x-5) + 1(3x-5)][3x(x-1) + 1(x-1)]$

$= (3x-5)(x+1)(3x+1)(x-1)$

Long Answer Type Questions

1. We have, $(a^2 - b^2)(c^2 - d^2) - 4abcd$

$= (a^2c^2 - b^2c^2 - a^2d^2 + b^2d^2) - 4abcd$

$= (a^2c^2 - b^2c^2 - a^2d^2 + b^2d^2) - 2abcd - 2abcd$

$= (a^2c^2 + b^2d^2 - 2abcd) + (-a^2d^2 - b^2c^2 - 2abcd)$

$= (a^2c^2 + b^2d^2 - 2abcd) - (a^2d^2 + b^2c^2 + 2abcd)$

$= [(ac)^2 + (bd)^2 - 2(ac)(bd)] - [(ad)^2 + (bc)^2 + 2(ad)(bc)]$

$= (ac - bd)^2 - (ad + bc)^2$

$[\because (a \pm b)^2 = a^2 \pm 2ab + b^2]$

$= (ac - bd + ad + bc)(ac - bd - ad - bc)$

$[\because a^2 - b^2 = (a+b)(a-b)]$

2. Given, $xya^2 = (x-y)^2(a+1)$

$\Rightarrow \frac{xy}{(x-y)^2} = \frac{a+1}{a^2}$

On multiplying by 4 both sides, we get

$\frac{4xy}{(x-y)^2} = \frac{4(a+1)}{a^2}$

$\Rightarrow \frac{4xy}{(x-y)^2} = \frac{4a+4}{a^2} \Rightarrow \frac{4xy}{(x-y)^2} = \frac{4}{a} + \frac{4}{a^2}$

Now, on adding 1 both sides, we get

$1 + \frac{4xy}{(x-y)^2} = 1 + \frac{4}{a} + \frac{4}{a^2}$

$\Rightarrow \frac{(x-y)^2 + 4xy}{(x-y)^2} = 1 + \frac{4}{a} + \frac{4}{a^2}$

$\Rightarrow \frac{x^2 + y^2 - 2xy + 4xy}{(x-y)^2} = 1 + \frac{4}{a} + \frac{4}{a^2}$

$[\because (a-b)^2 = a^2 + b^2 - 2ab]$

$\Rightarrow \frac{x^2 + y^2 + 2xy}{(x-y)^2} = 1 + \frac{4}{a} + \frac{4}{a^2}$

$\Rightarrow \frac{(x+y)^2}{(x-y)^2} = 1 + \frac{4}{a} + \frac{4}{a^2}$

$[\because a^2 + b^2 + 2ab = (a+b)^2]$

Hence, the value of $\left(1 + \frac{4}{a} + \frac{4}{a^2}\right) = \frac{(x+y)^2}{(x-y)^2} = \left(\frac{x+y}{x-y}\right)^2$

3. We have, $\left(2x - \frac{1}{2x}\right)^2 - 4x^2 + \frac{1}{4x^2}$

$= 4x^2 + \frac{1}{4x^2} - 2 - 4x^2 + \frac{1}{4x^2}$

$[\because (a-b)^2 = a^2 + b^2 - 2ab]$

$= \frac{1}{4x^2} + \frac{1}{4x^2} - 2$

$= \frac{1}{2x^2} - 2 = \frac{1}{2}\left(\frac{1}{x^2} - 4\right)$

$= \frac{1}{2}\left(\frac{1}{x} - 2\right)\left(\frac{1}{x} + 2\right)$

$[\because a^2 - b^2 = (a-b)(a+b)]$

4. Given, $a + \frac{1}{a} = \frac{9}{2}$ ...(a)

(i) We have, $a^2 + \frac{1}{a^2}$

On squaring both sides of Eq. (a), we get

$$\left(a + \frac{1}{a}\right)^2 = \left(\frac{9}{2}\right)^2 \Rightarrow a^2 + \frac{1}{a^2} + 2 \times a \times \frac{1}{a} = \frac{81}{4}$$

$$\Rightarrow a^2 + \frac{1}{a^2} + 2 = \frac{81}{4} \Rightarrow a^2 + \frac{1}{a^2} = \frac{81}{4} - 2$$

$$\therefore \quad a^2 + \frac{1}{a^2} = \frac{73}{4} \quad \text{...(b)}$$

(ii) We have, $a - \frac{1}{a}$

On squaring both sides, we get

$$\left(a - \frac{1}{a}\right)^2 = a^2 + \frac{1}{a^2} - 2 \times a \times \frac{1}{a}$$

$$[\because (a-b)^2 = a^2 + b^2 - 2ab]$$

$$= \frac{73}{4} - 2 \quad \text{[from Eq. (b)]}$$

$$= \frac{65}{4} = \sqrt{\frac{65}{4}}$$

$$\therefore \quad \left(a - \frac{1}{a}\right) = \frac{\sqrt{65}}{2} \quad \text{...(c)}$$

(iii) We have, $\left(a^4 - \frac{1}{a^4}\right)$

$$= \left[(a^2)^2 - \frac{1}{(a^2)^2}\right] = \left(a^2 + \frac{1}{a^2}\right)\left(a^2 - \frac{1}{a^2}\right)$$

$$[\because a^2 - b^2 = (a+b)(a-b)]$$

$$= \left(a^2 + \frac{1}{a^2}\right)\left(a + \frac{1}{a}\right)\left(a - \frac{1}{a}\right) = \frac{73}{4} \times \frac{9}{2} \times \frac{\sqrt{65}}{2}$$

[from Eqs. (a), (b) and (c)]

$$= \frac{657\sqrt{65}}{16}$$

(iv) We have, $\left(a - \frac{1}{a}\right)^3 = a^3 - \frac{1}{a^3} - 3 \times a \times \frac{1}{a}\left(a - \frac{1}{a}\right)$

$$[\because (a-b)^3 = a^3 - b^3 - 3ab(a-b)]$$

$$\Rightarrow \left(\frac{\sqrt{65}}{2}\right)^3 = a^3 - \frac{1}{a^3} - 3\left(\frac{\sqrt{65}}{2}\right)$$

[from Eq. (c)]

$$\Rightarrow \frac{65\sqrt{65}}{8} + \frac{3\sqrt{65}}{2} = a^3 - \frac{1}{a^3}$$

$$\Rightarrow \frac{77\sqrt{65}}{8} = a^3 - \frac{1}{a^3} \Rightarrow a^3 - \frac{1}{a^3} = \frac{77\sqrt{65}}{8}$$

5. We have, $27a^3 + \frac{1}{64b^3} + \frac{27a^2}{4b} + \frac{9a}{16b^2}$

$$= (3a)^3 + \frac{1}{(4b)^3} + \frac{9a}{4b}\left[3a + \frac{1}{4b}\right]$$

$$= \left(3a + \frac{1}{4b}\right)\left[(3a)^2 + \frac{1}{(4b)^2} - 3a \times \frac{1}{4b}\right] + \frac{9a}{4b}\left(3a + \frac{1}{4b}\right)$$

$$[\because (a^3 + b^3) = (a+b)(a^2 + b^2 - ab)]$$

Here, we see that $\left(3a + \frac{1}{4b}\right)$ is common factor in both groups.

$$\text{So, } \left(3a + \frac{1}{4b}\right)\left[(3a)^2 + \frac{1}{(4b)^2} - 3a \times \frac{1}{4b} + \frac{9a}{4b}\right]$$

$$= \left(3a + \frac{1}{4b}\right)\left[(3a)^2 + \frac{1}{(4b)^2} + \frac{6a}{4b}\right]$$

$$= \left(3a + \frac{1}{4b}\right)\left[(3a)^2 + \frac{1}{(4b)^2} + 2 \times 3a \times \frac{1}{4b}\right]$$

$$= \left(3a + \frac{1}{4b}\right)\left[3a + \frac{1}{4b}\right]^2 \quad [\because a^2 + b^2 + 2ab = (a+b)^2]$$

$$= \left(3a + \frac{1}{4b}\right)\left(3a + \frac{1}{4b}\right)\left(3a + \frac{1}{4b}\right)$$

SIMULTANEOUS LINEAR EQUATION IN TWO VARIABLES

Linear Equation in Two Variables

An equation $ax + by + c = 0$, where a, b and c are real numbers (a and b together cannot be zero) and x, y are variables (each with degree 1), is called a linear equation in two variables.

e.g. (i) $3x + 2y = 4$ (ii) $1.2s + 3t = 5$

System of Simultaneous Linear Equations

Two linear equations in the two variables say x and y, is said to form a system of simultaneous linear equations if the same values of x and y satisfy both the equations. The general form of system of simultaneous linear equation in two variables x and y is

$$a_1x + b_1y + c_1 = 0 \text{ and } a_2x + b_2y + c_2 = 0,$$

where a_1, b_1, c_1, a_2, b_2 and c_2 are all real numbers and $a_1^2 + b_1^2 \neq 0, a_2^2 + b_2^2 \neq 0$.

Solving a System of Simultaneous Linear Equations

Solving a system of simultaneous linear equations, we mean to find the values of variables, which simultaneously satisfy all the equations occurring in the system.

Consider $a_1x + b_1y + c_1 = 0$ and $a_2x + b_2y + c_2 = 0$

Solving this system of equations means to find the values of x and y, which satisfy both the equations simultaneously. Generally, this solution is written as an ordered pair (x, y).

Note If $x = a$ and $y = b$ is the solution of $a_1x + b_1y + c_1 = 0$ and $a_2x + b_2y + c_2 = 0$ then the values satisfy the given equations.

Methods of Solving System of Simultaneous Linear Equations

1. Substitution Method

In this method, value of one variable can be found out in terms of other variable from one of the given equation and this value is substituted in other equation, then we get an equation in one variable, which can be solved easily.

Example 1. Solve the system of linear equations $x + 8y = 19$ and $2x + 11y = 28$ by substitution method.

Sol. Suppose, given system of linear equations $x + 8y = 19$ ...(i)

and $2x + 11y = 28$ ...(ii)

From Eq. (i), $x = 19 - 8y$ ...(iii)

On substituting $x = 19 - 8y$ in Eq. (ii), we get

$$2(19 - 8y) + 11y = 28 \Rightarrow 38 - 16y + 11y = 28$$

$$\Rightarrow \quad 5y = 38 - 28 = 10 \Rightarrow y = \frac{10}{5} = 2$$

REVISION NOTES

On putting $y = 2$ in Eq. (iii), we get $x = 19 - 16 = 3$

Hence, $x = 3$ and $y = 2$ is the required solution.

2. Elimination Method

In this method, one variable out of the two variables is eliminated by making the coefficients of that variable equal in both the equations. After eliminating that variable, the left equation is an equation in one variable, which can be solved easily.

Value of one variable obtained in this way can be substituted in any one of the two given equations to find the value of other variable.

Example 2. Solve the pair of linear equations $x + y = 5$ and $2x - 3y = 4$ by elimination method.

Sol. Let pair of linear equations be $x + y = 5$ ...(i)

and $2x - 3y = 4$ ...(ii)

For making the coefficients of y numerically equal, multiply Eq. (i) by 3 and Eq. (ii) by 1, and write the above equations as

$3x + 3y = 15$ ...(iii)

and $2x - 3y = 4$ ...(iv)

On adding Eqs. (iii) and (iv), we get $3x + 2x = 15 + 4 = 19 \Rightarrow x = \frac{19}{5}$

On putting $x = \frac{19}{5}$ in Eq.(i), we get $\frac{19}{5} + y = 5 \Rightarrow y = 5 - \frac{19}{5} \Rightarrow y = \frac{25 - 19}{5} \Rightarrow y = \frac{6}{5}$

Hence, $x = \frac{19}{5}$ and $y = \frac{6}{5}$ is the required solution.

3. Cross-multiplication Method

According to this method, the solution of system of two linear equations

$a_1x + b_1y + c_1 = 0$ ...(i)

$a_2x + b_2y + c_2 = 0$ ...(ii)

is given by $x = \frac{(b_1c_2 - b_2c_1)}{(a_1b_2 - a_2b_1)}$ **and** $y = \frac{(c_1a_2 - c_2a_1)}{(a_1b_2 - a_2b_1)}$, **provided** $a_1b_2 - a_2b_1 \neq 0$.

Example 3. Solve the pair of linear equations $x + 4y - 5 = 0$ and $4x + 4y - 13 = 0$ by cross-multiplication method.

Sol. Let pair of linear equations be $x + 4y - 5 = 0$ ...(i)

and $4x + 4y - 13 = 0$ ...(ii)

Diagram for the above equations is

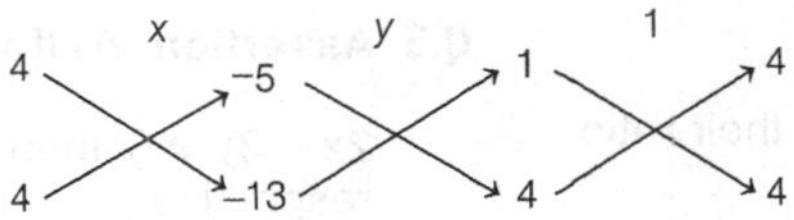

With the help of diagram, we get

$$\frac{x}{4(-13) - 4(-5)} = \frac{y}{-5(4) - (-13)(1)} = \frac{1}{(1)(4) - (4)(4)} \Rightarrow \frac{x}{-52 + 20} = \frac{y}{-20 + 13} = \frac{1}{4 - 16} \Rightarrow \underset{\text{I}}{\frac{x}{-32}} = \underset{\text{II}}{\frac{y}{-7}} = \underset{\text{III}}{\frac{1}{-12}}$$

On taking I and III terms, we get $\frac{x}{-32} = \frac{1}{-12} \Rightarrow x = \frac{-32}{-12} = \frac{8}{3}$

On taking II and III terms, we get $\frac{y}{-7} = \frac{1}{-12} \Rightarrow y = \frac{-7}{-12} = \frac{7}{12}$

Hence, $x = \frac{8}{3}$ and $y = \frac{7}{12}$ is the required solution.

Note *If the equations $a_1x + b_1y + c_1 = 0$ and $a_2x + b_2y + c_2 = 0$ are written in the form $a_1x + b_1y = -c_1$ and $a_2x + b_2y = -c_2$, then by cross-multiplication method, we have* $\frac{x}{b_2c_1 - b_1c_2} = \frac{y}{c_2a_1 - c_1a_2} = \frac{-1}{a_1b_2 - a_2b_1}$.

EXAM ORIENTED QUESTIONS

TYPE - 1   01 Mark

Multiple Choice Questions

Q.1 If x and y are the solutions of system of equations $0.5x + 1.7y = 4.4$ and $1.3x - 0.3y = 2$, then x and y are

(a) $x = 2, y = 2$ (b) $x = 2, y = 1$

(c) $y = 2, x = -1$ (d) $y = -2, x = -1$

Q.2 Solution of system of linear equations $2x + y = 15$ and $2x - y = -7$ is

(a) $x = 2, y = -11$ (b) $x = -2, y = 11$

(c) $x = -2, y = -11$ (d) $x = 2, y = 11$

Q.3 The values of x and y satisfying the two equations $32x + 33y = 34$ and $33x + 32y = 31$ respectively, are

(a) −1 and 2 (b) −1 and 4

(c) 1 and −2 (d) −1 and −4

Q.4 The solution of the pair of equations $x + y = -3$ and $3x - 5y = 8$ is

(a) $x = \frac{7}{8}, y = \frac{17}{8}$ (b) $x = \frac{-7}{8}, y = \frac{17}{8}$

(c) $x = \frac{-7}{8}, y = \frac{-17}{8}$ (d) $x = \frac{7}{8}, y = \frac{-17}{8}$

Q.5 3 chairs and 1 table cost ₹ 900; whereas 5 chairs and 3 tables cost ₹ 2100. If the cost of 1 chair is ₹ x and the cost of 1 table is ₹ y, then the situation can be represented algebraically as

(a) $3x + y = 900, 3x + 5y = 2100$

(b) $x + 3y = 900, 3x + 5y = 2100$

(c) $3x + y = 900, 5x + 3y = 2100$

(d) $x + 3y = 900, 5x + 3y = 2100$

Q.6 The sum of two natural numbers is 240 and their ratio is 3 : 5. Then, the greater number is

(a) 180 (b) 160 (c) 150 (d) 90

Q.7 The sum of two numbers is 12 and their difference is 2, then the numbers are

(a) 7 and 5 (b) 5 and 3

(c) 6 and 4 (d) None of these

Answers

1. (a) 2. (d) 3. (a) 4. (c) 5. (c)

6. (c) 7. (a)

TYPE - 2   01 Mark

Assertion-Reason Type Questions

Q.1 Assertion (A) The reducible form of equations $\frac{2}{x} + \frac{3}{y} = 13$ and $\frac{3}{x} - \frac{5}{y} = -9$ are $2a + 3b = 13$ and $3a - 5b = -9$, respectively.

Reason (R) If system of equations are in the form of $\frac{1}{x}$ and $\frac{1}{y}$, then put $\frac{1}{x} = a$ and $\frac{1}{y} = b$.

(a) A is true, R is false.

(b) A is false, R is true.

(c) Both A and R are true and R is the correct reason for A.

(d) Both A and R are true and R is incorrect reason for A.

Q.2 Assertion (A) If $4x - 3y = 10$ and $3x - 5y = 24$, then the solution of these equations is $x = 2$ and $y = 6$.

Reason (R) In substitution method, value of one variable can be found out in terms of other variable from one of the given equation and this value is substituted in other equation, then we get an equation in one variable.

(a) A is true, R is false.

(b) A is false, R is true.

(c) Both A and R are true and R is the correct reason for A.

(d) Both A and R are true and R is incorrect reason for A.

Q.3 Assertion (A) If $x + y = 2.2$ and $\frac{3.4}{2x - 3y} = 1$, $2x - 3y \neq 0$, then the values of x and y are 2 and 0.2, respectively.

Reason (R) In elimination method, value of one variable can be found out in terms of other variable from one of the given equation and this value is substituted in other equation.

(a) A is true, R is false.

(b) A is false, R is true.

(c) Both A and R are true and R is the correct reason for A.

(d) Both A and R are true and R is incorrect reason for A.

Q.4 **Assertion** (A) If (a, b) is the solution of system of equations $2x + 3y = 46$ and $3x + 5y = 74$, then $a = 8$ and $b = 10$.

Reason (R) The solution of system of two linear equations $a_1x + b_1y + c_1 = 0$ and $a_2x + b_2y + c_2 = 0$ is $x = \left(\frac{b_1c_2 - b_2c_1}{a_1b_2 - a_2b_1}\right)$ and $y = \left(\frac{c_1a_2 - a_1c_2}{a_1b_2 - a_2b_1}\right)$.

(a) A is true, R is false.
(b) A is false, R is true.
(c) Both A and R are true and R is the correct reason for A.
(d) Both A and R are true and R is incorrect reason for A.

Answers

1. (c) 2. (b) 3. (a) 4. (c)

TYPE - 3 01 Mark

Statement Based Questions

Q.1 **Statement I** The solution of system of equations $x + y = 8$ and $2x - 3y = 1$ is (5, 3).

Statement II Any pair of values of x and y which satisfied both the equations $a_1x + b_1y + c_1 = 0$ and $a_2x + b_2y + c_2 = 0$, is called a solution of a given pair of linear equations.

Which of the following is valid?
(a) Both the Statements are true.
(b) Both the Statements are false.
(c) Statement I is true and Statement II is false.
(d) Statement I is false and Statement II is true.

Q.2 **Statement I** The solution of system of equations $5x + 8y = 9$ and $2x + 3y = 4$ is $(-5, -2)$.

Statement II In elimination method, one variable out of the two variables is eliminated by making the coefficients of that variable equal in both the equations.

Which of the following is valid?
(a) Both the Statements are true.
(b) Both the Statements are false.
(c) Statement I is true and Statement II is false.
(d) Statement I is false and Statement II is true.

Q.3 If cost of 4 books and 3 copies is ₹ 210 and cost of 5 books and 2 copies is ₹ 175.

Statement I If the cost of 1 book is ₹ x and cost of 1 copy is ₹ y, then the algebraic forms of given situations are $4x + 3y = 210$ and $5x + 2y = 175$.

Statement II The cost of 1 book is ₹ 25 and cost of 1 copy is ₹ 50.

Which of the following is valid?
(a) Both the Statements are true.
(b) Both the Statements are false.
(c) Statement I is true and Statement II is false.
(d) Statement I is false and Statement II is true.

Answers

1. (a) 2. (d) 3. (c)

TYPE - 4 03 Marks

Short Answer Type Questions

Q.1 Show that $x = 5$, $y = 4$ is the solution of system of linear equations $4x - 3y = 8$ and $x - 2y = -3$.

Q.2 Solve the following system of equations $2x + 8y = 19$ and $2x + 11y = 28$, by substitution method.

Q.3 Solve the following pair of equations by substitution method.

$$3x + y - 30 = 0 \text{ and } 2x + 5y - 33 = 0$$

Q.4 Find the solution for the pair of equations $\frac{x}{10} + \frac{y}{5} - 1 = 0$ and $\frac{x}{8} + \frac{y}{6} = 15$.
Hence, find λ if $y = \lambda x + 5$.

Q.5 The expression $ax + by$ has value 7, when $x = 2$ and $y = 1$. When $x = -1$ and $y = 1$, it has value 1. Find the values of a and b.

Q.6 Use elimination method to find all possible solutions of the following pair of linear equations.

$$2x + 3y = 8 \text{ and } 4x + 6y = 7$$

Q.7 Solve the pair of equations

$$\frac{2}{x} + \frac{3}{y} = 13 \text{ and } \frac{5}{x} - \frac{4}{y} = -2.$$

Q.8 Solve the following pair of equations by reducing them to a pair of linear equations.

$$2x + \frac{9}{y} = 9 \text{ and } 4x + \frac{1}{y} = \frac{71}{3}$$

Q.9 Solve the following pair of equations by reducing them to a pair of linear equations.

$$\frac{10}{(x+y)} + \frac{2}{(x-y)} = 4 \text{ and } \frac{15}{(x+y)} - \frac{5}{(x-y)} = -2$$

Q.10 Use elimination method to find all possible solutions of the following pair of linear equations.

$$ax + by - a + b = 0 \text{ and } bx - ay - a - b = 0$$

Q.11 4 yr ago, a mother was four times as old as her daughter. 6 yr later, the mother will be two and a half times as old as her daughter at that time. Find the present ages of mother and her daughter.

Q.12 A fraction becomes $\frac{1}{3}$ when 1 is subtracted from the numerator. It becomes $\frac{1}{4}$ when 8 is added to the denominator. Find the fraction.

Q.13 The sum of two numbers is 24 and their difference is 4. Find the numbers.

Q.14 The sum of a two-digit number and number obtained by reversing the order of digits is 99. If the digits of the number differ by 3. Then, find the numbers.

Q.15 In ΔABC, $\angle C = 5\angle B = 3(\angle A + \angle B)$, find all angles of ΔABC.

Q.16 37 pens and 53 pencils together cost ₹ 320, while 53 pens and 37 pencils together cost ₹ 400. Find the cost of a pen and that of a pencil.

Q.17 Sabina went to a bank ATM to withdraw ₹ 2000. She received ₹ 50 and ₹ 100 notes only. If Sabina got 25 notes in all, how many notes of ₹ 50 and ₹ 100 did she receive?

Answers

2. $x = \frac{-5}{2}, y = 3$
3. $x = 9, y = 3$
4. $y = -165, x = 340$ and $\lambda = \frac{-1}{2}$
5. $a = 2$ and $b = 3$
6. no solution
7. $x = \frac{1}{2}$ and $y = \frac{1}{3}$
8. $x = 6, y = -3$
9. $x = 3, y = 2$
10. $x = 1$ and $y = -1$
11. The age of mother = 44 yr and the age of daughter = 14 yr
12. $\frac{5}{12}$
13. 14 and 10
14. 63 and 36
15. $\angle A = 18°$, $\angle B = 27°$ and $\angle C = 135°$
16. Cost of one pen is ₹ 6.5, cost of one pencil is ₹ 1.5.
17. Number of ₹ 50 notes = 10 and number of ₹ 100 notes = 15

TYPE - 5

4/5 Marks

Long Answer Type Questions

Q.1 Solve the following system of equations $3x - y = 3$ and $9x - 3y = 9$ by substitution method.

Q.2 Solve the simultaneous linear equations $3x - y = 5$ and $5x - 3y = -1$. Hence, find m, if $y = mx - 3$.

Q.3 Solve the following pair of linear equations by elimination method.

$5ax + 6by = 28$ and $3ax + 4by = 18$

Also, verify the solution.

Q.4 Solve the following pair of linear equations.
$41x + 53y = 135$ and $53x + 41y = 147$

Q.5 Solve the following pair of linear equations.
$x + y = 14xy$ and $2x - y = 4xy$

Q.6 Solve the following pair of linear equations by cross-multiplication method.

$$\frac{x}{7} + \frac{y}{3} = 5 \text{ and } \frac{x}{2} - \frac{y}{9} = 6$$

Q.7 Romila went to a stationary shop and purchased 2 pencils and 3 erasers for ₹ 9. Her friend Sonali saw the new variety of pencils and erasers with Romila and she also bought 4 pencils and 6 erasers of the same kind for ₹ 18. Find the cost of each pencil and each eraser.

Q.8 A milkman has two types of milk. In first container, the percentage of milk is 80% and in second container, the percentage of milk is 90%. If he mixes both types of milk, then percentage of milk in 30L of mixture is 85%. How many litres of each milk, he mixed?

Q.9 A fraction becomes 4/5, if 1 is added to both numerator and denominator. If however, 5 is subtracted from both numerator and denominator, the fraction becomes 1/2. What is the fraction?

Q.10 Two people are 16 km apart on a straight road. They start walking at the same time. If they walk towards each other with different speeds, they will meet in 2 h and if they walked in the same direction with same speeds as before, they would have met in 8 h. Find their walking speeds.

Q.11 The ratio of incomes of two persons is 9 : 7 and the ratio of their expenditures is 4 : 3. If each of them manages to save ₹ 2000 per month. To find their monthly incomes, form a pair of linear equations from the above data and solve them by elimination method.

Q.12 A train leaves Agra for Punjab, 420 km away, at 6 am. One hour later, another train leaves Punjab for Agra. They met at 9 am, if the second train had started at 6 am and the first train at 7 : 30 am, they would still have met at 9 am. Find the speed of each train.

Q.13 The area of a rectangle gets reduced by 9 sq units, if its length is reduced by 5 units and breadth is increased by 3 units. If we increase the length by 3 units and the breadth by 2 units, the area increases by 67 sq units. Find the dimensions of the rectangle.

Q.14 The sum of the digits of a 2-digit number is 9. Also, nine times this number is twice the number obtained by reversing the order of the digits. Find the number.

Q.15 Roohi travels 300 km to her home partly by train and partly by bus. She takes 4 h, if she travels 60 km by train and the remaining by bus. If she travels 100 km by train and the remaining by bus, she takes 10 min longer. Find the speed of the train and the bus separately.

Q.16 2 women and 5 men can together finish an embroidery work in 4 days, while 3 women and 6 men can finish it in 3 days. Find the time taken by one woman alone to finish the work and also that taken by one man alone.

Q.17 A boat goes 30 km upstream and 44 km downstream in 10 h. In 13 h, it can go 40 km upstream and 55 km downstream. Determine the speed of the stream and that of the boat in still water.

Answers

1. infinite solutions
2. $x = 4$, $y = 7$ and $m = \frac{5}{2}$
3. $x = \frac{2}{a}$, $y = \frac{3}{b}$
4. $x = 2$ and $y = 1$
5. $x = \frac{1}{8}$ and $y = \frac{1}{6}$
6. $x = 14$ and $y = 9$
7. We cannot find a unique cost of pencil and an eraser.
8. 15 litre
9. $\frac{7}{9}$
10. 5 km/h and 3 km/h
11. ₹ 18000, ₹ 14000
12. The speed of the first train is 70 km/h and that of second train is 105 km/h.
13. Length = 17 units and breadth = 9 units
14. 18
15. The speed of train is 60 km/h and the speed of bus is 80 km/h.
16. A single woman can finish the work in 18 days and a single man can finish the work in 36 days.
17. Speeds of boat and stream in still water are 8 km/h and 3 km/h, respectively.

TYPE - 6

Case Based Questions

Q.1 A book store shopkeeper gives books on rent for reading. He takes a fixed charge for the first two days and an additional charge for subsequent day. Amruta paid ₹ 22 for a book and kept 6 days. While Radhika paid ₹ 16 for keeping the book 4 days.

Assume that the fixed charge be ₹ x and additional charge (per day) be ₹ y.

(i) Represent both the situations algebraically.

(ii) What are the fixed charge and additional charge for a book? **(4 M)**

Q.2 The design and measurement have been made such that areas of two bedrooms and kitchen together is 95 m^2.

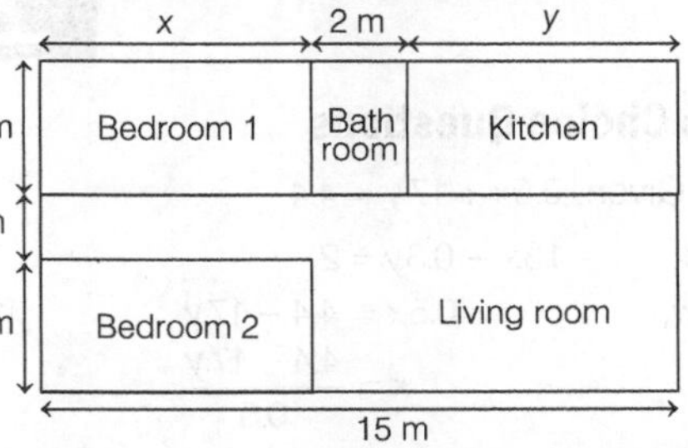

(i) Form the pair of linear equations in two variables from this situation.

(ii) Find the area of each bedroom and kitchen in the layout.

(iii) Find the cost of laying tiles in kitchen at the rate of ₹ 50 per m^2. **(3 M)**

Q.3 A coaching institute conducts Mathematics classes in two batches I and II and fee for rich and poor children are different. In batch I, there are 20 poor and 5 rich children, whereas in batch II, there are 5 poor and 25 rich children. The total monthly collection of fees from batch I is ₹ 9000 and from batch II is ₹ 26000. Assume that each poor child pays ₹ x per month and each rich child pays ₹ y per month.

Based on the above information, answer the following questions.

(i) Represent the information given above in terms of x and y.

(ii) Find the monthly fee paid by a poor child. Also, find the difference in the monthly fee paid by a poor child and a rich child.

(iii) If there are 10 poor and 20 rich children in batch II, what is the total monthly collection of fees from batch II? **(3 M)**

Answers

1. (i) Amruta paid = $x + 4y = 22$, Radhika paid = $x + 2y = 16$
   (ii) Fixed charge is ₹ 10 and additional charge is ₹ 3 per day.
2. (i) $2x + y = 19$ and $x + y = 13$
   (ii) area of each bedroom = 30 m^2
   and area of kitchen = 35 m^2 (iii) ₹ 1750
3. (i) **For batch I** $20x + 5y = 9000$
   For batch II $5x + 25y = 26000$
   (ii) ₹ 200, ₹ 800 (iii) ₹ 22000

EXPLANATIONS

Multiple Choice Questions

1. (a) Given, $0.5x + 1.7y = 4.4$ ...(i)

and $1.3x - 0.3y = 2$ ...(ii)

Now, $0.5x = 4.4 - 1.7y$ [from Eq. (i)]

$\Rightarrow x = \dfrac{4.4 - 1.7y}{0.5}$

On substituting the value of x in Eq. (ii), we get

$$1.3\left[\frac{4.4 - 1.7y}{0.5}\right] - 0.3y = 2$$

$\Rightarrow 5.72 - 2.21y - 0.15y = 1$

$\Rightarrow 4.72 = 2.36y$

$\Rightarrow y = 2$

On substituting $y = 2$ in Eq. (ii), we get

$1.3x - 0.3 \times 2 = 2$

$\Rightarrow x = \dfrac{2 + 0.6}{1.3}$

$\Rightarrow x = 2$

2. (d) Given, $2x + y = 15$ ...(i)

and $2x - y = -7$ ...(ii)

On adding Eqs. (i) and (ii), we get

$4x = 8$

$\Rightarrow x = 2$

On putting the value of x in Eq. (i), we get

$2(2) + y = 15$

$\Rightarrow 4 + y = 15 \Rightarrow y = 11$

3. (a) Given equations are

$32x + 33y = 34$ ...(i)

and $33x + 32y = 31$ ...(ii)

On adding Eqs. (i) and (ii), we get

$65x + 65y = 65 \Rightarrow x + y = 1$ ...(iii)

On subtracting Eq. (ii) from Eq. (i), we get

$-x + y = 3$ ...(iv)

Now, on adding Eqs. (iii) and (iv), we get

$2y = 4$

$\Rightarrow y = 2$

On substituting $y = 2$ in Eq. (iii), we get

$x = 1 - 2 \Rightarrow x = -1$

4. (c) Given, $x + y = -3 \Rightarrow x + y + 3 = 0$ ...(i)

and $3x - 5y = 8 \Rightarrow 3x - 5y - 8 = 0$ ...(ii)

On comparing with standard form of pair of linear equations, we get

$a_1 = 1, b_1 = 1, c_1 = 3, a_2 = 3, b_2 = -5$ and $c_2 = -8$

Now, $x = \dfrac{-8 - (-15)}{-5 - 3}$ $\left[\because x = \dfrac{b_1c_2 - b_2c_1}{a_1b_2 - a_2b_1}\right]$

$\Rightarrow x = \dfrac{-7}{8}$

and $y = \dfrac{9 - (-8)}{-5 - 3}$ $\left[\because y = \dfrac{c_1a_2 - c_2a_1}{a_1b_2 - a_2b_1}\right]$

$\Rightarrow y = -\dfrac{17}{8}$

5. (c) Given, cost of 1 chair = ₹ x

$\therefore$ Cost of 3 chairs = ₹ $3x$

and cost of 5 chairs = ₹ $5x$

Also given, cost of 1 table = ₹y

$\therefore$ Cost of 3 tables = ₹ $3y$

So, the given situation can be represented as

$3x + y = 900$ and $5x + 3y = 2100$

6. (c) Let the two numbers be x and y.

According to the question,

$x + y = 240$ ...(i)

and $x : y = 3 : 5 \Rightarrow x = \dfrac{3}{5}y$ ...(ii)

On substituting the value of x from Eq. (ii) in Eq. (i), we get

$\dfrac{3}{5}y + y = 240$

$\Rightarrow \dfrac{8}{5}y = 240$

$\Rightarrow y = \dfrac{240 \times 5}{8} \Rightarrow y = 150$

On substituting the value of y in Eq. (ii), we get

$x = \dfrac{3}{5} \times 150$

$\Rightarrow x = 90$

Hence, the greater number is 150.

7. (a) Let two numbers be x and y such that $x > y$.

According to the question,

$x + y = 12$ ...(i)

and $x - y = 2$ ...(ii)

On adding Eqs. (i) and (ii), we get

$2x = 14$

$\Rightarrow x = 7$

On substituting $x = 7$ in Eq. (i), we get

$y = 12 - 7 \Rightarrow y = 5$

Hence, the two numbers are 7 and 5.

Assertion-Reason Type Questions

1. (c) Given, $\frac{2}{x}+\frac{3}{y}=13$ and $\frac{3}{x}-\frac{5}{y}=-9$

On putting $\frac{1}{x}=a$ and $\frac{1}{y}=b$ in both equations, we get

$$2a+3b=13 \text{ and } 3a-5b=-9$$

Hence, A is true and R is also true and R is the correct reason for A.

2. (b) If $x=2$ and $y=6$ is the solution of given equations then it will be satisfy the given equations.

Here, $4x-3y=4\times2-3\times6=8-18=-10\neq10$

Hence, $x=2$ and $y=6$ is not the solution of the given equations.

Thus, Assertion is false.

Clearly, Reason is true.

3. (a) **Assertion** Given, $x+y=2.2$ ...(i)

and $\frac{3.4}{2x-3y}=1$

$\Rightarrow$ $2x-3y=3.4$ ...(ii)

For making the coefficients of y numerically equal, multiply Eq. (i) by 3.

$\therefore$ $3x+3y=6.6$ ...(iii)

On adding Eqs. (ii) and (iii), we get

$$3x+2x=6.6+3.4$$

$\Rightarrow$ $x=2$

On putting $x=2$ in Eq. (i), we get

$$2+y=2.2$$

$\Rightarrow$ $y=0.2$

Hence, A is true, R is false.

4. (c) Given, $2x+3y=46$ and $3x+5y=74$

On comparing the standard form of system of equations $a_1x+b_1y+c_1=0$ and $a_2x+b_2y+c_2=0$, we get

$$a_1=2, b_1=3, c_1=-46$$

and $a_2=3, b_2=5, c_2=-74$

Then, $x=\left[\frac{3(-74)-5(-46)}{2\times5-3\times3}\right]=\frac{-222+230}{10-9}=8$

and $y=\left[\frac{(-46)\times3-(-74)\times2}{2\times5-3\times3}\right]=\frac{-138+148}{10-9}=10$

Hence, A is true and R is also true and R is the correct reason for A.

Statement Based Questions

1. (a) We have, $x+y=8$ ...(i)

and $2x-3y=1$ ...(ii)

On multiplying Eq. (i) by 2, we get

$2x+2y=16$ ...(iii)

On subtracting Eq. (ii) from Eq. (iii), we get

$$5y=15 \Rightarrow y=3$$

On substituting $y=3$ in Eq. (i), we get

$$x=8-3\Rightarrow x=5$$

Hence, the solution of system of equations is (5, 3). Therefore, Statement I is true and Statement II is also true.

2. (d) **Statement I** Given, $5x+8y=9$ ...(i)

and $2x+3y=4$ ...(ii)

On multiplying Eq. (i) by 2 and Eq. (ii) by 5, we get

$10x+16y=18$ ...(iii)

$10x+15y=20$ ...(iv)

On subtracting Eqs. (iv) from Eq. (iii), we get

$$16y-15y=18-20$$

$\Rightarrow$ $y=-2$

On putting $y=-2$ in Eq. (i), we get

$$5x+8(-2)=9\Rightarrow 5x=25\Rightarrow x=5$$

Hence, Statement I is false and Statement II is true.

3. (c) Given, cost of 1 book is ₹ x and cost of 1 copy is ₹ y.

Then, according to the question,

$4x+3y=210$ ...(i)

and $5x+2y=175$ ...(ii)

Hence, Statement I is true.

On solving Eqs. (i) and (ii), we get

$$x=15 \text{ and } y=50$$

Therefore, the cost of 1 book is ₹ 15 and cost of 1 copy is ₹ 50. Hence, Statement II is false.

Short Answer Type Questions

1. Consider the given system of linear equations

$4x-3y=8$ ...(i)

and $x-2y=-3$ ...(ii)

Now, on substituting $x=5$, $y=4$ in LHS of Eq. (i), we get

LHS $=4(5)-3(4)=20-12=8=$ RHS of Eq. (i)

$\therefore$ $x=5$ and $y=4$ satisfy Eq. (i).

Now, on substituting $x=5$, $y=4$ in LHS of Eq. (ii), we get

LHS $=5-2(4)=5-8=-3=$ RHS of Eq. (ii)

$\therefore$ $x=5$, $y=4$ satisfy Eq. (ii).

Thus, $x=5$, $y=4$ satisfy both the equations.

Hence, $x=5$ and $y=4$ is the solution of given system of simultaneous linear equations.

2. Given equations are

$2x+8y=19$ ...(i)

$2x+11y=28$ ...(ii)

From Eq. (i), $x=\frac{19-8y}{2}$ ...(iii)

On substituting $x = \frac{19-8y}{2}$ in Eq. (ii), we get

$$2 \times \left(\frac{19-8y}{2}\right) + 11y = 28$$

$\Rightarrow$ $19 - 8y + 11y = 28$

$\Rightarrow$ $3y = 9$

$\Rightarrow$ $y = \frac{9}{3} = 3$

On putting $y = 3$ in Eq. (iii), we get

$$x = \frac{19 - 8 \times 3}{2} = \frac{19-24}{2} = \frac{-5}{2}$$

Hence, $x = \frac{-5}{2}$ and $y = 3$ is the required solution.

3. We have, $3x + y - 30 = 0 \Rightarrow 3x + y = 30$ ...(i)

and $2x + 5y - 33 = 0 \Rightarrow 2x + 5y = 33$ ...(ii)

From Eq. (i), we get

$$y = 30 - 3x$$

On substituting $y = 30 - 3x$ in Eq. (ii), we get

$$2x + 5(30 - 3x) = 33$$

$\Rightarrow$ $2x + 150 - 15x = 33$

$\Rightarrow$ $117 = 13x$

$\Rightarrow$ $x = 9$

On substituting $x = 9$ in Eq. (i), we get

$$27 + y = 30$$

$\Rightarrow$ $y = 3$

Hence, the required values of x and y are 9 and 3, respectively.

4. We have, $\frac{x}{10} + \frac{y}{5} = 1 \Rightarrow x + 2y = 10$ ...(i)

and $\frac{x}{8} + \frac{y}{6} = 15 \Rightarrow 3x + 4y = 360$ ...(ii)

From Eq. (i), we get

$$x = 10 - 2y$$

On substituting value of x in Eq. (ii), we get

$$3(10 - 2y) + 4y = 360$$

$\Rightarrow$ $30 - 6y + 4y = 360$

$\Rightarrow$ $-2y = 330 \Rightarrow y = -165$

On substituting $y = -165$ in Eq. (i), we get

$$x - 330 = 10 \Rightarrow x = 340$$

Hence, the values of x and y are 340 and -165, respectively.

Now, $y = \lambda x + 5$

$\Rightarrow$ $-165 = \lambda \times 340 + 5$ $[\because x = 340,\ y = -165]$

$\Rightarrow$ $340\lambda = -170$

$\Rightarrow$ $\lambda = \frac{-170}{340} \Rightarrow \lambda = \frac{-1}{2}$

Therefore, the value of λ is $-\frac{1}{2}$.

5. According to the question, we have

$2a + b = 7$ ...(i)

and $-a + b = 1$ ...(ii)

On subtracting Eq. (ii) from Eq. (i), we get

$$3a = 6 \Rightarrow a = 2$$

On putting $a = 2$ in Eq. (ii), we get

$$-2 + b = 1 \Rightarrow b = 1 + 2 = 3$$

Hence, $a = 2$ and $b = 3$.

6. Given, pair of linear equations is

$2x + 3y = 8$ ...(i)

and $4x + 6y = 7$ ...(ii)

On multiplying Eq. (i) by 2 to make the equal coefficients of x, we get the equations as

$4x + 6y = 16$ ...(iii)

and $4x + 6y = 7$ ...(iv)

On subtracting Eq. (iv) from Eq. (iii), we get

$$(4x - 4x) + (6y - 6y) = 16 - 7 \Rightarrow 0 \neq 9$$

which is a false equation involving no variable.

So, the given pair of linear equations has no solution.

7. Given, pair of linear equations is not linear.

On putting $\frac{1}{x} = p$ and $\frac{1}{y} = q$, we get

$2p + 3q = 13$ ...(i)

and $5p - 4q = -2$ ...(ii)

The pair obtained after substitution, is the pair of linear equations.

Now, let us solve these equations by elimination method.

On multiplying Eq. (i) by 4 and Eq. (ii) by 3 and then adding, we get

$$(8p + 12q) + (15p - 12q) = 52 - 6$$

$\Rightarrow$ $8p + 15p = 52 - 6$

$\Rightarrow$ $23p = 46$

$\Rightarrow$ $p = \frac{46}{23} = 2$

On putting $p = 2$ in Eq. (i), we get

$$2(2) + 3q = 13$$

$\Rightarrow$ $3q = 13 - 4 = 9$

$\Rightarrow$ $q = \frac{9}{3} = 3$

On putting $p = \frac{1}{x}$ and $q = \frac{1}{y}$, we get

$$2 = \frac{1}{x} \text{ and } 3 = \frac{1}{y}$$

$\Rightarrow$ $x = \frac{1}{2}$ and $y = \frac{1}{3}$,

which is the required solution.

8. Given, pair of linear equations is

$$2x + \frac{9}{y} = 9 \text{ and } 4x + \frac{1}{y} = \frac{71}{3}$$

On putting $\frac{1}{y} = p$, we get

$$2x + 9p = 9 \quad \text{...(i)}$$

and $$4x + p = \frac{71}{3} \quad \text{...(ii)}$$

On multiplying Eq. (i) by 2, we get

$$4x + 18p = 18 \quad \text{...(iii)}$$

On subtracting Eq. (iii) from Eq. (ii), we get

$$p - 18p = \frac{71}{3} - 18$$

$$\Rightarrow \quad -17p = \frac{17}{3} \Rightarrow p = \frac{-1}{3}$$

On substituting $p = \frac{-1}{3}$ in Eq. (i), we get

$$2x + 9\left(\frac{-1}{3}\right) = 9$$

$$\Rightarrow \quad 2x = 9 + 3$$

$$\Rightarrow \quad x = 6$$

Therefore, $p = \frac{1}{y} = \frac{-1}{3} \Rightarrow y = -3$

Hence, the required values of x and y are 6 and –3, respectively.

9. Given pair of linear equations is

$$\frac{10}{(x+y)} + \frac{2}{(x-y)} = 4$$

and $$\frac{15}{(x+y)} - \frac{5}{(x-y)} = -2$$

On putting $\frac{1}{x+y} = u$ and $\frac{1}{x-y} = v$, we get

$$10u + 2v = 4 \quad \text{...(i)}$$

and $$15u - 5v = -2 \quad \text{...(ii)}$$

On multiplying Eq. (i) by 5 and Eq. (ii) by 2 and then adding, we get

$$5(10u + 2v) + 2(15u - 5v) = 5 \times 4 + 2 \times (-2)$$

$$\Rightarrow \quad 50u + 10v + 30u - 10v = 20 - 4$$

$$\Rightarrow \quad 80u = 16$$

$$\Rightarrow \quad u = \frac{1}{5}$$

On substituting $u = \frac{1}{5}$ in Eq. (i), we get

$$10 \times \frac{1}{5} + 2v = 4$$

$$\Rightarrow \quad 2 + 2v = 4$$

$$\Rightarrow \quad 2v = 2$$

$$\Rightarrow \quad v = 1$$

If $u = \frac{1}{5}$ then by $\frac{1}{x+y} = u$, we get

$$\frac{1}{x+y} = \frac{1}{5} \Rightarrow x + y = 5 \quad \text{...(iii)}$$

If $v = 1$, then by $\frac{1}{x-y} = v$, we get

$$\frac{1}{x-y} = 1$$

$$\Rightarrow \quad x - y = 1 \quad \text{...(iv)}$$

On adding Eqs. (iii) and (iv), we get

$$2x = 6 \Rightarrow x = 3$$

On putting $x = 3$ in Eq. (iv), we get

$$3 - y = 1 \Rightarrow y = 2$$

Hence, $x = 3$ and $y = 2$, which is the required solution.

10. Given, pair of linear equations is

$$ax + by = a - b \quad \text{...(i)}$$

and $$bx - ay = a + b \quad \text{...(ii)}$$

On multiplying Eq. (i) by a and Eq. (ii) by b and adding them, we get

$$a^2x + aby + b^2x - aby = a^2 - ab + ba + b^2$$

$$\Rightarrow \quad (a^2 + b^2)x = (a^2 + b^2) \Rightarrow x = \frac{a^2 + b^2}{a^2 + b^2} = 1$$

On putting $x = 1$ in Eq. (i), we get

$$a + by = a - b \Rightarrow y = -\frac{b}{b} = -1$$

Hence, $x = 1$ and $y = -1$, which is the required unique solution.

11. Let the present age of mother = x yr

and present age of daughter = y yr

Four years ago,

the age of mother = $(x - 4)$ yr

and the age of daughter = $(y - 4)$ yr

According to the question,

$$(x - 4) = 4(y - 4) \Rightarrow x - 4y + 12 = 0 \quad \text{...(i)}$$

Six years later,

the age of mother = $(x + 6)$ yr

and the age of daughter = $(y + 6)$ yr

According to the question,

$$(x + 6) = 2\frac{1}{2}(y + 6) \Rightarrow (x + 6) = \frac{5}{2}(y + 6)$$

$$\Rightarrow \quad 2x - 5y - 18 = 0 \quad \text{...(ii)}$$

From Eq. (i), we get

$$x = 4y - 12 \quad \text{...(iii)}$$

On substituting value of x from Eq. (iii) in Eq. (ii), we get

$$2(4y - 12) - 5y - 18 = 0$$

$$\Rightarrow \quad 8y - 24 - 5y - 18 = 0$$

$$\Rightarrow \quad 3y = 42 \Rightarrow y = 14$$

On substituting $y = 14$ in Eq. (iii), we get

$$x = 4 \times 14 - 12 \Rightarrow x = 44$$

Hence, the age of mother = 44 yr and the age of daughter = 14 yr.

12. Let the numerator be x and the denominator be y.

So, the fraction $= \frac{x}{y}$

According to the question,

Condition I $\frac{x-1}{y} = \frac{1}{3} \Rightarrow 3(x-1) = y$

$$\Rightarrow \quad 3x - 3 = y \Rightarrow 3x - y - 3 = 0 \quad \text{...(i)}$$

Condition II $\frac{x}{y+8} = \frac{1}{4} \Rightarrow 4x = y + 8$

$$\Rightarrow \quad 4x - y = 8 \Rightarrow y = 4x - 8 \quad \text{...(ii)}$$

On substituting the value of y in Eq. (i), we get

$$3x - (4x - 8) - 3 = 0$$

$$\Rightarrow \quad 3x - 4x + 8 - 3 = 0 \Rightarrow x = 5$$

Now, on substituting the value of x in Eq. (ii), we get

$$y = 4(5) - 8 = 20 - 8 = 12$$

Hence, the fraction $\frac{x}{y}$ is $\frac{5}{12}$.

13. Let the numbers be x and y.

Then, we have

$$x + y = 24 \quad \text{...(i)}$$

and $\quad x - y = 4 \quad$ [assuming $x > y$] ...(ii)

On adding Eqs. (i) and (ii), we get

$$2x = 28 \Rightarrow x = 14$$

On substituting $x = 14$ in Eq. (i), we get

$$14 + y = 24 \Rightarrow y = 24 - 14 = 10$$

Hence, the required numbers are 14 and 10.

14. Let the unit's place digit be x and ten's place digit be y.

$\therefore$ Original number $= 10y + x$

Number obtained by reversing the order of digits $= 10x + y$

$\because$ Sum of both numbers = 99

$$\therefore \quad (10y + x) + (10x + y) = 99$$

$$\Rightarrow \quad 11x + 11y = 99$$

$$\Rightarrow \quad x + y = 9$$

[dividing both sides by 11] ...(i)

Also, given that the digits of the numbers differ by 3.

$\therefore$ If $y > x$, then $\quad y - x = 3$ ...(ii)

and if $y < x$, then $\quad x - y = 3$ ...(iii)

On adding Eqs. (i) and (ii), we get

$$2y = 12$$

$$\Rightarrow \quad y = \frac{12}{2} = 6$$

Then, from Eq. (i), we get

$$x = 9 - y = 9 - 6 = 3 \quad [\because y = 6]$$

$\therefore$ Number $= 10y + x = 10 \times 6 + 3 = 60 + 3 = 63$

On adding Eqs. (i) and (iii), we get

$$2x = 12 \Rightarrow x = \frac{12}{2} = 6$$

Then, from Eq. (i), we get

$$y = 9 - x = 9 - 6 = 3 \quad [\because x = 6]$$

$\therefore$ Number $= 10y + x = 10(3) + 6 = 36$

Hence, the required numbers are 63 and 36.

15. Let $\angle A$ and $\angle B$ be x and y, respectively.

Then, $\quad \angle C = 5\angle B = 3(\angle A + \angle B)$

$$\Rightarrow \quad \angle C = 5y \text{ and } \angle C = 3(x + y)$$

$$\Rightarrow \quad 5y = 3(x + y)$$

$$\Rightarrow \quad 2y - 3x = 0 \quad \text{...(i)}$$

Also, $\angle A + \angle B + \angle C = 180° \Rightarrow x + y + 5y = 180°$

$$\Rightarrow \quad x + 6y = 180° \quad \text{...(ii)}$$

Now, solve Eqs. (i) and (ii) to find $\angle A$ and $\angle B$.

On multiplying Eq. (ii) by 3, we get

$$3x + 18y = 540° \quad \text{...(iii)}$$

On adding Eqs. (i) and (iii), we get

$$20y = 540°$$

$$\Rightarrow \quad y = 27°$$

From Eq. (i), we get

$$2 \times 27° = 3x$$

$$x = \frac{2 \times 27°}{3} = 18°$$

Hence, $\angle A = 18°$, $\angle B = 27°$

and $\quad \angle C = 5 \times 27° = 135°$

16. Let the cost of a pen be ₹ x and that of a pencil be ₹ y.

According to the question,

$$37x + 53y = 320 \quad \text{...(i)}$$

and $\quad 53x + 37y = 400 \quad$ ...(ii)

On adding Eqs. (i) and (ii), we get

$$90x + 90y = 720$$

$$\Rightarrow \quad x + y = 8 \quad \text{...(iii)}$$

On subtracting Eq. (i) from Eq. (ii), we get

$$16x - 16y = 80$$

$$\Rightarrow \quad x - y = 5 \quad \text{...(iv)}$$

Now, on adding Eqs. (iii) and (iv), we get

$$2x = 13$$

$$\Rightarrow \quad x = 6.5$$

On substituting $x = 6.5$ in Eq. (iii), we get

$$6.5 + y = 8$$

$$\Rightarrow \quad y = 8 - 6.5 = 1.5$$

Hence, cost of one pen is ₹ 6.5 and cost of one pencil is ₹ 1.5.

17. Let number of ₹ 50 notes Sabina received be x and number of ₹ 100 notes be y.

According to the question,

total money withdrawn = ₹ 2000

$\Rightarrow \quad 50x + 100y = 2000 \Rightarrow x + 2y = 40$ ...(i)

and total number of notes = 25

$\Rightarrow \quad x + y = 25$ ...(ii)

On subtracting Eq. (ii) from Eq. (i), we get

$$y = 15$$

From Eq. (ii), $x = 25 - 15 = 10$

$\therefore$ Number of ₹ 50 notes = 10

and number of ₹ 100 notes = 15

Long Answer Type Questions

1. Given, system of equations is

$$3x - y = 3 \quad \text{...(i)}$$

and $\quad 9x - 3y = 9$ ...(ii)

Now, consider Eq. (i), i.e. $3x - y = 3$

$\Rightarrow \quad y = 3x - 3$ ...(iii)

Now, on substituting the value of y in Eq. (ii), we get

$$9x - 3(3x - 3) = 9$$

$\Rightarrow \quad 9x - 9x + 9 = 9 \Rightarrow 9 = 9$

This equation has no variable but it is true for all values of x. So, this system of linear equations has infinitely many solutions, which can be given by taking y (or x) = k in Eq. (iii), where k is an arbitrary real number.

Now, on taking $x = k$ in Eq. (iii), we get

$$y = 3k - 3$$

Hence, infinite solutions are given by $x = k$, $y = 3k - 3$, where k is an arbitrary real number.

2. Given, system of equations is

$$3x - y = 5 \quad \text{...(i)}$$

and $\quad 5x - 3y = -1$ ...(ii)

From Eq. (i), we have

$$y = 3x - 5 \quad \text{...(iii)}$$

On putting the value of y from Eq. (iii) in Eq. (ii), we get

$$5x - 3(3x - 5) = -1$$

$\Rightarrow \quad 5x - 9x + 15 = -1$

$\Rightarrow \quad -4x + 15 = -1$

$\Rightarrow \quad -4x = -1 - 15 = -16$

$\Rightarrow \quad x = 4$

On putting $x = 4$ in Eq. (iii), we get

$$y = 3(4) - 5 = 12 - 5 = 7$$

Hence, the required solution is $x = 4$ and $y = 7$.

Now, $\quad y = mx - 3 \Rightarrow 7 = 4m - 3$

$\Rightarrow \quad 10 = 4m \Rightarrow m = \frac{5}{2}$

3. Given, system of linear equations is

$$5ax + 6by = 28 \quad \text{...(i)}$$

and $\quad 3ax + 4by = 18$ ...(ii)

For making the coefficients of y numerically equal, multiply Eq. (i) by 2 and Eq. (ii) by 3 and write the above equations as

$$10ax + 12by = 56 \quad \text{...(iii)}$$

and $\quad 9ax + 12by = 54$ ...(iv)

On subtracting Eq. (iv) from Eq. (iii), we get

$$ax = 2$$

$$x = \frac{2}{a}$$

On putting $ax = 2$ in Eq. (i), we get

$$5 \times 2 + 6by = 28$$

$\Rightarrow \quad 6by = 28 - 10$

$\Rightarrow \quad 6by = 18$

$\Rightarrow \quad by = 3$

$\Rightarrow \quad y = \frac{3}{b}$

Hence, $x = \frac{2}{a}$ and $y = \frac{3}{b}$ is the required solution.

For verification

Put $x = \frac{2}{a}$ and $y = \frac{3}{b}$ in Eqs. (i) and (ii) respectively.

From Eq. (i), we get

$$\text{LHS} = 5ax + 6by = 5a \times \frac{2}{a} + 6 \times b \times \frac{3}{b}$$

$$= 28 = \text{RHS}$$

From Eq. (ii), we get

$$\text{LHS} = 3ax + 4by = 3 \times a \times \frac{2}{a} + 4 \times b \times \frac{3}{b}$$

$$= 18 = \text{RHS}$$

Hence, the solution is verified.

4. Given pair of linear equations is

$$41x + 53y = 135 \quad \text{...(i)}$$

and $\quad 53x + 41y = 147$ ...(ii)

On adding Eqs. (i) and (ii), we get

$$94x + 94y = 282$$

$\Rightarrow \quad x + y = 3$ ...(iii)

On subtracting Eq. (i) from Eq. (ii), we get

$$12x - 12y = 12$$

$\Rightarrow \quad x - y = 1$ ...(iv)

Now, on adding Eqs. (iii) and (iv), we get

$$2x = 4$$

$\Rightarrow \quad x = 2$

On substituting $x = 2$ in Eq. (iii), we get

$$y = 3 - x \Rightarrow y = 3 - 2 \Rightarrow y = 1$$

Hence, $x = 2$ and $y = 1$ is the required solution.

5. We have, $x+y=14xy \Rightarrow \frac{1}{y}+\frac{1}{x}=14$ ...(i)

and $2x-y=4xy \Rightarrow \frac{2}{y}-\frac{1}{x}=4$ ...(ii)

On substituting $\frac{1}{x}=p$ and $\frac{1}{y}=q$, we get

$$p+q=14 \quad ...(iii)$$

and $-p+2q=4$ ...(iv)

The pair obtained after substitution is the pair of linear equations.

On adding Eqs. (iii) and (iv), we get

$$3q=18$$

$\Rightarrow$ $q=6$

On substituting $q=6$ in Eq. (iii), we get

$$p+6=14$$

$\Rightarrow$ $p=8$

Since, $p=\frac{1}{x}$ and $q=\frac{1}{y}$

So, we put the values of p and q, we get

$$x=\frac{1}{8} \text{ and } y=\frac{1}{6}$$

6. Standard form of above equations are

$$\frac{x}{7}+\frac{y}{3}-5=0 \text{ and } \frac{x}{2}-\frac{y}{9}-6=0$$

Diagram for above equations is

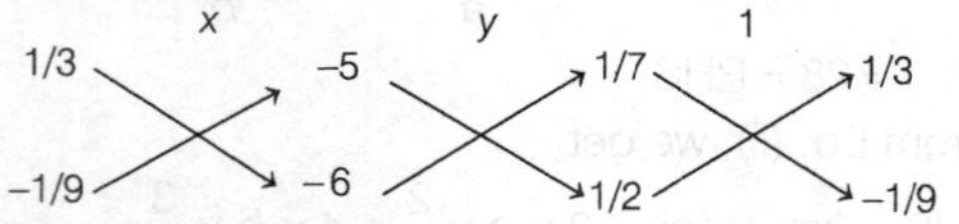

With the help of diagram, we get

$$\frac{x}{\frac{-6}{3}-\frac{5}{9}}=\frac{y}{\frac{-5}{2}+\frac{6}{7}}=\frac{1}{\frac{-1}{63}-\frac{1}{6}}$$

$\Rightarrow$ $\frac{x}{\frac{-23}{9}}=\frac{y}{\frac{-23}{14}}=\frac{1}{\frac{-23}{126}}$

I II III

On taking I and III terms, we get

$$\frac{x}{\frac{-23}{9}}=\frac{1}{\frac{-23}{126}} \Rightarrow x=\frac{\frac{-23}{9}}{\frac{-23}{126}}$$

$\Rightarrow$ $x=\frac{126}{9} \Rightarrow x=14$

On taking II and III terms, we get

$$\frac{y}{\frac{-23}{14}}=\frac{1}{\frac{-23}{126}} \Rightarrow y=\frac{\frac{-23}{14}}{\frac{-23}{126}}$$

$\Rightarrow$ $y=\frac{126}{14}$

$\Rightarrow$ $y=9$

Hence, $x=14$ and $y=9$ is the required solution.

7. Let cost of one pencil be ₹ x and cost of one eraser be ₹ y.

Then, according to given conditions, we get the following equations

$$2x+3y=9 \quad ...(i)$$

and $4x+6y=18$ ...(ii)

From Eq. (i), we get

$$x=\frac{9-3y}{2}$$

On substituting the value of x in Eq. (ii), we get

$$4\left(\frac{9-3y}{2}\right)+6y=18 \Rightarrow 2(9-3y)+6y=18$$

$\Rightarrow$ $18-6y+6y=18 \Rightarrow 18=18$

This equation has no variable but this is true for all values of y. [$\because$ LHS = RHS]

Thus, we do not get a specific value of y as a solution and so we cannot obtain a specific value of x.

Hence, Eqs. (i) and (ii) have infinitely many solutions and we cannot find a unique cost of pencil and an eraser.

Note This situation has arisen because both the given equations $2x+3y=9$ and $4x+6y=18$ (i.e. $2(2x+3y)=2\times 9$) are the same.

8. Let he mixed x litre of milk from first container and y litre of milk from second container.

Then, according to the question,

$$x+y=30 \quad ...(i)$$

and 80% of x + 90% of y = 85% of 30

$\Rightarrow$ $\frac{80}{100}\times x+\frac{90}{100}\times y=\frac{85}{100}\times 30$

$\Rightarrow$ $8x+9y=255$ ...(ii)

Now, $y=30-x$ [from Eq. (i)]

On putting $y=30-x$ in Eq. (ii), we get

$$8x+9(30-x)=255$$

$\Rightarrow$ $8x+270-9x=255 \Rightarrow x=15$

On substituting $x=15$ in Eq. (i), we get

$$y=15$$

Hence, he mixed 15 litre of each milk to get required mixture.

9. Let the numerator be x and denominator be y of the fraction.

Condition I When 1 is added to both numerator and denominator, then

new fraction $=\frac{x+1}{y+1}$

According to the question,

$$\frac{x+1}{y+1}=\frac{4}{5} \Rightarrow 5(x+1)=4(y+1)$$

$\Rightarrow \quad 5x+5=4y+4$

$\Rightarrow \quad 5x-4y=-1 \quad \ldots(i)$

Condition II When 5 is subtracted from both numerator and denominator, then

new fraction $=\dfrac{x-5}{y-5}$

According to the question,

$$\frac{x-5}{y-5}=\frac{1}{2} \Rightarrow 2(x-5)=1(y-5)$$

$\Rightarrow \quad 2x-10=y-5 \Rightarrow 2x-y=10-5$

$\Rightarrow \quad 2x-y=5 \quad \ldots(ii)$

On multiplying Eq. (ii) by 4, we get

$8x-4y=20 \quad \ldots(iii)$

On subtracting Eq. (i) from Eq. (iii), we get

$\Rightarrow \quad 3x=21 \Rightarrow x=7$

On putting $x=7$ in Eq. (i), we get

$5(7)-4y=-1 \Rightarrow 4y=35+1$

$\Rightarrow \quad y=\dfrac{36}{4}=9$

Hence, the required fraction is $\dfrac{7}{9}$.

10. Let the walking speed of 1st person be x km/h and of 2nd person be y km/h.

It is given that if they walk towards each other, they will meet in 2 h.

$\therefore$ Distance covered by 1st person in 2h + Distance covered by 2nd person in 2h = 16 km

$16=(x+y)\times 2$

$\Rightarrow \quad 16=2x+2y$ [$\because$ Distance = Speed × Time]

$\Rightarrow \quad x+y=8 \quad \ldots(i)$

Now, it is also given that if they walk in the same direction, then they will meet in 8 h.

$\therefore$ Distance covered by 1st person in 8 h = Distance covered by 2nd person in 8 h + 16 km

$\Rightarrow \quad 8x=8y+16$

$\Rightarrow \quad 8(x-y)=16$

$\Rightarrow \quad x-y=2 \quad \ldots(ii)$

On adding Eqs. (i) and (ii), we get

$2x=10$

$\Rightarrow \quad x=5$

From Eq. (ii), $5-y=2$

$\Rightarrow \quad y=3$

Hence, walking speeds of both persons are 5 km/h and 3 km/h, respectively.

11. Given, ratio of incomes = 9 : 7

and ratio of their expenditures = 4 : 3

Saving of each person = ₹ 2000

Let incomes of two persons be $9x$, $7x$ and their expenditures be $4y$, $3y$.

Then, linear equations so formed are

$9x-4y=2000 \quad \ldots(i)$

and $\quad 7x-3y=2000 \quad \ldots(ii)$

We make the coefficients of x numerically equal in both equations.

On multiplying Eq. (i) by 7 and Eq. (ii) by 9, we get

$63x-28y=14000 \quad \ldots(iii)$

and $\quad 63x-27y=18000 \quad \ldots(iv)$

On subtracting Eq. (iv) from Eq. (iii), we get

$-28y+27y=14000-18000$

$\Rightarrow \quad -y=-4000$

$\Rightarrow \quad y=4000$

On putting $y=4000$ in Eq. (i), we get

$9x-4\times 4000=2000$

$\Rightarrow \quad 9x=2000+16000$

$\Rightarrow \quad x=\dfrac{18000}{9}=2000$

Thus, monthly income of both persons are 9(2000) and 7(2000) i.e. ₹ 18000 and ₹ 14000, respectively.

12. Let the speed of the first train be x km/h and that of the second train be y km/h. The two trains meet at 9 am.

Let us consider the following chart

	Time (in hours)	**Speed** (in km/h)	**Distance** (in km)
First train	3	x	$3x$
Second train	2	y	$2y$
First train	1.5	x	$1.5x$
Second train	3	y	$3y$

Since, the two trains meet, therefore the sum of distances covered by them is 420 km.

$\therefore \quad 3x+2y=420 \quad \ldots(i)$

and $\quad 1.5x+3y=420 \quad \ldots(ii)$

On multiplying Eq. (ii) by 2, we get

$3x+6y=840 \quad \ldots(iii)$

On subtracting Eq. (i) from Eq. (iii), we get

$4y=420$

$\Rightarrow \quad y=105$

On substituting $y=105$ in Eq. (i), we get

$3x+210=420$

$\Rightarrow \quad 3x = 420 - 210$

$\Rightarrow \quad 3x = 210 \Rightarrow x = 70$

Hence, the speed of the first train is 70 km/h and that of second train is 105 km/h.

13. Let x units be the length and y units be the breadth of a rectangle. Then, area of rectangle $= xy$ sq units.

In the first case, area is reduced by 9 sq units, when length $= (x - 5)$ units and breadth $= (y + 3)$ units

i.e. $\quad xy - (x - 5) \times (y + 3) = 9$

$\Rightarrow xy - (xy + 3x - 5y - 15) = 9$

$\Rightarrow \quad -3x + 5y + 15 = 9$

$\Rightarrow \quad 3x - 5y = 6 \quad \ldots(i)$

In the second case, area is increased by 67 sq units, when length $= (x + 3)$ units and breadth $= (y + 2)$ units

i.e. $\quad (x + 3) \times (y + 2) - xy = 67$

$\Rightarrow \quad xy + 2x + 3y + 6 - xy = 67$

$\Rightarrow \quad 2x + 3y = 61 \quad \ldots(ii)$

On multiplying Eq. (i) by 3 and Eq. (ii) by 5, we get

$9x - 15y = 18 \quad \ldots(iii)$

and $\quad 10x + 15y = 305 \quad \ldots(iv)$

On adding Eqs. (iii) and (iv), we get

$19x = 323 \Rightarrow x = 17$

On substituting $x = 17$ in Eq. (ii), we get

$34 + 3y = 61 \Rightarrow 3y = 27 \Rightarrow y = 9$

Hence, the length of rectangle is 17 units and the breadth of rectangle is 9 units.

14. Let the number be $10x + y$.

Given, $\quad x + y = 9 \quad \ldots(i)$

According to the question,

$9(10x + y) = 2(10y + x)$

$\Rightarrow \quad 90x + 9y = 20y + 2x$

$\Rightarrow \quad 88x - 11y = 0$

$\Rightarrow \quad 8x - y = 0 \quad \ldots(ii)$

Diagram for Eqs. (i) and (ii)

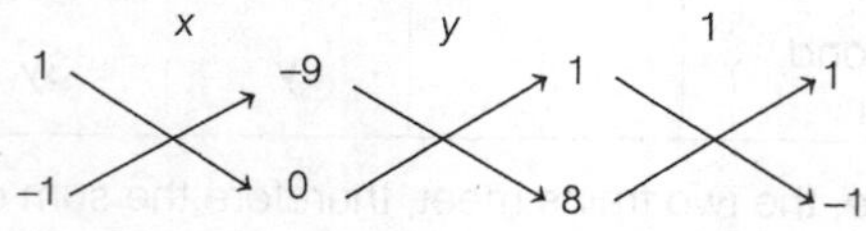

With the help of diagram, we get

$$\frac{x}{0 - 9} = \frac{y}{-72 - 0} = \frac{1}{-1 - 8} \Rightarrow \underset{\text{I}}{\frac{x}{-9}} = \underset{\text{II}}{\frac{y}{-72}} = \underset{\text{III}}{\frac{1}{-9}}$$

On taking I and III, we get

$$\frac{x}{-9} = \frac{1}{-9} \Rightarrow x = 1$$

On taking II and III, we get

$$\frac{y}{-72} = \frac{1}{-9} \Rightarrow y = 8$$

Hence, the required number is $10 \times 1 + 8 = 18$.

15. Let the speed of the train be x km/h and the speed of the bus be y km/h.

In first case, Roohi travels 60 km by train and 240 km by bus in 4 h.

Thus, $\quad \dfrac{60}{x} + \dfrac{240}{y} = 4 \quad \left[\because \text{Time} = \dfrac{\text{Distance}}{\text{Speed}}\right]$

$\Rightarrow \quad \dfrac{15}{x} + \dfrac{60}{y} = 1$ [dividing both sides by 4]...(i)

Similarly, in second case,

$\dfrac{100}{x} + \dfrac{200}{y} = 4 + \dfrac{1}{6} \quad \left[\because 10 \text{ min} = \dfrac{1}{6} \text{h}\right]$

$\Rightarrow \quad \dfrac{100}{x} + \dfrac{200}{y} = \dfrac{25}{6}$

$\Rightarrow \quad \dfrac{24}{x} + \dfrac{48}{y} = 1 \quad \ldots(ii)$

$\left[\text{multiplying both sides by } \dfrac{6}{25}\right]$

On putting $\dfrac{1}{x} = u$ and $\dfrac{1}{y} = v$ in Eqs. (i) and (ii), we get

$15u + 60v = 1 \quad \ldots(iii)$

and $\quad 24u + 48v = 1 \quad \ldots(iv)$

On multiplying Eq. (iii) by 4 and Eq. (iv) by 5 and then subtracting, we get

$4(15u + 60v) - 5(24u + 48v) = 4 \times 1 - 5 \times 1$

$\Rightarrow \quad 60u - 120u = -1$

$\Rightarrow \quad -60u = -1$

$\Rightarrow \quad u = \dfrac{1}{60}$

On putting $u = \dfrac{1}{60}$ in Eq. (iii), we get

$15 \times \dfrac{1}{60} + 60v = 1$

$\Rightarrow \quad 60v = 1 - \dfrac{1}{4} = \dfrac{3}{4}$

$\Rightarrow \quad v = \dfrac{1}{80}$

Thus, we get $u = \dfrac{1}{60}$ and $v = \dfrac{1}{80}$

$\Rightarrow \quad \dfrac{1}{x} = \dfrac{1}{60}$ and $\dfrac{1}{y} = \dfrac{1}{80}$

$\left[\because \text{putting } u = \dfrac{1}{x} \text{ and } v = \dfrac{1}{y}\right]$

$\therefore \quad x = 60$ and $y = 80$

Hence, the speed of train is 60 km/h and the speed of bus is 80 km/h.

16. Let one woman finishes the work in x days and one man finishes the work in y days.

Then, work done by one woman in one day $= \dfrac{1}{x}$

and work done by one man in one day $= \frac{1}{y}$

[assuming total work = 1]

∴ Work done by 2 women and 5 men in one day

$$= \frac{2}{x} + \frac{5}{y} = \frac{5x+2y}{xy}$$

∴ The number of days required for complete the work by 2 women and 5 men $= \frac{xy}{5x+2y}$.

According to the question, $\frac{xy}{5x+2y} = 4$ ...(i)

Similarly, in second case, $\frac{xy}{6x+3y} = 3$ ...(ii)

Eqs. (i) and (ii) can be rewritten as

$$\frac{5x+2y}{xy} = \frac{1}{4} \text{ and } \frac{6x+3y}{xy} = \frac{1}{3}$$

$$\Rightarrow \frac{20x+8y}{xy} = 1 \text{ and } \frac{18x+9y}{xy} = 1$$

$$\Rightarrow \frac{20}{y} + \frac{8}{x} = 1 \text{ and } \frac{18}{y} + \frac{9}{x} = 1$$

On putting $\frac{1}{x} = u$ and $\frac{1}{y} = v$ in given equations, we get

$$20v + 8u = 1 \quad \text{...(iii)}$$

and $$18v + 9u = 1 \quad \text{...(iv)}$$

On multiplying Eq. (iii) by 9 and Eq. (iv) by 8 and then subtracting, we get

$$(20v \times 9 + 8u \times 9) - (18v \times 8 + 9u \times 8) = 9 - 8$$

$$\Rightarrow 180v - 144v = 1$$

$$\Rightarrow 36v = 1$$

$$\Rightarrow v = \frac{1}{36}$$

On substituting $v = \frac{1}{36}$ in Eq. (iv), we get

$$18 \times \frac{1}{36} + 9u = 1 \Rightarrow \frac{1}{2} + 9u = 1 \Rightarrow u = \frac{1}{18}$$

Thus, we get $u = \frac{1}{18}$ and $v = \frac{1}{36}$

$$\Rightarrow \frac{1}{x} = \frac{1}{18} \text{ and } \frac{1}{y} = \frac{1}{36}$$

$$\left[\because u = \frac{1}{x} \text{ and } v = \frac{1}{y}\right]$$

∴ $x = 18$ and $y = 36$

Hence, a single woman can finish the work in 18 days and a single man can finish the work in 36 days.

17. Let speed of the boat in still water be x km/h and speed of the stream be y km/h.

Then speed of the boat downstream $= (x + y)$ km/h and speed of the boat upstream $= (x - y)$ km/h

Condition I When boat goes 30 km upstream, then the time taken,

$$t_1 = \frac{30}{x-y} \text{ h} \quad \left[\because \text{Time} = \frac{\text{Distance}}{\text{Speed}}\right]$$

When boat goes 44 km downstream, then the time taken,

$$t_2 = \frac{44}{x+y} \text{ h}$$

But total time taken = 10 h

$$\Rightarrow t_1 + t_2 = 10 \text{ h} \Rightarrow \frac{30}{x-y} + \frac{44}{x+y} = 10 \quad \text{...(i)}$$

Condition II When boat goes 40 km upstream, then the time taken,

$$T_1 = \frac{40}{x-y} \text{ h} \quad \left[\because \text{Time} = \frac{\text{Distance}}{\text{Speed}}\right]$$

When boat goes 55 km downstream, then the time taken,

$$T_2 = \frac{55}{x+y} \text{ h}$$

But total time taken = 13 h $\Rightarrow T_1 + T_2 = 13$ h

$$\Rightarrow \frac{40}{x-y} + \frac{55}{x+y} = 13 \quad \text{...(ii)}$$

Here, Eqs. (i) and (ii) are not in linear form, so we reduce them in linear form by putting

$\frac{1}{x-y} = u$ and $\frac{1}{x+y} = v$.

From Eq. (i), we get

$$30u + 44v = 10$$

$$\Rightarrow 30u + 44v - 10 = 0 \quad \text{...(iii)}$$

and from Eq. (ii), we get

$$40u + 55v = 13$$

$$\Rightarrow 40u + 55v - 13 = 0 \quad \text{...(iv)}$$

Eqs. (iii) and (iv) are in linear form.

Now, by cross-multiplication method, we get

$$\frac{u}{(44)(-13) - (55)(-10)} = \frac{v}{40(-10) - 30(-13)} = \frac{1}{30(55) - 44(40)}$$

$$\left[\because \frac{u}{b_1c_2 - b_2c_1} = \frac{v}{c_1a_2 - c_2a_1} = \frac{1}{a_1b_2 - a_2b_1}\right]$$

$$\Rightarrow \frac{u}{-572 + 550} = \frac{v}{-400 + 390} = \frac{1}{1650 - 1760}$$

$$\Rightarrow \underset{\text{I}}{\frac{u}{-22}} = \underset{\text{II}}{\frac{v}{-10}} = \underset{\text{III}}{\frac{1}{-110}}$$

On taking I and III terms, we get

$$\frac{u}{-22} = \frac{1}{-110} \Rightarrow u = \frac{22}{110} = \frac{1}{5}$$

On taking II and III terms, we get

$$\frac{v}{-10} = \frac{1}{-110}$$

$$\Rightarrow \quad v = \frac{10}{110} = \frac{1}{11}$$

Now, on putting the values of u and v in

$\frac{1}{x-y} = u$ and $\frac{1}{x+y} = v$, we get

$$\frac{1}{x-y} = \frac{1}{5} \Rightarrow x - y = 5 \quad \ldots(v)$$

and $\frac{1}{x+y} = \frac{1}{11} \Rightarrow x + y = 11 \quad \ldots(vi)$

On adding Eqs. (v) and (vi), we get

$$2x = 16 \Rightarrow x = \frac{16}{2} = 8$$

On putting $x = 8$ in Eq. (v), we get

$$8 - y = 5 \Rightarrow y = 8 - 5 = 3$$

Hence, speed of the boat in still water is 8 km/h and speed of the stream is 3 km/h.

Case Based Questions

1. (i) Given, fixed charge = ₹ x

and additional charge = ₹ y per day.

According to the question,

Amruta paid = ₹ $22 = x + (6-2)y \Rightarrow x + 4y = 22$ ...(a)

and Radhika paid = ₹ $16 = x + (4-2)y$

$\Rightarrow \quad x + 2y = 16$ ...(b)

(ii) On subtracting Eq. (b) from Eq. (a), we get

$$2y = 6$$

$\Rightarrow \quad y = 3$

Now, on substituting $y = 3$ in Eq. (b), we get

$$x + 6 = 16$$

$\Rightarrow \quad x = 10$

Hence, the fixed charge is ₹ 10 and additional charge is ₹ 3 per day.

2. (i) From the given figure, we see that area of two bedrooms = $2(5x) = 10x\, m^2$

∴ Area of kitchen = $5 \times y$

$= 5y\, m^2$

According to the question,

Area of the two bedrooms and area of kitchen $= 95\, m^2$

∴ $\quad 10x + 5y = 95$

$\Rightarrow \quad 2x + y = 19$ [dividing both sides by 5] ...(a)

Also, length of the home = 15 m

∴ $\quad x + 2 + y = 15$

$\Rightarrow \quad x + y = 13$ ...(b)

Hence, pair of linear equations is

$$2x + y = 19 \text{ and } x + y = 13$$

(ii) On subtracting Eq. (b) from Eq. (a), we get

$$x = 6$$

On substituting $x = 6$ in Eq. (b), we get

$$6 + y = 13 \Rightarrow y = 7$$

Now, area of each bedroom = $5x$

$= 30\, m^2$

and area of kitchen = $5y = 35\, m^2$

(iii) Since, area of kitchen = $35\, m^2$.

And it is also given, the cost of laying tiles in kitchen at the rate of ₹ 50 per m^2.

∴ Total cost of laying tiles in the kitchen = 35×50

= ₹ 1750

3. (i) According to given information,

For batch I

$$20x + 5y = 9000 \quad \ldots(a)$$

For batch II

$$5x + 25y = 26000 \quad \ldots(b)$$

(ii) On multiplying Eq. (a) by 5, we get

$$100x + 25y = 45000 \quad \ldots(c)$$

On subtracting Eq. (b) from Eq. (c), we get

$$100x - 5x = 45000 - 26000$$

$\Rightarrow \quad 95x = 19000$

$\Rightarrow \quad x = \frac{19000}{95} = 200$

On substituting $x = 200$ in Eq. (a), we get

$$20 \times 200 + 5y = 9000$$

$\Rightarrow \quad 5y = 9000 - 4000$

$\Rightarrow \quad y = \frac{5000}{5} = 1000$

∴ Difference in the monthly fee paid by a poor child and a rich child = $y - x = 1000 - 200 =$ ₹ 800

(iii) Total monthly collection of fees, if there are 10 poor and 20 rich children = $10x + 20y$.

On putting $x = 200$ and $y = 1000$, we get total monthly collection of fees

$= 10 \times 200 + 20 \times 1000$

$= 2000 + 20000$

= ₹ 22000

06

INDICES/EXPONENTS

Let a is the real number and n is any natural number, then $a \times a \times a$ ...... upto n times can be expressed as a^n. Here, a is called the base and n is called the **exponents** or **index** and a^n is called the exponential form of a.

a^n is read as 'a power n' or 'a raised to the power n'.

e.g. $9765625 = 5 \times 5 \times 5 \times \ldots$ upto 10 times $= 5^{10}$

Indices with Positive Integer If a is any non-zero real numbers and n is a positive integer, then $\sqrt[n]{a} = a^{1/n}$.

e.g. $\sqrt[2]{27} = (27)^{1/2}$.

Indices with Fractional/Rational Number If a is any non-zero real number and $\frac{m}{n}$ is a fractional/rational number.

Then, $a^{m/n} = (a^m)^{1/n} = \sqrt[n]{a^m}$.

e.g. $(2)^{5/3} = [(2)^5]^{1/3} = (32)^{1/3}$

Indices with Negative Integer If a is any non-zero real number and n is any positive integer, then $a^{-n} = \frac{1}{a^n}$.

e.g. $4^{-3} = \frac{1}{4^3} = \frac{1}{4 \times 4 \times 4} = \frac{1}{64}$

Indices with Zero For any non-zero number raised to the power zero, is always equal to 1.

i.e. $a^0 = 1$ e.g. $(-289)^0 = 1$ and $(7^5)^0 = 1$, etc.

Laws of Exponents

1. **Product Law** $a^m \times a^n = a^{m+n}$. **e.g.** $3^4 \times 3^5 = 3^{4+5} = 3^9$
2. **Division Law** $\frac{a^m}{a^n} = a^{m-n}$ or $a^m \div a^n = a^{m-n}$. **e.g.** $3^7 \div 3^5 = 3^{7-5} = 3^2 = 9$
3. **Power Law** (i) $(ab)^m = a^m \cdot b^m$ **e.g.** $(2 \times 5)^3 = 2^3 \times 5^3 = 8 \times 125 = 1000$

   (ii) $\left(\frac{a}{b}\right)^m = \frac{a^m}{b^m}$ **e.g.** $\left(\frac{10}{2}\right)^2 = \frac{10^2}{2^2} = \frac{100}{4} = 25$
4. **Power-to-Power Law** $(a^m)^n = a^{mn}$. **e.g.** $(2^2)^3 = 2^{2 \times 3} = 2^6 = 64$
5. **Reciprocal Law** $\left(\frac{a}{b}\right)^n = \left(\frac{b}{a}\right)^{-n}$. **e.g.** $\left(\frac{2}{3}\right)^4 = \left(\frac{3}{2}\right)^{-4}$

Note

(i) If $n \neq 0$ and $a^n = b^n$, then $a = b$. **e.g.** If $(x)^a = (5)^a$, then $x = 5$.

(ii) If $a \neq 1$ and $a^m = a^n$, then $m = n$. **e.g.** If $(5)^p = (5)^3$, then $p = 3$.

(iii) Why $a^0 = 1$? **Reason** We know that $\frac{a^m}{a^n} = a^{m-n}$. If $m = n$, then $\frac{a^m}{a^m} = a^{m-m} \Rightarrow 1 = a^0$

(iv) (I) $(-a)^m = a^m$, if m is even number. **e.g.** $(-3)^4 = 81 = (3)^4$

(II) $(-a)^m = -a^m$, if m is odd number. **e.g.** $(-3)^3 = -27 = -(3)^3$

EXAM ORIENTED QUESTIONS

TYPE - 1 — 01 Mark

Multiple Choice Questions

Q.1 Value of x, when $(13)^{\sqrt{x}} = 4^4 - 3^4 - 6$, is

(a) 4 (b) 3
(c) 2 (d) 5

$x = 4$

Q.2 Simplify $\frac{2^{n+4} - 2(2^n)}{2(2^{n+3})}$.

(a) $2^{n+1} - \frac{1}{8}$ (b) -2^{n+1}
(c) $1 - 2^n$ (d) $\frac{7}{8}$

Q.3 If x and y are positive real numbers, then $\sqrt[3]{xy^2} \div x^2y$ is equal to

(a) xy (b) $\frac{x^{\frac{5}{3}}}{y^{\frac{1}{3}}}$
(c) $\frac{1}{x^{\frac{5}{3}} \cdot y^{\frac{1}{3}}}$ (d) $x^{\frac{5}{3}} \cdot y^{\frac{1}{3}}$

Q.4 The value of $81^{0.16} \times 3^{0.09} \times 27^{\frac{0.36}{4}}$ is equal to

(a) 4 (b) 9
(c) 3 (d) 81.25

Q.5 Value of $\sqrt[5]{\sqrt[3]{9^2}}$ is

(a) $(9)^{1/5}$ (b) $3^{6/5}$
(c) $3^{4/15}$ (d) $9^{4/5}$

Q.6 Which one is the value of x, if $\sqrt{\frac{p}{q}} = \left(\frac{q}{p}\right)^{1-3x}$?

(a) $-\frac{3}{4}$ (b) $-\frac{4}{3}$
(c) $\frac{4}{3}$ (d) $\frac{1}{2}$

Q.7 $[\{(-1) \times (-1)\}^2]^3 - (1)^{(-2)}$

(a) 1 (b) 0
(c) 2 (d) 3

Answers

1. (a) 2. (d) 3. (c) 4. (c) 5. (c)
6. (d) 7. (b)

TYPE - 2 — 01 Mark

Assertion-Reason Type Questions

Q.1 Assertion (A) $(2)^4 \times (2)^{-2} = (2)^2$

Reason (R) When two powers with the same base are multiplied, then their exponents are added i.e. $a^m \times a^n = a^{m+n}$.

(a) A is true, R is false.
(b) A is false, R is true.
(c) Both A and R are true and R is the correct reason for A.
(d) Both A and R are true and R is incorrect reason for A.

Q.2 Assertion (A) $(3^4)^3 = (3)^{12}$

Reason (R) When raising a power to another power, we multiply the powers.

(a) A is true, R is false.
(b) A is false, R is true.
(c) Both A and R are true and R is the correct reason for A.
(d) Both A and R are true and R is incorrect reason for A.

Q.3 Assertion (A) If $x = 2^{1/3} + 2^{2/3}$, then $x^3 - 6x = 6$.

Reason (R) $(a-b)(a+b) = a^2 - b^2$.

(a) A is true, R is false.
(b) A is false, R is true.
(c) Both A and R are true and R is the correct reason for A.
(d) Both A and R are true and R is incorrect reason for A.

Q.4 Assertion (A) If $a^x = b$, $b^y = c$ and $c^z = a$, then $xyz = 1$.

Reason (R) $(a^m)^n = a^{mn}$.

(a) A is true, R is false.
(b) A is false, R is true.
(c) Both A and R are true and R is the correct reason for A.
(d) Both A and R are true and R is incorrect reason for A.

Q.5 Assertion (A) If $5^{14} = (125)^{2x}$, then $x = \frac{7}{3}$.

Reason (R) $a^m \times a^n = a^{m+n}$.

(a) A is true, R is false.
(b) A is false, R is true.
(c) Both A and R are true and R is the correct reason for A.
(d) Both A and R are true and R is incorrect reason for A.

Answers

1. (c) 2. (c) 3. (d) 4. (c) 5. (d)

TYPE - 3 — 01 Mark

Statement Based Questions

Q.1 Statement I $\sqrt[3]{27} - 7 \cdot \sqrt[3]{216} + 10 \cdot \sqrt[6]{64} = 19$

Statement II $\sqrt[n]{a^m} = a^{m/n}$

Which of the following is valid?
(a) Both the Statements are true.
(b) Both the Statements are false.
(c) Statement I is true and Statement II is false.
(d) Statement I is false and Statement II is true.

Q.2 Statement I $a^0 = 1$, where $a \neq 0$.

Statement II $\sqrt[m]{a^n} \neq (\sqrt[m]{a})^n$, $m > 0$.

Which of the following is valid?
(a) Both the Statements are true.
(b) Both the Statements are false.
(c) Statement I is true and Statement II is false.
(d) Statement I is false and Statement II is true.

Q.3 Statement I If $x = 2$ and $y = -3$, then xy^2 will be 18.

Statement II If a is any non-zero real number and n is a positive integer, then $\sqrt[n]{a} = a^{\frac{1}{n}}$.

Which of the following is valid?
(a) Both the Statements are true.
(b) Both the Statements are false.
(c) Statement I is true and Statement II is false.
(d) Statement I is false and Statement II is true.

Q.4 Statement I If $2^{7x} \div 4^x = \sqrt[5]{2^{15}}$, then $x = 3$.

Statement II $(-a)^m = a^m$, if m is an odd number.

Which of the following is valid?
(a) Both the Statements are true.
(b) Both the Statements are false.
(c) Statement I is true and Statement II is false.
(d) Statement I is false and Statement II is true.

Answers

1. (d) 2. (c) 3. (a) 4. (b)

TYPE - 4 — 03 Marks

Short Answer Type Questions

Q.1 Find the value of $3^{-a} \times 2^b \times 5^{-c} \times 7^d$, if $17640 = 2^a \cdot 3^b \cdot 5^c \cdot 7^d$.

Q.2 If $x = -3$ and $y = 2$, then find the value of $x^x + y^y + x^y + y^x$.

Q.3 Express $(a^{-1} + b^{-1}) \div (a^{-2} - b^{-2})$ in the simplest form.

Q.4 If $5^{3x} = 125$ and $10^y = 0.001$, then find $5x + y$.

Q.5 If $2^x = 3^y = 6^{-z}$, then show that $x^{-1} + y^{-1} + z^{-1} = 0$.

Q.6 Show that $\left[\left\{\frac{x^{l(l-m)}}{x^{l(l+m)}}\right\} \div \left\{\frac{x^{m(m-l)}}{x^{m(m+l)}}\right\}\right]^{a+b} = 1$.

Q.7 Find the value of $3^3 \times (243)^{-2/3} \times 9^{1/3}$.

Q.8 Evaluate $5^{-4} \times (125)^{5/3} \div (25)^{-1/2}$.

Q.9 Simplify $\dfrac{5 \cdot (25)^{m+1} - 25 \cdot (5)^{2m}}{5 \cdot (5)^{2m+3} - (25)^{m+1}}$.

Q.10 Evaluate $\dfrac{3 \times 27^{n+1} + 9 \times 3^{3n-1}}{8 \times 3^{3n} - 5 \times 27^n}$.

Q.11 Solve for y, if $(\sqrt[3]{4})^{2y+\frac{1}{2}} = (\sqrt[3]{8})^5$.

Q.12 Simplify $(x^{1/3} - x^{-1/3})(x^{2/3} + 1 + x^{-2/3})$.

Q.13 Find the value of x, when $\sqrt{\frac{2}{3}} = \left(\frac{3}{2}\right)^{1-2x}$.

Q.14 Simplify $\left(\frac{81}{16}\right)^{-3/4} \times \left[\left(\frac{25}{9}\right)^{-3/2} \div \left(\frac{5}{2}\right)^{-3}\right]$.

Answers

1. $1\frac{61}{135}$	2. 13.09	3. $\frac{ab}{b-a}$	4. 2
7. $3^{1/3}$	8. 25	9. $\frac{1}{6}$	10. 28
11. $3\frac{1}{2}$	12. $x - \frac{1}{x}$	13. $\frac{3}{4}$	14. 1

TYPE - 5 — 4/5 Marks

Long Answer Type Questions

Q.1 Prove that $\dfrac{x^{-1}}{x^{-1} + y^{-1}} + \dfrac{x^{-1}}{x^{-1} - y^{-1}} = \dfrac{2y^2}{y^2 - x^2}$.

Q.2 If $p^x = q^y = r^z$ and $q^2 = pr$, then show that $y = \dfrac{2xz}{z + x}$.

Q.3 Solve for x and y such that

$$3^x \times 3^{-y} = 9 \text{ and } 2^y \times 4^{-x} = \frac{1}{8}.$$

Q.4 Prove that

$$\frac{1}{1+x^{m-n}+x^{l-n}}+\frac{1}{1+x^{n-l}+x^{m-l}}+\frac{1}{1+x^{l-m}+x^{n-m}}=1.$$

Q.5 Find the value of x, when $\sqrt{\left(\frac{4}{5}\right)^{1-2x}} = 1\frac{9}{16}$.

Q.6 If $5^{2x-1} = 25^{x-1} + 100$, then find the value of 4^{3+x}.

Q.7 If $3^x = 9 \times 3^y$ and $8 \times 2^y = 4^x$, then find the value of $3x + 2y$.

Q.8 Find the value of x, when

$$3^3(7^0 + 4^{3x}) = 27\frac{27}{64}$$

Answers

3. $x = 1$ and $y = -1$ **5.** $\frac{5}{2}$

6. 1024 **7.** 1

8. -1

EXPLANATIONS

Multiple Choice Questions

1. (a) Given, $(13)^{\sqrt{x}} = 4^4 - 3^4 - 6$

$\Rightarrow \quad (13)^{\sqrt{x}} = 256 - 81 - 6$

$\Rightarrow \quad (13)^{\sqrt{x}} = 256 - 87$

$\Rightarrow \quad (13)^{\sqrt{x}} = 169$

$\Rightarrow \quad (13)^{\sqrt{x}} = (13)^2$

On comparing the exponents of 13 from both sides, we get

$$\sqrt{x} = 2$$

On squaring both sides, we get $x = 4$

2. (d) We have, $\dfrac{2^{n+4} - 2(2^n)}{2(2^{n+3})}$

$$= \frac{2^{n+4} - 2^{n+1}}{2^{n+3+1}} \quad [\because a^m \cdot a^n = a^{m+n}]$$

$$= \frac{2^{n+4} - 2^{n+1}}{2^{n+4}}$$

$$= \frac{2^{n+1}[2^3 - 1]}{2^{n+1} \cdot 2^3} = \frac{8-1}{8} = \frac{7}{8}$$

3. (c) We have, $\sqrt[3]{xy^2} \div x^2y$

$$= \frac{\sqrt[3]{xy^2}}{x^2y} = \frac{x^{\frac{1}{3}}y^{\frac{2}{3}}}{x^2y}$$

$$[\because \sqrt[n]{a} = a^{\frac{1}{n}} \text{ and } (ab)^m = a^m b^m]$$

$$= x^{\frac{1}{3}-2} \cdot y^{\frac{2}{3}-1} \quad \left[\because \frac{a^m}{a^n} = a^{m-n}\right]$$

$$= x^{\frac{-5}{3}} \cdot y^{\frac{-1}{3}}$$

$$= \frac{1}{x^{\frac{5}{3}} \cdot y^{\frac{1}{3}}}$$

4. (c) We have, $81^{0.16} \times 3^{0.09} \times 27^{\frac{0.36}{4}}$

$$= 81^{\frac{16}{100}} \times 3^{0.09} \times 27^{0.09}$$

$$= 81^{\frac{16}{100}} \times (3 \times 27)^{0.09} \quad [\because a^m \times a^n = a^{m+n}]$$

$$= (81)^{\frac{16}{100}} \times (81)^{\frac{9}{100}}$$

$$= (81)^{\frac{16}{100}+\frac{9}{100}} \quad [\because a^m \times a^n = a^{m+n}]$$

$$= (81)^{\frac{25}{100}} = (81)^{\frac{1}{4}} = 3$$

5. (c) We have, $\sqrt[5]{\sqrt[3]{9^2}} = \left((9^2)^{\frac{1}{3}}\right)^{\frac{1}{5}} \quad [\because \sqrt[n]{a} = (a)^{\frac{1}{n}}]$

$$= (9)^{2\times\frac{1}{3}\times\frac{1}{5}} \quad [\because (a^m)^n = a^{mn}]$$

$$= (9)^{\frac{2}{15}} = (3^2)^{\frac{2}{15}} = 3^{\frac{4}{15}}$$

6. (d) Given, $\sqrt{\frac{p}{q}} = \left(\frac{q}{p}\right)^{1-3x}$

$$\Rightarrow \quad \left(\frac{p}{q}\right)^{\frac{1}{2}} = \left(\frac{q}{p}\right)^{1-3x} \quad \left[\because \sqrt[2]{a} = (a)^{\frac{1}{n}}\right]$$

$$\Rightarrow \quad \left(\frac{q}{p}\right)^{\frac{-1}{2}} = \left(\frac{q}{p}\right)^{1-3x} \quad \left[\because \left(\frac{a}{b}\right)^n = \left(\frac{b}{a}\right)^{-n}\right]$$

On comparing the exponents of $\frac{q}{p}$ from both sides, we get

$$\frac{-1}{2} = 1 - 3x \Rightarrow 3x = 1 + \frac{1}{2}$$

$$\Rightarrow \quad 3x = \frac{2+1}{2} \Rightarrow x = \frac{3}{3\times 2} \Rightarrow x = \frac{1}{2}$$

7. (b) We have, $[\{(-1)\times(-1)\}^2]^3-(1)^{(-2)}$

$=[\{(-1)^{1+1}\}^2]^3-(1)^{(-2)}$ $[\because a^m \times a^n = a^{m+n}]$

$=[(-1)^{2\times 2}]^3-(1)^{(-2)}$ $[\because (a^m)^n = a^{mn}]$

$=(-1)^{4\times 3}-(1)^{(-2)}$

$=(-1)^{12}-\left(\frac{1}{1}\right)^2$ $\left[\because \left(\frac{a}{b}\right)^{-n}=\left(\frac{b}{a}\right)^n\right]$

$=1-1=0$

Assertion-Reason Type Questions

1. (c) Given, $(2)^4\times(2)^{-2}=(2)^2$

LHS $=(2)^4\times(2)^{-2}$

$=2^{4+(-2)}$ $[\because a^m\cdot a^n=a^{m+n}]$

$=(2)^2$

$=$ RHS

Hence, both A and R are true and R is the correct reason for A.

2. (c) We have, LHS $=(3^4)^3=(3)^{4\times 3}$ $[\because (a^m)^n=(a)^{mn}]$

$=(3)^{12}=$ RHS

Hence, A is true.

Now, when raising a power to another power, we multiply the powers i.e. $((a)^m)^n=a^{mn}$.

So, R is true and R is the correct reason for A.

3. (d) Given, $x=2^{1/3}+2^{2/3}$

On taking cube both sides, we get

$x^3=(2^{1/3}+2^{2/3})^3$

$\Rightarrow x^3=(2^{1/3})^3+(2^{2/3})^3+3\times 2^{1/3}\times 2^{2/3}(2^{1/3}+2^{2/3})$

$=2+4+3\times 2^{3/3}(x)$

$[\because a^m\cdot a^n=a^{m+n}$ and $(a^m)^n=a^{mn}]$

$=6+6x$

$\Rightarrow x^3-6x=6$

Hence, both A and R are true and R is incorrect reason for A.

4. (c) Given, $a^x=b$ ...(i)

$b^y=c$ ...(ii)

and $c^z=a$ ...(iii)

Now, $a^x=b$

$\Rightarrow (c^z)^x=b$ [from Eq. (iii)]

$\Rightarrow (c)^{zx}=b$ $[\because (a^m)^n=a^{mn}]$

$\Rightarrow (b^y)^{zx}=b$ [from Eq. (ii)]

$\Rightarrow (b)^{xyz}=b$

On comparing exponents of b both sides, we get

$xyz=1$

Hence, both A and R are true and R is the correct reason for A.

5. (d) Given, $5^{14}=(125)^{2x}$

$\Rightarrow 5^{14}=(5^3)^{2x}$

$\Rightarrow 5^{14}=5^{6x}$ $[\because (a^m)^n=a^{mn}]$

On comparing the exponents of 5 both sides, we get

$14=6x$

$\Rightarrow x=\frac{14}{6}=\frac{7}{3}$

Hence, both A and R are true and R is incorrect reason for A.

Statement Based Questions

1. (d) We have, $\sqrt[3]{27}-7\cdot\sqrt[3]{216}+10\cdot\sqrt[6]{64}$

$=\sqrt[3]{3^3}-7\cdot\sqrt[3]{6^3}+10\cdot\sqrt[6]{2^6}$

$=3^{3/3}-7\cdot 6^{3/3}+10\cdot 2^{6/6}$ $[\because \sqrt[n]{a^m}=a^{m/n}]$

$=3-7.6+10.2$

$=3-42+20$

$=-19$

Therefore, Statement I is false and Statement II is true.

2. (c) We know that

$a^0=1$ is for any $a\neq 0$.

So, Statement I is true and Statement II is false.

3. (a) We have, $x=2, y=-3$

Now, $xy^2=2\times(-3)^2=2\times 9=18$

Hence, Statement I is true and Statement II is also true.

4. (b) Given, $2^{7x}\div 4^x=\sqrt[5]{2^{15}}$

$\Rightarrow 2^{7x}\div 2^{2x}=2^{\frac{15}{5}}$ $[\because (a^m)^n=a^{mn}$ and $\sqrt[n]{a^m}=a^{\frac{m}{n}}]$

$\Rightarrow \frac{2^{7x}}{2^{2x}}=2^3$

$\Rightarrow 2^{7x-2x}=2^3$

$\Rightarrow 2^{5x}=2^3$

On comparing the exponents of 2 both sides, we get

$5x=3$

$\Rightarrow x=\frac{3}{5}$

Hence, Statement I is false

We know that $(-a)^m=a^m$, when m is an even number.

Therefore, Statement II is also false.

Short Answer Type Questions

1. We have, $17640=2^a.3^b.5^c.7^d$

$\Rightarrow 2^3\times 3^2\times 5^1\times 7^2=2^a.3^b.5^c.7^d$

On comparing the exponents of 2, 3, 5 and 7 both sides, we get

$a=3, b=2, c=1$ and $d=2$

$\therefore 3^{-a}\times 2^b\times 5^{-c}\times 7^d=3^{-3}\times 2^2\times 5^{-1}\times 7^2$

$=\frac{1}{27}\times 4\times\frac{1}{5}\times 49$ $\left[\because a^{-n}=\frac{1}{a^n}\right]$

$=\frac{196}{135}=1\frac{61}{135}$

2. We have, $x^x + y^y + x^y + y^x$

$$= (-3)^{-3} + (2)^2 + (-3)^2 + (2)^{-3}$$ [given, $x = -3$ and $y = 2$]

$$= \frac{1}{(-3)^3} + 4 + 9 + \frac{1}{2^3} \quad \left[\because a^{-n} = \frac{1}{a^n}\right]$$

$$= -\frac{1}{27} + 13 + \frac{1}{8}$$

$$= \frac{104+1}{8} - \frac{1}{27} = \frac{105 \times 27 - 8 \times 1}{27 \times 8}$$

$$= \frac{2835 - 8}{216} = \frac{2827}{216} = 13.09$$

3. We have, $(a^{-1} + b^{-1}) \div (a^{-2} - b^{-2})$

$$= \frac{a^{-1} + b^{-1}}{a^{-2} - b^{-2}} = \frac{\frac{1}{a} + \frac{1}{b}}{\frac{1}{a^2} - \frac{1}{b^2}} \quad \left[\because a^{-n} = \frac{1}{a^n}\right]$$

$$= \frac{\frac{b+a}{ab}}{\frac{b^2 - a^2}{a^2b^2}} = \frac{b+a}{ab} \times \frac{a^2b^2}{b^2 - a^2} \quad \left[\because \frac{a}{b} \div \frac{c}{d} = \frac{ad}{bc}\right]$$

$$= \frac{ab(b+a)}{(b+a)(b-a)} \quad [\because A^2 - B^2 = (A+B)(A-B)]$$

$$= \frac{ab}{b-a}$$

4. We have,

$$5^{3x} = 125 \Rightarrow 5^{3x} = 5^3$$

On comparing the exponents of 5 both sides, we get

$$3x = 3$$

$$\Rightarrow \quad x = 1 \quad \ldots \text{(i)}$$

Now, $10^y = 0.001$

$$\Rightarrow \quad 10^y = \frac{1}{1000} = \frac{1}{10^3}$$

$$\Rightarrow \quad 10^y = (10)^{-3} \quad \left[\because \frac{1}{a^n} = a^{-n}\right]$$

On comparing the exponents of 10 both sides, we get

$$y = -3 \quad \ldots \text{(ii)}$$

$$\therefore \quad 5x + y = 5 \times 1 - 3 \quad \text{[using Eqs. (i) and (ii)]}$$
$$= 5 - 3 = 2$$

5. Let $2^x = 3^y = 6^{-z} = k$

$$\therefore \quad 2^x = k \Rightarrow 2 = (k)^{\frac{1}{x}},$$

$$3^y = k \Rightarrow 3 = (k)^{\frac{1}{y}}$$

and $$6^{-z} = k \Rightarrow 6 = (k)^{\frac{-1}{z}}$$

Now, $$6 = 2 \times 3$$

$$\Rightarrow \quad (k)^{\frac{-1}{z}} = (k)^{\frac{1}{x}} \times (k)^{\frac{1}{y}}$$

$$\Rightarrow \quad (k)^{\frac{-1}{z}} = (k)^{\left(\frac{1}{x} + \frac{1}{y}\right)} \quad [\because a^m \times a^n = a^{m+n}]$$

On comparing the exponents of k both sides, we get

$$\frac{-1}{z} = \frac{1}{x} + \frac{1}{y}$$

$$\Rightarrow \quad \frac{1}{x} + \frac{1}{y} + \frac{1}{z} = 0$$

$$\Rightarrow x^{-1} + y^{-1} + z^{-1} = 0 \quad \left[\because \frac{1}{a^n} = a^{-n}\right]$$ **Hence proved.**

6. $$\text{LHS} = \left[\left\{\frac{x^{l(l-m)}}{x^{l(l+m)}}\right\} \div \left\{\frac{x^{m(m-l)}}{x^{m(m+l)}}\right\}\right]^{a+b}$$

$$= \left[\left\{\frac{x^{l^2 - ml}}{x^{l^2 + ml}}\right\} \div \left\{\frac{x^{m^2 - ml}}{x^{m^2 + ml}}\right\}\right]^{a+b}$$

$$= [x^{l^2 - ml - l^2 - ml} \div x^{m^2 - ml - m^2 - ml}]^{a+b} \quad \left[\because \frac{a^m}{a^n} = a^{m-n}\right]$$

$$= [x^{-2ml} \div x^{-2ml}]^{a+b}$$

$$= \left[\frac{x^{-2ml}}{x^{-2ml}}\right]^{a+b} = [1]^{a+b} \quad [\because 1^n = 1]$$

$$= 1 = \text{RHS}$$

7. We have, $3^3 \times (243)^{-2/3} \times 9^{1/3}$

$$= 3^3 \times (3 \times 3 \times 3 \times 3 \times 3)^{-2/3} \times (3 \times 3)^{1/3}$$

$$= 3^3 \times (3^5)^{-2/3} \times (3^2)^{1/3}$$

$$= 3^3 \times 3^{5 \times (-2/3)} \times 3^{2 \times 1/3} \quad [\because (a^m)^n = a^{m \times n}]$$

$$= 3^3 \times 3^{-10/3} \times 3^{2/3}$$

$$= 3^{3 - \frac{10}{3} + \frac{2}{3}} \quad [\because a^l \times a^m \times a^n = a^{l+m+n}]$$

$$= 3^{\frac{9-10+2}{3}} = 3^{\frac{11-10}{3}} = 3^{1/3}$$

8. We have, $5^{-4} \times (125)^{5/3} \div (25)^{-1/2}$

$$= 5^{-4} \times (5 \times 5 \times 5)^{5/3} \div (5 \times 5)^{-1/2}$$

$$= 5^{-4} \times (5^3)^{5/3} \div (5^2)^{-1/2}$$

$$= 5^{-4} \times 5^{3 \times \frac{5}{3}} \div 5^{2 \times \left(-\frac{1}{2}\right)} \quad [\because (a^m)^n = a^{m \times n}]$$

$$= \frac{5^{-4} \times 5^5}{5^{-1}} = \frac{5^{-4+5}}{5^{-1}} \quad [\because a^m \times a^n = a^{m+n}]$$

$$= \frac{5^1}{5^{-1}} = 5^{1-(-1)} \quad \left[\because \frac{a^m}{a^n} = a^{m-n}\right]$$

$$= 5^{1+1} = 5^2 = 25$$

9. We have, $$\frac{5 \cdot (25)^{m+1} - 25 \cdot (5)^{2m}}{5 \cdot (5)^{2m+3} - (25)^{m+1}}$$

$$= \frac{5 \times (5^2)^{m+1} - 5^2 \times 5^{2m}}{5 \times 5^{2m+3} - (5^2)^{m+1}}$$

$$= \frac{5 \times 5^{2(m+1)} - 5^2 \times 5^{2m}}{5 \times 5^{2m+3} - 5^{2(m+1)}} \quad [\because (a^m)^n = a^{m \times n}]$$

$$= \frac{5^1 \times 5^{2m+2} - 5^2 \times 5^{2m}}{5^1 \times 5^{2m+3} - 5^{2m+2}}$$

$$= \frac{5^{2m+2+1} - 5^{2+2m}}{5^{2m+3+1} - 5^{2m+2}} \quad [\because a^m \cdot a^n = a^{m+n}]$$

$$= \frac{5^{2m+3} - 5^{2m+2}}{5^{2m+4} - 5^{2m+2}} = \frac{5^{2m+2}(5-1)}{5^{2m+2}(5^2-1)}$$

[taking 5^{2m+2} common from both numerator and denominator]

$$= \frac{4}{(25-1)} = \frac{4}{24} = \frac{1}{6}$$

10. We have,

$$\frac{3 \times 27^{n+1} + 9 \times 3^{3n-1}}{8 \times 3^{3n} - 5 \times 27^n} = \frac{(3)^1 \times (3^3)^{n+1} + (3)^2 \times (3)^{3n-1}}{(2)^3 \times 3^{3n} - 5 \times (3^3)^n}$$

$$= \frac{3^{1+3n+3} + 3^{2+3n-1}}{(2)^3 \times 3^{3n} - 5 \times 3^{3n}}$$

$[\because (a^m)^n = a^{m \times n}$ and $a^m \cdot a^n = a^{m+n}]$

$$= \frac{3^{3n+4} + 3^{3n+1}}{3^{3n} \times (2)^3 - 3^{3n} \times 5} = \frac{3^{3n}(3^4 + 3^1)}{3^{3n}(2^3 - 5)}$$

[taking 3^{3n} common from both numerator and denominator]

$$= \frac{81+3}{8-5} = \frac{84}{3} = 28$$

11. We have, $(\sqrt[3]{4})^{2y+\frac{1}{2}} = (\sqrt[3]{8})^5$

$$\Rightarrow \left((4)^{\frac{1}{3}}\right)^{2y+\frac{1}{2}} = \left((8)^{\frac{1}{3}}\right)^5 \Rightarrow \left((2^2)^{\frac{1}{3}}\right)^{2y+\frac{1}{2}} = \left((2^3)^{\frac{1}{3}}\right)^5$$

$$\Rightarrow \left((2)^{\frac{2}{3}}\right)^{2y+\frac{1}{2}} = \left((2)^{\frac{3}{3}}\right)^5 \quad [\because (a^m)^n = a^{m \times n}]$$

$$\Rightarrow (2)^{\frac{4}{3}y+\frac{1}{3}} = (2)^5$$

On comparing the exponents of 2 both sides, we get

$$\frac{4}{3}y + \frac{1}{3} = 5$$

$$\Rightarrow 4y + 1 = 5 \times 3$$

$$\Rightarrow 4y = 15 - 1$$

$$\Rightarrow y = \frac{14}{4} = \frac{7}{2} \Rightarrow y = 3\frac{1}{2}$$

12. We have, $(x^{1/3} - x^{-1/3})(x^{2/3} + 1 + x^{-2/3})$

$$= \left(x^{\frac{1}{3}} - \frac{1}{x^{\frac{1}{3}}}\right)\left(\left(x^{\frac{1}{3}}\right)^2 + 1 + \left(x^{\frac{1}{3}}\right)^{-2}\right)$$

$$= \left(x^{\frac{1}{3}} - \frac{1}{x^{\frac{1}{3}}}\right)\left(\left(x^{\frac{1}{3}}\right)^2 + x^{\frac{1}{3}} \cdot \frac{1}{x^{\frac{1}{3}}} + \left(\frac{1}{x^{\frac{1}{3}}}\right)^2\right)$$

$$= \left(x^{\frac{1}{3}}\right)^3 - \left(\frac{1}{x^{\frac{1}{3}}}\right)^3 \quad [\because (a-b)(a^2+ab+b^2) = a^3 - b^3]$$

$$= x - \frac{1}{x} \quad [\because (a^m)^n = a^{m \times n}]$$

13. We have, $\sqrt{\frac{2}{3}} = \left(\frac{3}{2}\right)^{1-2x}$

We know that $\frac{a}{b} = \left(\frac{b}{a}\right)^{-1}$ [reciprocal law]

$$\therefore \sqrt{\frac{2}{3}} = \left[\left(\frac{2}{3}\right)^{-1}\right]^{1-2x}$$

$$\Rightarrow \left(\frac{2}{3}\right)^{1/2} = \left(\frac{2}{3}\right)^{-1(1-2x)} \quad [\because (a^m)^n = a^{m \times n}]$$

$$\Rightarrow \left(\frac{2}{3}\right)^{1/2} = \left(\frac{2}{3}\right)^{2x-1}$$

On comparing the exponents of $\frac{2}{3}$ from both sides, we get

$$2x - 1 = \frac{1}{2} \Rightarrow 2x = 1 + \frac{1}{2} = \frac{3}{2} \Rightarrow x = \frac{3}{4}$$

14. We have, $\left(\frac{81}{16}\right)^{-3/4} \times \left[\left(\frac{25}{9}\right)^{-3/2} \div \left(\frac{5}{2}\right)^{-3}\right]$

$$= \left(\frac{3^4}{2^4}\right)^{-3/4} \times \left[\left(\frac{5^2}{3^2}\right)^{-3/2} \div \left(\frac{5}{2}\right)^{-3}\right]$$

$$= \left(\frac{3}{2}\right)^{4 \times \left(\frac{-3}{4}\right)} \times \left[\left(\frac{5}{3}\right)^{2 \times \left(\frac{-3}{2}\right)} \div \left(\frac{5}{2}\right)^{-3}\right] \quad [\because (a^m)^n = a^{mn}]$$

$$= \left(\frac{3}{2}\right)^{-3} \times \left[\left(\frac{5}{3}\right)^{-3} \div \left(\frac{5}{2}\right)^{-3}\right]$$

$$= \left(\frac{2}{3}\right)^3 \times \left[\left(\frac{3}{5}\right)^3 \div \left(\frac{2}{5}\right)^3\right] \quad \left[\because \left(\frac{a}{b}\right)^n = \left(\frac{b}{a}\right)^{-n}\right]$$

$$= \left(\frac{2}{3}\right)^3 \times \left[\left(\frac{3}{5}\right)^3 \times \left(\frac{5}{2}\right)^3\right] \quad \left[\because \frac{a}{b} \div \frac{c}{d} = \frac{a}{b} \times \frac{d}{c}\right]$$

$$= \left(\frac{2}{3}\right)^3 \times \left[\left(\frac{3}{5} \times \frac{5}{2}\right)^3\right] \quad [\because a^m \times b^m = (ab)^m]$$

$$= \left(\frac{2}{3}\right)^3 \times \left(\frac{3}{2}\right)^3 = \left(\frac{2}{3} \times \frac{3}{2}\right)^3 = (1)^3 = 1$$

Long Answer Type Questions

1. LHS $= \frac{x^{-1}}{x^{-1} + y^{-1}} + \frac{x^{-1}}{x^{-1} - y^{-1}}$

$$= \frac{\frac{1}{x}}{\frac{1}{x} + \frac{1}{y}} + \frac{\frac{1}{x}}{\frac{1}{x} - \frac{1}{y}} \quad \left[\because a^{-n} = \frac{1}{a^n}\right]$$

$$= \frac{\frac{1}{x}}{\frac{y+x}{xy}} + \frac{\frac{1}{x}}{\frac{y-x}{xy}}$$

$$= \frac{xy}{(x+y)x} + \frac{xy}{(y-x)x} \quad \left[\because \frac{a}{b} \div \frac{c}{d} = \frac{ad}{bc}\right]$$

$$= \frac{y}{x+y} + \frac{y}{y-x} = \frac{y(y-x)+y(x+y)}{(y+x)(y-x)}$$

$$= \frac{y^2 - xy + xy + y^2}{y^2 - x^2} \quad [\because (a+b)(a-b) = a^2 - b^2]$$

$$= \frac{2y^2}{y^2 - x^2} = \text{RHS}$$ **Hence proved.**

2. Let $p^x = q^y = r^z = k$

$\therefore \quad p^x = k \Rightarrow p = (k)^{\frac{1}{x}}, q^y = k \Rightarrow q = (k)^{\frac{1}{y}}$

and $r^z = k \Rightarrow r = (k)^{\frac{1}{z}}$

Now, $q^2 = pr$

$$(k)^{2 \times \frac{1}{y}} = (k)^{\frac{1}{x}} \cdot (k)^{\frac{1}{z}}$$

$$\Rightarrow \quad (k)^{\frac{2}{y}} = (k)^{\frac{1}{x}+\frac{1}{z}} \quad [\because a^m \cdot a^n = a^{m+n}]$$

On comparing the exponents of k from both sides, we get

$$\frac{2}{y} = \frac{1}{x} + \frac{1}{z}$$

$$\Rightarrow \quad \frac{2}{y} = \frac{z+x}{xz}$$

$$\Rightarrow \quad \frac{2xz}{y} = z + x$$

$$\Rightarrow \quad y = \frac{2xz}{z+x}$$ **Hence proved.**

3. Given, $3^x \times 3^{-y} = 9$

$$\Rightarrow \quad 3^{x-y} = (3)^2 \quad [\because a^m \cdot a^n = a^{m+n}]$$

On comparing the exponents of 3 from both sides, we get

$$x - y = 2 \quad \ldots(i)$$

and $2^y \times 4^{-x} = \frac{1}{8}$

$$\Rightarrow \quad 2^y \times (2^2)^{-x} = \frac{1}{(2)^3}$$

$$\Rightarrow \quad (2)^{y-2x} = (2)^{-3}$$

On comparing the exponents of 2 from both sides, we get

$$y - 2x = -3$$

$$\Rightarrow \quad 2x - y = 3 \quad \ldots(ii)$$

On subtracting Eq. (i) from Eq. (ii), we get

$$x = 1$$

On putting $x = 1$ in Eq. (i), we get

$$y = -1$$

Hence, $x = 1$ and $y = -1$

4. LHS $= \dfrac{1}{1+x^{m-n}+x^{l-n}} + \dfrac{1}{1+x^{n-l}+x^{m-l}} + \dfrac{1}{1+x^{l-m}+x^{n-m}}$

$$= \frac{1}{1+\frac{x^m}{x^n}+\frac{x^l}{x^n}} + \frac{1}{1+\frac{x^n}{x^l}+\frac{x^m}{x^l}} + \frac{1}{1+\frac{x^l}{x^m}+\frac{x^n}{x^m}} \quad \left[\because a^{m-n} = \frac{a^m}{a^n}\right]$$

$$= \frac{1}{\frac{x^n+x^m+x^l}{x^n}} + \frac{1}{\frac{x^l+x^n+x^m}{x^l}} + \frac{1}{\frac{x^m+x^l+x^n}{x^m}}$$

$$= \frac{x^n}{x^l+x^m+x^n} + \frac{x^l}{x^l+x^m+x^n} + \frac{x^m}{x^l+x^m+x^n}$$

$$= \frac{x^l+x^m+x^n}{x^l+x^m+x^n} = 1 = \text{RHS}$$ **Hence proved.**

5. We have, $\sqrt{\left(\frac{4}{5}\right)^{1-2x}} = 1\frac{9}{16}$

$$\Rightarrow \quad \left(\left(\frac{4}{5}\right)^{1-2x}\right)^{1/2} = \frac{25}{16} \quad \left[\because \sqrt[n]{a} = (a)^{\frac{1}{n}}\right]$$

$$\Rightarrow \quad \left(\frac{4}{5}\right)^{\frac{1-2x}{2}} = \frac{5^2}{4^2} \quad [\because (a^m)^n = a^{m \times n}]$$

$$\Rightarrow \quad \left(\frac{4}{5}\right)^{\frac{1-2x}{2}} = \left(\frac{5}{4}\right)^2 \quad \left[\because \left(\frac{a}{b}\right)^m = \frac{a^m}{b^m}\right]$$

$$\therefore \quad \left(\frac{4}{5}\right)^{\frac{1-2x}{2}} = \left(\frac{4}{5}\right)^{-2} \quad \text{[reciprocal law]}$$

On comparing the exponents of $\frac{4}{5}$ from both sides,

we get $\dfrac{1-2x}{2} = -2$

$$\Rightarrow \quad 1 - 2x = -4 \Rightarrow -2x = -4 - 1$$

$$\Rightarrow \quad x = \frac{-5}{-2} \Rightarrow x = \frac{5}{2}$$

6. Given, $5^{2x-1} = 25^{x-1} + 100$

$$\Rightarrow \quad 5^{2x-1} = (5^2)^{x-1} + 100$$

$$\Rightarrow \quad 5^{2x-1} = 5^{2x-2} + 100 \quad [\because (a^m)^n = a^{m \times n}]$$

$$\Rightarrow \quad 5^{2x-1} - 5^{2x-2} = 100$$

$$\Rightarrow \quad 5^{2x-1}(1 - 5^{-1}) = 100$$

[taking 5^{2x-1} common from LHS]

$$\Rightarrow \quad 5^{2x-1} \times \frac{4}{5} = 100$$

$$\Rightarrow \quad 5^{2x-2} = 25$$

$$\Rightarrow \quad 5^{2x-2} = 5^2$$

On comparing the exponents of 5 from both sides, we get

$$2x - 2 = 2$$

$$\Rightarrow \quad 2x = 4$$

$$\Rightarrow \quad x = 2$$

Now. $4^{3+x} = 4^{3+2}$

$$= 4^5 = (2^2)^5 = 2^{10} = 1024$$

$[\because (a^m)^n = a^{mn}]$

7. We have,

$$3^x = 9 \times 3^y$$

$$\Rightarrow \quad 3^x = (3)^2 \times 3^y$$

$$\Rightarrow \quad 3^x = (3)^{2+y} \quad [\because a^m \times a^n = a^{m+n}]$$

On comparing the exponents of 3 both sides, we get

$$x = 2 + y$$

$$\Rightarrow \quad x - y = 2 \quad \ldots\text{(i)}$$

and $8 \times 2^y = 4^x$

$$\Rightarrow \quad (2)^3 \times 2^y = (2^2)^x$$

$$\Rightarrow \quad (2)^{3+y} = (2)^{2x} \quad [\because (a^m)^n = a^{m \times n}]$$

On comparing the exponents of 2 both sides, we get

$$3 + y = 2x$$

$$\Rightarrow \quad 2x - y = 3 \quad \ldots\text{(ii)}$$

On subtracting Eq. (i) from Eq. (ii), we get

$$x = 1 \text{ and } y = -1$$

Hence, $3x + 2y = 3 \times 1 + 2x(-1) = 3 - 2 = 1$

8. We have, $3^3(7^0 + 4^{3x}) = 27\frac{27}{64}$

$$\Rightarrow \quad 27(1 + 4^{3x}) = 27 + \frac{27}{64}$$

$$\Rightarrow \quad 27 + 27 \times 4^{3x} = 27 + \frac{27}{64}$$

$$\Rightarrow \quad 27 \times 4^{3x} = \frac{27}{64}$$

[subtracting 27 from both sides]

$$\Rightarrow \quad 4^{3x} = \frac{1}{64} \quad \text{[dividing both sides by 27]}$$

$$\Rightarrow \quad 4^{3x} = \frac{1}{4^3}$$

$$\Rightarrow \quad 4^{3x} = 4^{-3} \quad \left[\because \left(\frac{a}{b}\right)^n = \left(\frac{b}{a}\right)^{-n}\right]$$

On comparing the exponents of 4 from both sides, we get

$$3x = -3 \Rightarrow x = -1$$

07

LOGARITHMS

If a is any positive real number $(a \neq 1)$, m is any rational number and n be any real number such that

$$a^m = n$$

Then,

$$m = \log_a n$$

where m is called **logarithm** of n to the base a.

Thus, $a^m = n$ is called the **exponential form** and $m = \log_a n$ is called the **logarithmic form**.

Logarithmic form vis-a-vis expontential form

Exponential form	Logarithmic form
$2^4 = 16$	$4 = \log_2 16$
$5^0 = 1$	$0 = \log_5 1$
$3^{-4} = \frac{1}{3^4} = \frac{1}{81}$	$-4 = \log_3 \frac{1}{81}$
$(10)^{-4} = \frac{1}{(10)^4} = \frac{1}{10000}$	$-4 = \log_{10} \frac{1}{10000}$

Properties of Logarithms

1. $a^0 = 1 \Rightarrow \log_a 1 = 0, a \neq 1,$
2. $a^1 = a \Rightarrow \log_a a = 1,$
3. If $x = a^m$ and $y = a^m$, then $x = y$. Hence, $\log_a x = \log_a y \Rightarrow x = y$

Laws of Logarithms

(i) **Product Law** $\log_a(m \cdot n) = \log_a m + \log_a n$ **e.g.** $\log(10) = \log(2 \times 5) = \log 2 + \log 5$

(ii) **Quotient Law** $\log_a\left(\frac{m}{n}\right) = \log_a m - \log_a n$ **e.g.** $\log \frac{10}{3} = \log 10 - \log 3$

(iii) **Power Law** $\log_a(m)^n = n \log_a m$ **e.g.** $\log(10)^3 = 3 \log 10$

(iv) $\log_n m = \frac{\log_a m}{\log_a n}, m, n, a > 0, a \neq 1, n \neq 1$ **e.g.** $\log_2 3 = \frac{\log_{10} 3}{\log_{10} 2}$

(v) $a^{\log_a m} = m$ **e.g.** $4^{\log_4 64} = 64$

(vi) **Reciprocal Law** $\log_a b = \frac{1}{\log_b a}$ **e.g.** $\log_2 5 = \frac{1}{\log_5 2}$

Note *If base of logarithm is not given, then we always take 10 as a base. Logarithms to the base 10 are called* ***common logarithms***. **e.g.** $\log 50 = \log_{10} 50.$

EXAM ORIENTED QUESTIONS

TYPE - 1 01 Mark

Multiple Choice Questions

Q.1 Find the value of x, when $\log(97+\sqrt{x^2-16})=2$.

(a) 5 and –7 (b) 2 and –5
(c) –5 and 5 (d) –2 and –5

Q.2 If $\frac{1}{\log_a n}+\frac{1}{\log_c n}=\frac{2}{\log_b n}$, then the value of b^2 is

(a) nb (b) an
(c) ab (d) ac

Q.3 Solve $\log_5 2\times\log_2 5$.

(a) –1 (b) 2
(c) 0 (d) 1

Q.4 Simplify $\log_{10}\frac{a^2}{\sqrt{b}}$ in terms of $\log_{10} a$ and $\log_{10} b$.

(a) $2\log_{10} a-\frac{1}{2}\log_{10} b$ (b) $2\log_{10} a-\log_{10} b$
(c) $2\log_{10} a-2\log_{10} b$ (d) $\frac{1}{2}\log_{10} a-2\log_{10} b$

Answers

1. (c) 2. (d) 3. (d) 4. (a)

TYPE - 2 01 Mark

Assertion-Reason Type Questions

Q.1 Assertion (A) If $\log_2 x=a$, then 4^{2a-1} is $\frac{x^4}{4}$.

Reason (R) $\log_a n=m\Rightarrow a^m=n$

(a) A is true, R is false.
(b) A is false, R is true.
(c) Both A and R are true and R is the correct reason for A.
(d) Both A and R are true and R is incorrect reason for A.

Q.2 Assertion (A) If $2^{x+2}=2^x+10$, then the value of x is $\log_2\frac{10}{3}$.

Reason (R) $a^m=n\Rightarrow\log_n a=m$

(a) A is true, R is false.
(b) A is false, R is true.
(c) Both A and R are true and R is the correct reason for A.
(d) Both A and R are true and R is incorrect reason for A.

Q.3 Assertion (A) The value of $4+\log_{10}(0.001)$ is 1.

Reason (R) $\log_a\frac{m}{n}=\log_a m-\log_a n$.

(a) A is true, R is false.
(b) A is false, R is true.
(c) Both A and R are true and R is the correct reason for A.
(d) Both A and R are true and R is incorrect reason for A.

Q.4 Assertion (A) If $\log(20+5x)-\log(10-x)=1$, then the value of x is $\frac{17}{3}$.

Reason (R) $\log_a a=1$

(a) A is true, R is false.
(b) A is false, R is true.
(c) Both A and R are true and R is the correct reason for A.
(d) Both A and R are true and R is incorrect reason for A.

Answers

1. (c) 2. (a) 3. (d) 4. (b)

TYPE - 3 01 Mark

Statement Based Questions

Q.1 Statement I Logarithmic value of '64 to the base 4' i.e. $\log_4 64$ is 3.

Statement II $\log_a 1=1$, $a\neq 1$

Which of the following is valid?

(a) Both the Statements are true.
(b) Both the Statements are false.
(c) Statement I is true and Statement II is false.
(d) Statement I is false and Statement II is true.

Q.2 Statement I If $\log_{10} 2 = m$ and $\log_{10} 3 = n$, then $\log_{10} 120 = 2m + n + 1$.

Statement II $\log_a b \times \log_b a = 1$

Which of the following is valid?
(a) Both the Statements are true.
(b) Both the Statements are false.
(c) Statement I is true and Statement II is false.
(d) Statement I is false and Statement II is true.

Q.3 Statement I The equation $\log(x + 12) = 1 + \log(2 - x)$, then the value of x is -1.

Statement II The equation $\log(x - 8) + \log\frac{9}{2} = 1 + \log\left(\frac{x}{4}\right)$, then $x = 15$.

Which of the following is valid?
(a) Both the Statements are true.
(b) Both the Statements are false.
(c) Statement I is true and Statement II is false.
(d) Statement I is false and Statement II is true.

Q.4 Statement I Given that $\log_2 p = a$, $\log_8 q = b$ and $\frac{p}{q} = 2^c$, then $c = 4a - 3b$.

Statement II $\log_a b = \frac{\log b}{\log a}$.

Which of the following is valid?
(a) Both the Statements are true.
(b) Both the Statements are false.
(c) Statement I is true and Statement II is false.
(d) Statement I is false and Statement II is true.

Answers

1. (c) 2. (a) 3. (b) 4. (d)

TYPE - 4 — 03 Marks

Short Answer Type Questions

Q.1 Evaluate $\log_{2\sqrt{3}} 1728$.

Q.2 Find the logarithm of '$\frac{1}{81}$ to the base 27'.

Q.3 Solve the equation $3^{x+1} - 2 = 8 \times 3^{x-1}$.

Q.4 Evaluate $3 + \frac{1}{2}\log_{10} 9 - 2\log_{10} 5$.

Q.5 Express $\log 4.5 + \log\frac{25}{50}$ in terms of log 2 and log 3.

Q.6 Prove that $\log\frac{70}{33} + \log\frac{22}{135} - \log\frac{7}{18} = 3\log 2 - 2\log 3$.

Q.7 Simplify $\log_2(\log_2(\log_2 16))$.

Q.8 Solve for x, if $\log(x + 3) - \log(x - 3) = 1$.

Q.9 If $\log 2 = 0.3010$ and $\log 3 = 0.4771$, then find the value of $\log 3 + \log 8 - \log\sqrt{6}$.

Q.10 Simplify $\frac{\log_3 8}{\log_9 16 \log_4 10}$.

Q.11 Determine the logarithmic expansion of $y = \frac{5^p 7^q}{3^r}$.

Q.12 Find the value of $\log_3 2 \cdot \log_4 3 \cdot \log_5 4 \ldots \log_8 7$.

Q.13 If $x^2 + y^2 = 23xy$, then prove that $\log\left(\frac{x+y}{5}\right) = \frac{1}{2}(\log x + \log y)$.

Q.14 If $p = q^3 = r^2 = t^5$, then find the value of $\log_p p + \log_p q^2 + \log_p rt^4$.

Answers

1. 6 2. $-\frac{4}{3}$ 3. $x = \log_3 6$ 4. $\log_{10} 120$
5. $2(\log 3 - \log 2)$ 7. 1 8. $3\frac{2}{3}$
9. 0.99105 10. $3\log_{10} 2$ 11. $\log y = p\log 5 + q\log 7 - r\log 3$
12. $\frac{1}{3}$ 14. $\frac{89}{30}$

TYPE - 5 — 4/5 Marks

Long Answer Type Questions

Q.1 If $\log_5 x = p$ and $\log_5 y = q$, then
(i) express 5^{4p-5} in terms of x.
(ii) find the value of $5^{2-2q+3p}$ in terms of x and y.

Q.2 If $\log_5 m = p$ and $\log_7 n = p$, then find
(i) $\frac{n^3}{m^2}$ (ii) $(875)^p$

Q.3 Prove that $\log_{3^4} 4^3 = \frac{3}{4}\log_3 4$.

Q.4 Solve for x, if $(\log_{10} x)^2 - (\log_{10} x) - 2 = 0$.

Q.5 If $x = (100)^a$, $y = (10000)^b$ and $z = (10)^c$, then express $\log\left(\frac{10\sqrt{y}}{x^2 z^3}\right)$ in terms of a, b and c.

Q.6 Solve the equation $\log_3(2x - 1) - \log_9(x^2 - 2) = \frac{1}{\log_2 3}$.

Q.7 Given that $4\log(x\sqrt{y}) = 1.5 + \log x - \log y$, where x and y are both positive, express in its simplest form, y in terms of x.

Q.8 Solve the equation for x

$$\log_x 2 \times \log_{x/16} 2 = \log_{x/64} 2$$

Q.9 If $p = \log_x yz$, $q = \log_y zx$ and $r = \log_z xy$, then prove that $\frac{1}{1+p} + \frac{1}{1+q} + \frac{1}{1+r} = 1$.

Q.10 Solve for x and y, if

$$\frac{\log(x+y)}{\log 2} = \frac{\log(x-y)}{\log 5} = \frac{\log 4}{\log(0.5)}$$

Q.11 If $a = 1 + \log_x yz$, $b = 1 + \log_y zx$ and $c = 1 + \log_z xy$, then show that $ab + bc + ca = abc$.

Q.12 Prove that $\frac{\log_b p}{\log_{bc} p} = 1 + \log_b c = 1 + \frac{1}{\log_c b}$

Answers

1. (i) $\frac{x^4}{3125}$ (ii) $\frac{25x^3}{y^2}$ **2.** (i) $\left(\frac{343}{25}\right)^p$ (ii) $m^3 \cdot n$

4. $\frac{1}{10}$ and 100 **5.** $-4a + 2b - 3c + 1$ **6.** $x = \frac{9}{4}$

7. $y = \frac{(10)^{1/2}}{x}$ **8.** 8, 4

10. $x = \frac{29}{200}$ and $y = \frac{21}{200}$

EXPLANATIONS

Multiple Choice Questions

1. (c) We have,

$$\log(97 + \sqrt{x^2 - 16}) = 2$$

$$\Rightarrow 97 + \sqrt{x^2 - 16} = 10^2 \quad [\because \log_a n = m \Rightarrow a^m = n]$$

$$\Rightarrow \sqrt{x^2 - 16} = 100 - 97 = 3$$

On squaring both sides, we get

$$x^2 - 16 = 9$$

$$\Rightarrow x^2 = 25 \Rightarrow x = \pm 5$$

2. (d) We have,

$$\frac{1}{\log_a n} + \frac{1}{\log_c n} = \frac{2}{\log_b n}$$

$$\Rightarrow \log_n a + \log_n c = 2\log_n b \quad \left[\because \log_a b = \frac{1}{\log_b a}\right]$$

$$\Rightarrow \log_n a \cdot c = \log_n b^2$$

$[\because \log_a m + \log_a n = \log_a mn$ and $n \log_a m = \log_a m^n]$

On comparing both sides, we get

$$a \cdot c = b^2 \Rightarrow b^2 = ac$$

3. (d) We have, $\log_5 2 \times \log_2 5$

$$= \frac{\log_{10} 2}{\log_{10} 5} \times \frac{\log_{10} 5}{\log_{10} 2} \quad \left[\because \log_n m = \frac{\log_a m}{\log_a n}\right]$$

$$= 1$$

4. (a) We have, $\log_{10}\left(\frac{a^2}{\sqrt{b}}\right)$

$$= \log_{10} a^2 - \log_{10} \sqrt{b} \quad \left[\because \log \frac{m}{n} = \log m - \log n\right]$$

$$= 2\log_{10} a - \frac{1}{2}\log_{10} b \quad [\because \log_a m^n = n \log_a m]$$

Assertion-Reason Type Questions

1. (c) **Assertion** We have, $\log_2 x = a$

$$\Rightarrow 2^a = x$$

$$[\because \log_a n = m \Rightarrow a^m = n]$$

On squaring both sides, we get

$$(2^a)^2 = x^2$$

$$\Rightarrow 4^a = x^2$$

Again, on squaring both sides, we get

$$(4^a)^2 = (x^2)^2$$

$$\Rightarrow 4^{2a} = x^4$$

On dividing by 4 both sides, we get

$$\frac{4^{2a}}{4} = \frac{x^4}{4}$$

$$\Rightarrow 4^{2a-1} = \frac{x^4}{4}$$

Hence, A is true and R is also true and R is the correct reason for A.

2. (a) **Assertion** We have, $2^{x+2} = 2^x + 10$

$$\Rightarrow 2^x \cdot 2^2 = 2^x + 10$$

$$\Rightarrow 2^x \cdot 4 = 2^x + 10$$

Let $2^x = y$, then above expression reduces to

$$4y = y + 10$$

$$\Rightarrow y = \frac{10}{3}$$

$$\Rightarrow 2^x = \frac{10}{3}$$

$$\Rightarrow \log_2 \frac{10}{3} = x \quad [\because a^m = n \Rightarrow \log_a n = m]$$

Hence, A is true, R is false.

3. (d) We have,

$$4 + \log_{10}(0.001) = 4 + \log_{10}(10)^{-3}$$
$$= 4 - 3\log_{10} 10 \quad \text{[by power law]}$$
$$= 4 - 3 \times 1 \quad [\because \log_{10} 10 = 1]$$
$$= 1$$

Hence, A is true.

R is also true and R is incorrect reason for A.

4. (b) **Assertion** We have,

$$\log(20 + 5x) - \log(10 - x) = 1$$
$$\Rightarrow \log\frac{20 + 5x}{10 - x} = 1 \quad \left[\because \log m - \log n = \log\frac{m}{n}\right]$$
$$\Rightarrow \log\frac{20 + 5x}{10 - x} = \log 10 \quad [\because \log_a a = 1]$$
$$\Rightarrow \frac{20 + 5x}{10 - x} = 10$$
$$\Rightarrow 20 + 5x = 100 - 10x \Rightarrow 15x = 80$$
$$\Rightarrow x = \frac{80}{15} = \frac{16}{3}$$

Hence, A is false, R is true.

Statement Based Questions

1. (c) **Statement I**

Let $\log_4 64 = x$, then $64 = 4^x$ $[\because \log_a n = m \Rightarrow a^m = n]$

$\Rightarrow$ $4^x = 4 \times 4 \times 4$ $4^x = 4^3$

On comparing the exponents of 4 both sides, we get

$$x = 3$$

Hence, $\log_4 64 = 3$.

So, Statement I is true.

And we know that $\log_a 1 = 0$, when $a \neq 1$

So, Statement II is false.

2. (a) **Statement I** Given, $\log_{10} 2 = m$ and $\log_{10} 3 = n$

Now, $\log_{10} 120 = \log_{10} 4 \times 3 \times 10$

$$= \log_{10} 2^2 \times 3 \times 10$$
$$= 2\log_{10} 2 + \log_{10} 3 + \log_{10} 10$$
$$[\because \log_a p \cdot q \cdot r = \log_a p + \log_a q + \log_a r \text{ and } \log_a m^n = n\log_a m]$$
$$= 2m + n + 1$$
$$[\because \log_{10} 2 = m, \log_{10} 3 = n \text{ and } \log_a a = 1]$$

Hence, Statement I is true.

Statement II LHS $= \log_a b \times \log_b a$

$$= \log_a b \times \frac{1}{\log_a b} \quad \left[\because \log_p q = \frac{1}{\log_q p}\right]$$
$$= 1 = \text{RHS}$$

Hence, Statement II is also true.

3. (b) **Statement I** We have,

$$\log(x + 12) = 1 + \log(2 - x)$$
$$\Rightarrow \log(x + 12) - \log(2 - x) = 1$$
$$\Rightarrow \log\left(\frac{x + 12}{2 - x}\right) = 1 \quad \left[\because \log m - \log n = \log\frac{m}{n}\right]$$
$$\Rightarrow \log\left(\frac{x + 12}{2 - x}\right) = \log 10 \quad [\because \log_a a = 1]$$
$$\Rightarrow \frac{x + 12}{2 - x} = 10$$
$$\Rightarrow x + 12 = 20 - 10x$$
$$\Rightarrow 11x = 8 \Rightarrow x = \frac{8}{11}$$

Hence, Statement I is false.

Statement II We have,

$$\log(x - 8) + \log\frac{9}{2} = 1 + \log\frac{x}{4}$$
$$\Rightarrow \log\left[(x - 8) \times \frac{9}{2}\right] = 1 + \log\frac{x}{4} \quad [\because \log m + \log n = \log mn]$$
$$\Rightarrow \log\left[(x - 8) \times \frac{9}{2}\right] - \log\frac{x}{4} = 1$$
$$\Rightarrow \log\frac{\frac{9(x - 8)}{2}}{\frac{x}{4}} = \log 10 \quad \left[\because \log m - \log n = \log\frac{m}{n} \text{ and } \log_a a = 1\right]$$
$$\Rightarrow \frac{9(x - 8)}{2} \times \frac{4}{x} = 10$$
$$\Rightarrow 9x - 72 = 5x$$
$$\Rightarrow x = \frac{72}{4} = 18$$

Hence, Statement II is false.

4. (d) **Statement I** Given,

$$\log_2 p = a \Rightarrow 2^a = p$$

and $\log_8 q = b \Rightarrow 8^b = q$

Now, $\frac{p}{q} = 2^c$

$$\Rightarrow \frac{2^a}{8^b} = 2^c \quad [\because p = 2^a \text{ and } q = 8^b]$$
$$\Rightarrow \frac{2^a}{2^{3b}} = 2^c$$
$$\Rightarrow 2^{a - 3b} = 2^c$$

On comparing, we get

$$a - 3b = c$$

And we know that $\log_a b = \frac{\log b}{\log a}$

Hence, Statement I is false and Statement II is true.

Short Answer Type Questions

1. Let $x = \log_{2\sqrt{3}} 1728$

$\Rightarrow \quad (2\sqrt{3})^x = 1728 \qquad [\because \log_a n = m \Rightarrow a^m = n]$

$\Rightarrow \quad (2\sqrt{3})^x = (12)^3$

$\Rightarrow \quad (2\sqrt{3})^x = [(2\sqrt{3})^2]^3 \Rightarrow (2\sqrt{3})^x = (2\sqrt{3})^6$

On comparing the exponents of $2\sqrt{3}$ both sides, we get

$x = 6$

Hence, the value of $\log_{2\sqrt{3}} 1728$ is 6.

2. Let $\log_{27} \dfrac{1}{81} = x$

Then, $\dfrac{1}{81} = (27)^x \qquad [\because \log_a n = m \Rightarrow a^m = n]$

$\Rightarrow \quad \left(\dfrac{1}{3}\right)^4 = (3^3)^x$

$\Rightarrow \quad 3^{-4} = 3^{3x} \qquad \left[\because \dfrac{1}{a^n} = a^{-n} \text{ and } (a^m)^n = a^{mn}\right]$

On comparing the exponents of 3 both sides, we get

$3x = -4 \Rightarrow x = -\dfrac{4}{3}$

Hence, $\log_{27} \dfrac{1}{81} = -\dfrac{4}{3}$.

3. We have, $3^{x+1} - 2 = 8 \times 3^{x-1}$

$\Rightarrow \quad 3^x \cdot 3^1 - 2 = 8 \times 3^x \cdot 3^{-1}$

$\Rightarrow \quad y \cdot 3 - 2 = 8 \times y \times \dfrac{1}{3} \qquad [\because \text{let } 3^x = y]$

$\Rightarrow \quad 3y - 2 = \dfrac{8}{3} y$

$\Rightarrow \quad 3y - \dfrac{8}{3} y = 2 \Rightarrow y \times \dfrac{1}{3} = 2$

$\Rightarrow \quad y = 6$

Now, $y = 3^x \Rightarrow 6 = 3^x \Rightarrow x = \log_3 6$

4. We have, $3 + \dfrac{1}{2} \log_{10} 9 - 2 \log_{10} 5$

$= 3 \times 1 + \dfrac{1}{2} \log_{10} (3 \times 3) - 2 \log_{10} 5$

$= 3 \log_{10} 10 + \dfrac{1}{2} \log_{10} 3^2 - 2 \log_{10} 5$

$[\because 1 = \log_{10} 10]$

$= \log_{10} 10^3 + \log_{10} 3^{2 \times \frac{1}{2}} - \log_{10} (5)^2$

$[\because n \log m = \log m^n]$

$= \log_{10} 1000 + \log_{10} 3 - \log_{10} 25$

$= \log_{10} (1000 \times 3) - \log_{10} 25$

$[\because \log m + \log n = \log mn]$

$= \log_{10} \dfrac{3000}{25} \qquad \left[\because \log m - \log n = \log \dfrac{m}{n}\right]$

$= \log_{10} 120$

5. We have, $\log 4.5 + \log \dfrac{25}{50}$

$= \log \dfrac{45}{10} + \log \dfrac{25}{50} = \log \dfrac{9}{2} + \log \dfrac{1}{2}$

$= \log 9 - \log 2 + \log 1 - \log 2$

$\left[\because \log \dfrac{m}{n} = \log m - \log n\right]$

$= \log 3^2 - 2 \log 2 \qquad [\because \log 1 = 0]$

$= 2 \log 3 - 2 \log 2 \qquad [\because \log m^n = n \log m]$

$= 2(\log 3 - \log 2)$

6. LHS $= \log \dfrac{70}{33} + \log \dfrac{22}{135} - \log \dfrac{7}{18}$

$= \log \left(\dfrac{\dfrac{70}{33} \times \dfrac{22}{135}}{\dfrac{7}{18}} \right) \qquad [\because \log m + \log n = \log m \cdot n$

and $\log m - \log n = \log \dfrac{m}{n}]$

$= \log \left(\dfrac{70}{33} \times \dfrac{22}{135} \times \dfrac{18}{7} \right) = \log \left(\dfrac{8}{9} \right)$

$= \log 8 - \log 9 = \log 2^3 - \log 3^2$

$= 3 \log 2 - 2 \log 3 \qquad [\because \log m^n = n \log m]$

= RHS **Hence proved.**

7. We have, $\log_2 (\log_2 (\log_2 16))$

$= \log_2 (\log_2 (\log_2 2^4))$

$= \log_2 (\log_2 (4 \cdot \log_2 2)) \qquad [\because \log_a m^n = n \log_a m]$

$= \log_2 (\log_2 2^2) \qquad [\because \log_a a = 1]$

$= \log_2 (2 \cdot \log_2 2) = \log_2 2 = 1$

8. We have, $\log (x + 3) - \log (x - 3) = 1$

$\Rightarrow \quad \log \left(\dfrac{x+3}{x-3} \right) = 1 \qquad \left[\log m - \log n = \log \dfrac{m}{n}\right]$

$\Rightarrow \quad \log \left(\dfrac{x+3}{x-3} \right) = \log 10 \qquad [\because 1 = \log 10]$

$\Rightarrow \quad \left(\dfrac{x+3}{x-3} \right) = 10$

$\Rightarrow \quad x + 3 = 10(x - 3)$

$\Rightarrow \quad x + 3 = 10x - 30$

$\Rightarrow \quad x - 10x = -30 - 3$

$\Rightarrow \quad -9x = -33$

$\therefore \quad x = \dfrac{33}{9} = \dfrac{11}{3} = 3\dfrac{2}{3}$

9. We have, $\log 2 = 0.3010$ and $\log 3 = 0.4771$

Now, $\log 3 + \log 8 - \log \sqrt{6}$

$= \log 3 + \log 2^3 - \log (6)^{\frac{1}{2}}$

$= \log 3 + 3 \log 2 - \dfrac{1}{2} \log (2 \times 3)$

$[\because \log m^n = n \log m]$

$$= \log 3 + 3\log 2 - \frac{1}{2}[\log 2 + \log 3]$$
$$[\because \log m \cdot n = \log m + \log n]$$
$$= \frac{1}{2}\log 3 + \frac{5}{2}\log 2$$
$$= \frac{1}{2}[\log 3 + 5\log 2]$$
$$= \frac{1}{2}[0.4771 + 5 \times (0.3010)]$$
$$= \frac{1}{2}[0.4771 + 1.505] = 0.99105$$

10. We have, $\dfrac{\log_3 8}{\log_9 16 \; \log_4 10} = \dfrac{\dfrac{\log_{10} 8}{\log_{10} 3}}{\dfrac{\log_{10} 16}{\log_{10} 9} \times \dfrac{\log_{10} 10}{\log_{10} 4}}$
$$\left[\because \log_n m = \frac{\log_{10} m}{\log_{10} n}\right]$$
$$= \frac{\log_{10} 8 \times \log_{10} 9 \times \log_{10} 4}{\log_{10} 16 \times \log_{10} 3 \times \log_{10} 10}$$
$$\left[\because \frac{a/b}{c/d} = \frac{ad}{bc}\right]$$
$$= \frac{\log_{10} 2^3 \times \log_{10} 3^2 \times \log_{10} 2^2}{\log_{10} 2^4 \times \log_{10} 3 \times 1}$$
$$[\because \log_{10} 10 = 1]$$
$$= \frac{3\log_{10} 2 \times 2\log_{10} 3 \times 2\log_{10} 2}{4\log_{10} 2 \times \log_{10} 3} = 3\log_{10} 2$$

11. Given, $y = \dfrac{5^p 7^q}{3^r}$

On taking log both sides, we get
$$\log y = \log \frac{5^p\, 7^q}{3^r} \Rightarrow \log y = \log 5^p 7^q - \log 3^r$$
$$\left[\because \log \frac{m}{n} = \log m - \log n\right]$$
$$\Rightarrow \quad \log y = \log 5^p + \log 7^q - \log 3^r$$
$$[\because \log mn = \log m + \log n]$$
$$\Rightarrow \quad \log y = p\log 5 + q\log 7 - r\log 3$$
$$[\because \log m^n = n\log m]$$

Hence, $\log y = p\log 5 + q\log 7 - r\log 3$ is the logarithmic expansion of $y = \dfrac{5^p 7^q}{3^r}$.

12. We have, $\log_3 2 \cdot \log_4 3 \cdot \log_5 4 \ldots \log_8 7$

By base changing formula,
$$= \frac{\log 2}{\log 3} \cdot \frac{\log 3}{\log 4} \cdot \frac{\log 4}{\log 5} \ldots \frac{\log 7}{\log 8} = \frac{\log 2}{\log 8}$$
$$= \frac{\log 2}{3\log 2} = \frac{1}{3}$$

13. We have, $x^2 + y^2 = 23xy$

On adding $2xy$ both sides, we get
$$x^2 + y^2 + 2xy = 25xy$$
$$\Rightarrow \quad (x+y)^2 = 25xy \quad [\because a^2 + b^2 + 2ab = (a+b)^2]$$
$$\Rightarrow \quad \left(\frac{x+y}{5}\right)^2 = xy$$

On taking log both sides, we get
$$\log \left(\frac{x+y}{5}\right)^2 = \log xy$$
$$\Rightarrow \quad 2\log\left(\frac{x+y}{5}\right) = \log x + \log y$$
$$[\because \log m^n = n\log m \text{ and } \log m \cdot n = \log m + \log n]$$
$$\Rightarrow \quad \log\left(\frac{x+y}{5}\right) = \frac{1}{2}[\log x + \log y]$$ **Hence proved.**

14. Given, $p = q^3 = r^2 = t^5$
$$\Rightarrow \quad q = p^{\frac{1}{3}}, r = p^{\frac{1}{2}}, t = p^{\frac{1}{5}}$$

Now, $\log_p p + \log_p q^2 + \log_p rt^4 = \log_p pq^2rt^4$
$$[\because \log m + \log n + \log o = \log mno]$$
$$= \log_p p \cdot p^{\frac{2}{3}} \cdot p^{\frac{1}{2}} \cdot p^{\frac{4}{5}}$$
$$= \log_p p^{\left(1 + \frac{2}{3} + \frac{1}{2} + \frac{4}{5}\right)}$$
$$= \left(1 + \frac{2}{3} + \frac{1}{2} + \frac{4}{5}\right)\log_p p \quad [\because \log m^n = n\log m]$$
$$= \frac{30 + 20 + 15 + 24}{30} \times 1 \quad [\because \log_a a = 1]$$
$$= \frac{89}{30}$$

Long Answer Type Questions

1. We have, $\log_5 x = p$
$$\Rightarrow \quad 5^p = x \quad \ldots\text{(a)} \; [\because \log_a m = n \Rightarrow a^n = m]$$
and $\quad \log_5 y = q \Rightarrow 5^q = y \quad \ldots\text{(b)}$

(i) Now, $5^{4p-5} = \dfrac{5^{4p}}{5^5} = \dfrac{1}{5^5}(5^p)^4$
$$= \frac{1}{5^5} \cdot x^4 = \frac{x^4}{3125} \quad \text{[from Eq. (a)]}$$

(ii) Now, $5^{2-2q+3p} = \dfrac{5^2 \cdot 5^{3p}}{5^{2q}} = \dfrac{5^2 \cdot (5^p)^3}{(5^q)^2} = \dfrac{25 \cdot x^3}{y^2}$

[from Eqs. (a) and (b)]
$$= \frac{25x^3}{y^2}$$

2. We have, $\log_5 m = p$

$\Rightarrow \quad 5^p = m \quad \ldots(a)\ [\because \log_a m = n \Rightarrow a^n = m]$

and $\quad \log_7 n = p \Rightarrow 7^p = n \quad \ldots(b)$

(i) $\dfrac{n^3}{m^2} = \dfrac{(7^p)^3}{(5^p)^2}$ [from Eqs. (a) and (b)]

$= \dfrac{(7^3)^p}{(5^2)^p} = \left(\dfrac{343}{25}\right)^p$

(ii) Now, $(875)^p = (125 \times 7)^p = (5^3 \times 7)^p = (5^p)^3 \times 7^p$

$= m^3 \cdot n$ [from Eqs. (a) and (b)]

3. Let $\log_{3^4} 4^3 = x \Rightarrow (3^4)^x = 4^3$ $[\because \log_a n = m \Rightarrow a^m = n]$

$\Rightarrow \quad 3^{4x} = 4^3$

On taking log with base 3 both sides, we get

$\log_3 3^{4x} = \log_3 4^3$

$\Rightarrow \quad 4x = \log_3 4^3 \quad [\because \log_a a = 1]$

$\Rightarrow \quad 4x = 3\log_3 4 \Rightarrow x = \dfrac{3}{4}\log_3 4$

$\Rightarrow \log_{3^4} 4^3 = \dfrac{3}{4}\log_3 4 \quad [\because x = \log_{3^4} 4^3]$

Hence proved.

4. We have, $(\log_{10} x)^2 - (\log_{10} x) - 2 = 0$

Let $\log_{10} x = t$, then the given expression reduces to

$t^2 - t - 2 = 0$

Now, factorise by splitting the middle term, we get

$t^2 - 2t + t - 2 = 0$

$\Rightarrow \quad t(t-2) + 1(t-2) = 0 \Rightarrow (t-2)(t+1) = 0$

$t - 2 = 0$ or $t + 1 = 0$

$\Rightarrow \quad t = 2$ or $t = -1$

On putting the value of t, we get

$\log_{10} x = -1$ or $\log_{10} x = 2$

$\Rightarrow \quad x = (10)^{-1}$

or $\quad x = (10)^2 \quad [\because \log_a n = m \Rightarrow a^m = n]$

Hence, $x = \dfrac{1}{10}$ and 100.

5. We have, $x = (100)^a$, $y = (10000)^b$

and $z = (10)^c$

Now, $\log\left(\dfrac{10\sqrt{y}}{x^2 z^3}\right) = \log 10 + \log\sqrt{y} - \log x^2 - \log z^3$

$[\because \log\dfrac{m}{n} = \log m - \log n$ and $\log mn = \log m + \log n]$

$= 1 + \dfrac{1}{2}\log y - 2\log x - 3\log z \quad [\because \log_{10} 10 = 1]$

$= 1 + \dfrac{1}{2}\log(10000)^b - 2\log(100)^a - 3\log(10)^c$

$= 1 + \dfrac{b}{2}\log 10^4 - 2a\log 10^2 - 3c\log 10$

$[\because \log m^n = n\log m]$

$= 1 + \dfrac{4b}{2}\log 10 - 2a \cdot 2\log 10 - 3c\log 10$

$= 1 + 2b - 4a - 3c \quad [\because \log_{10} 10 = 1]$

$= -4a + 2b - 3c + 1$

6. We have, $\log_3(2x-1) - \log_9(x^2-2) = \dfrac{1}{\log_2 3}$

$\Rightarrow \quad \dfrac{\log(2x-1)}{\log 3} - \dfrac{\log(x^2-2)}{\log 9} = \dfrac{\log 2}{\log 3}$

$\left[\because \log_a b = \dfrac{\log a}{\log b}\right]$

$\Rightarrow \quad \dfrac{\log(2x-1)}{\log 3} - \dfrac{\log(x^2-2)}{2\log 3} = \dfrac{\log 2}{\log 3}$

$[\because \log m^n = n\log m]$

$\Rightarrow \quad \log(2x-1) - \log(x^2-2)^{\frac{1}{2}} = \log 2$

[multiplying by log 3 both sides]

$\Rightarrow \quad \log\dfrac{2x-1}{(x^2-2)^{\frac{1}{2}}} = \log 2$

$\left[\because \log m - \log n = \log\dfrac{m}{n}\right]$

$\Rightarrow \quad \dfrac{2x-1}{(x^2-2)^{\frac{1}{2}}} = 2$

$\Rightarrow \quad 2x - 1 = 2(x^2-2)^{\frac{1}{2}}$

On squaring both sides, we get

$4x^2 + 1 - 4x = 4x^2 - 8$

$\Rightarrow \quad -4x = -8 - 1 \Rightarrow x = \dfrac{9}{4}$

Hence, the value of x is $\dfrac{9}{4}$.

7. Given, $\quad 4\log(x\sqrt{y}) = 1.5 + \log x - \log y$

$\Rightarrow \quad 4\log(x\sqrt{y}) = \dfrac{3}{2} + \log\dfrac{x}{y}$

$\left[\because \log m - \log n = \log\dfrac{m}{n}\right]$

$\Rightarrow \quad \log(x\sqrt{y})^4 - \log\dfrac{x}{y} = \dfrac{3}{2} \quad [\because n\log m = \log m^n]$

$\Rightarrow \quad \log\dfrac{(x\sqrt{y})^4}{\dfrac{x}{y}} = \dfrac{3}{2} \Rightarrow \log x^4y^2 \times \dfrac{y}{x} = \dfrac{3}{2}$

$\Rightarrow \quad \log x^3y^3 = \dfrac{3}{2}$

$\Rightarrow \quad (10)^{\frac{3}{2}} = x^3y^3 \quad [\because \log_a m = n \Rightarrow a^n = m]$

$\Rightarrow \quad y = \left[\dfrac{(10)^{\frac{3}{2}}}{x^3}\right]^{\frac{1}{3}} \Rightarrow y = \dfrac{(10)^{1/2}}{x}$

8. Given, $\log_x 2 \times \log_{x/16} 2 = \log_{x/64} 2$

$$\Rightarrow \frac{1}{\log_2 x} \times \frac{1}{\log_2\left(\frac{x}{16}\right)} = \frac{1}{\log_2\left(\frac{x}{64}\right)} \quad \left[\because \log_a b = \frac{1}{\log_b a}\right]$$

By cross multiplication, we get

$$\log_2(x/64) = \log_2 x \times \log_2(x/16)$$

$$\Rightarrow \log_2 x - \log_2 64 = \log_2 x(\log_2 x - \log_2 16)$$

$$\left[\because \log_a \frac{m}{n} = \log_a m - \log_a n\right]$$

$$\Rightarrow \log_2 x - \log_2 2^6 = \log_2 x(\log_2 x - \log_2 2^4)$$

$$\Rightarrow \log_2 x - 6\log_2 2 = \log_2 x(\log_2 x - 4\log_2 2)$$

$$[\because \log_a m^n = n\log_a m]$$

$$\Rightarrow \log_2 x - 6 \times 1 = \log_2 x(\log_2 x - 4 \times 1)$$

$$[\because \log_a a = 1]$$

$$\Rightarrow (\log_2 x)^2 - 5\log_2 x + 6 = 0$$

Let $\quad y = \log_2 x \quad$ ...(i)

$$\Rightarrow y^2 - 5y + 6 = 0$$

$$\Rightarrow y^2 - 3y - 2y + 6 = 0$$

$$\Rightarrow y(y-3) - 2(y-3) = 0$$

$$\Rightarrow (y-3)(y-2) = 0$$

$$\Rightarrow y = 3 \text{ or } y = 2$$

On putting the values of y in Eq. (i), we get

$$\log_2 x = 3 \text{ or } \log_2 x = 2$$

$$\Rightarrow x = 2^3 \text{ or } x = 2^2$$

$$\Rightarrow x = 8 \text{ or } x = 4.$$

Hence, the solutions of the given equation are 8, 4.

9. Given, $p = \log_x yz, q = \log_y zx$ and $r = \log_z xy$

$$\therefore \frac{1}{1+p} = \frac{1}{1+\log_x yz} = \frac{1}{\log_x x + \log_x yz}$$

$$[\because 1 = \log_x x]$$

$$= \frac{1}{\log_x xyz} \quad [\because \log m + \log n = \log mn]$$

$$= \log_{xyz} x \quad \left[\because \frac{1}{\log_b a} = \log_a b\right]$$

Similarly, $\frac{1}{1+q} = \log_{xyz} y$ and $\frac{1}{1+r} = \log_{xyz} z$

$$\therefore \text{LHS} = \frac{1}{1+p} + \frac{1}{1+q} + \frac{1}{1+r}$$

$$= \log_{xyz} x + \log_{xyz} y + \log_{xyz} z$$

$$= \log_{xyz} xyz \quad [\because \log m + \log n = \log mn]$$

$$= 1 = \text{RHS}$$

Hence proved.

10. We have,

$$\underset{\text{I}}{\frac{\log(x+y)}{\log 2}} = \underset{\text{II}}{\frac{\log(x-y)}{\log 5}} = \underset{\text{III}}{\frac{\log 4}{\log(0.5)}} \quad \text{...(i)}$$

On taking I and III terms of Eq. (i), we get

$$\frac{\log(x+y)}{\log 2} = \frac{\log 4}{\log(0.5)} = \frac{\log 4}{\log\left(\frac{1}{2}\right)}$$

$$\Rightarrow \log(x+y) = \frac{\log 4 \cdot \log 2}{\log 1 - \log 2}$$

$$\left[\because \log \frac{m}{n} = \log m - \log n\right]$$

$$= \frac{\log 4 \cdot \log 2}{-\log 2} \quad [\because \log 1 = 0]$$

$$\Rightarrow \log(x+y) = -\log 4 = \log(4)^{-1} = \log\frac{1}{4}$$

On comparing both sides, we get

$$x + y = \frac{1}{4} \quad \text{...(ii)}$$

Now, on taking II and III terms of Eq. (i), we get

$$\frac{\log(x-y)}{\log 5} = \frac{\log 4}{\log(0.5)} = \frac{\log 4}{\log\left(\frac{1}{2}\right)}$$

$$\Rightarrow \log(x-y) = \frac{2\log 2 \cdot \log 5}{\log 1 - \log 2}$$

$$\left[\because \log m^n = n\log m \text{ and } \log\frac{m}{n} = \log m - \log n\right]$$

$$= \frac{2\log 2 \cdot \log 5}{-\log 2} \quad [\because \log 1 = 0]$$

$$\Rightarrow \log(x-y) = -2\log 5$$

$$= \log(5)^{-2}$$

$$= \log\left(\frac{1}{25}\right)$$

On comparing both sides, we get

$$x - y = \frac{1}{25} \quad \text{...(iii)}$$

On adding Eqs. (ii) and (iii), we get

$$2x = \frac{1}{4} + \frac{1}{25}$$

$$\Rightarrow 2x = \frac{29}{100}$$

$$\Rightarrow x = \frac{29}{200}$$

On substituting $x = \frac{29}{200}$ in Eq. (ii), we get

$$y = \frac{1}{4} - \frac{29}{200}$$

$$\Rightarrow y = \frac{21}{200}$$

Hence, the values of x and y are $\frac{29}{200}$ and $\frac{21}{200}$, respectively.

11. We have, $a = 1 + \log_x yz$

$\Rightarrow \quad a = \log_x x + \log_x yz \quad [\because \log_a a = 1]$

$\Rightarrow \quad a = \log_x xyz \quad [\because \log_a m + \log_a n = \log_a mn]$

$\Rightarrow \quad \frac{1}{a} = \log_{xyz} x \quad \ldots(i)$

$\left[\because \log_m n = \frac{1}{\log_n m}\right]$

Similarly, $\frac{1}{b} = \log_{xyz} y \quad \ldots(ii)$

and $\frac{1}{c} = \log_{xyz} z \quad \ldots(iii)$

On adding Eqs. (i), (ii) and (iii), we get

$$\frac{1}{a} + \frac{1}{b} + \frac{1}{c} = \log_{xyz} x + \log_{xyz} y + \log_{xyz} z$$

$$\Rightarrow \frac{bc + ac + ab}{abc} = \log_{xyz} x \cdot y \cdot z$$

$[\because \log a + \log b + \log c = \log abc]$

$$\Rightarrow \frac{ab + bc + ac}{abc} = 1 \quad [\because \log_a a = 1]$$

$\Rightarrow \quad ab + bc + ca = abc$ **Hence proved.**

12. We have,

$$\frac{\log_b p}{\log_{bc} p} = \frac{\frac{1}{\log_p b}}{\frac{1}{\log_p bc}} \quad \left[\because \log_n m = \frac{1}{\log_m n}\right]$$

$$= \frac{\log_p bc}{\log_p b}$$

$$= \log_b bc \quad \left[\because \log_n m = \frac{\log_a m}{\log_a n}\right]$$

$$= \log_b b + \log_b c$$

$[\because \log_a m \cdot n = \log_a m + \log_a n]$

$$\Rightarrow \frac{\log_b p}{\log_{bc} p} = 1 + \log_b c \quad \ldots(i)$$

$$\Rightarrow \frac{\log_b p}{\log_{bc} p} = 1 + \frac{1}{\log_c b} \quad \ldots(ii) \left[\because \log_n m = \frac{1}{\log_m n}\right]$$

From Eqs. (i) and (ii), we get

$$\frac{\log_b p}{\log_{bc} p} = 1 + \log_b c = 1 + \frac{1}{\log_c b}$$ **Hence proved.**

TRIANGLES

A plane figure closed by three intersecting lines is called a **triangle**. A triangle has three sides, three angles and three vertices and it is denoted by the symbol 'Δ'. A triangle *ABC* is shown in the given figure

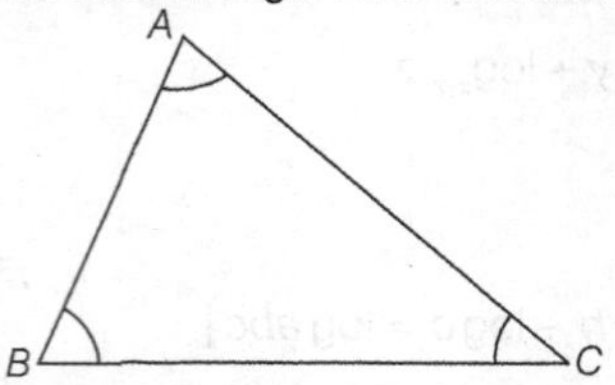

In given figure, three sides are *AB*, *BC* and *CA*, three vertices are *A*, *B* and *C* and three angles are $\angle A$, $\angle B$ and $\angle C$ i.e. $\angle ABC$, $\angle BAC$ and $\angle BCA$.

Types of Triangles

Triangles are classified according to the length of their sides and the measure of their angles.

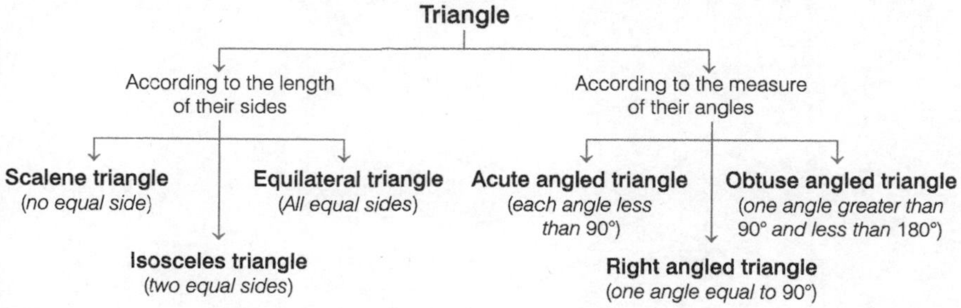

Important Properties of Triangles

(i) The sum of all angles of a triangle is 180°. It is called **angle sum property** of a triangle.

(ii) In an equilateral triangle, all sides and all angles are equal. So, each angle of an equilateral triangle is 60°.

(iii) A triangle cannot have more than one right angle.

(iv) A triangle cannot have more than one obtuse angle.

(v) In a right angled triangle, sum of the two acute angles is 90°.

(vi) If the side *BC* of a ΔABC is produced to *D*, then $\angle ACD$ so formed is called an **exterior angle** of ΔABC and it is equal to sum of its interior opposite angles i.e. $\angle ACD = \angle BAC + \angle ABC$.

This is called **exterior angle property** of a triangle.

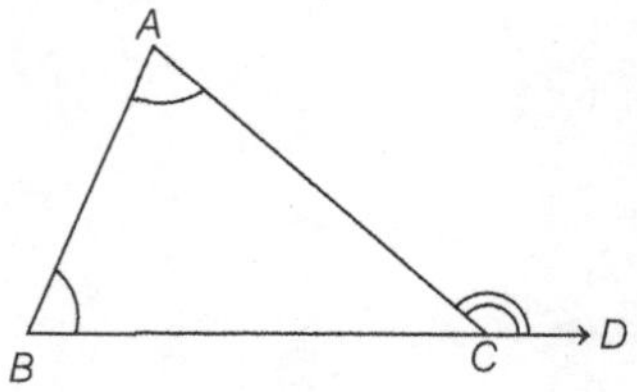

Congruence of Triangles

If a triangle superimposed on the other triangle and they cover each other completely, then the two triangles are congruent.

If ΔPQR is congruent to ΔABC, then we write $\Delta PQR \cong \Delta ABC$.

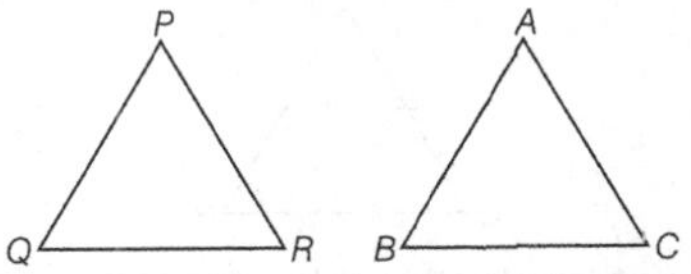

In congruent triangles, corresponding parts are equal and therefore we will write it in short as **CPCT**.

Criterias for Congruence of Triangles

(i) SAS (Side-Angle-Side) Congruence Rule

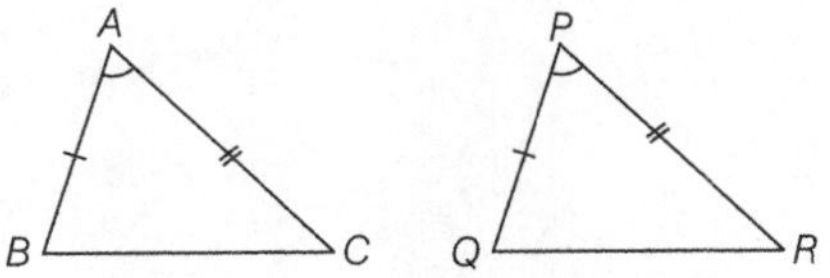

Two triangles are congruent, if two sides and the included angle of a triangle are equal to the two sides and the included angle of the other triangle.

In ΔABC and ΔPQR, if $AB = PQ$, $\angle A = \angle P$, $AC = PR$

or $AC = PR$, $\angle C = \angle R$, $CB = RQ$

or $CB = RQ$, $\angle B = \angle Q$, $BA = QP$.

Then, $\Delta ABC \cong \Delta PQR$.

(ii) ASA (Angle-Side-Angle) Congruence Rule

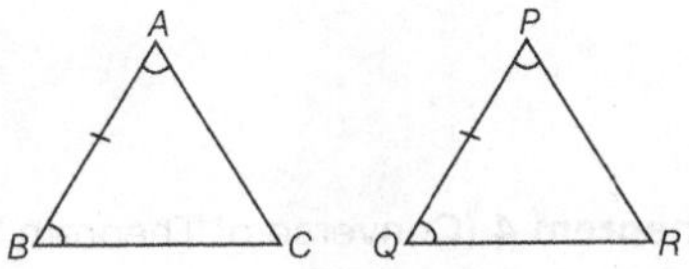

Two triangles are congruent, if two angles and the included side between two angles of one triangle are equal to the corresponding angles and included side of another triangle.

In ΔABC and ΔPQR, if $\angle A = \angle P$, $AB = PQ$ and $\angle B = \angle Q$

or $\angle B = \angle Q$, $BC = QR$ and $\angle C = \angle R$

or $\angle C = \angle R$, $AC = PR$ and $\angle A = \angle P$.

Then, $\Delta ABC \cong \Delta PQR$

(iii) AAS (Angle-Angle-Side) Congruence Rule

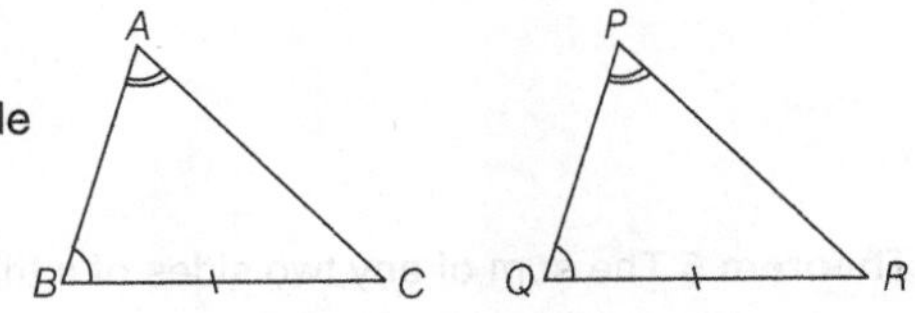

Two triangles are congruent, if any two angles and a side of one triangle are equal to two angles and the corresponding side of other triangle.

In ΔABC and ΔPQR, if $\angle A = \angle P$, $\angle B = \angle Q$ and $BC = QR$

or $\angle A = \angle P$, $\angle C = \angle R$ and $AB = PQ$

or $\angle B = \angle Q$, $\angle C = \angle R$ and $AC = PR$

Then, $\Delta ABC \cong \Delta PQR$.

(iv) SSS (Side-Side-Side) Congruence Rule

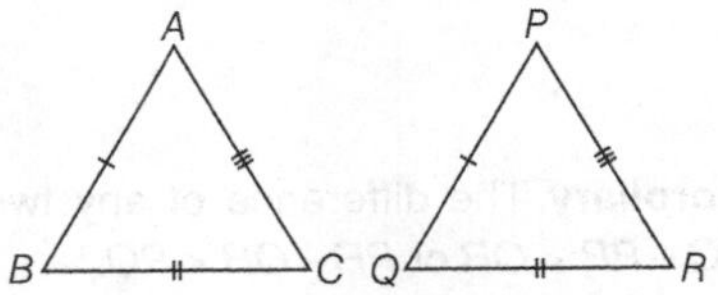

If three sides of one triangle are equal to the three sides of another triangle, then the triangles are congruent.

In ΔABC and ΔPQR, if $AB = PQ$, $BC = QR$ and $AC = PR$,

then $\Delta ABC \cong \Delta PQR$.

(v) RHS (Right Angle-Hypotenuse-Side) Congruence Rule

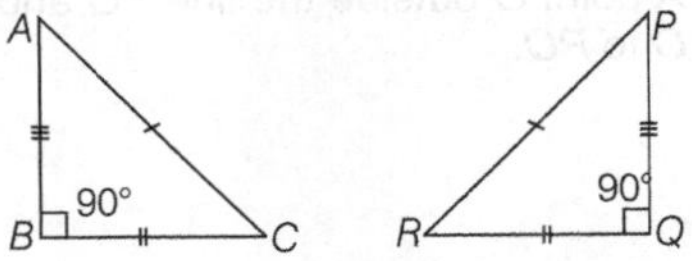

If in two right triangles, the hypotenuse and one side of one triangle are equal to the hypotenuse and one side of the other triangle, then the two triangles are congruent.

In ΔABC and ΔPQR, if $\angle B = \angle Q$, $AC = PR$ and $AB = PQ$

or $\angle B = \angle Q$, $AC = PR$ and $BC = RQ$.

Then, $\Delta ABC \cong \Delta PQR$.

Important Theorems Based on Triangles

Theorem 1 If two sides of a triangle are equal, then the angles opposite to the equal sides are equal.

In a ΔPQR, $PQ = PR$

$\therefore$ $\angle R = \angle Q$

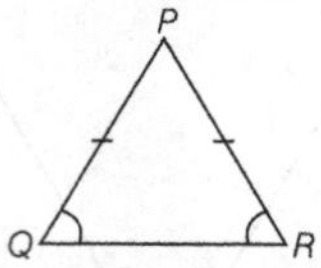

Theorem 2 (Converse of Theorem 1) In any triangle, the sides opposite to equal angles are equal.

In a ΔPQR, $\angle Q = \angle R$

$\therefore$ $PR = PQ$

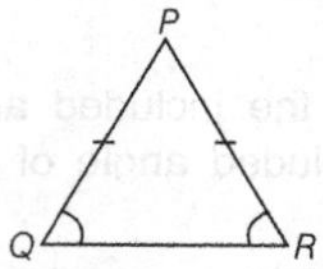

Theorem 3 If two sides of a triangle are unequal, then the angle opposite to longer side is larger (or greater).

A ΔPQR in which $PQ > PR$.

$\therefore$ $\angle PRQ > \angle Q$

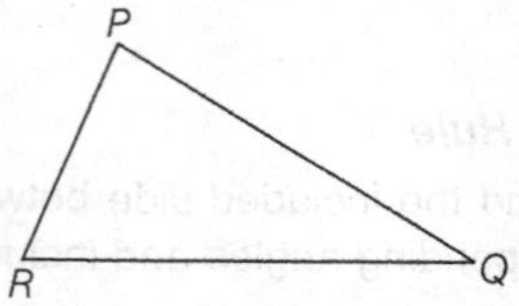

Theorem 4 (Converse of Theorem 3) In any triangle, the side opposite to the larger (or greater) angle is longer.

A ΔPQR in which $\angle RPQ > \angle Q$.

$\therefore$ $QR > PR$

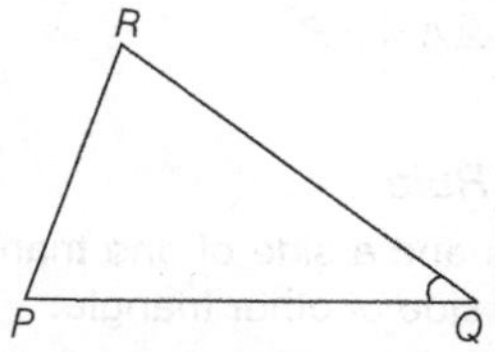

Theorem 5 The sum of any two sides of a triangle is greater than the third side.

In a ΔPQR, $PQ + QR > PR$ Or $PQ + PR > QR$ Or $PR + QR > PQ$

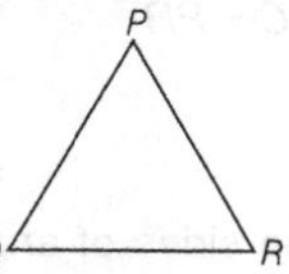

Corollary The difference of any two sides of a triangle is less than the third side. In a ΔPQR, $PQ - QR < PR$ or $PQ - PR < QR$ or $PR - QR < PQ$.

Theorem 6 Of all straight lines, that can be drawn to a given straight line from a point outside it, the perpendicular is the shortest line.

A point O outside the line PQ and OA perpendicular to PQ. OA is the shortest of all the lines that can be drawn from O to PQ.

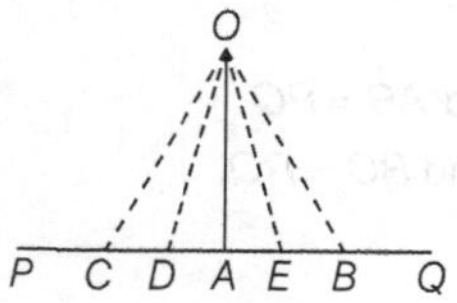

EXAM ORIENTED QUESTIONS

TYPE - 1   01 Mark

Multiple Choice Questions

Q.1 The three angles of a triangle are $a + 15°$, $2a - 20°$ and $a - 15°$. The angles are

(a) 65°, 70° and 45°   (b) 65°, 80° and 35°

(c) 45°, 100° and 35°   (d) 65°, 60° and 55°

Q.2 In the given figure, $AB = CD$, $\angle ABC = \angle BCD$ and $AC = 4$ units, then BD is equal to

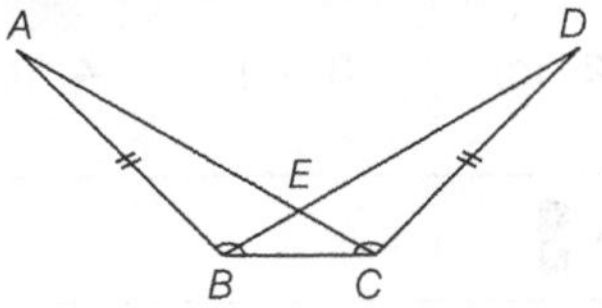

(a) 2 units   (b) 3 units

(c) 4 units   (d) 8 units

Q.3 In the given figures, the measure of $\angle B'A'C'$ is

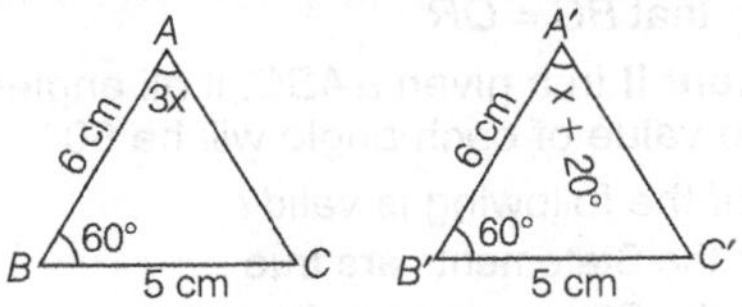

(a) 20°   (b) 30°

(c) 40°   (d) 35°

Q.4 In the given figure, BD bisects $\angle B$ and BD is perpendicular to AC. The values of x and y are

(a) $x = 8$ and $y = 8$

(b) $x = 8$ and $y = 16$

(c) $x = 16$ and $y = 16$

(d) $x = 16$ and $y = 8$

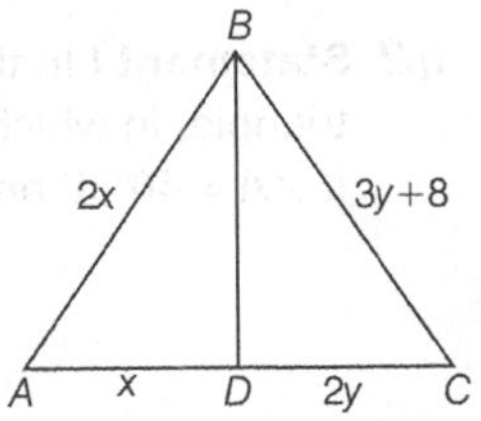

Q.5 In the given figure, if side $AO = 3$ cm, then the length of side AB is

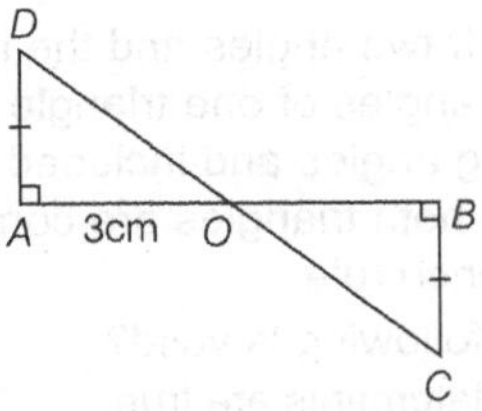

(a) 9 cm   (b) 6 cm

(c) 3 cm   (d) $\sqrt{3}$ cm

Q.6 In the given figure, the values of x and y are

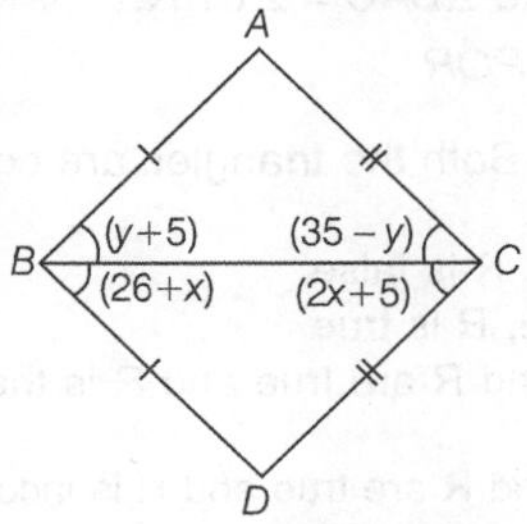

(a) 5 and 22   (b) 4 and 19

(c) 3 and 24   (d) 6 and 25

Q.7 If $\Delta PQR \cong \Delta ABC$ and given $PR = 6$, $AC = 6$ and $BC = 3$, then the value of QR is

(a) 3   (b) 4

(c) 5   (d) 6

Q.8 In a ΔABC, if $AB = 3$ cm, $AC = 3$ cm and $\angle A = 50°$, then $\angle B$ is

(a) 55°   (b) 80°

(c) 65°   (d) 60°

Q.9 In ΔABC, $\angle B = 35°$, $\angle C = 65°$ and the bisector of $\angle BAC$ meets BC in P.

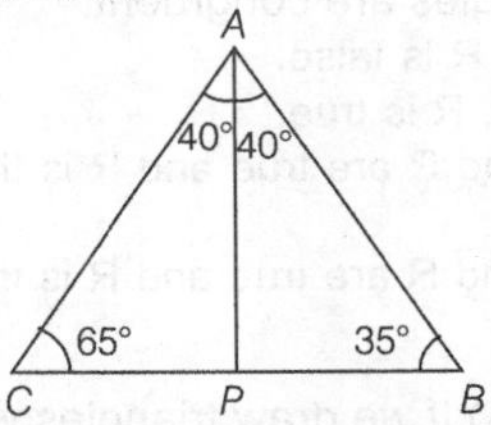

Choose the correct order of inequality.

(a) $AP > BP > CP$

(b) $BP > AP > CP$

(c) $CP > BP > AP$

(d) None of the above

Q.10 Which of the following does not represent the sides of a triangle?

(a) 2 cm, 3 cm, 6 cm

(b) 7 cm, 5 cm, 3 cm

(c) 3 cm, 2 cm, 4 cm

(d) 5 cm, 8 cm, 4 cm

Answers

1. (b)	**2.** (c)	**3.** (b)	**4.** (d)	**5.** (b)
6. (c)	**7.** (a)	**8.** (c)	**9.** (b)	**10.** (a)

TYPE - 2 01 Mark

Assertion-Reason Type Questions

Q.1 Assertion (A) In ΔABC and ΔPQR, $AB = PQ$, $AC = PR$ and $\angle BAC = \angle QPR$.

$\therefore \Delta ABC \cong \Delta PQR$

Reason (R) Both the triangles are congruent by SSA congruence.

(a) A is true, R is false.
(b) A is false, R is true.
(c) Both A and R are true and R is the correct reason for A.
(d) Both A and R are true and R is incorrect reason for A.

Q.2 Assertion (A) In the given figure, if AC is bisector of $\angle BAD$ such that $AD = AB = 3$ cm and $AC = 5$ cm, then $BC = CD$.

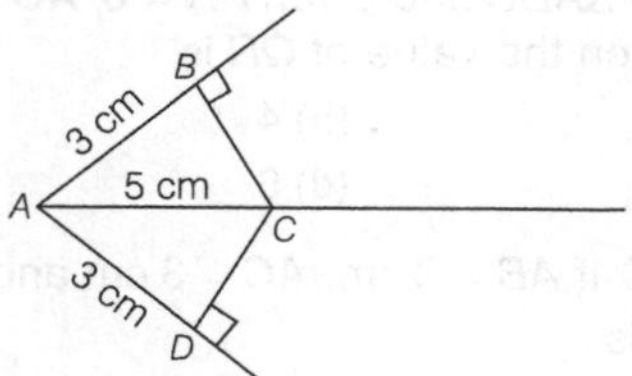

Reason (R) If in two right angled triangles, the hypotenuse and one side of one triangle are equal to hypotenuse and one side of the other triangle, then the two triangles are congruent.

(a) A is true, R is false.
(b) A is false, R is true.
(c) Both A and R are true and R is the correct reason for A.
(d) Both A and R are true and R is incorrect reason for A.

Q.3 Assertion (A) If we draw triangles with angles 30°, 70° and 80° and the length of the sides of one triangle be different from that of the corresponding sides of the other triangles, then they are not congruent.

Reason (R) If two triangles are constructed, which have all corresponding angles equal but have a pair of unequal corresponding sides, then two triangles cannot be congruent to each other.

(a) A is true, R is false.
(b) A is false, R is true.
(c) Both A and R are true and R is the correct reason for A.
(d) Both A and R are true and R is incorrect reason for A.

Q.4 Assertion (A) In ΔABC, $AB = AC$ and $\angle BAC = 70°$, then $\angle ABC = 50°$.

Reason (R) If two sides of a triangle are equal, then angles opposite to the equal sides are equal.

(a) A is true, R is false.
(b) A is false, R is true.
(c) Both A and R are true and R is the correct reason for A.
(d) Both A and R are true and R is incorrect reason for A.

Q.5 Assertion (A) In ΔABC, $AB = 8$ cm, $BC = 10.5$ cm and $CA = 6$ cm, then $\angle ABC$ is the greatest angle of ΔABC.

Reason (R) If two sides of a triangle are unequal, then the angle opposite to longer side is larger.

(a) A is true, R is false.
(b) A is false, R is true.
(c) Both A and R are true and R is the correct reason for A.
(d) Both A and R are true and R is incorrect reason for A.

Answers

1. (a) **2.** (c) **3.** (c) **4.** (b) **5.** (b)

TYPE - 3 01 Mark

Statement Based Questions

Q.1 Statement I It is given that $\Delta ABC \cong \Delta RPQ$, then we can say that $BC = QR$.

Statement II In a given ΔABC, if all angles are equal, then the value of each angle will be 60°.

Which of the following is valid?

(a) Both the Statements are true.
(b) Both the Statements are false.
(c) Statement I is true and Statement II is false.
(d) Statement I is false and Statement II is true.

Q.2 Statement I In the figure, ΔABC is an isosceles triangle, in which $AB = AC$ and PQ is parallel to BC. If $\angle A = 40°$, then $\angle PQC = 110°$.

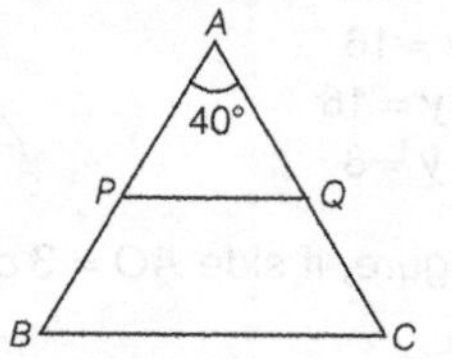

Statement II If two angles and the included side between two angles of one triangle are equal to the corresponding angles and included side of another triangle, then both triangles are congruent by ASA congruence rule.

Which of the following is valid?

(a) Both the Statements are true.
(b) Both the Statements are false.
(c) Statement I is true and Statement II is false.
(d) Statement I is false and Statement II is true.

Q.3 **Statement I** In any triangle, the sides opposite to equal angles are equal.

Statement II The sum of any two sides of a triangle is equal to third side.

Which of the following is valid?

(a) Both the Statements are true.
(b) Both the Statements are false.
(c) Statement I is true and Statement II is false.
(d) Statement I is false and Statement II is true.

Q.4 **Statement I** In ΔPQR, $\angle P = 70°$ and $\angle R = 30°$, then the longest side of this triangle is PR.

Statement II It is possible to construct a triangle with lengths of its sides as 4 cm, 3 cm and 7 cm.

Which of the following is valid?

(a) Both the Statements are true.
(b) Both the Statements are false.
(c) Statement I is true and Statement II is false.
(d) Statement I is false and Statement II is true.

Q.5 **Statement I** In any triangle, the side opposite to larger angle is shortest.

Statement II Perpendicular distance from a point to a line is the shortest distance between the point and the line.

Which of the following is valid?

(a) Both the Statements are true.
(b) Both the Statements are false.
(c) Statement I is true and Statement II is false.
(d) Statement I is false and Statement II is true.

Answers

1. (d) **2.** (a) **3.** (c) **4.** (c) **5.** (d)

TYPE - 4 03 Marks

Short Answer Type Questions

Q.1 If the base of an isosceles triangle is produced on both sides, then prove that the exterior angles, so formed are equal to each other.

Q.2 It is given that $\Delta ABC \cong \Delta FDE$. If $AB = 5$ cm, $\angle B = 40°$ and $\angle A = 80°$, then find the length of DF and also measurement of $\angle E$.

Q.3 In the given figure, $OB = OA$ and $OC = OD$.

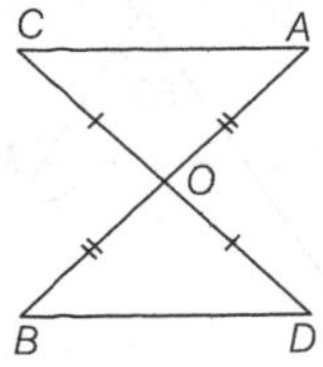

Show that

(i) $\Delta AOC \cong \Delta BOD$
(ii) $AC || BD$

Q.4 In a quadrilateral $ACBD$, $AC = AD$ and AB bisects $\angle A$ (see the figure). Show that $\Delta ABC \cong \Delta ABD$.

What can you say about BC and BD ?

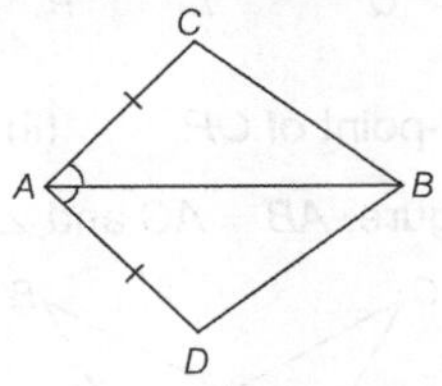

Q.5 AB is a line segment and line l is a perpendicular bisector of AB. If a point P lies on l, then show that P is equidistant from A and B.

Q.6 In right angled ΔABC, $\angle C = 90°$. M is the mid-point of hypotenuse AB. C is joined to M and produced to a point D such that $DM = CM$. Point D is joined to point B. Show that

(i) $\Delta AMC \cong \Delta BMD$
(ii) $\angle DBC = \angle ACB$

Q.7 In the given figure, $AC = AE$, $AB = AD$ and $\angle BAD = \angle EAC$. Show that $BC = DE$.

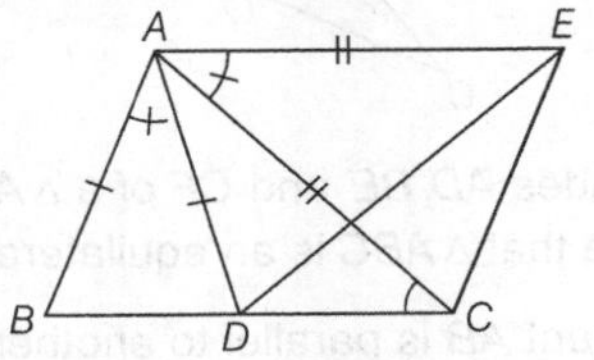

Q.8 In the given figure, $OP = OQ$, $OR = OS$ and $\angle POQ = \angle ROS$. Prove that $PR = QS$.

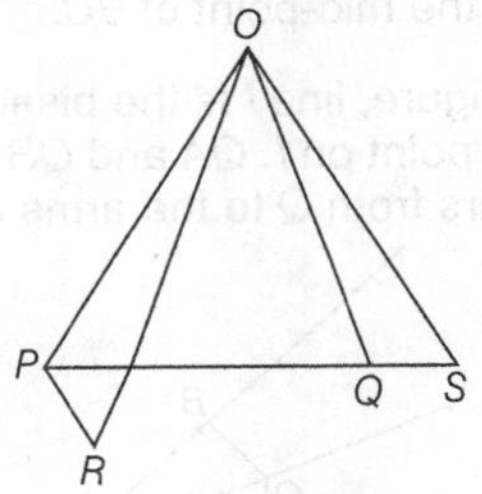

Q.9 In the given figure, ΔABC and ΔABD are such that $AD = BC$, $\angle 1 = \angle 2$ and $\angle 3 = \angle 4$. Prove that $BD = AC$.

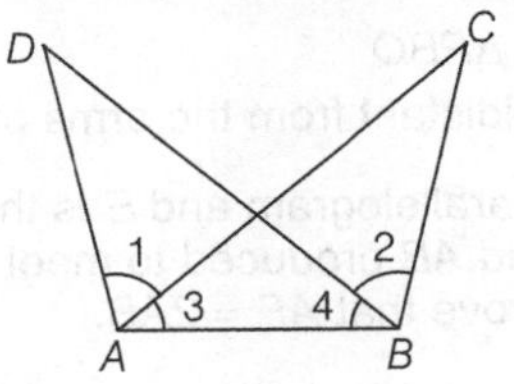

Q.10 In the given figure, $PQ = PR$ and PL is bisector of $\angle P$.

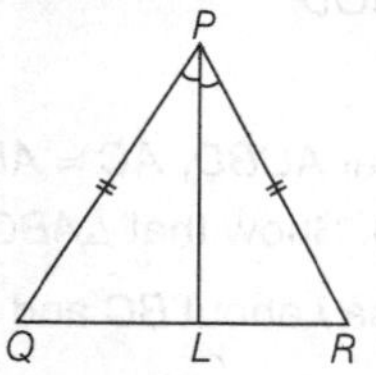

Prove that

(i) L is the mid-point of QR (ii) $PL \perp QR$

Q.11 In the given figure, $AB = AC$ and $\angle B = \angle C$. Prove that

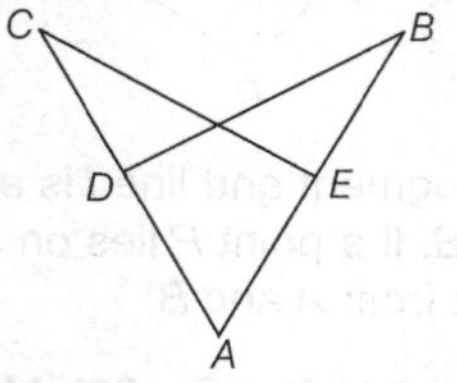

(i) $\Delta ABD \cong \Delta ACE$ (ii) $BD = CE$

Q.12 In the given figure, $AB = CB$ and $\angle x = \angle y$. Prove that $QA = PC$.

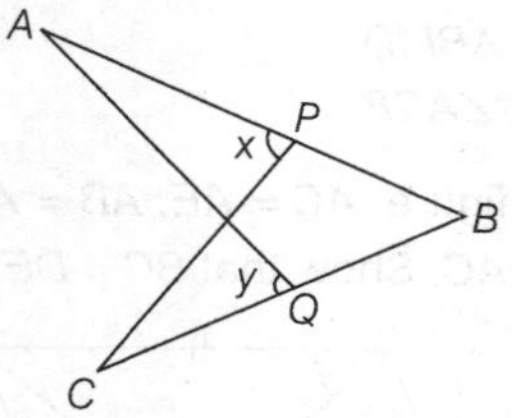

Q.13 If the altitudes AD, BE and CF of a ΔABC are equal, then prove that ΔABC is an equilateral triangle.

Q.14 Line segment AB is parallel to another line segment CD. O is the mid-point of AD. Show that

(i) $\Delta AOB \cong \Delta DOC$

(ii) O is also the mid-point of BC.

Q.15 In the given figure, line l is the bisector of an angle P and Q is any point on l. QA and QB are perpendiculars from Q to the arms of $\angle P$.

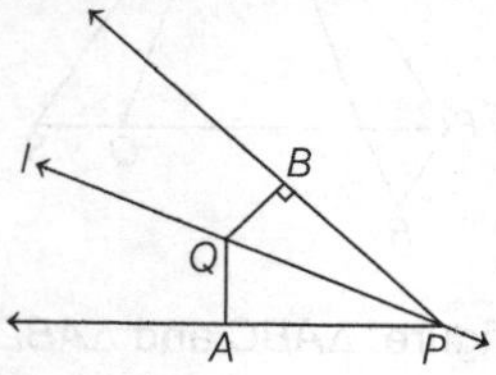

Show that

(i) $\Delta PAQ \cong \Delta PBQ$

(ii) Q is equidistant from the arms of $\angle P$.

Q.16 $ABCD$ is a parallelogram and E is the point on side BC. If DE and AB produced to meet at F such that $DE = EF$. Prove that $AF = 2AB$.

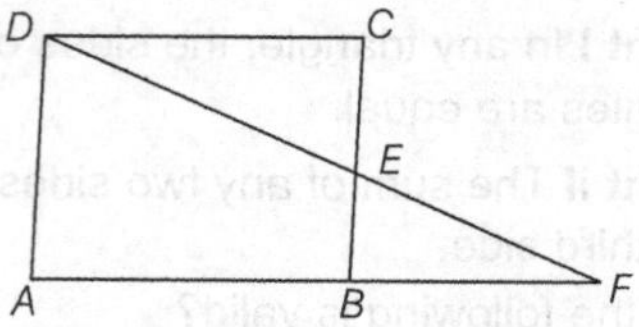

Q.17 In a quadrilateral $ABCD$, perpendiculars BM and DN are drawn to AC such that $BM = DN$. If $BR = 8$ cm, then find the length of BD.

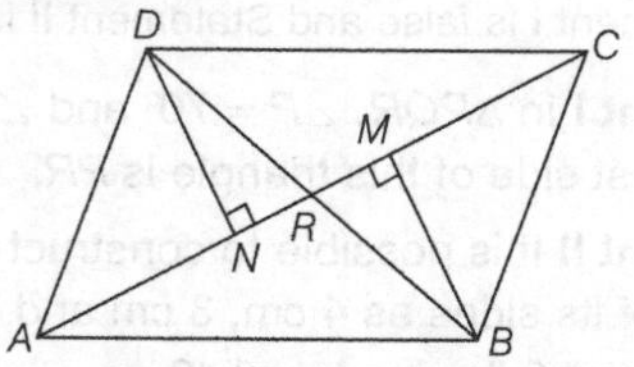

Q.18 AD is a median and BL, CM are perpendiculars drawn from B and C respectively on AD produced to M. Prove that $BL = CM$.

Q.19 AD is an altitude of an isosceles ΔABC in which $AB = AC$. Show that

(i) AD bisects BC (ii) AD bisects $\angle A$

Q.20 In the given figure, AB and CD are perpendiculars on BD. Also, $AB = CD$ and $AF = CE$. Prove that

(i) $\Delta ABF \cong \Delta CDE$ (ii) $BE = FD$

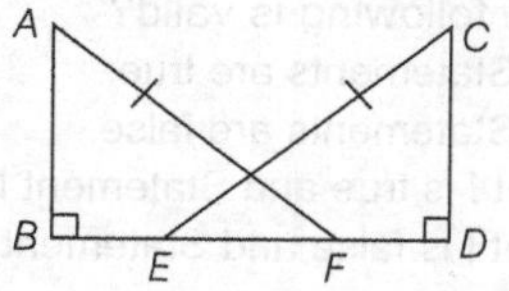

Q.21 In the given figure, ABC and DBC are two isosceles triangles on the same base BC. Show that $\angle ABD = \angle ACD$.

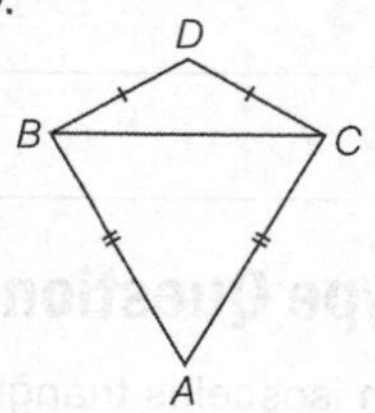

Q.22 PQR is an isosceles triangle in which perpendiculars QM and RN are drawn to equal sides PR and PQ, respectively. Show that these altitudes are equal.

Q.23 In the given figure, ΔABC is an isosceles triangle in which $AB = AC$ and LM is parallel to BC. If $\angle A = 50°$, then find $\angle LMC$.

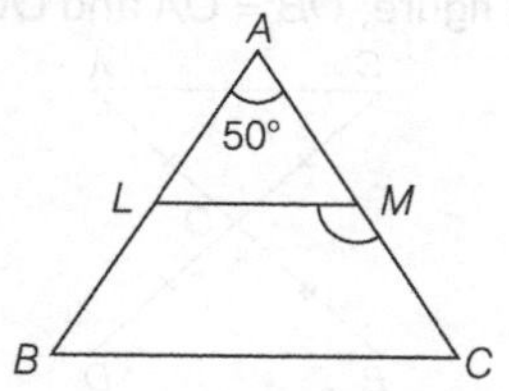

Q.24 In the given figure, find the value of P.

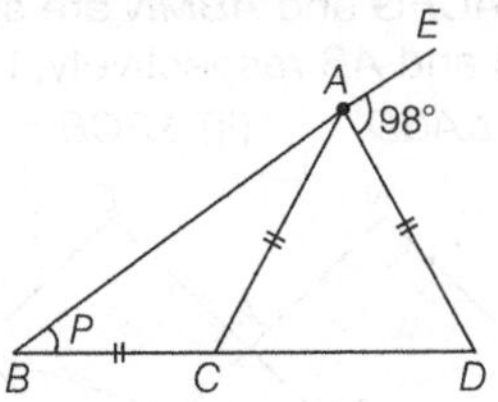

Q.25 In the given figure, $AB = BC$ and $AC = CD$. Prove that $\angle BAD : \angle ADB = 3:1$.

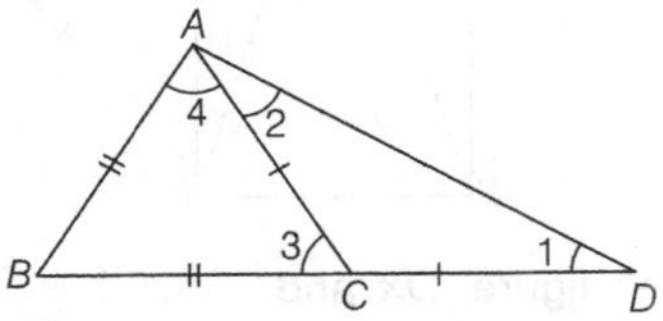

Q.26 In an isosceles ΔABC with $AB = AC$, D and E are the points on BC such that $BE = CD$. Show that $AD = AE$.

Q.27 In the given figure, AD bisects $\angle A$. Then, find the relation between the sides AB, AC and DC.

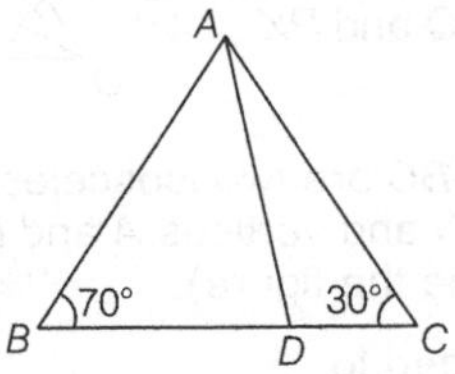

Q.28 ABC is a triangle, in which $AB = AC$ and D is any point on AB. Through D, a line parallel to AC intersects BC at E. If $DB = 1.5$ cm, then find the length of DE.

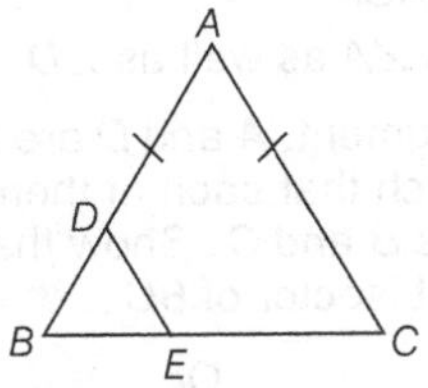

Q.29 It is given that $DE = EF$, $BE = EC$, $ED \perp AB$ and $EF \perp AC$. Prove that

(i) $AB = AC$ (ii) $AD = AF$

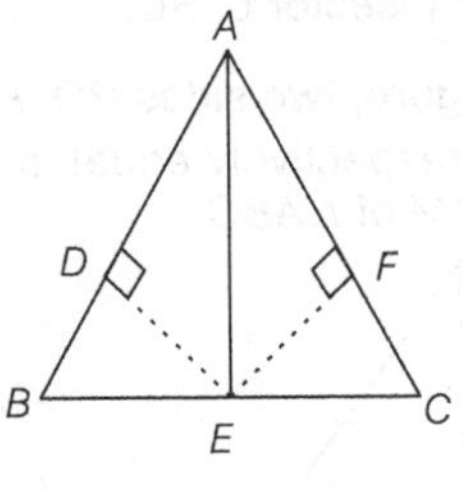

Q.30 In ΔABD, bisector of $\angle ADB$ meets opposite side AB at point O. If $OA = OB$, then prove that ΔABD is an isosceles.

Q.31 In the following figure, XZ and YZ are the bisectors of $\angle CXY$ and $\angle CYX$, respectively. AC is parallel to XZ and BC is parallel to YZ, then prove that AB is the perimeter of ΔXYC.

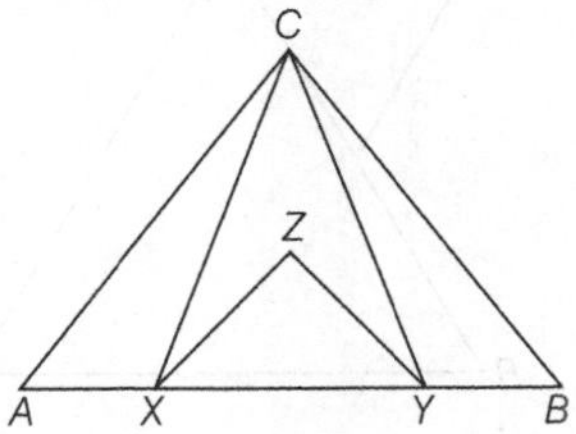

Q.32 In the given figure, $AB = 8.5$ cm, $BC = 6$ cm and $CA = 7.2$ cm. Write x, y and z in ascending order.

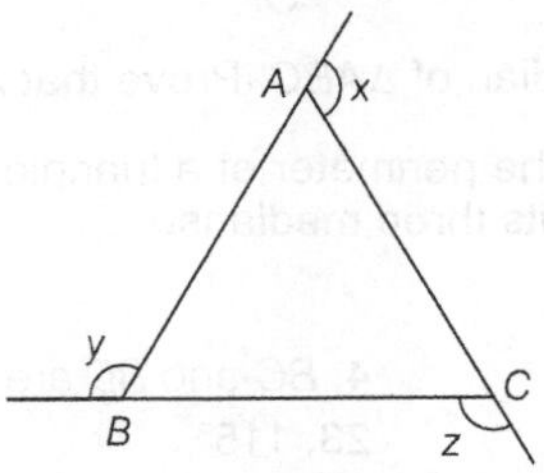

Q.33 AB and CD are the smallest and largest sides of a quadrilateral $ABCD$, respectively. Prove that $\angle B > \angle D$.

Q.34 D is a point on side BC of ΔABC such that $AD = AC$. Show that $AB > AD$.

Q.35 In the given figure, $PQ > PR$, QS and RS are the bisectors of $\angle Q$ and $\angle R$ respectively, then find the relation between the sides SQ and SR.

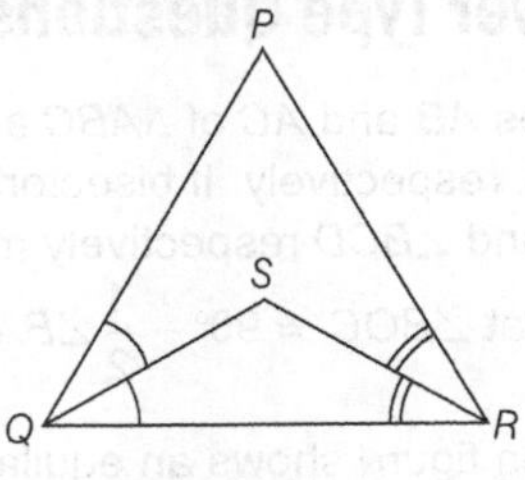

Q.36 Show that the sum of three altitudes of a triangle is less than the sum of the three sides of the triangle.

Q.37 Show that the difference of any two sides of a triangle is less than the third side.

Q.38 Show that in a quadrilateral $ABCD$,

$$AB + BC + CD + DA < 2(BD + AC).$$

Q.39 If S is any point on side QR of a ΔPQR, then show that $PQ + QR + RP > 2PS$.

Q.40 In the given figure, T is a mid-point of side QR of ΔPQR and S is a point such that $RT = ST$. Prove that $PQ + PR > QS$.

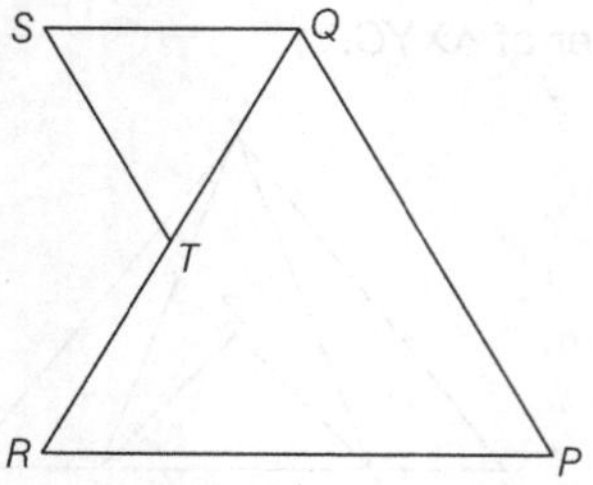

Q.41 Prove that the sum of any two sides of a triangle is greater than twice the median drawn to the third side.

Or

AD is a median of ΔABC. Prove that $AB + AC > 2AD$.

Q.42 Prove that the perimeter of a triangle is greater than the sum of its three medians.

Answers

2. 5 cm, 60° **4.** BC and BD are equal
17. 16 cm **23.** 115°
24. 32°40′
27. $AB < DC < AC$
28. 1.5 cm
32. $z < y < x$
35. $SQ > SR$

TYPE - 5 4/5 Marks

Long Answer Type Questions

Q.1 The sides AB and AC of ΔABC are produced to points E and D, respectively. If bisectors BO and CO of $\angle CBE$ and $\angle BCD$ respectively meet at point O, then prove that $\angle BOC = 90° - \frac{1}{2}\angle BAC$.

Q.2 The given figure shows an equilateral ΔPQR with each side 20 cm. Also, $DC \parallel PQ$, $DA \parallel RQ$ and $BC \parallel PR$. If $DC + DA + CB = 25$ cm, then find AB.

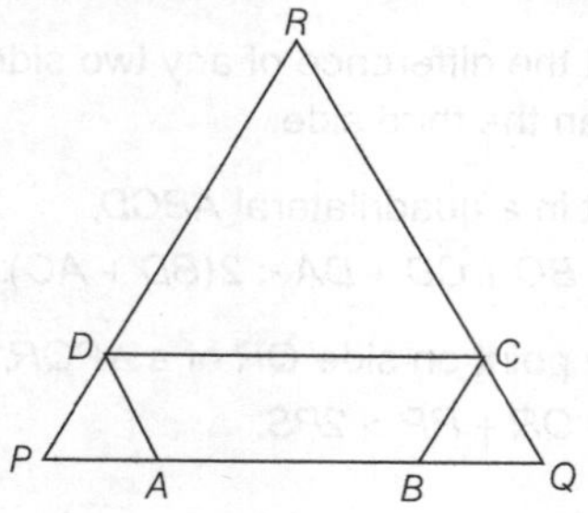

Q.3 In the following figure, ΔABC is a right angled triangle at A. $BCED$, $ACFG$ and $ABMN$ are squares on the sides BC, CA and AB respectively, then show that
(i) $\Delta MBC \cong \Delta ABD$ (ii) $\Delta FCB \cong \Delta ACE$

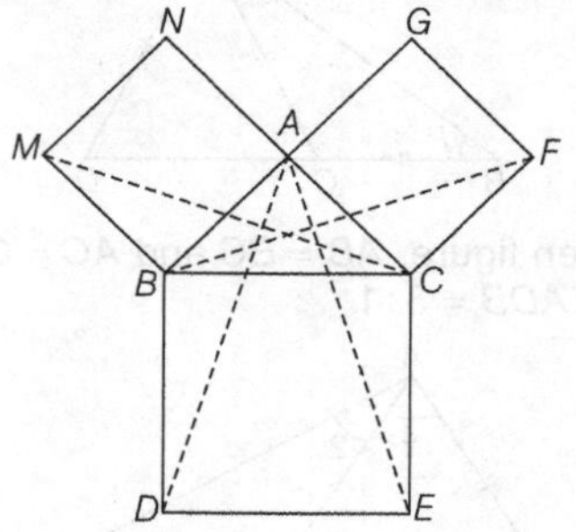

Q.4 In the given figure, QX and RX are the bisectors of $\angle PQR$ and $\angle PRQ$ respectively of ΔPQR. If $XS \perp QR$ and $XT \perp PQ$, then prove that $\Delta XTQ \cong \Delta XSQ$ and PX bisects $\angle P$.

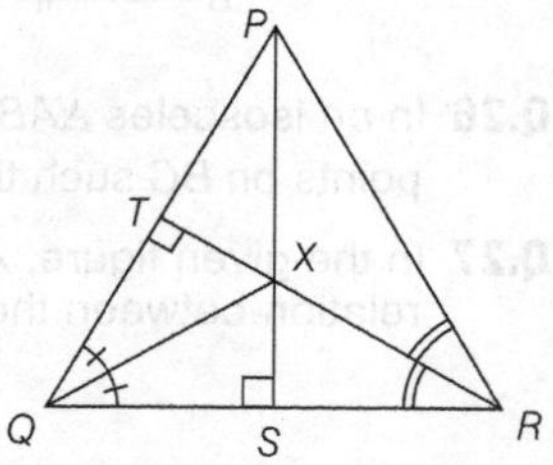

Q.5 ΔABC and ΔDBC are two isosceles triangles on the same base BC and vertices A and D are on the same side of BC (see the figure).

If AD is extended to intersect BC at P, then show that
(i) $\Delta ABD \cong \Delta ACD$
(ii) $\Delta ABP \cong \Delta ACP$
(iii) AP bisects $\angle A$ as well as $\angle D$

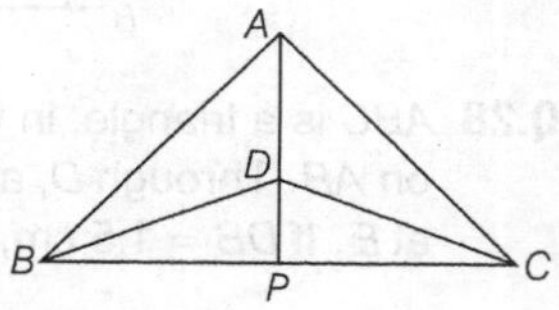

Q.6 BC is a line segment. A and D are points on opposite sides of BC such that each of them is equidistant from the points B and C. Show that the line AD is the perpendicular bisector of BC.

Or

ΔABC and ΔDBC are two triangles on the same base BC such that A and D lie on the opposite sides of BC, $AB = AC$ and $DB = DC$. Show that AD is the perpendicular bisector of BC.

Q.7 In the given figure, two sides PQ, PR and altitude PN of ΔPQR are respectively equal to two sides AB, AC and altitude AM of ΔABC.

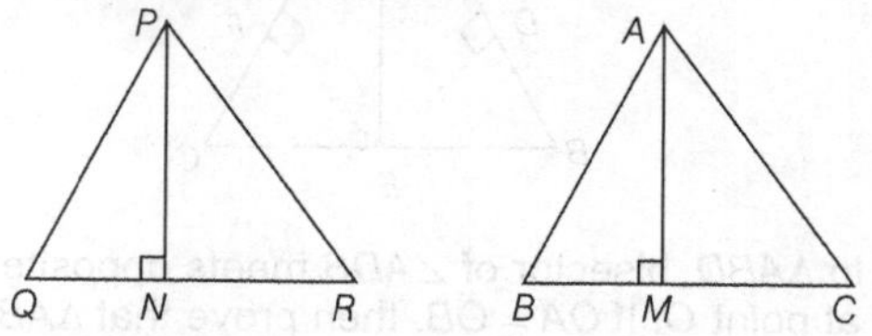

Prove that $\Delta PQR \cong \Delta ABC$.

Q.8 Find the measure of each lettered angle in the following figure.

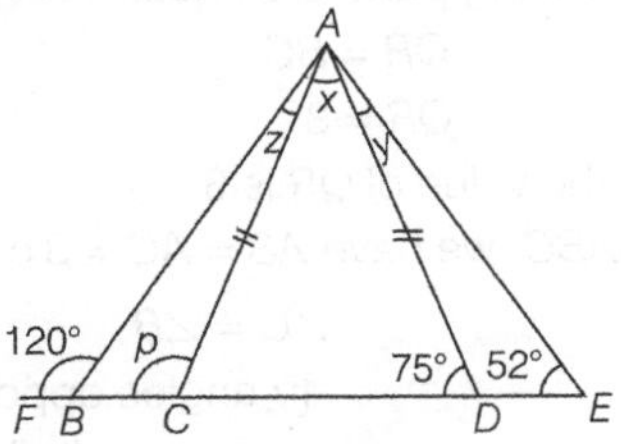

Q.9 ΔABC is a triangle in which $\angle B = 2\angle C$. D is a point on BC such that AD bisects $\angle BAC$ and $AB = CD$. Prove that $\angle BAC = 72°$.

Answers

2. 10 cm **8.** $x = 30°$, $y = 23°$, $z = 15°$ and $p = 105°$

TYPE - 6

Case Based Questions

Q.1 Pavan is studying in IX standard. His father purchases a square shape plot (shown in figure).

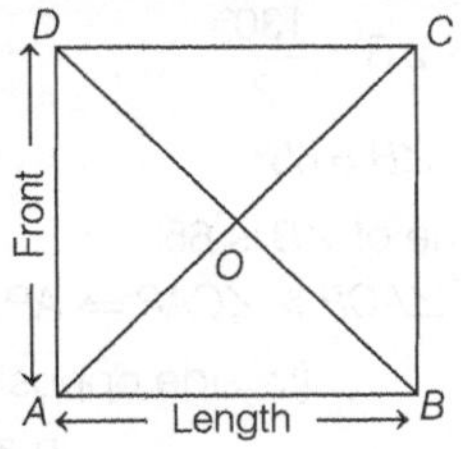

After visiting the land, few questions came in his mind, give answers to his questions by looking at the figure.

(i) Find measure of $\angle AOB$.

(ii) If $OA = 3$ cm, then find the value of OC.

(iii) Write the correct congruence rule applicable to prove $\Delta ABO \cong \Delta ADO$.

(iv) If $OB = 5$ cm, then find the value of BD. **(4 M)**

Q.2 Rajeev and Amit sit together at B. Their work places are at A and C respectively such that A, B and C form a triangle. BD is the bisector of $\angle ABC$, meets AC at right angle. Various distances are expressed in terms of x and y as shown in the figure.

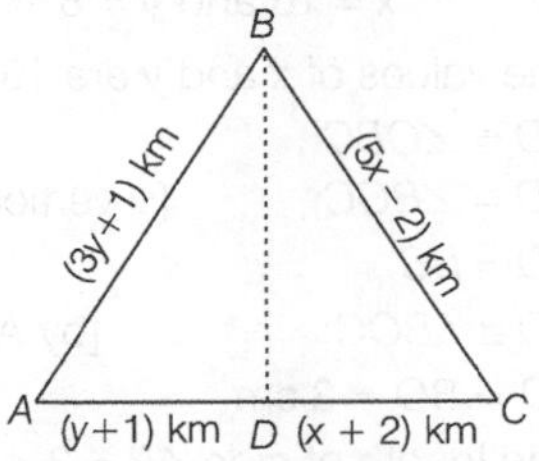

They used bicycles instead of bikes to go to their work places.

(i) Find the distance between A and C.

(ii) Using bicycles instead of bikes, which values are depicted by Rajeev and Amit? **(4 M)**

Answers

1. (i) 90° (ii) 3 cm (iii) SAS congruence rule (iv) 10 cm

2. (i) 10 km (ii) effort towards reducing pollution

EXPLANATIONS

Multiple Choice Questions

1. (b) We know that the sum of all three angles of a triangle is 180°.

Now, $a + 15° + 2a - 20° + a - 15° = 180°$

$\Rightarrow \quad 4a - 20° = 180°$

$\Rightarrow \quad 4a = 180° + 20°$

$\Rightarrow \quad 4a = 200°$

$\Rightarrow \quad a = 50°$

Hence, the angles of triangle are

$a + 15° = 50° + 15° = 65°$,

$2a - 20° = 2 \times 50° - 20° = 80°$

and $\quad a - 15° = 50° - 15° = 35°$

2. (c) In ΔABC and ΔBCD,

$AB = CD$ [given]

$\angle ABC = \angle BCD$ [given]

$BC = BC$ [common side]

$\therefore \quad \Delta ABC \cong \Delta DCB$ [by SAS congruency rule]

$\Rightarrow \quad AC = BD$ [by CPCT]

$\Rightarrow \quad BD = 4$ units [$\because AC = 4$ units]

Hence, BD is equal to 4 units.

3. (b) From ΔABC and $\Delta A'B'C'$,

$AB = A'B' = 6$ cm,

$\angle ABC = \angle A'B'C' = 60°$

and $\quad BC = B'C' = 5$ cm

$\therefore \quad \Delta ABC \cong \Delta A'B'C'$ [by SAS congruency rule]

$\Rightarrow \quad \angle BAC = \angle B'A'C'$ [by CPCT]

$\Rightarrow \quad 3x = x + 20°$ [from figure]

$\Rightarrow \quad 3x - x = 20°$

$\Rightarrow \quad 2x = 20° \Rightarrow x = 10°$

Hence, $\angle B'A'C' = x + 20°$

$= 10° + 20° = 30°$

4. (d) In ΔABD and ΔBCD,

$\angle BDA = \angle BDC$ [each 90°]

$BD = BD$ [common side]

$\angle ABD = \angle DBC$ [BD bisects $\angle B$]

$\therefore$ $\Delta ABD \cong \Delta CBD$ [by ASA congruency]

$\Rightarrow$ $AB = BC$ [by CPCT]

$\Rightarrow$ $2x = 3y + 8$

$\Rightarrow$ $2x - 3y = 8$ ...(i)

and $AD = DC$ [by CPCT]

$\Rightarrow$ $x = 2y$ ...(ii)

On putting $x = 2y$ in Eq. (i), we get

$x = 16$ and $y = 8$

Hence, the values of x and y are 16 and 8, respectively.

5. (b) $\angle OAD = \angle OBC$ [each 90°]

$\angle AOD = \angle BOC$ [$\because$ vertically opposite angles]

and $AD = BC$ [given]

$\therefore$ $\Delta AOD \cong \Delta BOC$ [by AAS congruency rule]

$\therefore$ $AO = BO = 3$ cm [by CPCT]

Hence, the length of side $AB = 3 + 3 = 6$ cm

6. (c) In ΔABC and ΔBDC,

$AB = BD$ [given]

$AC = DC$ [given]

$BC = BC$ [common side]

$\therefore$ $\Delta ABC \cong \Delta DBC$ [by SSS congruency rule]

Here, $\angle CBA = \angle CBD$ [by CPCT]

$\therefore$ $y + 5 = 26 + x$

$\Rightarrow$ $-x + y = 21$ ...(i)

and $\angle BCD = \angle BCA$ [by CPCT]

$\therefore$ $2x + 5 = 35 - y$

$\Rightarrow$ $2x + y = 30$ ...(ii)

On multiplying by 2 in Eq. (i) and then adding Eqs. (i) and (ii), we get

$$\begin{aligned} -2x + 2y &= 42 \\ 2x + y &= 30 \\ \hline 3y &= 72 \end{aligned}$$

$\Rightarrow$ $y = 24$

Now, put $y = 24$ in Eq. (i), we get

$-x + 24 = 21 \Rightarrow -x = -3 \Rightarrow x = 3$

Hence, the values of x and y are 3 and 24, respectively.

7. (a) Given, $\Delta PQR \cong \Delta ABC$

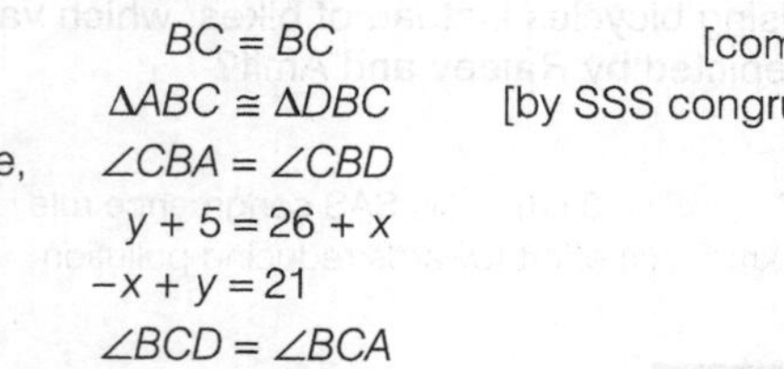

We know that if two triangles are congruent, then their corresponding parts are equal.

$\therefore$ $QR = BC$

$\Rightarrow$ $QR = 3$ [$\because BC = 3$]

Hence, the value of QR is 3.

8. (c) In ΔABC, we have $AB = AC = 3$ cm

$\therefore$ $\angle C = \angle B$

[$\because$ angles opposite to equal sides of a triangle are equal]

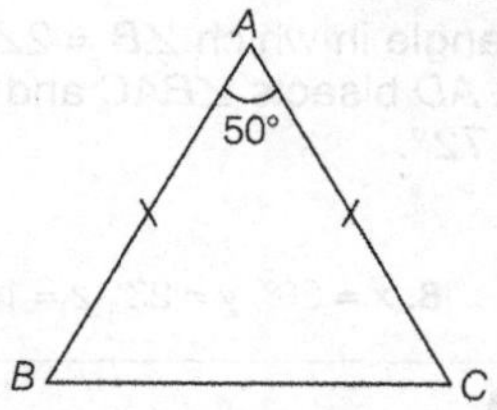

We know that $\angle A + \angle B + \angle C = 180°$

[by angle sum property of a triangle]

$\therefore$ $50° + \angle B + \angle B = 180°$ [$\because \angle A = 50°$ and $\angle C = \angle B$]

$\Rightarrow$ $50° + 2\angle B = 180°$

$\Rightarrow$ $2\angle B = 130°$

$\Rightarrow$ $\angle B = \dfrac{130°}{2}$

$\Rightarrow$ $\angle B = 65°$

Hence, the value of $\angle B$ is 65°.

9. (b) In ΔACP, $\angle ACP > \angle CAP \Rightarrow AP > CP$ ...(i)

[$\because$ side opposite to greater angle in a triangle is greater]

In ΔABP, $\angle BAP > \angle ABP$

$\Rightarrow$ $BP > AP$ ...(ii)

[$\because$ side opposite to greater angle in a triangle is greater]

Now, from Eqs. (i) and (ii), we get

$BP > AP > CP$

10. (a) We know that the sum of any two sides of a triangle is greater than its third side.

In option (a), $2 + 3 < 6$

Hence, it is not possible to construct a triangle with lengths of its sides as 2 cm, 3cm and 6 cm.

Assertion-Reason Type Questions

1. (a) **Assertion** In ΔABC and ΔPQR,

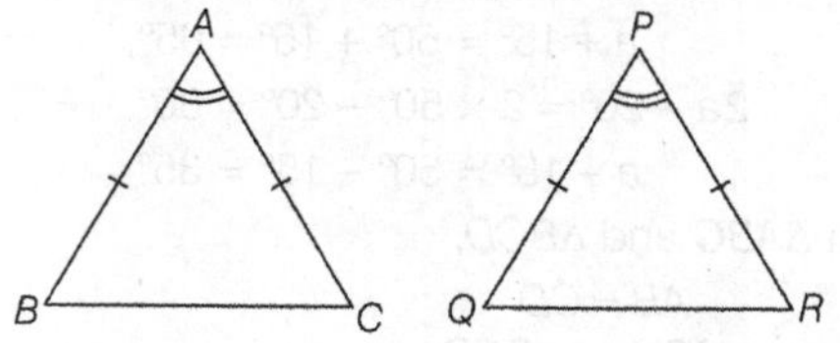

$AB = PQ$, $AC = PR$ and $\angle BAC = \angle QPR$

$\therefore \quad \Delta ABC \cong \Delta PQR$ [by SAS congruence rule]

$\therefore$ A is true.

R is false that both triangles are congruent by SSA congruence.

2. (c) In ΔABC and ΔADC,

$\angle ABC = \angle ADC$ [each 90°]

$AB = AD$ [given]

and $AC = AC$ [common]

$\therefore \quad \Delta ABC \cong \Delta ADC$ [by RHS congruency rule]

Then, $BC = DC$ [by CPCT]

Hence, both A and R are true and R is the correct reason for A.

3. (c) **Assertion** In ΔABC and ΔPQR,

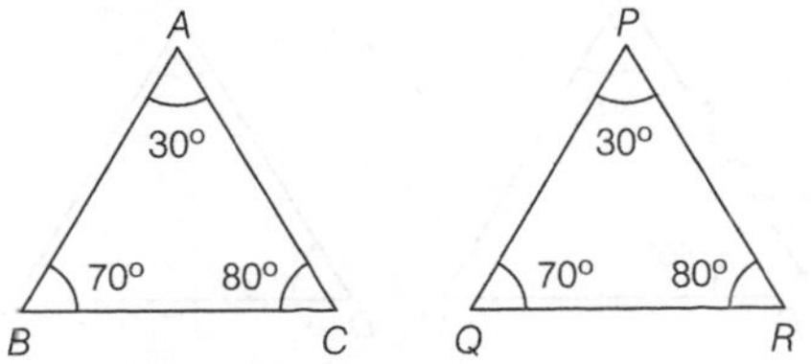

$\angle A = \angle P$, $\angle B = \angle Q$ and $\angle C = \angle R$

But sides are different.

Thus, there is no rule of congruence by AAA.

$\therefore$ ΔABC is not congruent to ΔPQR.

So, both A and R are true and R is the correct reason for A.

4. (b) Given, in ΔABC, $AB = AC$ and $\angle BAC = 70°$

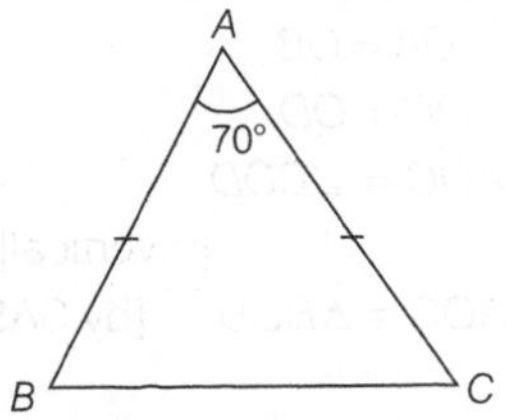

$\because \quad AB = AC$

$\therefore \quad \angle ACB = \angle ABC$ ...(i)

[$\because$ angles opposite to equal sides are equal]

Now, in ΔABC,

$\angle ABC + \angle BAC + \angle ACB = 180°$

[angle sum property of triangle]

$\Rightarrow \quad \angle ABC + 70° + \angle ABC = 180°$

[from Eq. (i) and $\angle BAC = 70°$ (given)]

$\Rightarrow \quad 2\angle ABC = 110°$

$\Rightarrow \quad \angle ABC = 55°$

Hence, A is false, R is true.

5. (b) Given, $AB = 8$ cm, $BC = 10.5$ cm and $AC = 6$ cm

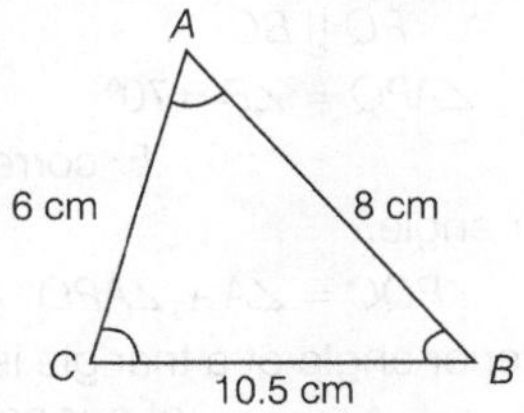

Here, $BC > AB > AC$

$\therefore \angle BAC > \angle ACB > \angle ABC$

[$\because$ angle opposite to longer side is greatest]

Hence, A is false, R is true.

Statement Based Questions

1. (d) **Statement I** We know that if two triangles are congruent, then the sides and angles of one triangle are equal to the corresponding sides and angles of other triangle.

Here, $\Delta ABC \cong \Delta RPQ$

$\therefore \quad AB = RP$, $BC = PQ$ and $AC = RQ$

Hence, it is not true to say that $BC = QR$.

$\therefore$ Statement I is false.

Statement II Given, in ΔABC,

$\angle A = \angle B = \angle C$ ...(i)

We know that the sum of all angles of triangle is 180°.

$\therefore \quad \angle A + \angle B + \angle C = 180°$

$\Rightarrow \quad \angle A + \angle A + \angle A = 180°$ [from Eq. (i)]

$\Rightarrow \quad 3\angle A = 180°$

$\Rightarrow \quad \angle A = 60°$

From Eq. (i), the value of each angle will be 60°.

Hence, Statement II is true.

2. (a) **Statement I** Given, $AB = AC$, $PQ \parallel BC$ and $\angle A = 40°$.

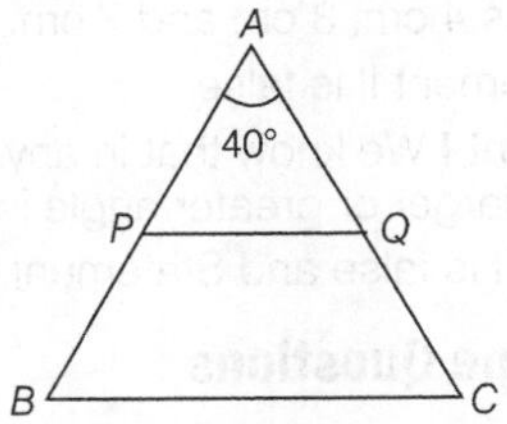

$\because \quad AB = AC$

$\therefore \quad \angle C = \angle B$ ...(i)

[$\because$ angles opposite to equal sides are equal]

Now, $\angle A + \angle B + \angle C = 180°$

[angle sum property of triangle]

$\Rightarrow \quad \angle B + \angle B = 180° - 40° = 140°$

[from Eq. (i) and $\angle A = 40°$ (given)]

$\Rightarrow \quad \angle B = 70^\circ$

$\because \quad PQ \parallel BC$

$\therefore \quad \angle APQ = \angle B = 70^\circ$

[$\because$ corresponding angles]

Now, exterior angle,

$\angle PQC = \angle A + \angle APQ$

[$\because$ exterior angle of a triangle is equal to the sum of opposite interior angles]

$\Rightarrow \quad \angle PQC = 40^\circ + 70^\circ = 110^\circ$

Hence, Statement I is true.

Statement II is also true.

3. (c) As we know that the sum of any two sides of a triangle is greater than the third side.

So, Statement II is false and Statement I is true.

4. (c) **Statement I** Given, in ΔPQR,

$\angle P = 70^\circ$ and $\angle R = 30^\circ$

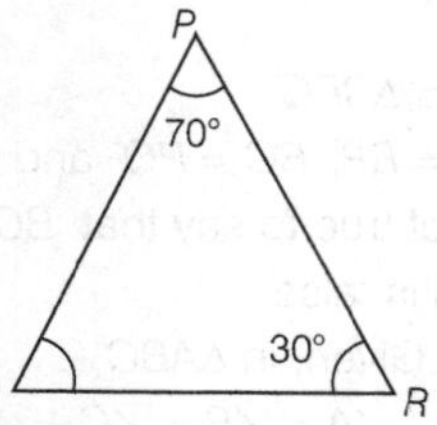

We know that the sum of angles of a triangle is 180°.

$\therefore \quad \angle P + \angle Q + \angle R = 180^\circ \Rightarrow 70^\circ + \angle Q + 30^\circ = 180^\circ$

$\Rightarrow \quad \angle Q = 180^\circ - (70^\circ + 30^\circ) = 80^\circ$

Here, $\angle Q$ is greatest, so side PR is longest.

[$\because$ side opposite to the greatest angle of a triangle is the longest]

Hence, Statement I is true.

Statement II The sum of any two sides of a triangle is greater than its third side.

So, it is not possible to construct a triangle with lengths of its sides as 4 cm, 3 cm and 7 cm.

Hence, Statement II is false.

5. (d) **Statement I** We know that in any triangle, the side opposite to larger or greater angle is largest.

$\therefore$ Statement I is false and Statement II is true.

Short Answer Type Questions

1. Given ΔABC is an isosceles triangle in which

$AB = AC$ and $\angle B = \angle C = \alpha$

Construction Extend the base BC on both sides. Let the points of extension be F and E, forming angles $\angle ABF$ and $\angle ACE$ with the extended lines.

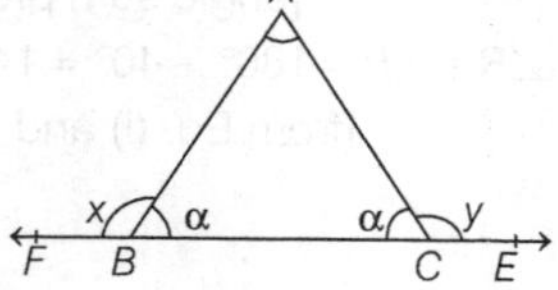

To prove $\angle ABF = \angle ACE \Rightarrow x = y$

Proof We know that the sum of angles on a straight line is 180°.

$\because BC$ is a straight line.

$\therefore \quad x + \alpha = 180^\circ$

$\Rightarrow \quad x = 180^\circ - \alpha \quad \ldots(i)$

and $\quad \alpha + y = 180^\circ \Rightarrow y = 180^\circ - \alpha \quad \ldots(ii)$

Now, from Eqs. (i) and (ii), we get

$x = y$

$\Rightarrow \quad \angle ABF = \angle ACE$ **Hence proved.**

2. Given, $AB = 5$ cm, $\angle B = 40^\circ$ and $\angle A = 80^\circ$

$\because \quad \Delta ABC \cong \Delta FDE$ [given]

$\therefore \quad FD = AB = 5$ cm, $\angle D = \angle B = 40^\circ$, $\angle F = \angle A = 80^\circ$ [by CPCT]

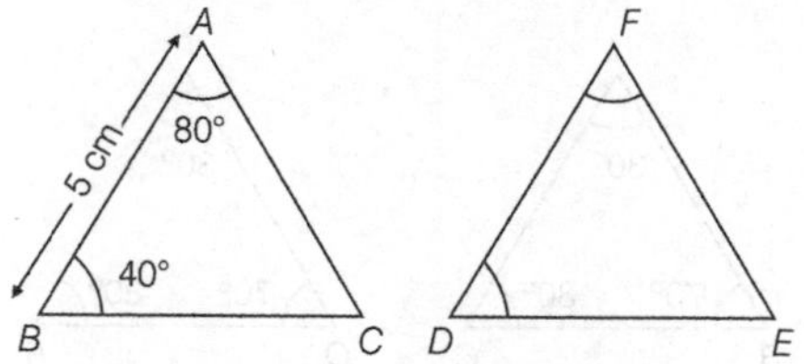

Also, in ΔFDE, $\angle F + \angle D + \angle E = 180^\circ$

[by angle sum property of a triangle]

$\Rightarrow \quad \angle E = 180^\circ - \angle F - \angle D$

$\therefore \quad \angle E = 180^\circ - 80^\circ - 40^\circ$

[$\because \angle D = 40^\circ$ and $\angle F = 80^\circ$]

$= 60^\circ$

Hence, $DF = 5$ cm and $\angle E = 60^\circ$.

3. (i) In ΔAOC and ΔBOD,

$OA = OB$ [given]

$OC = OD$ [given]

$\angle AOC = \angle BOD$

[$\because$ vertically opposite angles]

$\therefore \quad \Delta AOC \cong \Delta BOD$ [by SAS congruence rule]

Hence proved.

(ii) $\angle OBD = \angle OAC$ [by CPCT]

These forms a pair of alternate angles for line segment AC and BD.

Therefore, $AC \parallel BD$. **Hence proved.**

4. Given In quadrilateral $ACBD$,

$AC = AD$ and $\angle BAC = \angle BAD$

To prove $\Delta ABC \cong \Delta ABD$

Proof In ΔABC and ΔABD,

$AC = AD$ [given]

$\angle BAC = \angle BAD$ [given]

and $\quad AB = AB$ [common side]

Thus, $\quad \Delta ABC \cong \Delta ABD$ [by SAS congruence rule]

$\Rightarrow \quad BC = BD$ [by CPCT]

Hence, BC and BD are equal.

5. Given Line l is a perpendicular bisector of AB.

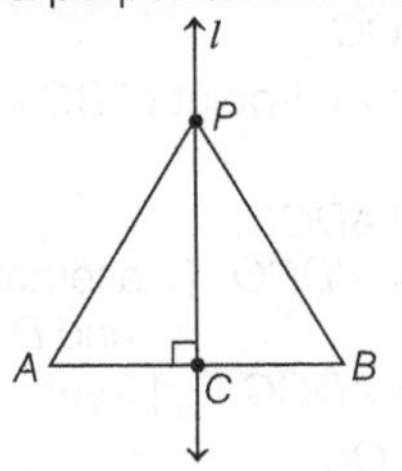

To prove P is equidistant from A and B.

i.e. to prove $PA = PB$

Proof Since, line l is perpendicular bisector of AB.

$\therefore \quad \angle ACP = \angle BCP = 90^\circ \quad \dots(i)$

and $\quad AC = BC \quad \dots(ii)$

[$\because$ C is the mid-point of AB]

In ΔPCA and ΔPCB,

$AC = BC$ [from Eq. (ii)]

$\angle ACP = \angle BCP$ [each 90°, from Eq. (i)]

and $PC = PC$ [common side]

$\therefore \quad \Delta PCA \cong \Delta PCB$ [by SAS congruence rule]

$\Rightarrow \quad PA = PB$ [by CPCT]

Hence proved.

6. (i) In ΔAMC and ΔBMD,

$AM = BM$ [$\because$ M is mid-point of line AB]

$CM = DM$ [given]

and $\angle AMC = \angle BMD$ [$\because$ vertically opposite angles]

$\Delta AMC \cong \Delta BMD$ [by SAS rule]

Hence proved.

(ii) $\angle CAM = \angle DBM$ [by CPCT]

These form a pair of alternate angles.

$\therefore \quad AC \parallel DB$

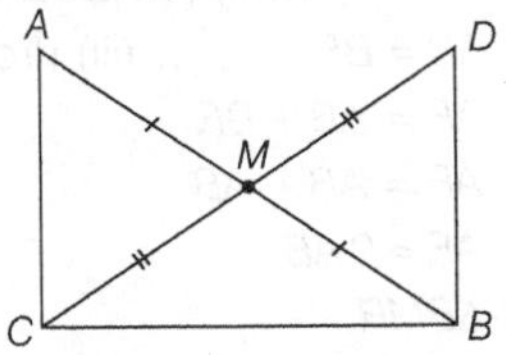

$\therefore \quad \angle C + \angle B = 180^\circ$

[$\because$ interior angles on the same side of transversal]

$\Rightarrow \quad \angle B = 90^\circ$ [$\because \angle C = 90^\circ$]

$\therefore \quad \angle B = \angle C = 90^\circ$ **Hence proved.**

7. In ΔABC and ΔADE,

$AB = AD$ [given]

$\angle BAD = \angle EAC$ [given] ...(i)

On adding $\angle DAC$ both sides of Eq. (i), we get

$\angle BAD + \angle DAC = \angle EAC + \angle DAC$

$\Rightarrow \quad \angle BAC = \angle EAD$

$AC = AE$ [given]

$\therefore \quad \Delta ABC \cong \Delta ADE$ [by SAS congruence rule]

$\Rightarrow \quad BC = DE$ [by CPCT]

Hence proved.

8. Given, $\angle POQ = \angle ROS$

$\Rightarrow \angle POQ - \angle ROQ = \angle ROS - \angle ROQ$

[subtracting $\angle ROQ$ from both sides]

$\Rightarrow \quad \angle POR = \angle QOS$

In ΔPOR and ΔQOS,

$OP = OQ$ [given]

$OR = OS$ [given]

$\angle POR = \angle QOS$ [proved above]

$\therefore \quad \Delta POR \cong \Delta QOS$ [by SAS congruence rule]

$\Rightarrow \quad PR = QS$ [by CPCT]

Hence proved.

9. Given $AD = BC$, $\angle 1 = \angle 2$ and $\angle 3 = \angle 4$

To prove $BD = AC$

Proof Since, $\angle 1 = \angle 2$ and $\angle 3 = \angle 4$

$\therefore \quad \angle 1 + \angle 3 = \angle 2 + \angle 4$

$\Rightarrow \quad \angle DAB = \angle CBA \quad \dots(i)$

Thus, in ΔABD and ΔABC, we have

$AB = AB$ [common side]

and $\angle DAB = \angle CBA$ [from Eq. (i)]

$AD = BC$ [given]

$\therefore \quad \Delta ABD \cong \Delta BAC$ [by SAS congruence rule]

$\Rightarrow \quad BD = AC$ [by CPCT]

Hence proved.

10. Given In ΔPQR, $PQ = PR$ and $\angle QPL = \angle RPL$

To prove (i) $QL = RL$ (ii) $\angle PLQ = 90^\circ$

Proof (i) In ΔQPL and ΔRPL,

$PQ = PR$ [given]

$\angle QPL = \angle RPL$ [$\because$ PL is bisector of $\angle P$]

$PL = PL$ [common]

$\Delta QPL \cong \Delta RPL$ [by SAS congruence rule]

$\Rightarrow \quad QL = RL$ [by CPCT]

Hence proved.

(ii) $\angle PLQ = \angle PLR$ [by CPCT]...(a)

Now, $\angle PLQ + \angle PLR = 180^\circ$ [$\because$ QLR is a straight line]

$\Rightarrow \quad \angle PLQ + \angle PLQ = 180^\circ$ [from Eq. (a)]

$\Rightarrow \quad 2\angle PLQ = 180^\circ$

$\Rightarrow \quad \angle PLQ = 90^\circ$ or $PL \perp QR$

Hence proved.

11. (i) In ΔABD and ΔACE, we have

$\angle B = \angle C$ [given]

$\angle A = \angle A$ [common]

and $AB = AC$ [given]

$\therefore \quad \Delta ABD \cong \Delta ACE$ [by ASA congruence rule]

(ii) $\because \quad \Delta ABD \cong \Delta ACE$

$\therefore \quad BD = CE$ [by CPCT] **Hence proved.**

12. For ΔPBC, $\angle x = \angle B + \angle PCB$

[$\because$ external angle = sum of two internal opposite angles]

For ΔQAB, $\angle y = \angle B + \angle QAB$

[$\because$ external angle = sum of two internal opposite angles]

But $\angle x = \angle y$ [given]

$\Rightarrow$ $\angle B + \angle PCB = \angle B + \angle QAB$

$\Rightarrow$ $\angle PCB = \angle QAB$

In ΔQAB and ΔPCB,

$\angle QAB = \angle PCB$ [proved above]

$\angle B = \angle B$ [common]

$AB = CB$ [given]

$\therefore$ $\Delta QAB \cong \Delta PCB$ [by ASA congruence rule]

$\therefore$ $QA = PC$ [by CPCT]

Hence proved.

13. Given In ΔABC, altitudes are equal

i.e. $AD = BE = CF$

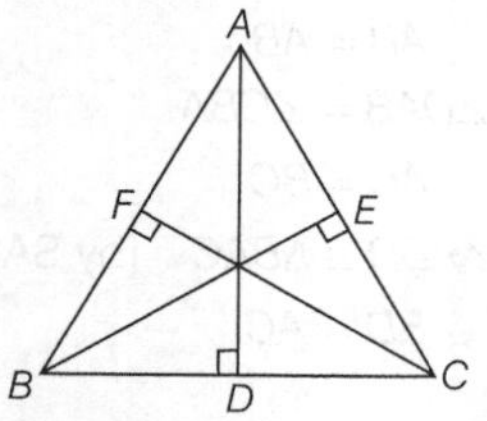

To prove ΔABC is an equilateral triangle i.e. to prove $AB = BC = CA$.

Proof In ΔADC and ΔBEC,

$\angle ADC = \angle BEC$ [each 90°]

$\angle ACD = \angle BCE$ [common angle]

and $AD = BE$ [given]

$\therefore$ $\Delta ADC \cong \Delta BEC$ [by AAS congruence rule]

$\Rightarrow$ $AC = BC$ [by CPCT] ...(i)

Similarly, we can prove that

$\Delta ADB \cong \Delta CFB$ [by AAS congruence rule]

$\Rightarrow$ $AB = CB$ ...(ii)

From Eqs. (i) and (ii), we get

$AB = BC = AC$

Thus, ΔABC is an equilateral triangle. **Hence proved.**

14. Given $AB || CD$ and O is the mid-point of AD.

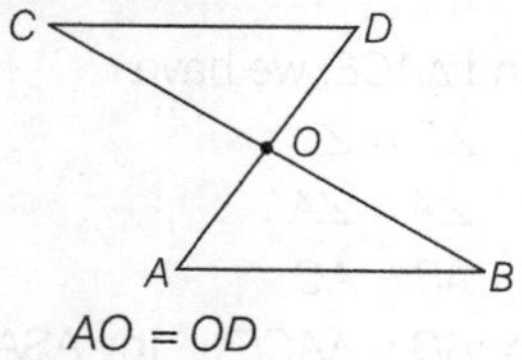

$\therefore$ $AO = OD$ ...(a)

To prove

(i) $\Delta AOB \cong \Delta DOC$

(ii) O is also the mid-point of BC i.e. to prove $OB = OC$.

Proof

(i) In ΔAOB and ΔDOC,

$\angle ABO = \angle DCO$ [$\because$ alternate angles as $AB || CD$ and BC is a transversal line]

$\angle AOB = \angle DOC$ [$\because$ vertically opposite angles]

and $OA = OD$ [from Eq. (a)]

$\therefore$ $\Delta AOB \cong \Delta DOC$ [by AAS congruence rule]

(ii) Using corresponding part of congruent triangles, we get

$OB = OC$

Thus, O is also the mid-point of BC. **Hence proved.**

15. (i) In ΔPAQ and ΔPBQ,

$\angle QPA = \angle QPB$ [$\because$ line l is bisector of $\angle P$]

$\angle PAQ = \angle PBQ$ [each 90°]

and $PQ = PQ$ [common]

$\therefore$ $\Delta PAQ \cong \Delta PBQ$ [by AAS congruence rule]

(ii) $QA = QB$ [by CPCT]

$\Rightarrow$ Q is equidistant from the arms of $\angle P$.

Hence proved.

16. In ΔECD and ΔEBF,

$\angle DEC = \angle FEB$ [vertically opposite angles]

$\angle DCB = \angle EBF$ [$\because$ alternate angles]

and $DE = EF$ [given]

$\therefore$ $\Delta ECD \cong \Delta EBF$ [by AAS congruence rule]

$\Rightarrow$ $CD = BF$ ...(i) [by CPCT]

$\because$ $CD = AB$

...(ii) [$\because$ $ABCD$ is a parallelogram]

$\therefore$ $AB = BF$ ...(iii) [from Eqs. (i) and (ii)]

Then, $AF = AB + BF$

$\Rightarrow$ $AF = AB + AB$ [from Eq. (iii)]

$\Rightarrow$ $AF = 2AB$ **Hence proved.**

17. In ΔDNR and ΔBMR,

$\angle DNR = \angle BMR$

[each 90° because $DN \perp AC$ and $BM \perp AC$]

and $\angle DRN = \angle BRM$

[$\because$ vertically opposite angles]

$DN = BM$ [given]

$\therefore$ $\Delta DNR \cong \Delta BMR$ [by AAS congruence rule]

$\Rightarrow$ $DR = BR$ [by CPCT]

$\Rightarrow$ $DR + BR = BR + BR$ [adding BR both sides]

$\Rightarrow$ $BD = 2BR$ [$\because$ $BD = DR + BR$]

$= 2 \times 8 = 16$ cm [$\because$ $BR = 8$ cm, given]

Hence, the length of BD is 16 cm.

18. Given AD is a median and BL, CM are perpendiculars drawn from B and C respectively on AD produced to M.

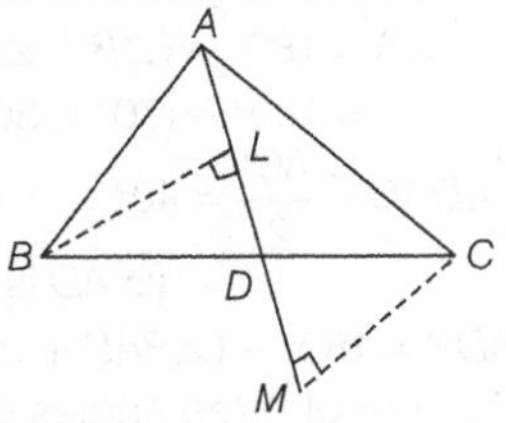

To prove $BL = CM$

Proof In ΔBDL and ΔCDM,

$\angle BLD = \angle CMD$ [each 90°]

$\angle BDL = \angle CDM$ [∵ vertically opposite angles]

and $BD = CD$ [∵ AD is a median, so D is the mid-point of BC]

∴ $\Delta BDL \cong \Delta CDM$ [by AAS congruence rule]

⇒ $BL = CM$ [by CPCT]

Hence proved.

19. Given, $AD \perp BC$ and $AB = AC$

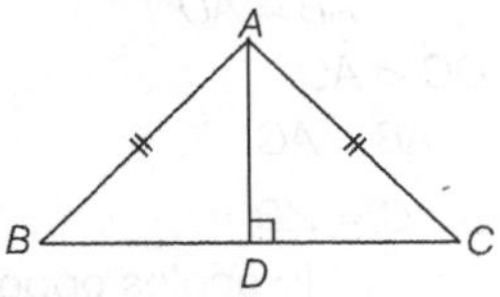

In ΔACB and ΔADC,

$AB = AC$ [given]

$\angle ADB = \angle ADC$ [each 90°]

and $AD = AD$ [common]

∴ $\Delta ADB \cong \Delta ADC$ [by RHS congruence rule]

⇒ $BD = DC$ [by CPCT]

and $\angle BAD = \angle CAD$ [by CPCT]

⇒ AC bisects BC and AD bisects $\angle A$. **Hence proved.**

20. Given $AB \perp BD$, $CD \perp BD$, $AB = CD$ and $AF = CE$.

To prove (i) $\Delta ABF \cong \Delta CDE$ (ii) $BE = FD$

Proof (i) In ΔABF and ΔCDE,

$AB = CD$ [given]

$AF = CE$ [given]

and $\angle ABF = \angle CDE$ [each 90°]

∴ $\Delta ABF \cong \Delta CDE$ [by RHS congruence rule]

Hence proved.

(ii) ∵ $\Delta ABF \cong \Delta CDE$

⇒ $BF = ED$ [by CPCT]

⇒ $BF - EF = ED - EF$ [subtracting EF from both sides]

⇒ $BE = FD$ **Hence proved.**

21. ∵ $CD = BD$ [given]

∴ $\angle CBD = \angle BCD$ ...(i) [∵ angles opposite to equal sides are equal]

and $AC = AB$ [given]

∴ $\angle ABC = \angle ACB$ ...(ii)

On adding Eqs. (i) and (ii), we get

$\angle CBD + \angle ABC = \angle BCD + \angle ACB$

⇒ $\angle ABD = \angle ACD$ **Hence proved.**

22. Given, $PR = PQ \Rightarrow \angle Q = \angle R$

[∵ angles opposite to equal sides are equal]

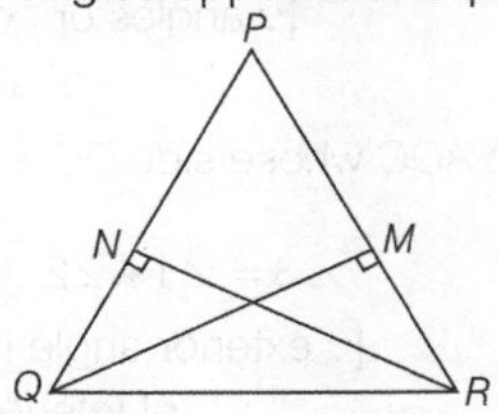

In ΔQMR and ΔRNQ,

$\angle R = \angle Q$ [from above]

$QR = RQ$ [common]

$\angle QMR = \angle RNQ$ [each 90°]

∴ $\Delta QMR \cong \Delta RNQ$ [by AAS congruence rule]

∴ $QM = RN$ [CPCT] **Hence proved.**

23. Given, ΔABC is an isosceles triangle with $AB = AC$.

∴ $\angle ACB = \angle ABC$ ...(i)

[∵ angles opposite to equal sides of a triangle are equal]

Using angle sum property of a triangle,

$\angle ABC + \angle ACB + \angle CAB = 180°$

⇒ $\angle ACB + \angle ACB + 50° = 180°$ [from Eq. (i)]

⇒ $2\angle ACB = 130° \Rightarrow \angle ACB = 65°$

Since, $LM \parallel BC$.

∴ $\angle LMC + \angle BCM = 180°$ [∵ co-interior angles]

⇒ $\angle LMC + 65° = 180°$ [∵ $\angle BCM = \angle ACB$]

⇒ $\angle LMC = 115°$

Hence, the value of $\angle LMC$ is 115°.

24. In ΔABC, $BC = AC$ [given]

∴ $\angle BAC = P$

[∵ angles opposite to equal sides are equal]

In ΔACD, $\angle ACD = P + P$

[∵ external angle = sum of two internal opposite angles]

⇒ $\angle ACD = 2P$ and $AC = AD$ [given]

∴ $\angle ADC = 2P$

[∵ angles opposite to equal sides are equal]

In ΔABD, $\angle EAD = \angle ABD + \angle ADB$

[∵ external angle = sum of two internal opposite angles]

⇒ $98° = P + 2P$ [∵ $\angle ADB = \angle ADC$]

⇒ $3P = 98° \Rightarrow P = \left(\frac{98}{3}\right)^{\circ} = 32°40'$

Hence, the value of P is 32°40′.

25. Given $AB = BC$ and $AC = CD$

To prove $\angle BAD : \angle ADB = 3 : 1$

Proof $\because CA = CD$ [given]

$\therefore \quad \angle 1 = \angle 2 = x$ (say) ...(i)

[$\because$ angles opposite to equal sides of a triangle are equal]

Considering ΔADC whose side DC is extended to B, we have

$$\angle 3 = \angle 1 + \angle 2$$

[$\because$ exterior angle is equal to the sum of interior opposite angles]

$\Rightarrow \quad \angle 3 = x + x = 2x$ ...(ii)

Also, $\quad BA = BC$ [given]

$\Rightarrow \quad \angle 3 = \angle 4$ ...(iii)

[$\because$ angles opposite to equal sides of a triangle are equal]

From Eqs. (ii) and (iii), we get

$\angle 4 = 2x$ ...(iv)

Now, $\angle BAD = \angle BAC + \angle CAD = \angle 4 + \angle 2$

$= 2x + x = 3x$ [from Eqs. (i) and (iv)]

Thus, $\angle BAD : \angle ADB = 3x : x$

$\Rightarrow \quad \angle BAD : \angle ADB = 3 : 1$ **Hence proved.**

26. Given, ΔABC is an isosceles triangle in which

$AB = AC$ ...(i)

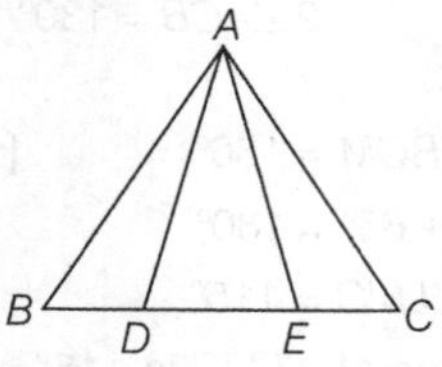

and D, E are points on BC such that

$BE = CD$ ...(ii)

Since, $\quad AB = AC$

So, $\quad \angle C = \angle B$ ...(iii)

[$\because$ angles opposite to equal sides are equal]

From Eq. (ii), we get

$BE = CD$

$\Rightarrow \quad BE - DE = CD - DE$

[subtracting DE from both sides]

$\Rightarrow \quad BD = CE$ ...(iv)

In ΔABD and ΔACE, $\quad AB = AC$ [from Eq. (i)]

$\angle B = \angle C$ [from Eq. (iii)]

and $\quad BD = CE$ [from Eq. (iv)]

$\therefore \quad \Delta ABD \cong \Delta ACE$

[by SAS congruence rule]

$\Rightarrow \quad AD = AE$ [by CPCT]

27. Given AD is the bisector of $\angle BAC$.

In ΔABC, sum of three angles of a triangle is 180°.

$\therefore \quad \angle A = 180° - (\angle B + \angle C)$

$= 180° - (70° + 30°) = 80°$

$\Rightarrow \quad \angle BAD = \angle DAC = \dfrac{80°}{2} = 40°$

[$\because AD$ is the bisector of $\angle A$]

In ΔABD, $\angle ADB = 180° - (\angle BAD + \angle ABD)$

[$\because$ sum of three angles of a triangle is 180°]

$= 180° - (40° + 70°) = 70°$

Thus, $\angle DBA = \angle ADB$

$\Rightarrow \quad AD = AB$ [$\because$ sides opposite to equal angles of a triangle are equal]

In ΔADC, $\angle ADC = 180° - (\angle DAC + \angle ACD)$

[$\because$ sum of three angles of a triangle is 180°]

$= 180° - (40° + 30°) = 110°$

Thus, in ΔADC, $\angle DCA < \angle CAD < \angle ADC$

[$\because \angle DCA = 30°$, $\angle CAD = 40°$ and $\angle ADC = 110°$]

$\Rightarrow \quad AD < DC < AC$

But $\quad AB = AD$

Hence, $AB < DC < AC$.

28. Given, $\quad AB = AC$

$\therefore \quad \angle C = \angle B$ ...(i)

[$\because$ angles opposite to equal sides of a triangle are equal]

Also, $\quad DE \parallel AC$

$\angle DEB = \angle C$ [$\because$ corresponding angles] ...(ii)

From Eqs. (i) and (ii), we get

$\angle B = \angle DEB$

Hence, $\quad DE = DB$ [$\because$ sides opposite to equal angles of a triangle are equal]

Thus, $\quad DE = 1.5$ cm [$\because DB = 1.5$ cm, given]

29. (i) In ΔBDE and ΔCEF,

$DE = FE$ [given]

$BE = CE$ [given]

and $\quad \angle EDB = \angle EFC$ [each 90°]

$\therefore \quad \Delta BDE \cong \Delta CFE$ [by RHS congruency rule]

$\therefore \quad \angle B = \angle C$ [by CPCT]

$\Rightarrow \quad AB = AC$

[$\because$ side opposite to equal angles are equal]

Hence proved.

(ii) In ΔAED and ΔAFE,

$\angle ADE = \angle AFE$ [each 90°]

$AE = AE$ [common side]

and $\quad DE = EF$ [given]

$\therefore \quad \Delta AED \cong \Delta AEF$ [by RHS congruency rule]

$\therefore \quad AD = AF$ [by CPCT]

Hence proved.

30. Given In ΔABD, $OA = OB$

To Prove ΔABD is an isosceles triangle.

Construction Produced DO upto C such that $OD = OC$.

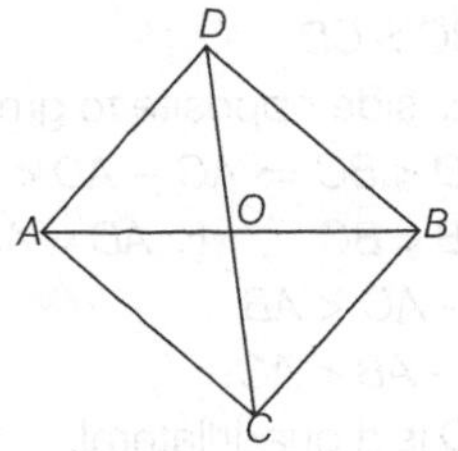

Proof In ΔAOD and ΔCOB,

$OD = OC$ [by construction]

$AO = OB$ [given]

$\angle DOA = \angle COB$

[$\because$ vertically opposite angles]

$\therefore$ $\Delta AOD \cong \Delta BOC$ [by SAS congruency rule]

$\Rightarrow$ $AD = BC$ ...(i) [by CPCT]

$\Rightarrow$ $\angle ADO = \angle BCO$ ...(ii) [by CPCT]

and $\angle ADO = \angle BDO$ ...(iii)

[$\because$ DO is the bisector of $\angle ADB$]

From Eqs. (ii) and (iii), we get

$\angle BCO = \angle BDO$

$\Rightarrow$ $BD = BC$ ...(iv)

[$\because$ sides opposite to equal angles are equal]

From Eqs. (i) and (iv), we get

$AD = BD$

Hence, ΔABD is an isosceles triangle.

31. $\angle CXZ = \angle YXZ$

[$\because$ XZ is the bisector of $\angle CXY$] ...(i)

$\because$ $XZ \parallel AC$ and XC is a transversal.

$\therefore$ $\angle CXZ = \angle ACX$

[$\because$ alternate interior angles] ...(ii)

Also, $XZ \parallel AC$ and AX is transversal.

$\therefore$ $\angle YXZ = \angle XAC$

[$\because$ corresponding angles] ...(iii)

Now, from Eqs. (i), (ii) and (iii), we get

$\angle XAC = \angle ACX$

$\Rightarrow$ $XC = AX$ ...(iv)

[$\because$ sides opposite to equal angles are equal]

Similarly, $YC = YB$ ...(v)

Now, $AB = AX + XY + YB$

$= XC + XY + YC$ [from Eqs. (iv) and (v)]

Hence, AB is the perimeter of ΔXYC. **Hence proved.**

32. Given, $AB = 8.5$ cm, $BC = 6$ cm and $CA = 7.2$ cm

$\therefore$ $AB > CA > BC \Rightarrow \angle C > \angle B > \angle A$

[$\because$ angle opposite to longer side is greater]

On multiplying each term of an inequality by -1, we get

$-\angle C < -\angle B < -\angle A$

[when we multiply the '–ve' sign, the sign of inequality will be reverse]

On adding 180° in each term, we get

$(180° - \angle C) < (180° - \angle B) < (180° - \angle A)$

$\Rightarrow$ $z < y < x$

Hence, angles in ascending order are z, y and x.

33. Given In quadrilateral $ABCD$, AB is the smallest and CD is the largest side.

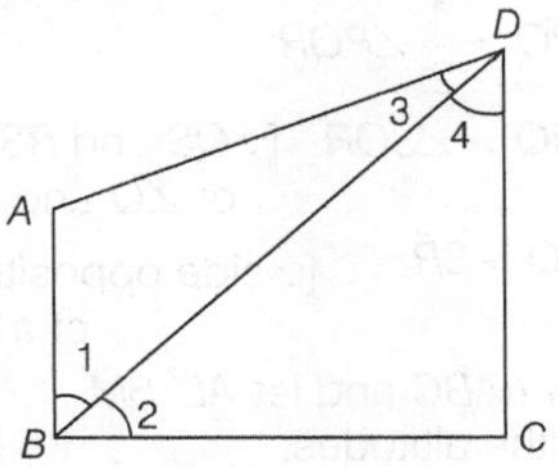

To prove $\angle D < \angle B$.

Construction Join BD.

Proof Now, in ΔABD, $AD > AB$

[$\because$ AB is the smallest side in $ABCD$]

$\Rightarrow$ $\angle 1 > \angle 3$ ...(i)

[$\because$ angle opposite to largest side of a triangle is greater]

In ΔBCD, $CD > BC$

[$\because$ CD is the largest side in $ABCD$]

$\Rightarrow$ $\angle 2 > \angle 4$ ...(ii)

[$\because$ angle opposite to larger side is greater]

On adding Eqs. (i) and (ii), we get

$\angle 1 + \angle 2 > \angle 3 + \angle 4$

$\Rightarrow$ $\angle B > \angle D$ **Hence proved.**

34. Given In ΔABC, $AD = AC$

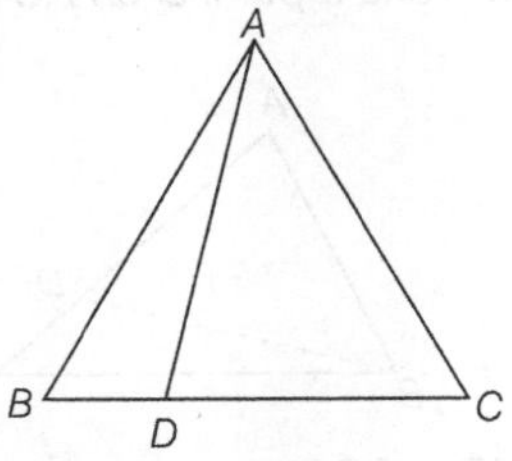

To prove $AB > AD$

Proof Since, $AD = AC$

$\therefore$ $\angle ACD = \angle ADC$ ...(i)

[$\because$ angles opposite to equal sides of a triangle are equal]

Now, $\angle ADC$ is an exterior angle of ΔABD.

$\therefore$ $\angle ADC > \angle ABD$

[$\because$ exterior angle is greater than interior opposite angles]

$\Rightarrow$ $\angle ACD > \angle ABD$ [from Eq. (i)]

$\Rightarrow \quad \angle ACB > \angle ABC$

[$\because \angle ABD = \angle ABC$ and $\angle ACD = \angle ACB$]

$\Rightarrow \quad AB > AC$ [$\because$ side opposite to greater angle in a triangle is greater]

$\therefore \quad AB > AD$ [$\because AD = AC$, given]

Hence proved.

35. Given, $PQ > PR$

$\Rightarrow \quad \angle PRQ > \angle PQR$ [$\because$ angle opposite to longer side is greater]

$\Rightarrow \quad \frac{1}{2}\angle PRQ > \frac{1}{2}\angle PQR$ [dividing by 2]

$\Rightarrow \quad \angle SRQ > \angle SQR$ [$\because QS$ and RS are the bisectors of $\angle Q$ and $\angle R$, respectively]

$\therefore \quad SQ > SR$ [$\because$ side opposite to greater angle of a triangle is longer]

36. Consider, a ΔABC and let AL, BM and CN be the altitudes.

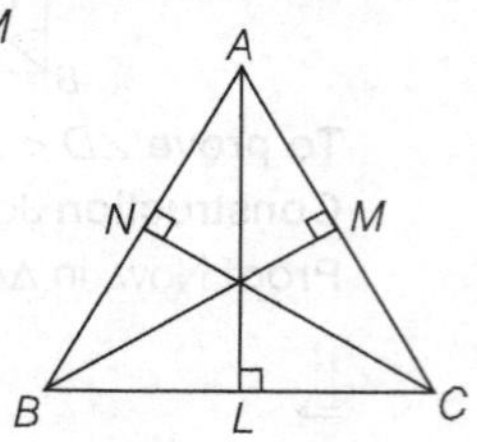

To prove

$AL + BM + CN < AB + BC + AC$

Proof Clearly, the perpendicular AL drawn from the point A to the line BC is shorter than the line segment AB drawn from point A to the line BC.

$\therefore \quad AL < AB$ ...(i)

Similarly, $\quad BM < BC$ ...(ii)

and $\quad CN < AC$ ...(iii)

On adding Eqs. (i), (ii) and (iii), we get

$AL + BM + CN < AB + BC + AC$ **Hence proved.**

37. Consider a ΔABC.

To prove $AC - AB < BC$, $BC - AC < AB$ and $BC - AB < AC$

Construction Take a point D on AC such that $AD = AB$ and join BD.

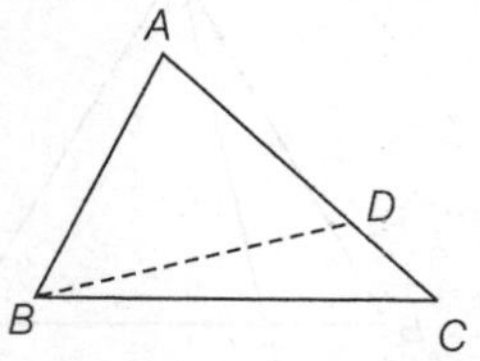

Proof In ΔABD, $\angle BDC$ is an exterior angle.

$\therefore \quad \angle BDC > \angle ABD$ ...(i)

[$\because$ exterior angle is greater than opposite interior angles]

In ΔBDC, $\angle ADB$ is an exterior angle.

$\therefore \quad \angle ADB > \angle DBC$ ...(ii)

[$\because$ exterior angle is greater than opposite interior angles]

In $\quad \Delta ABD, AB = AD$ [by construction]

$\Rightarrow \quad \angle ADB = \angle ABD$ ...(iii)

[$\because$ angles opposite to equal sides are equal]

From Eqs. (i) and (iii), we get

$\angle BDC > \angle ADB$ ...(iv)

$\Rightarrow \quad \angle BDC > \angle DBC$ [from Eq. (ii)]

$\Rightarrow \quad BC > CD$

[$\because$ side opposite to greater angle is larger]

$\Rightarrow \quad CD < BC \Rightarrow AC - AD < BC$

$\Rightarrow \quad AC - AB < BC$ [$\because AD = AB$, by construction]

Similarly, $BC - AC < AB$

and $\quad BC - AB < AC$. **Hence proved.**

38. Given $ABCD$ is a quadrilateral.

To prove $AB + BC + CD + DA < 2(BD + AC)$

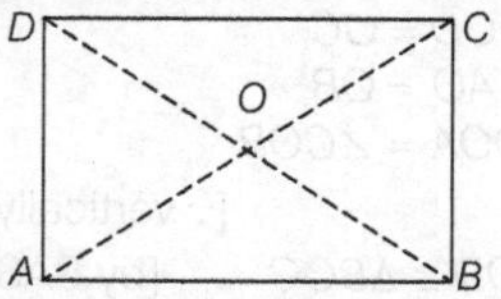

Proof In ΔOAB, $OA + OB > AB$ ...(i)

[$\because$ sum of any two sides of a triangle is greater than the third side]

Similarly, in ΔOBC,

$OB + OC > BC$ ...(ii)

In ΔOCD, $\quad OC + OD > CD$ ...(iii)

and in ΔODA, $OD + OA > DA$ ...(iv)

On adding Eqs. (i), (ii), (iii) and (iv), we get

$2[OA + OB + OC + OD] > AB + BC + CD + DA$

$\Rightarrow \quad 2[(OA + OC) + (OB + OD)] > AB + BC + CD + DA$

$\Rightarrow \quad 2(AC + BD) > AB + BC + CD + DA$

[$\because OA + OC = AC$ and $OB + OD = BD$]

$\Rightarrow AB + BC + CD + DA < 2(BD + AC)$ **Hence proved.**

39. Given In $\Delta PQR, S$ is any point on side QR.

To prove $PQ + QR + RP > 2PS$

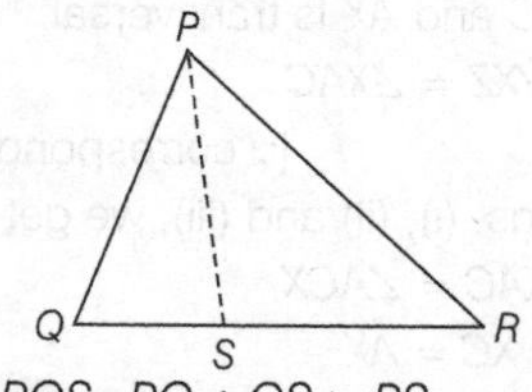

Proof In ΔPQS, $PQ + QS > PS$ ...(i)

[$\because$ sum of any two sides of a triangle is greater than the third side]

Similarly, in $\Delta PRS, SR + RP > PS$ ...(ii)

[$\because$ sum of any two sides of a triangle is greater than the third side]

On adding Eqs. (i) and (ii), we get

$PQ + QS + SR + RP > 2PS$

$\Rightarrow \quad PQ + (QS + SR) + RP > 2PS$

$\Rightarrow \quad PQ + QR + RP > 2PS$ [$\because QR = QS + SR$]

Hence proved.

40. Given T is a mid-point of side QR of ΔPQR and S is a point such that $RT = ST$.

To prove $PQ + PR > QS$

Proof In ΔPQR, $PQ + PR > QR$

[$\because$ sum of any two sides of a triangle is greater than the third side]

$\Rightarrow \quad PQ + PR > QT + RT \quad [\because QR = QT + RT]$

$\Rightarrow \quad PQ + PR > QT + ST \quad [\because RT = ST$, given$]$ ...(i)

In ΔQST, $QT + ST > QS$ ...(ii)

[$\because$ sum of any two sides of a triangle is greater than the third side]

From Eqs. (i) and (ii), we get

$PQ + PR > QS$ **Hence proved.**

41. Consider a ΔABC and let AD be the median drawn to side BC.

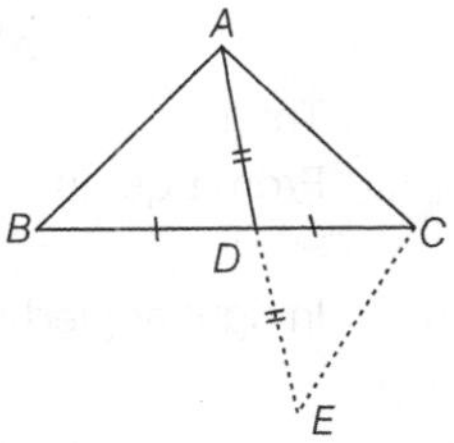

To prove $AB + AC > 2AD$

Construction Produce AD upto a point E such that $AD = DE$ i.e. $AE = 2AD$. Also, join C and E.

Proof As we know that sum of any two sides of a triangle is greater than the third side.

$\therefore$ In ΔACE, $AC + CE > AE$

i.e. $\quad AC + CE > 2AD$ ...(i)

Now, we will prove that $AB = CE$.

Consider ΔADB and ΔEDC

Clearly, $\angle ADB = \angle EDC$ [$\because$ vertically opposite angles]

$AD = DE$ [by construction]

and $\quad BD = DC$ [$\because D$ is mid-point of BC]

$\Rightarrow \quad \Delta ADB \cong \Delta EDC$ [by SAS congruence rule]

$\Rightarrow \quad AB = EC$ [by CPCT] ...(ii)

Now, from Eqs. (i) and (ii), we get

$AB + AC > 2AD$ **Hence proved.**

42. Consider a ΔABC and let AD, BE and CF are the medians of ΔABC.

We know that the sum of any two sides of a triangle is greater than twice the median drawn to the third side.

$\therefore \quad AB + AC > 2AD$ ...(i)

$AB + BC > 2BE$ ...(ii)

and $\quad BC + AC > 2CF$ ...(iii)

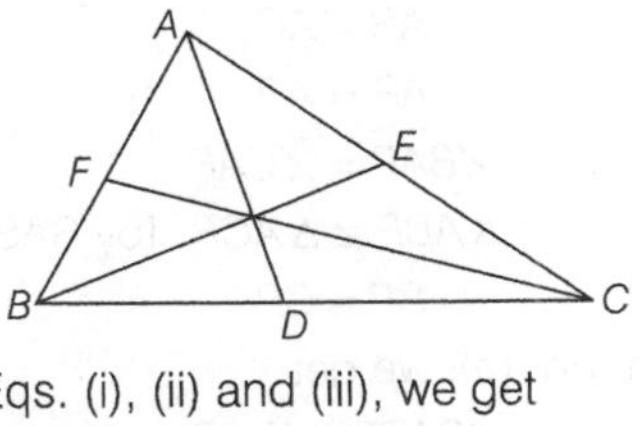

On adding Eqs. (i), (ii) and (iii), we get

$2(AB + BC + AC) > 2(AD + BE + CF)$

$\therefore \quad AB + BC + AC > AD + BE + CF$

Hence, the perimeter of a triangle is greater than the sum of its three medians. **Hence proved.**

Long Answer Type Questions

1.

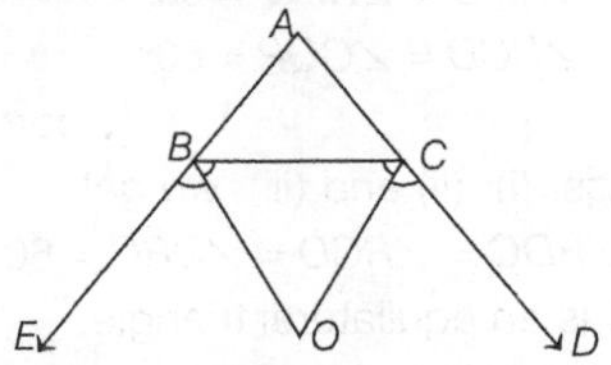

Now, $\angle CBE + \angle ABC = 180°$

[$\because$ the sum of the angles formed on a straight line is 180°]

$\Rightarrow \quad \angle CBE = 180° - \angle ABC$ ...(i)

$\Rightarrow \quad \angle CBO = \frac{1}{2} \times \angle CBE$

[$\because BO$ is the bisector of $\angle CBE$]

$\Rightarrow \quad \angle CBO = \frac{1}{2}[180° - \angle ABC]$ [from Eq. (i)]

$\Rightarrow \quad \angle CBO = 90° - \frac{1}{2}\angle ABC$ ...(ii)

Similarly, $\quad \angle BCD = 180° - \angle ACB$ ...(iii)

$\Rightarrow \quad \angle BCO = \frac{1}{2} \times \angle BCD$

[$\because CO$ is the bisector of $\angle BCD$]

$\Rightarrow \quad \angle BCO = \frac{1}{2}(180° - \angle ACB)$ [from Eq. (iii)]

$\Rightarrow \quad \angle BCO = 90° - \frac{1}{2} \times \angle ACB$ ...(iv)

Now, in ΔOBC,

$\angle BOC + \angle CBO + \angle BCO = 180°$

[$\because$ angle sum property of triangle]

$\Rightarrow \quad \angle BOC = 180° - (\angle CBO + \angle BCO)$

$\Rightarrow \quad \angle BOC = 180° - (90° - \frac{1}{2}\angle ABC + 90° - \frac{1}{2}\angle ACB)$

[from Eqs. (ii) and (iv)]

$\Rightarrow \quad \angle BOC = 180° - (180° - \frac{1}{2}\angle ABC - \frac{1}{2}\angle ACB)$

$\Rightarrow \quad \angle BOC = 180° - 180° + \frac{1}{2}(\angle ABC + \angle ACB)$

$\Rightarrow \quad \angle BOC = \frac{1}{2}(\angle ABC + \angle ACB)$ ...(v)

Now, in ΔABC, $\angle ABC + \angle ACB + \angle BAC = 180°$

[$\because$ angle sum property of triangle]

$\Rightarrow \quad \angle ABC + \angle ACB = 180° - \angle BAC$

Now, on putting the value of $\angle ABC + \angle ACB$ in Eq. (v), we get

$\angle BOC = \frac{1}{2}(180° - \angle BAC)$

$\Rightarrow \quad \angle BOC = 90° - \frac{1}{2}\angle BAC$ **Hence proved.**

2. Given, ΔPQR is an equilateral triangle.

$\therefore \quad PQ = QR = PR = 20$ cm

and $\quad \angle P = \angle Q = \angle R = 60^\circ \quad$ ...(i)

$\because DC \parallel PQ$ and PD and CQ are transversal.

$\therefore \quad \angle RDC = \angle RPQ = 60^\circ \quad$ ...(ii)

and $\quad \angle RCD = \angle CQP = 60^\circ \quad$ ...(iii)

[$\because$ corresponding angles]

From Eqs. (i), (ii) and (iii), we get

$\angle RDC = \angle RCD = \angle DRC = 60^\circ$

$\therefore \Delta RDC$ is an equilateral triangle.

Similarly, ΔPAD and ΔBQC are also equilateral triangles.

Now, let $DC = CR = RD = x \quad$ ...(iv)

$AD = AP = PD = y \quad$ ...(v)

and $\quad CQ = CB = BQ = z \quad$ ...(vi)

Now, $\quad DC + DA + CB = 25$ cm $\quad$ [given]

$\Rightarrow \quad x + y + z = 25$ cm $\quad$ ...(vii)

[from Eqs. (iv), (v) and (vi)]

Now, from figure

$PR + PQ + QR = PD + DR + PA + AB + BQ + QC + CR$

$\Rightarrow \quad 20 + 20 + 20 = y + x + y + AB + z + z + x$

$\Rightarrow \quad 60 = 2x + 2y + 2z + AB$

$\Rightarrow \quad 60 = 2(x + y + z) + AB$

$\Rightarrow \quad 60 = 2 \times 25 + AB \quad$ [from Eq. (vii)]

$\Rightarrow \quad 60 = 50 + AB \Rightarrow AB = 10$ cm

Hence, the value of AB is 10 cm.

3. (i) We know that each angle of a square is 90°.

$\therefore \angle ABM = \angle DBC = 90^\circ$

$\Rightarrow \angle ABM + \angle ABC = \angle DBC + \angle ABC$

[adding $\angle ABC$ on both sides]

$\Rightarrow \quad \angle MBC = \angle ABD \quad$ ...(a)

Now, in ΔMBC and ΔABD,

$\angle MBC = \angle ABD \quad$ [from Eq. (a)]

$MB = AB \quad$ [sides of square $ABMN$]

and $\quad BC = BD \quad$ [sides of square $BCDE$]

$\therefore \quad \Delta MBC \cong \Delta ABD$ [by SAS congruency rule]

(ii) We know that each angle of a square is 90°.

$\therefore \quad \angle FCA = \angle BCE = 90^\circ$

$\Rightarrow \quad \angle FCA + \angle ACB = \angle BCE + \angle ACB$

[adding $\angle ACB$ both on sides]

$\Rightarrow \quad \angle FCB = \angle ACE \quad$ ...(b)

Now, in ΔFCB and ΔACE,

$FC = AC \quad$ [sides of square $ACFG$]

$CB = CE \quad$ [sides of square $BCED$]

and $\quad \angle FCB = \angle ACE \quad$ [from Eq. (b)]

$\therefore \quad \Delta FCB \cong \Delta ACE$

[by SAS congruency rule]

Hence proved.

4. Given QX and RX are the bisectors of $\angle PQR$ and $\angle PRQ$, respectively. Also, $XS \perp QR$ and $XT \perp PQ$.

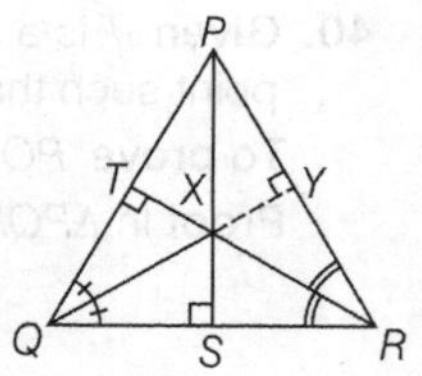

To prove $\Delta XTQ \cong \Delta XSQ$ and PX bisects $\angle P$.

Construction Draw $XY \perp PR$

Proof In ΔXTQ and ΔXSQ, we have

$\angle TQX = \angle SQX$

[$\because QX$ is the bisector of $\angle PQR$]

$\angle XTQ = \angle XSQ \quad$ [each 90°]

and $\quad QX = QX \quad$ [common side]

$\therefore \quad \Delta XTQ \cong \Delta XSQ$ [by AAS congruence rule]

Then, $\quad XT = XS \quad$ [by CPCT] ...(i)

Similarly, it can be proved that

$\Delta XSR \cong \Delta XYR$ [by AAS congruence rule]

Then, $\quad XS = XY \quad$ [by CPCT]...(ii)

From Eqs. (i) and (ii), we get

$XT = XY$

In right angled ΔXTP and ΔXYP, we have

$XT = XY \quad$ [proved above]

$\angle XTP = \angle XYP \quad$ [each 90°]

and $\quad XP = XP \quad$ [common side]

$\therefore \quad \Delta XTP \cong \Delta XYP$ [by RHS congruence rule]

Then, $\quad \angle XPT = \angle XPY \quad$ [by CPCT]

Therefore, PX bisects $\angle P$.

Hence, $\Delta XTQ \cong \Delta XSQ$ and PX bisects $\angle P$.

Hence proved.

5. Given ΔABC and ΔDBC are two isosceles triangles in which $AB = AC$ and $BD = DC$.

To prove

(i) $\Delta ABD \cong \Delta ACD$ (ii) $\Delta ABP \cong \Delta ACP$

(iii) AP bisects $\angle A$ as well as $\angle D$.

Proof (i) In ΔABD and ΔACD,

$AB = AC \quad$ [given]

$BD = DC \quad$ [given]

and $\quad AD = AD \quad$ [common side]

$\therefore \quad \Delta ABD \cong \Delta ACD$ [by SSS congruence rule]

Hence proved.

$\Rightarrow \quad \angle BAD = \angle CAD \quad$ [by CPCT] ...(a)

(ii) In ΔABP and ΔACP,

$AB = AC \quad$ [given]

$AP = AP \quad$ [common]

and $\quad \angle BAP = \angle CAP \quad$ [from Eq. (a)]

$\therefore \quad \Delta ABP \cong \Delta ACP$ [by SAS congruence rule]

$\Rightarrow \quad BP = CP \quad$ [by CPCT] ...(b)

(iii) From Eq. (a), we get

$\angle BAD = \angle CAD$

$\therefore AD$ bisects $\angle A \Rightarrow AP$ bisects $\angle A$

Now, in ΔBDP and ΔCDP,

$BP = CP$ [from Eq. (b)]

$DP = PD$ [common]

and $BD = DC$ [given]

$\therefore \Delta BDP \cong \Delta CDP$ [by SSS congruence rule]

$\Rightarrow \angle BDP = \angle CDP$ [by CPCT]

$\therefore DP$ bisects $\angle BDC$

$\Rightarrow AP$ bisects $\angle BDC$ **Hence proved.**

6. Given, BC is a line segment. A and D are points on opposite sides of BC such that

$AB = AC$ ...(i)

and $DB = DC$ ...(ii)

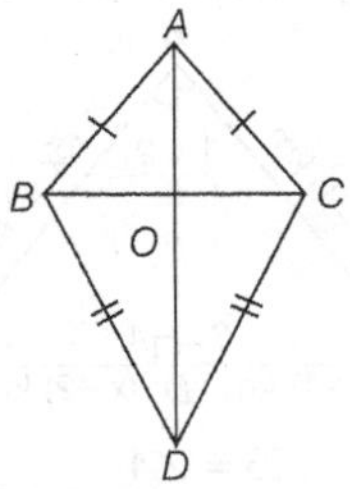

In ΔABD and ΔACD,

$AB = AC$ [from Eq. (i)]

$DB = DC$ [from Eq. (ii)]

and $AD = AD$ [common side]

$\therefore \Delta ABD \cong \Delta ACD$

[by SSS congruence rule]

Then, $\angle BAD = \angle CAD$ [by CPCT]

or $\angle BAO = \angle CAO$ ...(iii)

In ΔABO and ΔACO,

$AB = AC$ [from Eq. (i)]

$\angle BAO = \angle CAO$ [from Eq. (iii)]

and $AO = AO$ [common side]

$\therefore \Delta ABO \cong \Delta ACO$

[by SAS congruence rule]

Then, $BO = CO$ [by CPCT] ... (iv)

and $\angle AOB = \angle AOC$ [by CPCT] ...(v)

Since, BC is a line and OA is a ray on it.

$\therefore \angle AOB + \angle AOC = 180^\circ$ [by linear pair axiom]

$\Rightarrow \angle AOB + \angle AOB = 180^\circ$ [from Eq. (v)]

$\Rightarrow 2\angle AOB = 180^\circ$

$\Rightarrow \angle AOB = \dfrac{180^\circ}{2}$

$\Rightarrow \angle AOB = 90^\circ$

Thus, $BO = CO$ [from Eq. (iv)]

and $\angle AOB = 90^\circ = \angle AOC$

Hence, AD is the perpendicular bisector of BC.

Hence proved.

7. In ΔPQN and ΔABM,

$\angle PNQ = \angle AMB$ [each 90°]

$PQ = AB$ [given]

$PN = AM$ [given]

$\therefore \Delta PQN \cong \Delta ABM$

[by RHS congruence rule]

$\therefore QN = BM$ [CPCT] ...(i)

In ΔPNR and ΔAMC, we get

$\angle PNR = \angle AMC$ [each 90°]

$PR = AC$ [given]

$PN = AM$ [given]

$\therefore \Delta PNR \cong \Delta AMC$

[by RHS congruence rule]

$\therefore NR = MC$ [CPCT] ...(ii)

On adding Eqs. (i) and (ii), we get

$QN + NR = BM + MC$

$\Rightarrow QR = BC$ ...(iii)

In ΔPQR and ΔABC,

$PQ = AB$ [given]

$PR = AC$ [given]

$QR = BC$ [from Eq. (iii)]

$\therefore \Delta PQR \cong \Delta ABC$ [by SSS congruence rule]

Hence proved.

8. In ΔACD,

$\because AD = AC$ [given]

$\therefore \angle ACD = \angle ADC$

[$\because$ angles opposite to equal sides are equal]

$\Rightarrow \angle ACD = 75^\circ$ [$\because \angle ADC = 75^\circ$]

Now, in ΔACD,

$\angle CAD + \angle ACD + \angle ADC = 180^\circ$

[angle sum property of triangle]

$\Rightarrow x + 75^\circ + 75^\circ = 180^\circ$

$\Rightarrow x = 180^\circ - 150^\circ \Rightarrow x = 30^\circ$

Also, in ΔABC,

$120^\circ = p + z$ ...(i) [$\because$ exterior angle property]

and in ΔACD,

$p = x + 75^\circ$ ...(ii) [$\because$ exterior angle property]

and in ΔADE,

$75^\circ = y + 52^\circ$ ...(iii) [$\because$ exterior angle property]

$\Rightarrow y = 75^\circ - 52^\circ \Rightarrow y = 23^\circ$

On putting the value of x in Eq. (ii), we get

$p = 30^\circ + 75^\circ$

$p = 105^\circ$

Now, on putting the value of p in Eq. (i), we get

$120^\circ = 105^\circ + z$

$z = 120^\circ - 105^\circ = 15^\circ$

Hence, the values of x, y, z and p are 30°, 23°, 15° and 105°, respectively.

9. In ΔABC,

$$\angle B = 2\angle C$$

$\Rightarrow \quad \angle B = 2y \quad [\because \angle C = y]$

Since, AD is the bisector of $\angle BAC$.

So, let $\angle BAD = \angle CAD = x$

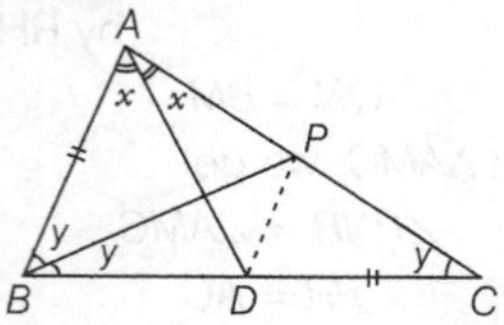

Let BP be the bisector of $\angle ABC$. Join PD.

In ΔBPC, $\angle CBP = \angle BCP = y$

$\Rightarrow \quad PC = BP \quad \ldots(i)$

[$\because$ sides opposite to equal angles of a triangle are equal]

In ΔABP and ΔDCP,

$\angle ABP = \angle DCP = y$

[$\because \angle ABP = \angle CBP = y$ and $\angle DCP = \angle BCP = y$]

$AB = DC$ [given]

and $BP = PC$ [from Eq. (i)]

$\therefore \quad \Delta ABP \cong \Delta DCP$ [by SAS congruence rule]

$\Rightarrow \quad \angle BAP = \angle CDP$ and $AP = DP$ [by CPCT]

$\Rightarrow \quad \angle CDP = 2x \quad [\because \angle BAP = 2x]$

and $\angle ADP = \angle DAP = x$

[$\because$ angles opposite to equal sides of a triangle are equal]

In ΔABD, $\angle ADC = \angle ABD + \angle BAD$

[$\because$ exterior angle of a triangle is equal to the sum of opposite interior angles]

$\Rightarrow \quad \angle ADP + \angle PDC = \angle ABD + \angle BAD$

[$\because \angle ADC = \angle ADP + \angle PDC$]

$\Rightarrow \quad x + 2x = 2y + x$

$\Rightarrow \quad x = y \quad \ldots(ii)$

In ΔABC, $\angle A + \angle B + \angle C = 180^\circ$

[by angle sum property of a triangle]

$\Rightarrow \quad 2x + 2y + y = 180^\circ$

$\Rightarrow \quad 2x + 2x + x = 180^\circ$ [from Eq. (ii)]

$\Rightarrow \quad 5x = 180^\circ \Rightarrow x = 36^\circ$

$\therefore \quad \angle BAC = 2x = 2 \times 36^\circ = 72^\circ$

Hence proved.

Case Based Questions

1. (i) Since, given quadrilateral $ABCD$ is a square.

$\therefore \quad AC \perp BD$

So, $\quad \angle AOB = \angle AOD = 90^\circ$

(ii) As we know that the diagonals of square bisect each others.

$\therefore \quad OC = AO = 3\text{ cm}$

(iii) In ΔABO and ΔADO,

$BO = OD$ [given]

$AO = AO$ [common]

$\angle AOB = \angle AOD = 90^\circ$ [given]

$\therefore \quad \Delta ABO \cong \Delta ADO$

[by SAS congruence rule]

Hence, ΔABO and ΔADO are congruent by SAS congruence rule.

(iv) Since, the diagonals of square bisect each others.

$\therefore \quad OB = OD$

So, $\quad OD = 5\text{ cm}$

$\therefore \quad BD = 10\text{ cm} \quad [\because BD = 2 \times OB]$

2. (i) In the given figure, BD is perpendicular to AC.

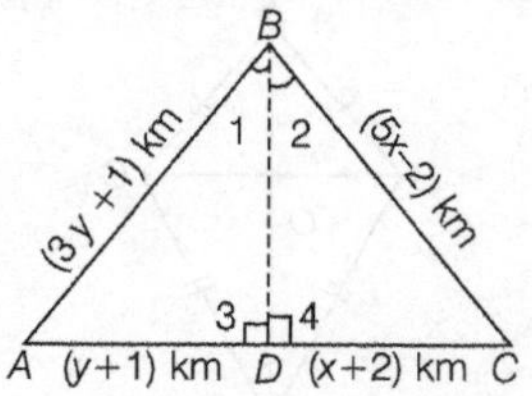

$\therefore \quad \angle 3 = \angle 4$ [each 90°]

Also, BD is the bisector of $\angle ABC$.

$\therefore \quad \angle 1 = \angle 2$

In ΔABD and ΔCBD,

$\angle 1 = \angle 2$ [proved above]

$\angle 3 = \angle 4$ [proved above]

and $BD = BD$ [common side]

$\therefore \quad \Delta ABD \cong \Delta CBD$

[by ASA congruence rule]

Then, $AB = CB$ [by CPCT]

$\Rightarrow \quad 3y + 1 = 5x - 2$

$\Rightarrow \quad 5x - 3y = 3 \quad \ldots(i)$

and $AD = CD$ [by CPCT]

$\Rightarrow \quad y + 1 = x + 2 \Rightarrow -x + y = 1 \quad \ldots(ii)$

On solving Eqs. (i) and (ii), we get

$x = 3, y = 4$

Now, distance between A and C

$= y + 1 + x + 2$

$= x + y + 3$

$= 3 + 4 + 3$

[$\because x = 3$ and $y = 4$]

$= 10\text{ km}$

(ii) Using bicycles instead of bikes by Rajeev and Amit, values shown by them are making an effort towards reducing pollution which helps in protecting the environment and maintaining their physical fitness.

09

MID-POINT AND PYTHAGORAS THEOREM

Mid-Point Theorem

The line segment joining the mid-points of any two sides of a triangle is parallel to the third side and equal to half of it.

In a ΔABC, if E and F are the mid-points of AB and AC respectively,

then $$EF \parallel BC$$

and then $$EF = \frac{1}{2} BC$$

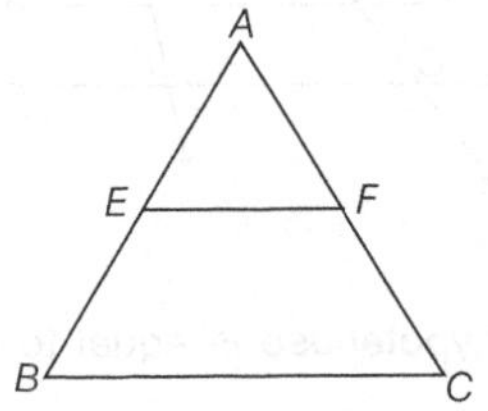

Converse of Mid-Point Theorem

The line drawn through the mid-point of one side of a triangle, parallel to another side bisects the third side.

In a ΔABC, E is the mid-point of AB and $EF \parallel BC$,

then F will be the mid-point of AC.

i.e. $$AF = FC$$

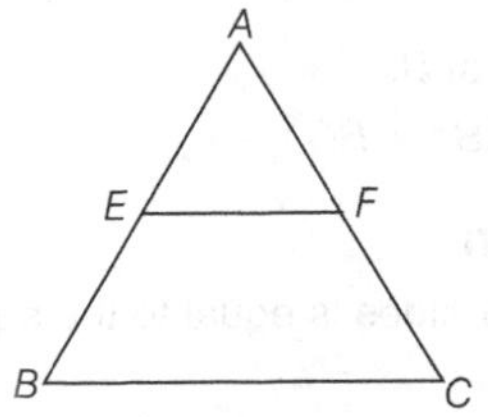

Intercept

If a line *l* cut two lines *m* and *n* (parallel or non-parallel) at points *A* and *B* respectively, then the line-segment *AB* is called intercept made on line *l* by the lines *m* and *n*.

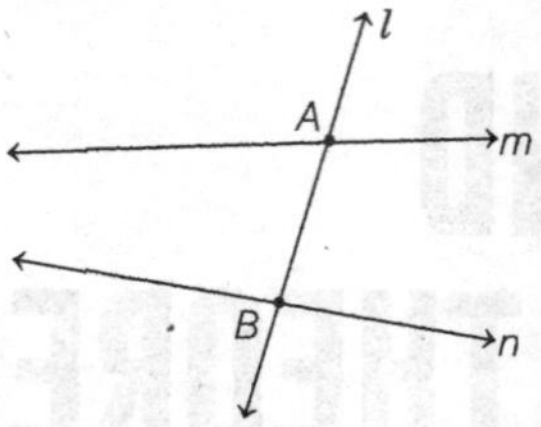

Equal Intercept Theorem

If a transversal makes equal intercepts on three (or more) parallel lines, then any other line cutting them will also makes equal intercepts.

If $l \parallel m \parallel n$ and a transversal *p* cutting them at points *A*, *B* and *C* respectively, such that $AB = BC$ and any other line *q* cuts them at points *D*, *E* and *F*, respectively.

Then, $DE = EF$.

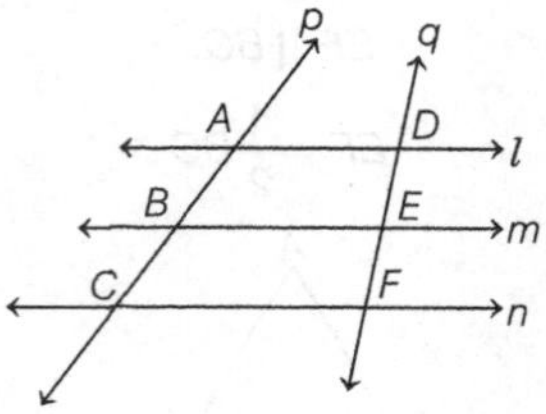

Pythagoras Theorem

In a right angled triangle, the square of the hypotenuse is equal to the sum of the squares of the remaining two sides.

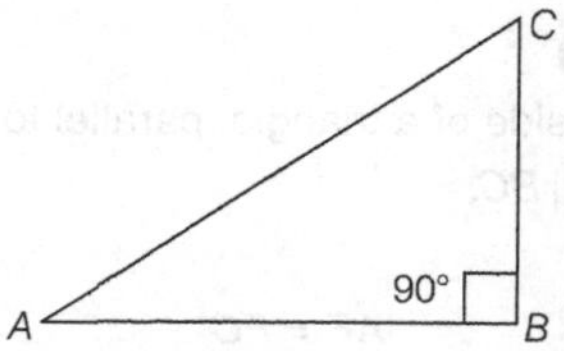

A ΔABC is a right angled triangle, right angled at *B*.

Then, $$AC^2 = AB^2 + BC^2$$

Converse of Pythagoras Theorem

In a triangle, the sum of squares of two smaller sides is equal to the square of third side, then the triangle is right angled triangle.

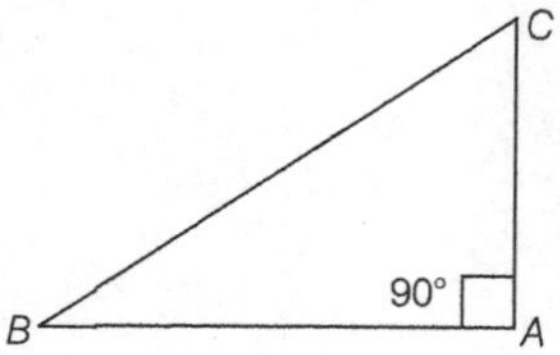

In ΔABC, if *BC* is the largest side and $BC^2 = AB^2 + AC^2$, then $\angle A = 90°$.

EXAM ORIENTED QUESTIONS

TYPE - 1 01 Mark

Multiple Choice Questions

Q.1 In ΔABC, P and Q are mid-points of sides AB and AC, respectively. If $BC = 4$ cm then PQ is equal to

(a) 4 cm (b) 2 cm
(c) 8 cm (d) 6 cm

Q.2 In the quadrilateral $MNOP$, if $MN \parallel OP \parallel AB$ and A and B are the mid-points of the sides MP and NO, respectively. If $MN = 10$ cm, $AB = 8$ cm, then the length of side PO is

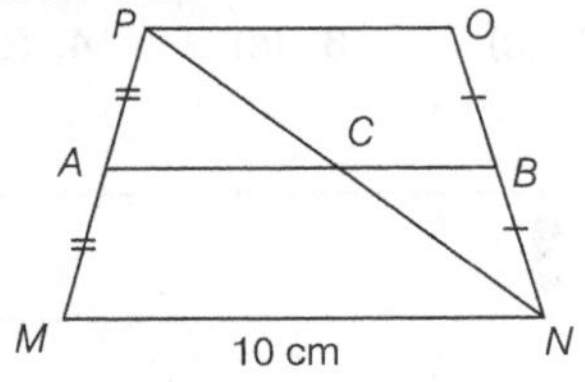

(a) 4 cm (b) 5 cm
(c) 6 cm (d) 8 cm

Q.3 In ΔABC, $AB = 5$ cm, $BC = 8$ cm and $CA = 7$ cm. If D and E are respectively the mid-points of AB and BC, then the length of DE is

(a) 4 cm
(b) 3.5 cm
(c) 2.5 cm
(d) 7 cm

Q.4 In the given figure, M is the mid-point of AB and $MN \parallel AD$, then BN is

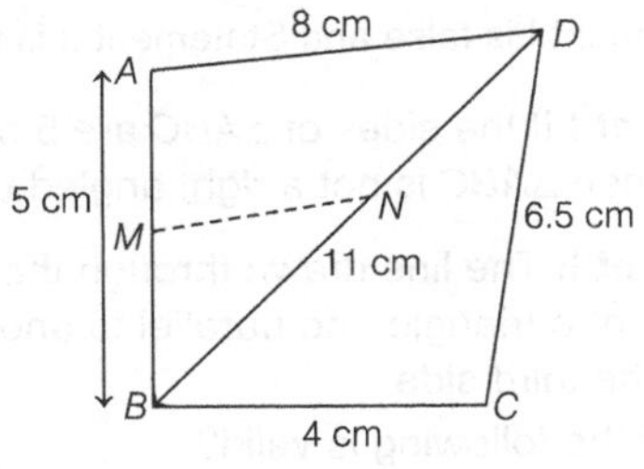

(a) 4 cm
(b) 5 cm
(c) 5.5 cm
(d) 6 cm

Q.5 In the following figure, $AB \parallel CD \parallel EF$ and $BD = DF$. If $AC = 2.5$ cm, then AE is

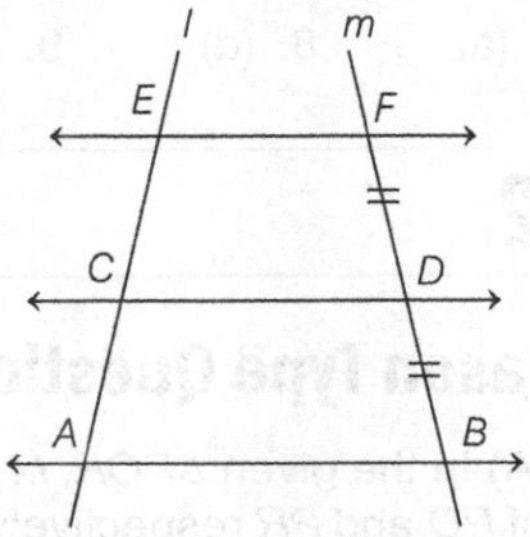

(a) 3 cm (b) 4 cm
(c) 6 cm (d) 5 cm

Q.6 In the given figure, $l \parallel m \parallel n$ and $AB = BC = 5$ cm. If $DG = 2DE$ and $DC = 18$ cm, then DE is

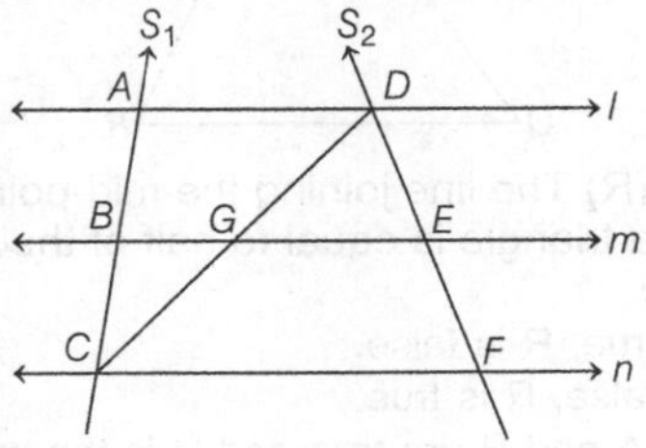

(a) 9 cm (b) 5 cm
(c) 18 cm (d) 4.5 cm

Q.7 Which of the following are the sides of right angled triangles?

(a) 7 cm, 24 cm, 25 cm
(b) 50 cm, 80 cm, 100 cm
(c) 8 cm, 40 cm, 41 cm
(d) 3 cm, 5 cm, 6 cm

Q.8 Which statement is true for the ΔABC, if AD is perpendicular to BC ?

(a) $AB^2 = AC^2 + BD^2$
(b) $AB^2 = CD^2 + AC^2 + BD^2$
(c) $AB^2 + AC^2 = CD^2 + BD^2$
(d) $AB^2 + CD^2 = AC^2 + BD^2$

Q.9 If the length of a side of rhombus is 11 cm and one of the diagonals is 18 cm, then the length of the other diagonal is

(a) 12 cm (b) $4\sqrt{10}$ cm
(c) $6\sqrt{10}$ cm (d) 20 cm

Q.10 In a ΔABC, if $(AB)^2 = (AC)^2 + (BC)^2$, then

(a) $\angle A = 90°$ and $\angle B < 90°$
(b) $\angle C = 90°$ and $\angle A < 90°$
(c) $\angle B = 90°$ and $\angle A < 90°$
(d) $\angle A = 90°$ and $\angle C < 90°$

Answers

1. (b)	2. (c)	3. (b)	4. (c)	5. (d)
6. (d)	7. (a)	8. (d)	9. (b)	10. (b)

TYPE - 2

01 Mark

Assertion-Reason Type Questions

Q.1 Assertion (A) In the given ΔPQR, M and N are the mid-points of PQ and PR respectively and $QR = 10$ cm then $MN = 5$ cm.

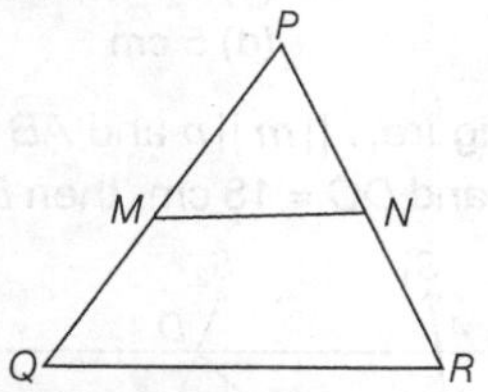

Reason (R) The line joining the mid-points of two sides of a triangle is equal to half of the length of the third side.

(a) A is true, R is false.
(b) A is false, R is true.
(c) Both A and R are true and R is the correct reason for A.
(d) Both A and R are true and R is incorrect reason for A.

Q.2 Assertion (A) In ΔABC, E and F are the mid-points of AC and AB, respectively. The altitude AP at BC intersects EF at Q. Then, $AQ = QP$.

Reason (R) The line drawn through the mid-point of one side of a triangle parallel to another side bisects the third side.

(a) A is true, R is false.
(b) A is false, R is true.
(c) Both A and R are true and R is the correct reason for A.
(d) Both A and R are true and R is incorrect reason for A.

Q.3 Assertion (A) In a right angled triangle, if height of triangle is 24 cm and base is 7 cm, then hypotenuse is 25 cm.

Reason (R) The Pythagoras theorem is applicable only in right angled triangles.

(a) A is true, R is false.
(b) A is false, R is true.
(c) Both A and R are true and R is the correct reason for A.
(d) Both A and R are true and R is incorrect reason for A.

Q.4 Assertion (A) If the sides of a triangle are 9 cm, 40 cm and 41 cm, then the triangle is right angled triangle.

Reason (R) In a triangle, the sum of squares of two smaller sides is equal to square of largest side, then the triangle is right angled triangle.

(a) A is true, R is false.
(b) A is false, R is true.
(c) Both A and R are true and R is the correct reason for A.
(d) Both A and R are true and R is incorrect reason for A.

Answers

1. (c)	2. (c)	3. (c)	4. (c)

TYPE - 3

01 Mark

Statement Based Questions

Q.1 Statement I In ΔPQR, $PQ = 8$ cm, $QR = 10$ cm and $RP = 6$ cm and points M and N are the mid-points of PQ and RP, respectively. Then, perimeter of ΔPMN is 12 cm.

Statement II The perimeter of a triangle is equal to the sum of all sides.

Which of the following is valid?

(a) Both the Statements are true.
(b) Both the Statements are false.
(c) Statement I is true and Statement II is false.
(d) Statement I is false and Statement II is true.

Q.2 Statement I If the sides of ΔABC are 5 cm, 6 cm and 10 cm, then ΔABC is not a right angled triangle.

Statement II The line drawn through the mid-point of one side of a triangle and parallel to another side bisects the third side.

Which of the following is valid?

(a) Both the Statements are true.
(b) Both the Statements are false.
(c) Statement I is true and Statement II is false.
(d) Statement I is false and Statement II is true.

Q.3 Statement I In the given figure, l, m and n are three lines parallel to each other. S_1 and S_2 are transversal such that $XY = YZ = 15$ cm and $DF = 24$ cm, then DE is 15 cm.

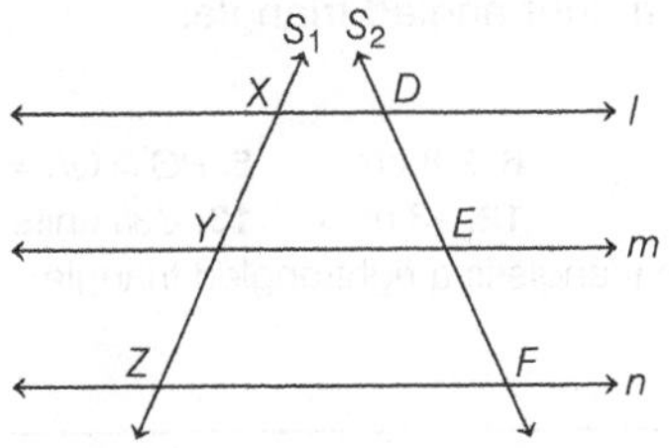

Statement II In a right angled ΔABC, the square of the hypotenuse AC is equal to the sum of the squares of AB and BC.

Which of the following is valid?

(a) Both the Statements are true.
(b) Both the Statements are false.
(c) Statement I is true and Statement II is false.
(d) Statement I is false and Statement II is true.

Q.4 Statement I Two buildings of height 5 m and 13 m stand vertically on the ground. If distance between their feet is 6 m, then distance between their tops be 10 m.

Statement II The Pythagoras theorem can be used in any type of triangle.

Which of the following is valid?

(a) Both the Statements are true.
(b) Both the Statements are false.
(c) Statement I is true and Statement II is false.
(d) Statement I is false and Statement II is true.

Answers

1. (a) **2.** (a) **3.** (d) **4.** (c)

TYPE - 4 03 Marks

Short Answer Type Questions

Q.1 ΔABC is an isosceles triangle in which $AB = AC$. D and E are the mid-points of sides AB and AC, respectively and $DE = 3.5$ cm. Find the perimeter of ΔABC when $AD = 4.5$ cm.

Q.2 ABC is an equilateral triangle and L, M and N are the mid-points of the sides AB, BC and CA, respectively. Prove that ΔLMN is an equilateral triangle.

Q.3 E and F are respectively the mid-points of non-parallel sides AD and BC of a trapezium $ABCD$. Prove that $EF \parallel AB$ and $EF = \frac{1}{2}(AB + CD)$.

Q.4 $ABCD$ is a trapezium in which $AB \parallel DC$ and $AD = BC$. If P, Q, R and S are the mid-points of BA, BD, CD and CA respectively, then show that $PQRS$ is a rhombus.

Q.5 In the following figure, AD is a median of ΔABC and E is the mid-point of AD. Also, BE produced meets AC at F. Prove that $AF = \frac{1}{3}AC$.

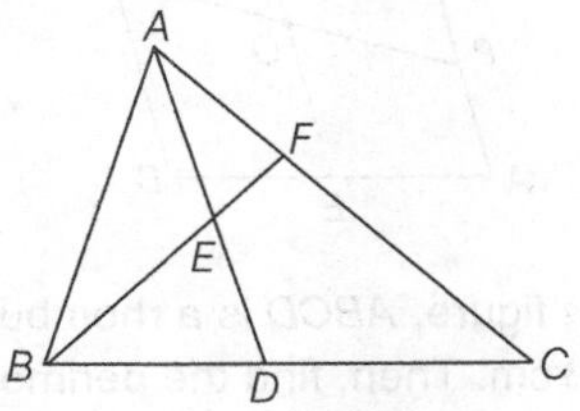

Q.6 In the given figure, $l \parallel m \parallel n$ and $AB = BC$. If $DC = 5.6$ cm, find DG.

Q.7 In the given figure, $ABCD$ is a parallelogram and E, F are the mid-points of the sides AB and CD, respectively. Show that the line segments AF and EC trisect the diagonal BD.

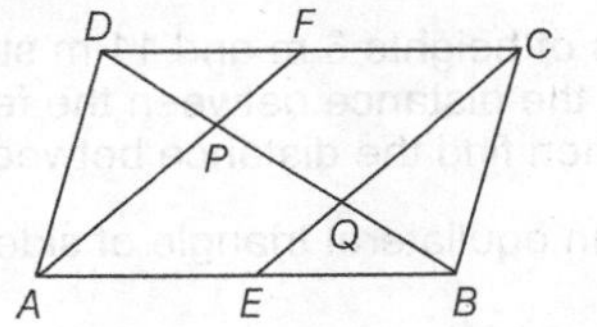

Q.8 In the given figure, l, m and n are the three lines parallel to each other. S_1 and S_2 are transversal such that $AB = BC = 5$ cm, find PQ and QR, if $PR = 12$ cm.

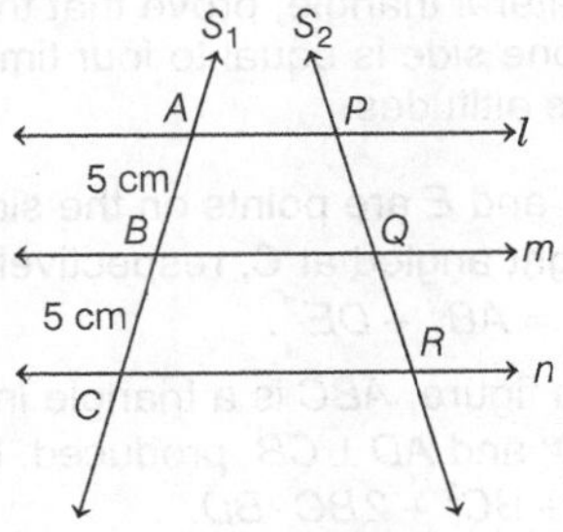

Q.9 In the given figure, M and N divide AB into three equal parts. Line segments MP and NQ are both parallel to BC and meet AC in P and Q, respectively. Prove that P and Q divide AC into three equal parts.

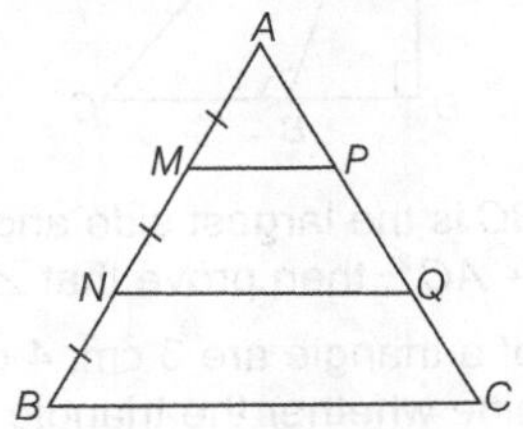

Q.10 In the given figure, $ABCD$ is a parallelogram. E and F are the mid-points of sides AB and CD, respectively. PQ is any line that meets AD, EF and BC in points P, O and Q, respectively. Prove that $PO = OQ$.

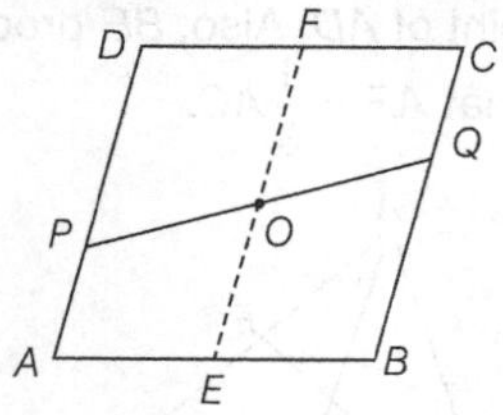

Q.11 In the given figure, $ABCD$ is a rhombus, $AO = 4$ cm and $DO = 3$ cm. Then, find the perimeter of the rhombus.

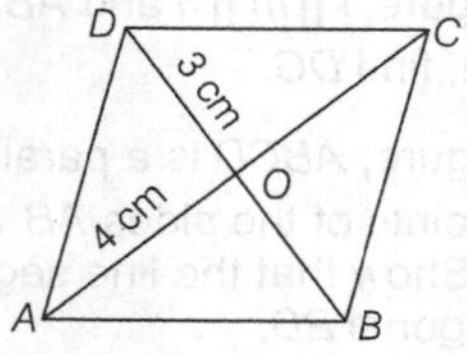

Q.12 Two poles of heights 6 m and 11 m stand on a plane ground. If the distance between the feet of the poles is 12 m, then find the distance between their tops.

Q.13 ΔABC is an equilateral triangle of side $2a$. Find its altitudes.

Q.14 Prove that the sum of the squares of the sides of a rhombus is equal to the sum of the squares of its diagonals.

Q.15 In an equilateral triangle, prove that three times the square of one side is equal to four times the square of one of its altitudes.

Q.16 Suppose D and E are points on the sides CA and CB of ΔABC right angled at C, respectively. Prove that $AE^2 + BD^2 = AB^2 + DE^2$.

Q.17 In the given figure, ABC is a triangle in which $\angle ABC > 90^\circ$ and $AD \perp CB$ produced. Prove that $AC^2 = AB^2 + BC^2 + 2BC \cdot BD$.

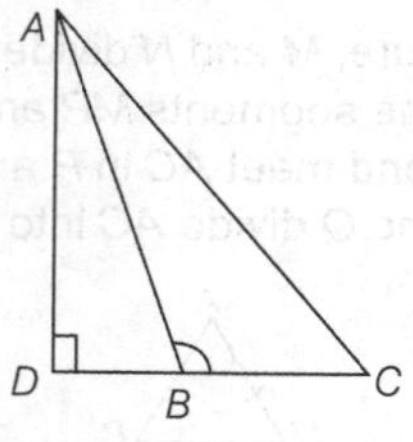

Q.18 In ΔABC, if BC is the largest side and $BC^2 = AB^2 + AC^2$, then prove that $\angle A = 90^\circ$.

Q.19 If the sides of a triangle are 3 cm, 4 cm and 5 cm long, determine whether the triangle is a right angled triangle.

Q.20 In ΔABC, if $AB = 6\sqrt{3}$ cm, $AC = 12$ cm and $BC = 6$ cm. Then, find the value of $\angle B$.

Q.21 In ΔPQR, $PS \perp QR$ and $PS^2 = QS \times RS$. Prove that ΔQPR is a right angled triangle.

Answers

1. 25 cm
6. 2.8 cm
8. $PQ = QR = 6$ cm
11. 20 cm
12. 13 m
13. $\sqrt{3}a$ units
19. Yes, given triangle is a right angled triangle
20. 90°

TYPE - 5 — 4/5 Marks

Long Answer Type Questions

Q.1 Suppose D, E and F are the mid-points of sides BC, CA and AB, respectively of ΔABC. If perimeter of ΔABC is 12.8 cm, then find the perimeter of ΔDEF.

Q.2 P, Q and R are the mid-points of the sides BC, CA and AB, respectively of a ΔABC. PR and BQ meet at X, CR and PQ meet at Y. Prove that $XY = \frac{1}{4}BC$.

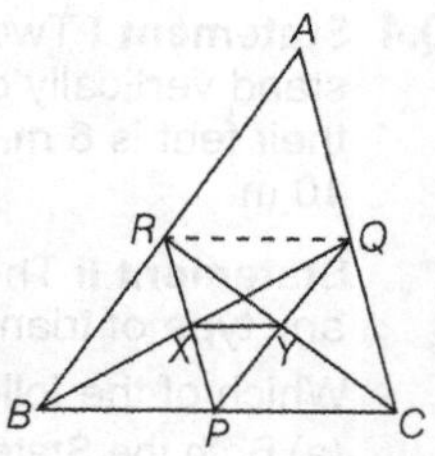

Q.3 $ABCD$ is a rectangle and P, Q, R and S are the mid-points of the sides AB, BC, CD and DA, respectively. Show that the quadrilateral $PQRS$ is a rhombus.

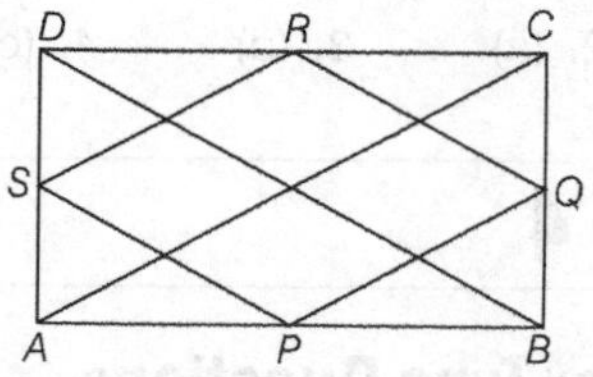

Q.4 $ABCD$ is a kite with $AB = AD$ and $CD = CB$. Prove that the figure formed by joining the mid-points of the consecutive sides is a rectangle.

Q.5 ABC is a triangle. D is a point on AB such that $AD = \frac{1}{4}AB$ and E is a point on AC such that $AE = \frac{1}{4}AC$. Prove that $DE = \frac{1}{4}BC$.

Q.6 In ΔABC, AD is the median and E is the mid-point of AD. BE produced meets AC at F. If $AC = 9$ cm, then find the length of AF.

Q.7 In the given figure, $PQRS$ is a parallelogram, L is the mid-point of sides SR and SN is drawn parallel to LQ which meets RQ produced at N and cut side PQ at M.

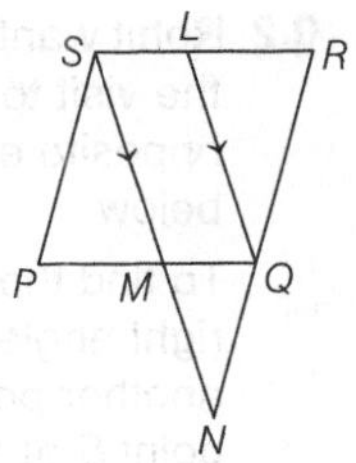

Prove that

(i) $SN = 2LQ$

(ii) $SP = \frac{1}{2}RN$

Q.8 In the given figure, AD is a median of ΔABC, E is the mid-point of AD and $DP \parallel AC$, prove that $BE : EQ = 3:1$.

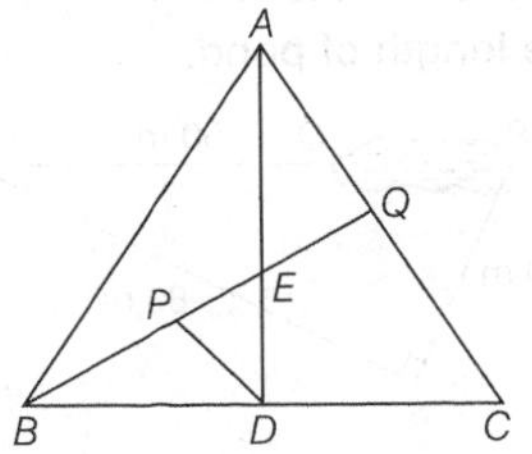

Q.9 Prove that if a transversal makes equal intercepts on three (or more) parallel lines, then any other line cutting them will also makes equal intercepts.

Q.10 In the given figure, $2XD = XY$, P is mid-point of XY, Q is mid-point of DR and $PR \parallel YS$. Prove that

(i) $XQ \parallel YS$ (ii) $DS = 3RS$

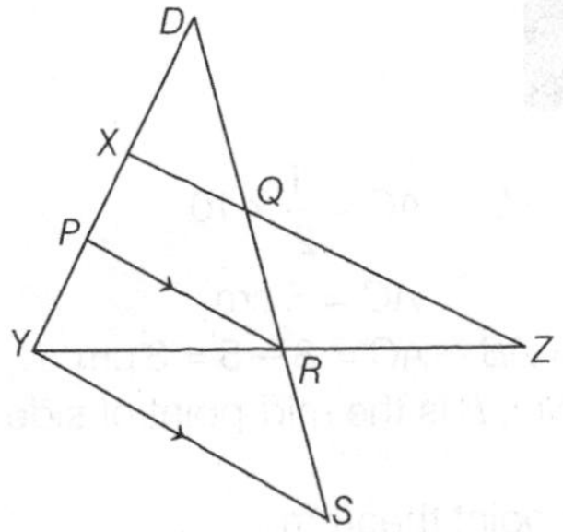

Q.11 Prove that in a right angled triangle, the square of the hypotenuse is equal to the sum of the squares of the remaining two sides.

Q.12 In the given figure, ABC is a right angled triangle at C and $CD \perp AB$, then prove that $\frac{1}{p^2} = \frac{1}{a^2} + \frac{1}{b^2}$.

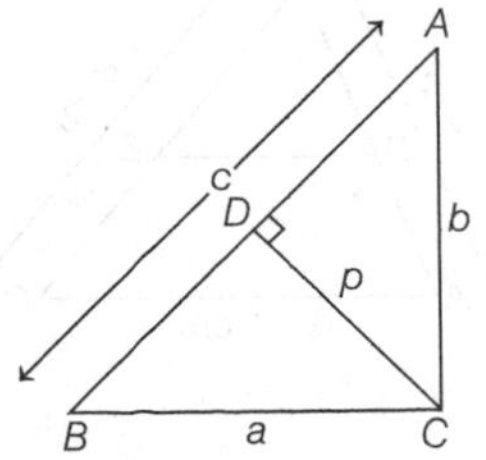

Q.13 In an equilateral ΔABC, D is a point on side BC such that $BD : DC = 2:1$. Prove that $9AD^2 = 7AB^2$.

Q.14 Let BL and CM are medians of a ΔABC right angled at A. Prove that $4(BL^2 + CM^2) = 5BC^2$.

Q.15 In ΔABC, $\angle B = 90°$. Find the sides of the triangle if $AB = (x-3)$ cm, $BC = (x+4)$ cm and $AC = (x+6)$ cm.

Q.16 In the given figure, ABC is a triangle with $AB = 8$ cm, $BC = 6$ cm and $AC = 3$ cm. Find the length of OC.

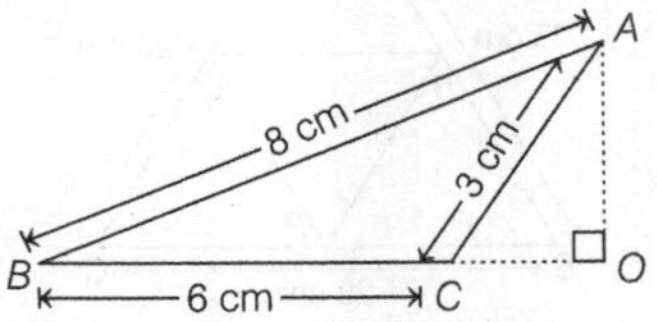

Q.17 Two poles of height 9 m and 14 m stand vertically on a plane ground. If the distance between their feet is 12 m.

(i) Find the distance between their tops.

(ii) Find the distance between the top of first pole and foot of second pole.

Q.18 In ΔABC, $\angle B = 90°$ and D is the mid-point of BC. Prove that $AC^2 = AD^2 + 3CD^2$.

Q.19 In the given figure, O is any point inside a rectangle $ABCD$. Prove that $OB^2 + OD^2 = OA^2 + OC^2$.

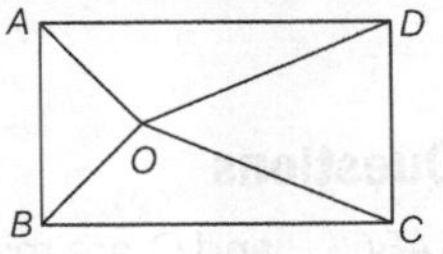

Q.20 In the given figure, OP, OQ and OR are drawn perpendiculars to the sides BC, CA and AB, respectively of ΔABC. Prove that $AR^2 + BP^2 + CQ^2 = AQ^2 + CP^2 + BR^2$.

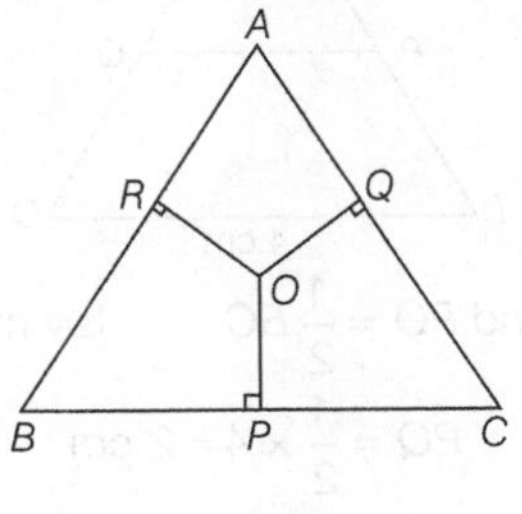

Answers

1. 6.4 cm
6. 3 cm
15. $AB = 8$ cm, $BC = 15$ cm and $CA = 17$ cm
16. $1\frac{7}{12}$ cm
17. (i) 13 m (ii) 15 m

TYPE - 6

Case Based Questions

Q.1 There is a visit of Director of Education in Nirja Modi school. To welcome the guest, girls were asked to prepare a rangoli in triangular shape.

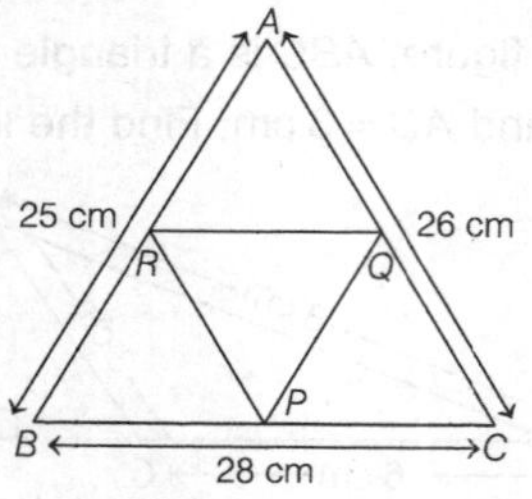

Dimensions of ΔABC are 26 cm, 28 cm, 25 cm.
Garland is to be placed along the side of ΔPQR, which is formed by joining mid-points of sides of ΔABC.
On the above information answer the following questions.

(i) Find the value of RQ. (ii) Find the value of PQ.
(iii) Find the length of garland. **(3 M)**

Q.2 Rohit wants to measure the distance of a pond during the visit to his native. He marks points P and Q on the opposite edge of a pond as shown in the figure below.

To find the distance between the points, he makes a right angled triangle using rope connecting Q with another point R at a distance 50 m, connecting R to point S at a distance of 80 m from point R and connecting S to the point P which is at a distance of 60 m from S such that $\angle PSR$ is a right angle.

(i) Which theorem will be used to find the distance PR?
(ii) What is the distance PR?
(iii) Find the length of pond. **(3 M)**

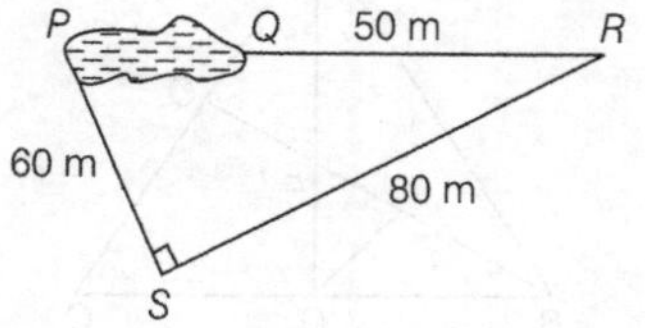

Answers

1. (i) 14 cm (ii) 12.5 cm (iii) 39.5 cm
2. (i) Pythagoras theorem (ii) 100 m (iii) 50 m

EXPLANATIONS

Multiple Choice Questions

1. (b) Given, in ΔABC, P and Q are mid-points of sides AB and AC, respectively.

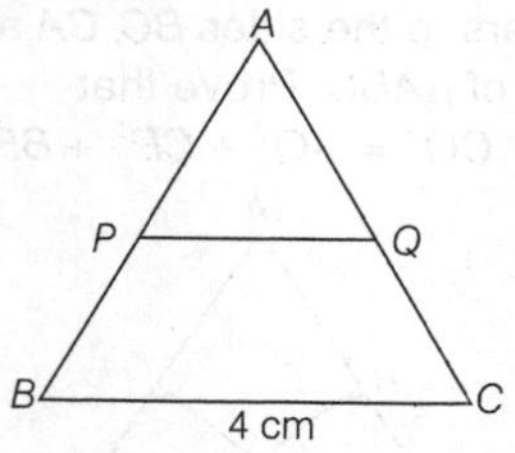

$\therefore PQ \parallel BC$ and $PQ = \frac{1}{2} BC$ [by mid-point theorem]

$\Rightarrow \quad PQ = \frac{1}{2} \times 4 = 2$ cm

2. (c) In ΔPMN, A is the mid-point of side PM and $AC \parallel MN$.
Using mid-point theorem,

$$AC = \frac{1}{2} MN$$

$\Rightarrow \quad AC = \frac{1}{2} \times 10$ [$\because MN = 10$ cm]

$\Rightarrow \quad AC = 5$ cm

Then, $CB = AB - AC = 8 - 5 = 3$ cm
and in ΔPNO, B is the mid-point of side NO and $PO \parallel CB$.
Using mid-point theorem,

$$CB = \frac{1}{2} PO \Rightarrow PO = 2CB$$

$\Rightarrow \quad PO = 2 \times 3$ [$\because CB = 3$ cm]

$\Rightarrow \quad PO = 6$ cm

3. (b) Given, in ΔABC,
$AB = 5$ cm, $BC = 8$ cm and $CA = 7$ cm

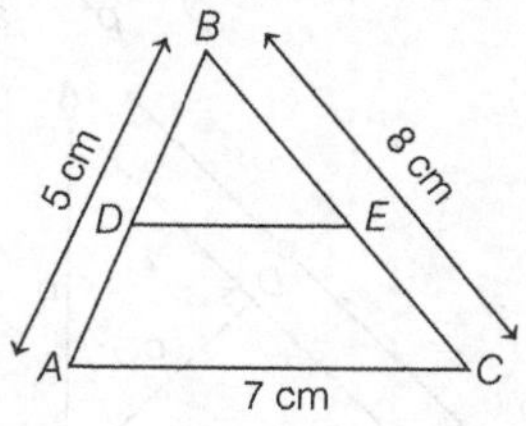

Since, D and E are the mid-points of AB and BC, respectively.

By mid-point theorem,

$$DE \parallel AC \text{ and } DE = \frac{1}{2} AC$$

$$\Rightarrow \quad DE = \frac{1}{2} \times 7 = 3.5 \text{ cm}$$

4. (c) In ΔABD, M is the mid-point of AB and $MN \parallel AD$.

By converse of mid-point theorem,

N is the mid-point of BD.

$$\therefore \quad BN = ND = \frac{1}{2} BD$$

$$\Rightarrow \quad BN = \frac{1}{2} \times 11 \quad [\because BD = 11 \text{cm}]$$

$$= 5.5 \text{ cm}$$

5. (d) Since, $AB \parallel CD \parallel EF$ and $BD = DF$

$\therefore$ By equal intercept theorem,

$$CE = AC$$

$$\Rightarrow \quad CE = 2.5 \text{ cm}$$

Now, $AE = AC + CE$

$$= 2.5 + 2.5 = 5 \text{ cm}$$

6. (d) Given, $l \parallel m \parallel n$, $AB = BC = 5$ cm, $DG = 2DE$ and $DC = 18$ cm

Since, the transversal S_1 makes equal intercepts AB and BC on parallel lines l, m and n, therefore by equal intercept theorem, we get

$$DG = GC$$

$$\because \quad DG + GC = DC$$

$$\therefore \quad DG + DG = 18 \text{ cm}$$

$$\Rightarrow \quad DG = 9 \text{ cm}$$

$$\because \quad DG = 2DE$$

$$\therefore \quad DE = \frac{DG}{2} = \frac{9}{2} = 4.5 \text{ cm}$$

7. (a) By converse of Pythagoras theorem, we know that in a triangle, the sum of squares of two smaller sides is equal to square of largest side, then the triangle is right angled triangle.

From option (a) Since, $(25)^2 = (7)^2 + (24)^2$

$$\Rightarrow \quad 625 = 49 + 576$$

$$\Rightarrow \quad 625 = 625$$

Hence, 7 cm, 24 cm and 25 cm are the sides of right angled triangle.

From option (b) Since, $(100)^2 \neq (50)^2 + (80)^2$

$$\Rightarrow \quad 10000 \neq 8900$$

Hence, 50 cm, 80 cm and 100 cm are not the sides of right angled triangle.

From option (c) Since, $(41)^2 \neq (8)^2 + (40)^2$

$$\Rightarrow \quad 1681 \neq 1664$$

Hence, 8 cm, 40 cm and 41 cm are not the sides of right angled triangle.

From option (d) Since, $(6)^2 \neq (3)^2 + (5)^2$

$$\Rightarrow \quad 36 \neq 34$$

Hence, 3 cm, 5 cm and 6 cm are not the sides of right angled triangle.

8. (d) We have, in ΔABC, $AD \perp BC$

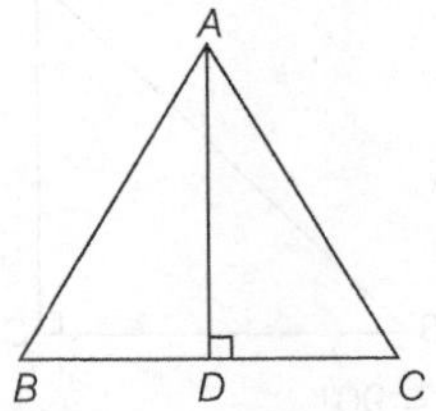

Now, in right angled ΔABD,

$$AB^2 = AD^2 + BD^2 \quad \text{[by Pythagoras theorem]}$$

$$\Rightarrow \quad AD^2 = AB^2 - BD^2 \quad \ldots\text{(i)}$$

Similarly, in right angled ΔACD,

$$AC^2 = AD^2 + CD^2 \quad \text{[by Pythagoras theorem]}$$

$$\Rightarrow \quad AD^2 = AC^2 - CD^2 \quad \ldots\text{(ii)}$$

From Eqs. (i) and (ii), we get

$$AB^2 - BD^2 = AC^2 - CD^2$$

$$\Rightarrow \quad AB^2 + CD^2 = AC^2 + BD^2$$

9. (b) Let $ABCD$ be a rhombus.

and $AB = BC = CD = DA = 11$cm,

diagonal $AC = 18$ cm

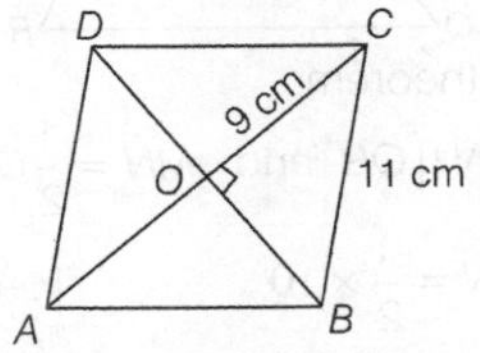

Since, diagonals fo rhombus bisect each other at right angle, then

$$OA = OC = \frac{1}{2} AC$$

$$\Rightarrow \quad OC = \frac{1}{2} \times 18$$

$$\Rightarrow \quad OC = 9 \text{ cm}$$

Now, in right angled ΔBOC,

$$OB^2 = BC^2 - OC^2 \quad \text{[by Pythagoras theorem]}$$

$$= (11)^2 - (9)^2$$

$$= (11 + 9)(11 - 9)$$

$$[\because a^2 - b^2 = (a + b)(a - b)]$$

$$= 20 \times 2$$

$$\Rightarrow \quad OB = \sqrt{40}$$

$$= 2\sqrt{10} \text{ cm}$$

Now, $BD = 2OB$

$$= 2 \times 2\sqrt{10}$$

$$BD = 4\sqrt{10} \text{ cm}$$

10. (b) We have, in a ΔABC,

$$AB^2 = AC^2 + BC^2,$$

which is the Pythagoras theorem.

$\therefore$ Side AB is the hypotenuse of right angled ΔABC.

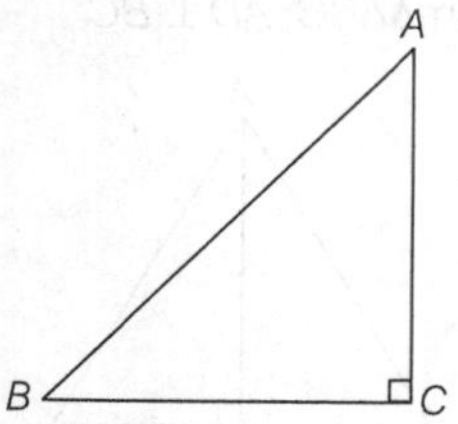

Therefore, $\angle C = 90^\circ$

and we know that in a right angled triangle, there are one right angle and two acute angles.

$\therefore \quad \angle A < 90^\circ$ and $\angle B < 90^\circ$

Assertion-Reason Type Questions

1. (c) In ΔPQR, M and N are the mid-points of sides PQ and PR, respectively.

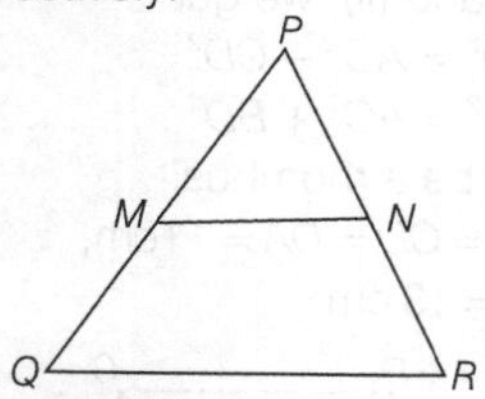

By mid-point theorem,

$$MN \parallel QR \text{ and } MN = \frac{1}{2}QR$$

$$\Rightarrow \quad MN = \frac{1}{2} \times 10 \qquad [\because QR = 10 \text{ cm, given}]$$

$$= 5 \text{ cm}$$

Hence, A is true.

R is also true and R is the correct reason for A.

2. (c) Given, E and F are the mid-points of AC and AB, respectively.

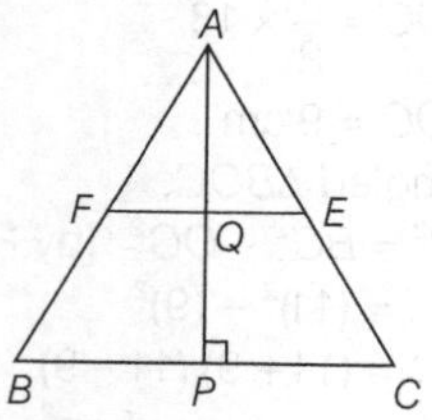

$\therefore FE \parallel BC$ and $FE = \frac{1}{2}BC$.

Now, in ΔABP,

F is the mid-point of AB and $FQ \parallel BC$.

$\therefore$ By converse of mid-point theorem,

Q is mid-point of AP.

$$\therefore \quad AQ = QP$$

Hence, both A and R are true and R is the correct reason for A.

3. (c) Let ΔABC is a right angled triangle in which $AB = 7$ cm and $BC = 24$ cm.

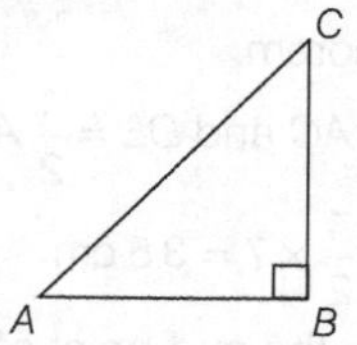

By Pythagoras theorem,

$$AC^2 = AB^2 + BC^2$$

$$\Rightarrow \quad AC^2 = 7^2 + 24^2 = 49 + 576 = 625$$

$$\Rightarrow \quad AC = 25 \text{ cm}$$

Hence, A is true.

And this theorem is applicable only in right angled triangles.

Hence, both A and R are true and R is the correct reason for A.

4. (c) We have, sides of a triangle are 9 cm, 40 cm and 41 cm.

By Pythagoras theorem,

$$(41)^2 = (9)^2 + (40)^2$$

$$\Rightarrow \quad 1681 = 81 + 1600$$

$$\Rightarrow \quad 1681 = 1681$$

Hence, the Pythagoras theorem is satisfied.

Therefore, it is a right angled triangle.

Hence, both A and R are true and R is the correct reason for A.

Statement Based Questions

1. (a) Given, in ΔPQR, $PQ = 8$ cm, $QR = 10$ cm and $RP = 6$ cm

Since, M and N are the mid-points of PQ and RP, respectively.

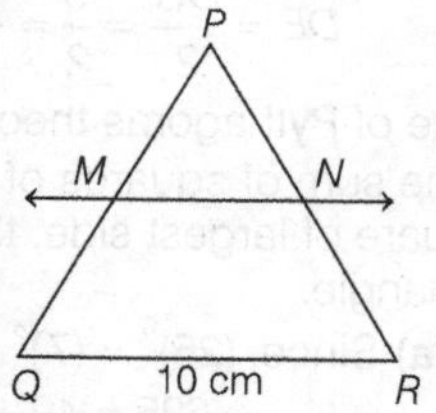

By mid-point theorem,

$$QR \parallel MN \text{ and } MN = \frac{1}{2}QR$$

$$PM = \frac{1}{2}PQ, \; PN = \frac{1}{2}RP$$

$$\Rightarrow \quad PM = \frac{1}{2} \times 8, \; PN = \frac{1}{2} \times 6$$

$$\Rightarrow \quad PM = 4 \text{ cm}, \; PN = 3 \text{ cm}$$

Now, $MN = \frac{1}{2}QR \Rightarrow MN = \frac{1}{2} \times 10 = 5$ cm

Perimeter of $\Delta PMN = PM + MN + PN$

$$= 4 + 5 + 3 = 12 \text{ cm}$$

Hence, both the Statements are true.

2. (a) Given, sides of ΔABC are 5 cm, 6 cm and 10 cm.
By converse of Pythagoras theorem, we know that in a triangle, the sum of squares of two smaller sides is equal to the square of largest side, then the triangle is a right angled triangle.

Since, $10^2 \neq 5^2 + 6^2$

$\Rightarrow \quad 100 \neq 25 + 36$

$\Rightarrow \quad 100 \neq 61$

$\therefore$ 5 cm, 6 cm and 10 cm are not the lengths of sides of a right angled triangle.

Hence, Statement I is true and Statement II is also true.

3. (d) We have, $l \parallel m \parallel n$, $XY = YZ = 15$ cm and $DF = 24$ cm

Since, transversal S_1 makes equal intercepts XY and YZ on parallel lines l, m and n, therefore by equal intercept theorem, we get

$$DE = EF$$

$\because \quad DE + EF = DF$

$\Rightarrow \quad DE + DE = 24$

$\Rightarrow \quad DE = 12$ cm

Hence Statement I is false.

In a right angled triangle, by Pythagoras theorem, square of hypotenuse is equal to the sum of the squares of other two sides.

Hence, Statement II is true.

4. (c) Let AB and CE be two buildings of height 5 m and 13 m, respectively.

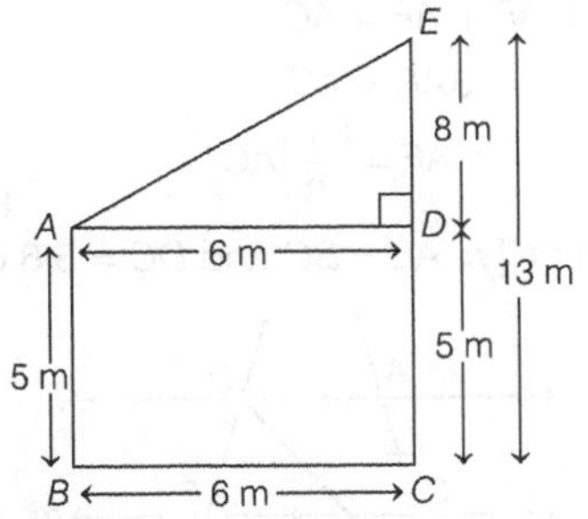

In figure, $AB = CD = 5$ m,

$CE = 13$ m

and $\quad BC = AD = 6$ m

Now, $\quad DE = CE - CD$

$= 13 - 5 = 8$ m

In right angled ΔADE,

$AE^2 = AD^2 + DE^2$ [by Pythagoras theorem]

$= (6)^2 + (8)^2 = 36 + 64 = 100$

$\Rightarrow \quad AE = 10$ m

Hence, the distance between buildings tops be 10 m.

Then, Statement I is true and Statement II is false.

Short Answer Type Questions

1. Given, a ΔABC, in which $AB = AC$ and D and E are the mid-points of AB and AC, respectively.

$\therefore AD = DB = 4.5$ cm [as D is the mid-point of AB]

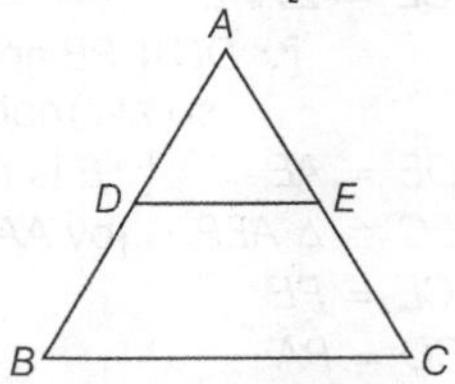

Then, $AB = 2AD = 2 \times 4.5 = 9$ cm

So, $\quad AB = AC = 9$ cm [given]

Since, D and E are the mid-points of AB and AC.

By mid-point theorem,

$$DE \parallel BC \text{ and } DE = \frac{1}{2} BC$$

Then, $\quad BC = 2DE = 2 \times 3.5 = 7$ cm

Now, perimeter of $\Delta ABC = AB + BC + CA$

$= 9 + 7 + 9 = 25$ cm

2. Given ΔABC is an equilateral triangle and L, M and N are the mid-points of the sides AB, BC and CA, respectively.

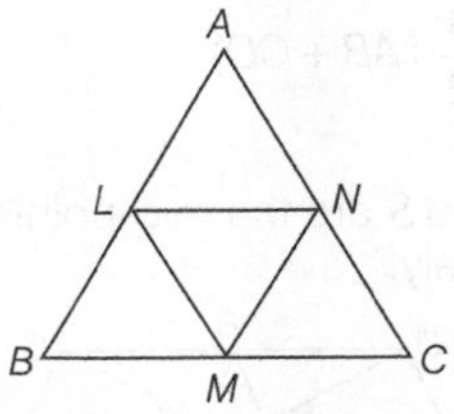

To prove ΔLMN is an equilateral triangle.

Proof Since, L and N are the mid-points of AB and AC, respectively.

By mid-point theorem, $LN = \frac{1}{2} BC$

Similarly, $LM = \frac{1}{2} AC$ and $MN = \frac{1}{2} AB$

$\because \Delta ABC$ is an equilateral triangle.

$\therefore \quad AB = BC = CA$

$\Rightarrow \quad \frac{1}{2} AB = \frac{1}{2} BC = \frac{1}{2} CA$

$\Rightarrow \quad MN = LN = LM$

Hence, ΔLMN is an equilateral triangle. **Hence proved.**

3. Given E and F are respectively the mid-points of non-parallel sides of AD and BC of trapezium $ABCD$.

To prove $EF \parallel AB$ and $EF = \frac{1}{2}(AB + CD)$

Construction Join CE and produce it to meet BA at P.

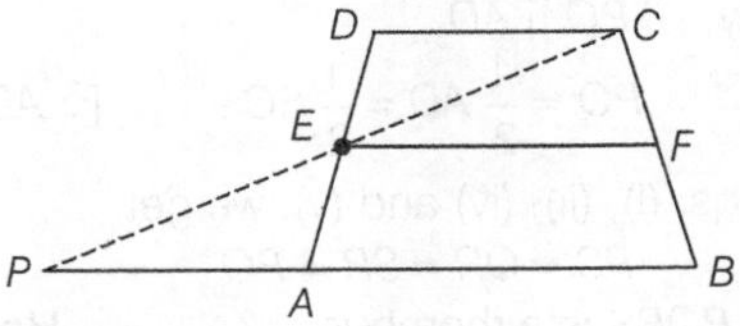

Proof In ΔDEC and ΔAEP, we have

$\angle DEC = \angle AEP$ [vertically opposite angles]

$\angle DCE = \angle APE$ [∵ $DC \parallel PB$ and PC is transversal, so alternate angles are equal]

$DE = AE$ [∵ E is the mid-point of AD]

∴ $\Delta DEC \cong \Delta AEP$ [by AAS congruence rule]

Then, $CE = PE$ [by CPCT]

and $CD = PA$ [by CPCT]

Now, in ΔCPB, E is the mid-point of CP. [∵ $CE = PE$]

Also, F is the mid-point of BC. [given]

So, by mid-point theorem,

$$EF \parallel PB \text{ and } EF = \frac{1}{2} PB$$

$\Rightarrow$ $EF \parallel AB$

and $EF = \frac{1}{2}(PA + AB)$

$= \frac{1}{2}(CD + AB)$ [∵ $PA = CD$]

Hence, $EF \parallel AB$

and $EF = \frac{1}{2}(AB + CD)$

Hence proved.

4. In ΔABC, P and S are the mid-points of sides AB and AC, respectively.

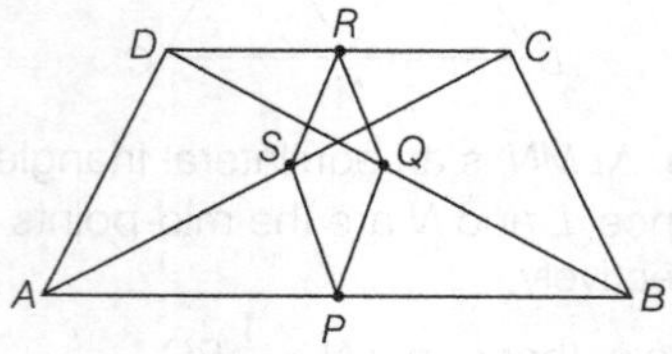

∴ $PS \parallel BC$ and $PS = \frac{1}{2} BC$

[by mid-point theorem] ...(i)

Similarly, $QR \parallel BC$ and $QR = \frac{1}{2} BC$ ...(ii)

Now, from Eqs. (i) and (ii), we get

$PS \parallel QR$ and $PS = QR$ ...(iii)

$\Rightarrow PQRS$ is a parallelogram.

[∵ one pair of opposite side are parallel and equal]

Further, in ΔACD, S and R are the mid-points of AC and CD, respectively.

∴ $SR \parallel AD$

and $SR = \frac{1}{2} AD = \frac{1}{2} BC$ [∵ $AD = BC$] ...(iv)

Similarly, $PQ \parallel AD$

and $PQ = \frac{1}{2} AD = \frac{1}{2} BC$ [∵ $AD = BC$] ...(v)

From Eqs. (i), (ii), (iv) and (v), we get

$PS = QR = SR = PQ$

Hence, $PQRS$ is a rhombus. **Hence proved.**

5. Given In ΔABC, AD is a median and E is mid-point of AD.

To prove $AF = \frac{1}{3} AC$

Construction Draw $DP \parallel BF$, which intersect AC at P.

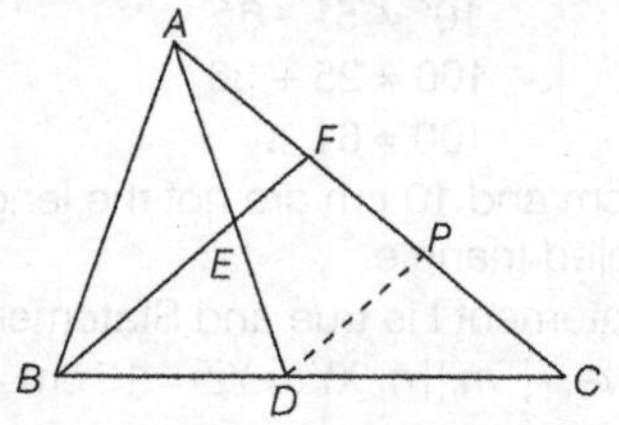

Proof In ΔADP, E is the mid-point of AD and $EF \parallel DP$. [by construction]

∴ F is the mid-point of AP.

[by converse of mid-point theorem]

$\Rightarrow$ $AF = FP$ ...(i)

In ΔFBC, D is the mid-point of BC and $DP \parallel BF$.

[∵ AD is a median of ΔABC]

∴ P is the mid-point of FC.

[by converse of mid-point theorem]

$\Rightarrow$ $FP = PC$ ...(ii)

From Eqs. (i) and (ii), we get

$AF = FP = PC$

Now, $AF + FP + PC = AC$

$AF + AF + AF = AC$

$3AF = AC$

∴ $AF = \left(\frac{1}{3}\right) AC$

Hence proved.

6. Given, $l \parallel m \parallel n$, $AB = BC$ and $DC = 5.6$ cm

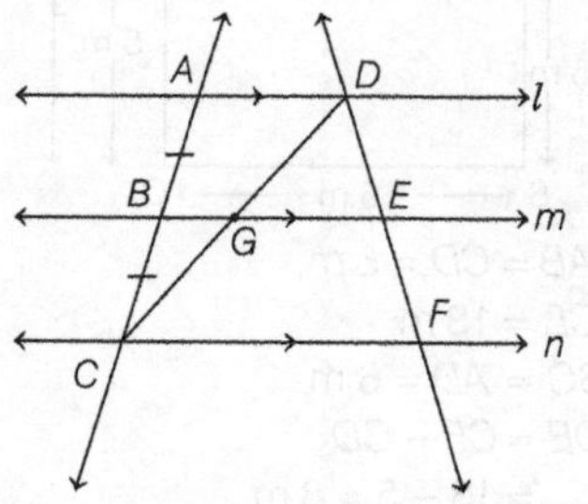

In ΔACD, B is a mid-point of AC and $BG \parallel AD$. [given]

∴ By converse of mid-point theorem, G is mid-point of CD.

$\Rightarrow$ $CG = GD$ ...(i)

Since, $CD = CG + GD$

$\Rightarrow$ $CD = GD + GD$ [from Eq. (i)]

$\Rightarrow$ $DG = \frac{1}{2} CD = \frac{1}{2} \times 5.6$

$= 2.8$ cm

7. As, $ABCD$ is a parallelogram, $AB \parallel DC$

$\Rightarrow \quad AE \parallel FC$

Also, $\quad AB = DC$

[$\because$ opposite sides of a parallelogram are equal]

$\Rightarrow \quad \frac{1}{2} AB = \frac{1}{2} DC$

$\Rightarrow \quad AE = FC$

Thus, in the quadrilateral $AECF$, $AE = FC$ and $AE \parallel FC$.

$\therefore$ $AECF$ is a parallelogram.

$\therefore \quad AF \parallel EC$

In ΔDQC, $\quad PF \parallel QC \quad$ [$\because AF \parallel EC$, proved above]

and F is mid-point of CD. [given]

$\therefore$ P is mid-point of DQ

[by converse of mid-point theorem]

$\Rightarrow \quad DP = PQ \quad$ ...(i)

In ΔABP, $\quad EQ \parallel AP \quad$ [$\because EC \parallel AF$, from above]

and E is mid-point of AB. [given]

$\therefore$ Q is mid-point of BP.

[by converse of mid-point theorem]

$\Rightarrow \quad BQ = PQ \quad$ ...(ii)

From Eqs. (i) and (ii), we get

$DP = PQ = BQ$

Hence, the line segments AF and EC trisect the diagonal BD.

8. Given, $l \parallel m \parallel n$, $AB = BC = 5$ cm and $PR = 12$ cm

Since, the transversal S_1 makes equal intercepts AB and BC on parallel lines l, m and n, therefore by equal intercept theorem, we have

$PQ = QR$

$\because \quad PR = PQ + QR$

$\Rightarrow \quad PQ + QR = 12$

$\Rightarrow \quad 2PQ = 12 \quad$ [$\because PQ = QR$]

$\Rightarrow \quad PQ = 6$ cm

Hence, $PQ = QR = 6$ cm

9. Given In ΔABC, $AM = MN = NB$; $MP \parallel BC$ and $NQ \parallel BC$.

To prove $AP = PQ = QC$

Construction Through A, draw a line DE parallel to BC.

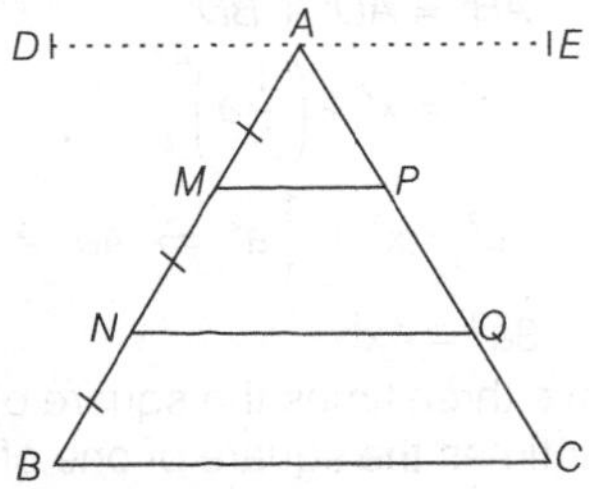

Proof Since, $DE \parallel BC$, $MP \parallel BC$ and $NQ \parallel BC$

Therefore, $DE \parallel MP \parallel NQ \parallel BC$.

Now, as the transversal AB makes equal intercepts AM, MN and NB on parallel lines DE, MP, NQ and BC into three equal parts.

Therefore, by equal intercept theorem, transversal AC also makes equal intercepts on these parallel lines.

Hence, $AP = PQ = QC$.

10. Given $ABCD$ is a parallelogram. E and F are the mid-points of AB and CD, respectively.

To prove $PO = OQ$

Proof Since, E and F are the mid-points of AB and CD, respectively.

$\therefore \quad AE = \frac{1}{2} AB \quad$ ...(i)

and $\quad DF = \frac{1}{2} CD \quad$ ...(ii)

Also, we know that opposite sides of parallelogram are equal,

$\therefore \quad AB = CD \quad$ ...(iii)

Now, from Eqs. (i), (ii) and (iii), we get

$AE = DF$

Also, $\quad AE \parallel DF \quad$ [$\because AB \parallel CD$]

$\Rightarrow$ $AEFD$ is a parallelogram.

[$\because$ if a pair of opposite sides of a quadrilateral are parallel and equal, then the quadrilateral is a parallelogram]

$\Rightarrow \quad AD \parallel EF$

Also, $\quad AD \parallel BC$

[$\because$ $ABCD$ is a parallelogram]

$\therefore \quad AD \parallel BC \parallel EF$

Now, E is the mid-point of AB.

$\therefore \quad AE = EB$

By equal intercept theorem, we can say that PQ also makes equal intercepts on these parallel lines,

i.e. $PO = OQ$ **Hence proved.**

11. We have, in rhombus $ABCD$. $AO = 4$ cm and $DO = 3$ cm.

We know that the diagonals of rhombus bisect each other at right angle.

$\therefore$ In right angled ΔAOD,

By Pythagoras theorem,

$AD^2 = AO^2 + DO^2$

$\Rightarrow \quad AD^2 = (4)^2 + (3)^2$

$\Rightarrow \quad AD^2 = 16 + 9$

$\Rightarrow \quad AD^2 = 25 \Rightarrow AD = 5$ cm

[$\because$ sides cannot be negative]

Now, the perimeter of the rhombus $= 4 \times$ Side

$= 4 \times AD = 4 \times 5$

[$\because AD = 5$ cm]

$= 20$ cm

12. Let x be the distance between top of the poles.
i.e. $DC = x$ m

Again, let $BC = 11$ m and $AD = 6$ m and $AB = 12$ m

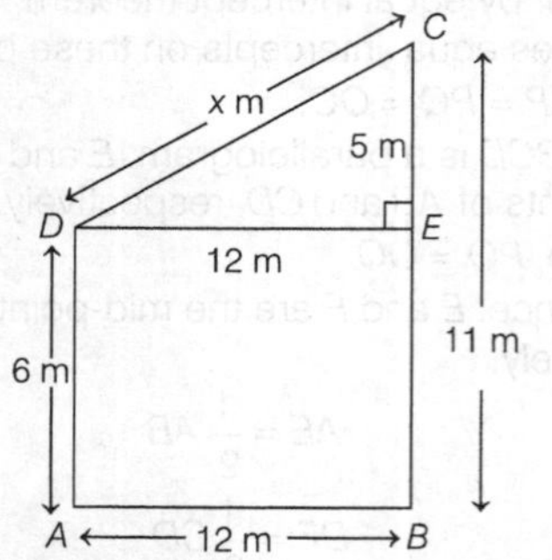

Then, $CE = BC - BE = 11 - 6 = 5$ m [$\because AD = BE$]

Also, $AB = 12$ m

$\therefore$ $DE = 12$ m

In ΔDEC, using Pythagoras theorem, we get

$$DC^2 = DE^2 + CE^2$$

$$\Rightarrow \quad x^2 = 12^2 + 5^2$$

$$= 144 + 25 = 169$$

$$\therefore \quad x = \sqrt{169} = 13$$

[taking positive square root]

Hence, the distance between the top of the poles is 13 m.

13. Draw an equilateral ΔABC having each side as $2a$. Also, draw $AD \perp BC$, where AD is an altitude.

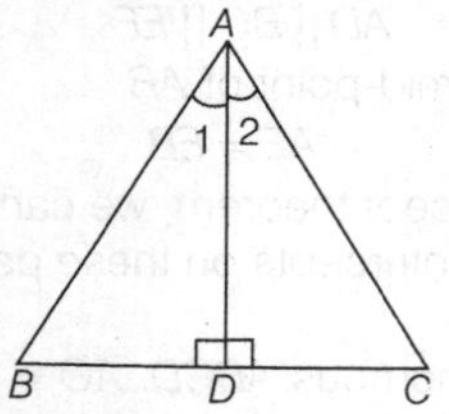

In ΔADB and ΔADC,

$AD = AD$ [common side]

$AB = AC$ [sides of an equilateral triangle]

and $\angle ADB = \angle ADC$ [each 90°]

$\therefore$ $\Delta ADB \cong \Delta ADC$ [by RHS congruency rule]

Then, $BD = CD = \frac{1}{2} BC = a$ [by CPCT]

In ΔADB, using Pythagoras theorem, we get

$$AB^2 = AD^2 + BD^2$$

$$\Rightarrow \quad (2a)^2 = AD^2 + a^2$$

$$\Rightarrow \quad 4a^2 = AD^2 + a^2$$

$$\Rightarrow \quad AD^2 = 3a^2$$

$$\therefore \quad AD = \sqrt{3}a$$

Hence, the altitude of ΔABC is $\sqrt{3}a$ units.

14. Suppose $ABCD$ is a rhombus, in which

$AB = BC = CD = DA = a$ [say]

Here, the diagonals AC and BD are perpendicular bisector of each other at O.

In ΔAOB, $\angle AOB = 90°$

$OA = \frac{1}{2} AC$ [$\because OA = OC$] ...(i)

and $OB = \frac{1}{2} BD$ [$\because OB = OD$] ...(ii)

By using Pythagoras theorem, we get

$$OA^2 + OB^2 = AB^2$$

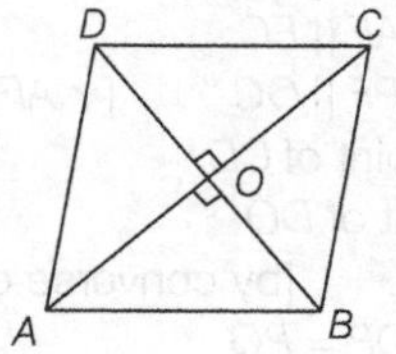

$$\left(\frac{1}{2} AC\right)^2 + \left(\frac{1}{2} BD\right)^2 = AB^2 \quad \text{[from Eqs. (i) and (ii)]}$$

$$\Rightarrow \quad AC^2 + BD^2 = 4AB^2$$

$$\Rightarrow \quad AB^2 + BC^2 + CD^2 + DA^2 = AC^2 + BD^2$$

[$\because AB = BC = CD = DA$] **Hence proved.**

15. Let ΔABC be an equilateral triangle of side a.
Draw $AD \perp BC$.
Again, let $AD = x$ be an altitude.

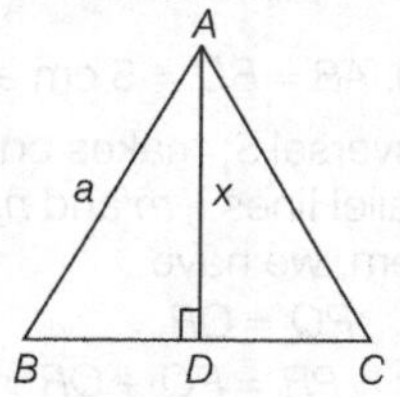

Now, $BD = CD$

[$\because$ in an equilateral triangle, altitude AD is perpendicular bisector of base BC]

$$= \frac{1}{2} BC = \frac{1}{2} a$$

[$\because$ each side of an equilateral triangle is a]

In right angled ΔADB, using Pythagoras theorem, we get

$$AB^2 = AD^2 + BD^2$$

$$\Rightarrow \quad a^2 = x^2 + \left(\frac{1}{2} a\right)^2$$

$$\Rightarrow \quad a^2 = x^2 + \frac{1}{4} a^2 \Rightarrow 4a^2 = 4x^2 + a^2$$

$$\therefore \quad 3a^2 = 4x^2$$

Thus, we have three times the square of one side (a) is equal to four times the square of one of its altitudes.

Hence proved.

16. Consider a right angled ΔABC, right angled at C. D and E are two points on sides CA and CB. Join ED, BD and EA.

By Pythagoras theorem,

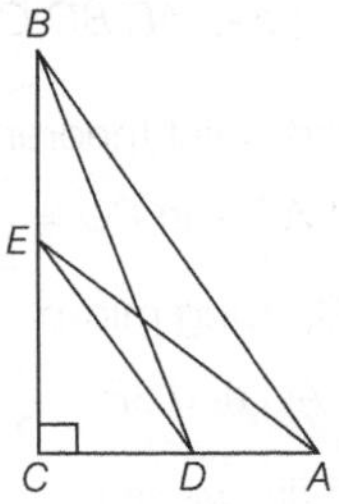

In ΔACE, $AE^2 = CA^2 + CE^2$ ...(i)

In ΔBCD, $BD^2 = BC^2 + CD^2$ ...(ii)

In ΔECD, $CD^2 + CE^2 = DE^2$ ...(iii)

and in ΔACB,

$CA^2 + CB^2 = BA^2$ ...(iv)

On adding Eqs. (i) and (ii), we get

$$AE^2 + BD^2 = (CA^2 + CE^2) + (BC^2 + CD^2)$$
$$= (BC^2 + CA^2) + (CD^2 + CE^2)$$

$\Rightarrow AE^2 + BD^2 = BA^2 + DE^2$ [from Eqs. (iii) and (iv)]

Hence proved.

17. Given In figure, ABC is a triangle in which $\angle ABC > 90^\circ$ and $AD \perp CB$ produced.

To prove $AC^2 = AB^2 + BC^2 + 2BC \cdot BD$

Proof In right angled ΔADC, $\angle D = 90^\circ$

By Pythagoras theorem,

$$AC^2 = AD^2 + DC^2$$
$$= AD^2 + (BD + BC)^2 \quad [\because DC = DB + BC]$$
$$= (AD^2 + BD^2) + BC^2 + 2BD \cdot BC$$
$$[\because (a + b)^2 = a^2 + b^2 + 2ab]$$

$\Rightarrow AC^2 = AB^2 + BC^2 + 2BC \cdot BD$

[$\because$ in right angled ΔADB, $AB^2 = AD^2 + DB^2$]

Hence proved.

18. Given In a ΔABC, $BC^2 = AB^2 + AC^2$

To prove $\angle A = 90^\circ$

Construction Construct an another ΔPQR such that $\angle P = 90^\circ$, $PQ = AB$ and $PR = AC$.

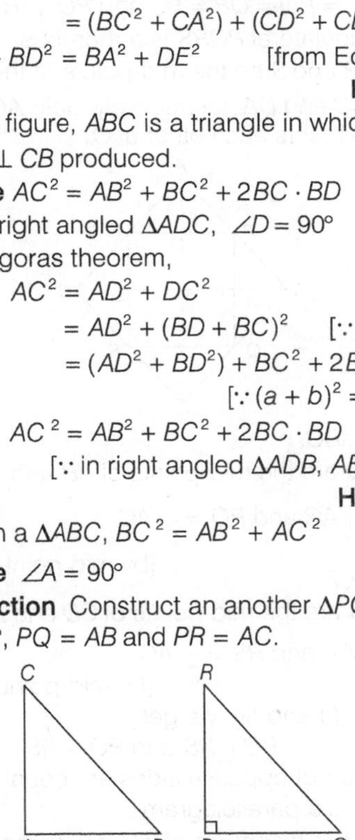

Proof In ΔPQR,

By Pythagoras theorem,

$QR^2 = PQ^2 + PR^2$

$\Rightarrow QR^2 = AB^2 + AC^2$ [by construction]

But $BC^2 = AB^2 + AC^2$ [given]

$\therefore QR^2 = BC^2$

$\Rightarrow QR = BC$

In ΔABC and ΔPQR,

$AB = PQ$ [by construction]

$AC = PR$ [by construction]

and $BC = QR$ [proved above]

$\therefore \Delta ABC \cong \Delta PQR$ [by SSS of congruence rule]

$\Rightarrow \angle A = \angle P$ [by CPCT]

$\Rightarrow \angle A = 90^\circ$

19. Let the sides of the triangle be $AB = 3$ cm, $BC = 4$ cm and $AC = 5$ cm.

$\therefore AB^2 = 3^2 = 9, BC^2 = 4^2 = 16$

and $AC^2 = 5^2 = 25$

Since, $AB^2 + BC^2 = AC^2$

Then, by converse of Pythagoras theorem, triangle is a right angled triangle.

20. Given, in ΔABC, $AB = 6\sqrt{3}$ cm, $AC = 12$ cm and $BC = 6$ cm

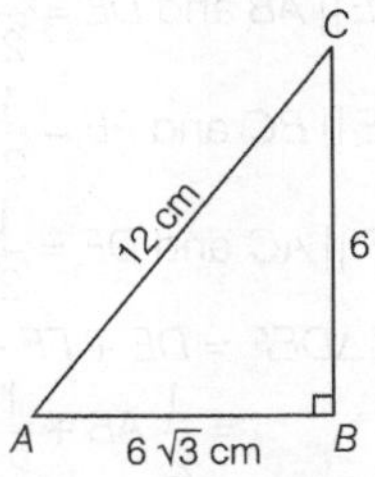

Now, $AB^2 = (6\sqrt{3})^2 = 108$

$AC^2 = (12)^2 = 144$

and $BC^2 = (6)^2 = 36$

Since, $AC^2 = AB^2 + BC^2$

Then, by converse of Pythagoras theorem, ΔABC is a right angled triangle i.e. $\angle B = 90^\circ$.

21. In right angled ΔPSQ and ΔPSR, we have

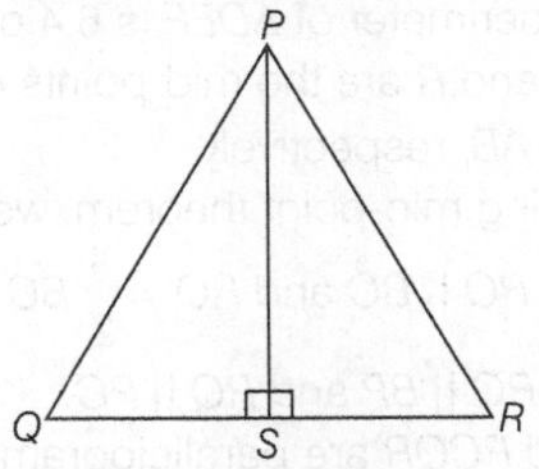

$PQ^2 = PS^2 + QS^2$ ...(i)

and $PR^2 = PS^2 + SR^2$ ...(ii)

On adding Eqs. (i) and (ii), we get

$$PQ^2 + PR^2 = 2PS^2 + QS^2 + SR^2$$
$$= 2(QS \times SR) + QS^2 + SR^2 \quad \text{[given]}$$
$$= (QS + SR)^2$$
$$[\because a^2 + b^2 + 2ab = (a + b)^2]$$

$\Rightarrow PQ^2 + PR^2 = QR^2$

Hence, ΔQPR is a right angled triangle.

[by converse of Pythagoras theorem]

Long Answer Type Questions

1. Given, D, E and F are the mid-points of sides BC, CA and AB, respectively.

And perimeter of $\Delta ABC = 12.8$ cm.

i.e. $AB + BC + CA = 12.8$ cm

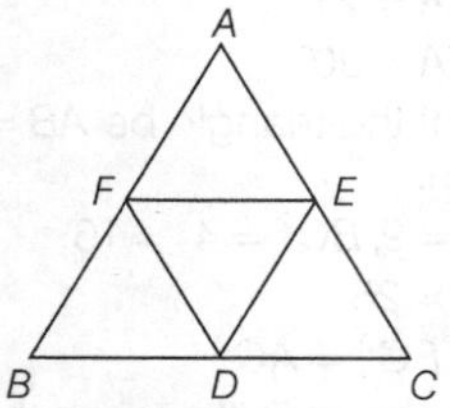

In ΔABC, D and E are the mid-points of sides BC and AC.

By mid-point theorem,

$$DE \parallel AB \text{ and } DE = \frac{1}{2} AB \quad \ldots(i)$$

Similarly, $$FE \parallel BC \text{ and } FE = \frac{1}{2} BC \quad \ldots(ii)$$

and $$DF \parallel AC \text{ and } DF = \frac{1}{2} AC \quad \ldots(iii)$$

Now, perimeter of $\Delta DEF = DE + FE + DF$

$$= \frac{1}{2} AB + \frac{1}{2} BC + \frac{1}{2} AC$$

[from Eqs. (i), (ii) and (iii)]

$$= \frac{1}{2}(AB + BC + AC)$$

$$= \frac{1}{2} \times 12.8$$

[$\because AB + BC + CA = 12.8$ cm]

$= 6.4$ cm

Hence, the perimeter of ΔDEF is 6.4 cm.

2. Given, P, Q and R are the mid-points of the sides BC, CA and AB, respectively.

In ΔABC, using mid-point theorem, we get

$$RQ \parallel BC \text{ and } RQ = \frac{1}{2} BC \quad \ldots(i)$$

$\Rightarrow$ $RQ \parallel BP$ and $RQ \parallel PC$.

$\therefore$ $BPQR$ and $PCQR$ are parallelograms.

We know that diagonals of parallelogram bisect each other.

$\therefore$ X and Y are the mid-points of PR and CR, respectively.

In ΔPQR, using mid-point theorem, we get

$$XY \parallel QR \text{ and } XY = \frac{1}{2} RQ \quad \ldots(ii)$$

From Eqs (i) and (ii), we get

$$XY = \frac{1}{2}\left(\frac{1}{2} BC\right)$$

$\Rightarrow$ $XY = \frac{1}{4} BC$ **Hence proved.**

3. Given, in rectangle $ABCD, P, Q, R$ and S are the mid-points of the sides AB, BC, CD and DA, respectively.

In ΔABC, using mid-point theorem, we get

$$PQ \parallel AC \text{ and } PQ = \frac{1}{2} AC \quad \ldots(i)$$

Similarly, in ΔADC, using mid-point theorem, we get

$$SR \parallel AC \text{ and } SR = \frac{1}{2} AC \quad \ldots(ii)$$

From Eqs. (i) and (ii), we get

$PQ \parallel SR$ and $PQ = SR$

Now, in ΔAPS and ΔBPQ,

$AP = BP$ [P is mid-point of AB]

$\angle SAP = \angle QBP$ [each 90°]

and $SA = QB$ [opposite sides of rectangle]

$\therefore$ $\Delta APS \cong \Delta BPQ$ [by SAS congruence rule]

$\therefore$ $SP = QP$ [by CPCT]

Hence, $SP = PQ = QR = RS$ and $PQ \parallel SR, PS \parallel QR$.

$\therefore$ The quadrilateral $PQRS$ is a rhombus.

4. Let P, Q, R and S be the mid-points of the sides AB, BC, CD and DA, respectively. Join AC and BD which intersects each other at O.

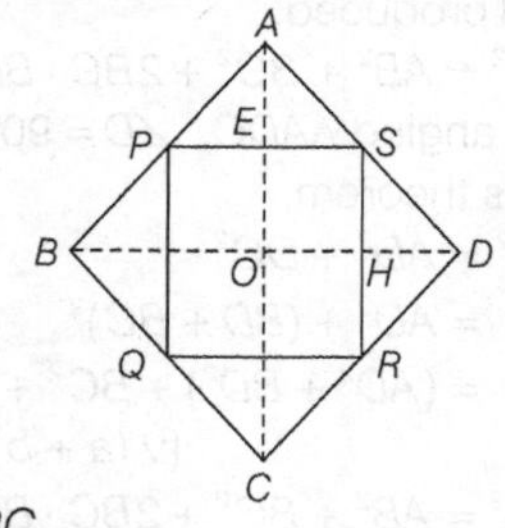

Now, in ΔABC,

$\because$ P and Q are the mid-points of AB and BC.

$\therefore$ $PQ \parallel AC$ and $PQ = \frac{1}{2} AC$

[by mid-point theorem] ...(i)

and in ΔACD,

$\because$ R and S are the mid-points of CD and DA.

$\therefore$ $RS \parallel AC$ and $RS = \frac{1}{2} AC$

[by mid-point theorem] ...(ii)

From Eqs. (i) and (ii), we get

$PQ \parallel RS$ and $PQ = RS$

Since, a pair of opposite sides are equal and parallel

So, $PQRS$ is a parallelogram.

We know that diagonals of kite are perpendicular to each other.

i.e. $AC \perp BD \Rightarrow \angle AOD = 90°$

Clearly, $HS \parallel OE$ and $SE \parallel OH$.

So, $SEOH$ is a parallelogram.

Hence, $\angle ESH = \angle EOH = 90°$

[$\because$ opposite angles of a parallelogram are equal]

So, parallelogram $PQRS$ is a rectangle as each angle is 90°. **Hence proved.**

5. Given In ΔABC, $AD = \frac{1}{4}AB$ and $AE = \frac{1}{4}AC$

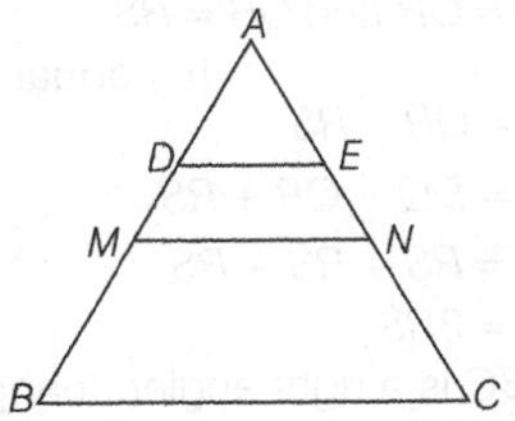

To prove $DE = \frac{1}{4}BC$

Proof Let M and N be the mid-points of sides AB and AC, respectively.

By mid-point theorem,

$$MN \parallel BC \text{ and } MN = \frac{1}{2}BC \quad \ldots\text{(i)}$$

We have,

$$AM = \frac{1}{2}AB \quad [\because M \text{ is mid-point of } AB]$$

$$\Rightarrow \quad \frac{1}{2}AM = \frac{1}{4}AB$$

$$\therefore \quad \frac{1}{2}AM = AD \quad \text{[given]}$$

So, D is mid-point of AM.

Similarly, $AN = \frac{1}{2}AC$ $\quad [\because N$ is mid-point of $AC]$

$$\Rightarrow \quad \frac{1}{2}AN = \frac{1}{4}AC$$

$$\Rightarrow \quad \frac{1}{2}AN = AE \quad \text{[given]}$$

So, E is mid-point of AN.

In ΔAMN, D and E are the mid-points of AM and AN, respectively.

By mid-point theorem,

$$DE \parallel MN \text{ and } DE = \frac{1}{2}MN$$

$$\Rightarrow \quad DE = \frac{1}{2}\left(\frac{1}{2}BC\right) \quad \text{[from Eq. (i)]}$$

$$\Rightarrow \quad DE = \frac{1}{4}BC$$

Hence proved.

6. Given, in ΔABC, AD is the median and E is the mid-point of AD.

Draw $DP \parallel BF$, which intersect AC at P.

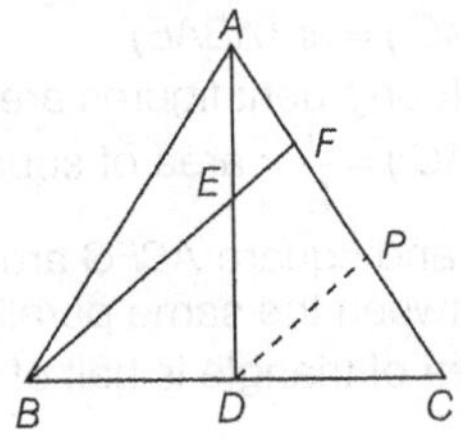

Now, in ΔADP, E is the mid-point of AD and $EF \parallel DP$.

By converse of mid-point theorem,

F is the mid-point of AP.

$$AF = FP \quad \ldots\text{(i)}$$

Similarly, in ΔFBC, D is the mid-point of BC and $DP \parallel BF$.

By converse of mid-point theorem,

P is the mid-point of FC.

$$FP = PC \quad \ldots\text{(ii)}$$

From Eqs. (i) and (ii), we get

$$AF = FP = PC$$

Now, $\quad AF + FP + PC = AC$

$$\Rightarrow \quad AF + AF + AF = 9 \quad [\because AC = 9\text{ cm}]$$

$$\Rightarrow \quad 3AF = 9 \Rightarrow AF = \frac{9}{3}$$

$$\therefore \quad AF = 3\text{ cm}$$

7. Given, $PQRS$ is a parallelogram, L is the mid-point of SR and $LQ \parallel SN$.

(i) In ΔRNS, L is the mid-point of SR and $LQ \parallel SN$.
Then, Q is the mid-point of RN.
[by converse of mid-point theorem]

i.e. $QN = QR = \frac{1}{2}RN$

and $LQ \parallel SN$, $LQ = \frac{1}{2}SN$ $\quad$ [by mid-point theorem]

$$\Rightarrow \quad SN = 2LQ$$

Hence proved.

(ii) Since, Q is the mid-point of RN.

$$QR = \frac{1}{2}RN \Rightarrow SP = \frac{1}{2}RN$$

$[\because SP = QR$, opposite sides of parallelogram$]$

Hence proved.

8. Given AD is a median of ΔABC, E is the mid-point of AD and $DP \parallel AC$.

To prove $BE : EQ = 3 : 1$

Proof In ΔBCQ, D is the mid-point of side BC and $PD \parallel CQ$.

Therefore, by converse of mid-point theorem,

P is the mid-point of BQ.

i.e. $\quad BP = PQ \quad \ldots\text{(i)}$

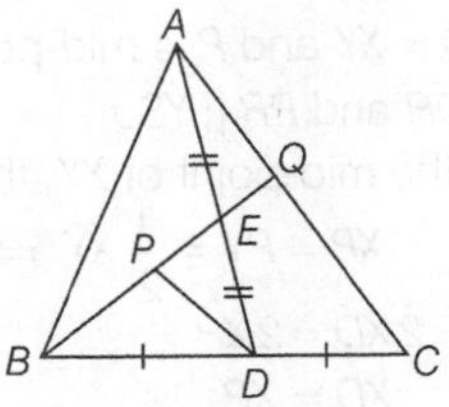

In ΔAEQ and ΔDEP,

$$\angle AEQ = \angle DEP \quad \text{[vertically opposite angles]}$$

$$\Rightarrow \quad AE = ED \quad \text{[given]}$$

$$\Rightarrow \quad \angle AQE = \angle DPE$$

[alternate angles as $PD \parallel AC$]

$$\therefore \quad \Delta AEQ \cong \Delta DEP \quad \text{[by AAS congruence rule]}$$

$\Rightarrow \quad EQ = PE$ [by CPCT]

i.e. E is the mid-point of PQ.

or $\quad EQ = \frac{1}{2}PQ$ ...(ii)

and $\quad PE = \frac{1}{2}PQ$ ...(iii)

On adding Eqs. (i) and (iii), we get

$$BP + PE = PQ + \frac{1}{2}PQ$$

$\Rightarrow \quad BE = \frac{3}{2}PQ = \frac{3}{2} \times 2EQ$ $[\because PQ = 2EQ]$

$\Rightarrow \quad BE = 3EQ$

$\Rightarrow \quad \frac{BE}{EQ} = \frac{3}{1}$

$\Rightarrow \quad BE : EQ = 3 : 1$

9. Given $l \parallel m \parallel n$ and a transversal p cutting them at points A, B and C respectively, such that $AB = BC$. Also, any other line q cuts them at points D, E and F, respectively.

To prove $DE = EF$

Construction Join AF which cuts BE at G.

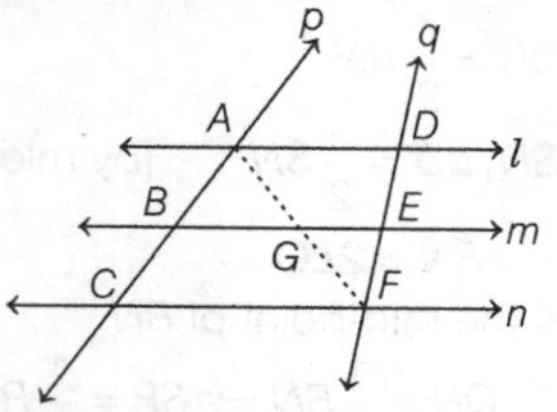

Proof In ΔACF, B is the mid-point of AC

$[\because AB = BC$, given$]$

and $\quad BG \parallel CF$ $[\because m \parallel n$, given$]$

By converse of mid-point theorem,

G is the mid-point of AF.

Now, in ΔAFD, G is the mid-point of AF.

and $\quad GE \parallel AD$ $[\because l \parallel m$, given$]$

By converse of mid-point theorem,

E is the mid-point of DF.

Then, $\quad DE = EF$

Hence, the line q makes equal intercept at l, m and n.

Hence proved.

10. We have, $2XD = XY$ and P is mid-point of XY, Q is mid-point of DR and $PR \parallel YS$.

(i) Since, P is the mid-point of XY, then

$$XP = PY = \frac{1}{2}XY \Rightarrow XY = 2XP$$

$\Rightarrow \quad 2XD = 2XP$ $[\because XY = 2XD]$

$\Rightarrow \quad XD = XP$

$\therefore$ X is the mid-point of PD

and Q is the mid-point of DR.

$XQ \parallel PR$ [by mid-point theorem] ...(a)

and $\quad PR \parallel YS$ [given] ...(b)

From Eqs. (a) and (b), we get

$XQ \parallel YS$ **Hence proved.**

(ii) Since, Q is the mid-point of DR.

Then, $DQ = QR$ and $QR = RS$

[by equal intercept theorem]

$\Rightarrow \quad DQ = QR = RS$

Now, $\quad DS = DQ + QR + RS$

$\Rightarrow \quad DS = RS + RS + RS$

$\Rightarrow \quad DS = 3RS$ **Hence proved.**

11. Given A ΔABC is a right angled triangle, right angled at B.

To prove $AC^2 = AB^2 + BC^2$

Construction Draw squares $ABFG$, $BCHI$ and $ACDE$ on sides AB, BC and AC, respectively. Draw $BN \perp DE$ which intersect AC at M, DE at N. Join GC and BE.

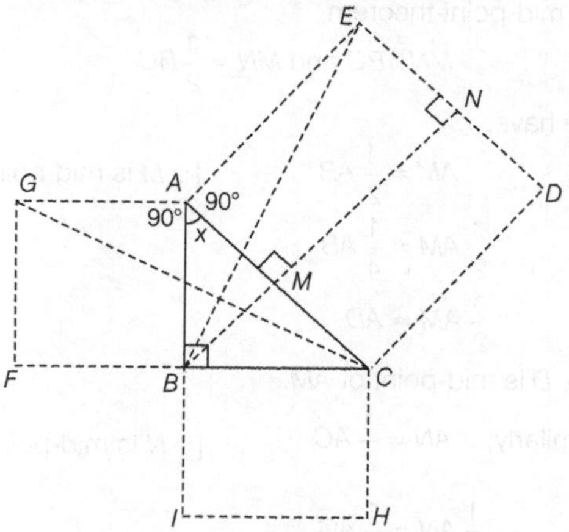

Proof $\angle FBC = \angle FBA + \angle ABC = 90° + 90° = 180°$

Hence, FBC is a straight line.

Since, GA and FB are opposite sides of a square.

$\therefore \quad GA \parallel FB$

$\Rightarrow \quad GA \parallel FC$

Since, $\quad BN \perp AC$ and $AE \perp AC$

$\Rightarrow \quad AE \parallel BN$

As each angle of quadrilateral $AMNE$ is 90°.

$\Rightarrow$ $AMNE$ is a rectangle.

Now, let $\angle BAC = x$

In ΔGAC and ΔBAE,

$AG = AB$ [sides of square]

$\angle GAC = \angle BAE = 90° + x$

and $\quad AC = AE$ [sides of square]

$\therefore \quad \Delta GAC \cong \Delta BAE$ [by SAS congruence rule]

$\therefore \quad$ ar (ΔGAC) = ar (ΔBAE)

[congruent figures are equal in area] ...(i)

Now, ar $(\Delta GAC) = \frac{1}{2} \times$ area of square $ABFG$ ...(ii)

$[\because \Delta GAC$ and square $ABFG$ are on same base AG and between the same parallel lines AG and CF, so area of triangle is half of the area of square$]$

Similarly, ar (ΔBAE) $= \frac{1}{2} \times$ area of rectangle $AMNE$ ...(iii)

From Eqs. (i), (ii) and (iii), we get

area of square $ABFG$ = area of rectangle $AMNE$ ...(iv)

Similarly, area of square $BCHI$

= area of rectangle $CMND$ ...(v)

On adding Eqs. (iv) and (v), we get

Area of square $ABFG$ + Area of square $BCHI$

= Area of rectangle $AMNE$ + Area of rectangle $CMND$

$\Rightarrow$ Area of square $ABFG$ + Area of square $BCHI$

= Area of square $ACDE$

$\Rightarrow \quad AB^2 + BC^2 = AC^2$

[$\because$ area of square = (side)^2]

$\Rightarrow \quad AC^2 = AB^2 + BC^2$

Hence proved.

12. (a) Given, $AB = c, BC = a, AC = b$ and $CD = p$

In right angled ΔABC, using Pythagoras theorem,

$$c^2 = a^2 + b^2 \quad \text{...(i)}$$

Now, area of $\Delta ABC = \frac{1}{2} \times (BC) \times (AC) = \frac{1}{2} ab$ ...(ii)

Again, area of $\Delta ABC = \frac{1}{2} \times (AB) \times (CD) = \frac{1}{2} cp$ ...(iii)

From Eqs. (ii) and (iii), we get

$$\frac{1}{2} ab = \frac{1}{2} cp \Rightarrow ab = cp$$

$$\Rightarrow \quad c = \left(\frac{ab}{p}\right)$$

On putting the value of c in Eq. (i), we get

$$\left(\frac{ab}{p}\right)^2 = a^2 + b^2$$

$$\Rightarrow \quad \frac{1}{p^2} = \frac{a^2}{a^2b^2} + \frac{b^2}{a^2b^2}$$

$$\Rightarrow \quad \frac{1}{p^2} = \frac{1}{b^2} + \frac{1}{a^2}$$

$$\Rightarrow \quad \frac{1}{p^2} = \frac{1}{a^2} + \frac{1}{b^2}$$

Hence proved.

13. Given A equilateral ΔABC, where D is a point on BC such that $BD : DC = 2 : 1$.

To prove $9\, AD^2 = 7\, AB^2$

Construction Draw $AE \perp BC$

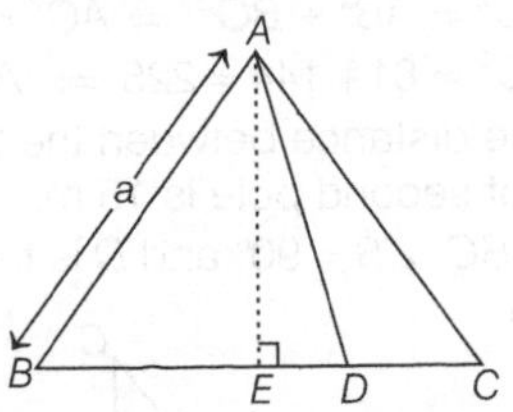

Proof Since, ABC is an equilateral triangle.

$\therefore \quad AB = BC = CA = a$ (say) ...(i)

Also, as $BD : DC = 2 : 1$, therefore

$$BD = \frac{2}{3} BC = \frac{2}{3} a \quad \text{...(ii)}$$

Now, since $AE \perp BC$

$\therefore \quad BE = EC = \frac{1}{2} a$

[in an equilateral triangle, altitude is a perpendicular bisector]

$\Rightarrow \quad DE = BD - BE$

$$= \frac{2}{3} a - \frac{1}{2} a$$

$$= \left(\frac{4-3}{6}\right) a = \frac{1}{6} a \quad \text{...(iii)}$$

Now, from ΔAED, we have

$$AD^2 = AE^2 + ED^2$$

[using Pythagoras theorem]

$\Rightarrow \quad AD^2 = AB^2 - BE^2 + ED^2$

[in ΔABE, $AB^2 = BE^2 + AE^2$]

$$= a^2 - \left(\frac{1}{2} a\right)^2 + \left(\frac{1}{6} a\right)^2$$

[using Eqs. (i), (ii) and (iii)]

$$\Rightarrow \quad AD^2 = a^2 - \frac{1}{4} a^2 + \frac{1}{36} a^2$$

$$\Rightarrow \quad AD^2 = a^2 \left(\frac{36 - 9 + 1}{36}\right)$$

$$= \frac{28}{36} \times a^2$$

$\Rightarrow \quad AD^2 = \frac{7}{9} \times AB^2$ [using Eq. (i)]

$\Rightarrow \quad 9AD^2 = 7AB^2$ **Hence proved.**

14. Since, BL and CM are medians, then lines BL and CM divides AC and AB into two equal parts.

$$\therefore \quad CL = AL = \frac{AC}{2} \quad \text{...(i)}$$

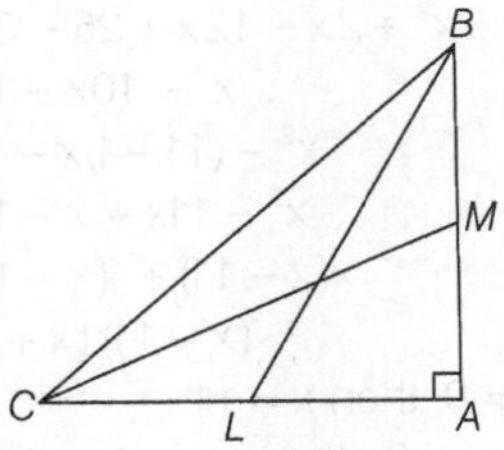

and $\quad AM = BM = \frac{AB}{2}$ ...(ii)

In ΔBAC, $\angle A = 90°$

By Pythagoras theorem, we get

$$BC^2 = AB^2 + AC^2 \quad \text{...(iii)}$$

In ΔBAL, $\angle A = 90°$

By Pythagoras theorem, we get

$$BL^2 = AB^2 + AL^2$$

$\Rightarrow \quad BL^2 = AB^2 + \left(\frac{AC}{2}\right)^2$ [using Eq. (i)]

$$\Rightarrow \quad BL^2 = AB^2 + \frac{AC^2}{4}$$

$$\Rightarrow \quad 4BL^2 = 4AB^2 + AC^2 \quad \text{...(iv)}$$

In ΔMAC, $\angle A = 90°$

By Pythagoras theorem, we get

$$CM^2 = AC^2 + AM^2$$

$$\Rightarrow \quad CM^2 = AC^2 + \left(\frac{AB}{2}\right)^2 \quad \text{[using Eq. (ii)]}$$

$$\Rightarrow \quad 4CM^2 = 4AC^2 + AB^2 \quad \text{...(v)}$$

On adding Eqs. (iv) and (v), we get

$$4(BL^2 + CM^2) = 5(AC^2 + AB^2)$$

$$\Rightarrow \quad 4(BL^2 + CM^2) = 5BC^2 \quad \text{[using Eq. (iii)]}$$

Hence proved.

15. In right angled ΔABC,

$AB = (x - 3)$ cm,

$BC = (x + 4)$ cm

and $AC = (x + 6)$ cm

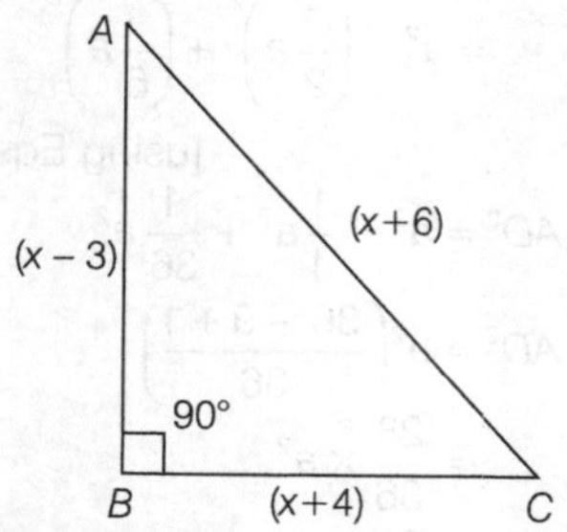

By Pythagoras theorem,

$$AC^2 = BC^2 + AB^2$$

$$\Rightarrow \quad (x + 6)^2 = (x + 4)^2 + (x - 3)^2$$

$$\Rightarrow x^2 + (6)^2 + 2(x)\cdot(6) = x^2 + (4)^2 + 2(x).(4) + x^2 + (3)^2 - 2(x).(3)$$

$$\Rightarrow \quad x^2 + 36 + 12x = 2x^2 + 16 + 8x + 9 - 6x$$

$$\Rightarrow \quad 2x^2 - x^2 + 2x - 12x + 25 - 36 = 0$$

$$\Rightarrow \quad x^2 - 10x - 11 = 0$$

$$\Rightarrow \quad x^2 - (11 - 1)x - 11 = 0$$

$$\Rightarrow \quad x^2 - 11x + x - 11 = 0$$

$$\Rightarrow \quad x(x - 11) + 1(x - 11) = 0$$

$$\Rightarrow \quad (x - 11)(x + 1) = 0$$

When $x - 11 = 0$, then $x = 11$

and when $x + 1 = 0$, then $x = -1$

On taking positive value of x, we get

$$AB = (x - 3) = (11 - 3) = 8 \text{ cm}$$

$$BC = (x + 4) = (11 + 4) = 15 \text{ cm}$$

and $\quad CA = (x + 6) = (11 + 6) = 17$ cm

16. Given, $AB = 8$ cm, $BC = 6$ cm and $AC = 3$ cm.

Let the length of OC be x cm.

Then, $OB = (x + 6)$ cm

Now, in right angled ΔAOB,

By Pythagoras theorem,

$$AB^2 = OB^2 + OA^2$$

$$\Rightarrow \quad OA^2 = AB^2 - OB^2$$

$$\Rightarrow \quad OA^2 = (8)^2 - (x + 6)^2 \quad \text{...(i)}$$

Similarly, in right angled ΔAOC,

$$AC^2 = OC^2 + OA^2$$

$$\Rightarrow \quad OA^2 = AC^2 - OC^2$$

$$\Rightarrow \quad OA^2 = (3)^2 - x^2 \quad \text{...(ii)}$$

From Eqs. (i) and (ii), we get

$$(8)^2 - (x + 6)^2 = (3)^2 - x^2$$

$$\Rightarrow \quad 64 - (x^2 + 36 + 12x) = 9 - x^2$$

$$\Rightarrow \quad 64 - x^2 - 36 - 12x = 9 - x^2$$

$$\Rightarrow \quad 28 - 9 - 12x = 0$$

$$\Rightarrow \quad 19 - 12x = 0$$

$$\Rightarrow \quad x = \frac{19}{12} = 1\frac{7}{12} \text{ cm}$$

17. (i) Let AB and CE are two poles of height 9 m and 14 m, respectively.

And distance between their feet BC be 12 m.

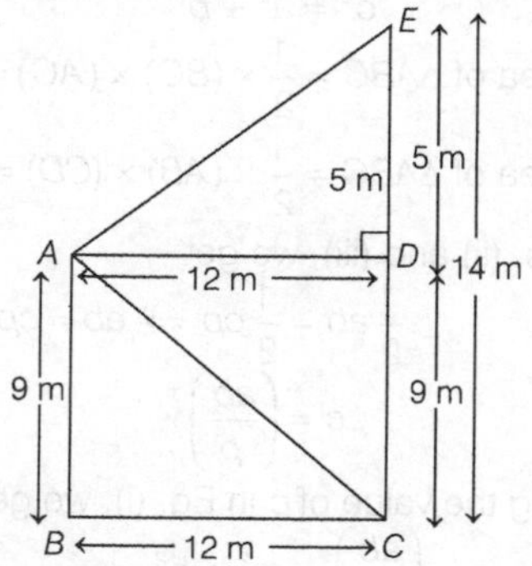

In figure, $AB = CD = 9$ m, $BC = AD = 12$ m,

$CE = 14$ m

and $\quad DE = CE - CD = 14 - 9 = 5$ m

Now, in right angle ΔADE,

By Pythagoras theorem,

$$AE^2 = AD^2 + DE^2$$

$$\Rightarrow \quad AE^2 = (12)^2 + (5)^2 \Rightarrow AE^2 = 144 + 25$$

$$\Rightarrow \quad AE^2 = 169 \Rightarrow AE = 13 \text{ m}$$

Hence, the distance between their tops be 13 m.

(ii) In right angled ΔABC,

by Pythagoras theorem,

$$AC^2 = AB^2 + BC^2 \Rightarrow AC^2 = (9)^2 + (12)^2$$

$$\Rightarrow \quad AC^2 = 81 + 144 = 225 \Rightarrow AC = 15 \text{ m}$$

Hence, the distance between the top of first pole and foot of second pole is 15 m.

18. Given, in ΔABC, $\angle B = 90°$ and D is the mid-point of BC, i.e. $BD = CD$

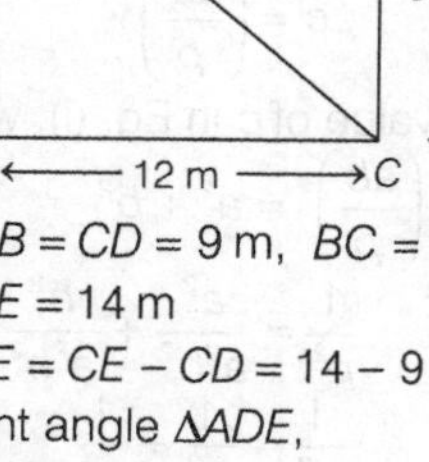

In ΔABC, using Pythagoras theorem, we get

$$AC^2 = AB^2 + BC^2$$

$\Rightarrow$ $AB^2 = AC^2 - BC^2$ ...(i)

In ΔABD, using Pythagoras theorem, we get

$$AD^2 = AB^2 + BD^2$$

$\Rightarrow$ $AB^2 = AD^2 - BD^2$ ...(ii)

From Eqs. (i) and (ii), we get

$$AC^2 - BC^2 = AD^2 - BD^2$$

$\Rightarrow$ $AC^2 = AD^2 + BC^2 - BD^2$

$\Rightarrow$ $AC^2 = AD^2 + (2CD)^2 - CD^2$ [$\because BC = 2CD, BD = CD$]

$\Rightarrow$ $AC^2 = AD^2 + 4CD^2 - CD^2$

$\Rightarrow$ $AC^2 = AD^2 + 3CD^2$ **Hence proved.**

19. Draw a line $PQ \parallel BC$ which passing through the point O and $PQ \perp AB$ and $PQ \perp CD$.

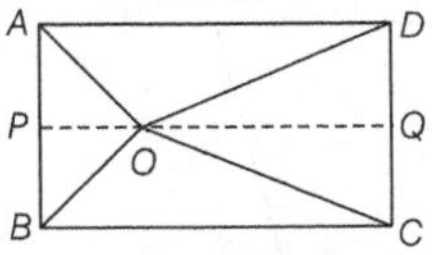

Now, in ΔOPB, using Pythagoras theorem, we get

$$OB^2 = OP^2 + PB^2$$ ...(i)

In ΔOAP, using Pythagoras theorem, we get

$$OA^2 = OP^2 + AP^2$$ ...(ii)

In ΔOQC, using Pythagoras theorem, we get

$$OC^2 = OQ^2 + CQ^2$$ ...(iii)

and in ΔOQD, using Pythagoras theorem, we get

$$OD^2 = OQ^2 + QD^2$$ ...(iv)

On adding Eqs. (i) and (iv), we get

$OB^2 + OD^2 = OP^2 + PB^2 + OQ^2 + QD^2$

$= OP^2 + CQ^2 + OQ^2 + AP^2$ [$\because BP = CQ$ and $QD = AP$, opposite sides of rectangles]

$= (OP^2 + AP^2) + (CQ^2 + OQ^2)$

$= OA^2 + OC^2$ [from Eqs. (ii) and (iii)]

$\Rightarrow$ $OB^2 + OD^2 = OA^2 + OC^2$ **Hence proved.**

20. Given, $OP \perp BC$, $OQ \perp AC$ and $OR \perp AB$.

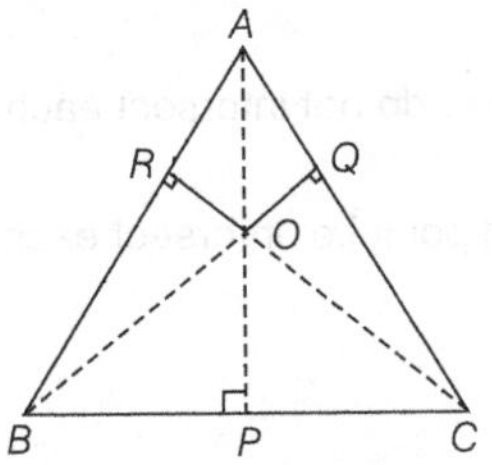

Join the point O to the points A, B and C, respectively.

Now, in ΔARO, using Pythagoras theorem, we get

$$AR^2 = OA^2 - OR^2$$ ...(i)

In ΔBPO, using Pythagoras theorem, we get

$$BP^2 = OB^2 - OP^2$$ ...(ii)

and in ΔCQO, using Pythagoras theorem, we get

$$CQ^2 = OC^2 - OQ^2$$ ...(iii)

On adding Eqs. (i), (ii) and (iii), we get

$AR^2 + BP^2 + CQ^2 = OA^2 - OR^2 + OB^2 - OP^2 + OC^2 - OQ^2$

$= (OA^2 - OQ^2) + (OB^2 - OR^2) + (OC^2 - OP^2)$

$= AQ^2 + BR^2 + CP^2$

$AR^2 + BP^2 + CQ^2 = AQ^2 + CP^2 + BR^2$

Hence proved.

Case Based Questions

1. (i) Since, R and Q are the mid-points of AB and CA, respectively.

$\therefore$ $RQ \parallel BC$ and $RQ = \frac{1}{2} BC$ [by mid-point theorem]

$RQ = \frac{1}{2} \times 28 = 14$ cm [$\because BC = 28$ cm] ...(a)

(ii) Since, P and Q are the mid-points of BC and CA, respectively.

$\therefore$ $PQ \parallel AB$ and $PQ = \frac{1}{2} AB$ [by mid-point theorem]

$\Rightarrow$ $PQ = \frac{1}{2} \times 25 = 12.5$ cm [$\because AB = 25$ cm] ...(b)

(iii) Since, P and R are the mid-points of BC and AB, respectively.

$\therefore$ $PR \parallel AC$ and $PR = \frac{1}{2} AC$ [by mid-point theorem]

$\Rightarrow$ $PR = \frac{1}{2} \times 26 = 13$ cm [$\because AC = 26$ cm]...(c)

Now, length of garland = Perimeter of ΔPQR

$= PQ + QR + PR$

$= 12.5 + 14 + 13$ [from Eqs. (a), (b) and (c)]

$= 39.5$ cm

2. (i) Since, PR is the hypotenuse of ΔPSR.

$\therefore$ Pythagoras theorem will be used.

(ii) In ΔPSR, using Pythagoras theorem, we get

$$(PR)^2 = (PS)^2 + (RS)^2$$

$\Rightarrow$ $PR^2 = (60)^2 + (80)^2$

$\Rightarrow$ $PR^2 = 3600 + 6400$

$\Rightarrow$ $PR^2 = 10000$

$\Rightarrow$ $PR = 100$ m

Hence, the distance PR is 100 m.

(iii) Let the length of pond p be x m. i.e. $PQ = x$ m

and $PR = 100$ m [from part (iii)]

$\Rightarrow$ $PQ + QR = 100$

$\Rightarrow$ $x + 50 = 100$ [$\because QR = 50$ m]

$\Rightarrow$ $x = 100 - 50 = 50$ m

Hence, the length of the pond is 50 m.

10

RECTILINEAR FIGURES

Rectilinear Figure

'Recti' means 'Straight' and 'Linear' means 'Line'. So, a rectilinear figure is a plane figure formed only by line segments. Some rectilinear figures are shown below

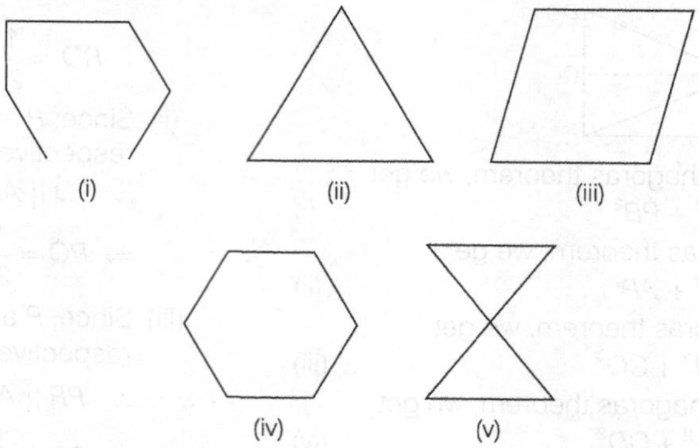

Quadrilaterals

'Quad' means 'Four' and 'Lateral' means 'Sides', so a closed figure having four sides, is called a quadrilateral.

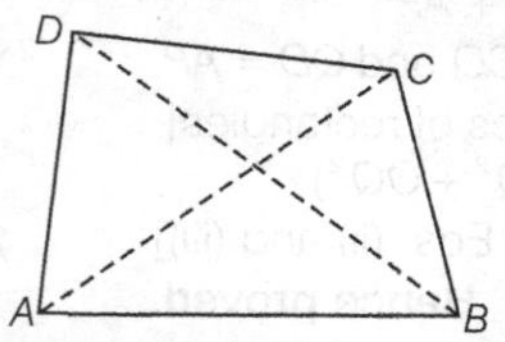

In a quadrilateral *ABCD, AB, BC, CD* and *DA* are the four sides, *A, B, C* and *D* are the four vertices and $\angle A$, $\angle B$, $\angle C$ and $\angle D$ are the four angles formed at the vertices.

(i) **Opposite Sides** Sides, which have no common end point (vertex) i.e. do not intersect each other.
e.g. *AB* and *DC*, *AD* and *BC*.

(ii) **Consecutive or Adjacent Sides** Sides, which have a common end point i.e. intersect each other.
e.g. *AB* and *BC*, *BC* and *CD*, *CD* and *AD*, *AD* and *AB*.

(iii) **Opposite Angles** Two angles, which do not have a common arm.
e.g. $\angle A = \angle C$ and $\angle B = \angle D$.

(iv) **Consecutive or Adjacent Angles** Two angles, which have a common arm.
e.g. $\angle A$ and $\angle B$, $\angle B$ and $\angle C$, $\angle C$ and $\angle D$, $\angle D$ and $\angle A$.

(v) **Diagonals** The line segment joining the opposite vertices.
e.g. *AC* and *BD*.

(vi) **Angle Sum Property of a Quadrilateral** The sum of all the four angles of a quadrilateral is 360°.
i.e. $\angle A + \angle B + \angle C + \angle D = 360°$.

Parallelogram

A quadrilateral in which both pairs of opposite sides are parallel, is called parallelogram.

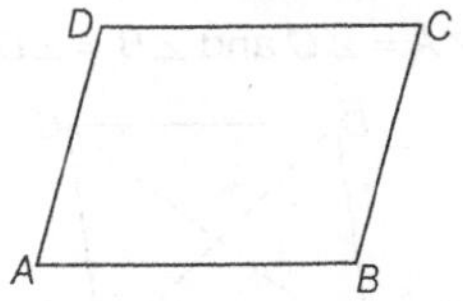

In the figure, *ABCD* is a parallelogram in which

$$AB \parallel DC \text{ and } AB = DC$$

$$BC \parallel AD \text{ and } BC = AD$$

$\therefore$ $$\angle A = \angle C \text{ and } \angle B = \angle D$$

Also, $\angle A + \angle B = 180°$, $\angle B + \angle C = 180°$, $\angle C + \angle D = 180°$ and $\angle D + \angle A = 180°$.

Properties of Parallelogram

(i) The opposite sides are parallel and equal.

(ii) The opposite angles are equal in measure.

(iii) The diagonals bisects each other.

(iv) The sum of adjacent angles of a parallelogram is 180°.

Theorems Based on Parallelogram and Their Uses

***Theorem* 1 A diagonal of a parallelogram divides it into two congruent triangles.**

Or Each diagonal of a parallelogram bisects the parallelogram.

ABCD is a parallelogram and *AC* is its diagonal, then

$$\Delta ABC \cong \Delta CDA$$

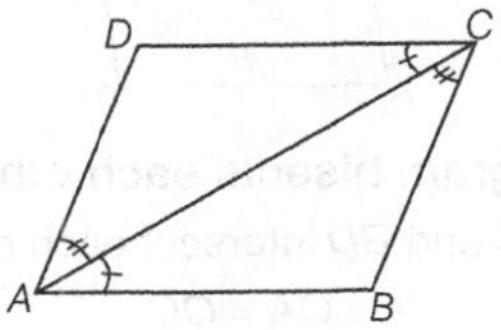

***Theorem* 2 In a parallelogram, opposite sides are equal.**

In a parallelogram *ABCD*, $AB = CD$ and $BC = AD$

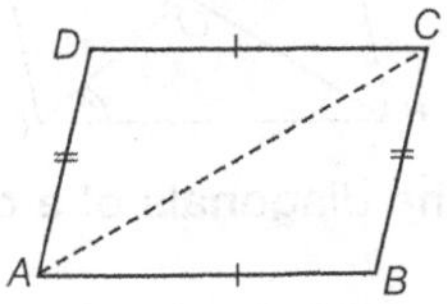

***Theorem* 3 (Converse of Theorem 2) If each pair of opposite sides of a quadrilateral is equal, then it is a parallelogram.**

In a quadrilateral *ABCD*, $AB = CD$ and $BC = AD$.

Then, *ABCD* is a parallelogram.

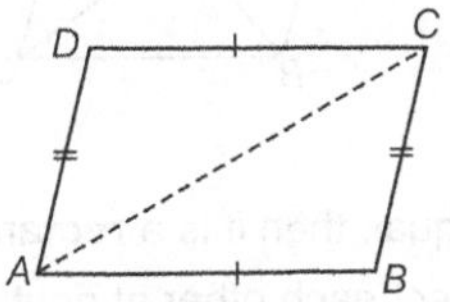

Theorem 4 In a parallelogram, opposite angles are equal.

ABCD is a parallelogram in which $AB \parallel CD$ and $BC \parallel AD$.

Then, $\angle A = \angle C$ and $\angle B = \angle D$

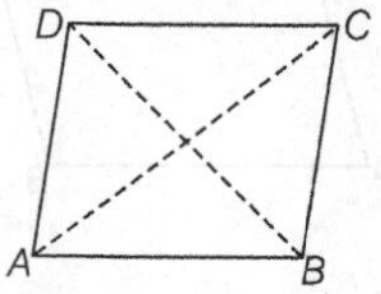

Theorem 5 (Converse of Theorem 4) If in a quadrilateral, each pair of opposite angles is equal, then it is a parallelogram.

In a quadrilateral, if $\angle A = \angle C$ and $\angle B = \angle D$, then that quadrilateral is parallelogram.

And $AB \parallel CD$ and $BC \parallel AD$

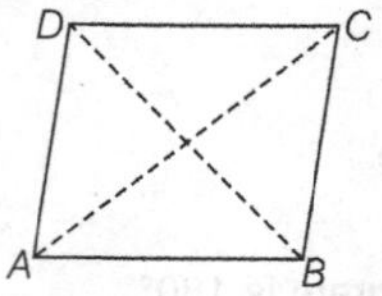

Theorem 6 A quadrilateral is a parallelogram, if a pair of opposite sides are equal and parallel.

ABCD is a quadrilateral, if $AB \parallel CD$ and $AB = CD$

$BC \parallel AD$ and $BC = AD$

Then, *ABCD* is a parallelogram.

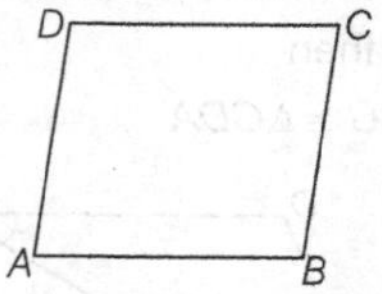

Theorem 7 The diagonals of a parallelogram bisects each other.

ABCD is a parallelogram, whose diagonals *AC* and *BD* intersect each other at *O*.

Then, $OA = OC$

and $OB = OD$

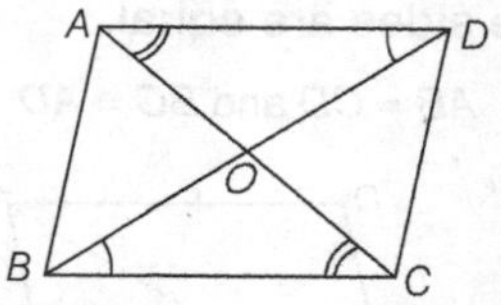

Theorem 8 (Converse of Theorem 7) If the diagonals of a quadrilateral bisect each other, then it is a parallelogram.

ABCD is a quadrilateral, whose diagonals *AC* and *BD* bisect each other.

i.e. $OA = OC$ and $OB = OD$. Then, *ABCD* is a parallelogram.

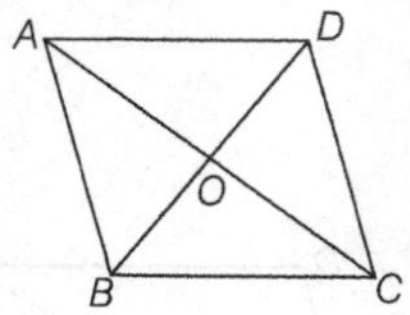

Important Results

(i) If the diagonals of a parallelogram are equal, then it is a **rectangle**.

(ii) If the diagonals of a parallelogram intersect each other at right angles, then it is a **rhombus**.

(iii) If the diagonals of a parallelogram are equal and intersect each other at right angles, then it is a **square**.

EXAM ORIENTED QUESTIONS

TYPE - 1   01 Mark

Multiple Choice Questions

Q.1 A diagonals of a parallelogram divides into two triangles. The triangles formed are
(a) congruent
(b) isosceles
(c) Don't have equal area
(d) None of the above

Q.2 In quadrilateral *PQRS*, $PQ \parallel SR$ and $QR \parallel PS$, then quadrilateral *PQRS* is a
(a) square (b) rectangle
(c) parallelogram (d) rhombus

Q.3 If the angles of a quadrilateral are in the ratio $3:5:9:13$, then angles are
(a) 36°, 60°, 120°, 156° (b) 36°, 60°, 108°, 156°
(c) 54°, 90°, 108°, 144° (d) 36°, 60°, 108°, 144°

Q.4 The measure of all the angles of a parallelogram, if an angle is 24° less than twice the smallest angle, are respectively
(a) 37°, 143°, 37°, 143° (b) 108°, 72°, 108°, 72°
(c) 68°, 112°, 68°, 112° (d) None of these

Q.5 In the given figure, if *ABCD* is a parallelogram, in which $\angle A = 60°$, then the value of $\angle B$ is

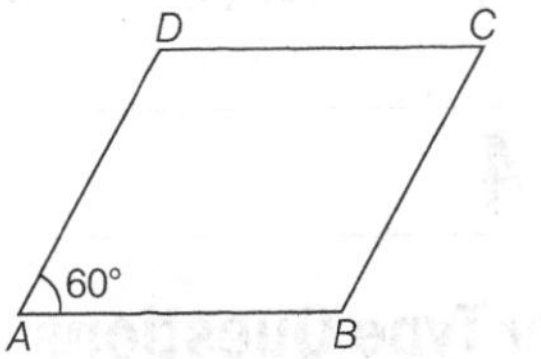

(a) 60° (b) 120°
(c) 50° (d) 100°

Q.6 The given figure shows a rhombus *ABCD*. Find the value of *y*.

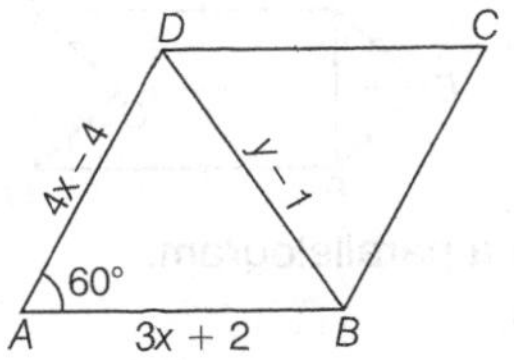

(a) 21 (b) 6
(c) 12 (d) 8

Q.7 If all the angles of a quadrilateral are equal, then the name of this quadrilateral is
(a) parallelogram (b) trapezium
(c) rhombus (d) rectangle

Q.8 Which of the following quadrilateral is not a square?
(a) All four sides are equal.
(b) All four interior angles are equal.
(c) Diagonals bisect each other.
(d) One angle between the diagonals is 30°.

Q.9 Two diagonals are not always equal in
(a) square (b) rectangle
(c) parallelogram (d) None of these

Q.10 In a quadrilateral *ABCD*, if $AB \parallel CD$, $BC \parallel AD$ and $\angle A = 90°$, then a quadrilateral *ABCD* is a
(a) square (b) rectangle
(c) parallelogram (d) rhombus

Answers

1. (a)	2. (c)	3. (b)	4. (c)	5. (b)
6. (a)	7. (d)	8. (d)	9. (c)	10. (b)

TYPE - 2   01 Mark

Assertion-Reason Type Questions

Q.1 **Assertion** (A) If an angle of a parallelogram is two third the adjacent angle, then the two angles of a parallelogram are 106° and 74°.

Reason (R) Adjacent angles of a parallelogram are supplementary.
(a) A is true, R is false.
(b) A is false, R is true.
(c) Both A and R are true and R is the correct reason for A.
(d) Both A and R are true and R is incorrect reason for A.

Q.2 **Assertion** (A) Three angles of a parallelogram are 85°, 95° and 85°, then the fourth angle is 95°.
Reason (R) The opposite angles of the parallelogram are unequal.
(a) A is true, R is false.
(b) A is false, R is true.
(c) Both A and R are true and R is the correct reason for A.
(d) Both A and R are true and R is incorrect reason for A.

Q.3 Assertion (A) In the given figure, if *ABCD* is a parallelogram, then the sum of the angles *x* and *z* is $180^\circ - y$.

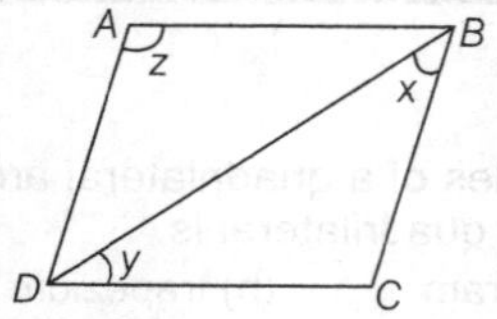

Reason (R) In a parallelogram, opposite angles are equal.

(a) A is true, R is false.
(b) A is false, R is true.
(c) Both A and R are true and R is the correct reason for A.
(d) Both A and R are true and R is incorrect reason for A.

Q.4 Assertion (A) If the side of a rhombus *ABCD* is 29 cm and one diagonal is 40 cm, then another diagonal is 42 cm.

Reason (R) In a right angled ΔABC,

$$AC^2 = AB^2 + BC^2.$$

(a) A is true, R is false.
(b) A is false, R is true.
(c) Both A and R are true and R is the correct reason for A.
(d) Both A and R are true and R is incorrect reason for A.

Answers

1. (b) **2.** (a) **3.** (c) **4.** (c)

TYPE - 3 01 Mark

Statement Based Questions

Q.1 Statement I The sum of adjacent angles of a parallelogram is 180°.

Statement II A quadrilateral is a parallelogram, if a pair of opposite sides are unequal and parallel.

Which of the following is valid?

(a) Both the Statements are true.
(b) Both the Statements are false.
(c) Statement I is true and Statement II is false.
(d) Statement I is false and Statement II is true.

Q.2 Statement I If the diagonals of a parallelogram intersect each other at right angles, then it is a rhombus.

Statement II All sides are equal in a rhombus.

Which of the following is valid?

(a) Both the Statements are true.
(b) Both the Statements are false.
(c) Statement I is true and Statement II is false.
(d) Statement I is false and Statement II is true.

Q.3 Statement I In a quadrilateral *PQRS*, $PQ = QR = RS = SP$, $\angle P = 90^\circ$, $PQ \parallel RS$ and $PS \parallel QR$. Then, *PQRS* is a rhombus.

Statement II Diagonals of a rhombus are perpendicular bisectors to each other.

Which of the following is valid?

(a) Both the Statements are true.
(b) Both the Statements are false.
(c) Statement I is true and Statement II is false.
(d) Statement I is false and Statement II is true.

Q.4 Statement I A diagonal of a parallelogram divides it into two congruent triangles.

Statement II If diagonals of a parallelogram are equal and perpendicular to each other, then it is a square.

Which of the following is valid?

(a) Both the Statements are true.
(b) Both the Statements are false.
(c) Statement I is true and Statement II is false.
(d) Statement I is false and Statement II is true.

Q.5 Statement I If the diagonals of a parallelogram are equal, then it is a rectangle.

Statement II The two diagonals are always unequal in square.

Which of the following is valid?

(a) Both the Statements are true.
(b) Both the Statements are false.
(c) Statement I is true and Statement II is false.
(d) Statement I is false and Statement II is true.

Answers

1. (c) **2.** (a) **3.** (d) **4.** (a) **5.** (c)

TYPE - 4 03 Marks

Short Answer Type Questions

Q.1 Prove that the sum of the four angles of a quadrilateral is 360°.

Q.2 In the given figure, *ABCD* and *PBCQ* are parallelograms. Prove that

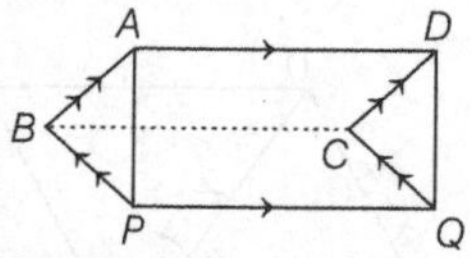

(i) *APQD* is a parallelogram.
(ii) $AP = DQ$.

Q.3 Prove that in a parallelogram, opposite angles are equal.

Q.4 In a parallelogram $ABCD$, if $\angle A = (3x - 20)^\circ$, $\angle B = (y + 15)^\circ$ and $\angle C = (x + 40)^\circ$, then find the values of x and y.

Q.5 Prove that if in a quadrilateral, each pair of opposite angles is equal, then it is a parallelogram.

Q.6 In the given figure, P is the mid-point of side BC of a parallelogram $ABCD$ such that $\angle BAP = \angle DAP$. Prove that $AD = 2CD$.

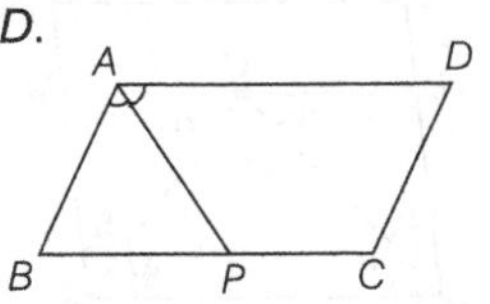

Q.7 Quadrilateral $ABCD$ is a parallelogram and AP and CQ are perpendicular from vertices A and C on diagonal BD (see the figure).

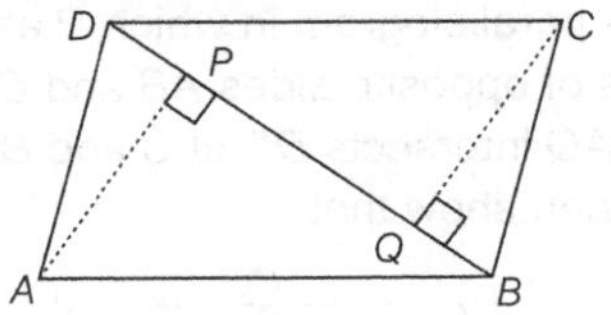

Show that

(i) $\Delta CQD \cong \Delta APB$ (ii) $AP = CQ$

Q.8 Prove that each diagonal of a parallelogram divides it into two congruent triangles.

Q.9 Prove that the diagonals of a parallelogram bisects each other.

Q.10 Prove that if the diagonals of a quadrilateral bisects each other, then it is a parallelogram.

Q.11 In the given figure, $ABCD$ is a rhombus. Then, find the value of x.

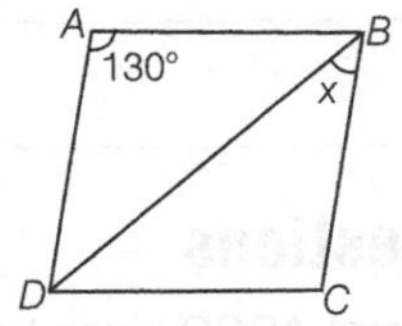

Q.12 In the following figure, $ABCD$ is a rhombus. If $\angle ABC = 54^\circ$, then determine $\angle ACD$.

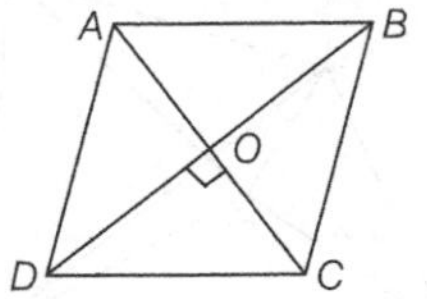

Q.13 Prove that if the diagonals of a parallelogram intersect each other at right angles, then it is a rhombus.

Q.14 A diagonal of a rectangle is inclined to the one side of the rectangle at 25°. Find the acute angle between the diagonals.

Q.15 If ΔBEC is an equilateral triangle in the square $ABCD$. Find the value of x in the figure.

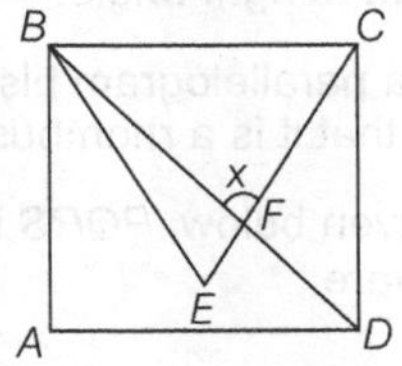

Q.16 In the following figure, $ABCD$ is a square. A line segment DX cuts the side BC at X and the diagonal AC at O such that $\angle COD = 105^\circ$. Find the value of x.

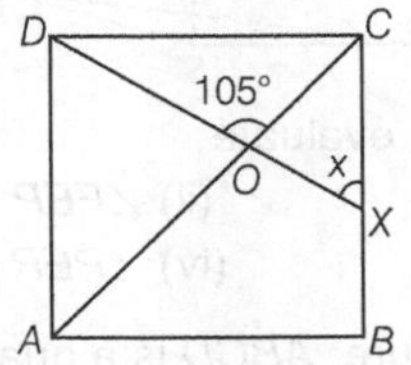

Q.17 In a parallelogram, show that the angle bisectors of two adjacent angles intersect at right angles.

Q.18 Prove that if the diagonals of a parallelogram are equal, then it is a rectangle.

Answers

4. $x = 30^\circ$, $y = 95^\circ$ **11.** 25° **12.** 63° **14.** 50° **15.** 75° **16.** 60°

TYPE - 5 4/5 Marks

Long Answer Type Questions

Q.1 In the given figure, $ABCD$ is a parallelogram and $\angle DAB = 60^\circ$. If the bisectors AP and BP of angles A and B respectively meets at P on CD. Prove that P is the mid-point of CD.

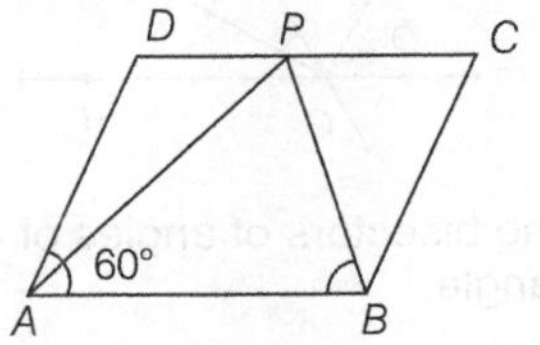

Q.2 $PQRS$ is a trapezium in which $PQ \parallel SR$ and $PS = QR$ [see figure].

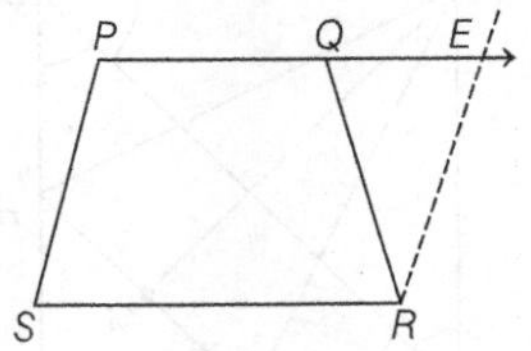

Show that

(i) $\angle P = \angle Q$ (ii) $\angle P + \angle R = \angle Q + \angle S$

Q.3 *ABCD* is a rhombus and *AB* is produced of *E* and *F* such that $AE = AB = BF$. Prove that *ED* and *FC*, when produced, meet at right angle.

Q.4 A diagonal of a parallelogram bisects one of its angles. Show that it is a rhombus.

Q.5 In the figure given below, *PQRS* is a rhombus and *SRFE* is a square.

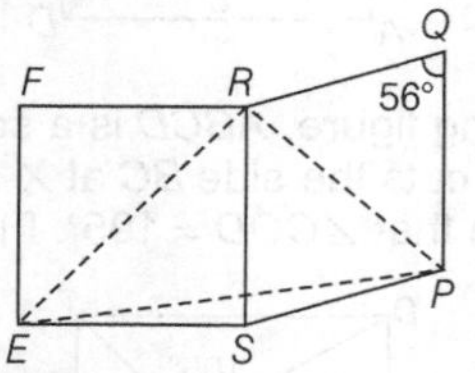

If $\angle PQR = 56°$, evaluate

(i) $\angle SPE$ (ii) $\angle FEP$

(iii) $\angle EPR$ (iv) $\angle PER$

Q.6 In the given figure, *ABCD* is a quadrilateral such that $AC = BD$ and *AC* and *BD* bisect each other at right angle. *O* is the intersection point of *AC* and *BD*. Show that the quadrilateral *ABCD* is a square.

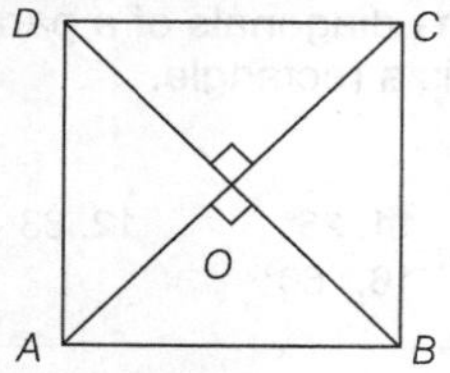

Q.7 In the given figure, two parallel lines *l* and *m* are intersected by a transversal *X*. Show that the quadrilateral formed by the bisectors of interior angles, is a rectangle.

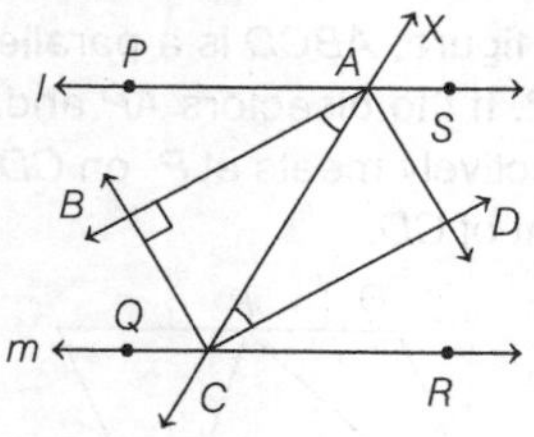

Q.8 Show that the bisectors of angles of a parallelogram form a rectangle.

Q.9 In the given figure, *ABCD* is a square and $EF \parallel BD$. *M* is the mid-point of *EF*. Prove that *AM* bisects $\angle BAD$.

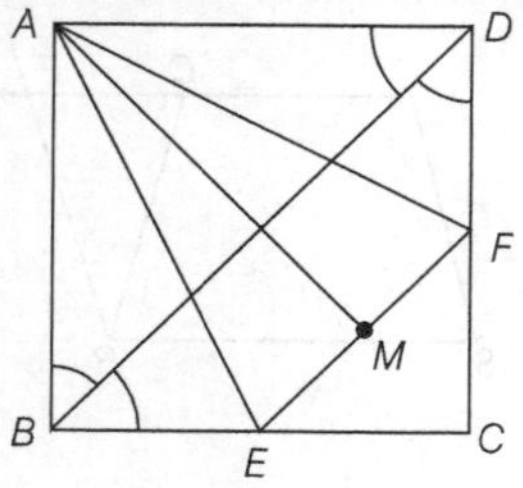

Q.10 Prove that if the diagonals of a parallelogram are equal and intersect each other at right angles, then it is a square.

Q.11 In the given figure, *PQRS* is a parallelogram, *PO* and *QO* are respectively, the angle bisectors of $\angle P$ and $\angle Q$. Line *LOM* is drawn parallel to *PQ*.

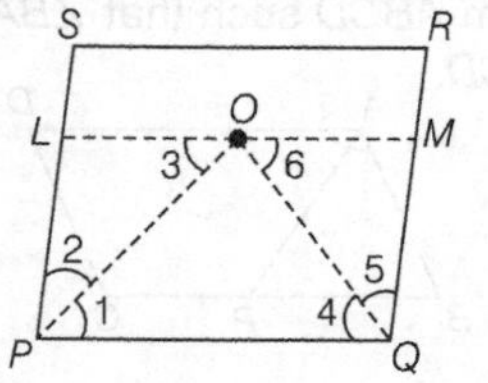

Prove that

(i) $PL = QM$ (ii) $LO = OM$

Q.12 *ABCD* is a parallelogram in which *P* and *Q* are the mid-points of opposite sides *AB* and *CD* (given in figure). If *AQ* intersects *DP* at *S* and *BQ* intersects *CP* at *R*, then show that

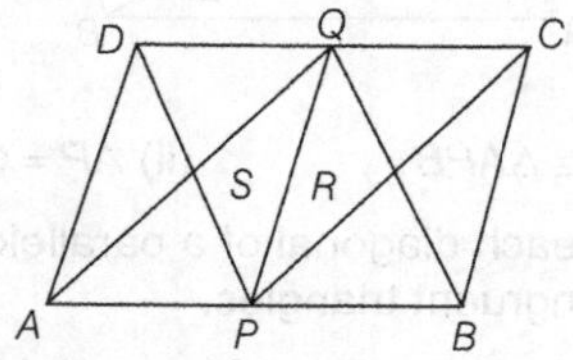

(i) *APCQ* is a parallelogram.

(ii) *DPBQ* is a parallelogram.

(iii) *PSQR* is a parallelogram.

Answers

5. (i) 17° (ii) 73° (iii) 45° (iv) 28°

TYPE - 6

Case Based Questions

Q.1 In the quadrilateral *ABCD* given below, $\angle DAC = 90°$ and $AB = AC = AD = DE = EB$.

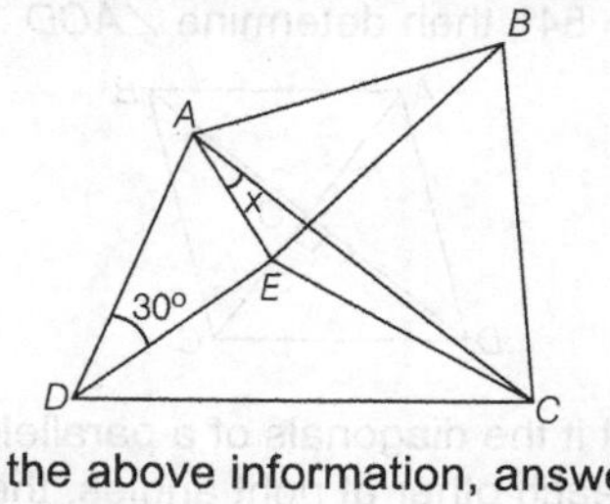

Based on the above information, answer the following questions.

(i) What is the value of $\angle EAC$?

(ii) Which type of quadrilateral is *ABED*?

(iii) What is the value of $\angle ABE$? **(3 M)**

Q.2 In the figure shown below, $WXYZ$ is a rhombus such that $\angle W = 65°$.

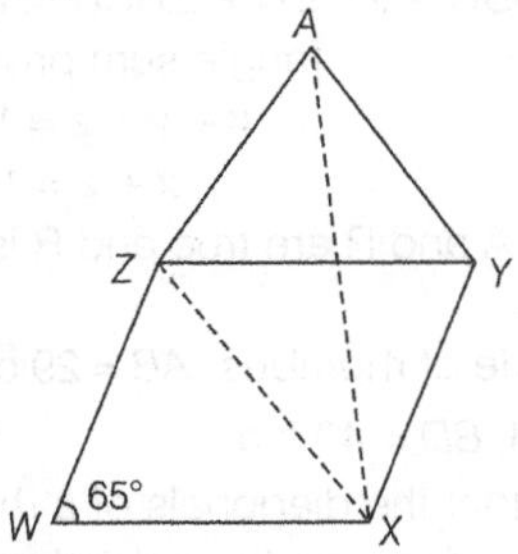

If ZAY is an equilateral triangle, determine

(i) $\angle YXA$ (ii) $\angle ZXA$ **(4 M)**

Q.3 In the parallelogram $ABCD$, M is mid-point of AC and X, Y are points on AB and DC, respectively such that $AX = CY$. Prove that

(i) ΔAXM is congruent to ΔCYM.

(ii) XMY is a straight line. **(4 M)**

Answers

1. (i) 15° (ii) rhombus (iii) 30°
2. (i) 27.5° (ii) 30°

EXPLANATIONS

Multiple Choice Questions

1. (a) We know that a diagonal of parallelogram divides it into two congruent triangles.

2. (c) Given, in quadrilateral $PQRS$, $PQ \parallel SR$ and $QR \parallel PS$. As we know that if opposite pairs of quadrilateral are parallel to each other, then it is a parallelogram.

3. (b) Given, the ratio of the angles of a quadrilateral is 3 : 5 : 9 : 13.
Let the angles of the quadrilateral be $3x$, $5x$, $9x$ and $13x$.
We know that sum of the angles of a quadrilateral is 360°.
$\therefore \quad 3x + 5x + 9x + 13x = 360° \Rightarrow 30x = 360°$
$\Rightarrow \quad x = \dfrac{360°}{30} = 12°$
Hence, angles of the quadrilateral are
$3x = 3 \times 12° = 36°$,
$5x = 5 \times 12° = 60°$,
$9x = 9 \times 12° = 108°$
and $13x = 13 \times 12° = 156°$.

4. (c) Let $ABCD$ be a parallelogram with smallest angle $\angle A = x$ and $\angle B = (2x - 24)°$.
Since, the adjacent angles of a parallelogram are supplementary.

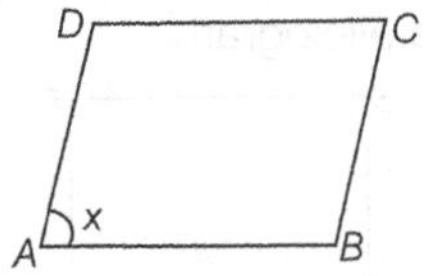

$\therefore \quad \angle A + \angle B = 180°$
$\Rightarrow \quad x + (2x - 24)° = 180°$
$\Rightarrow \quad 3x = 204$
$\Rightarrow \quad x = 68$
$\therefore \quad \angle A = x = 68°$
and $\angle B = (2x - 24)°$
$= (2 \times 68 - 24)° = 112°$
Since, the opposite angles of a parallelogram are ecual.
So, $\angle A = \angle C = 68°$
and $\angle B = \angle D = 112°$.

5. (b) We know that opposite angles of parallelogram are equal.
Therefore, $\angle C = \angle A = 60°$
and let $\angle B = \angle D = x$.
Now, using angle sum property of a quadrilateral, we get
$\angle A + \angle B + \angle C + \angle D = 360°$
$\Rightarrow \quad 60° + x + 60° + x = 360°$
$\Rightarrow \quad 120° + 2x = 360°$
$\Rightarrow \quad 2x = 360° - 120°$
$\Rightarrow \quad 2x = 240°$
$\Rightarrow \quad x = 120°$
Hence, the value of $\angle B$ is 120°.

6. (a) Given, $ABCD$ is a rhombus.
$\therefore \quad AB = AD$
$\Rightarrow \quad 3x + 2 = 4x - 4$
$\Rightarrow \quad x = 6$
Now, side $AB = 3 \times 6 + 2 = 20$ units
In ΔABD, $\quad \angle A = 60°$ and $AB = AD$
$\therefore \quad \angle ADB = \angle ABD \quad$ ...(i)
[$\because$ angles opposite to equal sides of a triangle are equal]
$\therefore \quad \angle ADB + \angle DAB + \angle ABD = 180°$
[$\because$ angle sum property of a triangle]
$\Rightarrow \quad \angle ADB + \angle ADB = 180° - 60° \quad$ [from Eq. (i)]
$\Rightarrow \quad \angle ADB = \dfrac{120°}{2} = 60°$
Now, ΔABD is an equilateral triangle.
$\therefore \quad AB = BD = DA = 20 \quad$ [$\because AB = 20$ units]
$\Rightarrow \quad y - 1 = 20$
$\Rightarrow \quad y = 21$ units

7. (d) We know that sum of all angles in a quadrilateral is 360°. If $ABCD$ is a quadrilateral, then

$$\angle A + \angle B + \angle C + \angle D = 360^\circ \quad \dots(i)$$

But it is given, $\angle A = \angle B = \angle C = \angle D$

From Eq. (i), we get

$$\angle A + \angle A + \angle A + \angle A = 360^\circ \Rightarrow 4\angle A = 360^\circ$$

$$\therefore \quad \angle A = 90^\circ$$

So, all angles of a quadrilateral are 90°.

Hence, given quadrilateral is a rectangle or square.

8. (d) As we know that in a square

(i) All sides are equal and opposite sides are parallel to each other.

(ii) All the interior angles are equal i.e. 90°.

(iii) Diagonals are perpendicular bisectors of each other.

Hence, one angle between the diagonals is 30°, is not true for a square.

9. (c) We know that two diagonals are always equal in square and rectangle but not in parallelogram.

10. (b) Given, in a quadrilateral $ABCD$, $AB \parallel CD$, $BC \parallel AD$ and $\angle A = 90^\circ$.

$\therefore$ $ABCD$ is a parallelogram.

$$AB \parallel CD \text{ and } AB = CD$$

$$BC \parallel AD \text{ and } BC = AD$$

$\therefore$ $ABCD$ is a rectangle.

Assertion-Reason Type Questions

1. (b) Let two adjacent angles of a parallelogram be x and y.

Since, adjacent angles of a parallelogram are supplementary.

$$\therefore \quad x + y = 180^\circ \quad \dots(i)$$

And according to Assertion,

$$x = \frac{2}{3}y \quad \dots(ii)$$

On substituting $x = \frac{2}{3}y$ in Eq. (i), we get

$$\frac{2}{3}y + y = 180^\circ \Rightarrow y = \frac{3 \times 180^\circ}{5} = 108^\circ$$

Now, on substituting $y = 108^\circ$ in Eq. (i), we get

$$x + 108^\circ = 180^\circ \Rightarrow x = 72^\circ$$

Hence, A is false, R is true.

2. (a) **Assertion** Given, three angles of a parallelogram are 85°, 95° and 85°.

Let the fourth angle be x.

We know that sum of the angles of a parallelogram is 360°.

$\therefore$ $85^\circ + 95^\circ + 85^\circ + x = 360^\circ \Rightarrow x = 360^\circ - 265^\circ = 95^\circ$

Also, the opposite angles of the parallelogram are equal. Hence, A is true, R is false.

3. (c) **Assertion** Given, $ABCD$ is a parallelogram.

$$\Rightarrow \quad \angle DAB = \angle DCB = z$$

[$\because$ opposite angles are equal]

In ΔBCD, $\angle DBC + \angle CDB + \angle BCD = 180^\circ$

[angle sum property of a triangle]

$$\Rightarrow \quad x + y + z = 180^\circ$$

$$\Rightarrow \quad x + z = 180^\circ - y$$

Hence, both A and R are true and R is the correct reason for A.

4. (c) Given, side of rhombus, $AB = 29$ cm and diagonal, $BD = 40$ cm

As we know that the diagonals of a rhombus are perpendicular bisectors to each other.

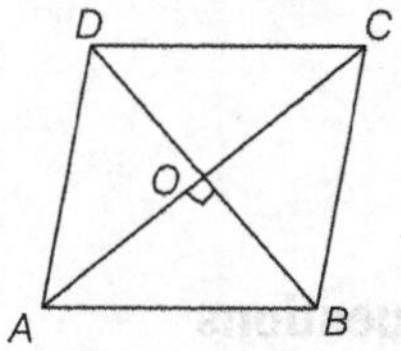

$$\therefore \quad OB = \frac{1}{2}BD = 20 \text{ cm}$$

and $$OA = \frac{AC}{2} \quad \dots(i)$$

In right angled ΔAOB,

$$(AB)^2 = (OA)^2 + (OB)^2$$

[by pythagoras theorem]

$$\Rightarrow \quad (29)^2 = (OA)^2 + (20)^2 \quad [\because OB = 20 \text{ cm}]$$

$$\Rightarrow \quad 841 - 400 = (OA)^2$$

$$\Rightarrow \quad OA = \pm 21 = 21 \text{ cm}$$

[$\because$ length cannot be negative]

$$\therefore \quad AC = 2 \cdot OA = 42 \text{ cm} \quad \text{[from Eq. (i)]}$$

Hence, A is true, R is also true and R is the correct reason for A.

Statement Based Questions

1. (c) We know that in a parallelogram, the sum of adjacent angles of a parallelogram is 180° and pairs of opposite sides are equal and parallel.

Hence, Statement I is true and Statement II is false.

2. (a) Clearly, both Statements are true.

3. (d) In quadrilateral $PQRS$, $PQ \parallel RS$ and $PS \parallel QR$.

$\therefore$ $PQRS$ is a parallelogram.

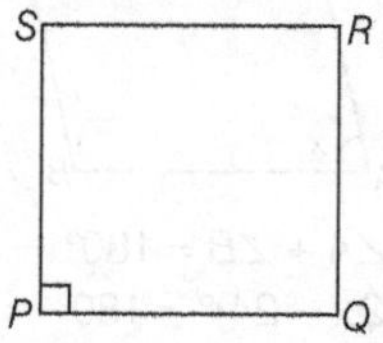

Now, $\angle P + \angle Q = 180^\circ$

[$\because$ adjacent angles of a parallelogram are supplementary]

$$\Rightarrow \quad \angle Q = 180^\circ - 90^\circ = 90^\circ$$

Similarly, $\angle R = 90^\circ$

and $\angle S = 90^\circ$

$\because$ Each angle of parallelogram $PQRS$ is 90° and all sides are equal.

$\therefore$ $PQRS$ is a square.

So, Statement I is false and Statement II is true.

4. (a) **Statement I** We know that in a parallelogram, diagonals bisect it into two congruent triangles.

So, Statement I is true.

Statement II We also know that diagonals of square are equal in length and perpendicular bisector to each other.

So, Statement II is also true.

5. (c) We know that the two diagonals are always equal in square.

Hence, Statement I is true and Statement II is false.

Short Answer Type Questions

1. Let $ABCD$ be a quadrilateral and AC be a diagonal.

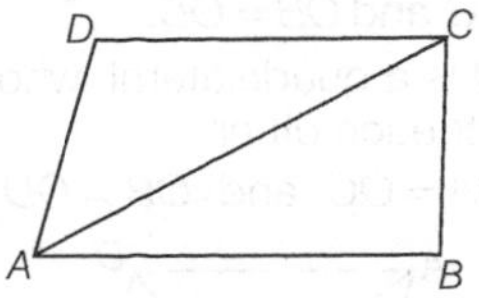

We know that in ΔADC,

$$\angle DAC + \angle ACD + \angle ADC = 180^\circ \quad \text{...(i)}$$

[$\because$ sum of angles of a triangle is 180°]

Similarly, in ΔABC,

$$\angle CAB + \angle ACB + \angle ABC = 180^\circ \quad \text{...(ii)}$$

[$\because$ sum of angles of a triangle is 180°]

On adding Eqs. (i) and (ii), we get

$$\angle DAC + \angle ACD + \angle ADC + \angle CAB + \angle ACB + \angle ABC = 180^\circ + 180^\circ = 360^\circ \quad \text{...(iii)}$$

Also, $\left.\begin{array}{l}\angle DAC + \angle CAB = \angle BAD \\ \text{and } \angle ACD + \angle ACB = \angle BCD\end{array}\right\}$ ...(iv)

From Eqs. (iii) and (iv), we get

$$\angle ABC + \angle BAD + \angle ADC + \angle BCD = 360^\circ$$

$\Rightarrow$ $\angle A + \angle B + \angle C + \angle D = 360^\circ$

2. Given, $ABCD$ and $PBCQ$ are parallelograms.

$\therefore$ $AD \parallel BC$ and $AD = BC$ ...(a)

and $PQ \parallel BC$ and $PQ = BC$ ...(b)

(i) From Eqs. (a) and (b), we get

$AD \parallel BC \parallel PQ$ and $AD = BC = PQ$

$\because$ $AD \parallel PQ$ and $AD = PQ$

$\therefore$ $APQD$ is a parallelogram.

[$\because$ opposite sides of a quadrilateral are equal and parallel, then it is a parallelogram]

(ii) $\because$ $APQD$ is a parallelogram.

$\therefore$ $AP \parallel QD$ and $AP = QD$ **Hence proved.**

3. Given $ABCD$ is a parallelogram.

$\therefore$ $AB \parallel CD$ and $BC \parallel AD$

To prove $\angle A = \angle C$ and $\angle B = \angle D$

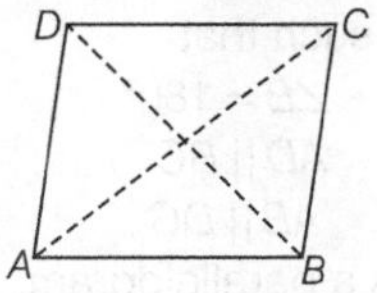

Proof Since, $AB \parallel CD$ and AD is a transversal, then

$$\angle A + \angle D = 180^\circ \quad [\because \text{co-interior angles}]\text{...(i)}$$

Similarly, $AD \parallel BC$ and CD is a transversal, then

$$\angle D + \angle C = 180^\circ \quad [\because \text{co-interior angles}]\text{ ...(ii)}$$

From Eqs. (i) and (ii), we get

$$\angle A + \angle D = \angle D + \angle C \Rightarrow \angle A = \angle C$$

Similarly, we can prove that $\angle B = \angle D$. **Hence proved.**

4. Given, $ABCD$ is a parallelogram.

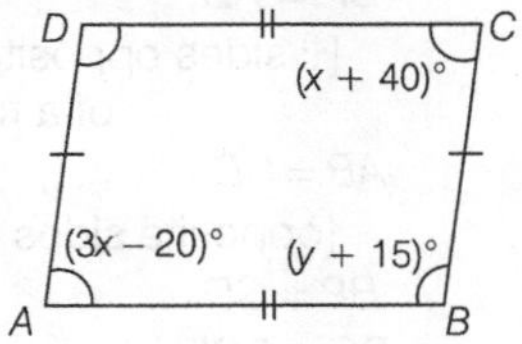

Then, $\angle A = \angle C$

[$\because$ opposite angles of a parallelogram are equal]

$\Rightarrow$ $(3x - 20)^\circ = (x + 40)^\circ$

$\Rightarrow$ $3x - x = 40^\circ + 20^\circ$

$\Rightarrow$ $2x = 60^\circ \Rightarrow x = 30^\circ$

Also, $\angle A + \angle B = 180^\circ$

[$\because$ the adjacent angles of a parallelogram are supplementary]

$\Rightarrow$ $3x - 20^\circ + y + 15^\circ = 180^\circ$

$\Rightarrow$ $3x + y = 185^\circ$

On putting $x = 30^\circ$, we get

$$3(30^\circ) + y = 185^\circ \Rightarrow y = 185^\circ - 90^\circ = 95^\circ$$

5. Given $ABCD$ is a quadrilateral, in which

$$\angle A = \angle C \quad \text{...(i)}$$

and $$\angle B = \angle D \quad \text{...(ii)}$$

To prove $ABCD$ is a parallelogram.

Proof On adding Eqs. (i) and (ii), we get

$$\angle A + \angle B = \angle C + \angle D \quad \text{...(iii)}$$

Now, by angle sum property of a quadrilateral, we have

$$\angle A + \angle B + \angle C + \angle D = 360^\circ \quad \text{...(iv)}$$

On putting the value from Eq. (iii), we get

$$\angle A + \angle B + \angle A + \angle B = 360^\circ$$

$\Rightarrow$ $2(\angle A + \angle B) = 360^\circ$

$\Rightarrow$ $\angle A + \angle B = 180^\circ$

$\therefore$ $\angle A + \angle B = \angle C + \angle D = 180^\circ$ [from Eq. (iii)]

Since, the line AB intersect AD and BC at points A and B, respectively such that

$\angle A + \angle B = 180^\circ$ [$\because$ co-interior angles]

$\therefore$ $AD \parallel BC$

Similarly, $AB \parallel DC$

Hence, $ABCD$ is a parallelogram.

6. Given, $ABCD$ is a parallelogram. P is the mid-point of BC i.e. $BC = 2BP$

$\Rightarrow$ $AD = 2BP$ [$\because BC = AD$]

and $\angle BAP = \angle DAP$

To prove $AD = 2\,CD$

Proof We have, $\angle BAP = \angle DAP$ [given] ...(i)

and $\angle DAP = \angle APB$

[$\because$ alternate interior angles] ...(ii)

$\Rightarrow$ $\angle BAP = \angle APB$ [from Eqs. (i) and (ii)]

$\Rightarrow$ $BP = AB$

[$\because$ sides opposite to equal angles of a triangle are equal]

and $AB = CD$

[opposite sides of parallelogram]

$\Rightarrow$ $BP = CD$ [$\because BP = AB$] ...(iii)

Also, $BC = 2BP$ [given]

$\Rightarrow$ $AD = 2BP$ ...(iv)

[$\because BC = AD$, opposite sides of parallelogram]

From Eqs. (iii) and (iv), we get

$AD = 2\,CD$ **Hence proved.**

7. Given, $ABCD$ is a parallelogram.

$\therefore$ $\angle CDB = \angle DBA$ ...(a)

[$\because$ alternate interior angles]

and AP and CQ are perpendicular from vertices A and C on diagonal BD.

(i) Now, in ΔCQD and ΔAPB, we have

$CD = AB$

[opposite sides of a parallelogram]

$\angle CQD = \angle APB = 90^\circ$ [given]

$\angle CDQ = \angle ABP$ [from Eq. (a)]

$\therefore$ $\Delta CQD \cong \Delta APB$ [by AAS congruence rule]

(ii) Since, $\Delta APB \cong \Delta CQD$

$\therefore$ $AP = CQ$ [by CPCT]

8. $ABCD$ is a parallelogram and AC is its diagonal.

$\therefore$ $AB \parallel CD$ and $BC \parallel AD$

To prove $\Delta ABC \cong \Delta CDA$

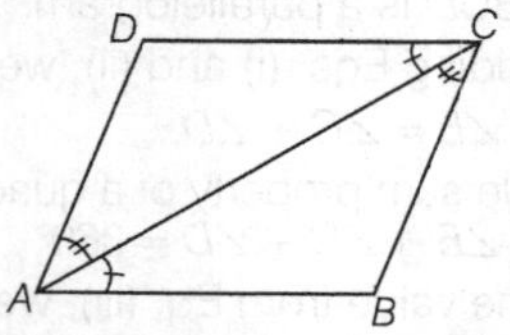

Proof In ΔABC and ΔCDA, $\angle BCA = \angle DAC$

[$\because$ alternate angles are equal]

$AC = AC$ [common]

$\angle BAC = \angle DCA$ [$\because$ alternate angles are equal]

$\therefore$ $\Delta ABC \cong \Delta CDA$ [by ASA congruence rule]

Similarly, we can prove that $\Delta ABD \cong \Delta CDB$

Hence, diagonal of a parallelogram divides it into two congruent triangles.

9. Given $ABCD$ is a parallelogram, whose diagonals AC and BD intersect each other at O.

To prove $OA = OC$ and $OB = OD$.

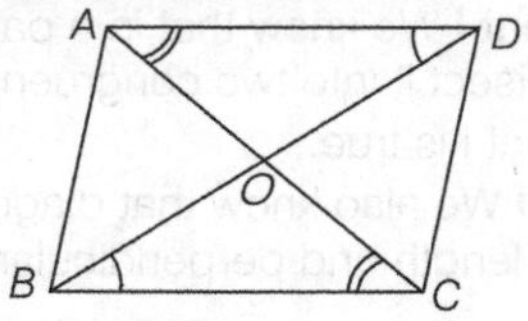

Proof In ΔAOD and ΔCOB,

$\angle ODA = \angle OBC$ [$\because$ alternate angles]

$\angle OAD = \angle OCB$ [$\because$ alternate angles]

and $AD = BC$

[$\because$ opposite sides of a parallelogram are equal]

$\therefore$ $\Delta AOD \cong \Delta COB$ [by ASA congruence rule]

Then, $OA = OC$ and $OB = OD$. [by CPCT]

10. Given $ABCD$ is a quadrilateral, whose diagonals AC and BD bisect each other

i.e. $OA = OC$ and $OB = OD$

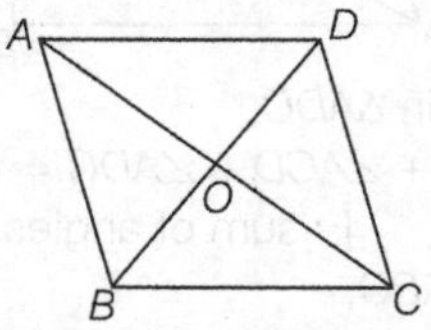

To prove $ABCD$ is a parallelogram.

Proof In ΔAOB and ΔCOD,

$OA = OC$ [given]

$\angle AOB = \angle COD$

[$\because$ vertically opposite angles]

$OB = OD$ [given]

$\therefore$ $\Delta AOB \cong \Delta COD$

[by SAS congruence rule]

Then, $\angle ODC = \angle OBA$ [by CPCT]

But these are alternate angles, which are formed, when transversal BD intersects lines AB and DC.

$\therefore$ $AB \parallel CD$

Similarly, we can prove that $BC \parallel AD$.

Hence, $ABCD$ is a parallelogram.

11. Given, $ABCD$ is a rhombus in which $\angle BAD = 130^\circ$ and $\angle DBC = x$.

$\therefore$ $\angle B = 2\angle DBC = 2x$

[$\because$ diagonals bisect the angles in rhombus]

Now, $\angle DAB + \angle B = 180^\circ$

[$\because$ the adjacent angles of a parallelogram are supplementary]

$\Rightarrow$ $130^\circ + 2x = 180^\circ$ [from figure]

$\Rightarrow$ $2x = 180^\circ - 130^\circ = 50^\circ$

$\therefore$ $x = 25^\circ$

12. Given, $ABCD$ is a rhombus

$\Rightarrow ABCD$ is a parallelogram.

$\Rightarrow \angle ADC = \angle ABC = 54^\circ$ ...(i)

[$\because$ opposite angles of a parallelogram are equal]

Here, $\angle ODC = \frac{1}{2} \angle ADC$

[$\because$ diagonal DB of rhombus $ABCD$, bisects $\angle ABC$ and $\angle ADC$]

$\Rightarrow \quad \angle ODC = \frac{1}{2} \times 54^\circ = 27^\circ$ [from Eq. (i)]

Now, in ΔCOD,

$\angle OCD + \angle ODC + \angle COD = 180^\circ$

[$\because$ angle sum property of a triangle]

$\Rightarrow \quad \angle OCD + 27^\circ + 90^\circ = 180^\circ$

[$\because \angle COD = 90^\circ$, diagonals of a rhombus bisect each other at right angles]

$\Rightarrow \quad \angle OCD + 117^\circ = 180^\circ$

$\Rightarrow \quad \angle OCD = 180^\circ - 117^\circ$

$\Rightarrow \quad \angle OCD = 63^\circ$

or $\quad \angle ACD = 63^\circ$

13. A parallelogram $ABCD$, whose diagonals AC and BD intersect each other at right angles.

i.e. $\angle AOD = \angle AOB = \angle COD = \angle BOC = 90^\circ$

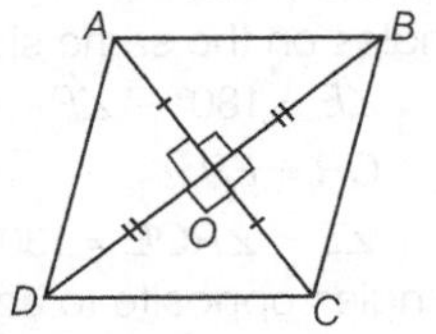

To prove $ABCD$ is a rhombus.

Proof $\because ABCD$ is a parallelogram.

$\therefore \quad AD = BC$ ...(i)

and $\quad AB = CD$ ... (ii)

[$\because$ opposite sides of parallelogram]

Now, in ΔAOD and ΔAOB,

$\angle AOD = \angle AOB$ [each 90°]

$AO = AO$ [common]

$OD = OB$

[$\because$ diagonals of a parallelogram bisect each other]

$\therefore \quad \Delta AOD \cong \Delta AOB$ [by SAS congruence rule]

$\Rightarrow \quad AD = AB$ [by CPCT] ... (iii)

From Eqs. (i), (ii) and (iii), we get

$AB = BC = AD = CD$

Hence, $ABCD$ is a rhombus. **Hence proved.**

14. Given, diagonal inclined to the one side of the rectangle at 25°.

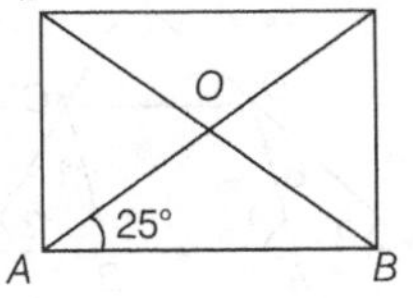

Let $\angle CAB = 25^\circ$

$\because$ Diagonals of a rectangle are equal in length and bisect each other.

$\therefore \quad OA = OB$

In ΔOAB,

$\because \quad OA = OB$

$\therefore \quad \angle OAB = \angle OBA$

[$\because$ angles opposite to equal sides are equal]

$\therefore \quad \angle OBA = 25^\circ$

and $\angle OAB + \angle AOB + \angle OBA = 180^\circ$

[$\because$ angle sum property of a triangle]

$\Rightarrow \quad \angle AOB = 180^\circ - 25^\circ - 25^\circ = 130^\circ$

Now, $\angle AOB + \angle AOD = 180^\circ$ [$\because$ linear pair]

$\Rightarrow \quad \angle AOD = 180^\circ - 130^\circ = 50^\circ$

Hence, the acute angle between the diagonals is 50°.

15. Given, $ABCD$ is a square and ΔBEC is an equilateral triangle.

$\because BD$ is a diagonal of square $ABCD$.

$\therefore \quad \angle CBD = \frac{1}{2} \angle ABC = 45^\circ$ [$\because \angle ABC = 90^\circ$]

and $\quad \angle BCE = 60^\circ$ [$\because \Delta BEC$ is an equilateral triangle]

Now, in ΔBFC,

$\angle FBC + \angle BCF + \angle BFC = 180^\circ$

[$\because$ angle sum property of triangle]

$\Rightarrow \quad 45^\circ + 60^\circ + x = 180^\circ$

[$\because \angle CBD = \angle FBC = 45^\circ$ and $\angle BCE = \angle BCF = 60^\circ$]

$\Rightarrow \quad x = 180^\circ - 105^\circ = 75^\circ$

16. Given, $ABCD$ is a square in which $\angle COD = 105^\circ$.

We know that the diagonal AC of square $ABCD$ will bisect the $\angle C$.

$\therefore \quad \angle OCX = \frac{1}{2} \angle C = \frac{1}{2} \times 90^\circ = 45^\circ$ ...(i)

Now, we have

$\angle COD + \angle COX = 180^\circ$ [$\because$ linear pair]

$\Rightarrow \quad 105^\circ + \angle COX = 180^\circ$

$\Rightarrow \quad \angle COX = 180^\circ - 105^\circ$

$\Rightarrow \quad \angle COX = 75^\circ$ ...(ii)

Now, in ΔCOX,

$\angle COX + \angle OXC + \angle OCX = 180^\circ$

[$\because$ angle sum property of a triangle]

$\Rightarrow \quad 75^\circ + x + 45^\circ = 180^\circ$

[using Eqs. (i) and (ii)]

$\Rightarrow \quad x = 180^\circ - 120^\circ$

$\therefore \quad x = 60^\circ$

17. Let $ABCD$ be a parallelogram such that angle bisectors of adjacent angle A and B intersect at point P.

To show that $\angle APB = 90^\circ$

Here, $\quad \angle A + \angle B = 180^\circ$

[$\because AD || BC$ and $\angle A$ and $\angle B$ are consecutive interior angles]

$\Rightarrow \quad \frac{1}{2}\angle A + \frac{1}{2}\angle B = 90^\circ$

[dividing both sides by 2] ...(i)

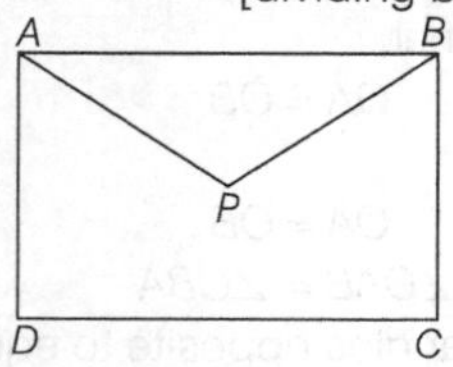

But in ΔAPB, we have

$$\frac{1}{2}\angle A + \frac{1}{2}\angle B + \angle APB = 180^\circ$$

[by angle sum property of a triangle]

$\Rightarrow \quad 90^\circ + \angle APB = 180^\circ$ [using Eq. (i)]

$\therefore \quad \angle APB = 90^\circ$ **Hence proved.**

18. Let parallelogram be $ABCD$, whose diagonals AC and BD are equal i.e. $AC = BD$.

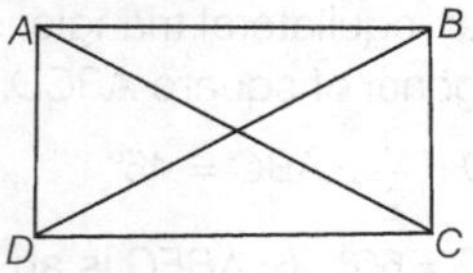

To prove $ABCD$ is a rectangle.

Proof In ΔABC and ΔDCB, we have

$AB = CD$

[$\because$ opposite sides of parallelogram]

$BC = CB$ [common]

and $AC = BD$ [given]

$\therefore \quad \Delta ABC \cong \Delta DCB$

[by SSS congruence rule]

So, $\angle ABC = \angle DCB$ ...(i) [by CPCT]

But $DC \parallel AB$ and transversal CB intersects them.

$\therefore \quad \angle ABC + \angle DCB = 180^\circ$ [co-interior angles]

$\Rightarrow \quad \angle ABC + \angle ABC = 180^\circ$ [from Eq. (i)]

$\Rightarrow \quad 2\angle ABC = 180^\circ$

$\Rightarrow \quad \angle ABC = 90^\circ = \angle DCB$

Thus, $ABCD$ is a parallelogram and one of its angle is 90°.

Hence, $ABCD$ is a rectangle. **Hence proved.**

Long Answer Type Questions

1. Given, $ABCD$ is a parallelogram i.e. $AB \parallel CD$ and $AD \parallel BC$ and $\angle DAB = 60^\circ$. AP and BP are the bisectors of $\angle A$ and $\angle B$, respectively.

$\therefore \quad \angle PAB = \angle DAP = \frac{1}{2}\angle DAB = \frac{1}{2} \times 60^\circ = 30^\circ$

$\Rightarrow \angle PAB = \angle DAP = 30^\circ$

and $\angle B = 180^\circ - \angle A$

[$\because$ co-interior angles of parallelogram]

$= 180^\circ - 60^\circ = 120^\circ$ [$\because \angle A = 60^\circ$]

$\Rightarrow \angle PBA = \angle CBP = \frac{1}{2}\angle B = 60^\circ$ [$\because \angle B = 120^\circ$]

We have, $AB \parallel DC$ and PA is a transversal.

$\therefore \quad \angle DPA = \angle PAB = 30^\circ$

[$\because$ alternate angle] ...(i)

Also, $\angle DAP = \angle PAB = 30^\circ$ [given] ...(ii)

From Eqs. (i) and (ii), we get

$\angle DAP = \angle DPA$

$\Rightarrow \quad DP = DA$ ...(iii)

[$\because$ sides opposite to equal angles of a triangle are also equal]

Similarly, $CB = PC$ ...(iv)

Also, $DA = CB$ ...(v)

[$\because$ opposite sides of a parallelogram]

From Eq. (iii), (iv) and (v), we get

$DP = PC$

Hence, P is the mid-point of CD. **Hence proved.**

2. (i) $PQRS$ is a trapezium in which $PQ \parallel SR$, $PS = QR$.

Now, extend PQ and draw a line through R parallel to PS intersecting extended PQ at E.

$\therefore \quad PS \parallel ER$

So, $PSRE$ is a parallelogram.

$\therefore \quad PS = ER$ and $PE = SR$

But $PS = QR$ [given]

$\therefore \quad PS = QR = ER$

Now, $\angle P + \angle E = 180^\circ$

[$\because$ interior angles on the same side of transversal PE]

$\Rightarrow \quad \angle E = 180^\circ - \angle P$

Also, $QR = ER$

$\Rightarrow \quad \angle E = \angle RQE = 180^\circ - \angle P$

[$\because$ angles opposite to equal sides are equal]

But $\angle PQR = 180^\circ - \angle RQE$

[$\because PQE$ is a straight line]

$= 180^\circ - 180^\circ + \angle P = \angle P$

$\Rightarrow \quad \angle Q = \angle P$ ... (a)

(ii) Now, $\angle P + \angle S = 180^\circ$ [$\because$ co-interior angles]

$\Rightarrow \quad \angle S = 180^\circ - \angle P = 180^\circ - \angle Q$

[from Eq. (a)] ... (b)

Also, $\angle Q + \angle R = 180^\circ$ [$\because$ co-interior angles]

$\Rightarrow \quad \angle R = 180^\circ - \angle Q$ ... (c)

From Eqs. (b) and (c), we get

$\angle S = \angle R$ ... (d)

On adding Eqs. (a) and (d), we get

$\angle Q + \angle S = \angle P + \angle R$

3. Given $ABCD$ is a rhombus. AB produced to E and F such that

$AE = AB = BF$ ...(i)

Construction Join ED and CF and produced it to meet at G.

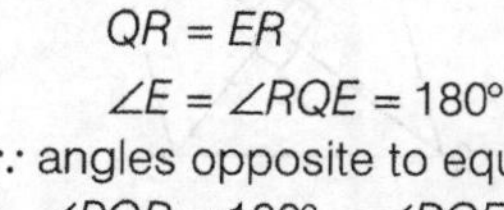

To prove $EG \perp FG$

Proof Since, $ABCD$ is a rhombus.

$\therefore \quad AB = CD = BC = AD \quad \ldots(ii)$

Now, in ΔBCF, we have

$BC = BF \quad$ [from Eqs. (i) and (ii)]

$\Rightarrow \quad \angle 2 = \angle 1$

[$\because$ angles opposite to equal sides are equal]

and $\quad \angle 3 = \angle 1 + \angle 2 \quad$ [$\because$ exterior angles]

$\Rightarrow \quad \angle 3 = 2\angle 2 \quad \ldots(iii)$

Similarly, in ΔADE, we have

$AE = AD \Rightarrow \angle 6 = \angle 5$

[from Eqs. (i) and (ii)]

and $\quad \angle 4 = \angle 5 + \angle 6 = 2\angle 5 \quad \ldots(iv)$

[$\because$ exterior angles]

On adding Eqs. (iii) and (iv), we get

$\angle 4 + \angle 3 = 2\angle 5 + 2\angle 2$

$\Rightarrow \quad 180° = 2(\angle 5 + \angle 2)$

[$\because$ $\angle 4$ and $\angle 3$ are consecutive interior angles]

$\Rightarrow \quad \angle 5 + \angle 2 = 90° \quad \ldots(v)$

Now, in ΔEGF, we have

$\angle 5 + \angle 2 + \angle EGF = 180°$

$\Rightarrow \quad 90° + \angle EGF = 180° \quad$ [from Eq. (v)]

$\therefore \quad \angle EGF = 90°$

Hence, $EG \perp FG$. **Hence proved.**

4. $ABCD$ is a parallelogram, in which diagonal AC bisects the $\angle A$.

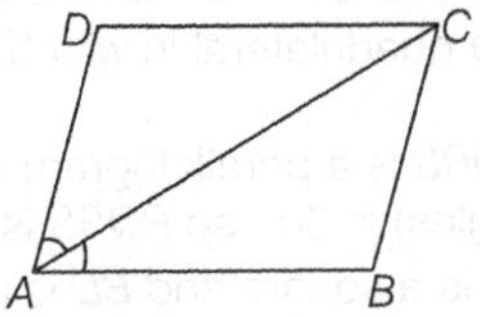

To show $ABCD$ is a rhombus.

Proof Since, diagonal AC bisects $\angle A$.

$\therefore \quad \angle CAB = \angle CAD \quad \ldots(i)$

Since, $AB \parallel CD$ and AC is a transversal.

$\therefore \quad \angle CAB = \angle ACD \quad \ldots(ii)$

[$\because$ alternate interior angles]

Again $AD \parallel BC$ and AC is a transversal.

$\angle DAC = \angle ACB \quad \ldots(iii)$

[$\because$ alternate interior angles]

From Eqs. (i), (ii) and (iii), we get

$\therefore \quad \angle ACD = \angle ACB$

$\Rightarrow$ AC bisects $\angle C$.

Now, $\quad \angle A = \angle C$

[$\because$ opposite angles of a parallelogram]

$\Rightarrow \quad \frac{1}{2}\angle A = \frac{1}{2}\angle C \Rightarrow \angle DAC = \angle DCA$

$\Rightarrow \quad CD = AD \quad \ldots(iv)$

[$\because$ sides opposite to equal angles of a triangle are equal]

But $AB = CD$ and $AD = BC$

[$\because$ opposite sides of parallelogram]

$\therefore \quad AB = BC = CD = AD \quad$ [$\because$ from Eq. (iv)]

Hence, $ABCD$ is a rhombus.

5. Given, $PQRS$ is a rhombus.

$\therefore$ $PS = RS$ and $\angle PSR = \angle PQR = 56°$

Also, $SRFE$ is a square.

$\therefore \quad ES = RS$

and $\angle FES = \angle ESR = \angle SRF = \angle RFE = 90°$

$\Rightarrow \quad PS = RS = ES$

(i) In ΔPES, $\quad PS = ES$

$\Rightarrow \quad \angle SPE = \angle PES \quad \ldots(a)$

[$\because$ angles opposite to equal sides of a triangle are equal]

$\therefore$ $\angle SPE + \angle PES + \angle PSE = 180°$

[$\because$ angle sum property of a triangle]

$\Rightarrow \quad 2\angle SPE + 146° = 180°$

[$\because$ $\angle PSE = \angle ESR + \angle PSR = 90° + 56° = 146°$]

$\Rightarrow \quad 2\angle SPE = 34°$

$\Rightarrow \quad \angle SPE = 17°$

(ii) $\angle SEP = 17° \quad \ldots$(b) [using Eq. (a)]

$\angle FEP = \angle FES - \angle SEP = 90° - 17° = 73°$

[using Eq. (b) and each angle of a square is 90°]

(iii) In rhombus $PQRS$,

$\angle PQR + \angle QRS + \angle RSP + \angle SPQ = 360°$

[$\because$ angle sum property of a quadrilateral]

$\Rightarrow \quad 56° + 56° + 2SPQ = 360°$

[$\because$ opposite angles of a rhombus are equal i.e. $\angle SPQ = \angle QRS$]

$\Rightarrow \quad 2\angle SPQ = 360° - 112°$

$\Rightarrow \quad \angle SPQ = 124°$

$\therefore \quad \angle SPR = \frac{124°}{2} = 62° \quad \ldots(c)$

[$\because$ diagonals of a rhombus bisect its angles]

$\therefore \quad \angle EPR = \angle SPR - \angle SPE = 62° - 17° = 45°$

[from Eq. (c)]

(iv) $\angle RES = \frac{90°}{2} = 45°$

[$\because$ the diagonals of a square bisect its angles]

$\therefore \quad \angle PER = \angle RES - \angle SEP$

$= 45° - 17° = 28°$

6. Given, $ABCD$ is a quadrilateral such that $AC = BD$ and AC and BD bisect each other at right angle at point O.

$\therefore \quad OA = OB = OC = OD \quad$ [$\because$ $AC = BD$] ...(i)

and $\angle AOB = \angle BOC = \angle COD = \angle DOA = 90° \quad \ldots(ii)$

We have to show that quadrilateral $ABCD$ is a square.

Now, in ΔAOB, $\quad OA = OB \quad$ [given]

and $\quad \angle AOB = 90° \quad$ [given]

$\therefore \quad \angle OAB = \angle OBA = 45°$

[$\because$ angles opposite to equal sides are also equal]

Similarly, we can prove that
$\angle OAD = \angle ODA = 45°$
$\angle OBC = \angle OCB = 45°$
Then, $\angle A = \angle BAD = \angle BAO + \angle OAD = 45° + 45°$
$\angle A = 90°$
Similarly, $\angle B = \angle ABC = \angle OBA + \angle OBC$
$= 45° + 45° = 90°$
Also, $\angle C = 90°$ and $\angle D = 90°$
In ΔAOB and ΔCOB,
$OA = OC$ [given]
$OB = OB$ [common]
and $\angle AOB = \angle BOC$ [given]
$\therefore$ $\Delta AOB \cong \Delta COB$ [by SAS congruence rule]
Then, $AB = BC$ [by CPCT]
Similarly, we can prove that
$BC = CD$ and $CD = AD$
Thus, we get
$AB = BC = CD = AD$
and $\angle A = \angle B = \angle C = \angle D = 90°$
Hence, quadrilateral $ABCD$ is a square.

Hence proved.

7. Given, lines l and m are parallel i.e. $PS \parallel QR$ and transversal X intersects PS and QR at points A and C, respectively.
The bisectors of $\angle PAC$ and $\angle ACQ$ intersect each other at B and bisectors of $\angle ACR$ and $\angle SAC$ intersect each other at D.
Now, we have to show that quadrilateral $ABCD$ is a rectangle.
Since, $PS \parallel CR$ and X is a transversal.
$\therefore$ $\angle PAC = \angle ACR$ [$\because$ alternate angles]
$\Rightarrow$ $\frac{1}{2}\angle PAC = \frac{1}{2}\angle ACR$
[dividing by 2 both sides]
$\Rightarrow$ $\angle BAC = \angle ACD$
These form a pair of alternate angles for lines AB and CD with AC as transversal.
So, $AB \parallel CD$
Similarly, $BC \parallel AD$
Therefore, quadrilateral $ABCD$ is a parallelogram.
Now, PS is a straight line.
So, $\angle PAC + \angle SAC = 180°$ [$\because$ linear pair]
$\Rightarrow \frac{1}{2}\angle PAC + \frac{1}{2}\angle SAC = \frac{1}{2} \times 180°$
[dividing by 2 both sides]
$\Rightarrow$ $\angle BAC + \angle DAC = 90°$
$\Rightarrow$ $\angle BAD = 90°$
Similarly, QR is a straight line.
So, $\angle BCD = 90°$
Thus, two angles of parallelogram $ABCD$ is a right angle.
Hence, $ABCD$ is a rectangle. **Hence proved.**

8. Let P, Q, R and S be the points of intersection of the bisectors of $\angle A$ and $\angle B$, $\angle B$ and $\angle C$, $\angle C$ and $\angle D$ and $\angle D$ and $\angle A$ respectively of parallelogram $ABCD$ (see figure).

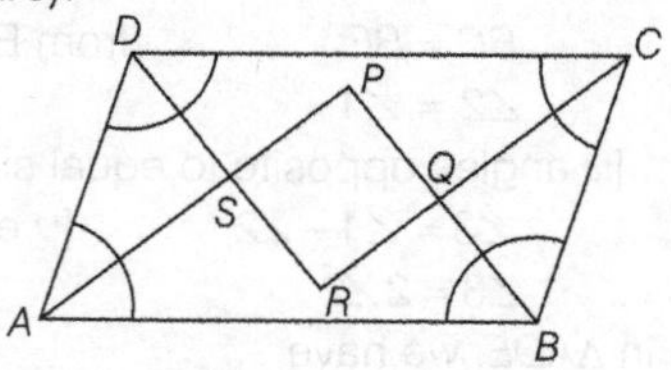

In ΔASD, we observe
DS bisects $\angle D$ and AS bisects $\angle A$, therefore
$\angle DAS + \angle ADS = \frac{1}{2}\angle A + \frac{1}{2}\angle D$
$= \frac{1}{2}(\angle A + \angle D) = \frac{1}{2} \times 180°$
$= 90°$
[$\because$ $\angle A$ and $\angle D$ are interior angles on the same side of the transversal]
Also, $\angle DAS + \angle ADS + \angle DSA = 180°$
[$\because$ angle sum property of a triangle]
$\Rightarrow$ $90° + \angle DSA = 180°$
$\Rightarrow$ $\angle DSA = 90°$
$\Rightarrow$ $\angle PSR = 90°$
[$\because$ vertically opposite angles, $\angle DSA = \angle PSR$]
Similarly, it can be shown that $\angle APB = 90°$ or $\angle SPQ = 90°$, $\angle PQR = 90°$ and $\angle SRQ = 90°$.
So, $PQRS$ is a quadrilateral in which all angles are right angles.
Therefore, $PQRS$ is a parallelogram in which one angle (in fact all angles) is 90°, so $PQRS$ is a rectangle.

9. Given, $ABCD$ is a square and BD is a diagonal.
$\therefore$ $\angle CBD = \angle CDB = \frac{1}{2} \times 90° = 45°$
[$\because$ diagonal of a square bisect each angle at the vertex]
Also, $EF \parallel BD$ [given]
So, $\angle CEF = \angle CBD = 45°$ [$\because$ corresponding angles]
and $\angle CFE = \angle CDB = 45°$ [$\because$ corresponding angles]
$\Rightarrow$ $CE = CF$
[$\because$ sides opposite to equal angles are equal]
$\Rightarrow BC - CE = CD - CF$ [$\because BC = CD$]
$\Rightarrow$ $BE = DF$ ... (i)
Now, in ΔABE and ΔADF,
$AB = AD$ [$\because$ adjacent sides of a square]
$\angle ABE = \angle ADF$ [each 90°]
$BE = DF$ [from Eq. (i)]
So, $\Delta ABE \cong \Delta ADF$ [by SAS congruence rule]
Then, $AE = AF$ [by CPCT] ... (ii)
and $\angle BAE = \angle DAF$ [by CPCT] ... (iii)
Now, in ΔAEM and ΔAFM,
$AE = AF$ [from Eq. (ii)]

$ME = MF$ [M is mid-point of EF]
$AM = AM$ [common side]
$\therefore \quad \Delta AEM \cong \Delta AFM$ [by SSS congruence rule]
So, $\angle EAM = \angle FAM$ [by CPCT]...(iv)
On adding Eqs. (iii) and (iv), we get
$\angle BAE + \angle EAM = \angle DAF + \angle FAM$
$\Rightarrow \quad \angle BAM = \angle DAM$
i.e. AM bisects $\angle BAD$. **Hence proved.**

10. Given A parallelogram $ABCD$, in which $AC = BD$ and $AC \perp BD$.

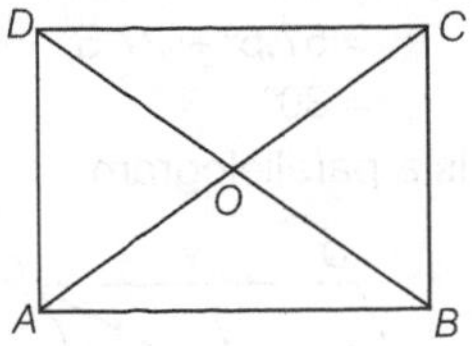

To prove $ABCD$ is a square.
Proof Let AC and BD intersect at a point O.
In ΔAOB and ΔAOD, we have
$BO = OD$
[∵ diagonals of parallelogram bisect each other]
$AO = OA$ [common]
$\angle AOB = \angle AOD = 90^\circ$ [given]
$\therefore \quad \Delta AOB \cong \Delta AOD$ [by SAS congruence rule]
Then, $AB = AD$ [by CPCT]
Also, $AB = DC$ and $AD = BC$
[∵ opposite sides of a parallelogram are equal]
$\therefore \quad AB = BC = DC = AD$ ...(i)
Again, in ΔABC and ΔBAD, we have
$AB = BA$ [common sides]
$AC = BD$ [given]
$BC = AD$ [from Eq. (i)]
$\therefore \quad \Delta ABC \cong \Delta BAD$ [by SSS congruence rule]
Then, $\angle ABC = \angle BAD$ [by CPCT] ...(ii)
Also, $\angle ABC + \angle BAD = 180^\circ$ [∵ co-interior angles]
$\therefore \quad \angle ABC = \angle BAD = 90^\circ$ [using Eq. (ii)]
Thus, $AB = BC = CD = DA$ and $\angle A = 90^\circ$
Hence, $ABCD$ is a square. **Hence proved.**

11. (i)

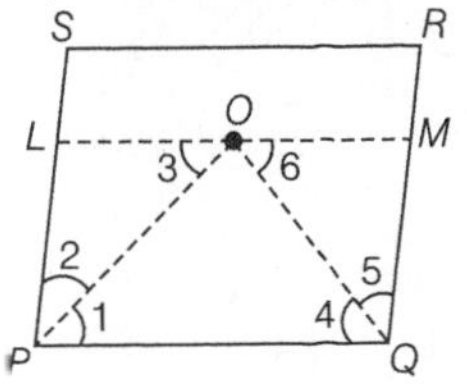

$\angle 1 = \angle 2$ and $\angle 4 = \angle 5$
[∵ PO and QO are the angle bisectors of $\angle P$ and $\angle Q$ respectively]

Now, $PS \parallel RQ \Rightarrow PL \parallel QM$
Also, $PQ \parallel SR \Rightarrow PQ \parallel LM$
$\therefore PQML$ is a parallelogram.
$\therefore \quad PL = QM$
[opposite sides of parallelogram are equal]... (a)

(ii) Now, $PQ \parallel LM$ and OP is transversal.
$\therefore \quad \angle 1 = \angle 3$ [alternate interior angles]
$\therefore \quad \angle 2 = \angle 3$ [∵ $\angle 1 = \angle 2$]
In ΔOPL, $\angle 2 = \angle 3$
$\Rightarrow \quad OL = PL$ ...(b)
[∵ opposite sides of equal angles are equal]
Also, $PL \parallel QM$ and OQ is transversal.
$\therefore \quad \angle 4 = \angle 6 \Rightarrow \angle 5 = \angle 6$
In ΔOQM, $\angle 5 = \angle 6$
$OM = QM$ ...(c)
[∵ opposite sides of equal angles are equal]
$\therefore$ From Eqs. (a), (b) and (c), we have
$OL = OM$

12. Given, $ABCD$ is a parallelogram.
$\therefore \quad AB \parallel CD, \ AB = CD$
and $AD \parallel BC, \ AD = BC$
Also, given P and Q are the mid-points of sides AB and CD, respectively.

(i) In quadrilateral $APCQ$,
$AP \parallel CQ$ [∵ $AB \parallel CD$] ...(a)
Now, $AP = \frac{1}{2}AB$
and $CQ = \frac{1}{2}CD$ ...(b)
Since, $AB = CD$ [given]
$\Rightarrow \quad \frac{1}{2}AB = \frac{1}{2}CD$
$\Rightarrow \quad AP = CQ$ [using Eq. (b)]
Thus, we have $AP \parallel CQ$ and $AP = CQ$.
Hence, $APCQ$ is a parallelogram.

(ii) Similarly, in quadrilateral $DPBQ$,
$BP \parallel QD$ and $BP = QD$
$\therefore DPBQ$ is a parallelogram.

(iii) Since, $DPBQ$ is a parallelogram.
$\therefore \quad DP \parallel BQ$
$\Rightarrow \quad PS \parallel QR$ ...(c)
and $APCQ$ is also a parallelogram.
$\therefore \quad AQ \parallel PC$
$\Rightarrow \quad SQ \parallel PR$ ...(d)
From Eqs. (c) and (d), we have
$PS \parallel QR$
and $SQ \parallel PR$
Hence, $PSQR$ is also a parallelogram.

Case Based Questions

1. (i) In ΔADE, $\angle ADE = 30°$

$AD = DE$ [given]

$\Rightarrow \angle DAE = \angle DEA$

[$\because$ angles opposite to equal sides are equal]

Let $\angle DAE = \angle DEA = y$

Now, $y + y + 30° = 180°$

[$\because$ angle sum property of a triangle]

$\Rightarrow 2y = 150°$

$\Rightarrow y = 75°$ ...(a)

Also, $\angle DAC = 90°$ [given]

$\therefore x + y = 90°$

$\Rightarrow x = 90° - 75° = 15°$ [from Eq. (a)]

(ii) $\because$ All the sides of quadrilateral $ABED$ are equal.

$\therefore$ It is a square or rhombus.

But one of the angle i.e. $\angle ADE$ is not 90°.

So, it is a rhombus.

(iii) Since, $ABED$ is a rhombus

$\therefore \angle ABE = \angle ADE = 30°$ [$\because$ opposite angles]

2. Given, $WXYZ$ is a rhombus and $\angle W = 65°$.

(i) $\angle XYZ = \angle ZWX = 65°$

[$\because$ opposite angles of a rhombus]

If ΔZAY is an equilateral triangle, then

$\angle AYZ = 60°$

$\therefore \angle AYX = \angle AYZ + \angle XYZ$

$= 60° + 65° = 125°$

Now, $AY = XY$ [$\because AY = YZ$ and $YZ = XY$]

$\therefore \angle YAX = \angle YXA$

[$\because$ angles opposite to equal sides are equal]

In ΔAYX, $\angle YXA + \angle YAX + \angle AYX = 180°$

[$\because$ angle sum property]

$\Rightarrow 2\angle YXA = 180° - 125°$

[$\because \angle AYX = 125°$ and $\angle YAX = \angle YXA$]

$\Rightarrow \angle YXA = \frac{55°}{2} = 27.5°$

(ii) We know that the sum of adjacent angles of a parallelogram is 180°.

$\therefore \angle YXW + \angle XYZ = 180°$

$\Rightarrow \angle YXW = 180° - 65° = 115°$

[$\because \angle XYZ = 65°$]

In a rhombus, diagonal XZ bisects $\angle YXW$.

$\therefore \angle YXZ = \frac{1}{2} \times \angle YXW = \frac{1}{2} \times 115° = 57.5°$

Now, in ΔXZY,

$\angle ZXA = \angle ZXY - \angle YXA$

$= 57.5° - 27.5°$

$= 30°$

3. Given $ABCD$ is a parallelogram.

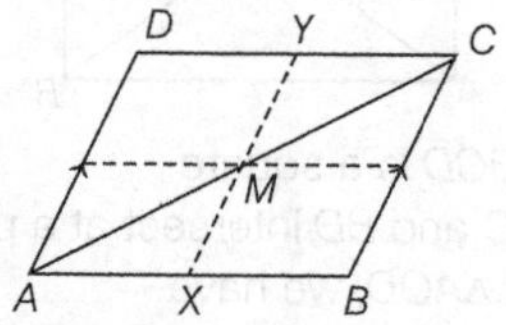

Construction Join XM and MY.

(i) In ΔAXM and ΔCYM, we have

$AM = MC$ [$\because M$ is mid-point of AC]

$AX = CY$ [given]

$\angle XAM = \angle YCM$ [$\because$ alternate angles]

$\therefore \Delta AXM \cong \Delta CYM$

[by SAS congruency rule]

$\angle YMC = \angle XMA$ ...(a) [by CPCT]

(ii) Now, in ΔYMC,

$\angle YMA = \angle MYC + \angle MCY$ ...(b)

[$\because$ exterior angle is equal to the sum of the two opposite interior angles]

Also, $\angle YMC + \angle MYC + \angle MCY = 180°$

$\Rightarrow \angle YMC + \angle YMA = 180°$ [from Eq. (b)]

$\Rightarrow \angle AMX + \angle YMA = 180°$ [from Eq. (a)]

Hence, XMY is a straight line.

11

CONSTRUCTION OF POLYGONS

TYPE - 1 03 Mark

Construction 1 *To construct a quadrilateral, when its four sides and one angle are given.*

Q.1 Construct a quadrilateral $ABCD$, where $AB = 7.0$ cm, $BC = 5.8$ cm, $CD = 6.3$ cm, $DA = 4.3$ cm and $\angle A = 75°$.

Sol. Given, a quadrilateral $ABCD$, in which $AB = 7.0$ cm, $BC = 5.8$ cm, $CD = 6.3$ cm, $DA = 4.3$ cm and $\angle A = 75°$.

Steps of construction

1. Draw a line segment AB of length 7.0 cm.

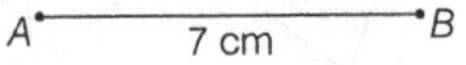

2. At point A, construct $\angle PAB = 75°$ $[\because 75° = 60° + 15°]$

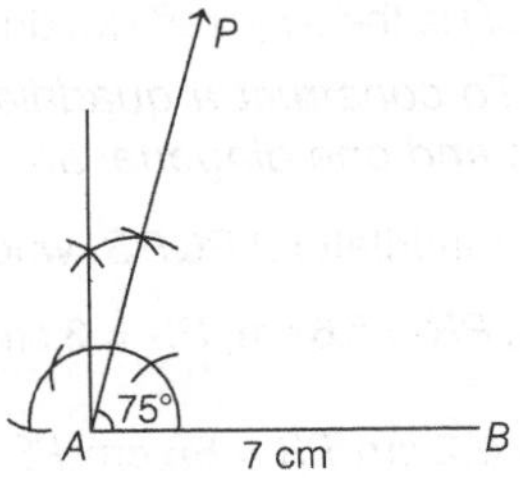

3. Taking A as centre, make an arc of radius 4.3 cm, which cuts AP at D.

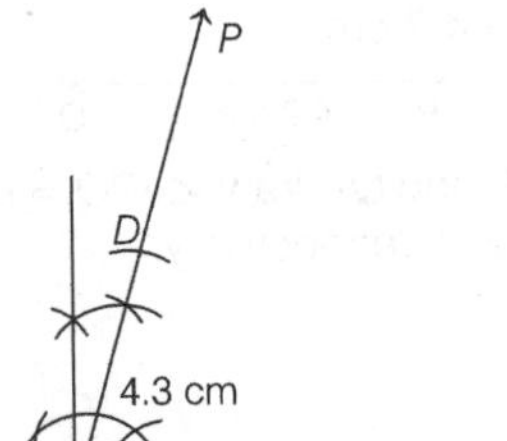

4. Taking B and D as centres, make arcs of radii 5.8 cm and 6.3 cm respectively, which cut each other at C and then join BC and CD.

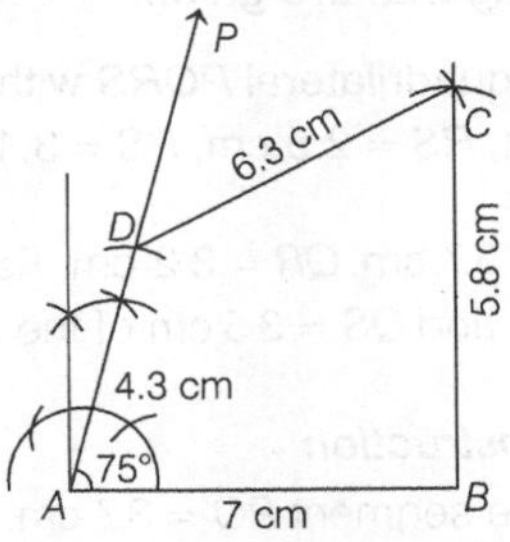

Thus, $ABCD$ is the required quadrilateral.

Construction 2 *To construct a quadrilateral, when three sides and two angles are given.*

Q.2 Construct a quadrilateral $KITE$, given that $KI = 3.8$ cm, $IT = 2.9$ cm, $KE = 4.2$ cm, $\angle K = 90°$ and $\angle I = 120°$.

Sol. Given, $KI = 3.8$cm, $IT = 2.9$ cm, $KE = 42$ cm, $\angle K = 90°$ and $\angle I = 120°$ of the quadrilateral $KITE$.

Steps of construction

1. Draw a line segment KI of length 3.8 cm.

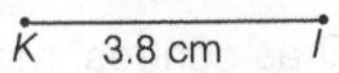

2. At points K and I, construct $\angle XKI$ and $\angle YIK$ of 90° and 120°, respectively.

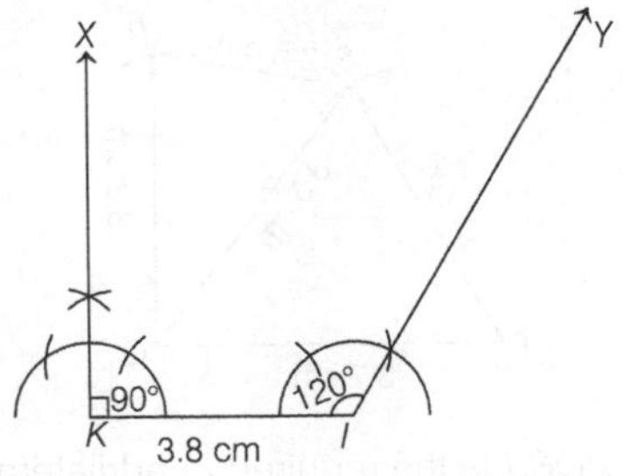

3. Taking K and I as centres, make arcs of radii 4.2 cm and 2.9 cm respectively, which cut KX and IY at E and T respectively and join T and E.

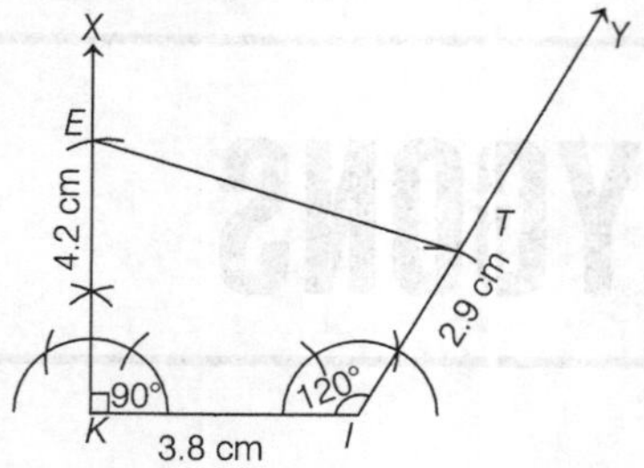

Thus, $KITE$ is the required quadrilateral.

Construction 3 *To construct a quadrilateral, when four sides and one diagonal are given.*

Q.3 Construct a quadrilateral $PQRS$ with $PQ = 3.7$ cm, $QR = 3.2$ cm, $RS = 2.5$ cm, $PS = 3.1$ cm and $QS = 3.5$ cm.

Sol. Given, $PQ = 3.7$ cm, $QR = 3.2$ cm, $RS = 2.5$ cm, $PS = 3.1$ cm and $QS = 3.5$ cm of the quadrilateral $PQRS$.

Steps of construction

1. Draw a line segment $PQ = 3.7$ cm.

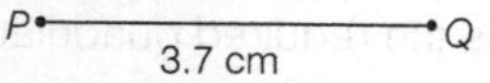

2. Taking P and Q as centres, make arcs of radii 3.1cm and 3.5 cm respectively, which cut each other at S.

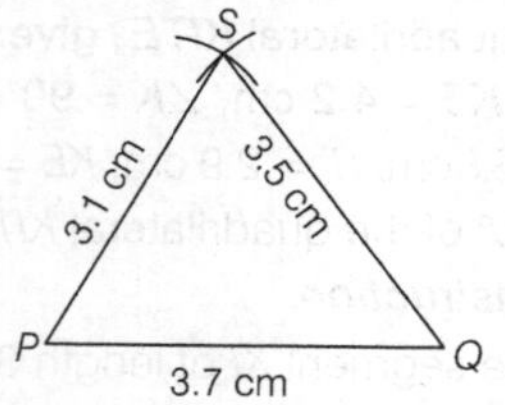

3. Taking S and Q as centres, make arcs of radii 2.5 cm and 3.2 cm respectively, which cut each other at R and join SR and QR.

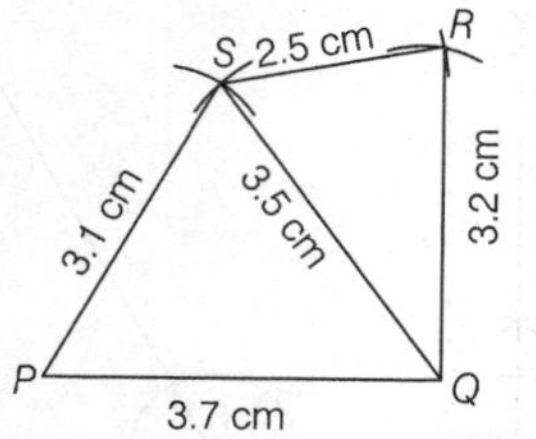

Thus, $PQRS$ is the required quadrilateral.

Construction 4 *To construct a quadrilateral, whose three sides and two diagonals are given.*

Q.4 Construct a quadrilateral $ABCD$ whose three sides i.e. $AB = 2.7$ cm, $BC = 1.9$ cm, $AD = 3.6$ cm and two diagonals i.e. $AC = 3.5$ cm, $BD = 5.3$ cm are given.

Sol. Given, $AB = 2.7$ cm, $BC = 1.9$ cm, $AD = 3.6$ cm, $AC = 3.5$ cm and $BD = 5.3$ cm of the quadrilateral $ABCD$.

Steps of construction

1. Draw a line segment $AB = 2.7$ cm.

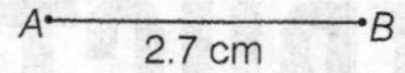

2. Taking A and B as centres, make arcs of radii 3.5 cm and 1.9 cm respectively, which cut each other at C.

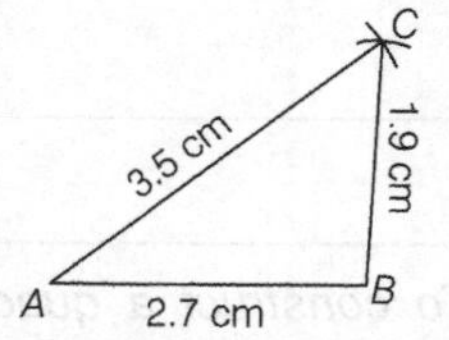

3. Again, taking A and B as centres, make arcs of radii 3.6 cm and 5.3 cm respectively, which cut each other at D and join BD, CD and DA.

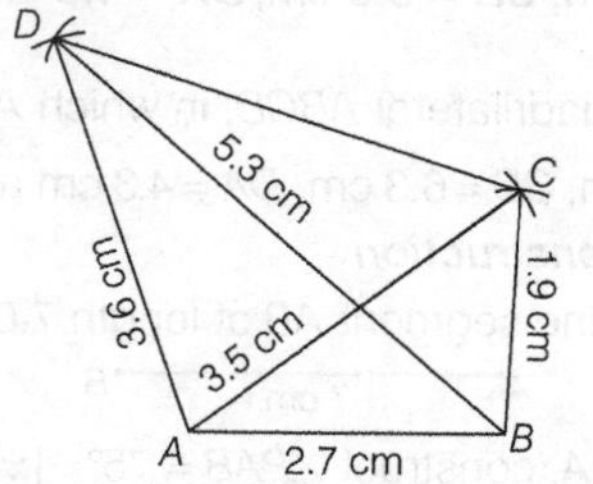

Thus, $ABCD$ is the required quadrilateral.

Construction 5 *To construct a quadrilateral, whose two sides, two angles and one diagonal are given.*

Q.5 Construct a quadrilateral $PQRS$, when

$PQ = 4.2$ cm, $PR = 5.6$ cm, $PS = 3$ cm, $\angle P = 90°$ and $\angle Q = 120°$.

Sol. Given, $PQ = 4.2$ cm, $PR = 5.6$ cm, $PS = 3$ cm, $\angle P = 90°$ and $\angle Q = 120°$

Steps of construction

1. Draw $PQ = 4.2$ cm

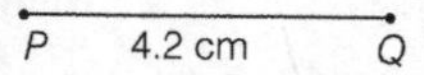

2. At points P and Q, draw $\angle APQ = 90°$ and $\angle BQP = 120°$, respectively.

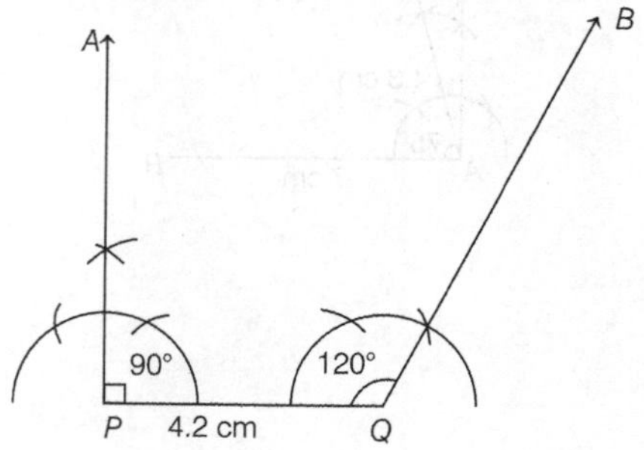

3. Taking P as centre, make arcs of radius 3 cm and 5.6 cm, which cut AP and BQ at points S and R respectively and join RS.

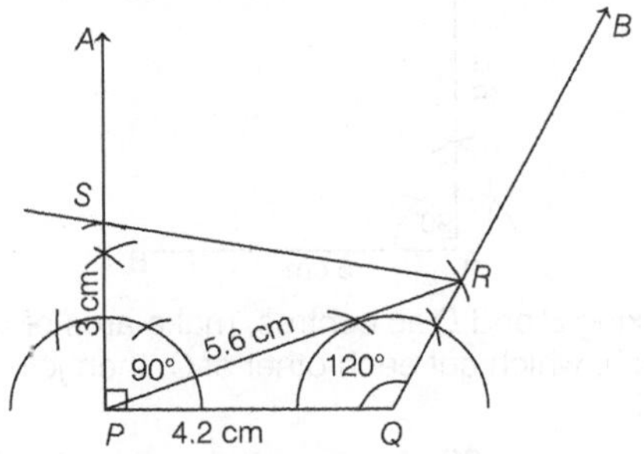

Thus, $PQRS$ is required quadrilateral.

Construction 6 *To construct a parallelogram, when two adjacent sides and the including angle are given.*

Q.6 **Construct a parallelogram, whose adjacent sides $AB = 3.6$ cm, $BC = 5.4$ cm and including angle $\angle B = 60^\circ$ are given.**

Sol. Given, $AB = 3.6$ cm, $BC = 5.4$ cm and $\angle B = 60^\circ$ of the parallelogram $ABCD$.

Steps of construction

1. Draw a line segment BC of length 5.4 cm.

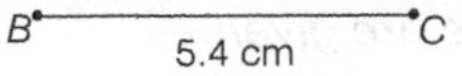

2. At B as centre, construct $\angle MBC = 60^\circ$.

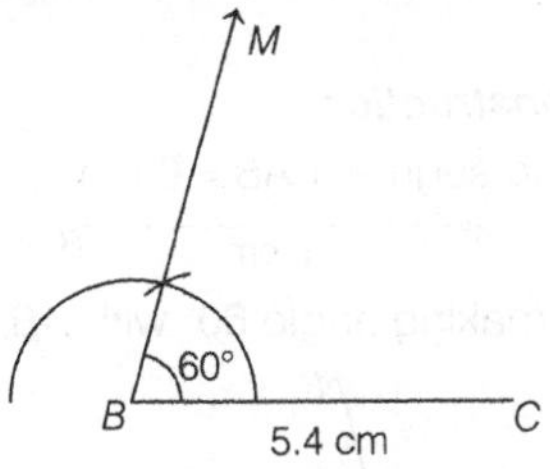

3. Taking B as centre, cut an arc of radius 3.6 cm, which cuts the line BM at A.

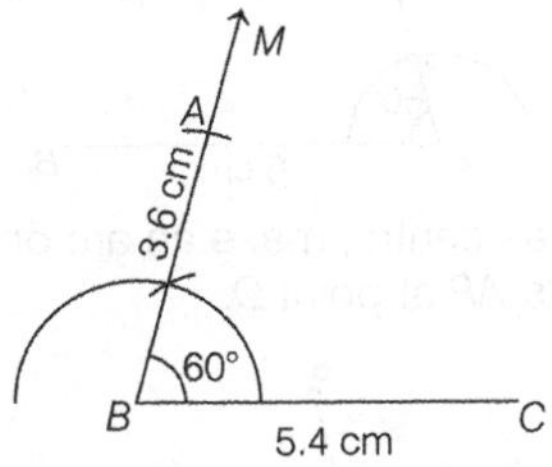

4. Taking A as centre, make an arc of radius 5.4 cm.

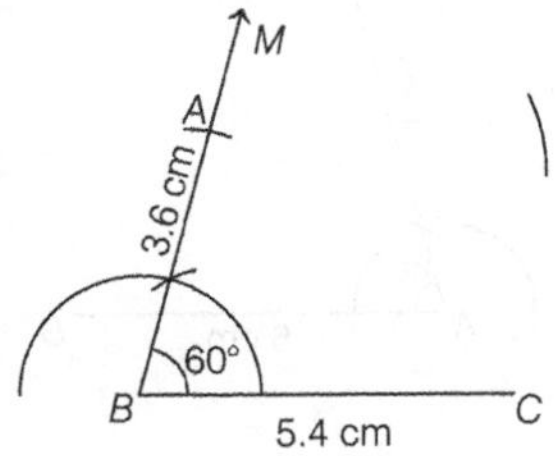

5. Taking C as centre, make another arc of radius 3.6 cm, which cuts previous arc at D and join AD and CD.

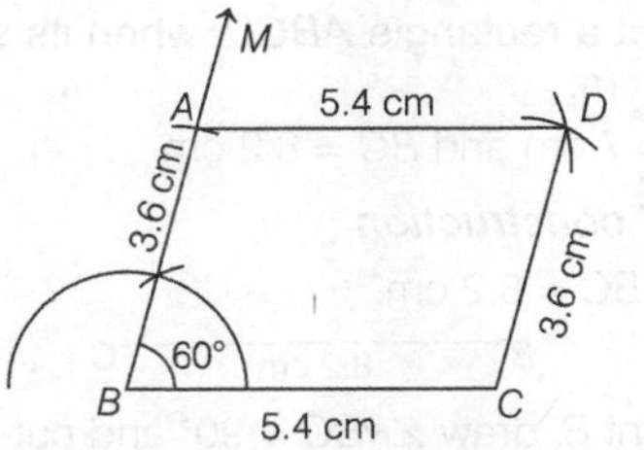

Thus, $ABCD$ is the required parallelogram.

Construction 7 *To construct a parallelogram, when two diagonals and an included angle are given.*

Q.7 **Given that $AC = 6$ cm, $BD = 5.2$ cm and $\angle COD = 60^\circ$, where O is the point of intersection of diagonals, then construct a parallelogram $ABCD$.**

Sol. Given, a parallelogram $ABCD$, in which $AC = 6$ cm, $BD = 5.2$ cm and $\angle COD = 60^\circ$, where O is the point of intersection of diagonals.

Steps of construction

1. Draw a line segment AO, which is the half of the line AC i.e. 3 cm and produce AO to C such that $OC = OA$.

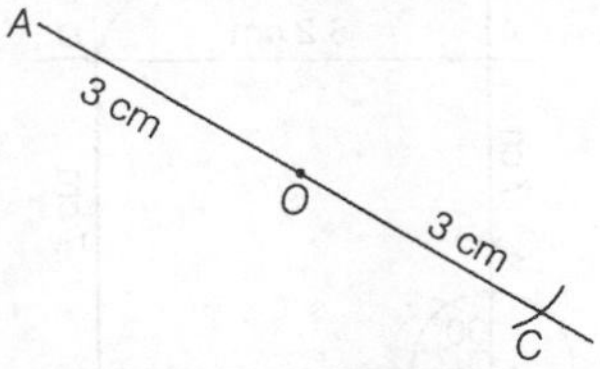

2. Taking O as centre, construct $\angle COP = 60^\circ$ and produce PO to Q.

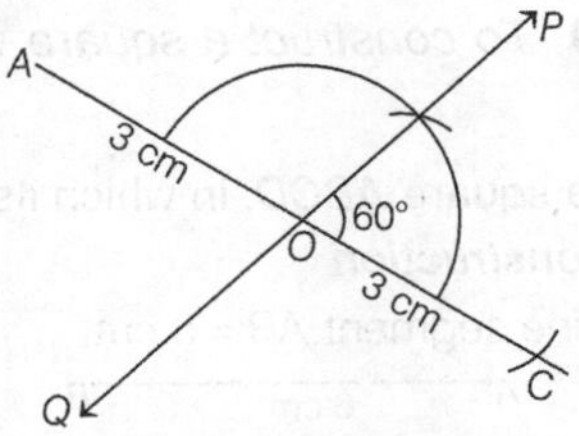

3. Taking O as centre, make arcs of radii 2.6 cm to line PQ, where $OB = OD = 2.6$ cm and join AB, BC, CD and DA.

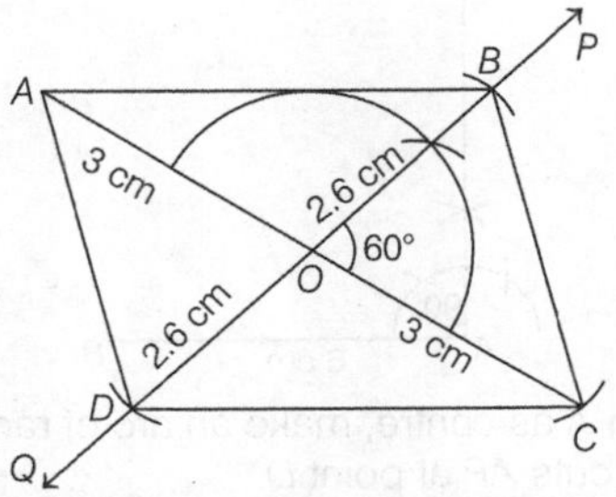

Thus, $ABCD$ is the required parallelogram.

Construction 8 *To construct a rectangle, when its sides are given.*

Q.8 Construct a rectangle *ABCD*, when its sides are 7cm and 8.2 cm.

Sol. Let *AB* = 7 cm and *BC* = 8.2 cm

Steps of construction

1. Draw *BC* = 8.2 cm.

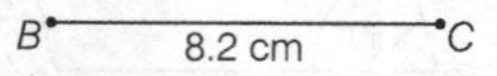

2. At point *B*, draw ∠*PBC* = 90° and cut-off an arc of radius 7cm, which cuts *PB* at *A*.

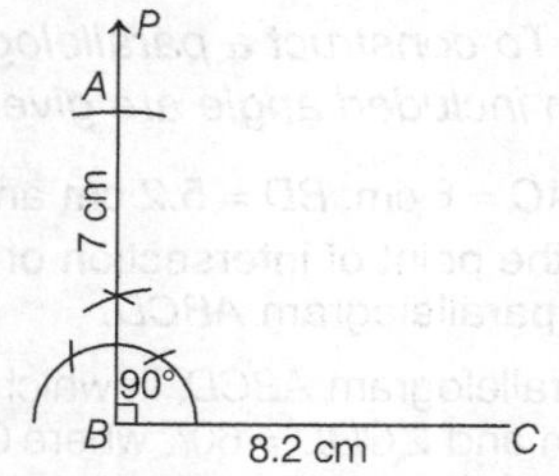

3. Taking points *A* and *C* as centres, make arcs of radii 8.2cm and 7cm respectively, which meet at point *D*, then join *AD* and *CD*.

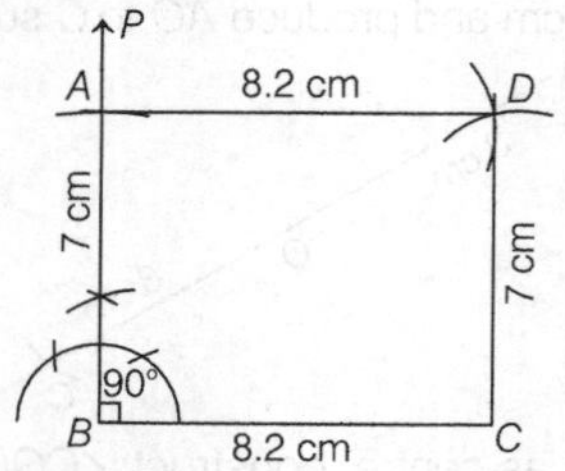

Thus, *ABCD* is the required rectangle.

Construction 9 *To construct a square whose one side is given.*

Q.9 Construct a square *ABCD*, in which its side is 6 cm.

Sol. ***Steps of construction***

1. Draw a line segment *AB* = 6 cm.

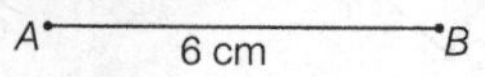

2. Draw *AP*⊥ *AB* at point *A*.

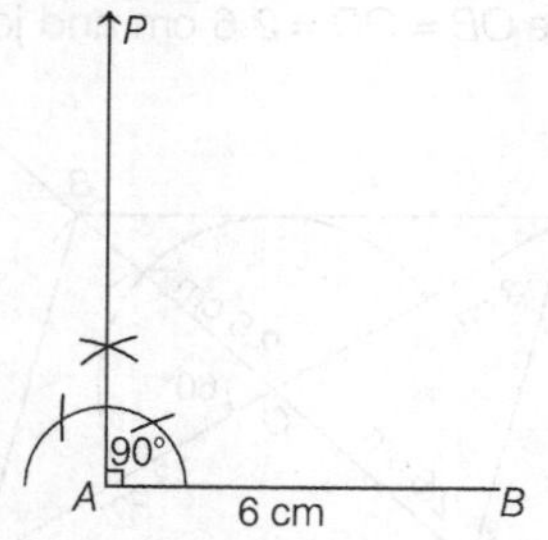

3. Taking *A* as centre, make an arc of radius 6 cm, which cuts *AP* at point *D*.

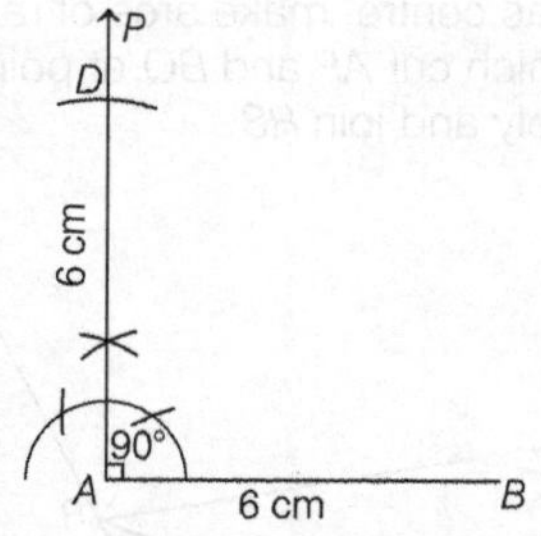

4. Taking *B* and *D* as centres, make arcs of radii 6 cm each, which cut each other at *C*, then join *BC* and *DC*.

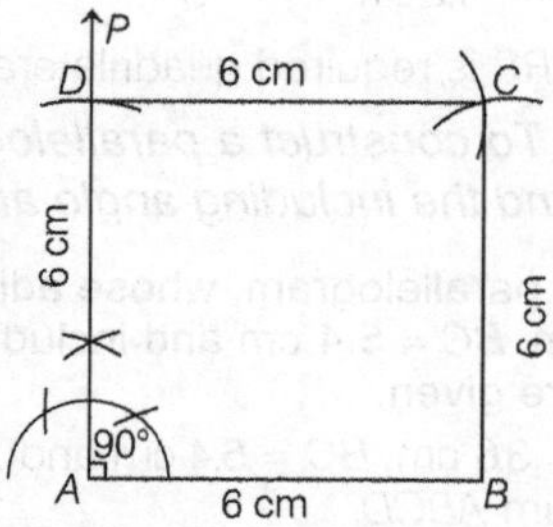

Thus, *ABCD* is the required square.

Construction 10 *To construct a rhombus whose one side and one angle are given.*

Q.10 Construct a rhombus *ABCD*, when its side = 6 cm and ∠*A* = 60°.

Sol. ***Steps of construction***

1. Draw a line segment *AB* = 6 cm.

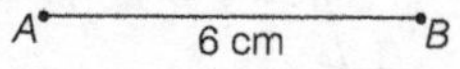

2. Draw *AP* making angle 60° with *AB*.

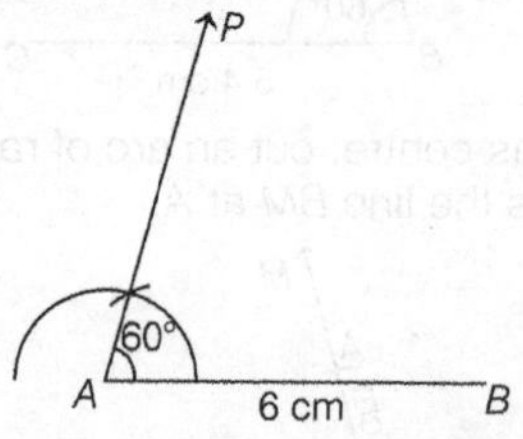

3. Taking *A* as centre, make an arc of radius 6 cm, which cuts *AP* at point *D*.

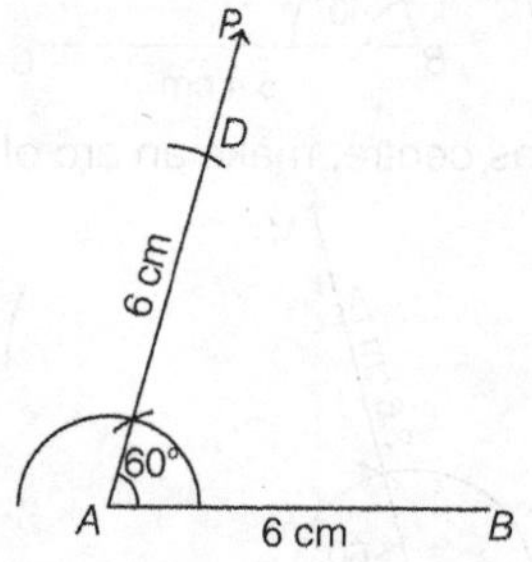

4. Taking B and D as centres, make arcs of radii 6cm each, which cut each other at C, then join BC and CD.

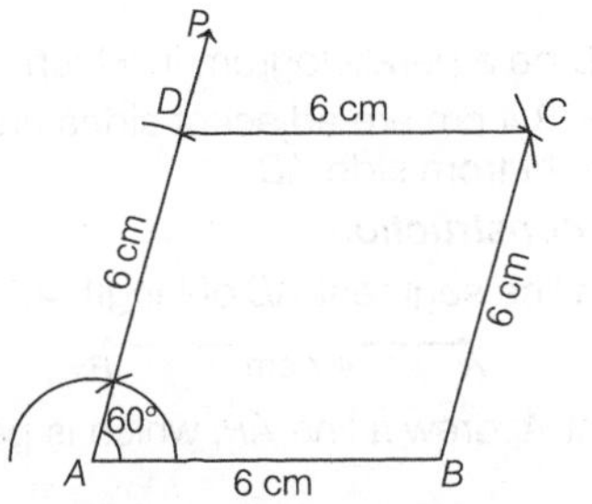

Thus, $ABCD$ is the required rhombus.

Construction 11 ***To construct a quadrilateral, when two sides, two diagonals and one angle are given.***

Q.11 Construct a quadrilateral $ABCD$ when $\angle A = 90°$, diagonals AC and BD are 5.2 cm and 6.1 cm, respectively and sides AB and CD are 4.2 cm and 4.5 cm, respectively.

Sol. ***Steps of construction***

1. Draw $AB = 4.2$ cm

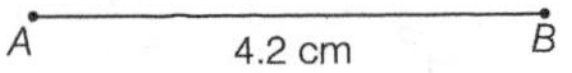

2. At point A, draw $AP \perp AB$.

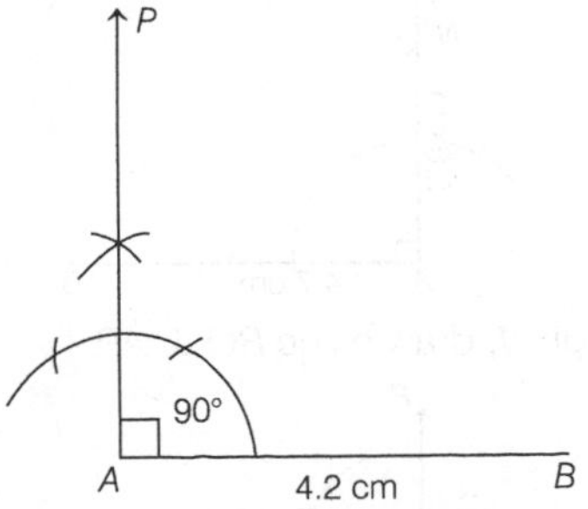

3. Taking B as centre, make an arc of radius 6.1 cm, which cuts AP at point D.

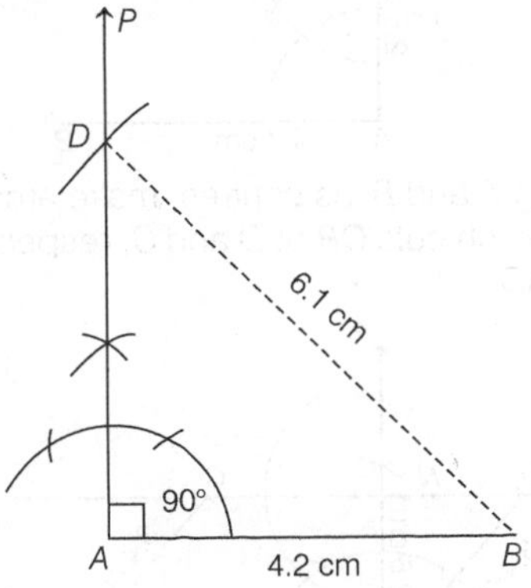

4. Taking A and D as centres, make arcs of radii 5.2 cm and 4.5 cm respectively, which meet at point C. Then, join BC and CD.

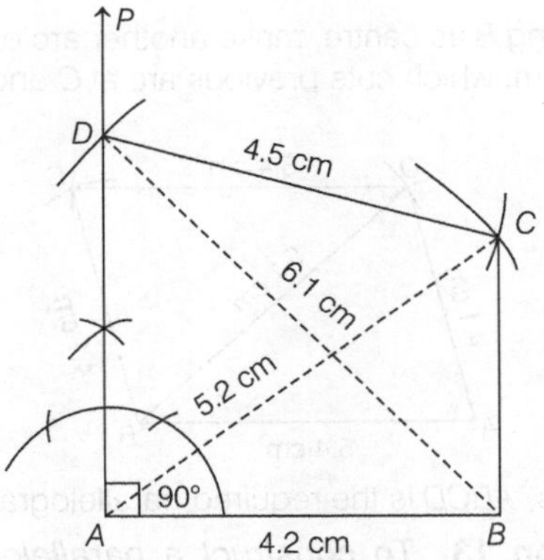

Thus, $ABCD$ is the required quadrilateral.

Construction 12 ***To construct a parallelogram, when two adjacent sides and one diagonal are given.***

Q.12 If $AB = 5.4$ cm, $AD = 4.1$ cm and $BD = 5.1$ cm, then construct a parallelogram $ABCD$.

Sol. Given, a parallelogram $ABCD$, in which $AB = 5.4$ cm, $AD = 4.1$ cm and diagonal $BD = 5.1$ cm.

Steps of construction

1. Draw a line segment AB of length 5.4 cm.

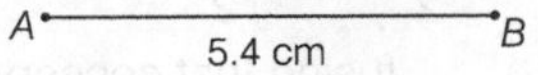

2. Taking A as centre, make an arc 4.1 cm.

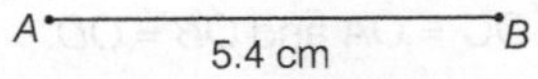

3. Taking B as centre, make another arc of radius 5.1 cm, which cuts previous arc at D.

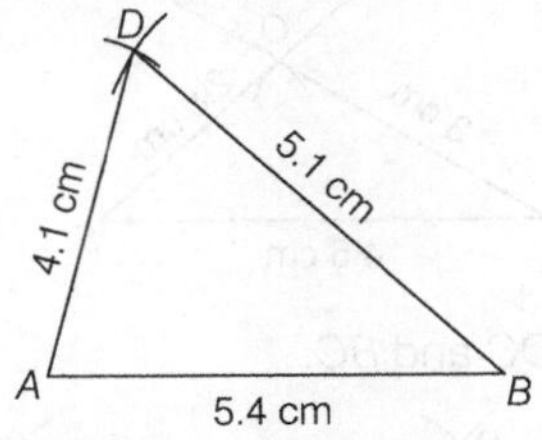

4. Taking D as centre, make an arc of radius 5.4 cm.

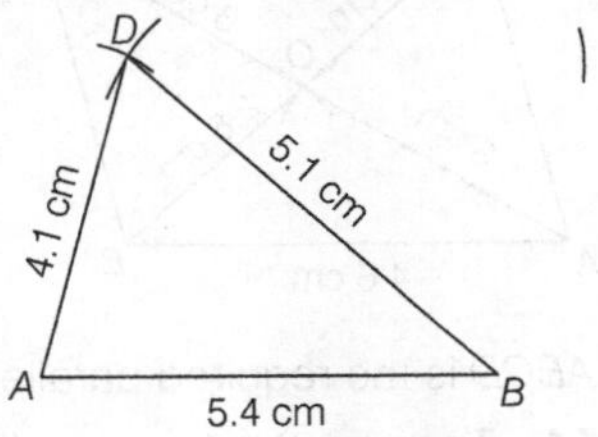

5. Taking B as centre, make another arc of radius 4.1cm, which cuts previous arc at C and join BC and CD.

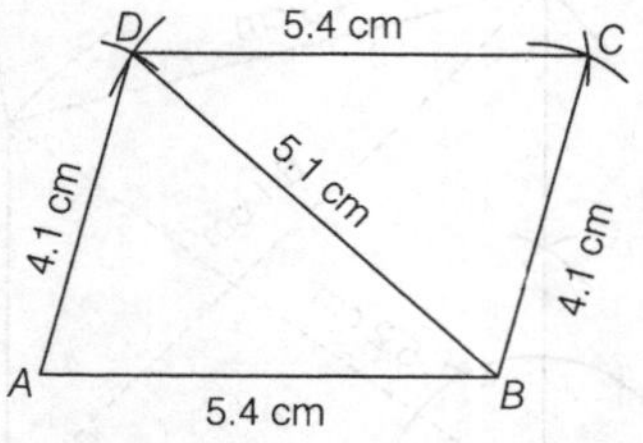

Thus, $ABCD$ is the required parallelogram.

Construction 13 *To construct a parallelogram, when one side and both diagonals are given.*

Q.13 Construct a parallelogram, whose one side is 4.5 cm and diagonals are 6.0 cm and 5.6 cm.

Sol. Let $AB = 4.5$ cm, $AC = 6.0$ cm and $BD = 5.6$ cm

Steps of construction

1. Draw a ΔAOB having base $AB = 4.5$ cm

$$OA = \frac{1}{2} \times AC = \frac{1}{2} \times 6.0 = 3 \text{ cm}$$

and $$OB = \frac{1}{2} \times BD = \frac{1}{2} \times 5.6 = 2.8 \text{ cm}$$

[using that concept that diagonals of parallelogram bisect each other]

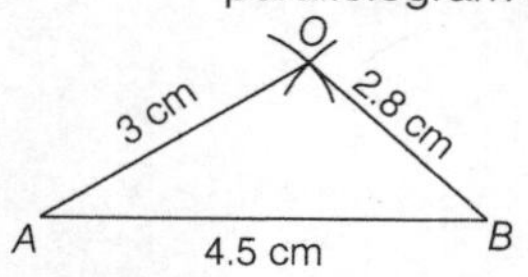

2. Now, produce the side AO to C and side BO to D such that $OC = OA$ and $OB = OD$.

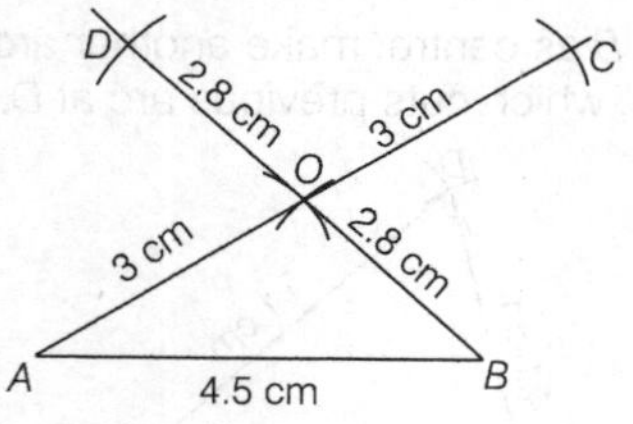

3. Join AD, DC and BC.

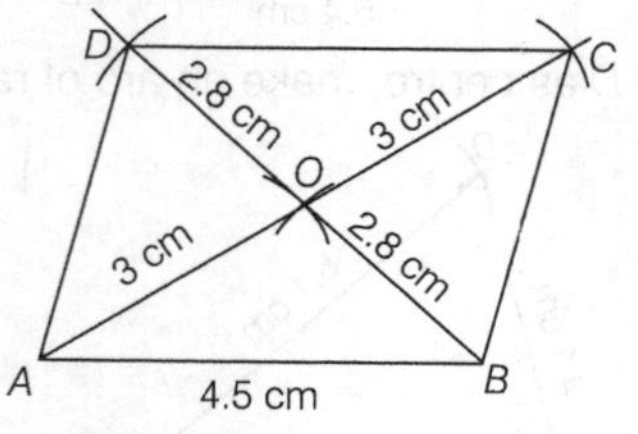

Hence, $ABCD$ is the required parallelogram.

Construction 14 *To construct a parallelogram, when two adjacent sides and height are given.*

Q.14 Construct a parallelogram, whose adjacent sides are 4.7 cm and 3.4 cm. Also, height from 4.7 cm side, is 2.6 cm.

Sol. Let $ABCD$ be a parallelogram in which $AB = 4.7$ cm and $BC = 3.4$ cm are adjacent sides and $AN = 2.6$ cm is the height from side AB.

Steps of construction

1. Draw a line segment AB of length 4.7 cm.

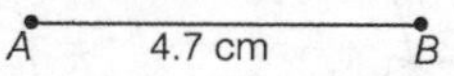

2. At point A, draw a line AP, which is perpendicular to AB.

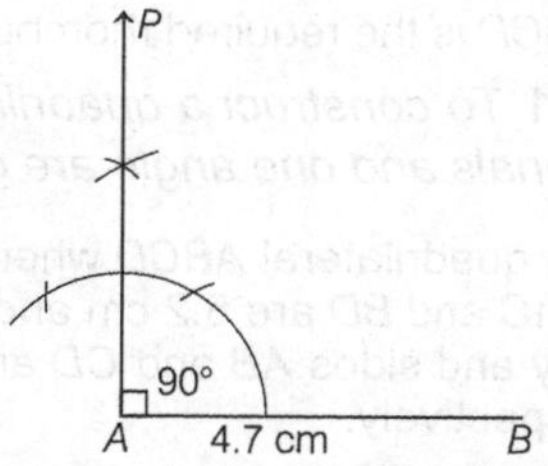

3. Taking A as centre, draw an arc of radius 2.6 cm, which cuts AP at N.

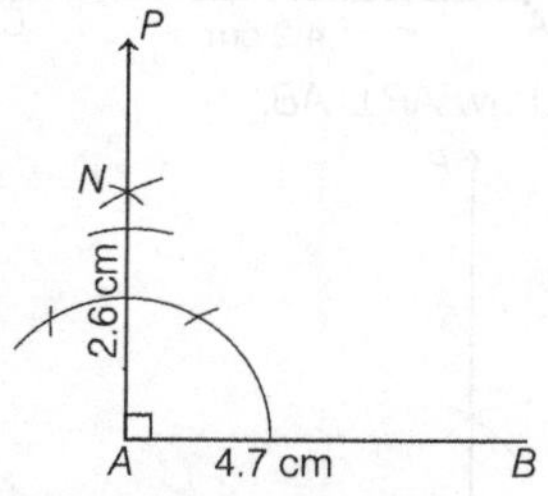

4. Through N, draw a line $RQ \perp AP$.

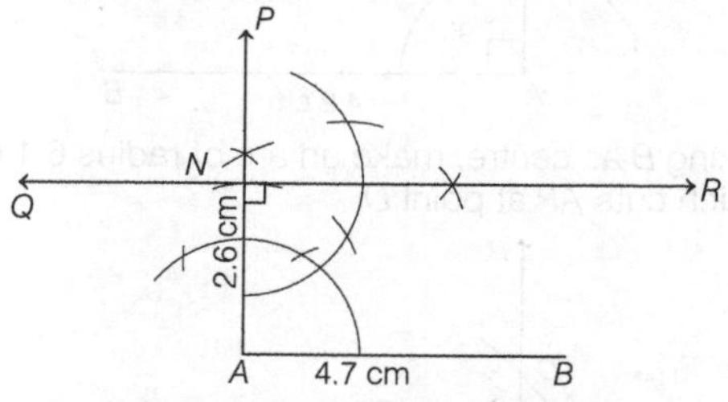

5. Taking A and B as centres, make arcs of radii 3.4 cm, which cuts QR at D and C, respectively. Join BC and AD.

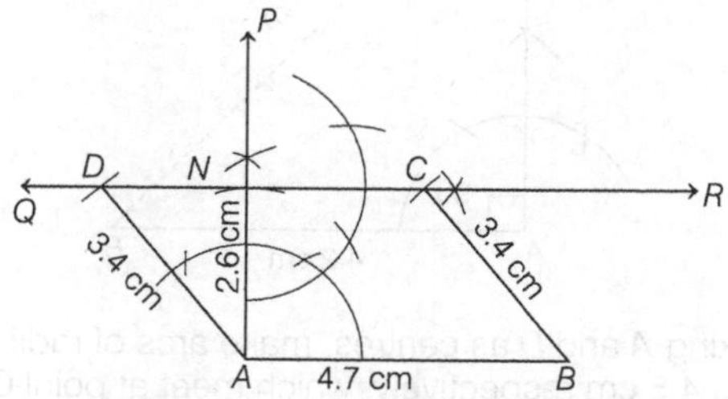

Thus, $ABCD$ is the required parallelogram.

Construction 15 *To construct a parallelogram, when one side, one diagonal and one height are given.*

Q.15 **Construct a parallelogram, whose one side, one diagonal and height from the given sides are respectively 4 cm, 3.5 cm and 2 cm.**

Sol. Let $AB = 4$ cm, $AC = 3.5$ cm and height from $AB = 2$ cm.

Steps of construction

1. Draw $AB = 4$ cm.

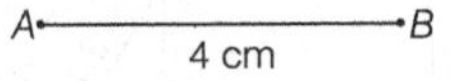

2. At point A, draw $AP \perp AB$.
   From AP, cut-off $AN = 2$ cm.

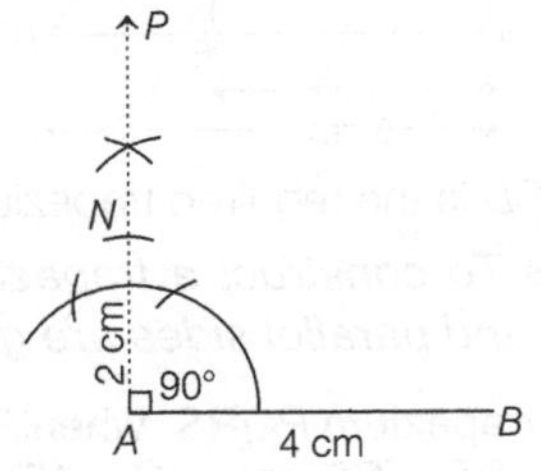

3. Through N, draw a line $QR \perp AP$.

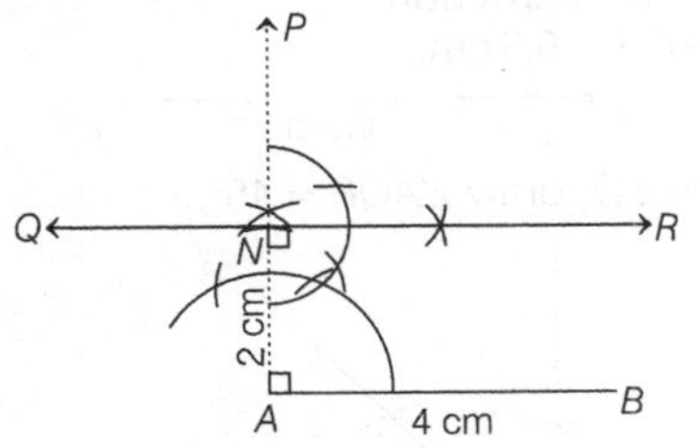

4. Taking A as centre, draw an arc of radius 3.5 cm, which cuts QR at C.

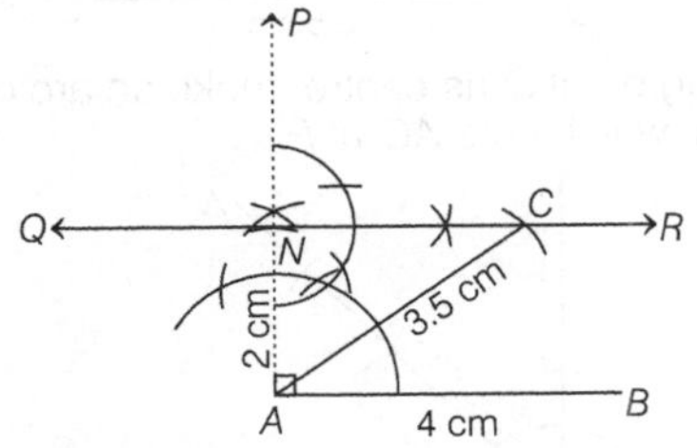

5. Taking C as centre, draw an arc of radius 4cm, which cuts QR at D. Join BC and AD.

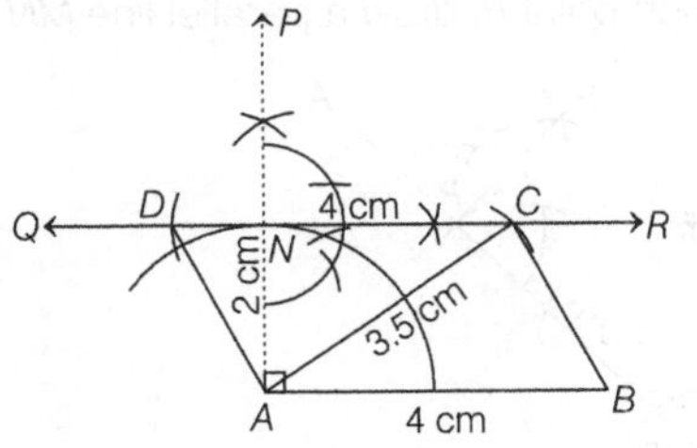

Thus, $ABCD$ is the required parallelogram.

Construction 16 *To construct a parallelogram, when both heights and the angle between two sides are given.*

Q.16 **Construct a parallelogram $ABCD$, whose height from AB is 2.3 cm and height from BC is 4.2 cm. Also, $\angle BAD = 60°$.**

Sol. Given, the heights from $AB = 2.3$ cm and from $BC = 4.2$ cm and $\angle BAD = 60°$.

Steps of construction

1. Draw a line segment PQ of any length and take a point A on it.

2. At point A, construct $\angle QAF$ of 60°.

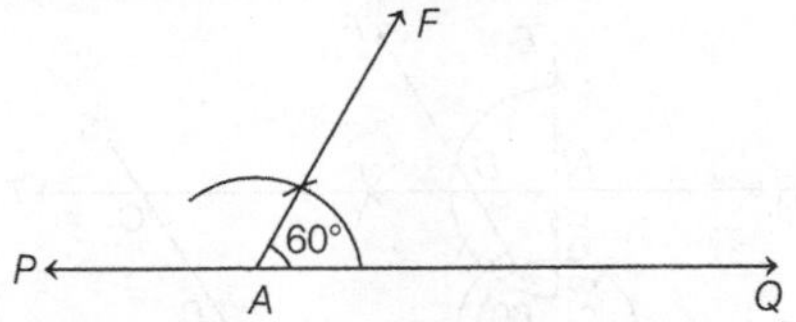

3. At point A, draw a line AE perpendicular to PQ.

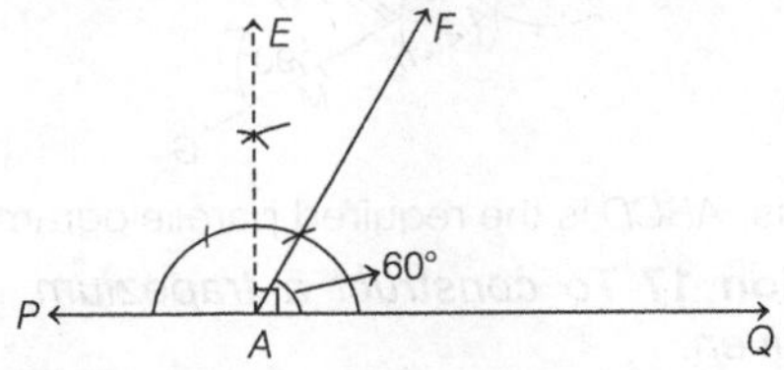

4. Taking A as centre, draw an arc of radius 2.3 cm, which cuts AE at N.

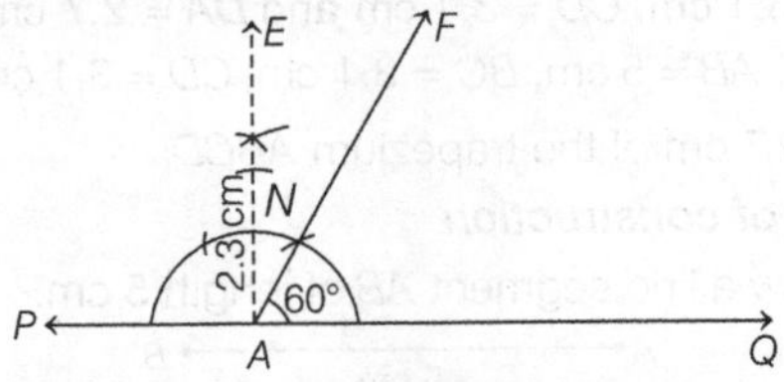

5. Through N, draw a line $RT \parallel PQ$ to meet AF at D.

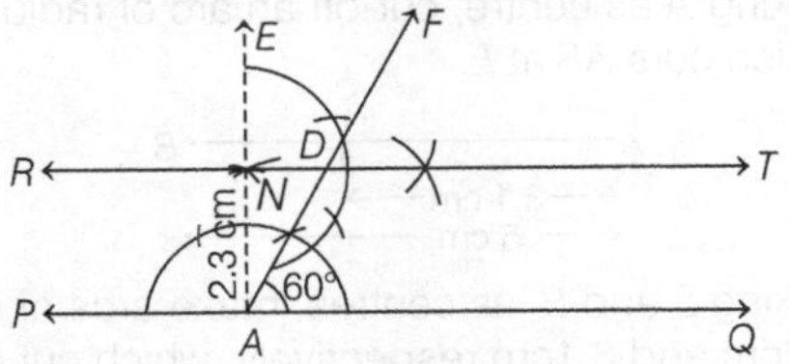

6. At point A, draw a line AG perpendicular to AD.

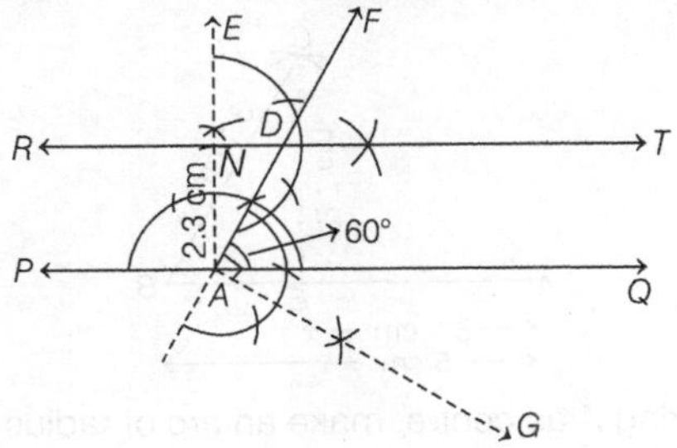

7. Taking A as centre, make an arc of radius 4.2 cm, which cuts AG at M.

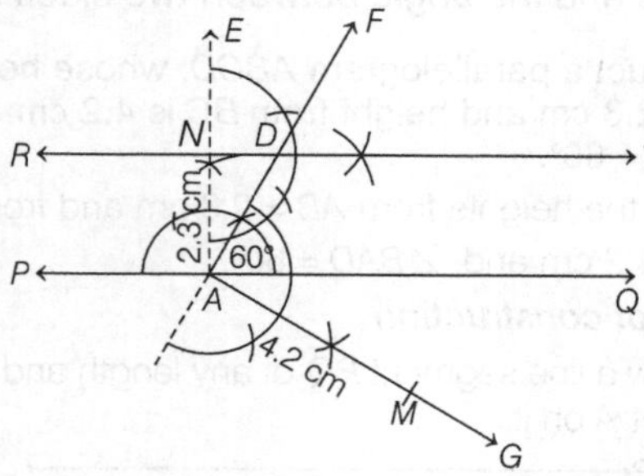

8. Through M, draw a line $MS \perp AG$ to meet AQ at B and DT at C.

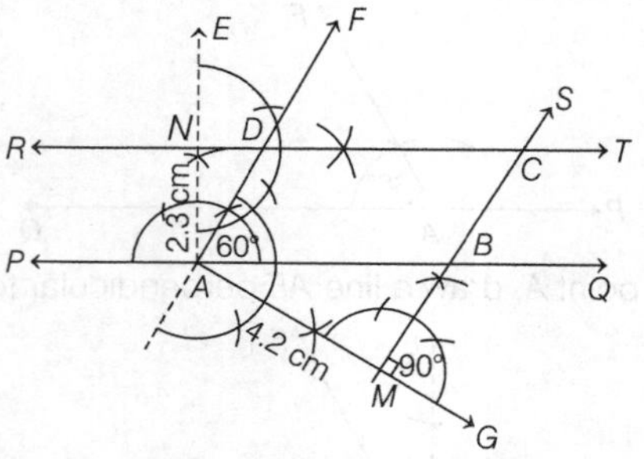

Thus, $ABCD$ is the required parallelogram.

Construction 17 ***To construct a trapezium, when four sides are given.***

Q.17 Construct a trapezium $ABCD$, where $AB = 5$ cm, $BC = 3.1$ cm, $CD = 3.1$ cm and $DA = 2.7$ cm.

Sol. Given, $AB = 5$ cm, $BC = 3.1$ cm, $CD = 3.1$ cm and $DA = 2.7$ cm of the trapezium $ABCD$.

Steps of construction

1. Draw a line segment AB of length 5 cm.

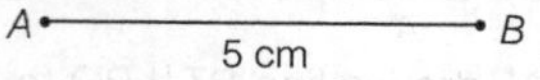

2. Taking A as centre, cut-off an arc of radius 3.1cm, which cuts AB at E.

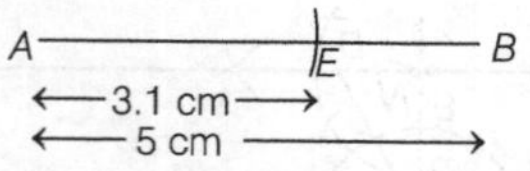

3. Taking E and B as centres, make arcs of radii 2.7cm and 3.1cm respectively, which cut each other at C and complete ΔEBC.

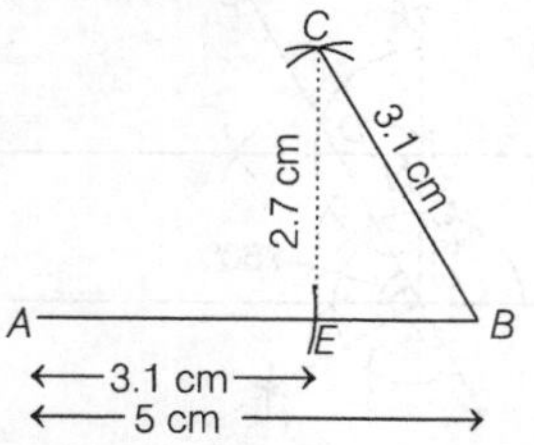

4. Taking A as centre, make an arc of radius 2.7 cm.

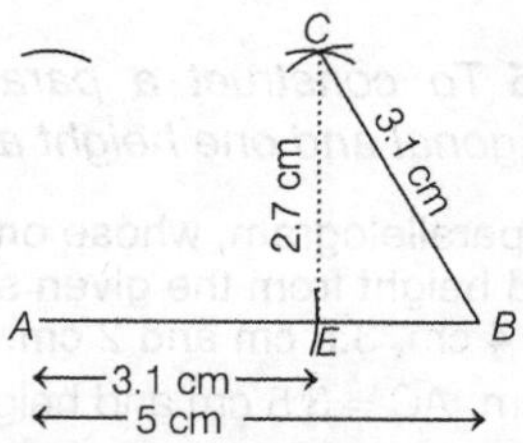

5. Taking C as centre, make another arc of radius 3.1cm, which cuts previous arc at D. Join AD and DC.

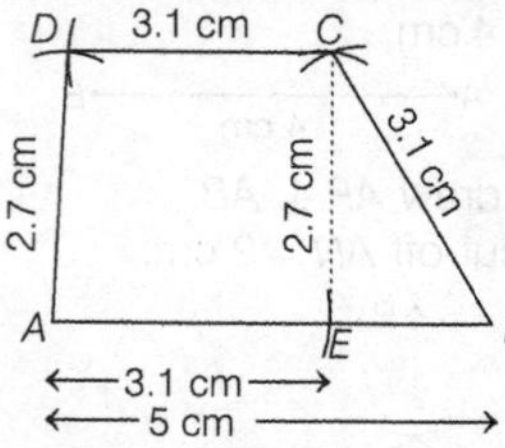

Thus, $ABCD$ is the required trapezium.

Construction 18 ***To construct a trapezium, when three sides, one angle and parallel sides are given.***

Q.18 Construct a trapezium $PQRS$, when $PQ = 5$ cm, $QR = 6.5$ cm, $RS = 5.5$ cm, $\angle Q = 45°$ and $PS || QR$.

Sol. ***Steps of construction***

1. Draw $QR = 6.5$ cm.

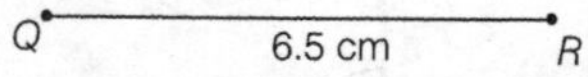

2. At point Q, draw $\angle AQR = 45°$.

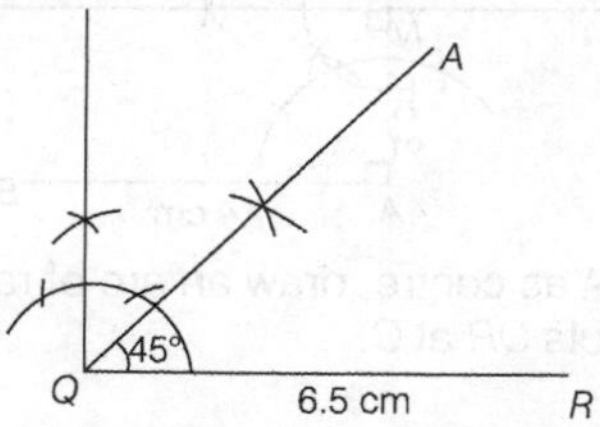

3. Taking point Q as centre, make an arc of radius 5 cm, which cuts AQ at P.

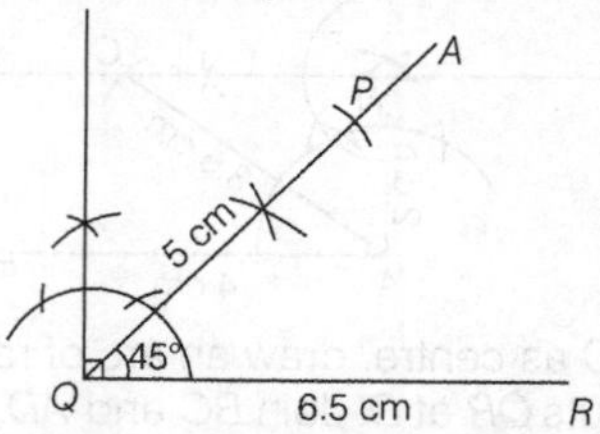

4. Through point P, draw a parallel line MN to QR.

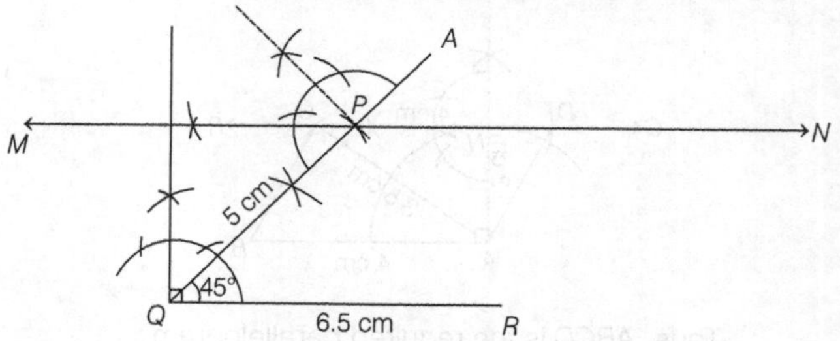

5. Taking R as centre, make an arc of radius 5.5 cm, which cuts MN at S. Then, join RS.

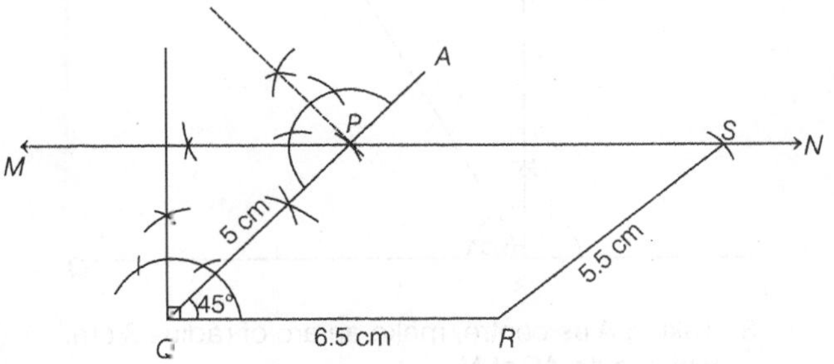

Thus, $PQRS$ is the required trapezium.

Construction 19 ***To construct a rectangle, when one side and one diagonal are given.***

Q.19 **If AB = 5.2 cm and AC = 5.7 cm, then construct a rectangle $ABCD$.**

Sol. Given, AB = 5.2 cm and AC = 5.7 cm of the rectangle $ABCD$.

Steps of construction

1. Draw a line segment AB = 5.2 cm.

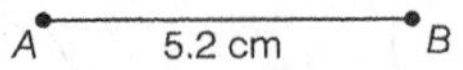

2. At point B, construct a line BP, which is perpendicular to AB.

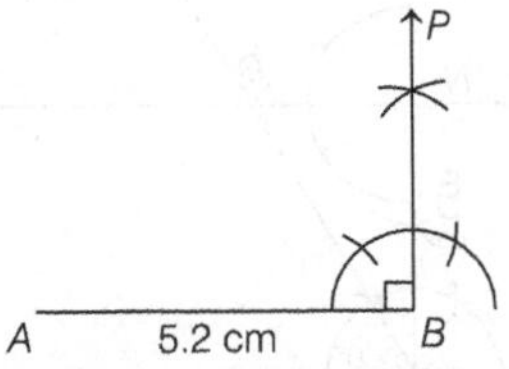

3. Taking A as centre, make an arc of radius 5.7 cm, which cuts BP at C.

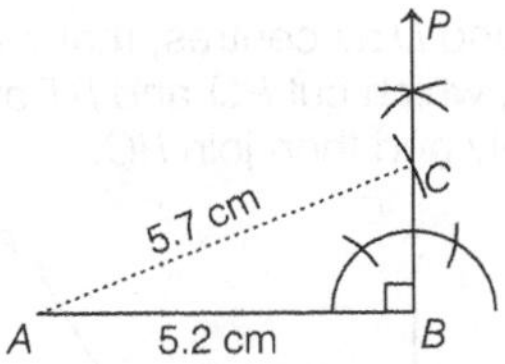

4. Taking C and B as centres, make arcs of radii 5.2 cm and 5.7 cm respectively, which cut each other at point D.

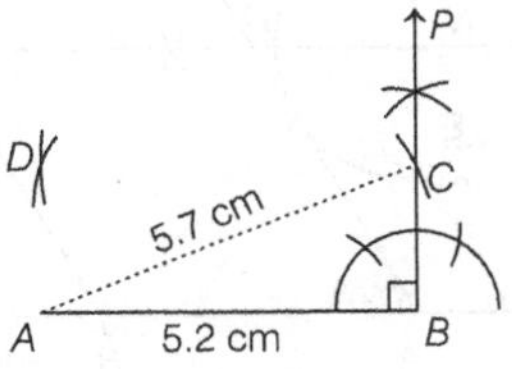

5. Join AD and DC.

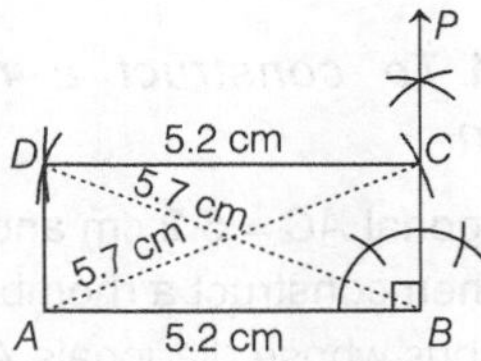

Thus, $ABCD$ is the required rectangle.

Construction 20 ***To construct a square, when one diagonal is given.***

Q.20 **Construct a square $ABCD$, whose one diagonal AC = 5.2 cm.**

Sol. Given, a square $ABCD$, whose length of a diagonal AC is 5.2 cm.

Steps of construction

1. Make a line segment AO, which is the half of AC i.e. 2.6 cm and produce AO to C such that $AO = OC$.

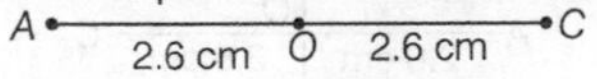

2. At point O, construct $\angle AOX = 90°$.

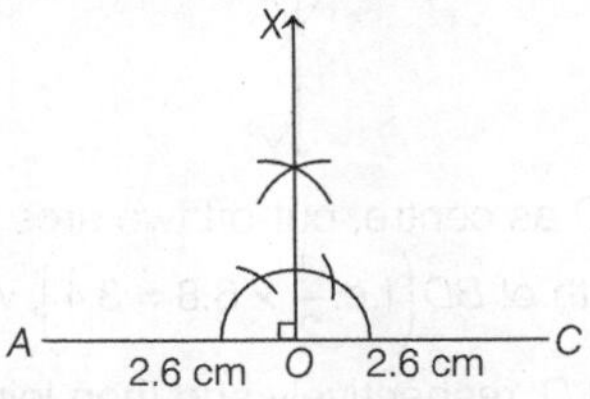

3. Taking O as centre, cut-off an arc of radius equal to the half of AC i.e. $\left(\frac{1}{2} \times 5.2 = 2.6\right)$, which cuts OX at D.

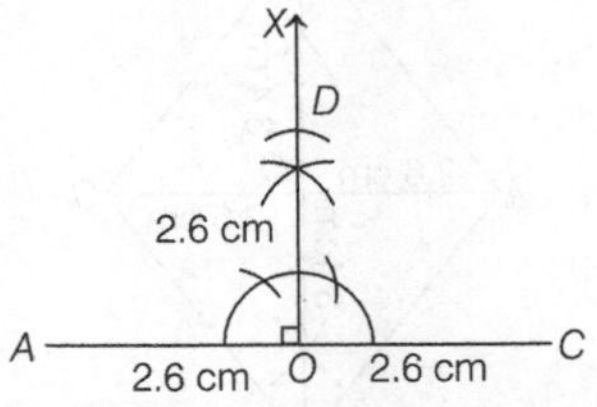

4. Produce DO to B such that $DO = OB$. Join AB, BC, CD and DA.

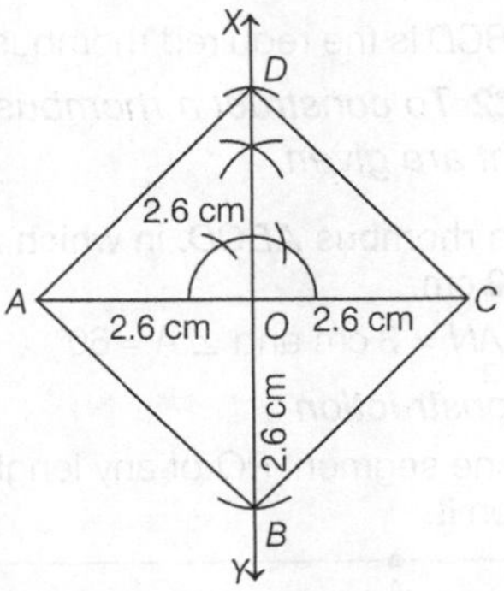

Thus, $ABCD$ is the required square.

Construction 21 *To construct a rhombus, when diagonals are given.*

Q.21 Given that diagonal $AC = 5.2$ cm and diagonal $BD = 6.8$ cm, then construct a rhombus $ABCD$.

Sol. Given, a rhombus whose diagonals $AC = 5.2$ cm and $BD = 6.8$ cm.

Steps of construction

1. Draw a line segment AC of length 5.2 cm.

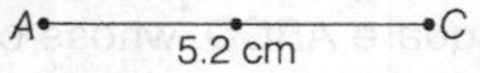

2. Draw perpendicular bisector XY of AC, which cut each other at O.

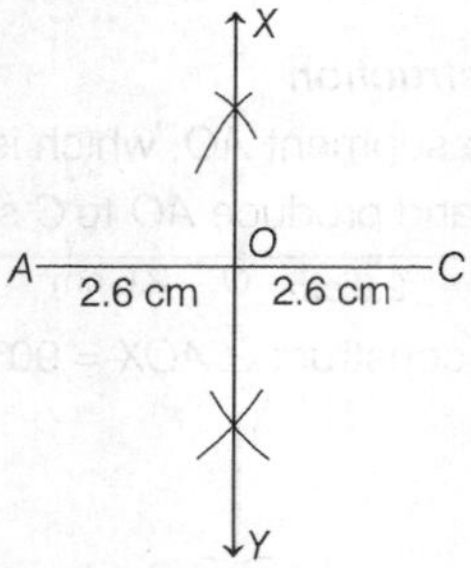

3. Taking O as centre, cut-off two arcs of length half of the length of $BD\left(\text{i.e.} \frac{1}{2} \times 6.8 = 3.4\right)$, which cut line XY at B and D respectively and then join AB, BC, CD and DA.

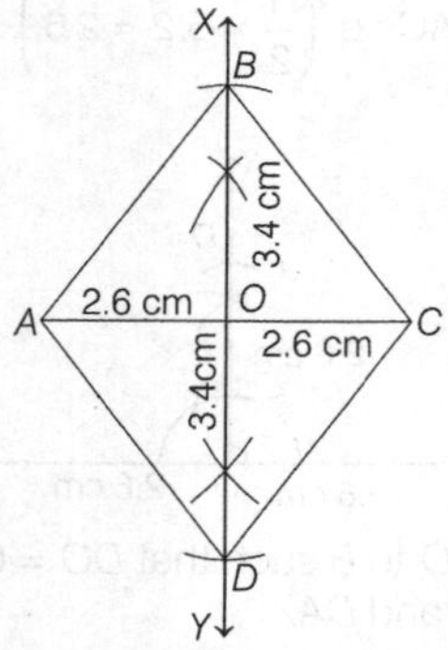

Thus, $ABCD$ is the required rhombus.

Construction 22 *To construct a rhombus, when one angle and height are given.*

Q.22 Construct a rhombus $ABCD$, in which $\angle A = 60°$ and height = 3.0 cm.

Sol. Let height $AN = 3$ cm and $\angle A = 60°$

Steps of construction

1. Draw a line segment PQ of any length and take a point A on it.

2. At point A, construct $\angle QAF = 60°$ and $AE \perp PQ$.

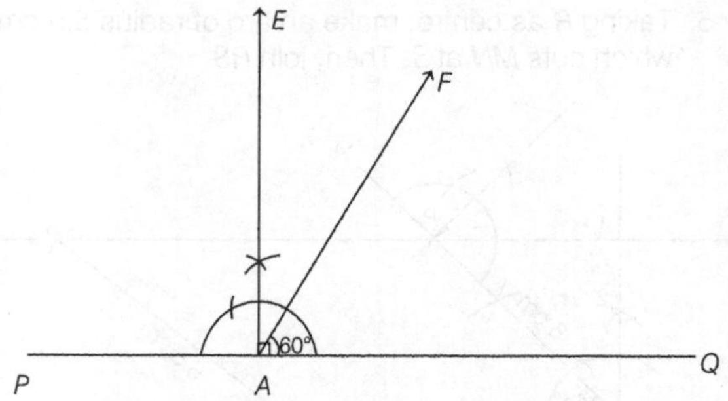

3. Taking A as centre, make an arc of radius 3 cm, which cuts AE at N.

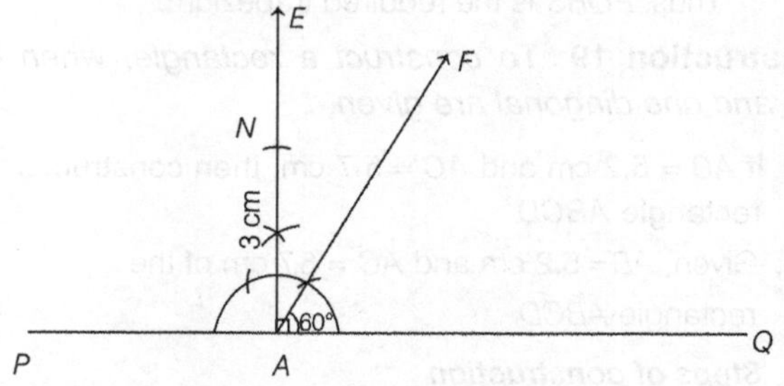

4. Through N, draw a line $RT \parallel PQ$ to meet AF at D.

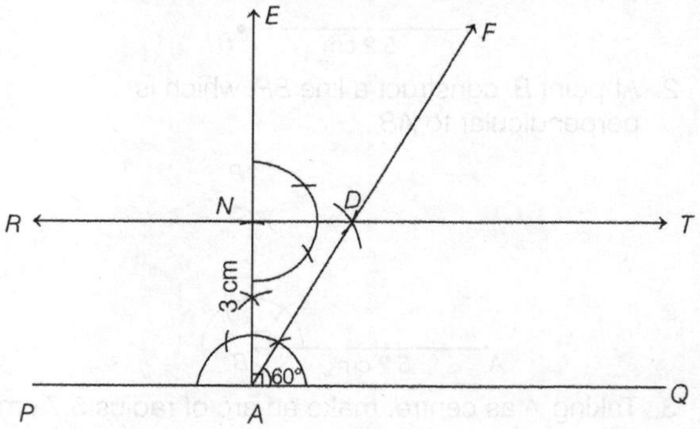

5. Measure the length of AD by compass.
   Taking A and D as centres, make arcs of radii of length AD, which cut PQ and RT at B and C respectively and then join BC.

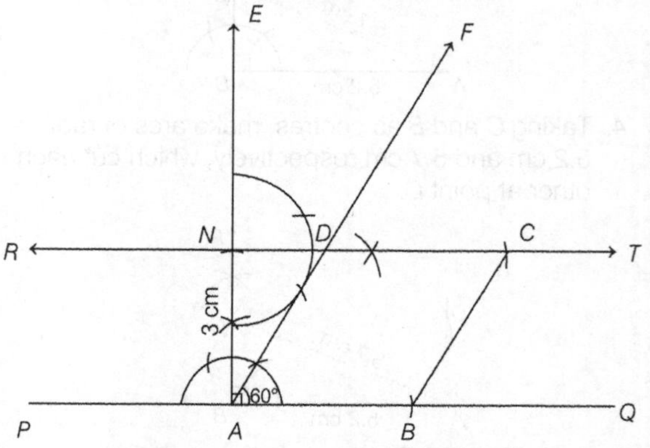

Thus, $ABCD$ is the required rhombus.

Construction 23 *To construct a regular hexagon, when side is given.*

Q.23 If each side of regular hexagon is 2.8 cm, then construct a regular hexagon.

Sol. Let each side of regular hexagon *ABCDEF* is 2.8 cm.

Steps of construction

1. Draw a line segment *AB* = 2.8 cm.

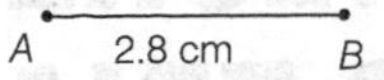

2. At point *B*, draw ∠*ABP* = 120° and cut-off an arc of racius 2.8 cm, which cuts *BP* at *C*.

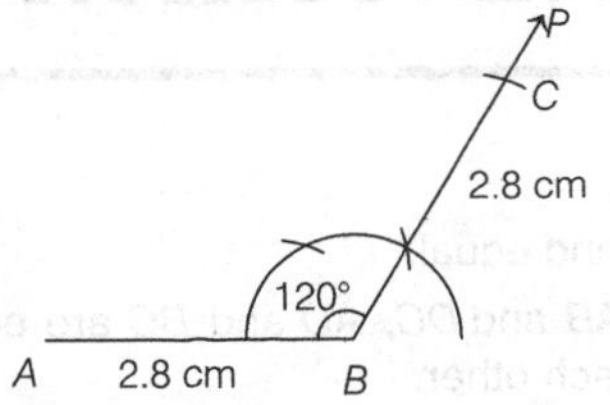

3. At point *C*, draw ∠*BCQ* = 120° and cut-off an arc of radius 2.8 cm, which cuts *CQ* at *D*.

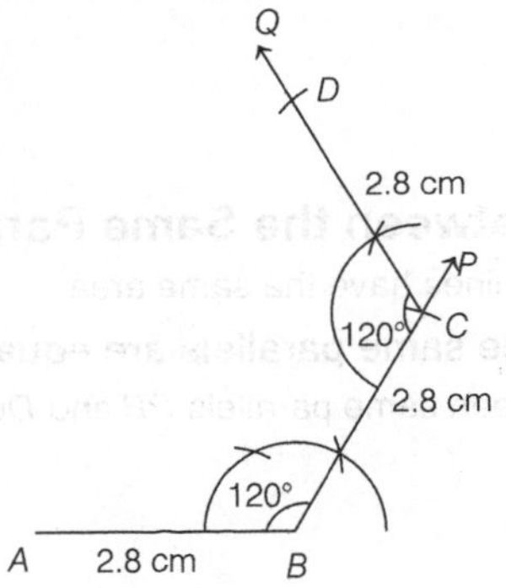

4. At point *D*, draw ∠*CDR* = 120° and cut-off an arc of radius 2.8 cm, which cuts *DR* at *E*.

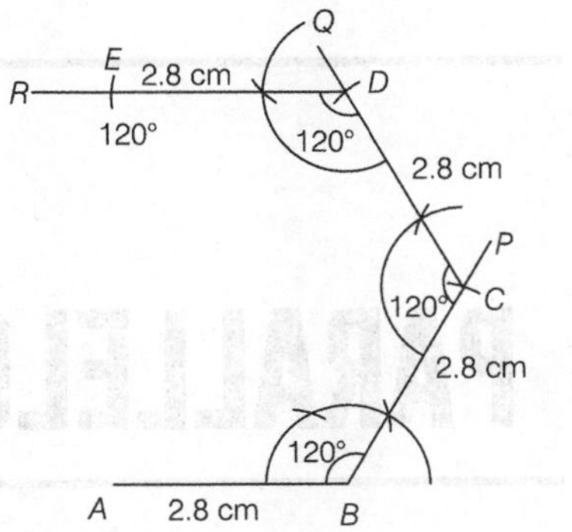

5. At point *E*, draw ∠*DES* = 120° and cut-off an arc of radius 2.8 cm, which cuts *ES* at *F* and then join *AF*.

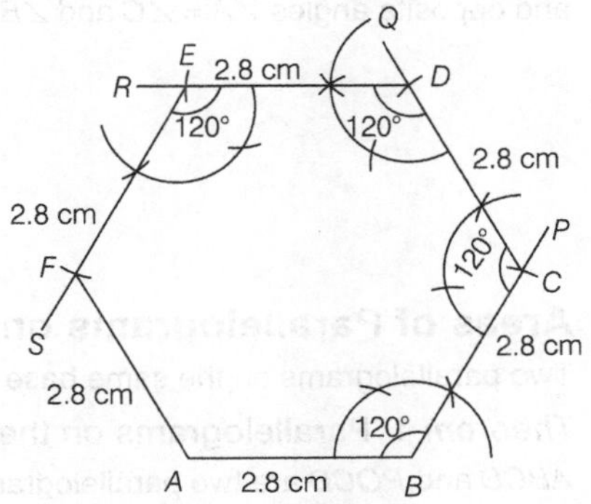

Thus, *ABCDEF* is the required regular hexagon.

12

AREAS THEOREMS ON PARALLELOGRAMS AND TRIANGLES

Parallelogram

A parallelogram is a quadrilateral in which opposite sides are parallel and equal.

In the given figure, *ABCD* is a parallelogram whose opposite sides *AB* and *DC*, *AD* and *BC* are equal and parallel and opposite angles $\angle A = \angle C$ and $\angle B = \angle D$. Also, diagonals bisect each other.

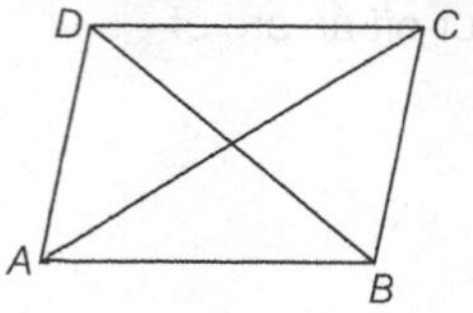

Areas of Parallelograms on the Same Base and between the Same Parallels

Two parallelograms on the same base and between the same parallel lines have the same area.

***Theorem* 1 Parallelograms on the same base and between the same parallels are equal in area.**

ABCD and *PQCD* are two parallelograms on same base *DC* and between same parallels *PB* and *DC*.

Then, area of parallelogram *ABCD* = Area of parallelogram *PQCD*.

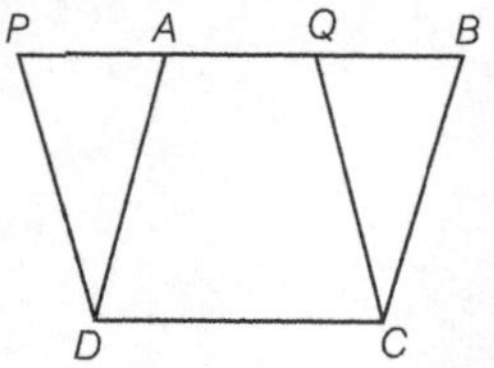

***Theorem* 2 (Converse of theorem 1) Parallelograms on the same base and having equal areas lie between same parallel lines.**

Suppose, *ABCD* and *PQCD* are two parallelograms on the same base *DC* and having same area.

i.e. area of parallelogram *ABCD* = area of parallelogram *PQCD*.

Then, both parallelogram lie between the same parallel line.

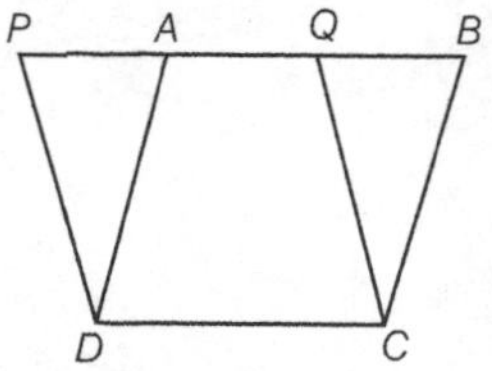

- **Corollary 1** If a parallelogram and a rectangle are on the same base and between the same parallel lines, then they are equal in area.

REVISION NOTES

- **Corollary 2** Area of a parallelogram = Base × Height
- **Corollary 3** Parallelograms with equal bases and between the same parallels are equal in area.

***Theorem* 3 If a triangle and a parallelogram are on the same base and between the same parallels, then the area of the triangle is equal to half the area of the parallelogram.**

ΔABP and parallelogram *ABCD* are on the same base *AB* and between the same parallels *AB* and *PC*.

Then, ar (ΔABP) = $\frac{1}{2}$ × ar (parallelogram *ABCD*)

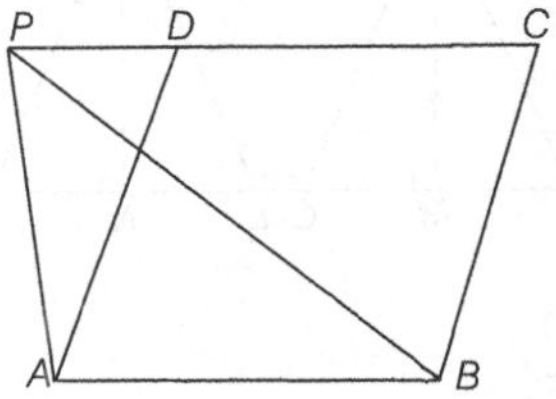

- **Corollary 1** Area of triangle = $\frac{1}{2}$ × Base × Height
- **Corollary 2** A triangle is divided into two triangles of equal area by its median.
- **Corollary 3** Area of a trapezium = $\frac{1}{2}$ × (Sum of parallel sides) × Height

Triangles on the Same Base and between the Same Parallels

Theorem 4

(i) Two triangles on the same base (or equal bases) and between the same parallels are equal in area.

Or

In other words, if ΔABC and ΔABD are on the same base AB and between the same parallel lines *AB* and CD, then ar (ΔABC) = ar (ΔABD).

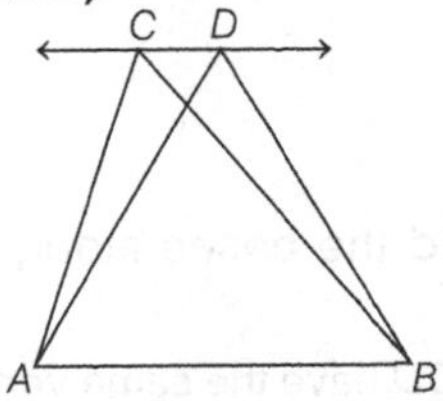

(ii) Also, if ΔABC and ΔPQR are two triangles with equal bases *BC* = *QR* and between the same parallel lines AP and BR, then ar (ΔABC) = ar (ΔPQR).

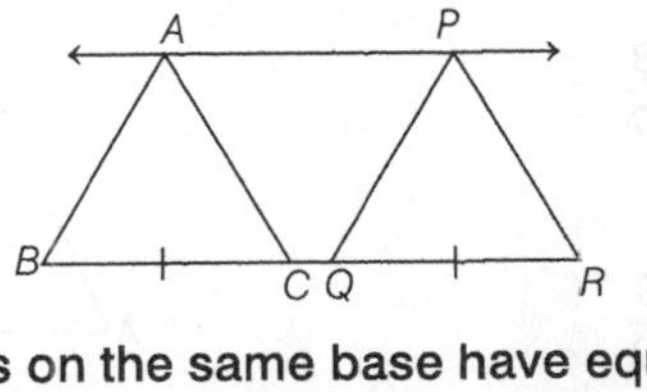

***Theorem* 5 Triangles with equal areas on the same base have equal corresponding altitudes.**

Two triangles, ΔABC and ΔABD are on the same base *AB* and ar (ΔABC) = ar (ΔABD).

Also, $CM \perp AB$ and $DN \perp AB$. Then, $CM = DN$.

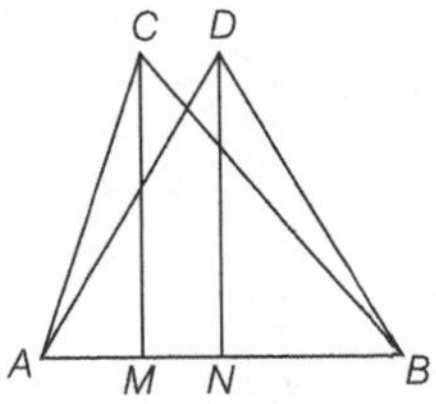

Corollary Triangles on the same base and having equal areas lie between the same parallel lines.

Some Important Results

1. **If two triangles lie between the same parallels (i.e. have equal altitudes), then the ratio of their areas equals the ratio of their bases.**

In the given figure, ΔABC and ΔDEF lie between the same parallel AD and BF.

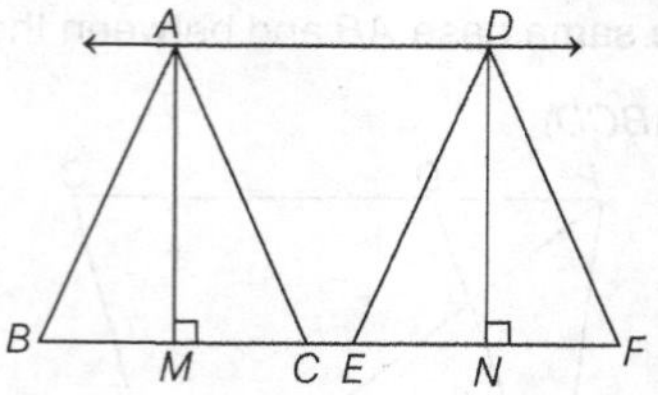

Then, $\dfrac{\text{ar }(\Delta ABC)}{\text{ar }(\Delta DEF)} = \dfrac{\frac{1}{2} \times BC \times AM}{\frac{1}{2} \times EF \times DN} = \dfrac{BC}{EF}$ $[\because AM = DN]$

2. **If two triangles have same base (or equal bases), then the ratio of their areas equals the ratio of their altitudes.**

In the given figure, ΔABC and ΔABD are on the same base AB.

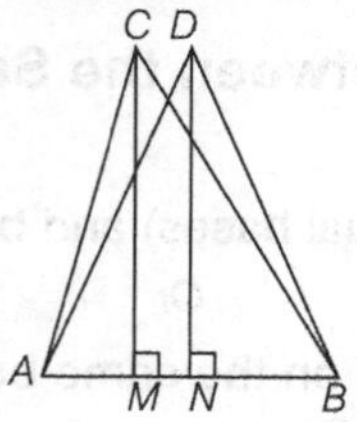

Then, $\dfrac{\text{ar }(\Delta ABC)}{\text{ar }(\Delta ABD)} = \dfrac{\frac{1}{2} \times AB \times CM}{\frac{1}{2} \times AB \times DN} = \dfrac{CM}{DN}$

3. **If the triangles have same vertex and the bases along the same line, then the areas of triangles are in the ratio of their bases.**

In the given figure, ΔABD, ΔBCD and ΔACD have the same vertex D and bases along the same straight line AC. So, they have the same height.

In such a case, we have the following ratios

(i) $\dfrac{\text{ar }(\Delta ABD)}{\text{ar }(\Delta BCD)} = \dfrac{\frac{1}{2} \times AB \times DN}{\frac{1}{2} \times BC \times DN} = \dfrac{AB}{BC}$

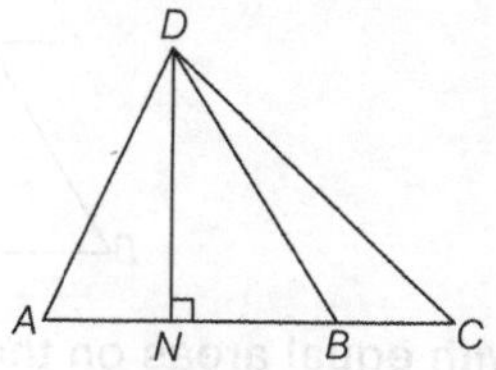

(ii) $\dfrac{\text{ar }(\Delta ABD)}{\text{ar }(\Delta ACD)} = \dfrac{\frac{1}{2} \times AB \times DN}{\frac{1}{2} \times AC \times DN} = \dfrac{AB}{AC}$

(iii) $\dfrac{\text{ar }(\Delta BCD)}{\text{ar }(\Delta ACD)} = \dfrac{\frac{1}{2} \times BC \times DN}{\frac{1}{2} \times AC \times DN} = \dfrac{BC}{AC}$

EXAM ORIENTED QUESTIONS

TYPE - 1 01 Mark

Multiple Choice Questions

Q.1 In the given figure, the area of parallelogram *ABCD* is 140 cm^2 then the area of parallelogram *ABEF* is

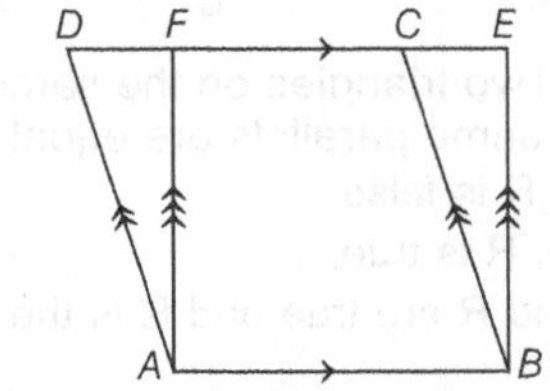

(a) 148 cm^2 (b) 140 cm^2
(c) 70 cm^2 (d) 280 cm^2

Q.2 In the given figure, $l \| m$ and $AB = PQ$. If area of parallelogram *ABCD* is 40 cm^2, then area of parallelogram *PQRS* is

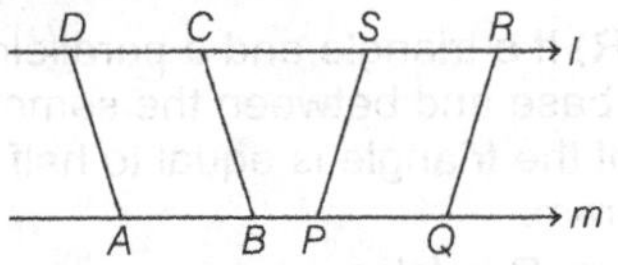

(a) 80 cm^2 (b) 20 cm^2 (c) 40 cm^2 (d) 60 cm^2

Q.3 In the given figure, *P* is a point in the interior of parallelogram *ABCD*. If the area of parallelogram *ABCD* is 60 cm^2, then [ar(ΔADP) + ar(ΔBPC)] is equal to

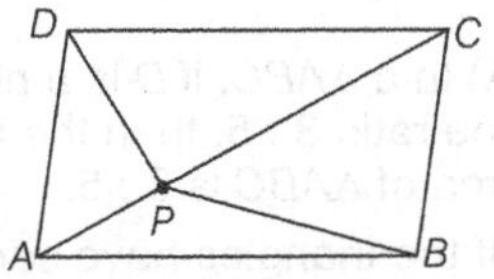

(a) 15 cm^2 (b) 30 cm^2 (c) 45 cm^2 (d) 20 cm^2

Q.4 *ABCD* is a rhombus and *P* and *Q* are any points on *AB* and *BC*. If area of rhombus is 90 cm^2. then ar (ΔAQD) + ar (ΔCPD) is

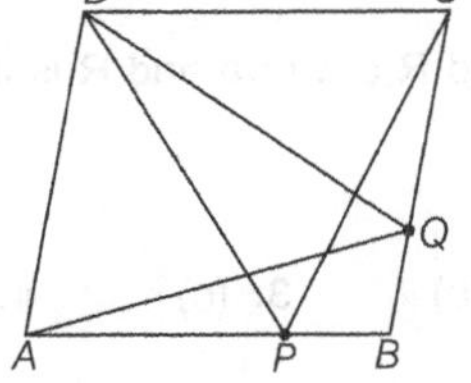

(a) 45 cm^2 (b) 90 cm^2 (c) $\frac{45}{2}$ cm^2 (d) 60 cm^2

Q.5 In the given figure, areas of parallelograms *ABCD* and *FECG* are equal. If ar (ΔAQE) = 12 cm^2, then ar (parallelogram *FGBQ*) is equal to

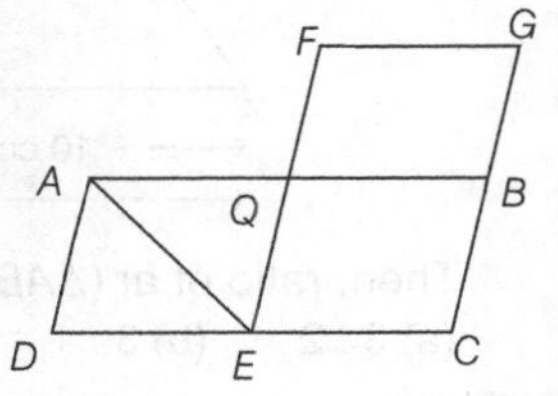

(a) 12 cm^2
(b) 20 cm^2
(c) 24 cm^2
(d) 36 cm^2

Q.6 A median of a triangle divides it into two
(a) right angled triangles (b) isosceles triangles
(c) triangles of equal area (d) congruent triangles

Q.7 If *ABCD* is a trapezium with $AB \| DC$, then ar(ΔDAO) is equal to

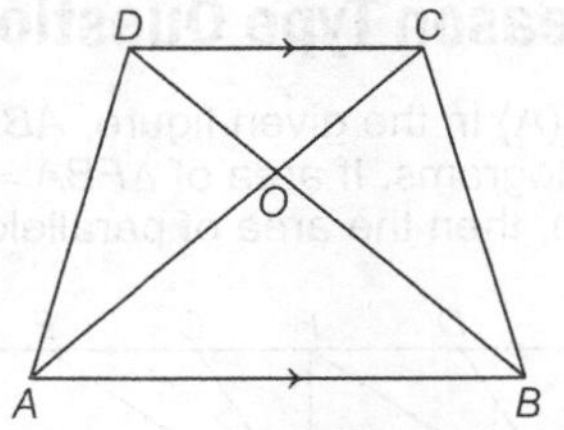

(a) ar(ΔOAB) (b) ar(ΔOBC)
(c) ar(ΔODC) (d) ar(ΔABC)

Q.8 In the given figure, two isosceles right angled triangles ΔDEF and ΔHGI are on the equal bases *DE* and *GH*, which are parallel to *FI*. If *DE* = *GH* = 9 cm and *DH* = 20 cm, then the area of the quadrilateral *FEGI* is equal to

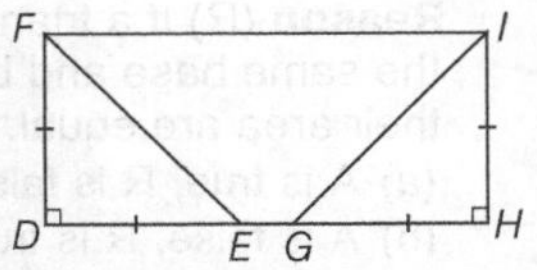

(a) 95 cm^2 (b) 99 cm^2
(c) 92 cm^2 (d) 90 cm^2

Q.9 If *BD* = 2*DC* and ar (ΔABC) = 60 cm^2, then ar(ΔADC) is

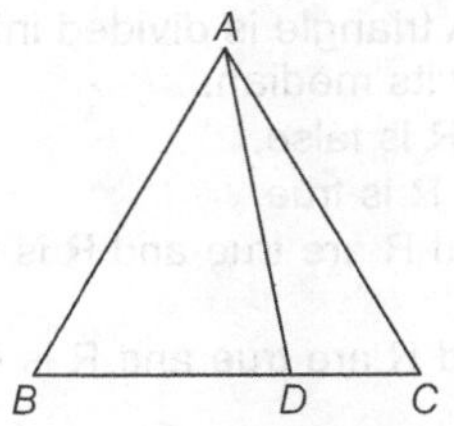

(a) 180 cm^2 (b) 20 cm^2
(c) 30 cm^2 (d) 10 cm^2

Q.10 In the given figure, $AB = 10$ cm and $AC = 15$ cm.

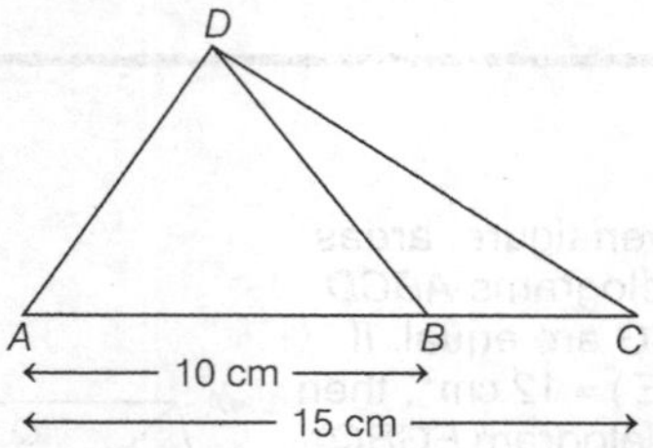

Then, ratio of ar (ΔABD) and ar (ΔBCD) is
(a) 3 : 2 (b) 3 : 1 (c) 4 : 3 (d) 2 : 1

Answers

1. (b)	**2.** (c)	**3.** (b)	**4.** (b)	**5.** (c)
6. (c)	**7.** (b)	**8.** (b)	**9.** (b)	**10.** (d)

TYPE - 2

01 Mark

Assertion-Reason Type Questions

Q.1 Assertion (A) In the given figure, $ABCD$ and $ABEF$ are parallelograms. If area of $\Delta FBA = 130\text{ cm}^2$ and $AB = 15$ cm, then the area of parallelogram $ABCD$ is 260 cm^2.

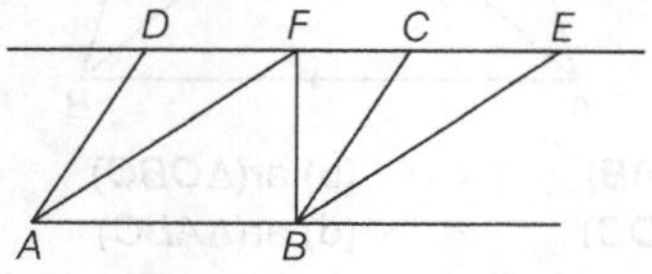

Reason (R) If a triangle and a parallelogram are on the same base and between the same parallels, then their area are equal.
(a) A is true, R is false.
(b) A is false, R is true.
(c) Both A and R are true and R is the correct reason for A.
(d) Both A and R are true and R is incorrect reason for A.

Q.2 Assertion (A) In ΔPQR, PM is one of its median and area of triangle ΔPQR is 38 cm^2, then the area of ΔPQM is equal to 19 cm^2.

Reason (R) A triangle is divided into two triangles of equal area by its median.
(a) A is true, R is false.
(b) A is false, R is true.
(c) Both A and R are true and R is the correct reason for A.
(d) Both A and R are true and R is incorrect reason for A.

Q.3 Assertion (A) In the given figure, $ABCD$ is a quadrilateral. If BP is drawn parallel to AC and BP meets DC produced at P, then ar (ΔADP) = ar (quadrilateral $ABCD$).

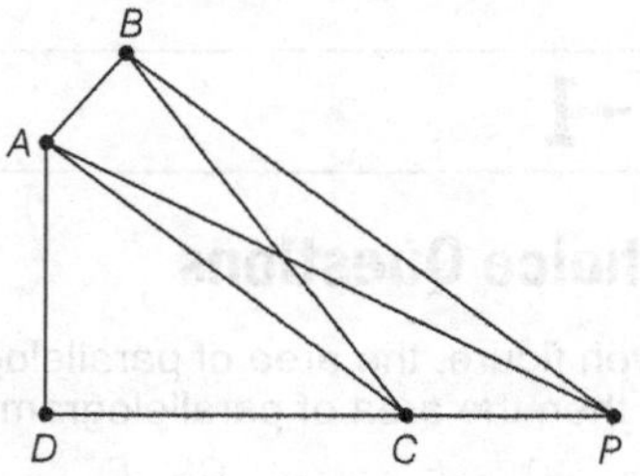

Reason (R) Two triangles on the same base and between the same parallels are equal in area.
(a) A is true, R is false.
(b) A is false, R is true.
(c) Both A and R are true and R is the correct reason for A.
(d) Both A and R are true and R is incorrect reason for A.

Q.4 Assertion (A) ΔABC and ΔABD lie between two parallel lines AB and CD and on the same base AB. If area of $\Delta ABC = 20\text{ cm}^2$, then area of ΔABD is 20 cm^2.

Reason (R) If a triangle and a parallelogram are on the same base and between the same parallels, then the area of the triangle is equal to half the area of the parallelogram.
(a) A is true, R is false.
(b) A is false, R is true.
(c) Both A and R are true and R is the correct reason for A.
(d) Both A and R are true and R is incorrect reason for A.

Q.5 Assertion (A) In a ΔABC, if D is a point on BC and divides it in the ratio 3 : 5, then the ratio of area of ΔADC and area of ΔABC is 3 : 5.

Reason (R) If the triangles have same vertex and the bases along the same line, then the areas of triangles are in the ratio of their bases.
(a) A is true, R is false.
(b) A is false, R is true.
(c) Both A and R are true and R is the correct reason for A.
(d) Both A and R are true and R is incorrect reason for A.

Answers

1. (a)	**2.** (c)	**3.** (c)	**4.** (d)	**5.** (b)

TYPE - 3 (01 Mark)

Statement Based Questions

Q.1 **Statement I** If parallelogram and a rectangle are on the same base and between the same parallel lines, then they are equal in area.

Statement II A parallelogram and a triangle lie on the same base and between the same parallels. If area of triangle is 20 cm^2, then area of parallelogram will be 40 cm^2.

Which of the following is valid?
(a) Both the Statements are true.
(b) Both the Statements are false.
(c) Statement I is true and Statement II is false.
(d) Statement I is false and Statement II is true.

Q.2 **Statement I** Area of a trapezium

$$= \frac{1}{2} \times \text{(Sum of parallel sides)} \times \text{Height}$$

Statement II A triangle is divided into two triangles of equal area by its altitude.

Which of the following is valid?
(a) Both the Statements are true.
(b) Both the Statements are false.
(c) Statement I is true and Statement II is false.
(d) Statement I is false and Statement II is true.

Q.3 **Statement I** A trapezium, whose parallel sides are 9 cm and 6 cm and the distance between these sides is 8 cm. Then, area of trapezium is 60 cm^2.

Statement II Triangles with equal areas on the same base have equal corresponding altitudes.

Which of the following is valid?
(a) Both the Statements are true.
(b) Both the Statements are false.
(c) Statement I is true and Statement II is false.
(d) Statement I is false and Statement II is true.

Q.4 **Statement I** If the area, base and corresponding altitude of a parallelogram are x^2, $x-3$ and $x+4$, respectively, then value of x is 6.

Statement II If two triangles have same base (or equal bases), then the ratio of their areas equals the ratio of their altitudes.

Which of the following is valid?
(a) Both the Statements are true.
(b) Both the Statements are false.
(c) Statement I is true and Statement II is false.
(d) Statement I is false and Statement II is true.

Answers

1. (a) 2. (c) 3. (a) 4. (d)

TYPE - 4 (03 Marks)

Short Answer Type Questions

Q.1 The perimeter of an isosceles triangle is 32 cm and its base is 12 cm. One of its equal side forms the diagonal of a parallelogram. Find the area of parallelogram.

Q.2 In the given figure, $ABCD$ and $ABFE$ are two parallelograms and ar (quadrilateral $EABC$) = 17 cm^2 and ar (parallelogram $ABCD$) = 25 cm^2. Then, find ar (ΔBCF).

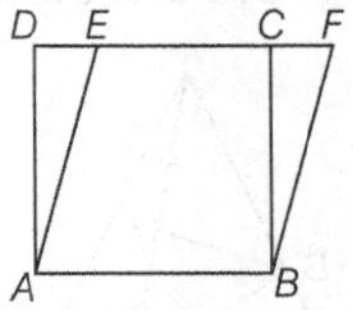

Q.3 In the given figure, $ABCD$ and $PBCQ$ are given parallelograms. If R is a mid-point on PB, then show that

$$ar(\Delta QRC) = \frac{1}{2} ar(\text{parallelogram } ABCD).$$

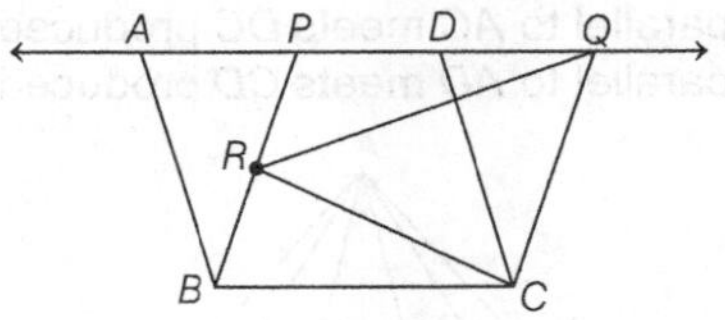

Q.4 $PQRS$ is a parallelogram, a line through Q cuts RS at M and meets PS produced at N.

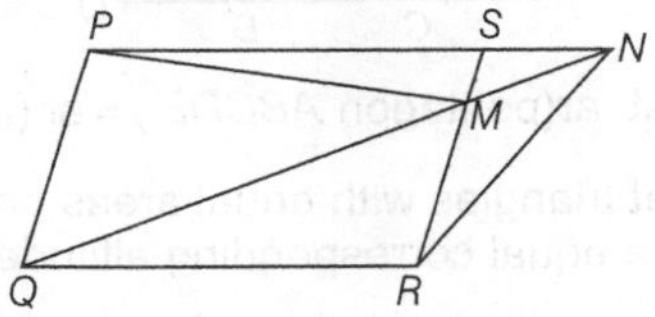

Show that ar (ΔPMS) = ar (ΔMNR).

Q.5 The medians BE and CF of a ΔABC intersect at G. Prove that ar (ΔGBC) = ar (quadrilateral $AFGE$).

Q.6 In the given figure, E is any point on median AD of a ΔABC. Show that ar (ΔABE) = ar (ΔACE).

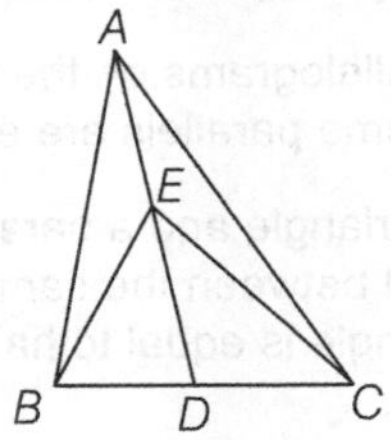

Q.7 Let O be any point on the diagonal PR of a parallelogram $PQRS$ (see the figure). Prove that ar (ΔPSO) = ar (ΔPQO).

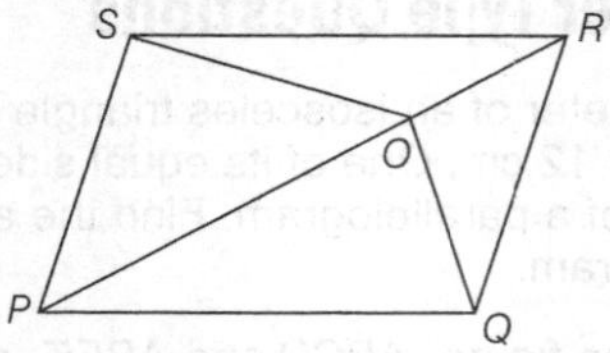

Q.8 In the given figure, D is the mid-point of side AB of the ΔABC. E is the mid-point of CD and F is the mid-point of AE. Prove that $8\text{ar}(\Delta AFD) = \text{ar}(\Delta ABC)$.

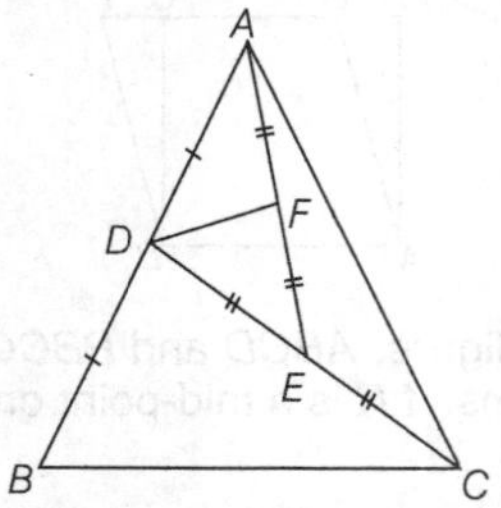

Q.9 In the given figure, $ABCDE$ is any pentagon. BP drawn parallel to AC meets DC produced at P and EQ drawn parallel to AD meets CD produced at Q.

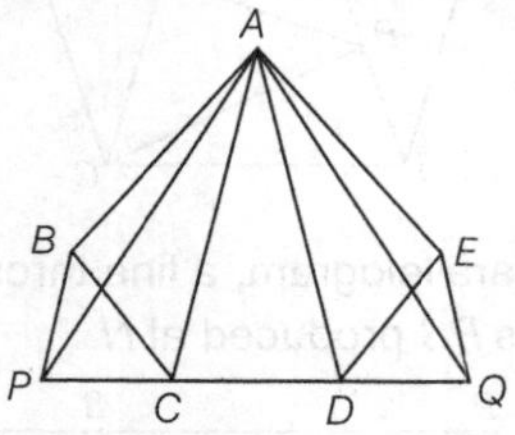

Prove that ar(pentagon $ABCDE$) = ar (ΔAPQ).

Q.10 Prove that triangles with equal areas on the same base have equal corresponding altitudes.

Answers

1. 96 cm^2 2. 8 cm^2

TYPE - 5

4/5 Marks

Long Answer Type Questions

Q.1 Prove that parallelograms on the same base and between the same parallels are equal in area.

Q.2 Prove that if a triangle and a parallelogram are on the same base and between the same parallels, then the area of the triangle is equal to half the area of the parallelogram.

Q.3 The area of the parallelogram $ABCD$ is 90 cm^2.

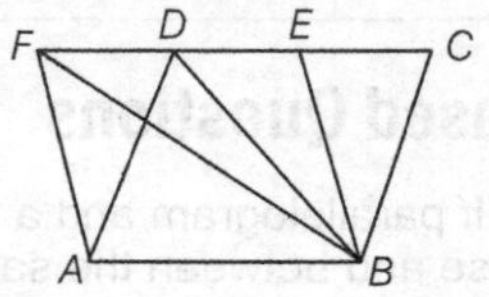

Find

(i) ar $(ABEF)$ (ii) ar (ΔABD) (iii) ar (ΔBEF)

Q.4 In the given figure, P is a point in the interior of a parallelogram $ABCD$.

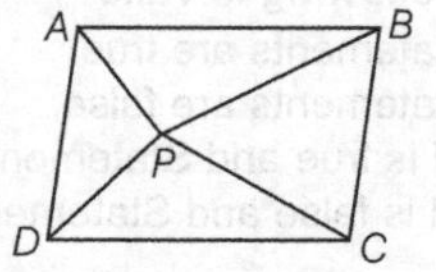

Show that

(i) $\text{ar}(\Delta APB) + \text{ar}(\Delta PCD) = \frac{1}{2}\text{ar}(\text{parallelogram } ABCD)$

(ii) $\text{ar}(\Delta APD) + \text{ar}(\Delta PBC) = \text{ar}(\Delta APB) + \text{ar}(\Delta PCD)$.

Q.5 In the given figure, ABC is a right angled triangle, right angled at A, $BCED$ and $ABMN$ are squares on the sides BC and AB respectively. Line segment $AX \perp DE$ meets BC at Y.

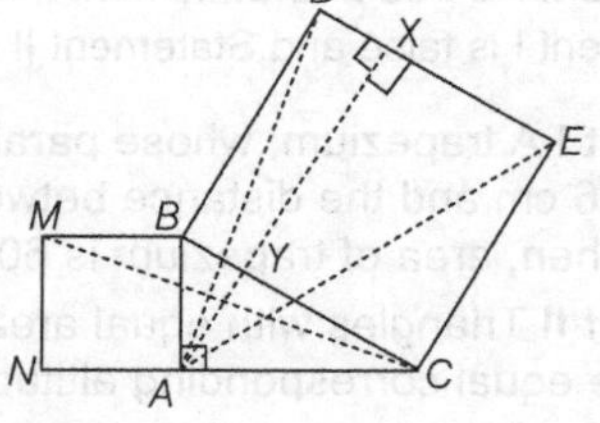

Show that

(i) $\Delta MBC \cong \Delta ABD$ (ii) ar $(BYXD) = 2$ ar (ΔMBC)

(iii) ar $(BYXD)$ = ar $(ABMN)$

Q.6 Show that the area of the quadrilateral made by connecting the mid-points of the adjacent sides of a quadrilateral is half the area of the given quadrilateral.

Q.7 In the given figure, ABC is a triangle and D is the mid-point of AB. P is any point on BC. Line CQ is drawn parallel to PD to intersect AB at Q. PQ is joined. Show that ar $(\Delta BPQ) = \frac{1}{2}$ ar (ΔABC).

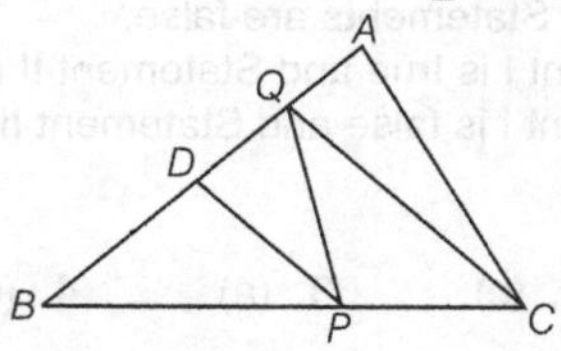

Q.8 The medians of a ΔABC intersect each other at point G. If one of its median is AD, then prove that

(i) $ar(\Delta ABD) = 3\,ar(\Delta BGD)$

(ii) $ar(\Delta ACD) = 3\,ar(\Delta CGD)$

(iii) $ar(\Delta BGC) = \frac{1}{3} ar(\Delta ABC)$

Answers

3. (i) 90 cm^2 (ii) 45 cm^2 (iii) 45 cm^2

TYPE - 6

Case Based Questions

Q.1 There was a deserted land near a colony where people used to throw garbage. Colony people united to construct a pond in triangular shape as given in the figure.

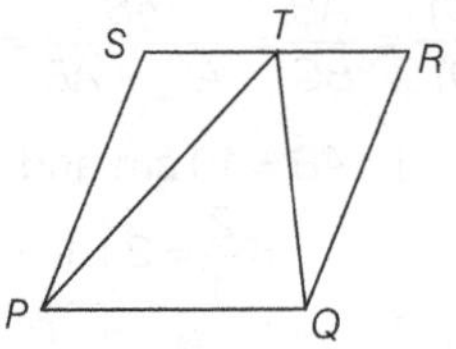

The land is in the shape of parallelogram $PQRS$. In rest of the area, medicinal plants were grown. If area of the land is 300 m^2, then

(i) find the area occupied by the pond.

(ii) find the area where medicinal plants were grown. **(4 M)**

Q.2 A rally was organised by a school for 'Sarva Shiksha Abhiyan'. Students were given triangular cardboard pieces to write slogan. They divided the triangular shape into three equal parts by constructing medians as given in figure.

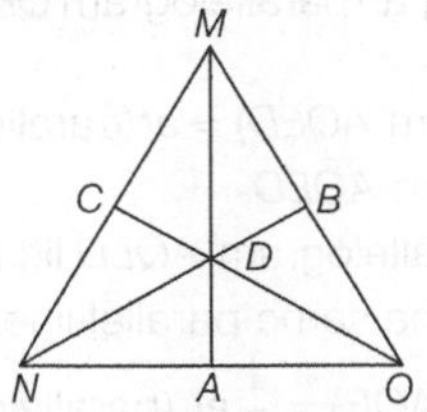

(i) Show that $ar(\Delta MNO) = 3\,ar(\Delta NDM)$

(ii) If $ar(\Delta NAD) = 40\ cm^2$, then find $ar(\Delta NDO)$. **(4 M)**

Answers

1. (i) 150 m^2 (ii) 150 m^2
2. (ii) 80 cm^2

EXPLANATIONS

Multiple Choice Questions

1. (b) Given, ar (parallelogram $ABCD$) = 140 cm^2

   As we know that two parallelograms with equal bases and between same parallels are equal in area.

   $\therefore$ ar (parallelogram $ABCD$) = ar (parallelogram $ABEF$)

   $\Rightarrow$ ar (parallelogram $ABEF$) = 140 cm^2

2. (c) Given, $l \parallel m$ and $AB = PQ$

   and ar(parallelogram $ABCD$) = 40 cm^2

   As we know that two parallelograms with equal bases and between the same parallels are equal in area.

   $\therefore$ ar(parallelogram $ABCD$) = ar(parallelogram $PQRS$)

   $\Rightarrow$ ar(parallelogram $PQRS$) = 40 cm^2

3. (b) Given, ar(parallelogram) = 60 cm^2

   Now, draw a line XY through P parallel to AD.

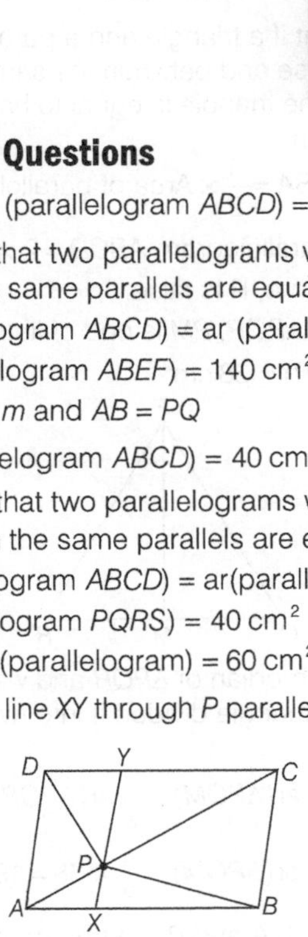

   $\because XY \parallel AD$ and $AX \parallel DY$

   $\therefore AXYD$ is a parallelogram.

   Now, ΔAPD and parallelogram $AXYD$ are on the same base AD and between the same parallels AD and XY.

   $\therefore ar(\Delta APD) = \frac{1}{2}$ ar (parallelogram $AXYD$) ...(i)

   Similarly, $ar(\Delta PBC) = \frac{1}{2}$ ar(parallelogram $BXYC$) ...(ii)

   On adding Eqs. (i) and (ii), we get

   $ar(\Delta APD) + ar(\Delta PBC)$

   $= \frac{1}{2}$ ar(parallelogram $AXYD$) $+ \frac{1}{2}$ ar(parallelogram $BXYC$)

   $= \frac{1}{2}$ ar(parallelogram $ABCD$) $= \frac{1}{2} \times 60 = 30\ cm^2$

4. (b) Given, area of rhombus $ABCD$ = 90 cm^2

   $\because ABCD$ is a rhombus.

   $\therefore AB \parallel CD$ and $AD \parallel BC$

   As we know that if a triangle and a parallelogram are on the same base and between the same parallels, then the area of the triangle is equal to half the area of the parallelogram.

$\therefore \quad ar(\Delta CPD) = \frac{1}{2} ar(\text{rhombus } ABCD)$ ...(i)

[$\because$ base = CD and AB || CD]

and $ar(\Delta AQD) = \frac{1}{2} ar(\text{rhombus } ABCD)$ ...(ii)

[$\because$ base = AD and AD || BC]

On adding Eqs. (i) and (ii), we get

$ar(\Delta CPD) + ar(\Delta AQD) = ar(\text{rhombus } ABCD) = 90 \text{ cm}^2$

5. (c) Given, $ar(\Delta AQE) = 12 \text{ cm}^2$

and ar(parallelogram ABCD) = ar(parallelogram FECG)

On subtracting ar(parallelogram QBEC) from both sides, we get

ar(parallelogram AQED) = ar(parallelogram FGBQ)...(i)

In parallelogram AQED,

ΔAQE and parallelogram AQED lie on same base AQ and between the same parallel lines AQ || ED.

$\therefore \quad ar(\Delta AQE) = \frac{1}{2} ar(\text{parallelogram } AQED)$

$\Rightarrow \quad ar(\text{parallelogram } AQED) = 2 \times 12 = 24 \text{ cm}^2$ ...(ii)

From Eqs. (i) and (ii), we get

$ar(\text{parallelogram } FGBQ) = 24 \text{ cm}^2$

6. (c) We know that a triangle is divided into two triangles of equal area by its median.

7. (b) Since, ΔABC and ΔABD lie on the same base AB and between the same parallel lines AB || DC.

$\therefore \quad ar(\Delta ABD) = ar(\Delta ABC)$

$\Rightarrow ar(\Delta ABD) - ar(\Delta AOB) = ar(\Delta ABC) - ar(\Delta AOB)$

[subtracting $ar(\Delta AOB)$ from both sides]

$\Rightarrow \quad ar(\Delta DAO) = ar(\Delta OBC)$

8. (b) In the given figure,

$DE = GH = 9 \text{ cm}$ ...(i)

and $DH = 20 \text{ cm}$

$\because \Delta EDF$ and ΔIHG are isosceles right angled triangles.

$\therefore FD = DE$ and $IH = GH$

From Eq. (i), $FD = DE = IH = GH = 9 \text{ cm}$

Now, area of right angled $\Delta FDE = \frac{1}{2} \times FD \times DE$

$= \frac{9 \times 9}{2} = \frac{81}{2} \text{ cm}^2$

As we know that two triangles with equal bases and between the same parallel lines are equal in area.

$\therefore$ Area of $\Delta GHI = ar(\Delta FDE) = \frac{81}{2} \text{ cm}^2$

Now, ar (quadrilateral FEGI) = ar (rectangle FIHD) − ar (ΔFDE) − ar (GHI)

$= 20 \times 9 - \frac{81}{2} - \frac{81}{2}$

$= 180 - 81 = 99 \text{ cm}^2$

9. (b) We have, $BD = 2DC$

and $ar(\Delta ABC) = 60 \text{ cm}^2$

and $BC = BD + DC$

$\Rightarrow \quad BC = 2DC + DC$

$\Rightarrow \quad BC = 3DC$ ...(i)

Since, ΔABC and ΔADC have the same vertex A and bases (BC and DC) along the same line.

$\therefore \quad \frac{ar(\Delta ABC)}{ar(\Delta ADC)} = \frac{BC}{DC}$

$\Rightarrow \quad \frac{60}{ar(\Delta ADC)} = \frac{3DC}{DC}$ [from Eq. (i)]

$\Rightarrow \quad ar(\Delta ADC) = \frac{60}{3} = 20 \text{ cm}^2$

10. (d) We know that if the triangles have same vertices and bases along the same line, then the areas of triangles are in the ratio of their bases.

$\therefore \quad \frac{ar(\Delta ABD)}{ar(\Delta BCD)} = \frac{AB}{BC} = \frac{AB}{AC - AB} = \frac{10}{15 - 10} = \frac{10}{5}$

[$\because$ AB = 10 cm and AC = 15 cm (given)]

$= \frac{2}{1} = 2 : 1$

Assertion-Reason Type Questions

1. (a) Given, $AB = 15$ cm and area of $\Delta FBA = 130 \text{ cm}^2$

We know that if a triangle and a parallelogram are on the same base and between the same parallels, then the area of the triangle is equal to half the area of the parallelogram.

$\therefore$ Area of $\Delta FBA = \frac{1}{2} \times$ Area of parallelogram ABCD

$\Rightarrow$ Area of parallelogram $ABCD = 2 \times 130 = 260 \text{ cm}^2$

Hence, A is true, R is false.

2. (c) Given, in ΔPQR, PM is one of its median and $ar(\Delta PQR) = 38 \text{ cm}^2$

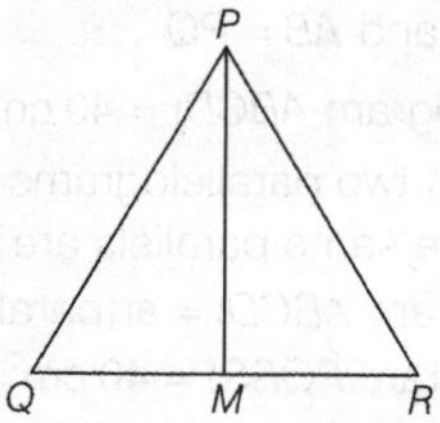

Since, PM is median of ΔPQR and we know that median of a triangle divided it into two triangles of equal area.

$\therefore \quad ar(\Delta PQM) = \frac{1}{2} ar(\Delta PQR)$

$\Rightarrow \quad ar(\Delta PQM) = \frac{1}{2} \times 38 = 19 \text{ cm}^2$

Therefore, both A and R are true and R is the correct reason for A.

3. (c) Given, $ABCD$ is a quadrilateral and $BP \parallel AC$.

Here, ΔACB and ΔACP lie on the same base AC and between the same parallel lines AC and BP.

So, ar (ΔACB) = ar (ΔACP)

On adding ar (ΔADC) both sides, we get

$$\text{ar}(\Delta ACB) + \text{ar}(\Delta ADC) = \text{ar}(\Delta ACP) + \text{ar}(\Delta ADC)$$

$$\Rightarrow \quad \text{ar}(ABCD) = \text{ar}(\Delta ADP)$$

Hence, both A and R are true and R is the correct reason for A.

4. (d) Clearly, $\text{ar}(\Delta ABC) = \text{ar}(\Delta ABD)$

$$= 20\text{ cm}^2$$

Because both triangles lie on the same base and between the same parallel lines.

And area of a triangle is equal to half the area of a parallelogram, if both lie on the same base and between the same parallel lines.

Hence, both A and R are true and R is incorrect reason for A.

5. (b) Given, D is a point on BC such that

$$BD : DC = 3 : 5$$

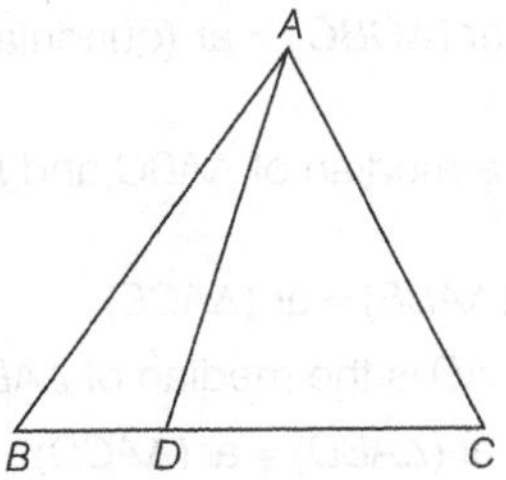

Since, ΔADC and ΔABC have same vertex A and bases (DC and BC) along the same line, therefore

$$\frac{\text{ar}(\Delta ADC)}{\text{ar}(\Delta ABC)} = \frac{DC}{BC} \quad \ldots \text{(i)}$$

Now, consider $\dfrac{BD}{DC} = \dfrac{3}{5}$

$$\Rightarrow \quad \frac{BD}{DC} + 1 = \frac{3}{5} + 1$$

$$\Rightarrow \quad \frac{BD + DC}{DC} = \frac{3+5}{5}$$

$$\Rightarrow \quad \frac{BC}{DC} = \frac{8}{5}$$

$$\Rightarrow \quad \frac{DC}{BC} = \frac{5}{8} \quad \ldots \text{(ii)}$$

From Eqs. (i) and (ii), we get

$$\frac{\text{ar}(\Delta ADC)}{\text{ar}(\Delta ABC)} = \frac{5}{8}$$

Hence, A is false, R is true.

Statement Based Questions

1. (a) As we know that if a rectangle and a parallelogram are on the same base and between the same parallel lines, then they are equal in area.

So, Statement I is true.

Since, area of a triangle is half of the area of parallelogram, if both lie on the same base and between the same parallel lines.

$$\therefore \text{ Area of triangle} = \frac{1}{2} \times \text{Area of parallelogram}$$

$$\Rightarrow \text{ Area of parallelogram} = 2 \times \text{Area of triangle}$$

$$= 2 \times 20 = 40\text{ cm}^2$$

So, Statement II is also true.

2. (c) Clearly, Statement I is correct but Statement II is incorrect because median of a triangle divides it into two triangles of equal area.

3. (a) We know that

Area of trapezium

$$= \frac{1}{2}(\text{Sum of parallel sides}) \times \text{Height}$$

$$= \frac{1}{2} \times (9 + 6) \times 8$$

$$= 15 \times 4 = 60\text{ cm}^2$$

Hence, Statement I is true and Statement II is also true.

4. (d) Given, area of parallelogram = x^2,

base of parallelogram = $x - 3$

and altitude of parallelogram = $x + 4$

As we know that

$$\text{Area of parallelogram} = \text{Base} \times \text{Height}$$

$$\Rightarrow \quad x^2 = (x-3)(x+4)$$

$$\Rightarrow \quad x^2 = x^2 + x - 12$$

$$\Rightarrow \quad x = 12$$

Hence, Statement I is false but Statement II is true.

Short Answer Type Questions

1. Let ABC be an isosceles triangle with base BC = 12 cm, perimeter = 32 cm and AC is a diagonal of a parallelogram $ABCD$.

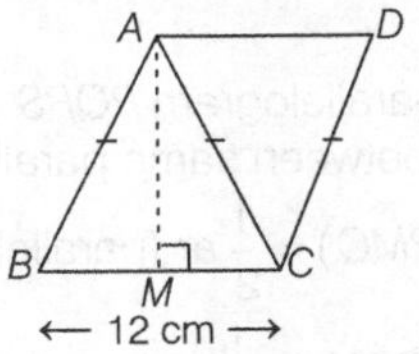

Draw $AM \perp BC$.

So, $BM = CM = \dfrac{12}{2} = 6$ cm

[$\because \Delta AMB \cong \Delta AMC$, by RHS congruence rule]

Also, $AB = AC = \frac{32 - 12}{2} = 10$ cm

In ΔAMC, $AM = \sqrt{AC^2 - CM^2} = \sqrt{10^2 - 6^2}$

$= \sqrt{100 - 36} = \sqrt{64} = 8$ cm

$\therefore$ Area of parallelogram $ABCD = BC \times AM$

$= 12 \times 8 = 96$ cm^2

2. Given, *ABCD* and *ABFE* are two parallelograms on the same base *AB* and between same parallel lines *AB* and *DF*.

Also, ar(quadrilateral *EABC*) = 17 cm^2

and ar(parallelogram *ABCD*) = 25 cm^2

We have, ar(parallelogram *ABCD*)

= ar(parallelogram *ABFE*)

[$\because$ parallelograms on the same base and between same parallels are equal in area]

$\Rightarrow$ ar (parallelogram *ABFE*)

= ar (parallelogram *ABCD*) = 25 cm^2

$\therefore$ ar (ΔBCF) = ar (parallelogram *ABFE*)

− ar (quadrilateral *EABC*)

= 25 − 17 = 8 cm^2

Hence, the area of ΔBCF is 8 cm^2.

3. Given *ABCD* and *PBCQ* are two parallelograms and *R* is a mid-point on *PB*.

To prove ar(ΔQRC) = $\frac{1}{2}$ ar(parallelogram *ABCD*)

Proof Here, parallelograms *PBCQ* and *ABCD* lie on the same base *BC* and between the same parallels *BC* and *AQ*.

So, ar (parallelogram *PBCQ*)

= ar (parallelogram *ABCD*) ...(i)

Now, ΔQRC and parallelogram *PBCQ* lie on the same base *CQ* and between the same parallels *CQ* and *BP*.

So, ar (ΔQRC) = $\frac{1}{2}$ ar (parallelogram *PBCQ*) ...(ii)

From Eqs. (i) and (ii), we get

ar (ΔQRC) = $\frac{1}{2}$ ar (parallelogram *ABCD*)

Hence proved.

4. $\because$ ΔPMQ and parallelogram *PQRS* are on the same base *PQ* and between same parallels *PQ* || *SR*.

$\therefore$ ar (ΔPMQ) = $\frac{1}{2}$ ar (parallelogram *PQRS*) ...(i)

Similarly, ar (ΔQRN) = $\frac{1}{2}$ ar (parallelogram *PQRS*) ...(ii)

On adding Eqs. (i) and (ii), we get

ar (ΔPMQ) + ar (ΔQRN) = ar (parallelogram *PQRS*)

$\Rightarrow$ ar (ΔPMQ) + ar (ΔQRM) + ar (ΔRMN)

= ar (ΔQRM) + ar (ΔPMQ) + ar (ΔPMS)

$\Rightarrow$ ar (ΔRMN) = ar (ΔPMS) **Hence proved.**

5. Given *BE* and *CF* are medians of a ΔABC and they intersect at *G*.

To prove ar (ΔGBC) = ar (quadrilateral *AFGE*)

Proof We know that median of a triangle divide it into two triangles of equal areas.

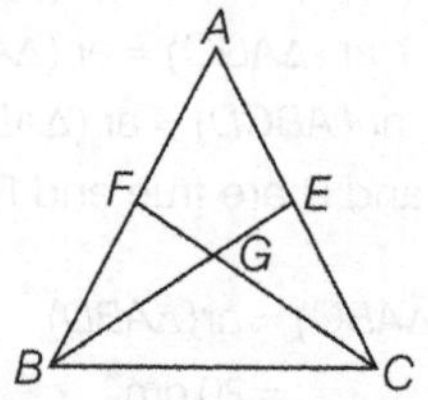

$\therefore$ ar (ΔFBC) = ar (ΔAFC)

$\Rightarrow$ ar (ΔFBC) = $\frac{1}{2}$ ar (ΔABC) ...(i)

Similarly, ar (ΔAEB) = $\frac{1}{2}$ ar (ΔABC) ...(ii)

From Eqs. (i) and (ii), we get

ar (ΔFBC) = ar (ΔAEB)

On subtracting ar (ΔGBF) from both sides, we get

ar (ΔFBC) − ar (ΔGBF) = ar (ΔAEB) − ar (ΔGBF)

$\Rightarrow$ ar (ΔGBC) = ar (quadrilateral *AFGE*)

Hence proved.

6. Given *AD* is a median of ΔABC and *E* is any point on *AD*.

To prove ar (ΔABE) = ar (ΔACE)

Proof Since, *AD* is the median of ΔABC.

$\therefore$ ar (ΔABD) = ar (ΔACD) ...(i)

[$\because$ a median of a triangle divides it into two triangles of equal areas]

Also, *ED* is the median of ΔEBC.

$\therefore$ ar (ΔBED) = ar (ΔCED) ...(ii)

On subtracting Eq. (ii) from Eq. (i), we get

ar (ΔABD) − ar (ΔBED) = ar (ΔACD) − ar (ΔCED)

$\Rightarrow$ ar (ΔABE) = ar (ΔACE) **Hence proved.**

7. Given *PQRS* is a parallelogram and *O* is any point on the diagonal *PR*.

To prove ar (ΔPSO) = ar (ΔPQO)

Construction Join *SQ* to intersect *PR* at *B*.

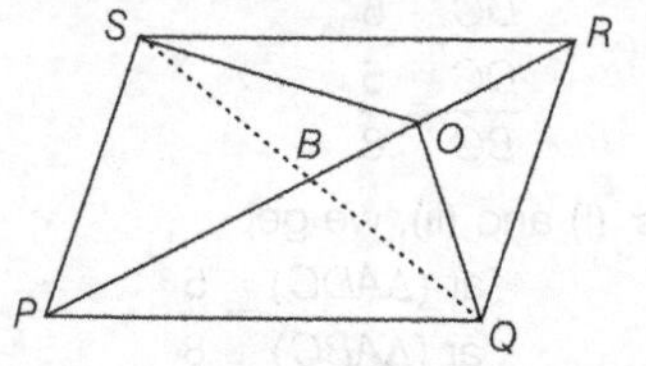

Proof We know that the diagonals of a parallelogram bisect each other, so *B* is the mid-point of *SQ*.

Thus, *PB* is a median of ΔQPS and median of a triangle divides it into two triangles of equal areas.

∴ ar (ΔBPQ) = ar (ΔBPS) ...(i)

Also, OB is a median of ΔOSQ.

∴ ar (ΔOBQ) = ar (ΔOBS) ...(ii)

On adding Eqs. (i) and (ii), we get

ar (ΔBPQ) + ar (ΔOBQ) = ar (ΔBPS) + ar (ΔOSB)

⇒ ar (ΔPQO) = ar (ΔPSO) **Hence proved.**

8. Since, DF is median of a ΔADE.

[∵ F is the mid-point of AE]

∴ $ar(\Delta AFD) = \frac{1}{2} ar(\Delta ADE)$ ...(i)

Since E is the mid-point of CD.

∴ AE is median of a ΔACD, then

$ar(\Delta ADE) = \frac{1}{2} ar(\Delta ACD)$ ...(ii)

Similarly, D is the mid-point of AB.

∴ CD is median of a ΔABC, then

$ar(\Delta ACD) = \frac{1}{2} ar(\Delta ABC)$ ...(iii)

From Eqs. (i), (ii) and (iii), we get

$ar(\Delta AFD) = \frac{1}{2} \times \frac{1}{2} \times \frac{1}{2} ar(\Delta ABC)$

⇒ $ar(\Delta AFD) = \frac{1}{8} ar(\Delta ABC)$

⇒ $8\, ar(\Delta AFD) = ar(\Delta ABC)$ **Hence proved.**

9. Given $ABCDE$ is a pentagon, $BP \parallel AC$ and $EQ \parallel AD$.

To prove ar (pentagon $ABCDE$) = ar (ΔAPQ)

Proof We know that triangles on the same base and between the same parallels are equal in area.

∴ ar (ΔADE) = ar (ΔADQ) ...(i)

Similarly, ar (ΔCAB) = ar (ΔCAP) ...(ii)

On adding Eqs. (i) and (ii), we get

ar (ΔADE) + ar (ΔCAB) = ar (ΔADQ) + ar (ΔCAP)

On adding ar (ΔCDA) both sides, we get

ar (ΔADE) + ar (ΔCAB) + ar (ΔCDA)

= ar (ΔADQ) + ar (ΔCAP) + ar(ΔCDA)

⇒ ar ($ABCDE$) = ar (ΔAPQ) **Hence proved.**

10. Given ΔABC and ΔABD are on the same base AB and ar(ΔABC) = ar(ΔABD).

Further, $CM \perp AB$ and $DN \perp AB$.

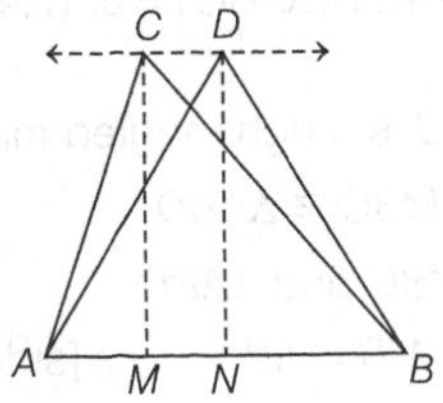

To prove $CM = DN$

Proof Clearly, ar (ΔABC) = $\frac{1}{2} \times AB \times CM$ ...(i)

and ar (ΔABD) = $\frac{1}{2} \times AB \times DN$ ...(ii)

∵ ar (ΔABC) = ar (ΔABD)

∴ $\frac{1}{2} \times AB \times CM = \frac{1}{2} \times AB \times DN$

[using Eqs. (i) and (ii)]

⇒ $CM = DN$ **Hence proved.**

Long Answer Type Questions

1. Given $ABCD$ and $PQCD$ are two parallelograms on same base DC and between same parallels PB and DC.

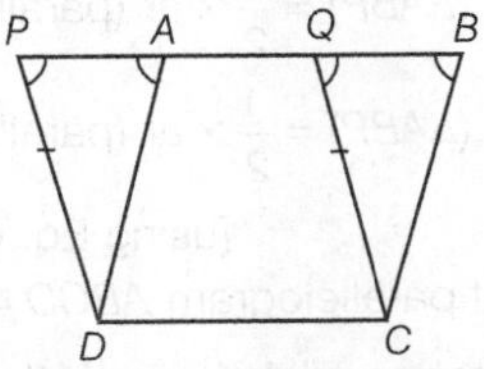

To prove Area of parallelogram $ABCD$

= Area of parallelogram $PQCD$

Proof In ΔPDA and ΔQCB,

$\angle DPA = \angle CQB$ [∵ corresponding angles]

$\angle DAP = \angle CBQ$ [∵ corresponding angles]

Also, $PD = QC$

[∵ opposite sides of the parallelogram are equal]

So, $\Delta PDA \cong \Delta QCB$ [by AAS congruence rule]

⇒ ar (ΔPDA) = ar (ΔQCB) ...(i)

[congruent figures have equal areas]

On adding area of trapezium $AQCD$ both sides, we get

ar (ΔPDA) + ar (trapezium $AQCD$)

= ar (ΔQCB) + ar (trapezium $AQCD$)

⇒ ar (parallelogram $PQCD$) = ar (parallelogram $ABCD$)

Hence, parallelograms on the same base and between the same parallels are equal in area. **Hence proved.**

2. Given ΔABP and parallelogram $ABCD$ are on the same base AB and between the same parallels AB and PC.

To prove ar (ΔABP) = $\frac{1}{2}$ × ar (parallelogram $ABCD$)

Construction Draw $BQ \parallel AP$ to get another parallelogram $ABQP$.

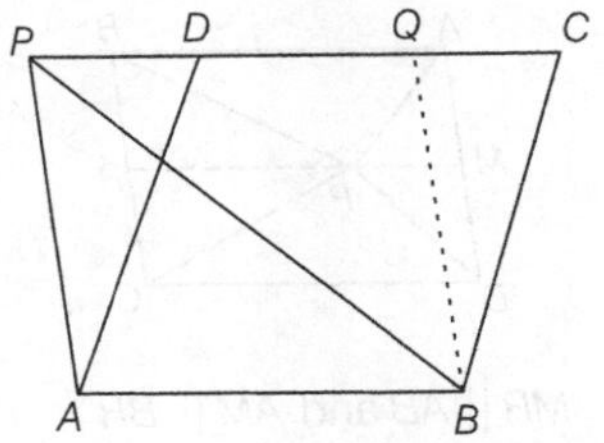

Proof Since, parallelograms $ABCD$ and $ABQP$ lie on the same base AB and between the same parallels AB and PC.

$\therefore$ ar (parallelogram $ABCD$)

$$= \text{ar (parallelogram } ABQP) \quad \ldots\text{(i)}$$

Now, diagonal PB of parallelogram $ABQP$ divides it into two congruent triangles i.e. ΔABP and ΔQPB.

$\therefore$ ar (ΔABP) = ar (ΔBPQ) ...(ii)

Now, ar (ΔABP) + ar (ΔBPQ) = ar(parallelogram $ABQP$)

$\Rightarrow$ ar (ΔABP) + ar (ΔABP) = ar (parallelogram $ABQP$) [using Eq. (ii)]

$\Rightarrow$ $2 \times$ ar (ΔABP) = ar (parallelogram $ABQP$)

$\Rightarrow$ ar (ΔABP) $= \frac{1}{2} \times$ ar (parallelogram $ABQP$)

$\Rightarrow$ ar (ΔABP) $= \frac{1}{2} \times$ ar (parallelogram $ABCD$)

[using Eq. (i)] **Hence proved.**

3. Given, area of parallelogram $ABCD = 90 \text{ cm}^2$

(i) We know that parallelogram on the same base and between the same parallel lines are equal in area.

$\therefore$ ar ($ABEF$) = ar (parallelogram $ABCD$) = 90 cm^2

(ii) We know that if a triangle and a parallelogram are on the same base and between the same parallels, then area of triangle is equal to half of the area of the parallelogram.

$\therefore$ ar (ΔABD) $= \frac{1}{2} \times$ ar (parallelogram $ABEF$)

$$= \frac{1}{2} \times 90$$

$\Rightarrow$ ar (ΔABD) = 45 cm^2

(iii) Similarly, ΔBEF and parallelogram $ABEF$ are on the same base EF and $EF \parallel AB$.

$\therefore$ ar (ΔBEF) $= \frac{1}{2} \times$ ar ($ABEF$) $= \frac{1}{2} \times 90 = 45 \text{ cm}^2$

4. Given $ABCD$ is a parallelogram.

So, $AB \parallel CD$ and $AD \parallel BC$.

To prove

(i) ar (ΔAPB) + ar (ΔPCD) $= \frac{1}{2}$ ar (parallelogram $ABCD$)

(ii) ar (ΔAPD) + ar (ΔPBC) = ar (ΔAPB) + ar (ΔPCD)

Proof

(i) Through the point P, draw MR parallel to AB.

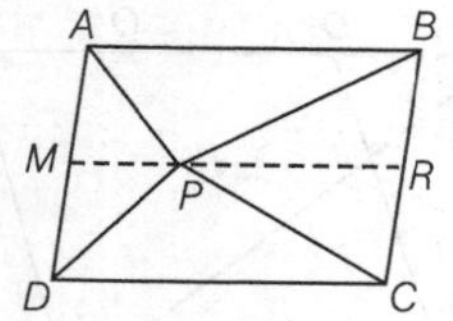

$\because$ $MR \parallel AB$ and $AM \parallel BR$

So, $ABRM$ is a parallelogram.

Now, as ΔAPB and parallelogram $ABRM$ are on the same base AB and between the same parallel lines AB and MR.

$\therefore$ ar (ΔAPB) $= \frac{1}{2}$ ar (parallelogram $ABRM$)

Similarly, ar (ΔPCD) $= \frac{1}{2}$ ar (parallelogram $MRCD$)

Now, ar (ΔAPB) + ar (ΔPCD)

$$= \frac{1}{2} \text{ ar (parallelogram } ABRM)$$

$$+ \frac{1}{2} \text{ ar (parallelogram } MRCD)$$

$$= \frac{1}{2} \text{ ar (parallelogram } ABCD) \ldots\text{(a)}$$

Hence proved.

(ii) Draw a line XY through P parallel to AD.

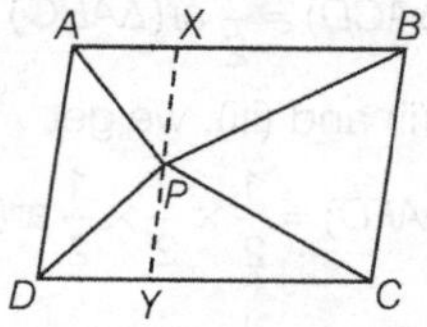

$\because$ $XY \parallel AD$ and $AX \parallel DY$.

So, $AXYD$ is a parallelogram.

Now, ΔAPD and parallelogram $AXYD$ are on the same base AD and between the same parallels AD and XY.

$\therefore$ ar (ΔAPD) $= \frac{1}{2}$ ar (parallelogram $AXYD$)

Similarly, ar (ΔPBC) $= \frac{1}{2}$ ar (parallelogram $BXYC$)

Now, ar (ΔAPD) + ar (ΔPBC)

$$= \frac{1}{2} \text{ ar (parallelogram } AXYD)$$

$$+ \frac{1}{2} \text{ ar (parallelogram } BXYC)$$

$\Rightarrow$ ar(ΔAPD) + ar (ΔPBC)

$$= \frac{1}{2} \text{ ar (parallelogram } ABCD) \quad \ldots\text{(b)}$$

From Eqs. (a) and (b), we get

ar (ΔAPD) + ar (ΔPBC) = ar (ΔAPB) + ar (ΔPCD)

Hence proved.

5. (i) **Given** ΔABC is a right angled triangle and $AX \perp DE$.

To prove $\Delta MBC \cong \Delta ABD$

Proof In ΔMBC and ΔABD,

$MB = AB$ [sides of square $ABMN$]

$BC = BD$ [sides of square $BCED$]

and $\angle MBA = \angle CBD$ [each 90°]

$\angle MBA + \angle ABC = \angle CBD + \angle ABC$ [adding $\angle ABC$ both sides]

$\Rightarrow \quad \angle MBC = \angle ABD$

Hence, $\Delta MBC \cong \Delta ABD$ [by SAS congruence rule]

(ii) From part (i), we have

$\Delta MBC \cong \Delta ABD$

$\therefore \quad ar(\Delta MBC) = ar(\Delta ABD)$ ...(a)

It is given that $AX \perp DE$ and $BD \perp DE$, then

$BD \parallel AX$

Since, ΔABD and parallelogram $BYXD$ are on the same base BD and between the same parallels BD and AX.

$\therefore \quad ar(\Delta ABD) = \frac{1}{2} ar(BYXD)$

$\Rightarrow \quad ar(BYXD) = 2\, ar(\Delta ABD)$

$\Rightarrow \quad ar(BYXD) = 2\, ar(\Delta MBC)$ [from Eq. (a)] ...(b)

(iii) Since, ΔMBC and parallelogram $ABMN$ lie on the same base MB and between the same parallels MB and NC.

$\therefore \quad ar(\Delta MBC) = \frac{1}{2} ar(ABMN)$

$\Rightarrow \quad ar(ABMN) = 2\, ar(\Delta MBC)$ ...(c)

From Eqs. (b) and (c), we get

$ar(BYXD) = ar(ABMN)$ **Hence proved.**

6. Given A quadrilateral $WXYZ$ and $ABCD$ is the quadrilateral made by joining mid-points of the sides WX, XY, YZ and ZW, respectively.

To prove $ar\,(ABCD) = \frac{1}{2} ar\,(WXYZ)$

Construction Join WY and WC.

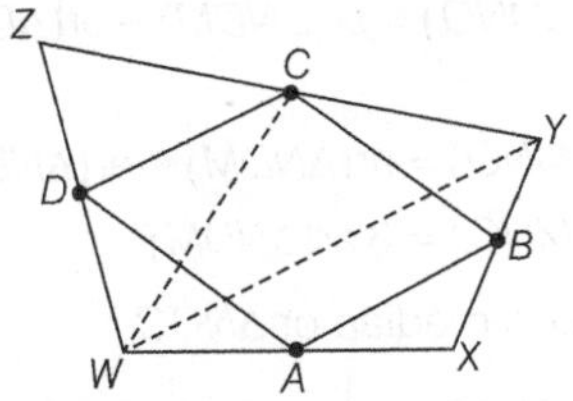

Proof We know that a triangle is divided by its median in two triangles of equal area.

$\therefore \quad ar\,(\Delta WCZ) = \frac{1}{2} ar\,(\Delta WYZ)$ ...(i)

and $\quad ar\,(\Delta DCZ) = \frac{1}{2} ar\,(\Delta WCZ)$ ...(ii)

From Eqs. (i) and (ii), we get

$ar\,(\Delta DCZ) = \frac{1}{4} ar\,(\Delta WYZ)$ ...(iii)

Similarly, $ar\,(\Delta AXB) = \frac{1}{4} ar\,(\Delta WXY)$ ...(iv)

On adding Eqs. (iii) and (iv), we get

$ar\,(\Delta DCZ) + ar\,(\Delta AXB)$

$= \frac{1}{4}[ar\,(\Delta WYZ) + ar\,(\Delta WXY)]$ ...(v)

$\therefore$ $ar\,(\Delta DCZ) + ar\,(\Delta AXB) = \frac{1}{4} ar\,(WXYZ)$ ...(vi)

Similarly,

$ar\,(\Delta WAD) + ar\,(\Delta BYC) = \frac{1}{4} ar\,(WXYZ)$ ...(vii)

On adding Eqs. (vi) and (vii), we get

$ar\,(\Delta WAD) + ar\,(\Delta AXB) + ar\,(\Delta BYC)$

$+ ar\,(\Delta DCZ) = \frac{1}{2} ar\,(WXYZ)$ ...(viii)

Now, $ar\,(\Delta WAD) + ar\,(\Delta AXB) + ar\,(\Delta BYC)$

$+ ar\,(\Delta DCZ) + ar\,(ABCD) = ar\,(WXYZ)$ ...(ix)

On subtracting Eq. (viii) from Eq. (ix), we get

$ar\,(ABCD) = \frac{1}{2} ar\,(WXYZ)$ **Hence proved.**

7. Given ΔABC in which D is the mid-point of AB and $CQ \parallel PD$.

To prove $ar\,(\Delta BPQ) = \frac{1}{2} ar\,(\Delta ABC)$

Construction Join CD.

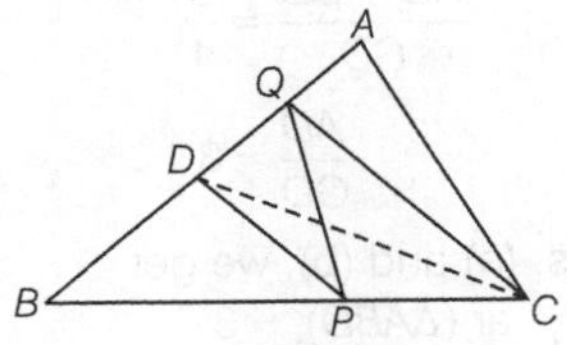

Proof Since, D is the mid-point of AB.

So, in ΔABC, CD is the median.

$\Rightarrow \quad ar\,(\Delta BCD) = \frac{1}{2} ar\,(\Delta ABC)$ ...(i)

Since, ΔPDQ and ΔPDC are on the same base PD and between same parallels PD and CQ.

$\therefore \quad ar\,(\Delta PDQ) = ar\,(\Delta PDC)$ ...(ii)

Now, from Eq. (i), $ar\,(\Delta BCD) = \frac{1}{2} ar\,(\Delta ABC)$

$\Rightarrow \quad ar\,(\Delta BDP) + ar\,(\Delta PDC) = \frac{1}{2} ar\,(\Delta ABC)$

$\Rightarrow \quad ar(\Delta BDP) + ar(\Delta PDQ) = \frac{1}{2} ar\,(\Delta ABC)$ [from Eq. (ii)]

$\Rightarrow \quad ar\,(\Delta BPQ) = \frac{1}{2} ar\,(\Delta ABC)$

Hence proved.

8. Given A ΔABC in which G is centroid of the triangle and AD is one of its median.

To prove (i) ar $(\Delta ABD) = 3 \times$ ar (ΔBGD)

(ii) ar $(\Delta ACD) = 3 \times$ ar (ΔCGD)

(iii) ar $(\Delta BGC) = \frac{1}{3} \times$ ar (ΔABC)

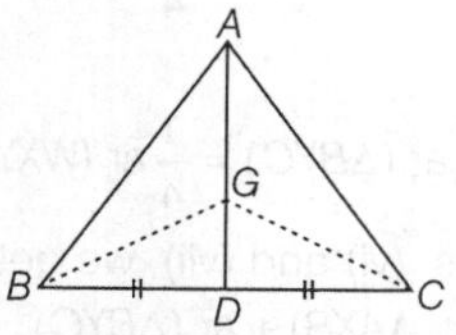

Proof We know that centroid divides each median in the ratio 2 : 1.

$\therefore AG : GD = 2 : 1$

(i) Since, ΔABD and ΔBGD have the same vertex B and bases (AD and DG) along the same line.

$$\therefore \quad \frac{\text{ar}(\Delta ABD)}{\text{ar}(\Delta BGD)} = \frac{AD}{DG} \quad \text{...(a)}$$

We have, $\frac{AG}{GD} = \frac{2}{1}$

$$\Rightarrow \quad \frac{AG}{GD} + 1 = \frac{2}{1} + 1$$

$$\Rightarrow \quad \frac{AG + GD}{GD} = \frac{3}{1}$$

$$\Rightarrow \quad \frac{AD}{GD} = 3 \quad \text{...(b)}$$

From Eqs. (a) and (b), we get

$$\frac{\text{ar}(\Delta ABD)}{\text{ar}(\Delta BGD)} = \frac{3}{1}$$

$$\Rightarrow \quad \text{ar}(\Delta ABD) = 3 \times \text{ar}(\Delta BGD) \quad \text{...(c)}$$

(ii) Since, ΔACD and ΔCGD have the same vertex C and bases (AD and DG) along the same line.

$$\therefore \quad \frac{\text{ar}(\Delta ACD)}{\text{ar}(\Delta CGD)} = \frac{AD}{DG} = \frac{3}{1} \quad \text{[using Eq. (b)]}$$

$$\Rightarrow \quad \text{ar}(\Delta ACD) = 3 \times \text{ar}(\Delta CGD) \quad \text{...(d)}$$

(iii) On adding Eqs. (c) and (d), we get

$$\text{ar}(\Delta ABD) + \text{ar}(\Delta ACD) = 3 \times \text{ar}(\Delta BGD) + 3 \times \text{ar}(\Delta CGD)$$

$$\Rightarrow \quad \text{ar}(\Delta ABC) = 3[\text{ar}(\Delta BGD) + \text{ar}(\Delta CGD)]$$

$$= 3[\text{ar}(\Delta BGC)]$$

$$\Rightarrow \quad \text{ar}(\Delta BGC) = \frac{1}{3}\text{ar}(\Delta ABC)$$

Hence proved.

Case Based Questions

1. (i) Given, area of the land = 300 m^2

i.e. area of parallelogram $PQRS = 300 \text{ m}^2$

Since, triangular pond PTQ and parallelogram $PQRS$ lie on the same base PQ and between the same parallel lines $PQ \parallel SR$.

$$\therefore \text{ Area of } \Delta PTQ = \frac{1}{2} \times \text{Area of parallelogram } PQRS$$

$$= \frac{1}{2} \times 300 = 150 \text{ m}^2$$

The area occupied by the pond = Area of ΔPTQ

$$= \frac{1}{2} \times 300 = 150 \text{ m}^2$$

(ii) Now, the area where medicinal plants were grown

= Area of parallelogram $PQRS$ − Area of ΔPTQ

$= 300 - 150 = 150 \text{ m}^2$

2. (i) Since, MA is the median of ΔMNO.

$$\therefore \quad \text{ar}(\Delta MAN) = \text{ar}(\Delta MAO) \quad \text{...(a)}$$

Also, $\text{ar}(\Delta DAN) = \text{ar}(\Delta DAO)$ ...(b)

On subtracting Eq. (b) from Eq. (a), we get

$$\text{ar}(\Delta MAN) - \text{ar}(\Delta DAN) = \text{ar}(\Delta MAO) - \text{ar}(\Delta DAO)$$

$$\Rightarrow \quad \text{ar}(\Delta NDM) = \text{ar}(\Delta MDO)$$

Similarly, $\text{ar}(\Delta NDM) = \text{ar}(\Delta DNO)$

Now, $\text{ar}(\Delta MNO) = \text{ar}(\Delta NDM) + \text{ar}(\Delta DNO) + \text{ar}(\Delta MDO)$

$$\Rightarrow \quad \text{ar}(\Delta MNO) = \text{ar}(\Delta NDM) + \text{ar}(\Delta NDM) + \text{ar}(\Delta NDM)$$

$$\Rightarrow \quad \text{ar}(\Delta MNO) = 3\,\text{ar}(\Delta NDM)$$

Hence proved.

(ii) Since, AD is median of ΔNDO.

$$\therefore \quad \text{ar}(\Delta NAD) = \frac{1}{2}\text{ar}(\Delta NDO)$$

$$\Rightarrow \quad \text{ar}(\Delta NDO) = 2\,\text{ar}(\Delta NAD)$$

$$= 2 \times 40 \quad [\because \text{ar}(\Delta NAD) = 40 \text{ cm}^2]$$

$$= 80 \text{ cm}^2$$

13

CIRCLES

The collection of all the points in a plane, which are at a fixed distance from a fixed point in the plane, is called a **circle**. The fixed point is called the **centre** of the circle and the fixed distance is called the **radius** of the circle.

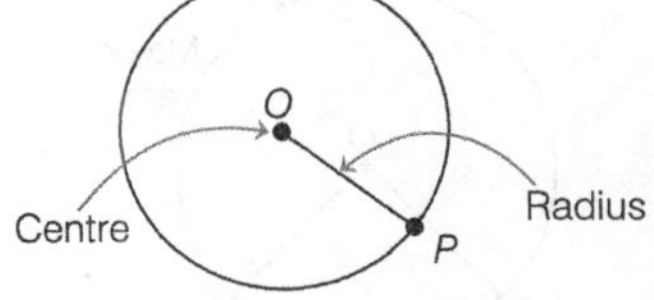

Important Terms Related to a Circle

Chord

A line segment joining two points on the circumference of a circle is called a chord of the circle. In figure, *PQ* is a chord of the circle.

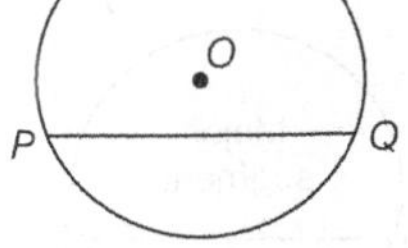

Diameter

A chord, which passes through the centre of the circle, is called a diameter of the circle. In figure, *AB* is the diameter of the circle.

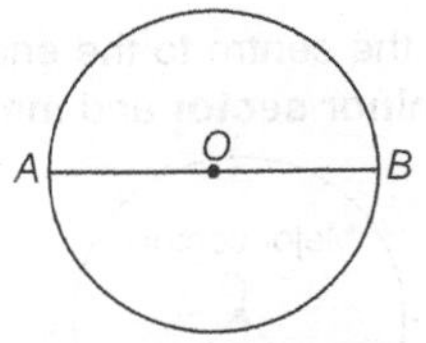

Diameter is the longest chord and all diameters have the same length, which is equal to two times the radius.

i.e. diameter = 2 × radius.

Circumference

The length of the complete circle is called its circumference.

Circumference $= \pi \times$ diameter $= \pi \times 2r = \mathbf{2\pi r}$

where, r is the radius of the circle.

Secant of a Circle

A line, which meets a circle in two points, is called a secant of the circle.

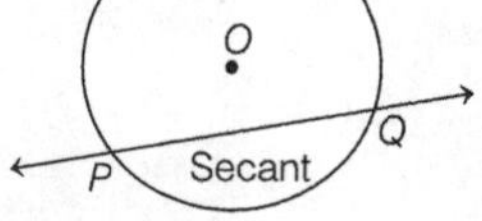

In figure, line *PQ* is a secant of the circle with centre *O*.

Arc

Any part of the circumference of a circle is called an arc of that circle. In the adjoining figure, there are two pieces, one longer and the other smaller. The longer one is called the **major arc** *PRQ* and the smaller one is called the **minor arc** *PQ*.

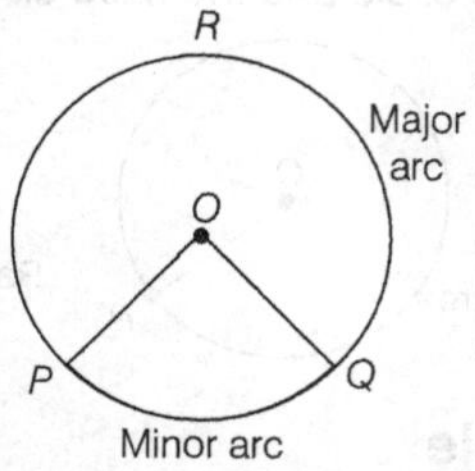

The minor arc *PQ* is denoted by $\overset{\frown}{PQ}$ and the major arc *PRQ* is denoted by $\overset{\frown}{PRQ}$.

Segment

The region between a chord and an arc is called a segment of the circle. This chord is called the **base** of the segment. The segment formed by minor arc along with chord, is called **minor segment** and the segment formed by major arc alongwith chord, is called the **major segment**.

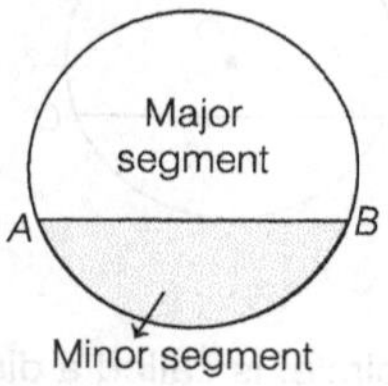

Sector

The region between an arc and two radii joining the centre to the end points of the arc is called a sector. The sector corresponding to minor and major arc is called **minor sector** and **major sector**, respectively.

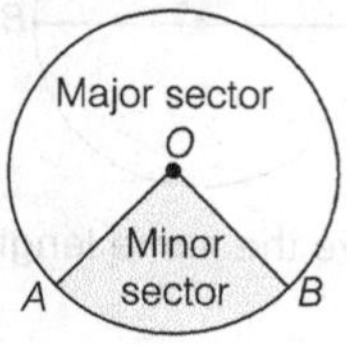

Concentric Circles

Two or more circles having common centre are called concentric circles.

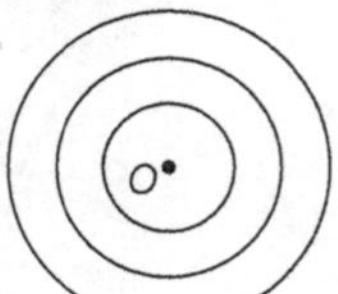

Congruent Circles

Two circles are said to be congruent, iff either they can superimposed or their radii are equal.

Chord Properties

***Theorem* 1 The line drawn through the centre of a circle to bisect a chord, which is not a diameter, is perpendicular to the chord.**

AB is a chord of a circle with centre *O*. A line *OM* is drawn through the centre *O* to the chord *AB* such that *M* is the mid-point of *AB*. i.e. $AM = MB$ then *OM* is perpendicular to *AB*.

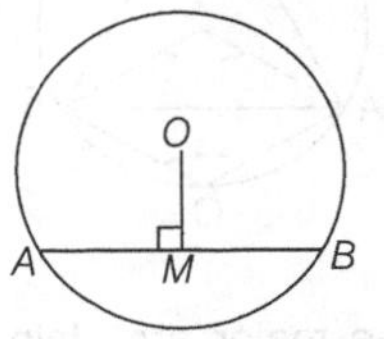

***Theorem* 2 (Converse of Theorem 1) The perpendicular from the centre of a circle to a chord, bisects the chord.**

If *AB* is a chord of a circle with centre *O* and $OM \perp AB$, then $AM = MB$.

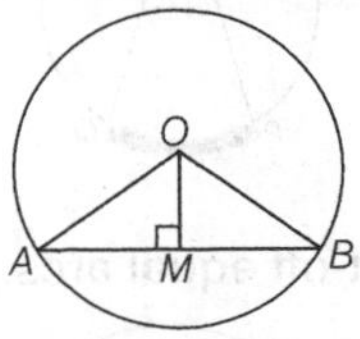

***Theorem* 3 Equal chords of a circle are equidistant from the centre.**

A circle with centre *O* and two equal chords *AB* and *PQ*, then $OM = ON$ i.e. *AB* and *PQ* are equidistant from the centre *O*.

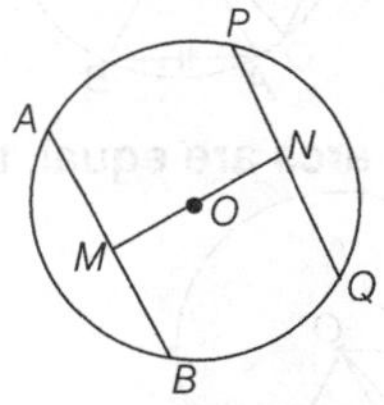

***Theorem* 4 (Converse of Theorem 3) Chords equidistant from the centre of a circle are equal in length.**

If in a circle with centre *O*, *OM* and *ON* are equal, then $AB = CD$.

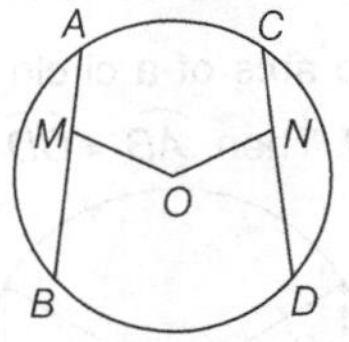

***Theorem* 5 There is one and only one circle, passing through three given non-collinear points.**

Three non-collinear points are *A*, *B* and *C*. Then, there is one and only one circle, passing through the points *A*, *B* and *C*.

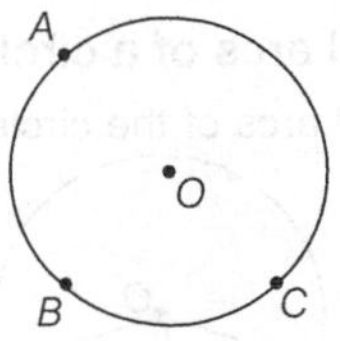

REVISION NOTES

Angle Subtended by a Chord

Let AB be a chord and points P and Q on the circle and join PA, PB, QA and QB. Then, $\angle APB$ and $\angle AQB$ are called the angles subtended by the chord AB.

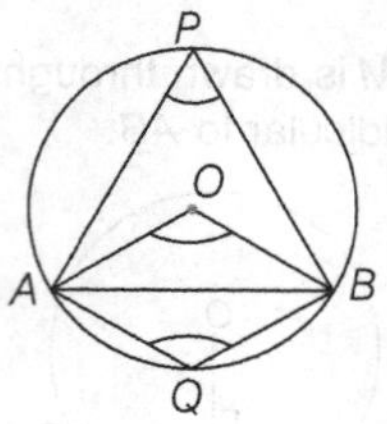

Angle Subtended by an Arc

Let PQ be the minor arc and the point R on the major arc. Join PR and RQ. Then, $\angle PRQ$ is called the angle subtended by an arc PQ.

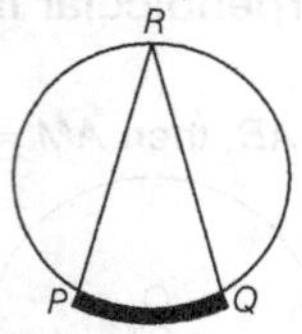

Arc Properties

***Theorem* 6 If two chords are equal, they cut-off equal arcs.**

If $PQ = AB$, then $\overparen{PQ} = \overparen{AB}$.

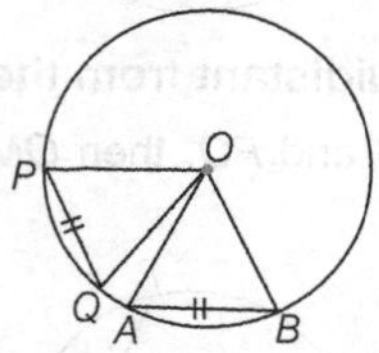

***Theorem* 7 (Converse of Theorem 6) If two arcs are equal, then their chords are equal.**

i.e. if $\overparen{PQ} = \overparen{AB}$, then $PQ = AB$.

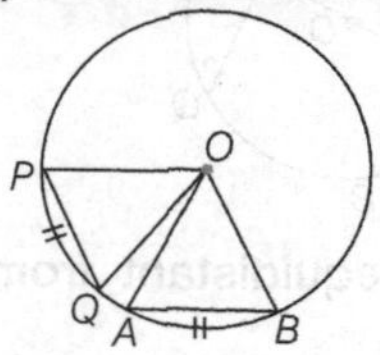

***Theorem* 8 If two arcs subtend equal angles at the centre, then the arcs are equal.**

If in a circle with centre O, let AB and CD be two arcs of a circle such that angles subtended by these arcs at the centre O of a circle are equal. i.e. $\angle AOB = \angle COD$. Then, $\overparen{AB} = \overparen{CD}$

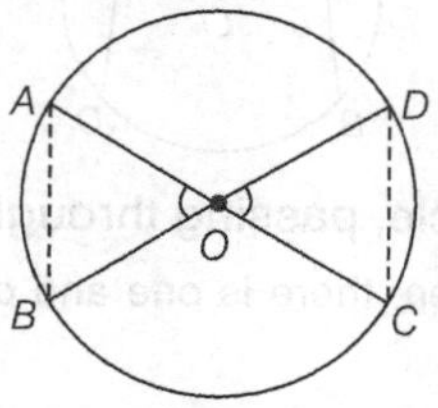

***Theorem* 9 (Converse of Theorem 8) Equal arcs of a circle subtend equal angles at the centre.**

If in circle with centre O, AB and CD are two equal arcs of the circle, which subtend $\angle AOB$ and $\angle COD$ at the centre O. Then, $\angle AOB = \angle COD$

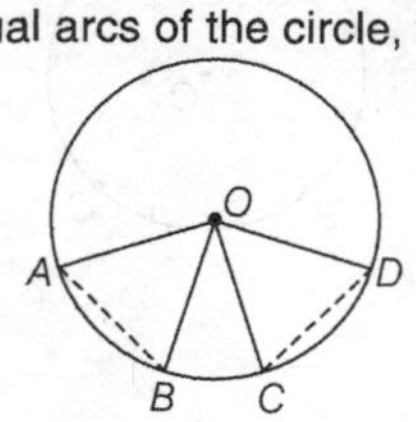

EXAM ORIENTED QUESTIONS

TYPE - 1 (01 Mark)

Multiple Choice Questions

Q.1 The region between a chord and either of the arc is called a

(a) segment (b) sector
(c) centre (d) radius

Q.2 The region between an arc and the two radii joining the centre to the ends of the arc is called

(a) sector (b) segment
(c) chord (d) circumference

Q.3 Let P be the mid-point of an arc of circle such that $m\widehat{APB} = 185°$. If the region bounded by the arc APB and line segment AB is denoted by Z, then the centre O of the circle lies

(a) on the segment AB. (b) on AB and bisects AB.
(c) in the interior of Z. (d) in the exterior of Z.

Q.4 In given figure, M is the mid-point of PQ, $OP = 13$ cm and $PQ = 24$ cm, then the length of OM is

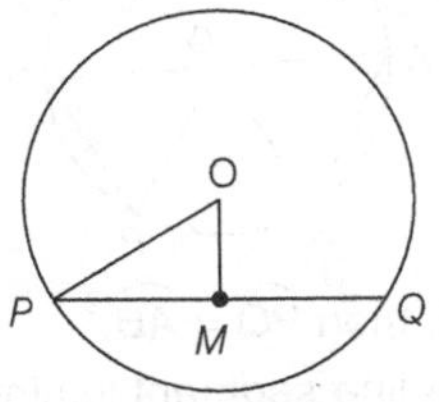

(a) 8 cm (b) 10 cm
(c) 5.6 cm (d) 5 cm

Q.5 Perpendicular bisector of every chord of a circle always passes through its

(a) chord (b) segment
(c) sector (d) centre

Q.6 In given figure, if $OD = 9$ units and $PQ = 80$ units. Then, length of OQ is

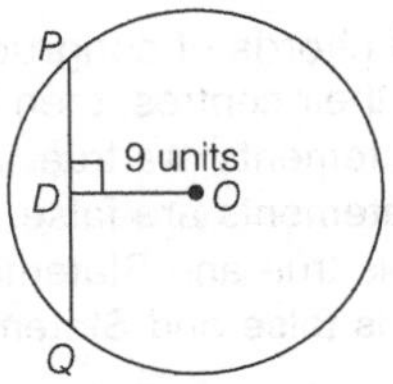

(a) 41 units (b) 48 units
(c) 45 units (d) 42 units

Q.7 In given figure, if $MN = 8$ cm and $AB = 6$ cm, then the length of CD is

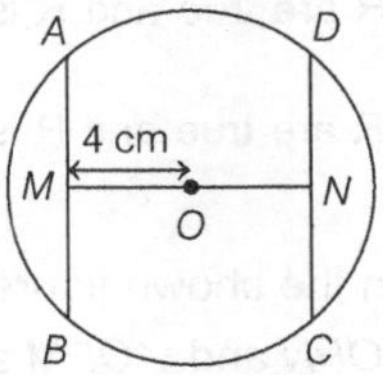

(a) 4 cm
(b) 6 cm
(c) 10 cm
(d) 8 cm

Q.8 In two congruent circles, having centres O and O', arc ABC and arc PQR subtend equal angles at the centres O and O', then the ratio of AC and PR is

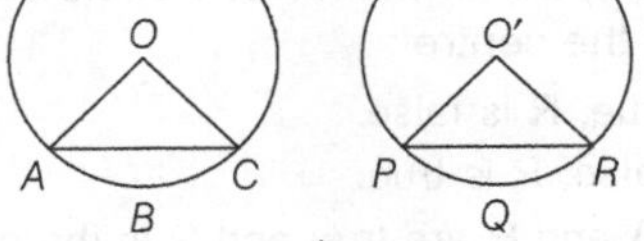

(a) 7 : 5 (b) 1 : 2
(c) 5 : 5 (d) 1 : 1

Answers

1. (a) 2. (a) 3. (c) 4. (d) 5. (d)
6. (a) 7. (b) 8. (d)

TYPE - 2 (01 Mark)

Assertion-Reason Type Questions

Q.1 Assertion (A) The length of a chord which is at a distance of 5 cm from the centre of a circle of radius 10 cm is 17.32 cm.

Reason (R) The perpendicular from the centre of a circle to a chord bisects the chord.

(a) A is true, R is false.
(b) A is false, R is true.
(c) Both A and R are true and R is the correct reason for A.
(d) Both A and R are true and R is incorrect reason for A.

Q.2 **Assertion** (A) The radius of a circle is 5 cm and the length of one of its chords is 8 cm, then the distance of chord from the centre is 3 cm.

Reason (R) The perpendicular drawn from the centre of a circle to a chord bisects the chord.

(a) A is true, R is false.
(b) A is false, R is true.
(c) Both A and R are true and R is the correct reason for A.
(d) Both A and R are true and R is incorrect reason for A.

Q.3 **Assertion** (A) In the shown figure, if $MP = PN$, then the values of $\angle OPN$ and $\angle OPM$ are same i.e. $90°$.

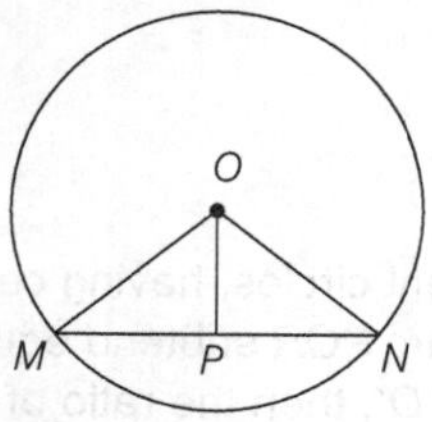

Reason (R) Equal chords of a circle subtend equal angles at the centre.

(a) A is true, R is false.
(b) A is false, R is true.
(c) Both A and R are true and R is the correct reason for A.
(d) Both A and R are true and R is incorrect reason for A.

Q.4 **Assertion** (A) In the given figure, if $\widehat{AB} = \widehat{CD}$, then $\angle AOB \neq \angle COD$.

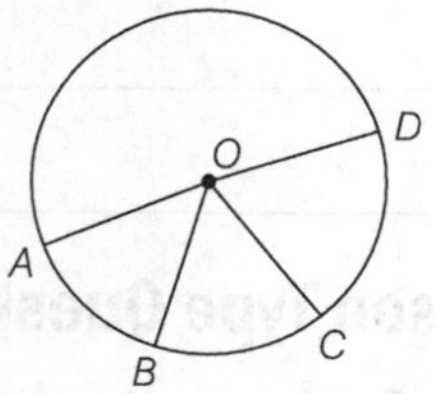

Reason (R) If two arcs of the same circle subtend equal angles at the centre, then they are equal.

(a) A is true, R is false.
(b) A is false, R is true.
(c) Both A and R are true and R is the correct reason for A.
(d) Both A and R are true and R is incorrect reason for A.

Answers

1. (c) **2.** (c) **3.** (d) **4.** (b)

TYPE - 3 — 01 Mark

Statement Based Questions

Q.1 **Statement I** The region between an arc and two radii joining the centre to the end points of the arc is called a segment.

Statement II The region between a chord and an arc is called a sector.

Which of the following is valid?

(a) Both the Statements are true.
(b) Both the Statements are false.
(c) Statement I is true and Statement II is false.
(d) Statement I is false and Statement II is true.

Q.2 **Statement I** Two or more circles having common centre are called concentric circles.

Statement II Equal chords of a circle are equidistant from the centre.

Which of the following is valid?

(a) Both the Statements are true.
(b) Both the Statements are false.
(c) Statement I is true and Statement II is false.
(d) Statement I is false and Statement II is true.

Q.3 **Statement I** If two chords are equal, they cut-off equal arcs.

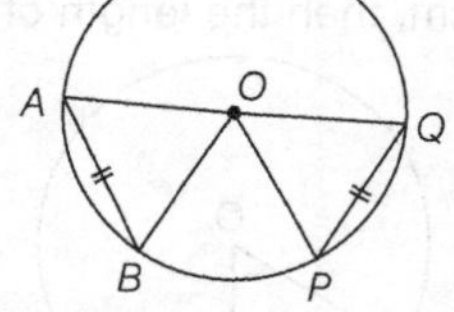

i.e. if $PQ = AB$, then $\widehat{PQ} = \widehat{AB}$.

Statement II A line segment joining two points on the circumference of a circle is called a chord of the circle.

Which of the following is valid?

(a) Both the Statements are true.
(b) Both the Statements are false.
(c) Statement I is true and Statement II is false.
(d) Statement I is false and Statement II is true.

Q.4 **Statement I** AB and CD are equal chords of a circle with centre O. If $OM \perp AB$ and $ON \perp CD$, then we can say $\angle OMN = \angle ONM$.

Statement II If chords of congruent circles subtend equal angles at their centres, then the chords are equal.

(a) Both the Statements are true.
(b) Both the Statements are false.
(c) Statement I is true and Statement II is false.
(d) Statement I is false and Statement II is true.

Answers

1. (b) **2.** (a) **3.** (a) **4.** (a)

TYPE - 4

03 Marks

Short Answer Type Questions

Q.1 In the given figure, equal chords AB and CD of a circle with centre O, cut at right angle at E. If M and N are the mid-points of AB and CD respectively, then prove that $OMEN$ is a square.

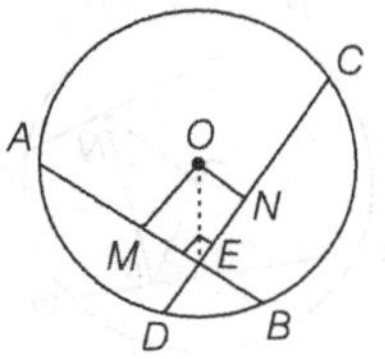

Q.2 A chord of a circle is 10 cm long and 20 cm away from the centre. Find the length of another chord of the circle, which is 5 cm away from the centre.

Q.3 In the given figure, if $OA = 5$ cm, $AB = 8$ cm and OD is perpendicular to AB, then find the length of CD.

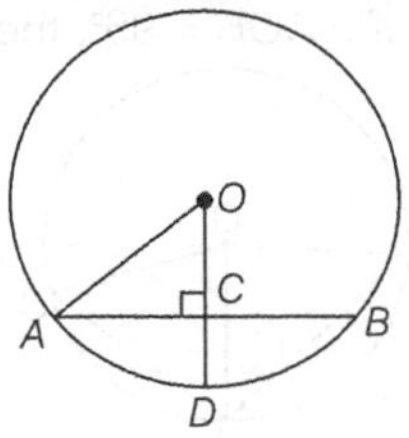

Q.4 Two concentric circles with centre O have A, B, C and D as points of intersection with a line l as shown in the figure. If $AD = 12$ cm and $BC = 8$ cm, then find the lengths of AB and CD.

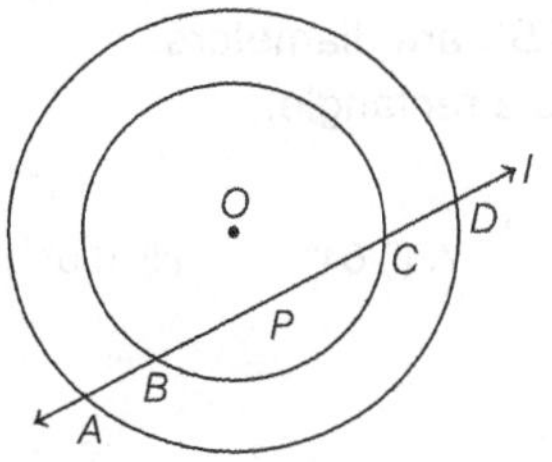

Q.5 AB and CD are two chords of a circle such that $AB = 6$ cm, $CD = 12$ cm and $AB \parallel CD$. OM is perpendicular to AB. If the distance between AB and CD is 3 cm, then find the radius of the circle.

Q.6 In the given figure, lengths of two parallel chords of a circle are 6 cm and 8 cm. If the smaller chord is at a distance of 4 cm from the centre, then what is the distance of the other chord from the centre?

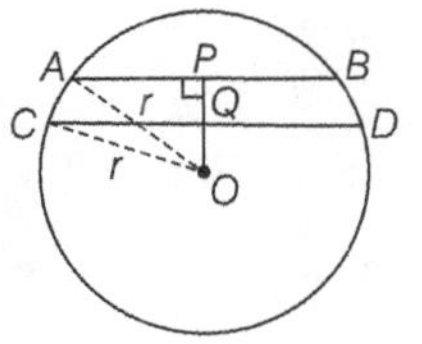

Q.7 In isosceles ΔPQR inscribed in a circle $PQ = PR = 7$ cm and $QR = 6$ cm. Find the radius of the circle.

Q.8 Two circles of radii 10 cm and 8 cm intersect each other and the length of the common chord is 12 cm. Find the distance between their centres.

Q.9 AB and CD are two equal chords of a circle with centre O.

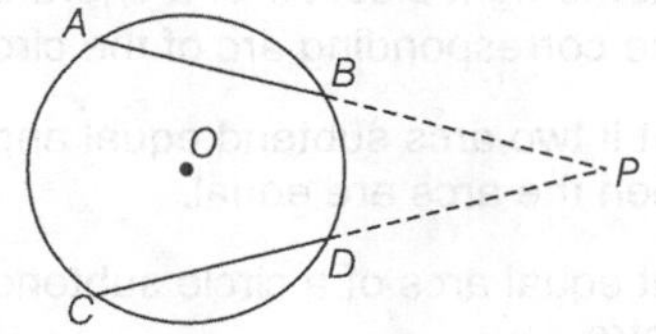

If AB and CD, on being produced, meet at a point P outside the circle, prove that

(i) $PA = PC$ (ii) $PB = PD$

Q.10 If two chords intersect inside the circle, make equal angles with the line passing through the centre and their point of intersection (see the figure), then prove that the chords are equal.

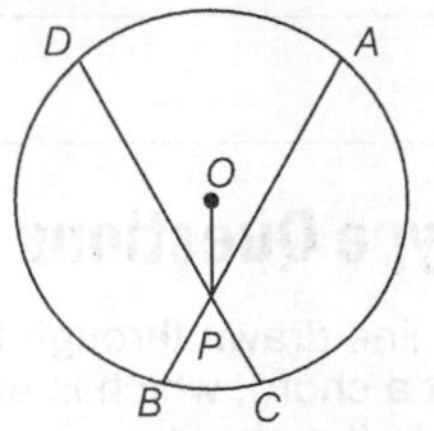

Or

In the given figure, O is the centre of a circle and PO bisects $\angle APD$. Prove that $AB = CD$.

Q.11 In the given figure, chords AB and CD are equal. If $\angle OBA = 55°$, then find $\angle COD$.

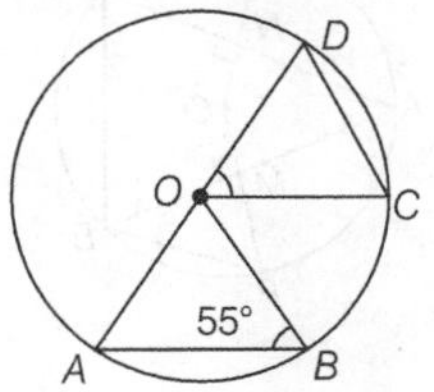

Q.12 If A, B and C are three points on a circle such that $AB = BC = CA$ and O is the centre of the circle, then find the angle subtended by the chords AB, BC and CA at the centre O.

Q.13 If arcs AXB and CYD of a circle are congruent, then find the ratio of AB and CD.

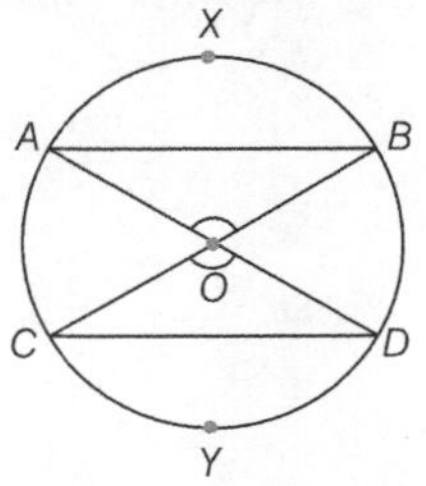

Q.14 If O is the centre of a circle and points A, B, C, D, E, F, G and H are on the circle such that $AB = BC = CD = DE = EF = FG = GH = HA$, then find $\angle AOB$, $\angle AOC$, $\angle DOF$ and $\angle EOH$.

Q.15 Prove that the right bisector of a chord of a circle bisects the corresponding arc of the circle.

Q.16 Prove that if two arcs subtend equal angles at the centre, then the arcs are equal.

Q.17 Prove that equal arcs of a circle subtend equal angles at the centre.

Answers

2. 40 cm **3.** 2 cm **4.** 2 cm **5.** 6.71 cm
6. 3 cm **7.** $\frac{49\sqrt{10}}{40}$ cm **8.** 13.29 cm **11.** 70°
12. 120° **13.** 1 : 1
14. $\angle AOB = 45°$, $\angle AOC = 90°$, $\angle DOF = 90°$ and $\angle EOH = 135°$

TYPE - 5 — 4/5 Marks

Long Answer Type Questions

Q.1 Prove that the line drawn through the centre of a circle to bisect a chord, which is not a diameter, is perpendicular to the chord.

Q.2 In the given figure, O is the centre of a circle. If AB and AC are chords of the circle such that $AB = AC$, $OP \perp AB$ and $OQ \perp AC$, then prove that $PB = QC$.

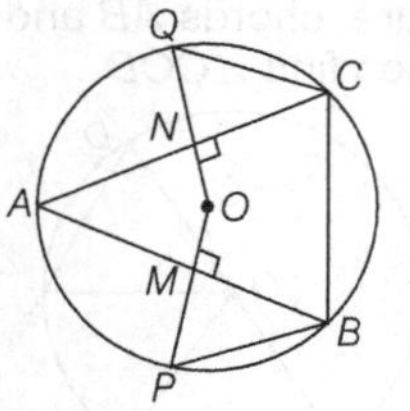

Q.3 If two equal chords of a circle intersect within the circle, then prove that the segments of one chord are equal to corresponding segments of the other chord.

Q.4 In the given figure, PQ and RS are two chords of a circle having its centre O and N is the mid-point of chord RS. If $PQ = RS$ and $ON = 3$ cm, find OM and if $\angle NOM = 140°$, then find the value of $\angle SNM$.

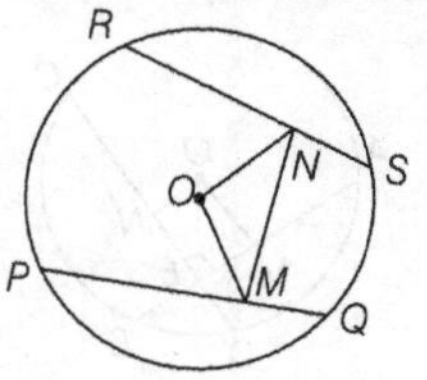

Q.5 Prove that equal chords of a circle are equidistant from the centre.

Q.6 Prove that there is one and only one circle, passing through three given non-collinear points.

Q.7 In the given figure, the length of arcs AB and BC are in the ratio 3 : 2. If $\angle AOB = 96°$, then find

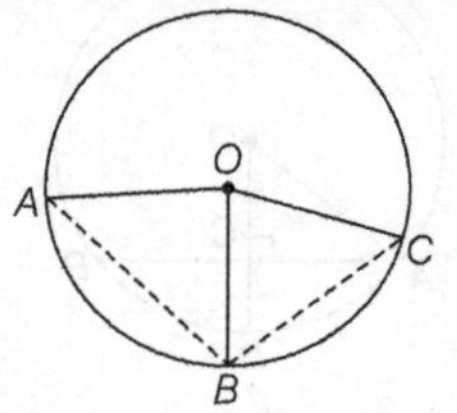

(i) $\angle BOC$ (ii) $\angle ABC$.

Q.8 AC and BD are chords of a circle, which bisect each other. Prove that

(i) AC and BD are diameters.

(ii) $ABCD$ is a rectangle.

Answers

4. 3 cm, 70° **7.** (i) 64° (ii) 100°

EXPLANATIONS

Multiple Choice Questions

1. (a) We know that the region between a chord and an arc is called a segment of the circle.

2. (a) We know that the region between an arc and two radii joining the centre to the end points of the arc is called a sector.

3. (c)

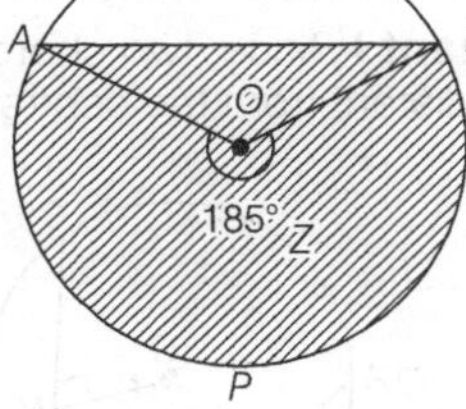

$\because m\widehat{APB} = 185°$, which is greater than 180°.

$\therefore APB$ is a major arc.

Hence, the centre O of the circle lies in the interior of the region Z.

4. (d) Given, $OP = 13$ cm

and $\quad PQ = 24$ cm

$\because \quad PM = \frac{1}{2} \times PQ \quad [\because M$ is the mid-point of $PQ]$

$\therefore \quad PM = \frac{1}{2} \times 24 = 12$ cm

The line drawn through the centre of a circle to bisect a chord, is perpendicular to the chord.

$\therefore \quad \angle OMP = 90°$

Now in ΔOMP,

$(OP)^2 = (OM)^2 + (PM)^2$ [by Pythagoras theorem]

$\Rightarrow \quad (13)^2 = (OM)^2 + (12)^2$

$\Rightarrow \quad 169 = (OM)^2 + 144$

$\Rightarrow 169 - 144 = (OM)^2 \Rightarrow (OM)^2 = 25$

$\Rightarrow \quad OM = 5$ cm [taking +ve value]

Hence, the length of $OM = 5$ cm

5. (d) We know that the perpendicular to a chord from the centre of circle bisects the chord.

Then, we say that perpendicular bisector of every chord of a circle always passes through its centre.

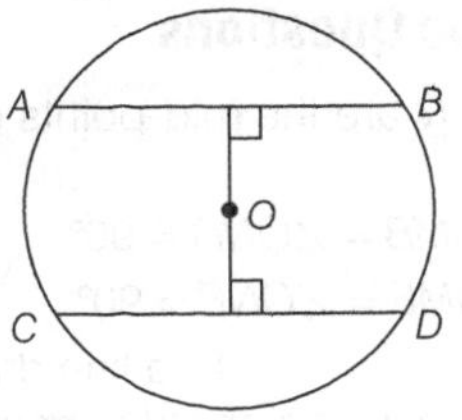

6. (a) Given, $OD = 9$ units and $PQ = 80$ units

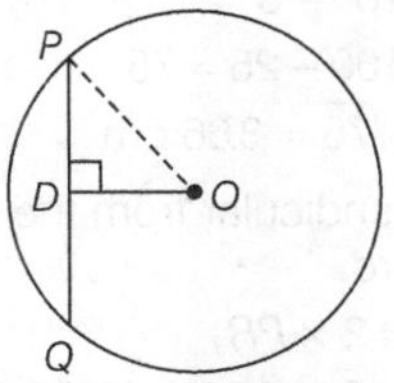

We know that the perpendicular to a chord from the centre of circle bisects the chord.

$\therefore \quad PD = \frac{1}{2} \times PQ = \frac{1}{2} \times 80 = 40$ units

Now, in right angled ΔODP,

$(OP)^2 = (OD)^2 + (PD)^2$

[by Pythagoras theorem]

$= (9)^2 + (40)^2 = 81 + 1600 = 1681$

$\therefore \quad OP = 41$ units [taking +ve value]

Therefore, $\quad OP = OQ$ [radii of same circle]

$OQ = 41$ units

7. (b) Given, $MN = 8$ cm and $AB = 6$ cm

From figure, $OM = 4$ cm $= ON$ $\quad [\because MN = 8$ cm$]$

We know that chords equidistant from the centre of a circle are equal in length.

Therefore, $AB = CD = 6$ cm

8. (d) In ΔAOC and $\Delta PO'R$,

$AO = PO'$ [radii of congruent circle]

$CO = RO'$ [radii of congruent circle]

and $\angle AOC = \angle PO'R$ [equal arcs of congruent circles subtend equal angles at their centres]

$\therefore \quad \Delta AOC \cong \Delta PO'R$ [by SAS congruency rule]

$\therefore \quad AC = PR$ [by CPCT]

$\Rightarrow \quad \frac{AC}{PR} = \frac{1}{1} \Rightarrow AC : PR = 1 : 1$

Hence, the ratio of AC and PR is 1 : 1.

Assertion-Reason Type Questions

1. (c) Let PQ be a chord of a circle with centre O and radius 10 cm. Draw $OR \perp PQ$.

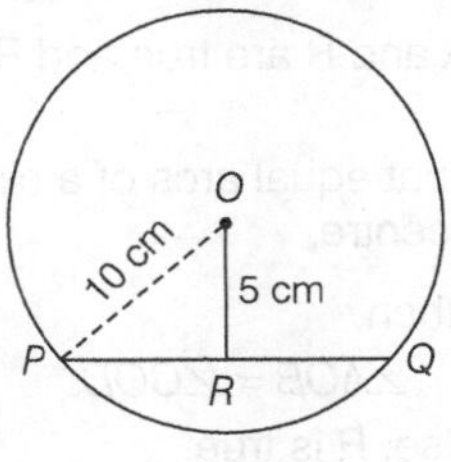

Now, $OP = 10$ cm and $OR = 5$ cm

In right angled ΔORP,

$$OP^2 = PR^2 + OR^2 \quad \text{[by Pythagoras theorem]}$$

$$\Rightarrow \quad PR^2 = OP^2 - OR^2$$

$$\Rightarrow \quad PR^2 = 10^2 - 5^2$$

$$= 100 - 25 = 75$$

$$\Rightarrow \quad PR = \sqrt{75} = 8.66 \text{ cm}$$

Since, the perpendicular from the centre to a chord bisects the chord.

Therefore, $PQ = 2 \times PR$

$$= 2 \times 8.66 = 17.32 \text{ cm}$$

So, A is true.

Also, R is true and R is the correct reason for of A.

2. (c) **Assertion** Let AB be a chord of the given circle with centre O.

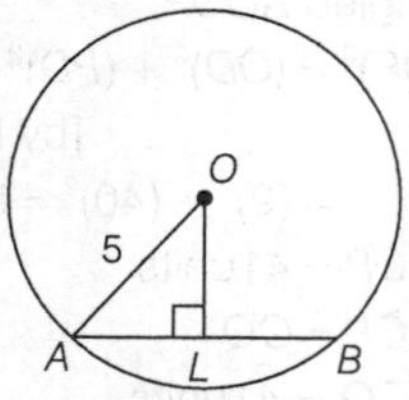

Given, radius $(OA) = 5$ cm and $AB = 8$ cm

From O, draw $OL \perp AB$.

We know that the perpendicular drawn from the centre of a circle to a chord bisects the chord.

$$\therefore \quad AL = \frac{1}{2} AB = \frac{1}{2} \times 8 = 4 \text{ cm}$$

Now, in right angled ΔOLA,

$$OA^2 = OL^2 + AL^2 \quad \text{[by Pythagoras theorem]}$$

$$\Rightarrow \quad 5^2 = OL^2 + 4^2$$

$$\Rightarrow \quad OL^2 = 25 - 16 = 9$$

$$\therefore \quad OL = 3 \quad \text{[taking +ve value]}$$

Hence, both A and R are true and R is the correct reason for A.

3. (d) Since, $MP = PN$ and MN is a chord.

Therefore, line OP bisects the chord.

We know that if line drawn through the centre of a circle bisects a chord, then it is perpendicular to the chord.

$\therefore$ Line OP is perpendicular to the chord MN.

$$\therefore \quad \angle OPN = \angle OPM = 90^\circ$$

Hence, both A and R are true and R is incorrect reason for A.

4. (b) We know that equal arcs of a circle subtend equal angles at the centre.

$\therefore$ If $\overset{\frown}{AB} = \overset{\frown}{CD}$, then

$$\angle AOB = \angle COD.$$

Hence, A is false, R is true.

Statement Based Questions

1. (b) We know that the region between an arc and two radii joining the centre to the end points of the arc is called a sector. And the region between a chord and an arc is called a segment.

Hence, both the Statements are false.

2. (a) We know that two or more circles having common centre are called concentric circles and equal chords of a circle are equidistant from the centre.

Hence, both the Statements are true.

3. (a) Clearly, both the Statements are true.

4. (a) **Statement I** Since, two chords are equal, so both are at equidistant from the centre.

$\therefore OM = ON$

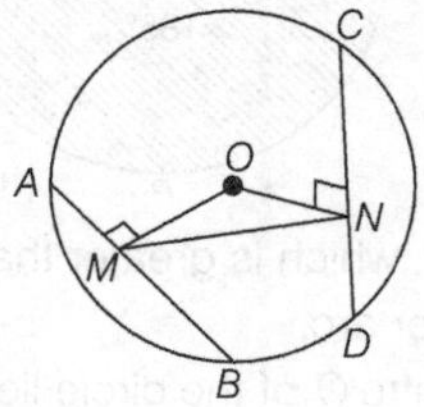

In ΔOMN, $\angle ONM = \angle OMN$

[$\because$ opposite angles of equal sides are equal]

Hence, Statement I is true.

Statement II Let MN and PQ be two chords of congruent circles such that angles subtended by these chords at the centres O and O' of the circles are equal i.e. $\angle MON = \angle PO'Q$.

In ΔMON and $\Delta PO'Q$, we have

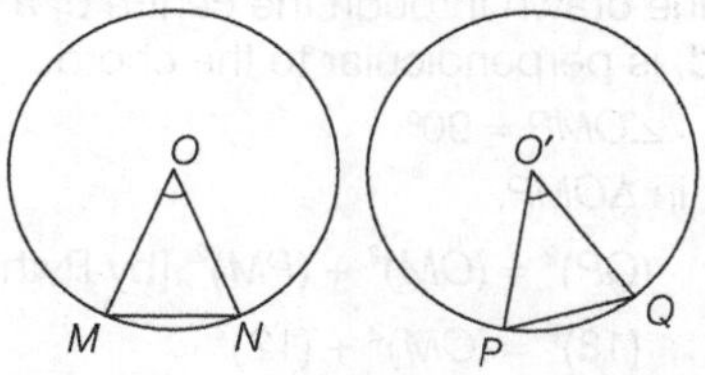

$MO = PO'$ [radii of congruent circles]

$\angle MON = \angle PO'Q$ [given]

and $NO = QO'$ [radii of congruent circles]

$\therefore$ $\Delta MON \cong \Delta PO'Q$ [by SAS congruence rule]

So, $MN = PQ$ [by CPCT]

Hence, chords are equal if they subtend equal angles at their centres.

Hence, Statement II is true.

Short Answer Type Questions

1. Since, M and N are the mid-points of AB and CD, respectively.

$$\therefore \quad \angle OMB = \angle OND = 90^\circ$$

$$\Rightarrow \quad \angle OME = \angle ONE = 90^\circ \quad \ldots(i)$$

[$\because$ a line drawn from the centre to bisect a chord is perpendicular to chord] and $\angle MEN = 90^\circ$ [given] ...(ii)

Now, in quadrilateral $OMEN$,

$\angle OME + \angle ONE + \angle MEN + \angle MON = 360^\circ$

[$\because$ angle sum property of quadrilateral]

$\Rightarrow \quad 90^\circ + 90^\circ + 90^\circ + \angle MON = 360^\circ$

[from Eqs. (i) and (ii)]

$\Rightarrow \quad \angle MON = 360^\circ - 270^\circ$

$\Rightarrow \quad \angle MON = 90^\circ$

Since, equal chords of a circle are equidistance from the centre.

$\therefore \quad OM = ON$

Therefore, adjacent sides are equal and all angles are 90° of quadrilateral $OMEN$.

Hence, $OMEN$ is a square. **Hence proved.**

2. Let CD and AB are the chords of the circle.

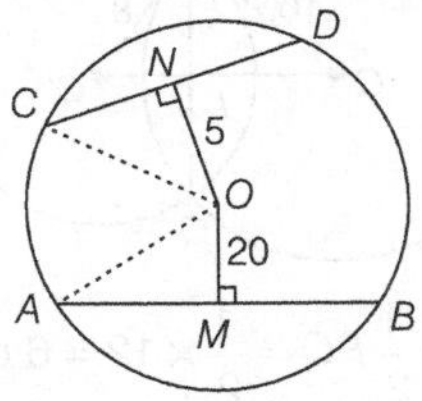

Draw $OM \perp AB$ and $ON \perp CD$

We know that perpendicular from the centre to a chord, bisects the chord.

$AM = MB$ and $CN = ND$ ...(i)

Since, $ON = 5$ cm

$\because \quad AM = \frac{1}{2}AB$

$\therefore \quad AM = \frac{10}{2}$ cm $= 5$ cm $= ON$ [$\because AB = 10$ cm]

In right angled ΔAMO and ΔCNO,

$AO = CO$ [radii]

$AM = ON$ [proved above]

$\angle OMA = \angle ONC$ [each 90°]

$\therefore \quad \Delta AMO \cong \Delta CNO$ [by RHS congruence rule]

$\Rightarrow \quad CN = OM = 20$ [by CPCT]

$CD = 2 \times CN = 2 \times 20 = 40$ cm

Hence, the length of another chord is 40 cm.

3. We know that the perpendicular from the centre of a circle to a chord, bisects the chord.

$\therefore \quad AC = CB = \frac{1}{2}AB = \frac{1}{2} \times 8 = 4$ cm [$\because AB = 8$ cm]

$\because \quad OA = 5$ cm [given]

In right angled ΔOCA, we have

$AO^2 = AC^2 + OC^2$ [by Pythagoras theorem]

$\Rightarrow \quad 5^2 = 4^2 + OC^2$

$\Rightarrow \quad 25 = 16 + OC^2$

$\Rightarrow \quad OC^2 = 25 - 16 = 9$

$\Rightarrow \quad OC = 3$ cm [taking +ve value]

Now, $\quad OA = OD$ [radii of same circle]

$\Rightarrow \quad OD = 5$ cm

$\therefore \quad CD = OD - OC = 5 - 3 = 2$ cm

Hence, the length of CD is 2 cm.

4. Draw $OP \perp BC$

Also, $OP \perp AD$

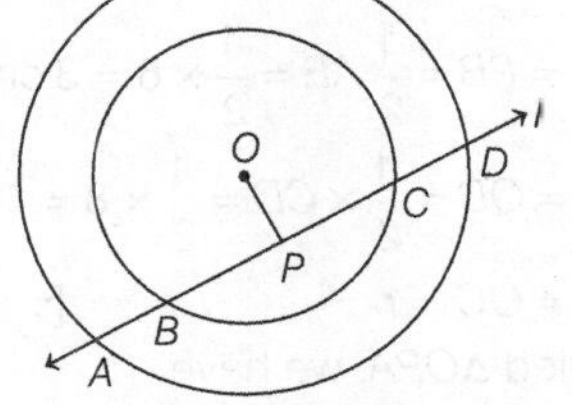

We know that the perpendicular to a chord from the centre of circle bisects the chord.

$\therefore \quad BP = PC = \frac{1}{2} \times BC = \frac{8}{2} = 4$ cm [$\because BC = 8$ cm]

and $\quad AP = PD = \frac{1}{2} \times AD = \frac{12}{2} = 6$ cm

[$\because AD = 12$ cm]

Now, $\quad AB = AP - BP$

$\Rightarrow \quad AB = 6 - 4$

$\Rightarrow \quad AB = 2$ cm

and $\quad CD = PD - PC$

$\Rightarrow \quad CD = 6 - 4 \Rightarrow CD = 2$ cm

Hence, the lengths of AB and CD are same i.e. 2 cm.

5. Given, $AB = 6$ cm, $CD = 12$ cm and $PM = 3$ cm

Clearly, $AM = MB = \frac{1}{2}AB = \frac{1}{2} \times 6 = 3$ cm

and $\quad CP = PD = \frac{1}{2}CD = \frac{1}{2} \times 12 = 6$ cm

[$\because$ line drawn through the centre of a circle bisect a chord]

Let radius $= r = OC = OD$ and $OP = y$ cm.

Then, $OM = OP + PM = (y + 3)$ cm

In right angled ΔOPC and ΔAMO,

$CP^2 + OP^2 = r^2$ and $AM^2 + OM^2 = r^2$

[by Pythagoras theorem]

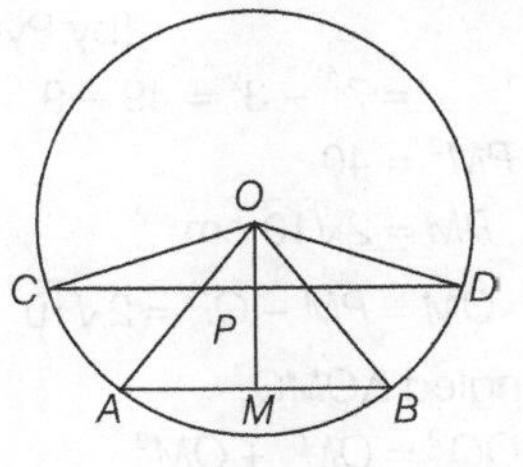

$\therefore \quad CP^2 + OP^2 = AM^2 + OM^2 = r^2$

$\Rightarrow \quad 6^2 + y^2 = 3^2 + (3 + y)^2 = r^2$ ...(i)

$\Rightarrow \quad 36 + y^2 = 9 + 9 + y^2 + 6y$

$[\because (a+b)^2 = a^2 + b^2 + 2ab]$

$\Rightarrow \quad 6y = 18$

$\Rightarrow \quad y = 3$ cm

$\therefore \quad r^2 = 6^2 + y^2 = 36 + 9 = 45$ [from Eq. (i)]

$\Rightarrow \quad r = 3\sqrt{5}$ cm $= 6.708 \approx 6.71$ cm

Hence, the radius of the circle is 6.71 cm.

6. Given, $AB = 6$ cm, $CD = 8$ cm and $OP = 4$ cm

Clearly, $AP = PB = \frac{1}{2}AB = \frac{1}{2} \times 6 = 3$ cm $\quad [\because OP \perp AB]$

and $\quad CQ = QD = \frac{1}{2} \times CD = \frac{1}{2} \times 8 = 4$ cm $[\because OQ \perp CD]$

Let $\quad OA = OC = r$ $\quad$ [$\because$ radii of the circle]

In right angled ΔOPA, we have

$OA^2 = OP^2 + AP^2$ $\quad$ [by Pythagoras theorem]

$\Rightarrow \quad (r)^2 = (4)^2 + (3)^2$

$[\because OP = 4$ cm and $AP = 3$ cm$]$

$\Rightarrow \quad r = \sqrt{16 + 9} = \sqrt{25}$

$\therefore \quad r = 5$ cm $\quad$ [taking +ve value]

In right angled ΔOQC, we have

$OC^2 = OQ^2 + QC^2$

$\Rightarrow \quad r^2 = OQ^2 + (4)^2$

$\Rightarrow \quad OQ = \sqrt{25 - 16} = \sqrt{9}$

$\therefore \quad OQ = 3$ cm $\quad$ [taking +ve value]

7. Let isosceles ΔPQR be inscribed in a circle with centre O and $PQ = PR = 7$ cm, $QR = 6$ cm.

Draw $OM \perp QR$.

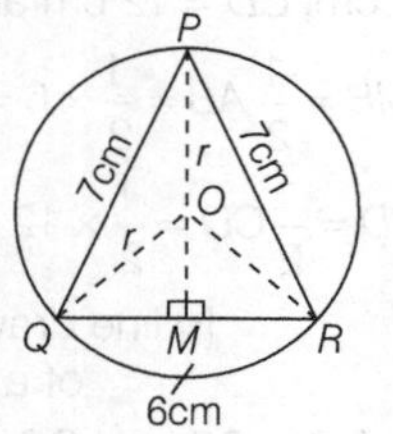

Now, $\quad QM = \frac{1}{2}QR = \frac{1}{2} \times 6 = 3$ cm $\quad [\because OM \perp QR]$

From right angled ΔPMQ,

$PM^2 = PQ^2 - QM^2$

[by Pythagoras theorem]

$= 7^2 - 3^2 = 49 - 9$

$PM^2 = 40$

$\therefore \quad PM = 2\sqrt{10}$ cm

$\therefore \quad OM = PM - OP = 2\sqrt{10} - r$

From right angled ΔOMQ,

$OQ^2 = QM^2 + OM^2$

$\Rightarrow \quad r^2 = 3^2 + (2\sqrt{10} - r)^2$

$\Rightarrow \quad r^2 = 9 + 40 + r^2 - 4\sqrt{10}r$

$[\because (a-b)^2 = a^2 - 2ab + b^2]$

$\Rightarrow \quad 4\sqrt{10}r = 49$

$\Rightarrow \quad r = \frac{49}{4\sqrt{10}}$

$\Rightarrow \quad r = \frac{49}{4\sqrt{10}} \times \frac{\sqrt{10}}{\sqrt{10}} = \frac{49\sqrt{10}}{40}$ cm

Hence, the radius of circle is $\frac{49\sqrt{10}}{40}$ cm.

8. Let O and O' be the centres of the circles of radii 10 cm and 8 cm respectively and PQ be their common chord of length 12 cm.

We have, $OP = 10$ cm, $O'P = 8$ cm and $PQ = 12$ cm

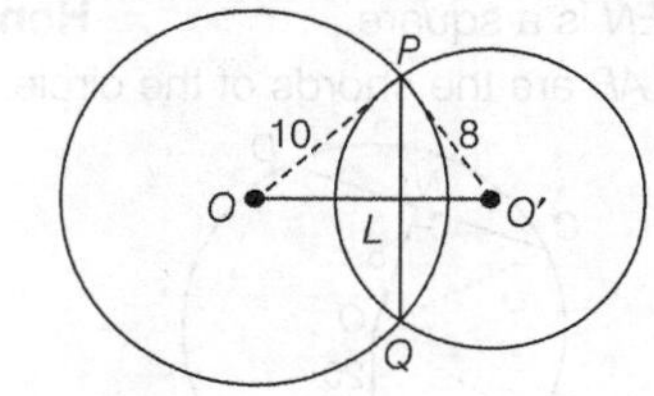

$\therefore \quad PL = \frac{1}{2}PQ = \frac{1}{2} \times 12 = 6$ cm

[when two circles intersect at two points, then their centres lie on the perpendicular bisector of the common chord]

In right angled ΔOLP,

$OP^2 = OL^2 + LP^2$ $\quad$ [by Pythagoras theorem]

$\Rightarrow \quad OL = \sqrt{OP^2 - LP^2}$

[taking +ve value]

$= \sqrt{10^2 - 6^2} = \sqrt{100 - 36} = \sqrt{64} = 8$ cm

Similarly, in right angled $\Delta O'LP$,

$O'P^2 = O'L^2 + LP^2$ $\quad$ [by Pythagoras theorem]

$\Rightarrow \quad O'L = \sqrt{O'P^2 - LP^2}$

$= \sqrt{8^2 - 6^2} = \sqrt{64 - 36}$

$= \sqrt{28} = 5.29$ cm $\quad$ [taking +ve value]

Hence, distance between their centres,

$OO' = OL + LO'$

$= (8 + 5.29) = 13.29$ cm

9. Given, AB and CD are two equal chords of a circle with centre O.

Draw $OM \perp AB$, $ON \perp CD$ and join OP.

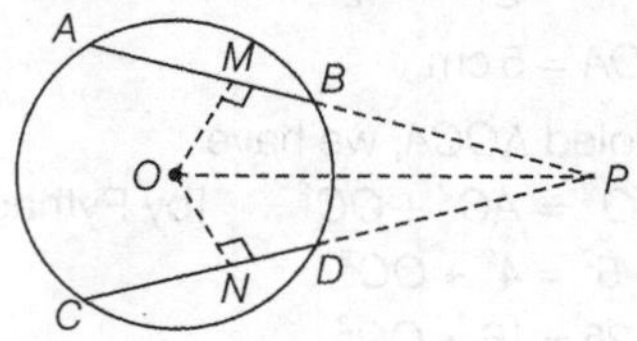

(i) We know that the perpendicular from the centre of a circle to a chord, bisects the chord.

$\therefore \quad AM = \frac{1}{2} AB = BM$

and $\quad CN = DN = \frac{1}{2} CD$

Thus, $AM = BM = CN = DN$ $\quad [\because AB = CD]$

In ΔOMP and ΔONP, we have

$\angle OMP = \angle ONP$ $[\because OM \perp AB$ and $ON \perp CD]$

$OP = OP$ $\quad$ [common]

$OM = ON$

[$\because$ equal chords of a circle are equidistant from the centre]

$\therefore \quad \Delta OMP \cong \Delta ONP$ $\quad$ [by RHS congruence rule]

$\Rightarrow \quad MP = NP$ $\quad$ [by CPCT]

Thus, $PA = PC$ $\quad [\because AM = CN]$

(ii) Since, $\quad PA = PC$

$\Rightarrow \quad AB + PB = CD + PD \Rightarrow PB = PD$ $\quad [\because AB = CD]$

10. Given, AB and CD are two chords of a circle with centre O, intersecting at a point P.

To prove $AB = CD$

Construction Draw $OE \perp AB$ and $OF \perp CD$

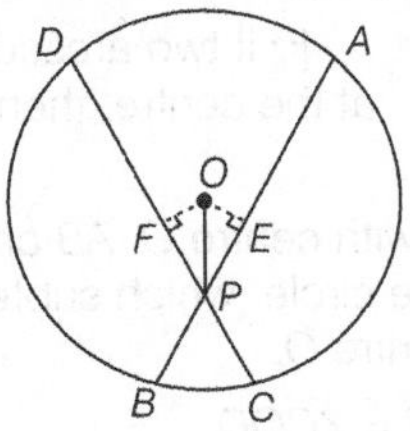

Proof In ΔOEP and ΔOFP,

$\angle OEP = \angle OFP$ $\quad$ [each 90°]

$OP = OP$ $\quad$ [common]

and $\quad \angle OPE = \angle OPF$ $\quad [\because OP$ bisects $\angle APD]$

$\therefore \quad \Delta OEP \cong \Delta OFP$ $\quad$ [by AAS congruence rule]

Then, $\quad OE = OF$ $\quad$ [by CPCT]

Thus, chords AB and CD are equidistant from the centre O of the circle, then we know that chords of a circle, which are equidistant from the centre, are equal.

$\therefore \quad AB = CD$ $\quad$ **Hence proved.**

11. We know that two equal chords of circles such that angles subtended by these chords at the centre O of the circle are equal.

i.e. $\quad \angle AOB = \angle COD$ $\quad$ ...(i)

Now, ΔAOB is isosceles triangle $\quad [\because AO = BO = \text{radius}]$

$\therefore \quad \angle OAB = \angle OBA$ $\quad$ [$\because$ angles opposite to equal sides of a triangle are equal]

$\therefore \quad \angle OAB = 55°$ $\quad$ ...(ii) $[\because \angle OBA = 55°]$

Now, we know that the sum of all angles of triangle is 180°.

In ΔAOB,

$\angle AOB + \angle OAB + \angle OBA = 180°$

$\Rightarrow \quad \angle AOB + 55° + 55° = 180°$ $\quad$ [from Eq. (ii)]

$\Rightarrow \quad \angle AOB = 180° - 110°$

$\Rightarrow \quad \angle AOB = 70°$

Now, from Eq. (i),

$\angle COD = 70°$

Hence, the measure of $\angle COD$ is 70°.

12. Given, three points A, B and C are on a circle such that $AB = BC = CA$.

We know that equal chords of a circle subtend equal angles at the centre of circle.

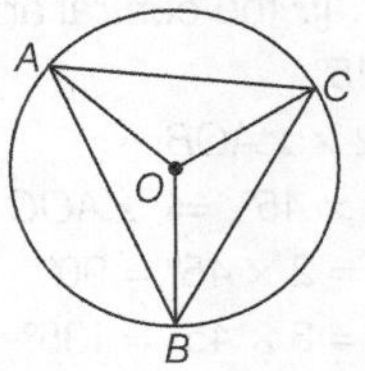

So, $\angle AOB = \angle BOC = \angle AOC$ $\quad$ ...(i)

Now, $\angle AOB + \angle BOC + \angle AOC = 360°$

[$\because$ sum of angles at a point is 360°]

$\Rightarrow \quad 3\angle AOB = 360°$ $\quad$ [from Eq. (i)]

$\Rightarrow \quad \angle AOB = \frac{360°}{3} = 120°$

Hence, the angle subtended by the chords AB, BC and CA at the centre O is 120°.

13. Let AXB and CYD be arcs of circle whose centre and radius are O and r units, respectively.

So, $\quad OA = OB = OC = OD = r$ $\quad$ ...(i)

$\because \quad$ arc $AXB \cong$ arc CYD

$\therefore \quad \angle AOB = \angle COD$ $\quad$ ...(ii)

[congruent arcs of a circle subtend equal angles at the centre]

In ΔAOB and ΔCOD,

$\Rightarrow \quad AO = CO$ $\quad$ [from Eq. (i)]

$BO = DO$ $\quad$ [from Eq. (i)]

and $\quad \angle AOB = \angle COD$ $\quad$ [from Eq. (ii)]

$\therefore \quad \Delta AOB \cong \Delta COD$ $\quad$ [by SAS congruence rule]

$\Rightarrow \quad AB = CD$ $\quad$ [by CPCT]

$\Rightarrow \quad \frac{AB}{CD} = \frac{1}{1}$

Hence, the ratio of AB and CD is 1 : 1.

14. Given, $AB = BC = CD = DE = EF = FG = GH = HA$

We know that equal arcs subtend equal angles at the centre of circle.

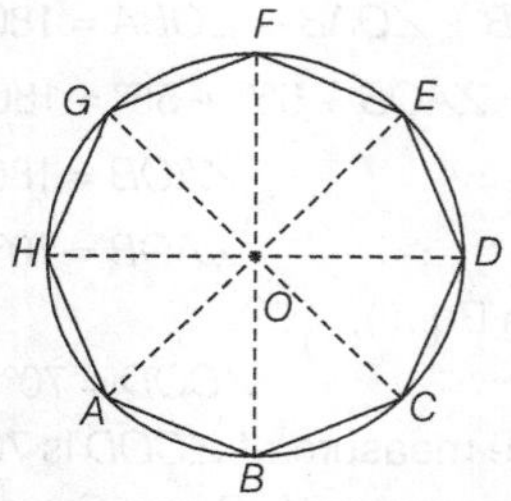

$\therefore \quad \angle AOB = \angle BOC = \angle COD = \angle DOE$

$= \angle EOF = \angle FOG = \angle GOH = \angle HOA$

$\Rightarrow 8 \times \angle AOB = 360°$

[∵ the central angle of a circle is 360°]

$\Rightarrow \quad \angle AOB = 45°$

Now, $\angle AOC = 2 \times \angle AOB$

$\Rightarrow \quad \angle AOC = 2 \times 45° \Rightarrow \angle AOC = 90°$

Similarly, $\angle DOF = 2 \times 45° = 90°$

and $\quad \angle EOH = 3 \times 45° = 135°$

Hence, the values of $\angle AOB$, $\angle AOC$, $\angle DOF$ and $\angle EOH$ are 45°, 90°, 90° and 135°, respectively.

15. Let AB be a chord of a circle having its centre O. Let PQ be the right bisector of the chord AB, intersecting AB at L and the arc AB at Q.

Since, the right bisector of a chord always passes through the centre.

So, PQ must pass through the centre O.

Join OA and OB.

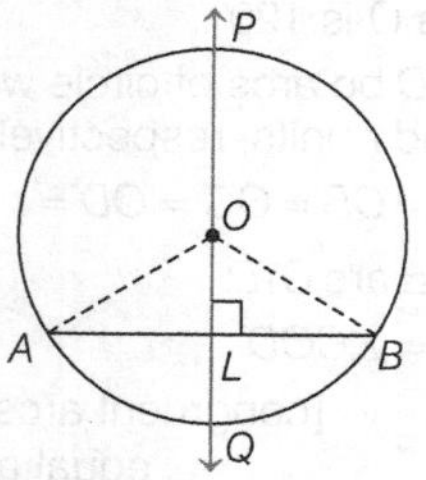

In ΔOLA and ΔOLB, we have

$OA = OB$ [radii of same circle]

$\angle ALO = \angle BLO = 90°$ [given]

$OL = OL$ [common]

$\therefore \quad \Delta OLA \cong \Delta OLB$ [by RHS congruence rule]

Then, $\angle AOL = \angle BOL$ [by CPCT]

$\therefore \quad \widehat{AQ} = \widehat{BQ}$ [∵ if two arcs subtend equal angles at the centre then the arcs are equal]

Hence proved.

16. Given A circle with centre O. Let AB and CD be two arcs of a circle such that angles subtended by these arcs at the centre O of a circle are equal i.e. $\angle AOB = \angle COD$.

To prove $\widehat{AB} = \widehat{CD}$

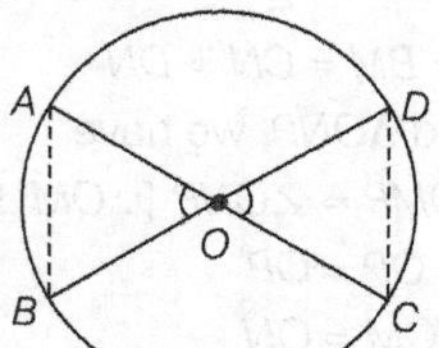

Construction Join AB and CD.

Proof In ΔAOB and ΔCOD, we have

$AO = CO$ [radii of same circle]

$\angle AOB = \angle COD$ [given]

and $\quad OB = OD$ [radii of same circle]

$\therefore \quad \Delta AOB \cong \Delta COD$ [by SAS congruence rule]

So, $\quad AB = CD$ [by CPCT]

We know that if two chords are equal, they cut-off equal arcs.

$\therefore \quad \widehat{AB} = \widehat{CD}$

[∵ if two arcssubtend equal angles at the centre, then the arcs are equal]

Hence proved.

17. Given A circle with centre O. AB and CD are two equal arcs of the circle, which subtend $\angle AOB$ and $\angle COD$ at the centre O.

To prove $\angle AOB = \angle COD$

Construction Join AB and CD.

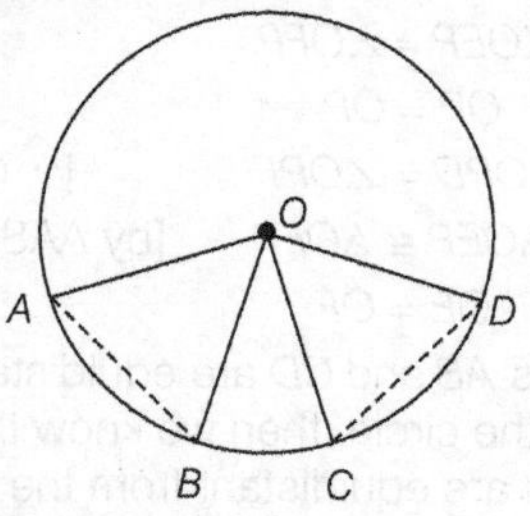

Proof In ΔAOB and ΔCOD,

$OA = OC$ [radii of same circle]

$OB = OD$ [radii of same circle]

$AB = CD$ [∵ $\widehat{AB} = \widehat{CD}$]

$\therefore \quad \Delta AOB \cong \Delta COD$ [by SSS congruence rule]

Then, $\quad \angle AOB = \angle COD$ [by CPCT] **Hence proved.**

Long Answer Type Questions

1. Given AB is a chord of a circle with centre O. A line OM is drawn through the centre O to the chord AB such that M is the mid-point of AB i.e. $AM = MB$.

To prove $OM \perp AB$

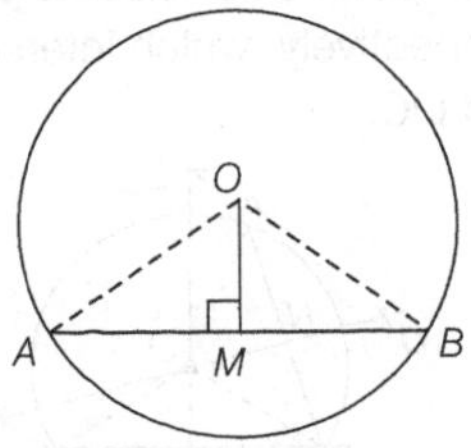

Construction Join OA and OB.

Proof In ΔOMA and ΔOMB, we have

$AM = MB$ [$\because$ M is the mid-point of AB]

$OA = OB$ [radii of same circle]

$OM = OM$ [common]

$\therefore \Delta OMA \cong \Delta OMB$ [by SSS congruence rule]

Then, $\angle OMA = \angle OMB$ [by CPCT] ...(i)

Now, AB is a straight line. So, by linear pair axiom,

$\angle OMA + \angle OMB = 180°$

$\Rightarrow 2\angle OMA = 180°$ [using Eq. (i)]

$\Rightarrow \angle OMA = \frac{180°}{2} = 90°$

Thus $\angle OMA = \angle OMB = 90°$

$\therefore OM \perp AB$ **Hence proved.**

2. Given AB and AC are two equal chords of circle with centre O. Also, $OP \perp AB$ at M and $OQ \perp AC$ at N.

To prove $PB = QC$

Proof We know that the perpendicular from the centre of a circle to a chord, bisects the chord.

$\therefore AM = MB = \frac{1}{2} AB$ [$\because OP \perp AB$]

and $AN = NC = \frac{1}{2} AC$ [$\because OQ \perp AC$]

Since, $AB = AC$

$\therefore \frac{1}{2} AB = \frac{1}{2} AC$

$\Rightarrow AM = MB = AN = NC$ ...(i)

$OM = ON$ ...(ii)

[$\because$ equal chords are equidistant from the centre]

$OP = OQ$ [radii of same circle] ...(iii)

$\Rightarrow OP - OM = OQ - ON$

[subtracting Eq. (ii) from Eq. (iii)]

$\Rightarrow PM = QN$ ...(iv)

Now, in ΔPMB and ΔQNC, we have

$MB = NC$ [from Eq. (i)]

$\angle PMB = \angle QNC$ [each 90°]

$\Rightarrow PM = QN$ [from Eq. (iv)]

$\therefore \Delta PMB \cong \Delta QNC$ [by SAS congruence rule]

$\Rightarrow PB = QC$ [by CPCT]

Hence proved.

3. Let MN and AB be two equal chords of a circle with centre O. AB and MN intersect at P and $MN = AB$.

To prove $MP = PB$ and $PN = AP$

Construction Draw $OD \perp MN$ and $OC \perp AB$. Join OP.

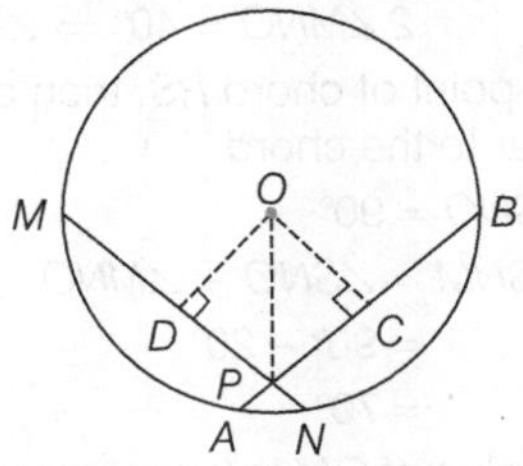

Proof Here, $DM = DN = \frac{1}{2} MN$

[$\because$ perpendicular from centre on the chord bisects the chord]

and $AC = CB = \frac{1}{2} AB$

[$\because$ perpendicular from centre on the chord bisects the chord]

Since, $MN = AB$, so we get

$DM = CB = DN = AC$ ...(i)

In right angled ΔODP and ΔOCP,

$OD = OC$ [$\because$ equal chords of a circle are equidistant from the centre]

$\angle ODP = \angle OCP$ [each 90°]

$OP = OP$ [common]

$\therefore \Delta ODP \cong \Delta OCP$ [by RHS congruence rule]

Then, $DP = PC$ [by CPCT] ...(ii)

On adding DM both sides, we get

$DM + DP = DM + PC$

$\Rightarrow DM + DP = CB + PC$ [from Eq. (i)]

$\Rightarrow MP = PB$

On subtracting Eq. (ii) from DN, we get

$DN - DP = DN - PC$

$\Rightarrow DN - DP = AC - PC$ [from Eq. (i)]

$\Rightarrow PN = AP$

Hence, $MP = PB$ and $PN = AP$ **Hence proved.**

4. Given, chord PQ = chord RS

$\because$ Two chords are equal, so both are at equidistant from the centre of the circle.

$\therefore OM = ON$

$\therefore OM = 3$ cm [$\because ON = 3$ cm]

and $\angle OMN = \angle MNO$ ...(i)

[$\because$ angles opposite to equal sides are equal]

Now, in ΔOMN,

$\angle OMN + \angle MNO + \angle NOM = 180°$

[$\because$ angle sum property of triangle]

$\Rightarrow \angle MNO + \angle MNO + 140° = 180°$

[from Eq. (i) and $\angle NOM = 140°$]

$\Rightarrow \quad 2\angle MNO = 180° - 140°$

$\Rightarrow \quad 2\angle MNO = 40° \Rightarrow \angle MNO = 20°$

N is the mid-point of chord RS, then centre of circle is perpendicular to the chord.

$\therefore \quad \angle SNO = 90°$

Now, $\quad \angle SNM = \angle SNO - \angle MNO$

$= 90° - 20° \quad [\because \angle MNO = 20°]$

$= 70°$

Hence, the value of OM is 3 cm and value of $\angle SNM$ is 70°.

5. Given A circle with centre O and two equal chords AB and PQ.

To Prove AB and PQ are equidistant from the centre O.

Construction Draw $OM \perp AB$ and $ON \perp PQ$.

Join OA, OB, OP and OQ.

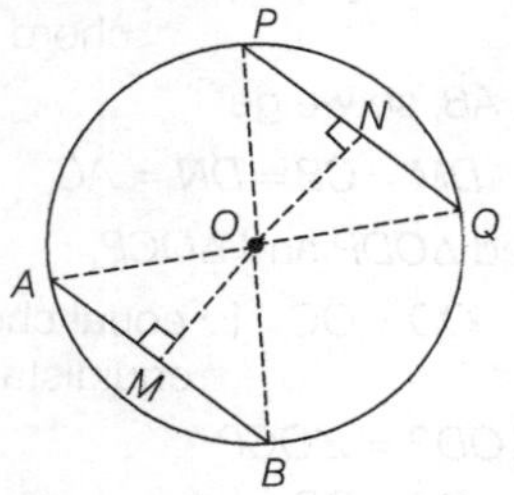

Proof We know that a perpendicular from the centre to a chord, bisects the chord.

$\therefore \quad AM = MB = \frac{1}{2} AB \quad [\because OM \perp AB]$

and $\quad PN = NQ = \frac{1}{2} PQ \quad [\because ON \perp PQ]$

Since, chord AB = Chord PQ [given]

$\Rightarrow \quad \frac{1}{2} AB = \frac{1}{2} PQ$

Then, $AM = MB = PN = NQ$

In right angled ΔOMA and ΔONQ,

$OA = OQ$ [radii of same circle]

$AM = NQ$ [proved above]

$\angle OMA = \angle ONQ$ [each 90°]

$\therefore \quad \Delta OMA \cong \Delta ONQ$ [by RHS congruence rule]

$\Rightarrow \quad OM = ON$ [by CPCT]

Hence, PQ and AB are equidistant from the centre O.

Hence proved.

6. Given Three non-collinear points A, B and C.

To prove There is one and only one circle, passing through the points A, B and C.

Construction Draw line segments AB and BC and then draw perpendicular bisectors DP and EQ of AB and BC, respectively, which intersect at point O. Join OA, OB and OC.

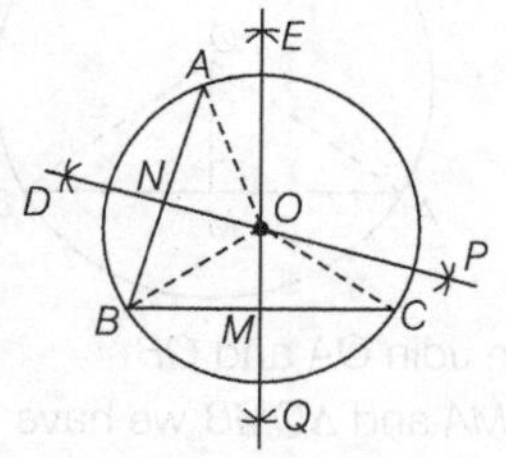

Proof Let perpendicular bisectors EQ and DP intersect BC and AB at M and N, respectively.

In ΔOMB and ΔOMC,

$BM = MC$

[$\because EQ$ is perpendicular bisector of BC]

$\angle OMB = \angle OMC$ [each 90°]

$OM = OM$ [common]

$\therefore \quad \Delta OMB \cong \Delta OMC$ [by SAS congruence rule]

Then, $\quad OB = OC$ [by CPCT] ...(i)

Similarly, $\Delta ONA \cong \Delta ONB$

Then, $\quad OA = OB$ ...(ii)

From Eqs. (i) and (ii), we get

$OA = OB = OC$ = Radius

Thus, circle of radius $OA = r$ with centre O passes through three non-collinear points A, B and C.

Hence proved.

7. (i) Given, $\overparen{AB} : \overparen{BC} = 3:2$

We know that equal arcs of a circle subtend equal angles at the centre.

$\therefore \quad \angle AOB : \angle BOC = 3:2$

$\Rightarrow \angle AOB = 3x$ and $\angle BOC = 2x$

and $\quad \angle AOB = 96°$ [given] ...(a)

$3x = 96°$

$x = 32$

Now, $\quad \angle BOC = 2x$

$\Rightarrow \quad \angle BOC = 2 \times 32$

$\Rightarrow \quad \angle BOC = 64°$ ...(b)

(ii) ΔBOC is an isosceles.

$OB = OC$ [radii of the same circle]

$\therefore \quad \angle OCB = \angle OBC$ ...(c)

[$\because$ opposite angles of equal sides are equal]

We know that the sum of all angles of triangle is 180°.

$\therefore \quad \angle BOC + \angle OBC + \angle OCB = 180°$

$\Rightarrow \quad 64° + \angle OBC + \angle OBC = 180°$ [from Eqs. (b) and (c)]

$\Rightarrow \quad 2\angle OBC = 180° - 64°$

$\Rightarrow \quad 2\angle OBC = 116°$

$\Rightarrow \quad \angle OBC = 58°$ ...(d)

Now, ΔOAB is also an isosceles.

$OB = OA$ [radii of the circle]

$\therefore \quad \angle BAO = \angle OBA$ ...(e)

[$\because$ opposite angles of equal sides are equal]

Now, $\angle AOB + \angle BAO + \angle OBA = 180°$

[$\because$ angle sum property of triangle]

$\Rightarrow \quad 96° + \angle OBA + \angle OBA = 180°$ [from Eqs. (a) and (e)]

$\Rightarrow \quad 96° + 2\angle OBA = 180°$

$\Rightarrow \quad 2\angle OBA = 180° - 96°$

$\Rightarrow \quad 2\angle OBA = 84°$

$\Rightarrow \quad \angle OBA = 42°$ ...(f)

Now, $\angle ABC = \angle OBA + \angle OBC$

$\angle ABC = 42° + 58°$ [from Eqs. (d) and (f)]

$\angle ABC = 100°$

Hence, the values of $\angle BOC$ and $\angle ABC$ are 64° and 100°, respectively.

8. (i) Let *BD* and *AC* be two chords of a circle, bisect at *P*.

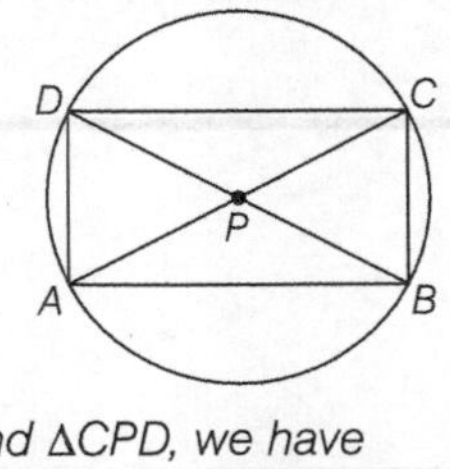

In ΔAPB and ΔCPD, we have

$PA = PC$ [$\because$ *P* is the mid-point of *AC*]

$\angle APB = \angle CPD$ [vertically opposite angles]

and $PB = PD$ [$\because$ *P* is the mid-point of *BD*]

$\therefore \quad \Delta CPD \cong \Delta APB$ [by SAS congruence rule]

Then, $CD = AB$ [by CPCT]

$\Rightarrow \quad \overset{\frown}{CD} = \overset{\frown}{AB}$ ...(a)

Similarly, in ΔCPB and ΔAPD,

$\overset{\frown}{CB} = \overset{\frown}{AD}$ ...(b)

On adding Eqs. (a) and (b), we get

$\Rightarrow \quad \overset{\frown}{CD} + \overset{\frown}{CB} = \overset{\frown}{AB} + \overset{\frown}{AD}$

$\Rightarrow \quad \overset{\frown}{BCD} = \overset{\frown}{BAD}$

Thus, *BD* divides the circle into two equal parts.

So, *BD* is a diameter.

Similarly, *AC* is a diameter.

(ii) Now, *BD* and *AC* bisect each other. So, *ABCD* is a parallelogram.

Also, $AC = BD$

Hence, *ABCD* is a rectangle. **Hence proved.**

14

STATISTICS

Data

The facts or figures (i.e. observation/information) which are numerical or otherwise; collected with a definite purpose, are called data.

We can define the two types of data on the basis of their sources.

- **Primary data** The data collected by the investigator himself for a definite plan or purpose, is known as primary data.
- **Secondary data** The data which are not collected directly but obtained from some other sources (published or unpublished), is known as secondary data.

Raw Data and Grouped Data

The data obtained in the original form is called **raw data**. When raw data is arranged as classes or grouped is called **grouped data**.

Important Terms Related to Statistics

- **Variable** The quantity which is being measured through the data is called variable.
  e.g. Height of students of a class.
  (i) **Continuous Variable** A variable which can take any numerical values between two given values.
  e.g. Weight of indiviual can be 50 kg, 50.5 kg, 50.8 kg etc.
  (ii) **Discontinuous** (or Discrete) **Variable** A variable which cannot take all possible numerical values between two given values.
  e.g. Number of member in a group can be 1, 2, 3 only not 1.5 or 2.5.
- **Variate** A particular value of a variable is called variate (observation).
- **Range** The difference between the maximum and minimum values of a variable is called its range.
- **Tabulation** Representation of data in the table form is called tabulation of the given data.
  e.g.

Class IX	Boys	Girls	Total
Section A	3	2	5
Section B	1	3	4
Section C	4	2	6
Total	8	7	15

- **Frequency** The frequency is the number which indicates how many times a variate appear in the given set of data.
- **Frequency Distribution** A tabular arrangement of given numerical data showing the frequency of different variates and the table itself is called frequency distribution table.

Presentation of Data

Presentation of data means to present or organise the collected data in a simple form which can be easily analysed and interpreted by the user. There are various ways to represent a collected data.

Some of them are given below

Presentation of Data in Ascending or Descending Order

Consider the marks obtained by 10 students in a Mathematics test as given below

55, 36, 95, 73, 60, 42, 25, 78, 75, 62

The data in this form is called **raw data.** Now, arrange this raw data in ascending order as

25, 36, 42, 55, 60, 62, 73, 75, 78, 95

Now, we can clearly see that the lowest mark is 25 and the highest mark is 95.

Here, range $= 95 - 25 = 70$

If the raw data is arranged in ascending or descending order of magnitude, then it is called an **array** or **arranged data**

Presentation of Data in the Form of Ungrouped Frequency Distribution

If the number of observations (in a data) is large, then it takes much time to arrange them in ascending or descending order.

In this case of observations, data can be easily presented by using frequency distribution method. To present given data in the form of ungrouped frequency distribution or simply a frequency distribution table, we write observations in one column and the corresponding frequency in second column.

The number of occurrence of an observation is called **frequency** of the observation.

e.g. Consider the marks obtained (out of 100 marks) by 30 students of Class IX of a school are

10, 20, 36, 92, 95, 40, 50, 56, 60, 70, 92, 88, 80, 70, 72, 70, 36, 40, 36, 40, 92, 40, 50, 50, 56, 60, 70, 60, 60, 88

The representation of this data in the form of a frequency distribution table is

Marks	Number of students (Frequency)	Marks	Number of students (Frequency)
10	1	70	4
20	1	72	1
36	3	80	1
40	4	88	2
50	3	92	3
56	2	95	1
60	4	**Total**	30

Data Presented by using Tally Marks

To represent data using tally marks, we use following steps

Step I We take each observation from the data, one at a time and represent the frequency by small line or stroke called tally marks.

Step II We write tally marks in bunches of five lines, the fifth one crossing the four vertical lines diagonally.

e.g. 5 represented as 𝍸 and 7 represented as 𝍸 ||.

Step III In table, sum of all frequencies is equal to the total number of observations in the given data.

e.g. Three coins tossed 30 times. Each time the number of heads occurring was noted down as follows

0, 1, 2, 2, 1, 2, 3, 1, 3, 0, 1, 3, 3, 0, 1

0, 1, 1, 2, 1, 2, 2, 0, 3, 1, 2, 2, 2, 1, 0

To construct a frequency distribution table by using tally marks is given below

Number of heads	Tally marks	Frequency
0	𝍸 |	6
1	𝍸 𝍸	10
2	𝍸 ||||	9
3	𝍸	5
Total		30

Presentation of Data in the Form of Grouped Frequency Distribution

When a data has a large number of values (entries) as $x_1, x_2, \ldots, x_n$ and most of them are distinct, it becomes inconvenient to present this data in the form of ungrouped frequency distribution.

Here, we condense the data into finite number of groups as 20-29, 30-39, ... etc.

These groupings are called **classes** or **class intervals.** In each of these classes, the least number is called the **lower class limit** and the greatest number is called the **upper class limit**.

The difference between the upper class limit and lower class limit is called **class size** or **class width.**

The number midway between the lower and upper limits is called **classmark.**

$$\text{Class mark} = \frac{\text{Lower limit} + \text{Upper limit}}{2}$$

The number of entries of the data having their values lying in a class is defined as the frequency of the class. The table in which the corresponding frequencies are written against each class, is called the **frequency distribution** of given data.

Types of Grouped Frequency Distribution

- **Exclusive form** (*Continuous form*) A frequency distribution in which upper limit of each class is excluded and lower limit is included, is called an *exclusive form.*

  e.g. In class 0-10, we include 0 and exclude 10 and in class 10-20, we include 10 and exclude 20.
- **Inclusive form** (*Discontinuous form*) A frequency distribution in which each upper limit as well as lower limit are included, is called an *inclusive form.*

  e.g. In 0-10, both 0 and 10 are included; in class 11-20, both 11 and 20 are included, etc.

To Convert Discontinuous Form in Continuous Form

To convert the intervals in continuous form, firstly we find the difference between the upper limit of a class and the lower limit of its succeeding class that is adjustment factor, then add and subtract half of this difference to upper limit and lower limit, respectively.

e.g. Consider the intervals 11-20 and 21-30.

Here, lower limit of 21-30 = 21

and upper limit of 11-20 = 20

Now, difference = 21 − 20 = 1

$\therefore$ Half of the difference $= \frac{1}{2} = 0.5$

So, the new class interval formed from 11-20 is

(11 − 0.5)-(20 + 0.5) i.e. 10.5-20.5

Similarly, the new class interval formed from 21-30 is

(21 − 0.5)-(30 + 0.5) i.e. 20.5-30.5.

Thus, we get the continuous classes as 10.5-20.5 and 20.5-30.5.

Cumulative Frequency

The sum of frequency of all the previous classes and that particular class is called the cumulative frequency of the class. Suppose the marks of 72 students in a test were recorded as follows :

Marks	10-19	20-29	30-39	40-49	50-59
Number of Students	7	11	20	16	18

Now, we can draw the cumulative frequency table for above record as

Marks	Tally	Number of Students (Frequency)	Cumulative Frequency
10-19	𝍸 ||	7	7
20-29	𝍸 𝍸 |	11	7 + 11 = 18
30-39	𝍸 𝍸 𝍸 𝍸	20	18 + 20 = 38
40-49	𝍸 𝍸 𝍸 |	16	38 + 16 = 54
50-59	𝍸 𝍸 𝍸 |||	18	54 + 18 = 72

Mean or Arithmetic Mean

The average of a given set of numbers, is called the arithmetic mean or the mean and denoted by $\bar{x}$.

$$\therefore \quad \text{Mean, } \bar{x} = \frac{\text{Sum of all observations}}{\text{Number of observations}}$$

Thus, the mean of n observations $x_1, x_2, x_3, \ldots, x_n$ is given by

$$\bar{x} = \frac{(x_1 + x_2 + \ldots + x_n)}{n} = \frac{\sum_{i=1}^{n} x_i}{n} = \frac{\sum x}{n}$$

Example 1. If following are the marks obtained by 5 students of a class, then find their mean.

10, 5, 20, 25, 15

Sol. Mean, $\bar{x} = \frac{\Sigma x}{n} = \frac{10 + 5 + 20 + 25 + 15}{5} = \frac{75}{5} = 15$

Mean of Ungrouped Frequency Distribution

If $x_1, x_2, \ldots, x_n$ are n observations whose corresponding frequencies are $f_1, f_2, \ldots, f_n$, then mean is given by

$$\bar{x} = \frac{x_1 f_1 + x_2 f_2 + \ldots + x_n f_n}{f_1 + f_2 + \ldots + f_n} = \frac{\sum_{i=1}^{n} f_i x_i}{\sum_{i=1}^{n} f_i}$$

Example 2. Find the mean of the following distribution.

Variable	5	6	7	8	9
Frequency	4	8	14	11	3

Sol. Mean $= \frac{\Sigma f_i x_i}{\Sigma f_i} = \frac{5 \times 4 + 6 \times 8 + 7 \times 14 + 8 \times 11 + 9 \times 3}{4 + 8 + 14 + 11 + 3}$

$= \frac{20 + 48 + 98 + 88 + 27}{40}$

$= \frac{281}{40} = 7.025$

Median

The value of the middle most observation when data is arranged in ascending / descending order, is called the median of the data.

Median of Ungrouped Data

Suppose there are n observations, first arrange the given observations in ascending or descending order.

(i) If n is odd, then Median = Value of $\left(\frac{n+1}{2}\right)$th observation

(ii) If n is even, then Median $=\frac{1}{2}\left[\text{Value of }\left(\frac{n}{2}\right)\text{th observation} + \text{Value of }\left(\frac{n}{2}+1\right)\text{th observation}\right]$

Example 3. The percentage of marks obtained by students of a class in Mathematics are 65, 35, 37, 23, 0, 18, 82, 92, 72, 32, 10, 5. Find the median.

Sol. First, we write the given data in ascending order.

0, 5, 10, 18, 23, 32, 35, 37, 65, 72, 82, 92

Here, the number of observations is even, i.e. $n = 12$

$\therefore$ There are two middle terms $\frac{12}{2}$th and $\left(\frac{12}{2}+1\right)$th i.e. 6th and 7th terms.

So, the median is the mean of the values of the 6th and 7th terms.

$\therefore$ Median $=\frac{1}{2}$ [value of 6th observation + value of 7th observation]

$\therefore$ Median $=\frac{32+35}{2}=\frac{67}{2}=33.5$ [$\because$ 6th term = 32, 7th term = 35]

Frequency Polygon

A frequency polygon is the polygon obtained by joining the mid-points of upper horizontal sides of all the rectangles in the histogram. Frequency polygons can also be drawn independently without drawing histograms.

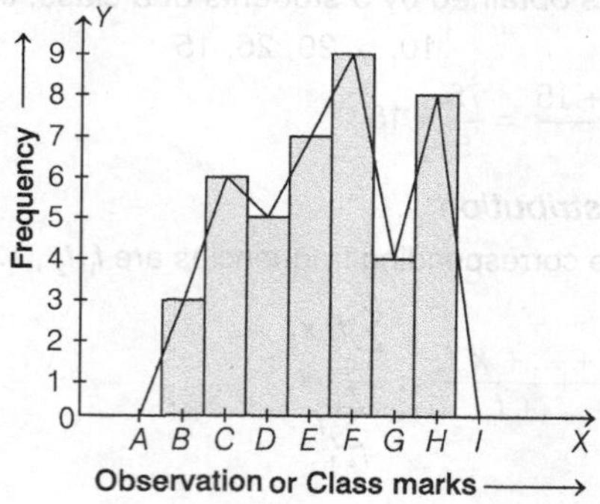

EXAM ORIENTED QUESTIONS

TYPE - 1 01 Mark

Multiple Choice Questions

Q.1 The points scored by a basketball team in a series of matches are follows

17, 7, 10, 25, 5, 10, 18, 10 and 24

Then, the range is

(a) 24 (b) 25 (c) 21 (d) 20

Q.2 The raw data, arranged in ascending or descending order is

(a) primary data (b) grouped data
(c) arrayed data (d) secondary data

Q.3 If m is the mid-point and l is the upper limit of a class in a continuous frequency distribution, then lower limit of the class is

(a) $m-2l$ (b) $2m-l$
(c) $m+2l$ (d) $2m+l$

Q.4 If lower limit of a class is 10 and upper limit of previous class is 8, then adjustment factor is

(a) 9 (b) 1
(c) 2 (d) 0.5

Q.5 A frequency distribution is given below.

Class interval	Frequency
10-15	5
15-20	8
20-25	3
25-30	11
30-35	6

The cumulative frequency of class (25-30) is

(a) 11 (b) 33
(c) 16 (d) 27

Q.6 If the mean of the data 6, 8, 10, 3, 7 and m is 7, then the value of m is

(a) 6 (b) 7
(c) 8 (d) 9

Q.7 The mean of the factors of 24 is

(a) 7.6 (b) 7.5
(c) 5.7 (d) 5.6

Q.8 The mean of prime numbers between 20 and 30 is

(a) 26 (b) 27
(c) 28 (d) 25

Q.9 If the mean of the data $x_1, x_2, x_3, \ldots, x_n$ is α, then the mean of the data $x_1+a, x_2+a, x_3+a, \ldots, x_n+a$ is

(a) $\alpha-a$ (b) $\alpha+a$
(c) $\alpha-2a$ (d) $2\alpha+a$

Q.10 The mean of 16 numbers is 50. If 3 is multiplied to every number, then the new mean is

(a) 150 (b) 53
(c) 47 (d) 48

Q.11 The mean of 100 observations was found to be 30. If two observations were wrongly taken as 32 and 12 instead of 23 and 11, then the correct mean is

(a) 29 (b) 30
(c) 29.90 (d) 28

Q.12 The weight (in kg) of 7 students are given below

32.5, 36.4, 39.2, 41.3, 42.9, 37.2, 41.2

Then, its median is

(a) 39.2 (b) 41.3
(c) 42.9 (d) 41.2

Q.13 The data 32, 35, 54, 56, x, $x+2$, 78, 84, 90 and 100 are arranged in ascending order, if their median is 63, then the value of x is

(a) 61 (b) 62
(c) 63 (d) 64

Q.14 The numbers are given below

2, 5, 9, 6, 4, 8, 5, 13, 2, 31.

Which of the following is true?

(a) Mean = Median (b) Mean < Median
(c) Mean > Median (d) None of these

Q.15 A frequency polygon is constructed by plotting frequency of the class interval and the

(a) mid value of the class.
(b) lower limit of the class.
(c) upper limit of the class.
(d) None of the above

Answers

1. (d)	2. (c)	3. (b)	4. (b)	5. (d)
6. (c)	7. (b)	8. (a)	9. (b)	10. (a)
11. (c)	12. (a)	13. (b)	14. (c)	15. (a)

TYPE - 2 01 Mark

Assertion-Reason Type Questions

Q.1 Assertion (A) The range of the data 16, 19, 23, 13, 11, 25, 18 is 14.

Reason (R) The difference between the maximum and minimum values of a variable is called its range.

(a) A is true, R is false.
(b) A is false, R is true.
(c) Both A and R are true and R is the correct reason for A.
(d) Both A and R are true and R is incorrect reason for A.

Q.2 Assertion (A) If two overlapping intervals of equal size are 10-20 and 20-30, then the class marks are 15 and 25, respectively.

Reason (R) The class mark of a class interval

$$= \frac{\text{Lower limit} + \text{Upper limit}}{2}$$

(a) A is true, R is false.
(b) A is false, R is true.
(c) Both A and R are true and R is the correct reason for A.
(d) Both A and R are true and R is incorrect reason for A.

Q.3 Assertion (A) The adjustment factor for the class intervals 0-5, 6-11, 12-17, 18-23 and 24-29 is 1.5.

Reason (R) Adjustment factor

$$= \frac{\text{Lower limit of one class} - \text{Upper limit of previous class}}{2}$$

(a) A is true, R is false.
(b) A is false, R is true.
(c) Both A and R are true and R is the correct reason for A.
(d) Both A and R are true and R is incorrect reason for A.

Q.4 Assertion (A) The mean of the observations 2, 4, 6, 8, 10, 12, 14 is 8.

Reason (R) The mean of the first n even natural numbers is given by $\left(\frac{n+1}{2}\right)$.

(a) A is true, R is false.
(b) A is false, R is true.
(c) Both A and R are true and R is the correct reason for A.
(d) Both A and R are true and R is incorrect reason for A.

Q.5 Assertion (A) The median of the observations 15, 40, 25, 16, 28, 32, 36, 42, 16, 19, 28 is 28.

Reason (R) If $\overline{x}$ is the mean of n numbers of observations $x_1, x_2, x_3 \ldots . x_n$, then the mean of observations $x_1 + a, x_2 + a, x_3 + a, \ldots . x_n + a$ is $\overline{x} + a$.

(a) A is true, R is false.
(b) A is false, R is true.
(c) Both A and R are true and R is the correct reason for A.
(d) Both A and R are true and R is incorrect reason for A.

Answers

1. (c) **2.** (c) **3.** (b) **4.** (a) **5.** (d)

TYPE - 3 01 Mark

Statement Based Questions

Q.1 Statement I The mean of the first five prime numbers is 5.6.

Statement II The adjustment factor for class 0-10 and 11-20 will be 5.

Which of the following is valid?
(a) Both the Statements are true.
(b) Both the Statements are false.
(c) Statement I is true and Statement II is false.
(d) Statement I is false and Statement II is true.

Q.2 Statement I The observations 24, 27, 43, 48, $x - 1$, $x + 3$, 68, 73, 80 90, have been arranged in ascending order. If the median of these observations is 58, then the value of x is 59.

Statement II The mean of 25 numbers is 12. If 2 is subtracted from each number, then new mean will be 10.

Which of the following is valid?
(a) Both the Statements are true.
(b) Both the Statements are false.
(c) Statement I is true and Statement II is false.
(d) Statement I is false and Statement II is true.

Q.3 Statement I The median of the following data. 2.0025, 2.0205, – 2.206, – 2.006 is – 0.00185.

Statement II The weight (in kg) of 7 students are 32.5, 36.4, 39.2, 41.3, 42.9, 37.2 and 41.2, then its median is 41.2.

Which of the following is valid?
(a) Both the Statements are true.
(b) Both the Statements are false.
(c) Statement I is true and Statement II is false.
(d) Statement I is false and Statement II is true.

Q.4 Statement I The mid-value of a class interval is 25 and the class size is 8. The class interval is 21-29.

Statement II A frequency polygon is constructed by plotting frequency of the class interval and the mid-value of the class.

Which of the following is valid?

(a) Both the Statements are true.
(b) Both the Statements are false.
(c) Statement I is true and Statement II is false.
(d) Statement I is false and Statement II is true.

Answers

1. (c) 2. (d) 3. (b) 4. (a)

TYPE - 4 — 03 Marks

Short Answer Type Questions

Q.1 The heights of 50 students, measured to the nearest centimetres have been found to be as follows

161, 150, 154, 165, 168, 161, 154, 162, 150, 151, 162, 164, 171, 165, 158, 154, 156, 172, 160, 170, 153, 159, 161, 170, 162, 165, 166, 168, 165, 164, 154, 152, 153, 156, 158, 162, 160, 161, 173, 166, 161, 159, 162, 167, 168, 159, 158, 153, 154, 159

(i) Represent the data given above by a grouped frequency distribution table, taking class intervals as 160-165, 165-170 etc., using tally marks.

(ii) What can you conclude about their heights from the table?

Q.2 The distance (in km) between workplace and the residence of 40 engineers are given below

5, 3, 10, 20, 25, 11, 13, 7, 12, 31, 19, 10, 12, 17, 18, 11, 32, 17, 16, 2, 7, 9, 7, 8, 3, 5, 12, 15, 18, 3, 12, 14, 2, 9, 6, 15, 15, 7, 6, 12

Construct a grouped frequency distribution table with class size 5 for the data given above taking the first interval as 0-5 (5 is not included). What main features do you observe from this tabular representation?

Q.3 The relative humidity (in %) of a certain city for a month of 30 days was as follows

98.1, 98.6, 99.2, 90.3, 86.5, 95.3, 92.9, 96.3, 94.2, 95.1, 89.2, 92.3, 97.1, 93.5, 92.7, 95.1, 97.2, 93.3, 95.2, 97.3, 96.2, 92.1, 84.9, 90.2, 95.7, 98.3, 97.3, 96.1, 92.1, 89.0

(i) Construct a grouped frequency distribution table with classes 84-86, 86-88 etc.

(ii) Which month or season do you think this data is about?

Q.4 (i) Find the mean $(\overline{x})$ of first 5 even natural numbers.

(ii) If x denotes the even natural numbers, taken in part (i), show that $\Sigma(x - \overline{x}) = 0$.

Q.5 If the mean of observations p, $p + 2$, $p + 4$, $p + 6$ and $p + 8$ is 11, then find

(i) the value of p.
(ii) the mean of first three observations.

Q.6 Find the mean of 8, 12, 16, 22, 10 and 4. Find the resulting mean, if each of the observations, given above be

(i) increased by 25%
(ii) decreased by 40%

Q.7 If the mean of the following data is 18.75, then find the value of p.

x_i	10	15	p	25	30
f_i	5	10	7	8	2

Q.8 If the mean of the following data is 20.2, then find the value of p.

x_i	10	15	20	25	30
f_i	6	8	p	10	6

Q.9 The mean of the following distribution is 50.

x	10	30	50	70	90
f	17	$5a + 3$	32	$7a - 11$	19

Find the value of a.

Q.10 The pass percentage in different subjects and the number of students who appeared in the subjects are given below.

Subjects	Number of students	Pass percentage
English	45	66
Hindi	40	95
Sanskrit	20	80
Mathematics	60	55
Science and Technology	55	70
Social Science	60	60

Find the arithmetic mean of pass percentage.

Q.11 The following table presents the number of illiterate females in the age group (10-34) in a town.

Number of females	300	980	800	580	290
Age group	10-14	15-19	20-24	25-29	30-34

Draw a histogram to represent the above data.

Q.12 The length of 40 leaves of a plant measured correct to one millimetre and the obtained data is represented in the following table.

Length (in mm)	Number of leaves
118-126	3
127-135	5
136-144	9
145-153	12
154-162	5
163-171	4
172-180	2

(i) Draw a histogram to represent the given data.
(ii) Is there any other suitable graphical representation for the same data?
(iii) Is it correct to conclude that the maximum number of leaves are 153 mm long and why?

Q.13 The water bills (in rupees) of 32 houses in a locality are given below

30, 48, 52, 78, 103, 85, 37, 94, 72, 73, 66, 52, 92, 65, 78, 81, 64, 60, 75, 78, 108, 63, 71, 54, 59, 75, 100, 103, 35, 89, 95, 73 taking class intervals 30-40, 40-50, 50-60, ... form frequency distribution table. Construct a combined histogram and frequency polygon.

Answers

1. (ii) more than 50% of students (i.e. 12 + 9 + 14 = 35) are shorter than 165 cm height.
3. (ii) the data appears to be taken in the rainy season as the relative humidity is high.
4. (i) 6
5. (i) 7 (ii) 9
6. 12 (i) 15 (ii) 7.2
7. 20
8. 20
9. 5
10. 68.28
12. (ii) Frequency polygon
(iii) No, because the maximum number of leaves have their lengths lying in the interval 145-153.

TYPE - 5 4/5 Marks

Long Answer Type Questions

Q.1 Use the following table to find

Class	Frequency
18-22	5
23-27	8
28-32	13
33-37	9
38-42	7
43-47	5
48-52	2

(i) upper and lower limits of 5th class.
(ii) true class limits of the 5th class.
(iii) class boundaries of 3rd class.
(iv) class mark of 4th class.
(v) width of 6th class.

Q.2 The following table gives the life-times of 400 neon lamps.

Life-times (in hours)	Number of lamps
300-400	14
400-500	56
500-600	60
600-700	86
700-800	74
800-900	62
900-1000	48

(i) Represent the given information with the help of a histogram.
(ii) How many lamps have a life-time of more than 700 h?

Q.3 Draw a frequency polygon for each of the following frequency distribution.
(i) Using histogram
(ii) Without using histogram

Class interval	10-30	30-50	50-70	70-90	90-110	110-130	130-150
Frequency	4	7	5	9	5	6	4

Q.4 Draw a frequency polygon for the following frequency distribution.

Class interval	Frequency
1-10	8
11-20	3
21-30	6
31-40	12
41-50	2
51-60	7

Q.5 The following table gives the distribution of students of two sections according to the marks obtained by them.

Section A		Section B	
Marks	Frequency	Marks	Frequency
0-10	3	0-10	5
10-20	9	10-20	19
20-30	17	20-30	15
30-40	12	30-40	10
40-50	9	40-50	1

Represent the marks of the students of both on the same graph by two frequency polygons. From the two polygons, compare the performance of the two sections.

Q.6 Draw a frequency polygon representing the following frequency distribution.

Class intervals	30-34	35-39	40-44	45-49	50-54	55-59
Frequency	12	16	20	8	10	4

Q.7 Given below are the marks obtained by 30 students in Mathematics exam

2, 7, 11, 13, 10, 18, 20, 23, 17, 18, 16, 11, 13, 18, 24, 25, 27, 30, 31, 36, 37, 8, 11, 13, 16, 15, 18, 27, 20, 3

Arrange the data in increasing order and present the same as a grouped data in

(i) discontinuous interval form, taking class intervals as 1-5, 6-10, 11-15, etc.

(ii) continuous interval form, taking class intervals as 1-5, 5-9, 9-13, etc.

Q.8 A company analysed the weekly working hours of its employees and record the following data.

Weekly working hours	Number of hours
20-30	5
30-40	10
40-50	20
50-60	25
60-70	15
70-80	30

(i) Draw a frequency polygon representing the data.

(ii) Find the cumulative frequency of class 50-60.

Answers

1. (i) Upper limit = 42 and lower limit = 38
(ii) 37.5 and 42.5 (iii) 27.5 and 32.5
(iv) 35 (v) 5

2. (ii) 184

7. (i) Discontinuous interval form

Class interval	Frequency
1-5	2
6-10	3
11-15	7
16-20	9
21-25	3
26-30	3
31-35	1
36-40	2

(ii) Continuous interval form

Class interval	Frequency
1-5	2
5-9	2
9-13	4
13-17	6
17-21	7
21-25	2
25-29	3
29-33	2
33-37	1
37-41	1

8. (ii) 60

EXPLANATIONS

Multiple Choice Questions

1. (d) Given, 17, 7, 10, 25, 5, 10, 18, 10 and 24

Now, range = Maximum value − Minimum value

$= 25 - 5 = 20$

2. (c) We know that the raw data, arranged in ascending or descending order is called the arrayed data.

3. (b) We know that

$$\text{Class mark} = \frac{\text{Lower limit} + \text{Upper limit}}{2}$$

$$\Rightarrow \quad m = \frac{\text{Lower limit} + l}{2}$$

$$\Rightarrow \quad 2m = \text{Lower limit} + l$$

$$\Rightarrow \quad \text{Lower limit} = 2m - l$$

4. (b) Given, lower limit of a class = 10

and upper limit of previous class = 8

Now, adjustment factor

$$= \frac{\text{Lower limit of one class} - \text{Upper limit of previous class}}{2}$$

$$= \frac{10-8}{2} = 1$$

5. (d) The cumulative frequency table is

Class interval	Frequency	Cumulative frequency
10-15	5	5
15-20	8	13
20-25	3	16
25-30	11	27
30-35	6	33

Hence, cumulative frequency of class (25-30) is 27.

6. (c) We have, 6, 8, 10, 3, 7 and m

and mean = 7

$$\because \quad \text{Mean} = \frac{\text{Sum of all observations}}{\text{Number of observations}}$$

$$\therefore \quad 7 = \frac{6+8+10+3+7+m}{6}$$

$$\Rightarrow \quad 42 = 34 + m$$

$$\Rightarrow \quad m = 8$$

7. (b) Factors of 24 are 1, 2, 3, 4, 6, 8, 12, 24.

Now, mean of the factors

$$= \frac{1+2+3+4+6+8+12+24}{8} = \frac{60}{8} = 7.5$$

8. (a) The prime numbers between 20 and 30 are 23 and 29.

Now, mean of 23 and 29 $= \frac{23+29}{2} = \frac{52}{2} = 26$

9. (b) Given, the mean of the data $x_1, x_2, x_3, \ldots x_n$ is α.

We know that if each observation under consideration is increased by quantity a, then their mean is also increased by the same quantity a.

$\therefore$ The mean of the data,

$x_1 + a, x_2 + a, x_3 + a, \ldots x_n + a$ is $\alpha + a$.

10. (a) Let the given numbers be $x_1, x_2, \ldots\ldots x_{16}$.

$$\therefore \quad \text{Mean} = \frac{x_1 + x_2 + x_3 + \ldots + x_{16}}{16}$$

$$\Rightarrow \quad 50 = \frac{x_1 + x_2 + x_3 + \ldots + x_{16}}{16}$$

[$\because$ mean = 50 (given)]

$$\Rightarrow \quad x_1 + x_2 + \ldots\ldots + x_{16} = 800 \quad \ldots(i)$$

$\because$ 3 is multiplied to every number.

$\therefore$ New numbers are $3x_1, 3x_2, 3x_3, \ldots\ldots 3x_{16}$.

$$\text{Mean of new numbers} = \frac{3x_1 + 3x_2 + 3x_3 + \ldots + 3x_{16}}{16}$$

$$= \frac{3}{16}(x_1 + x_2 + \ldots + x_{16})$$

$$= \frac{3}{16} \times 800 \quad \text{[from Eq. (i)]}$$

$$= 150$$

Hence, the new mean is 150.

11. (c) Given, number of observations, $n = 100$

and mean of the observations = 30

$$\because \text{Mean} = \frac{\text{Sum of all observations}}{\text{Number of observations}}$$

$\therefore$ Sum of 100 observations $= 30 \times 100$

$= 3000$

According to the question,

two observations were wrongly taken as 32 and 12 instead of 23 and 11.

$\therefore$ Correct sum of 100 observations

$= 3000 - (32 + 12) + (23 + 11)$

$= 2990$

Now, correct mean $= \frac{2990}{100} = 29.9$

12. (a) On arranging the given data in ascending order, we get

32.5, 36.4, 37.2, 39.2, 41.2, 41.3, 42.9

So, the number of observations, $n = 7$, which is odd.

$\therefore$ Median = Value of $\left(\frac{n+1}{2}\right)$th term

$= $ Value of $\left(\frac{7+1}{2}\right)$th term

$=$ Value of 4th term

$= 39.2$

13. (b) Given, number of observations, $n = 10$, which is an even number.

$\therefore$ Median

$$= \frac{\left(\frac{n}{2}\right)\text{th observation} + \left(\frac{n}{2}+1\right)\text{th observation}}{2}$$

$$= \frac{\left(\frac{10}{2}\right)\text{th observation} + \left(\frac{10}{2}+1\right)\text{th observation}}{2}$$

$$= \frac{\text{5th observation} + \text{6th observation}}{2}$$

$$= \frac{x + (x+2)}{2} = x + 1$$

According to the question, median = 63

$\therefore \quad x + 1 = 63$

$\Rightarrow \quad x = 62$

14. (c) Given numbers are

2, 5, 9, 6, 4, 8, 5, 13, 2, 31.

The ascending order of numbers is

2, 2, 4, 5, 5, 6, 8, 9, 13, 31

Number of observations, $n = 10$

Mean of given data

$$= \frac{2+2+4+5+5+6+8+9+13+31}{10}$$

$$= \frac{85}{10} = 8.5$$

$\because n = 10$ (even)

$$\therefore \text{ Median} = \frac{\left(\frac{n}{2}\right)\text{th term} + \left(\frac{n}{2}+1\right)\text{th term}}{2}$$

$$= \frac{\text{5th term} + \text{6th term}}{2} = \frac{5+6}{2} = 5.5$$

Hence, $8.5 > 5.5$

Therefore, mean > median.

15. (a) As we know that frequency polygon is constructed by plotting frequency of the class interval and the mid value of class.

Assertion-Reason Type Questions

1. (c) We have, 16, 19, 23, 13, 11, 25 and 18.

The maximum value of given data = 25

and minimum value of given data = 11

Now, we know that

Range = Maximum value of data − Minimum value of data

$= 25 - 11 = 14$

Hence, both A and R are true and R is the correct reason for A.

2. (c) We have, class intervals are 10-20 and 20-30.

Class mark for interval (10-20)

$$= \frac{\text{Lower limit} + \text{Upper limit}}{2}$$

$$= \frac{10+20}{2} = 15$$

and class mark for interval (20-30) $= \frac{20+30}{2} = 25$

Hence, both A and R are true and R is the correct reason for A.

3. (b) We know that

Adjustment factor

$$= \frac{\text{Lower limit of one class} - \text{Upper limit of previous class}}{2}$$

$\therefore$ Adjustment factor for the class intervals 0-5, 6-11, 12-17, 18-23 and 24-29

$$= \frac{6-5}{2} = \frac{12-11}{2} = \frac{18-17}{2} = \frac{24-23}{2} = \frac{1}{2} = 0.5$$

Hence, A is false, R is true.

4. (a) Given, the observations are 2, 4, 6, 8, 10, 12, 14.

$$\therefore \text{ Mean} = \frac{2+4+6+8+10+12+14}{7} = \frac{56}{7} = 8$$

Hence, A is true.

Now, first n even natural numbers 2, 4, 6, 8, ..., $2n$.

$$\therefore \text{ Mean} = \frac{2+4+6+8+\ldots\ldots+2n}{n}$$

$$= \frac{2(1+2+3+4+\ldots.+n)}{n}$$

$$= \frac{2 \times \frac{n(n+1)}{2}}{n} = (n+1)$$

$$\left[\because 1+2+3\ldots.+n = \frac{n(n+1)}{2}\right]$$

$\therefore$ R is false.

5. (d) On arranging the given data in ascending order, we get

15, 16, 16, 19, 25, 28, 28, 32, 36, 40, 42

Here, $n = 11$, which is odd number.

$\therefore \quad$ Median $= \left(\frac{11+1}{2}\right)$th observation = 28

Hence, both A and R are true and R is incorrect reason for A.

Statement Based Questions

1. (c) The first five prime numbers are 2, 3, 5, 7, 11.

$\therefore$ Mean $= \dfrac{2+3+5+7+11}{5}$

$= \dfrac{28}{5} = 5.6$

and the adjustment factor for class 0-10 and 11-20

$= \dfrac{11-10}{2}$

$= \dfrac{1}{2} = 0.5$

Hence, Statement I is true and Statement II is false.

2. (d) **Statement I** Given observations are 24, 27, 43, 48, $x-1$, $x+3$, 68, 73, 80 and 90.

Here, number of observations, $n = 10$, which is an even number.

$$\therefore \text{Median} = \frac{\left(\frac{n}{2}\right)\text{th observation} + \left(\frac{n}{2}+1\right)\text{th observation}}{2}$$

$$\Rightarrow \quad 58 = \frac{\left(\frac{10}{2}\right)\text{th observation} + \left(\frac{10}{2}+1\right)\text{th observation}}{2}$$

$$\Rightarrow \quad 58 = \frac{(x-1)+(x+3)}{2}$$

$\Rightarrow \quad 58 = (x+1)$

$\Rightarrow \quad x = 57$

$\therefore$ Statement I is false.

Statement II Given, mean of 25 numbers = 12.

As we know that if each observation under consideration is increased or decreased by quantity a, then their mean is also increased or decreased by same quantity a, respectively.

$\therefore$ If 2 is subtracted to each number, then

New mean = Original mean $-2 = 12 - 2$

$= 10$

Hence, Statement I is false and Statement II is true.

3. (b) **Statement I** On arranging the given data in ascending order, we get

$-2.206, -2.006, 2.0025, 2.0205$

Here, $n = 4$, which is even.

$$\therefore \text{Median} = \frac{\left(\frac{4}{2}\right)\text{th observation} + \left(\frac{4}{2}+1\right)\text{th observation}}{2}$$

$$= \frac{-2.006 + 2.0025}{2} = \frac{-0.0035}{2} = -0.00175$$

$\therefore$ Statement I is false.

Statement II On arranging the given data in ascending order, we get

32.5, 36.4, 37.2, 39.2, 41.2, 41.3, 42.9

Here, $n = 7$, which is odd.

$\therefore$ Median $= \left(\dfrac{7+1}{2}\right)$th observation

= 4th observation = 39.2

$\therefore$ Statement II is also false.

4. (a) Let the class interval be x-y.

Mid-value of a class interval $= \dfrac{x+y}{2}$

$\Rightarrow \quad 25 = \dfrac{x+y}{2}$ [$\because$ mid-value = 25 (given)]

$\Rightarrow \quad x + y = 50$ ...(i)

Now, class size of $(x$-$y) = y - x$

$\Rightarrow \quad 8 = y - x$ ...(ii)

[$\because$ class size = 8 (given)]

On adding Eqs. (i) and (ii), we get

$2y = 58$

$\Rightarrow \quad y = 29$

On substituting $y = 29$ in Eq. (ii), we get

$8 = 29 - x$

$\Rightarrow \quad x = 21$

Hence, the class interval is 21-29.

$\therefore$ Statement I is true.

Clearly, Statement II is also true.

Short Answer Type Questions

1. (i) We condense the given data into groups, like 150-155, 155-160, ..., 170-175. The class width in this case is 5.

Heights (in cm)	Tally marks	Number of students (Frequency)
150-155	𝍸 𝍸 ||	12
155-160	𝍸 ||||	9
160-165	𝍸 𝍸 ||||	14
165-170	𝍸 𝍸	10
170-175	𝍸	5
Total		50

(ii) From the table, our conclusion is that more than 50% of students (i.e. $12 + 9 + 14 = 35$) are shorter than 165 cm height.

2. We convert the given data into groups, like 0-5, 5-10, 15-20, ... , 30-35. The class width in this case is 5.

Distance (in km)	**Tally marks**	**Number of engineers** (Frequency)
0-5	$\cancel{||||}$	5
5-10	$\cancel{||||}$ $\cancel{||||}$ $|$	11
10-15	$\cancel{||||}$ $\cancel{||||}$ $|$	11
15-20	$\cancel{||||}$ $||||$	9
20-25	$|$	1
25-30	$|$	1
30-35	$||$	2
Total		40

(i) Frequencies of class intervals 5-10 and 10-15 are equal and maximum i.e. 11 each. It shows that maximum number of engineers have their residence within the distance of 5 km to 15 km from their workplace.

(ii) Frequencies of class intervals 20-25 and 25-30 are also equal and minimum i.e. 1 each. It shows that minimum number of engineers have their residences within 20 km to 30 km from their workplace.

3. (i) We convert the given data into groups like 84-86, 86-88, ... 98-100. The class width in this case is 2.

Relative humidity (in %)	**Tally marks**	**Number of days** (Frequency)
84-86	$|$	1
86-88	$|$	1
88-90	$||$	2
90-92	$||$	2
92-94	$\cancel{||||}$ $||$	7
94-96	$\cancel{||||}$ $|$	6
96-98	$\cancel{||||}$ $||$	7
98-100	$||||$	4
Total		30

(ii) From the table, we observe that the data appears to be taken in the rainy season as the relative humidity is high.

4. (i) The first 5 even natural numbers are 2, 4, 6, 8 and 10.

$$\therefore \text{ Mean} = \frac{2+4+6+8+10}{5}$$

$$\left[\because \text{mean} = \frac{\text{sum of observations}}{\text{number of observations}}\right]$$

$$\Rightarrow \quad \bar{x} = \frac{30}{5} = 6$$

(ii) Now,

x	**$x - \bar{x}$**
2	$2-6=-4$
4	$4-6=-2$
6	$6-6=0$
8	$8-6=2$
10	$10-6=4$

$$\therefore \ \Sigma(x-\bar{x}) = -4-2+0+2+4 = 0$$

5. (i) We have, number of observations,

$n = 5$ and mean $= 11$

$$\therefore \text{ Mean } = \frac{p+(p+2)+(p+4)+(p+6)+(p+8)}{5}$$

$$\left[\because \text{mean} = \frac{\text{sum of observations}}{\text{number of observations}}\right]$$

$$\Rightarrow \quad 11 = \frac{5p+20}{5}$$

$$\Rightarrow \quad 11 = p+4$$

$$\Rightarrow \quad p = 7$$

Hence, the value of p is 7.

(ii) The first three observations are $p, (p+2), (p+4)$ i.e. 7, 9, 11

$$\therefore \text{ Mean} = \frac{7+9+11}{3} = \frac{27}{3} = 9$$

6. Given observations are 8, 12, 16, 22, 10 and 4.

$$\therefore \quad \text{Mean} = \frac{8+12+16+22+10+4}{6} = \frac{72}{6} = 12$$

(i) **Increased by 25%**

New mean = Original mean + 25% of original mean

$$= 12 + \frac{25 \times 12}{100}$$

$$= 12 + 3 = 15$$

(ii) **Decreased by 40%**

New mean = Original mean − 40% of original mean

$$= 12 - \frac{40 \times 12}{100}$$

$$= 12 - 4.8 = 7.2$$

7. The product of observation and frequency is given in the table below.

x_i	f_i	$f_i x_i$
10	5	50
15	10	150
p	7	$7p$
25	8	200
30	2	60
Total	$\Sigma f_i = 32$	$\Sigma f_i x_i = (460 + 7p)$

Now, mean $= \dfrac{\Sigma f_i x_i}{\Sigma f_i}$

$= \dfrac{460 + 7p}{32}$

Also, mean $= 18.75$ [given]

$\Rightarrow \dfrac{460 + 7p}{32} = 18.75$

$\Rightarrow 460 + 7p = 18.75 \times 32$

$\Rightarrow 460 + 7p = 600$

$\Rightarrow 7p = 140$

$\therefore p = 20$

8. The product of observation and frequency is given in the table below.

x_i	f_i	$f_i x_i$
10	6	60
15	8	120
20	p	$20p$
25	10	250
30	6	180
Total	$\Sigma f_i = 30 + p$	$\Sigma f_i x_i = 610 + 20p$

Now, mean $= \dfrac{\Sigma f_i x_i}{\Sigma f_i}$

$= \dfrac{610 + 20p}{30 + p}$

Also, mean $= 20.2$

$\Rightarrow \dfrac{610 + 20p}{30 + p} = 20.2$

$\Rightarrow 610 + 20p = 606 + 20.2p$

$\Rightarrow 20p - 20.2p = 606 - 610$

$\Rightarrow -0.2p = -4$

$\Rightarrow p = \dfrac{4}{0.2}$

$\Rightarrow p = 20$

9. The product of observation and frequency is given in the table below.

x	f	fx
10	17	170
30	$5a + 3$	$150a + 90$
50	32	1600
70	$7a - 11$	$490a - 770$
90	19	1710
Total	$12a + 60$	$640a + 2800$

Given, mean $= 50$

$\therefore \dfrac{640a + 2800}{12a + 60} = 50$

$\Rightarrow 640a + 2800 = 600a + 3000$

$\Rightarrow 640a - 600a = 3000 - 2800$

$\Rightarrow 40a = 200$

$\Rightarrow a = \dfrac{200}{40} = 5$

Hence, the value of a is 5.

10. The product of observation and frequency is given in the table below.

Subjects	Number of Students (f_i)	Pass Percentage (x_i)	$f_i x_i$
English	45	66	2970
Hindi	40	95	3800
Sanskrit	20	80	1600
Mathematics	60	55	3300
Science and Technology	55	70	3850
Social Science	60	60	3600
Total	$\Sigma f_i = 280$		$\Sigma f_i x_i = 19120$

Now, mean $= \dfrac{\Sigma f_i x_i}{\Sigma f_i}$

$= \dfrac{19120}{280} = 68.28$

11. The given frequency distribution is not continuous. So, we will first convert it into a continuous frequency distribution.

Now, adjustment factor $= \dfrac{15 - 14}{2} = 0.5$

So, we subtract 0.5 from lower limit and add 0.5 to upper limit of each class interval.

Thus, we get continuous frequency distribution.

The distribution so obtained is as given below

Age group	Number of females
9.5-14.5	300
14.5-19.5	980
19.5-24.5	800
24.5-29.5	580
29.5-34.5	290

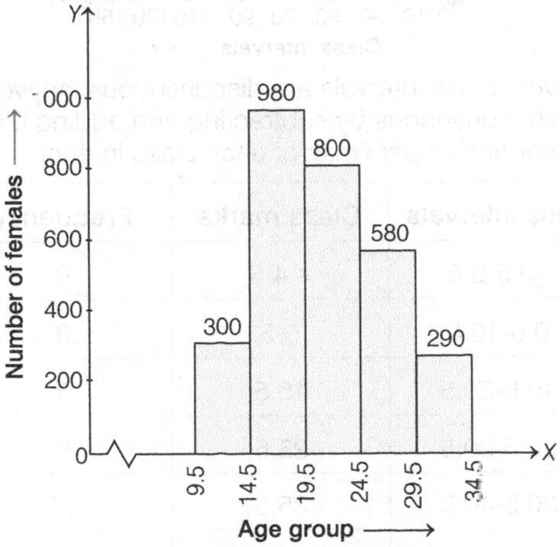

12. (i) Since, the given distribution is not continuous.

So, we will first convert it into a continuous frequency distribution.

Now, adjustment factor $= \dfrac{127 - 126}{2} = 0.5$

So, we add 0.5 to upper limit and subtract 0.5 from lower limit of each class interval.

Thus, we get continuous frequency distribution

Length (in mm)	Number of leaves
117.5-126.5	3
126.5-135.5	5
135.5-144.5	9
144.5-153.5	12
153.5-162.5	5
162.5-171.5	4
171.5-180.5	2

Take the length along the X-axis choosing any scale and the number of leaves along the Y-axis.

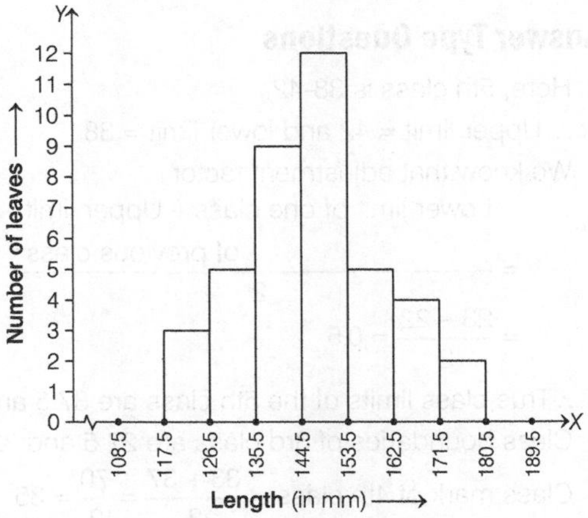

(ii) Frequency polygon

(iii) No, because the maximum number of leaves have their lengths lying in the interval 145-153.

13. Given, class intervals are 30-40, 40-50, 50-60 ....

Now, form a frequency distribution table.

Class Intervals	Class marks	Frequency
30-40	35	3
40-50	45	1
50-60	55	4
60-70	65	5
70-80	75	9
80-90	85	3
90-100	95	3
100-110	105	4

Along the X-axis, we take class intervals (30-40), (40-50), (50-60), ... and (100-110) with a suitable scale.

Along the Y-axis, we take frequencies with a suitable scale.

Now, plot the points $A(25, 0)$, $B(35, 3)$, $C(45, 1)$, $D(55, 4)$, $E(65, 5)$, $F(75, 9)$, $G(85, 3)$, $H(95, 3)$, $I(105, 4)$ and $J(115, 0)$.

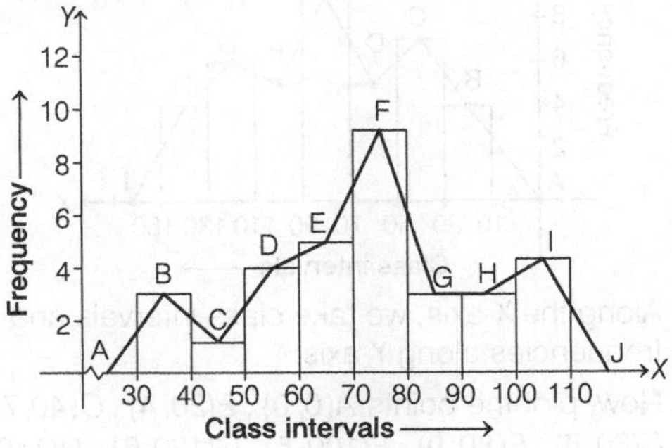

Long Answer Type Questions

1. (i) Here, 5th class is 38-42.

$\therefore$ Upper limit = 42 and lower limit = 38

(ii) We know that adjustment factor

$$= \frac{\text{Lower limit of one class} - \text{Upper limit of previous class}}{2}$$

$$= \frac{23 - 22}{2} = 0.5$$

$\therefore$ True class limits of the 5th class are 37.5 and 42.5.

(iii) Class boundaries of 3rd class are 27.5 and 32.5.

(iv) Class mark of 4th class $= \frac{33 + 37}{2} = \frac{70}{2} = 35$

(v) Width of 6th class = 47.5 − 42.5 = 5

2. (i) Take scale

At X-axis, 1 cm = 100 units

At Y-axis, 1 cm = 10 lamps

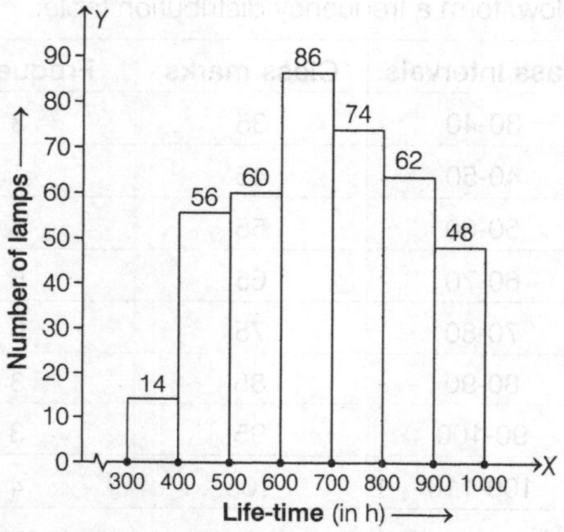

(ii) Number of lamps have a life-time of more than 700 h = 74 + 62 + 48 = 184

3. (i) We represent the class intervals along the *X*-axis on suitable scale and the corresponding frequencies along the *Y*-axis on a suitable scale.

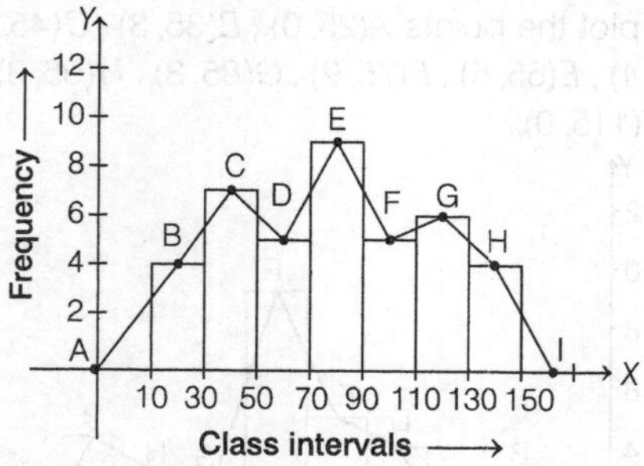

(ii) Along the *X*-axis, we take class intervals and frequencies along *Y*-axis.

Now, plot the points $A(0, 0)$, $B(20, 4)$, $C(40, 7)$, $D(60, 5)$, $E(80, 9)$, $F(100, 5)$, $G(120, 6)$, $H(140, 4)$ and $I(160, 0)$.

We join the line segments *AB*, *BC*, *CD*, *DE*, EF, *FG* and *GH* to obtain the required frequency polygon as shown below.

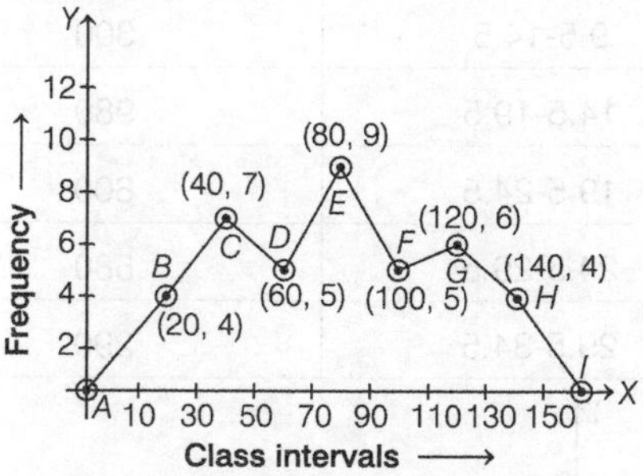

4. Given, class intervals are discontinuous, so we make them continuous by subtracting and adding 0.5 in lower and upper limits of each class interval.

Class intervals	Class marks	Frequency
-9.5-0.5	− 4.5	0
0.5-10.5	5.5	8
10.5-20.5	15.5	3
20.5-30.5	25.5	6
30.5-40.5	35.5	12
40.5-50.5	45.5	2
50.5-60.5	55.5	7
60.5-70.5	65.5	0

Along the X-axis, we take class marks − 4.5, 5.5, 15.5, 25.5, 30.5, 40.5, 50.5 and 60.5 with a suitable scale. Along the *Y*-axis, we take corresponding frequencies 0, 8, 3, 6, 12, 2, 7 and 0 with a suitable scale. Now, plot the points $A(-4.5, 0)$, $B(5.5, 8)$, $C(15.5, 3)$, $D(25.5, 6)$, $E(35.5, 12)$, $F(45.5, 2)$, $G(55.5, 7)$ and $H(65.5, 0)$. We join line segments *AB*, *BC*, *CD*, *DE*, *EF*, *FG*, *GH* to obtain the required frequency polygon.

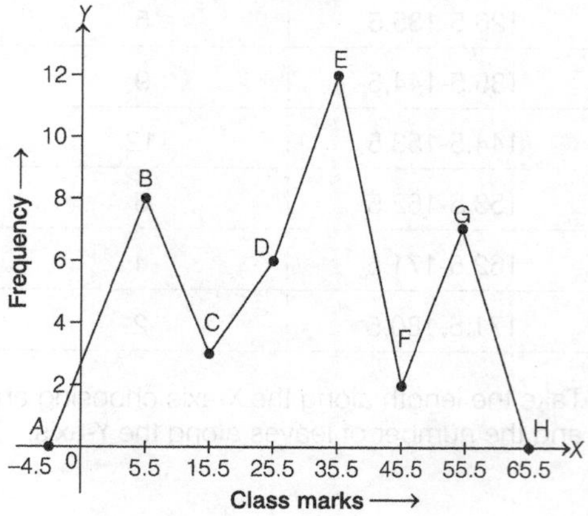

5.

Class	Class Marks	Section *A* (Number of students)	Section *B* (Number of students)
0-10	5	3	5
10-20	15	9	19
20-30	25	17	15
30-40	35	12	10
40-50	45	9	1

Along the *X*-axis, we take class intervals and frequencies along the *Y*-axis.

Now, plot the points for each section.

For section *A* (5, 3), (15, 9), (25, 17) (35, 12) and (45, 9)

For section *B* (5, 5), (15, 19), (25, 15) (35, 10) and (45, 1)

The required frequency polygon as shown below.

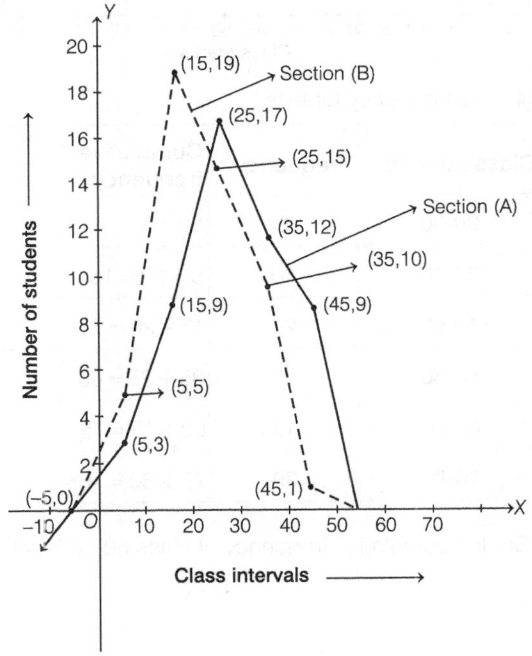

6. Given, class intervals are discontinuous, so we make them continuous by subtracting and adding 0.5 in lower and upper limits of each class interval.

Class intervals	Class marks	Frequency
24.5-29.5	$\frac{24.5+29.5}{2}=27$	0
29.5-34.5	32	12
34.5-39.5	37	16
39.5-44.5	42	20
44.5-49.5	47	8
49.5-54.5	52	10
54.5-59.5	57	4
59.5-64.5	62	0

Along the *X*-axis, we take class marks 27, 32, 37, 42, 47, 52, 57 and 62 with a suitable scale and along *Y*-axis, we take frequencies.

Now, plot the points *A*(27, 0), *B*(32, 12), *C*(37, 16), *D*(42, 20), *E*(47, 8), *F*(52, 10), *G*(57, 4) and *H* (62, 0).

We join line segments *AB*, *BC*, *CD*, *DE*, *EF*, *FG* and *GH* to obtain the required frequency polygon as shown below.

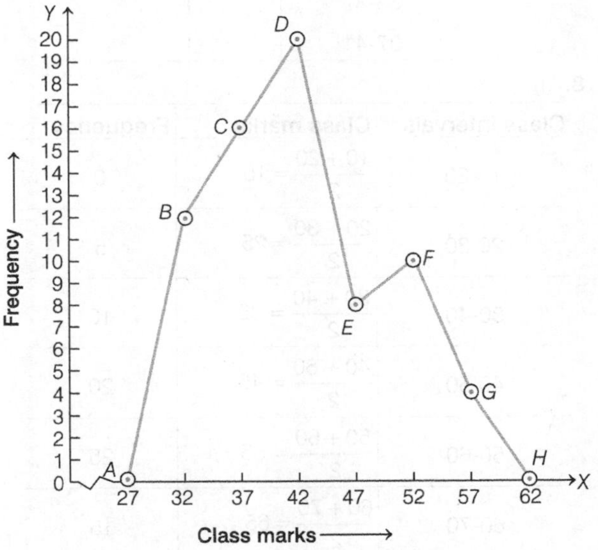

7. Given data in increasing order is given below

2, 3, 7, 8, 10, 11, 11, 11, 13, 13, 13, 15, 16, 16, 17, 18, 18, 18, 18, 20, 20, 23, 24, 25, 27, 27, 30, 31, 36, 37

We can classify the given data into group as given below

(i) **Discontinuous interval form**

Class Interval	Frequency
1-5	2
6-10	3
11-15	7
16-20	9
21-25	3
26-30	3
31-35	1
36-40	2

(ii) **Continuous interval form**

Class Interval	Frequency
1-5	2
5-9	2
9-13	4
13-17	6
17-21	7
21-25	2
25-29	3
29-33	2
33-37	1
37-41	1

8. (i)

Class intervals	Class marks	Frequency
10-20	$\frac{10+20}{2}=15$	0
20-30	$\frac{20+30}{2}=25$	5
30-40	$\frac{30+40}{2}=35$	10
40-50	$\frac{40+50}{2}=45$	20
50-60	$\frac{50+60}{2}=55$	25
60-70	$\frac{60+70}{2}=65$	15
70-80	$\frac{70+80}{2}=75$	30
80-90	$\frac{80+90}{2}=85$	0

Along X-axis, we take class marks 25, 35, 45, 55, 65 and 75 with a suitable class.

Along Y-axis, we take corresponding frequencies 0, 5, 10, 20, 25, 15, 10 and 0 with a suitable scale.

Now, plot the points A (15, 0), B (25, 5), C (35,10), D (45, 20), E (55, 25), F (65, 15), G (75, 10) and H (85, 0).

We join line segments AB, BC, CD, DE, EF, GH to obtain the required frequency polygon.

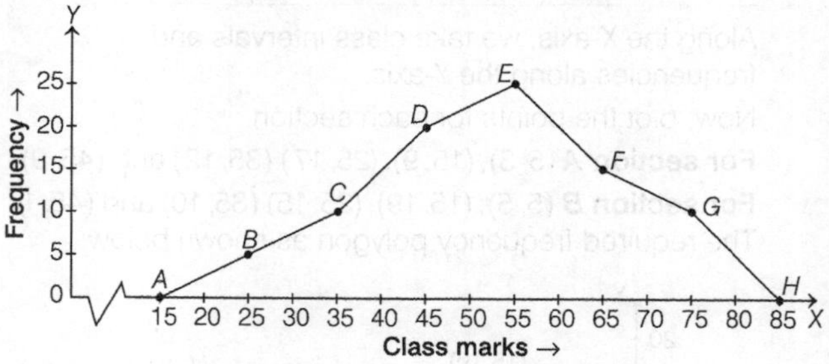

(ii) The frequency table is

Class interval	Frequency	Cumulative frequency
20-30	5	5
30-40	10	5 + 10 = 15
40-50	20	15 + 20 = 35
50-60	25	35 + 25 = 60
60-70	15	60 + 15 = 75
70-80	30	75 + 30 = 105

So, the cumulative frequency of class 50-60 is 60.

15

PERIMETER AND AREA

The total length of boundary of a plane figure is called its **perimeter**. The units of perimeter are cm, m etc. The measurement of the region enclosed by a plane figure is called its **area**. The units of area are cm^2, m^2 etc.

Perimeter and Area of a Triangle

In ΔABC, BC is taken as base and AD is the corresponding height (altitude).

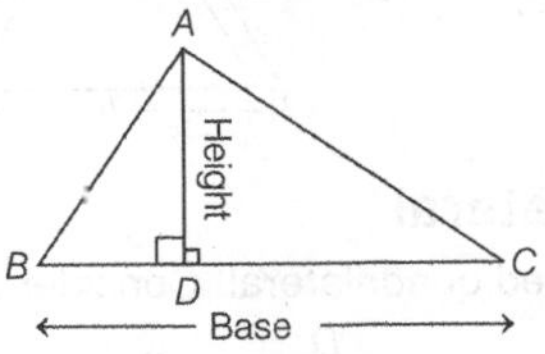

Then, Area of $\Delta ABC = \frac{1}{2} \times \text{Base} \times \text{Corresponding height} = \frac{1}{2} \times BC \times AD$

In ΔABC, BC is taken as base and AD is the corresponding height (altitude).

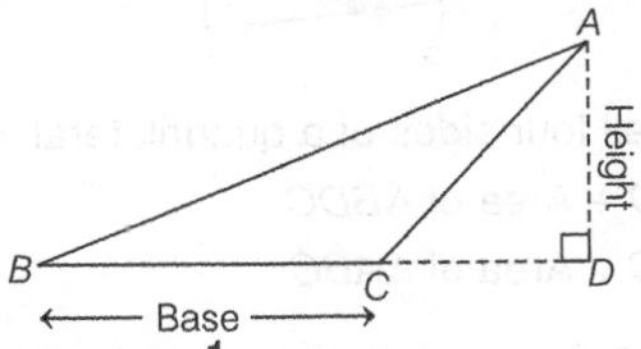

Then, Area of $\Delta ABC = \frac{1}{2} \times \text{Base} \times \text{Height (altitude)} = \frac{1}{2} \times BC \times AD$

Heron's Formula

For any triangle with its sides a, b and c,

the area of $\Delta ABC = \sqrt{s(s-a)(s-b)(s-c)}$.

This formula is called Heron's formula, where a, b and c are the sides of triangle and s = semi-perimeter = $\frac{a+b+c}{2}$.

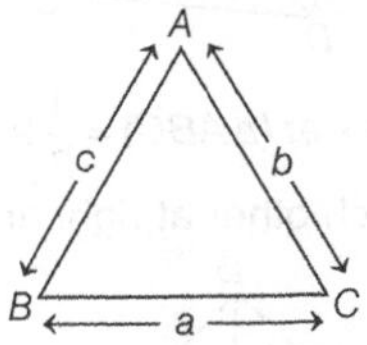

Area and Perimeter of Different Types of Triangles

1. **Right angled triangle**

   The triangle whose one angle is right angle is called right angled triangle. The sides of the triangle making right angle with each other are called base (horizontal side) and altitude(vertical side) respectively.

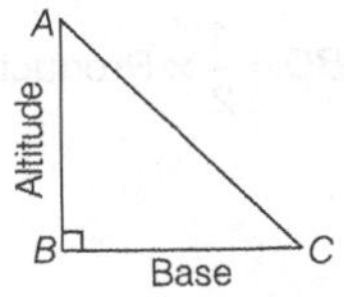

Area of $\Delta ABC = \frac{1}{2} \times BC \times AB = \frac{1}{2} \times$ Base $\times$ altitude and Perimeter of $\Delta ABC = AB + BC + CA$.

2. **Equilateral triangle** The triangle whose all the three sides are equal, is called an equilateral triangle.

   Area of $\Delta ABC = \frac{\sqrt{3}}{4} a^2$ sq units.

   Perimeter of $\Delta ABC = 3a$ units.

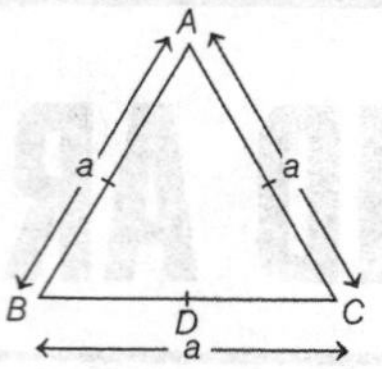

3. **Isosceles triangle** The triangle whose two sides are equal, is called an isosceles triangle.

   Area of an isosceles $\Delta ABC = \frac{1}{4} b\sqrt{4a^2 - b^2}$ sq units

   Perimeter of $\Delta ABC = a + a + b = (2a + b)$ units

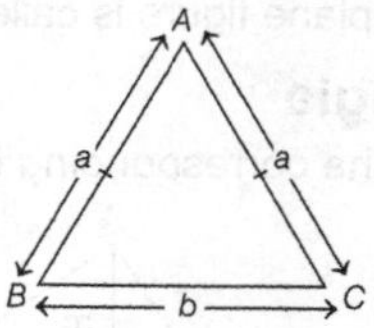

Perimeter and Area of a Quadrilateral

A closed plane figure having four sides is called quadrilateral. Consider a quadrilateral *ABCD*.

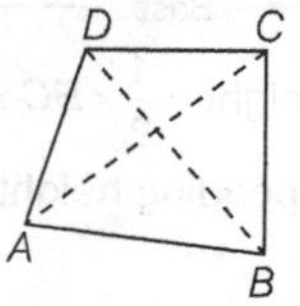

Perimeter of quadrilateral *ABCD* = Sum of all four sides of a quadrilateral $= AB + BC + CD + DA$

Area of quadrilateral *ABCD* = Area of ΔABD + Area of ΔBDC

Or Area of ΔADC + Area of ΔABC

Area of Quadrilateral in Special Cases

(i) When one diagonal and the perpendicular drawn from the remaining vertices to this diagonal are given.

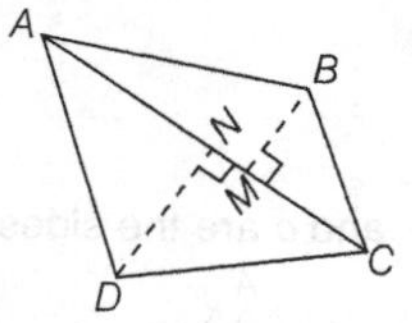

Then, area of quadrilateral $ABCD = \text{ar}(\Delta ADC) + \text{ar}(\Delta ABC) = \frac{1}{2} \times AC \times (DN + BM)$

(ii) When diagonals of a quadrilateral intersect each other at right angles.

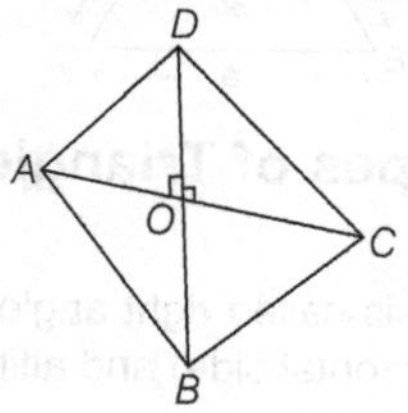

Then, area of quadrilateral $ABCD = \frac{1}{2} \times AC \times BD = \frac{1}{2} \times$ Product of diagonals

Area and Perimeter of Different types of Quadrilaterals

S.No.	Name	Figure	Perimeter	Area
1.	Trapezium	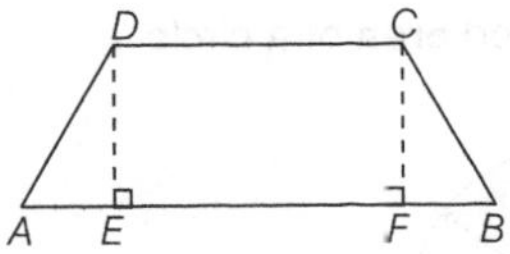	Sum of all sides of trapezium *Or* $AB + BC + CD + DA$	$\frac{1}{2} \times$ (Sum of parallel sides) $\times$ (Distance between them) *Or* $\frac{1}{2} \times (AB + DC) \times DE$ *Or* $\frac{1}{2} \times (AB + DC) \times CF$
2.	Parallelogram	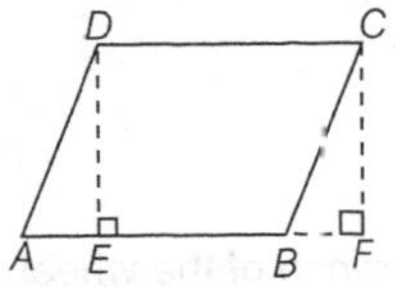	Sum of all sides of parallelogram *Or* $AB + BC + CD + DA$	Base $\times$ Height *Or* $AB \times DE$ *Or* $AB \times CF$
3.	Rectangle	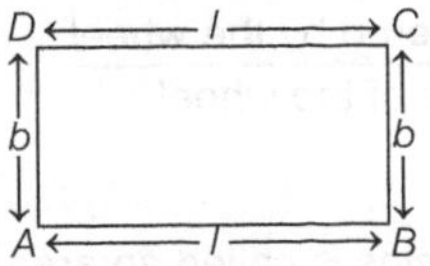	$2(l + b)$	$l \times b$
4.	Square	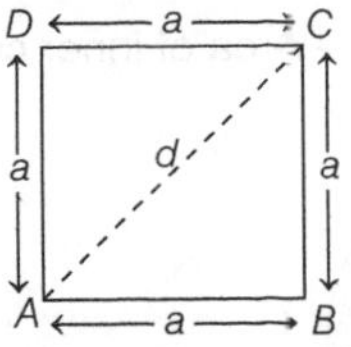	$4a$ *Or* $4 \times$ (Side)	a^2 *Or* $(\text{Side})^2$
5.	Rhombus	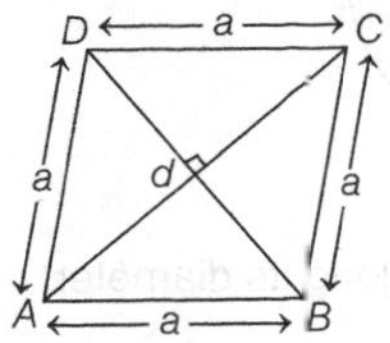	$4a$ *Or* $4 \times$ (Side)	$\frac{1}{2} \times$ Product of diagonals

Circle

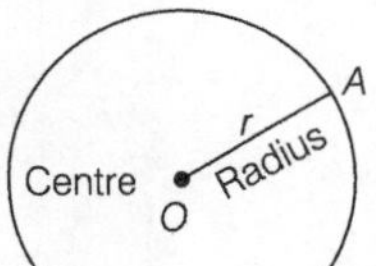

A circle is the locus of a point that moves in a plane in such a way that its distance from a fixed point remains same. This fixed point is called the **centre** and the constant distance is called the **radius** of the circle.

Diameter of a Circle

A line-segment joining any two points on a circle and passing through its centre is called a **diameter** of the circle.

$\therefore$ Diameter $= 2 \times$ Radius

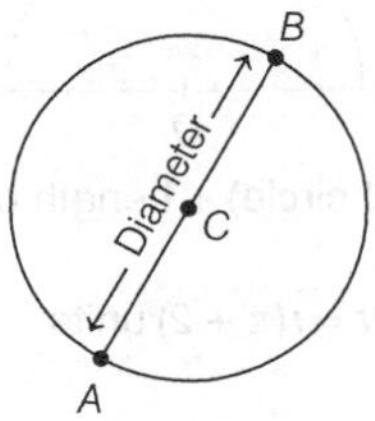

Circumference of a Circle

The length of the boundary of a circle is known as circumference (or perimeter) of a circle.

$$\text{Circumference} = \pi \times \text{Diameter} = \pi \times 2r = 2\pi r$$

Area of a Circle

The surface enclosed by the circumference of the circle is called **area** of a circle.
Area of circle = πr^2, where r is radius of a circle.

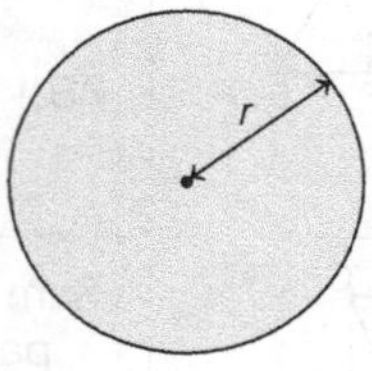

Some Important Facts Related to Circle

(i) Distance covered by a circular wheel in 1 rotation = Circumference of the wheel

(ii) Number of rotations taken by wheel $(n) = \dfrac{\text{Total distance covered by the wheel}}{\text{Circumference of the wheel}}$

Area of a Circular Ring

The region bounded by the circumferences of two concentric circles is called an area of a circular ring.

Area of circular ring = Area of shaded region = Area of outer circle – Area of inner circle

$$= \pi R^2 - \pi r^2 = \pi(R^2 - r^2)$$

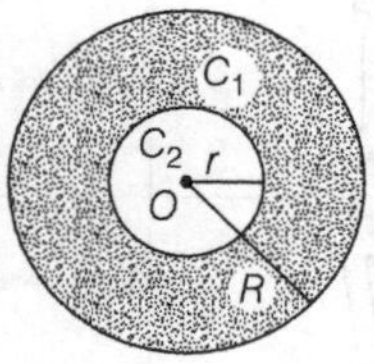

Semi-circle

A semi-circle is a half circle, formed by dividing the whole circle along its diameter.

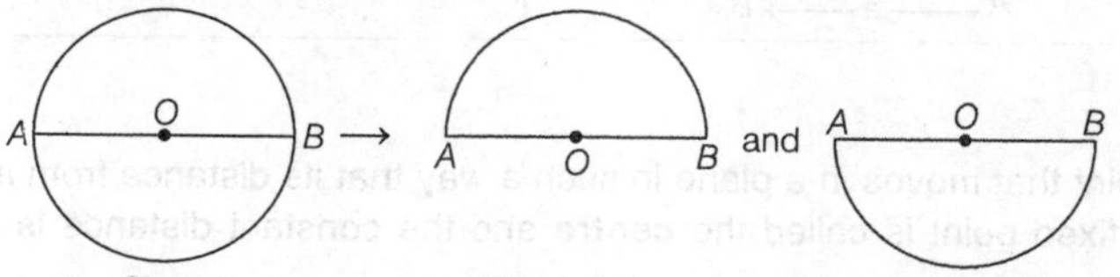

Circle Semi-circle Semi-circle

Perimeter of a Semi-circle

The perimeter of a semi-circle is equal to the sum of half circumference of a circle and length of the diameter.

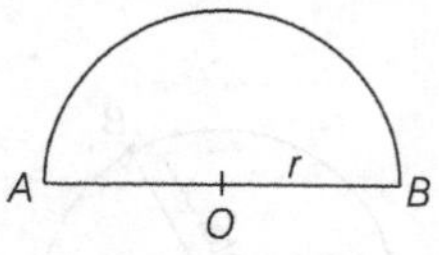

i.e. Perimeter of semi-circle = $\frac{1}{2}$ (Circumference of circle) + Length of the diameter

$$= \frac{1}{2}(2\pi r) + 2r = \pi r + 2r = r(\pi + 2) \text{ units}$$

Area of a Semi-circle

The area of semi-circle is equal to the half of area of circle.

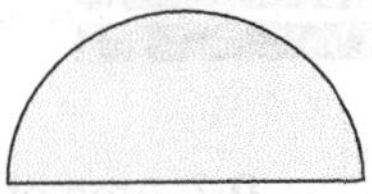

i.e. area of semi-circle $= \frac{1}{2}$ (area of a circle) $= \frac{1}{2}(\pi r^2) = \frac{\pi r^2}{2}$ sq units

Quarter circle

A quarter circle refers to one-fourth of a full circle also known as a quadrant, formed by two perpendicular radii and a curved arc that is one-fourth of the circle's circumference.

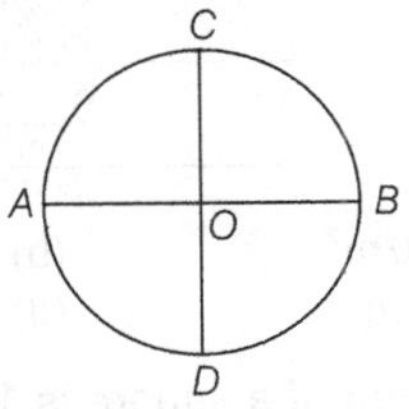

Circle

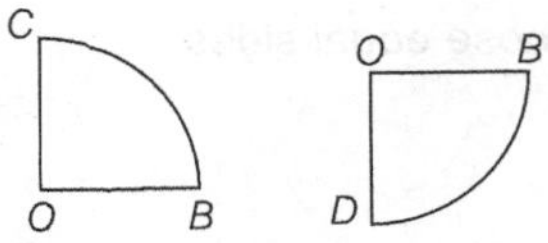

Quarter circle

Perimeter of a Quarter circle

Perimeter of a quarter circle is equal to the sum of arc length (one fourth of circumference) and two radii.

Perimeter of quarter circle $= \frac{1}{4}$(Circumference of circle) $+ 2r$

$$= \frac{1}{4}(2\pi r) + 2r = \frac{\pi r}{2} + 2r = r\left(\frac{\pi}{2} + 2\right) \text{ units}$$

Area of Quarter circle

The area of quarter circle is equal to the one-fourth of area of circle.

i.e. area of quarter circle $= \frac{1}{4}$ (area of circle) $= \frac{1}{4}(\pi r^2) = \frac{\pi r^2}{4}$ sq units

Problems Based on Inner and Outer Circles

Circumscribed circle

The circle passing through vertices of a square *ABCD* is called circumscribed circle. Its radius *R* is called the **circumradius** and its centre is known as **circumcentre** of a circle.

Inscribed circle

The circle touching all sides of square *ABCD* internally is known as an inscribed circle. Its radius *r* is called the **inradius** and its centre is called **incentre** of a circle.

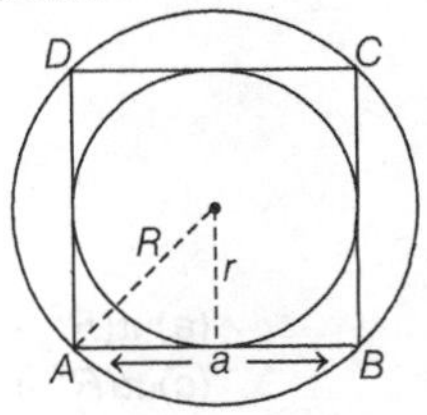

Let *ABCD* be a square of side *a* unit.

Let *R* and *r* be the radii of circumscribed and inscribed circle, respectively.

Then, $2r = a \Rightarrow r = \frac{a}{2}$ and $2R = \sqrt{a^2 + a^2} \Rightarrow R = \frac{a}{2}\sqrt{2} = \frac{a}{\sqrt{2}}$

(i) Area of inscribed circle $= \pi r^2 = \pi\left(\frac{a}{2}\right)^2 = \frac{\pi a^2}{4}$

(ii) Area of circumscribed circle $= \pi R^2 = \pi\left(\frac{a}{\sqrt{2}}\right)^2 = \frac{\pi a^2}{2}$

EXAM ORIENTED QUESTIONS

TYPE - 1 — 01 Mark

Multiple Choice Questions

Q.1 Area of a triangle whose sides are 12 cm, 16 cm and 20 cm, respectively is

(a) 120 cm^2 (b) 96 cm^2
(c) 160 cm^2 (d) 192 cm^2

Q.2 The area of an isosceles triangle whose equal sides are 5 cm each and base is 6 cm, is

(a) 30 cm^2 (b) 15 cm^2
(c) 12 cm^2 (d) 18 cm^2

Q.3 A rhombus and a equilateral triangle have equal perimeters. If the perimeter of rhombus is 36 cm, then area of triangle is

(a) 72 cm^2
(b) 144 cm^2
(c) $36\sqrt{3}$ cm^2
(d) $72\sqrt{3}$ cm^2

Q.4 The area of an equilateral triangle is $16\sqrt{3}\ m^2$, then its side will be

(a) 16 m (b) $8\sqrt{3}$ m (c) 8 m (d) $8\sqrt{2}$ m

Q.5 The area of the trapezium *PQRS*, with height *PQ* given in the figure, is

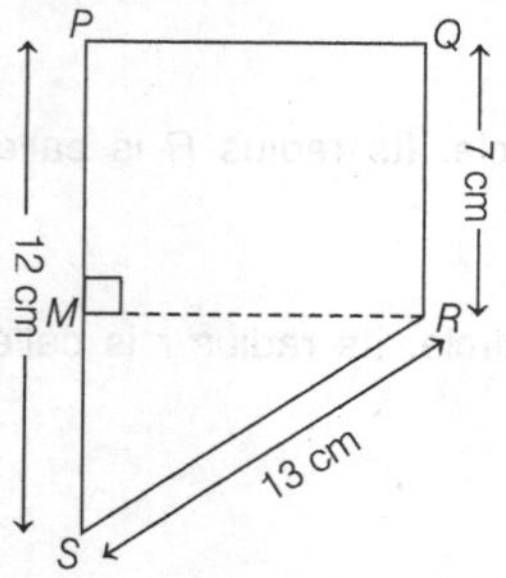

(a) 228 cm^2 (b) 114 cm^2
(c) 144 cm^2 (d) 91 cm^2

Q.6 The area of a parallelogram is 392 cm^2. If its altitude is twice the corresponding base, then its base and altitude are

(a) 14 cm, 28 cm
(b) 28 cm, 14 cm
(c) $14\sqrt{2}$ cm, $28\sqrt{2}$ cm
(d) 14 cm, 42 cm

Q.7 Area of the unshaded region is

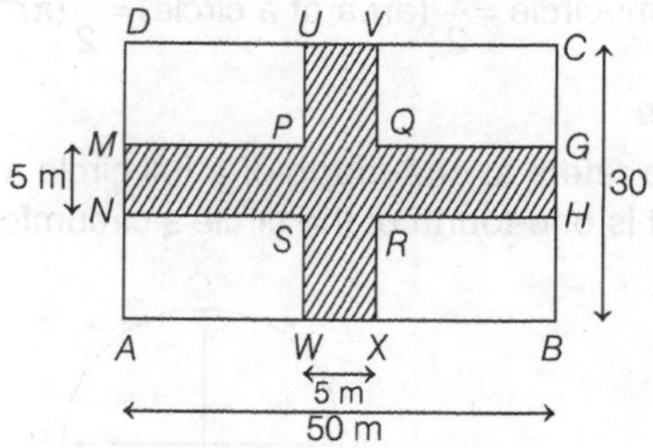

(a) 1100 m^2 (b) 1150 m^2
(c) 375 m^2 (d) 1125 m^2

Q.8 If the area of a square is 16 cm^2, then its diagonal will be

(a) 4 cm (b) 8 cm
(c) $2\sqrt{2}$ cm (d) $4\sqrt{2}$ cm

Q.9 In a given figure, *ABCD* is a rhombus, then the value of *a* is

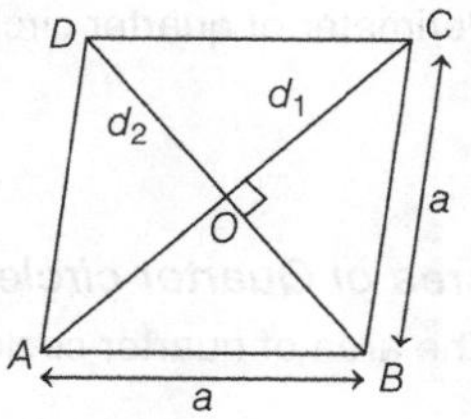

(a) $a = \sqrt{\left(\frac{d_1}{2}\right)^2 - \left(\frac{d_2}{2}\right)^2}$ unit

(b) $a = \frac{1}{4}\sqrt{d_1^2 + d_2^2}$ unit

(c) $a = \frac{1}{2}\sqrt{d_1^2 + d_2^2}$ sq unit

(d) $a = \sqrt{\left(\frac{d_1}{2}\right)^2 + \left(\frac{d_2}{2}\right)^2}$ unit

Q.10 In a given figure, two circles having radii *R* and *r*. Then, area of circular ring is

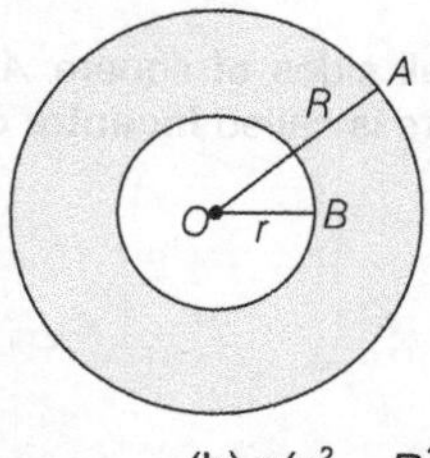

(a) $\pi(R^2 - r^2)$ (b) $\pi(r^2 - R^2)$
(c) $\pi(R^2 + r^2)$ (d) $\pi(2r^2 - R^2)$

Q.11 If perimeter of a circle is 96π cm, then find the perimeter of semi-circle.

(a) 26.472 cm (b) 24.672 cm
(c) 264.72 cm (d) 246.72 cm

Q.12 If the area of the quadrant of a circle is $\frac{1}{4}\pi r^2$, then the perimeter of the quadrant of the circle is

(a) $\left(\frac{\pi}{2}+2\right)r$

(b) $(\pi+4)r$

(c) $\left(\frac{\pi}{2}+4\right)r$

(d) $\left(\frac{\pi}{4}+2\right)r$

Answers

1. (b) 2. (c) 3. (c) 4. (c) 5. (b)
6. (a) 7. (d) 8. (d) 9. (d) 10. (a)
11. (d) 12. (a)

TYPE - 2 — 01 Mark

Assertion-Reason Type Questions

Q.1 Assertion (A) The sides of a ΔABC are consecutive odd numbers. If longest side of ΔABC is equal to side of an equilateral triangle having perimeter 57 cm, then the perimeter of ΔABC is 51 cm.

Reason (R) Area of triangle $= \sqrt{s(s-a)(s-b)(s-c)}$.

(a) A is true, R is false.
(b) A is false, R is true.
(c) Both A and R are true and R is the correct reason for A.
(d) Both A and R are true and R is incorrect reason for A.

Q.2 Assertion (A) In an isosceles ΔABC, $AB = 5$ cm $= AC$ and $BC = 6$ cm, then the area of ΔABC is 12 cm^2.

Reason (R) Area of an isosceles ΔABC is $\frac{1}{4}b\sqrt{4a^2-b^2}$, if $AB = AC = a$ cm and $BC = b$ cm.

(a) A is true, R is false.
(b) A is false, R is true.
(c) Both A and R are true and R is the correct reason for A.
(d) Both A and R are true and R is incorrect reason for A.

Q.3 Assertion (A) In a quadrilateral, one diagonal is 20 cm long and lengths of perpendicular from the other two vertices on it are 16.4 cm and 11.6 cm respectively, then area of quadrilateral is 280 cm^2.

Reason (R) Area of quadrilateral $ABCD$ is $\frac{1}{2}\times AC(DN+BM)$.

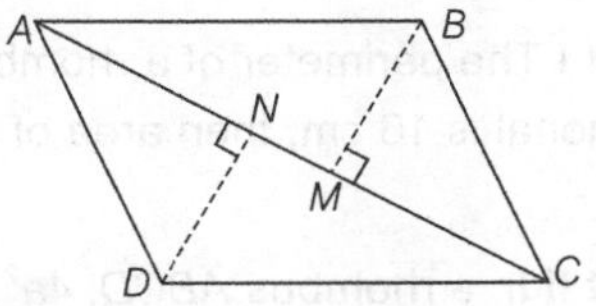

(a) A is true, R is false.
(b) A is false, R is true.
(c) Both A and R are true and R is the correct reason for A.
(d) Both A and R are true and R is incorrect reason for A.

Q.4 Assertion (A) If perimeter and area of the circle are numerically equal, then area of circle is 4 sq units.

Reason (R) Area of the circle $= \frac{\pi}{4}\times(\text{Diameter})^2$

(a) A is true, R is false.
(b) A is false, R is true.
(c) Both A and R are true and R is the correct reason for A.
(d) Both A and R are true and R is incorrect reason for A.

Q.5 Assertion (A) If the side of square is a cm, then the circumradius of a circle will be $\frac{a}{\sqrt{2}}$.

Reason (R) The circle passing through vertices of a square is called circumscribed circle and its radius is called the circumradius.

(a) A is true, R is false.
(b) A is false, R is true.
(c) Both A and R are true and R is the correct reason for A.
(d) Both A and R are true and R is incorrect reason for A.

Answers

1. (d) 2. (c) 3. (c) 4. (b) 5. (c)

TYPE - 3 — 01 Mark

Statement Based Questions

Q.1 Statement I The sides of a right angled triangle containing the right angle are $5x$ cm and $(3x-1)$ cm. If its area is 60 cm^2, then its perimeter is 60 cm.

Statement II Area of right angled triangle $= \frac{1}{2}\times \text{Base}\times\text{Height}$.

Which of the following is valid?

(a) Both the Statements are true.
(b) Both the Statements are false.
(c) Statement I is true and Statement II is false.
(d) Statement I is false and Statement II is true.

Q.2 Statement I The perimeter of a rhombus is 68cm. If one diagonal is 16 cm, then area of rhombus is 240 cm^2.

Statement II In a rhombus $ABCD$, $4a^2 = d_1^2 + d_2^2$

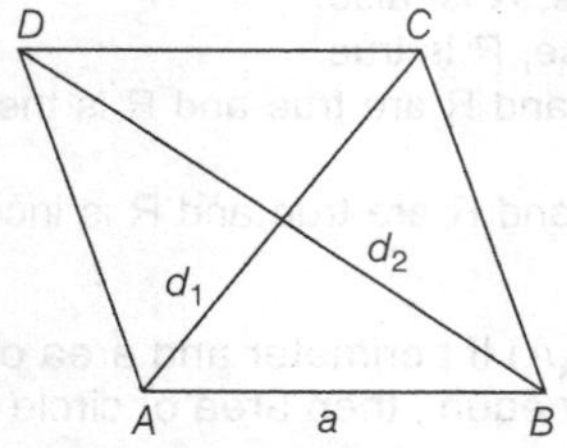

Which of the following is valid?

(a) Both the Statements are true.

(b) Both the Statements are false.

(c) Statement I is true and Statement II is false.

(d) Statement I is false and Statement II is true.

Q.3 Statement I The area of the shaded portion is 65.94 cm^2.

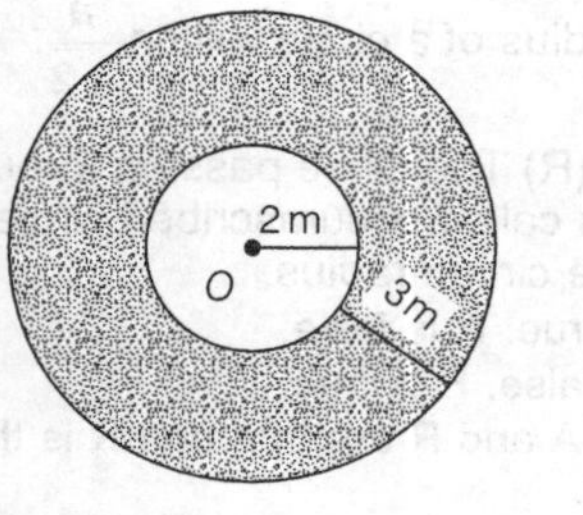

Statement II Area of the circle = πr^2.

Which of the following is valid?

(a) Both the Statements are true.

(b) Both the Statements are false.

(c) Statement I is true and Statement II is false.

(d) Statement I is false and Statement II is true.

Q.4 Statement I If the area of quadrant of a circle is πr^2, then the perimeter of quadrant is $r(4 + \pi)$.

Statement II The perimeter of quadrant is $\frac{2\pi r}{4} + r$.

Which of the following is valid?

(a) Both the Statements are true.

(b) Both the Statements are false.

(c) Statement I is true and Statement II is false.

(d) Statement I is false and Statement II is true.

Answers

1. (d) 2. (a) 3. (a) 4. (c)

TYPE - 4 03 Marks

Short Answer Type Questions

Q.1 Calculate the area of triangle, whose sides are in the ratio 7 : 5 : 4 and perimeter equal to 32 cm.

Q.2 Rakesh wants to make a triangular shape painting on the wall in his room. The height of the painting is 2 times its base. If the cost of making the painting is ₹ 30 per square feet and total cost of making the painting is ₹ 4320, then find its base and height.

Q.3 The base and hypotenuse of a right angled triangle are, respectively 5 cm and 13 cm long. Find its area.

Q.4 Find the area of an equilateral triangle, whose height is 5 cm. [take, $\sqrt{3} = 1.73$]

Q.5 In the trapezium $ABCD$, $AB \parallel DC$ and $\angle ADC = 90°$, $AB = 10$ cm, $DC = 40$ cm and the diagonal $AC = 41$ cm. Then, find the area of trapezium.

Q.6 A triangle and a parallelogram have the same base and the same area. If the sides of the triangle are 15cm, 14cm and 13cm and the parallelogram stands on the base 15cm, find the height of the parallelogram.

Q.7 There is a rectangular park in a society with dimensions 60m × 80m, a footpath uniform width of 5m is made around the park. Find the area of path.

Q.8 The radii of two circles are 13 cm and 6 cm, respectively. Find the radius of the circle which has circumference equal to sum of the circumferences of the two circles.

Q.9 The radius of the wheel of a bus is 25 cm. If the speed of the bus is 33 km/h, then how many revolutions will the wheel make in 1 min?

Q.10 The cost of fencing a circular field at the rate of ₹ 24 per m is ₹ 5280. The field is to be ploughed at the rate of ₹ 0.50 per m^2. Find the cost of ploughing the field. [take, $\pi = 22/7$]

Q.11 Find the area of the shaded region in figure as shown below, where $ABCD$ is a square of side 12 cm.

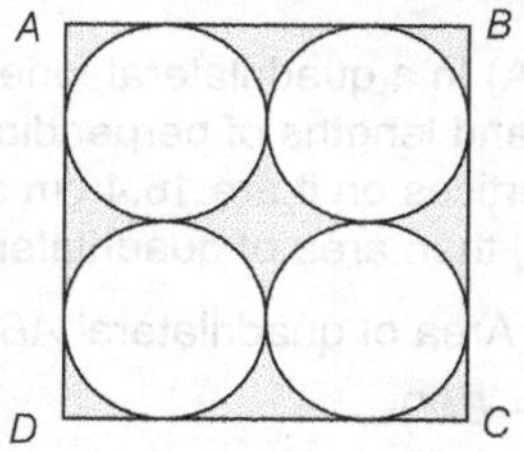

Q.12 A square *OABC* is inscribed in a quadrant *OPBQ* of a circle as shown in figure.

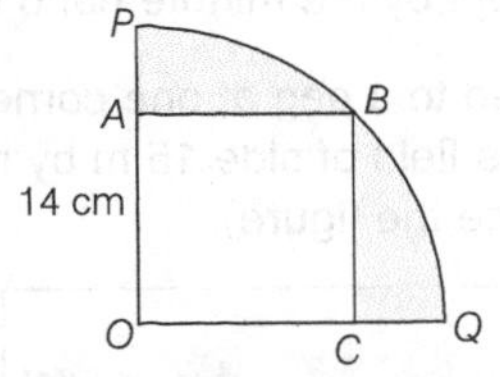

If *OA* = 14 cm, then find the area of shaded region. [take, $\pi = 22/7$]

Q.13 In the given figure, *ABCD* is a square of side 14 cm. With centres *A*, *B*, *C* and *D*, four circles are drawn such that each circle touch externally two of the remaining three circles. Find the area of the shaded region.

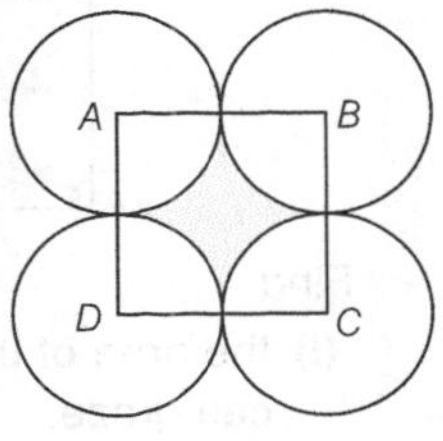

Q.14 There are three semi-circles *A*, *B* and *C* having diameter 3 cm each and another semi-circle *E* having a circle *D* with diameter 4.5 cm as shown in the figure below. Find the area of the shaded region.

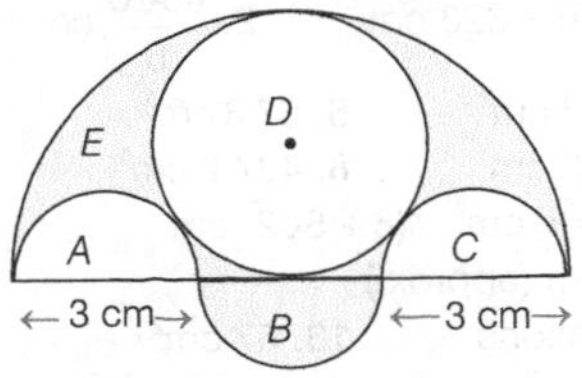

Q.15 In the given figure, *AB* and *CD* are two diameters of a circle (with centre *O*) perpendicular to each other and *OD* is the diameter of the smaller circle. If *OA* = 7 cm, then find the area of the shaded region.

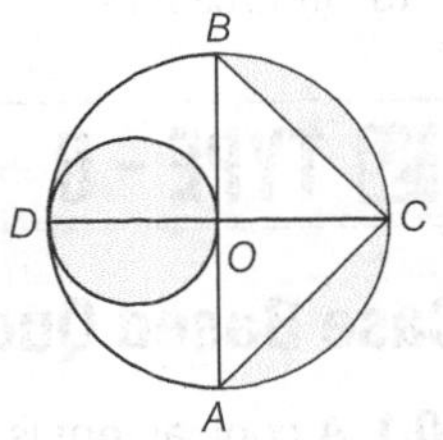

Q.16 Calculate the area of the designed region in figure, common between the two quadrants of circles of radius 8 cm each.

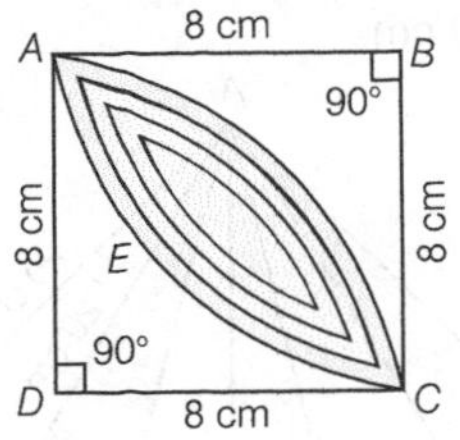

Answers

1. $16\sqrt{6}$ cm² 2. Base = 12 feet, height = 24 feet
3. 30 cm² 4. 14.45 cm² 5. 225 cm² 6. 5.6 cm
7. 1500 m² 8. 19 cm 9. 350 10. ₹1925
11. 30.86 cm² 12. 112 cm² 13. 42 cm² 14. 12.36 cm²
15. 66.5 cm² 16. $\frac{256}{7}$ cm²

TYPE - 5 4/5 Marks

Long Answer Type Questions

Q.1 ΔABC is a triangle, in which $AB = AC = 4$ cm and $\angle A = 90°$. Find

(i) the area of ΔABC.

(ii) the length of perpendicular from *A* to *BC*.

Q.2 If the sides of a triangle are in the ratio 5 : 6 : 7 and its perimeter is 72 cm, then find the length of longest altitude.

Q.3 The given figure shows an equilateral ΔABC, whose each side is 10 cm and a right angled ΔBDC whose side *BD* = 8 cm and $\angle D = 90°$. Find the area of the shaded portion.

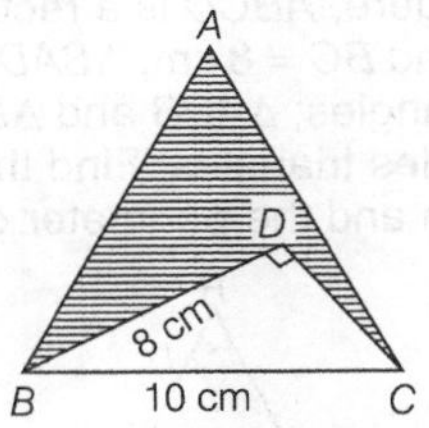

Q.4 Each of equal sides of an isosceles triangle is 4cm greater than its height. If the base of the triangle is 24 cm, then calculate the perimeter and area of triangle.

Q.5 Calculate the area of quadrilateral *ABCD*, in which ΔBCD is an equilateral with each side equal to 10 cm, $\angle A = 90°$ and *AD* = 8 cm.

Q.6 Find the area of a parallelogram given in the following figure. Also, find the length of the altitude from vertex *A* on the side *DC*.

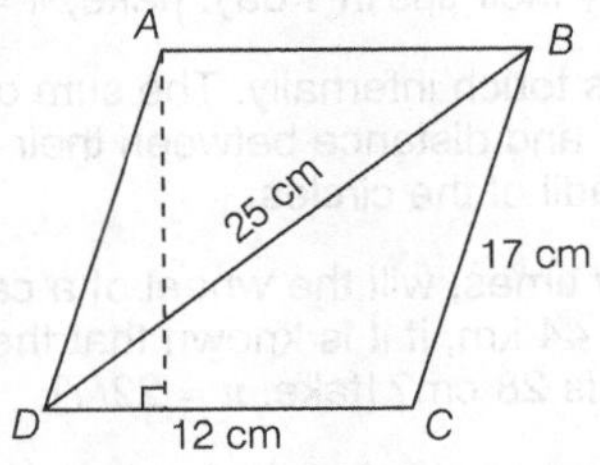

Q.7 In the given figure, triangle is drawn inside the rectangle. Find the area and perimeter of the shaded region.

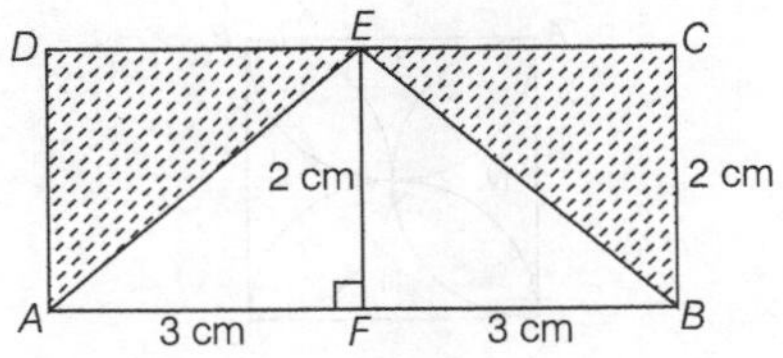

Q.8 A kite is made as shown alongside in which ΔABC is an equilateral triangle with side 20 cm, ΔBOC is an isosceles triangle with $OB = OC = 26$ cm and ΔODE is an isosceles triangle with base $DE = 8$ cm and height 6 cm. Find the whole area of the kite.

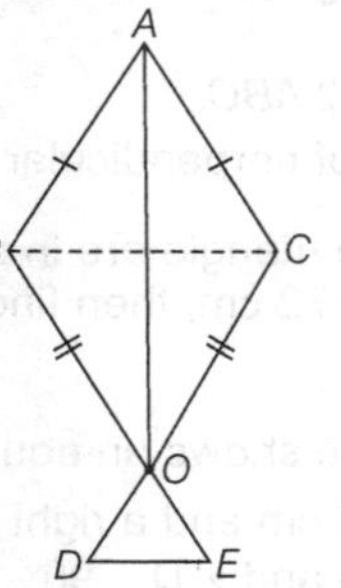

Q.9 In the given figure, $ABCD$ is a rectangle with sides $AB = 10$ cm and $BC = 8$ cm, ΔSAD and ΔBQC are equilateral triangles; ΔAPB and ΔDRC are right angled isosceles triangles. Find the area of the shaded region and the perimeter of the figure.

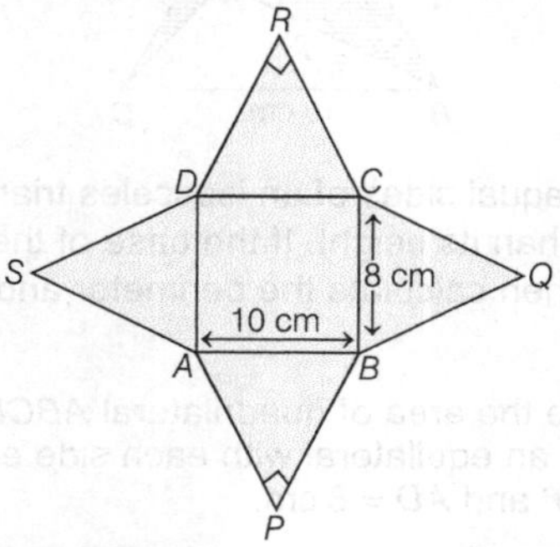

Q.10 The short and long hands of a clock are 6 cm and 8 cm long, respectively. Find the sum of the distance travelled by their tips in 1 day. [take, $\pi = 22/7$]

Q.11 Two circles touch internally. The sum of their areas is $116\,\pi$ cm^2 and distance between their centres is 6 cm. Find the radii of the circles.

Q.12 How many times, will the wheel of a car rotate in a journey of 44 km, if it is known that the diameter of the wheel is 28 cm? [take, $\pi = 22/7$]

Q.13 Find the area of shaded design in the given figure, where $ABCD$ is a square of side 10 cm and semi-circles are drawn with each of the side as diameter. [take, $\pi = 3.14$]

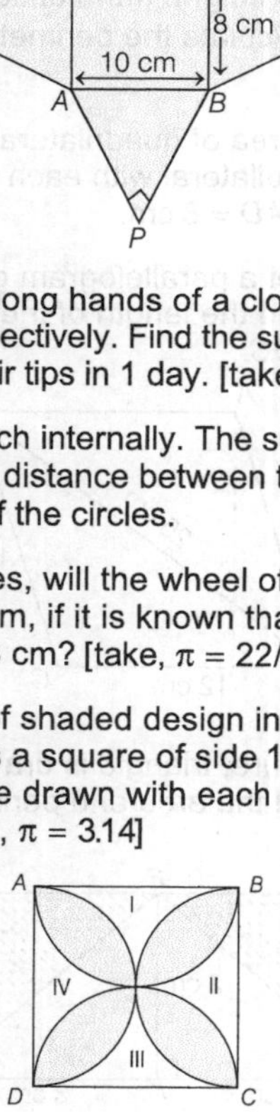

Q.14 The length of minute hand of a clock is 14cm. Find the area swept by the minute hand in 30 min.

Q.15 A horse is tied to a peg at one corner of a square shaped grass field of side 15 m by means of a 5m long rope (see the figure).

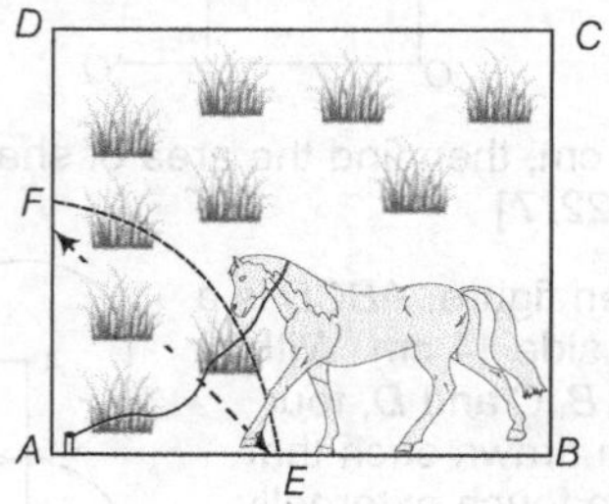

Find

(i) the area of the part of the field in which the horse can graze.

(ii) the increase in the grazing area if the rope were 10m long instead of 5m. [take, $\pi = 3.14$]

Answers

1. (i) 8 cm^2 (ii) 2.828 cm
2. $\frac{48\sqrt{6}}{5}$ cm
3. 19.30 cm^2
4. 64 cm, 192 cm^2
5. 67.3 cm^2
6. 180 cm^2, 15 cm
7. 6 cm^2, 17.2 cm
8. 437.2 cm^2
9. $(130 + 32\sqrt{3})$ cm^2, $4(8 + 5\sqrt{2})$ cm
10. 1282.29 cm (approx.)
11. 10 cm, 4 cm
12. 50000 rotations
13. 57 cm^2
14. 308 cm^2
15. (i) 19.625 cm^2 (ii) 58.875 cm^2

TYPE - 6

Case Based Questions

Q.1 A conical tent is made by stitching 12 triangular pieces of cloth of two different colours, black and white alternately, each piece measuring 10 cm, 20 cm and 20 cm.

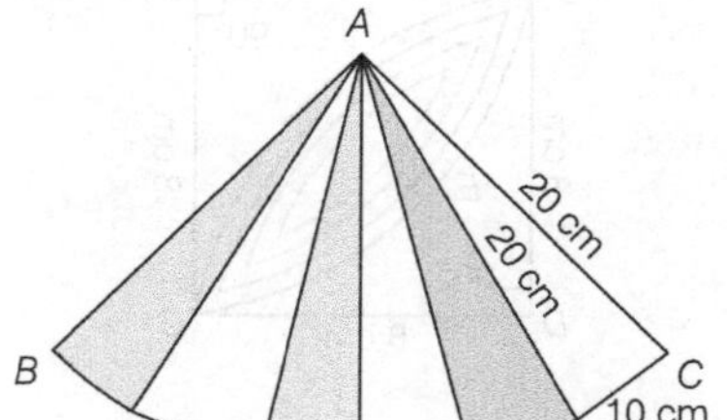

(i) How much cloth of black colour is required to make a conical tent?

(ii) Find the total length of triangular pieces of white colour. **(4 M)**

Q.2 In the given figure, a circle is inscribed and circumscribed in a square of side 14 cm.

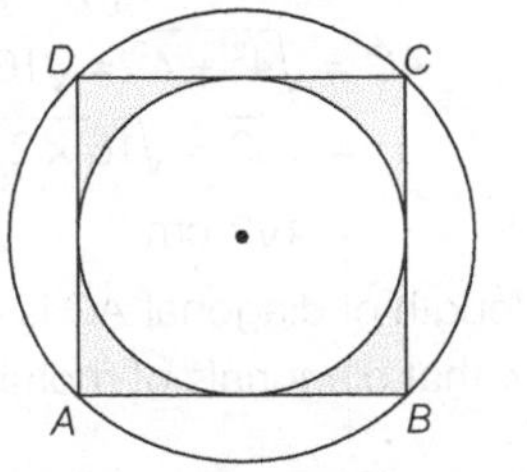

(i) Determine the inradius and circumradius of a circle.

(ii) Find the area of inscribed and circumscribed of circle.

(iii) Find the area of the shaded region. **(3 M)**

Q.3 In the given figure, O is the centre and AOC is a diameter of the circle.

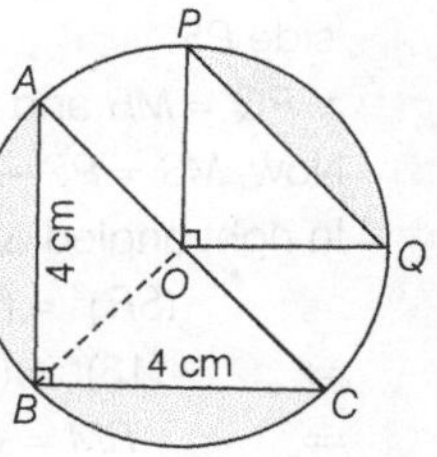

Find

(i) the sum of the areas of the two shaded segments made by the chords AB and BC.

(ii) the area of the shaded segment made by the chord PQ. $\left[\text{take, } \pi = \frac{22}{7}\right]$ **(4 M)**

Answers

1. (i) $150\sqrt{15}$ cm² (ii) 300 cm
2. (i) Inradius = 7 cm, Circumradius = $7\sqrt{2}$ cm (ii) 154 cm² and 308 cm² (iii) 42 cm² **3.** (i) $\frac{32}{7}$ cm² (ii) $\frac{16}{7}$ cm²

EXPLANATIONS

Multiple Choice Questions

1. (b) Let the sides of triangle be

$a = 12$ cm, $b = 16$ cm and $c = 20$ cm.

We know that semi-perimeter,

$$s = \frac{a+b+c}{2} = \frac{12+16+20}{2} = \frac{48}{2} = 24 \text{ cm}$$

By Heron's formula,

$$\text{area of triangle} = \sqrt{s(s-a)(s-b)(s-c)}$$
$$= \sqrt{24(24-12)(24-16)(24-20)}$$
$$= \sqrt{24 \times 12 \times 8 \times 4}$$
$$= \sqrt{9216}$$
$$= 96 \text{ cm}^2$$

Hence, the area of the given triangle is 96 cm².

2. (c) Draw $AD \perp BC \Rightarrow BD = DC = 3$ cm

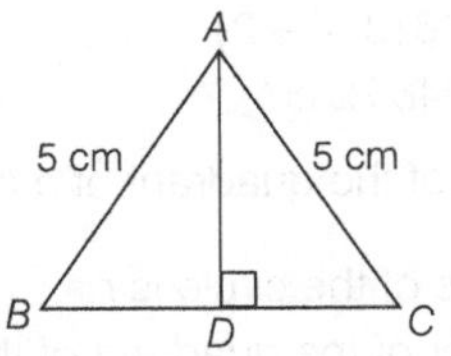

By Pythagoras theorem,

$$AD = \sqrt{AC^2 - DC^2}$$
$$= \sqrt{(5)^2 - (3)^2}$$

[$\because AC = 5$ cm and $DC = 3$ cm]

$AD = 4$ cm [taking +ve value]

$$\text{Area of } \Delta ABC = \frac{1}{2} \times BC \times AD$$
$$= \frac{1}{2} \times 6 \times 4$$

$\left[\because \text{area of triangle} = \frac{1}{2} \times \text{base} \times \text{height}\right]$

$$= 12 \text{ cm}^2$$

3. (c) Given, perimeter of rhombus

= perimeter of equilateral triangle

= 36 cm

Let side of equilateral triangle be a cm.

$\therefore$ $3a = 36$ cm

$\Rightarrow$ $a = 12$ cm

We know that

$$\text{Area of an equilateral triangle} = \frac{\sqrt{3}}{4}(\text{Side})^2$$
$$= \frac{\sqrt{3}}{4} \times 12^2$$
$$= 36\sqrt{3} \text{ cm}^2$$

4. (c) Given, area of an equilateral triangle is $16\sqrt{3}$ m².

We know that

$$\text{Area of an equilateral triangle} = \frac{\sqrt{3}}{4}(\text{Side})^2$$

$\Rightarrow$ $16\sqrt{3} = \frac{\sqrt{3}}{4}(\text{Side})^2$

$\Rightarrow$ $\text{Side} = \sqrt{16 \times 4} = 8$ m

Hence, the side of an equilateral triangle is 8 m.

5. (b) Let us draw a perpendicular RM parallel to PQ on side PS.

$\therefore PQ = MR$ and $QR = PM$

Now, $MS = PS - PM = 12 - 7 = 5$ cm $[\because PM = QR]$

In right angled ΔRMS,

$(SR)^2 = (MS)^2 + (RM)^2$ [by Pythagoras theorem]

$\Rightarrow (13)^2 = (5)^2 + (RM)^2$

$\Rightarrow RM = \sqrt{169 - 25} = 12$ cm

$\therefore PQ = MR = 12$ cm

Now, area of trapezium,

$$PQRS = \frac{1}{2}(QR + PS) \times PQ = \frac{1}{2} \times (7 + 12) \times 12$$

$$= 19 \times 6 = 114 \text{ cm}^2$$

6. (a) Let DE be the altitude.

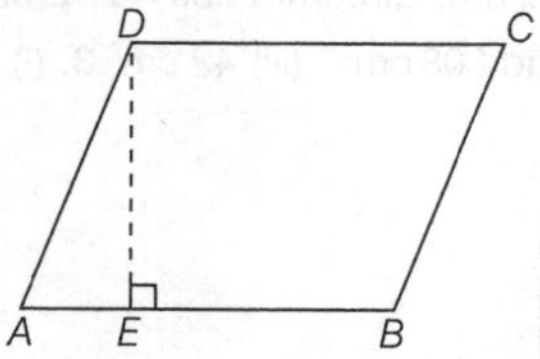

According to the question, $DE = 2\,AB$

$\because$ Area of parallelogram $ABCD = 392$ cm^2.

$\therefore AB \times DE = 392$

[$\because$ area of parallelogram = base × height]

$\Rightarrow AB \times 2\,AB = 392 \Rightarrow 2(AB)^2 = 392$

$\Rightarrow (AB)^2 = \frac{392}{2} = 196 \Rightarrow AB = 14$ cm

[taking positive square root as side cannot be negative]

Hence, the required base is 14 cm and altitude is 28 cm.

7. (d) From figure,

Area of shaded region

= Area of rectangle $MNHG$ + Area of rectangle $UVXW$ – Area of square $PQRS$

$= 50 \times 5 + 30 \times 5 - 5^2$

$= 250 + 150 - 25 = 375 \text{ m}^2$

Area of unshaded region

= Area of rectangle – Area of shaded region

$= 50 \times 30 - 375 = 1125 \text{ m}^2$

8. (d) Given, area of a square = 16 cm^2

Let side of a square be a.

$\therefore a^2 = 16 \Rightarrow a = 4$ cm [taking +ve value]

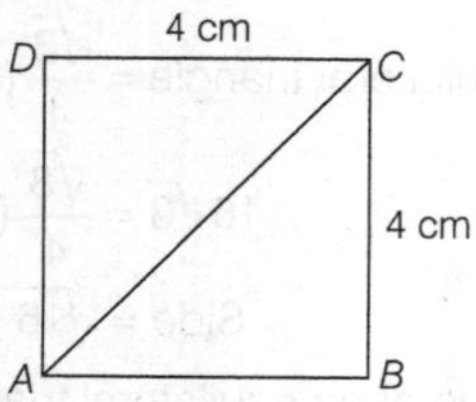

In ΔABC, we have

$AC^2 = AB^2 + BC^2$

[by Pythagoras theorem]

$\Rightarrow AC = \sqrt{4^2 + 4^2} = \sqrt{16 + 16}$

$= \sqrt{32} = \sqrt{16 \times 2}$

$= 4\sqrt{2}$ cm

Hence, the length of diagonal AC is $4\sqrt{2}$ cm.

9. (d) We know that diagonals of rhombus bisect each other at 90°.

$\therefore OB = \frac{d_2}{2}$ unit

and $OC = \frac{d_1}{2}$ unit

In ΔBOC, $BC^2 = OB^2 + OC^2$ [by Pythagoras theorem]

$$\Rightarrow a^2 = \left(\frac{d_2}{2}\right)^2 + \left(\frac{d_1}{2}\right)^2$$

$$\Rightarrow a = \sqrt{\left(\frac{d_2}{2}\right)^2 + \left(\frac{d_1}{2}\right)^2}$$

10. (a) In a given figure, two circles having radii R and r.

Then, area of circular ring

= Area of shaded region

= Area of outer circle – Area of inner circle

$= \pi R^2 - \pi r^2$

$= \pi (R^2 - r^2)$

11. (d) Given, perimeter of a circle = 96π cm

Let radius of the circle be r cm.

$\therefore 2\pi r = 96\pi$

$\Rightarrow r = 48$ cm

[$\because$ perimeter (circumference of a circle) = $2\pi r$]

Now, perimeter of semi-circle

$$= \frac{\text{Perimeter of circle}}{2} + \text{Diameter}$$

$$= \frac{96\pi}{2} + 2 \times 48 \quad [\because d = 2r]$$

$= 48(\pi + 2)$

$= 48(3.14 + 2)$ $[\because \pi = 3.14]$

$= 246.72$ cm

12. (a) If the area of the quadrant of a circle is $\frac{1}{4}\pi r^2$, then the radius of the circle is r.

Now, perimeter of the quadrant of the circle

$$= \frac{2\pi r}{4} + 2 \times \text{Radius}$$

$$= \frac{\pi r}{2} + 2r$$

$$= \left(\frac{\pi}{2} + 2\right)r$$

Assertion-Reason Type Questions

1. (d) Given, perimeter of an equilateral triangle = 57 cm

So, side of an equilateral triangle $= \frac{57}{3} = 19$ cm

Let three consecutive odd numbers be $(2n+1), (2n+3)$ and $(2n+5)$.

Now, perimeter of ΔABC

$$= 2n + 1 + 2n + 3 + 2n + 5$$
$$= (6n + 9) \text{ cm} \quad \ldots\text{(i)}$$

According to the question,

Longest side of ΔABC = Side of an equilateral triangle

$$\Rightarrow \quad 2n + 5 = 19$$
$$\Rightarrow \quad n = \frac{19-5}{2} = 7$$

Perimeter of $\Delta ABC = 6 \times 7 + 9$ [from Eq. (i)]

$$= 42 + 9$$
$$= 51 \text{ cm}$$

Hence, both A and R are true and R is incorrect reason for A.

2. (c) **Assertion** Given, in an isosceles ΔABC,

$$AB = AC = 5 \text{ cm and } BC = 6 \text{ cm}$$

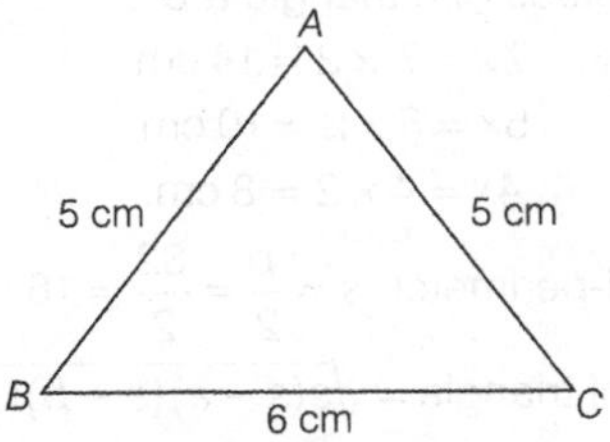

Now, area of an isosceles ΔABC

$$= \frac{1}{4} b\sqrt{4a^2 - b^2}$$
$$= \frac{1}{4} \times 6\sqrt{4 \times (5)^2 - (6)^2}$$
$$[\because a = 5 \text{ cm and } b = 6 \text{ cm}]$$
$$= \frac{1}{4} \times 6 \times \sqrt{100 - 36}$$
$$= \frac{1}{4} \times 6 \times 8 = 12 \text{ cm}^2$$

Hence, both A and R are true and R is the correct reason for A.

3. (c) Let $AC = 20$ cm, $BM = 16.4$ cm and $DN = 11.6$ cm.

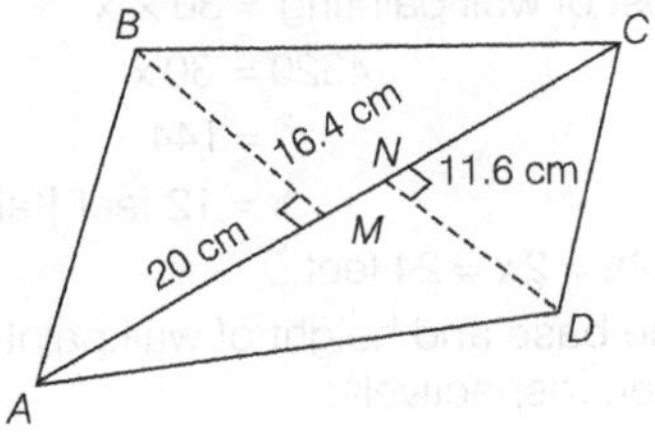

$\therefore$ Area of quadrilateral $ABCD$

$$= \frac{1}{2} \times AC \times (BM + DN)$$
$$= \frac{1}{2} \times 20 \times (16.4 + 11.6) = \frac{1}{2} \times 20 \times 28 = 280 \text{ cm}^2$$

Hence, both A and R are true and R is the correct reason for A.

4. (b) Given, perimeter of circle = Area of the circle [numerically]

Let the radius of the circle be r.

$$\therefore \quad 2\pi r = \pi r^2 \Rightarrow r = 2 \text{ units}$$

Now, area of the circle $= \pi r^2 = \pi \times 2^2 = 4\pi$ sq units

Hence, A is false, R is true.

5. (c) We know that the circle passing through vertices of a square $ABCD$ is called circumscribed circle and its radius R is called the circumradius.

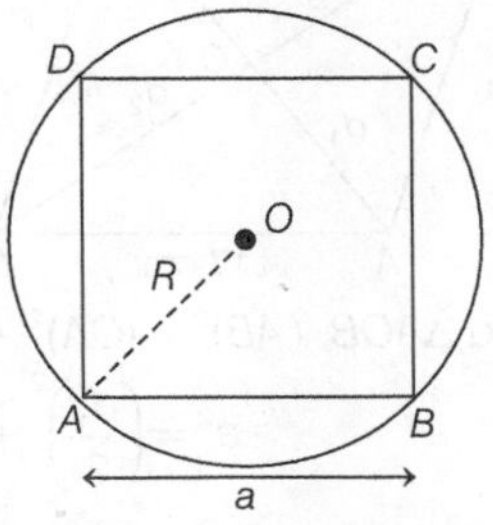

Therefore, diagonal of square $= a\sqrt{2}$

$$\Rightarrow \quad 2R = a\sqrt{2}$$
$$[\because \text{diagonal of square} = 2R]$$
$$\Rightarrow \quad R = \frac{a}{\sqrt{2}}$$

Hence, both A and R are true and R is the correct reason for A.

Statement Based Questions

1. (d) Given, sides of right angled triangle are $5x$ cm and $(3x - 1)$ cm

and area of triangle = 60 cm^2

$$\Rightarrow \quad \frac{1}{2} \times 5x(3x - 1) = 60$$
$$\left[\because \text{area of triangle} = \frac{1}{2} \times \text{base} \times \text{height}\right]$$
$$\Rightarrow \quad 3x^2 - x = 24$$
$$\Rightarrow \quad 3x^2 - x - 24 = 0$$
$$\Rightarrow \quad 3x^2 - 9x + 8x - 24 = 0$$
$$\Rightarrow \quad 3x(x - 3) + 8(x - 3) = 0$$
$$\Rightarrow \quad (3x + 8)(x - 3) = 0 \Rightarrow x = 3, \frac{-8}{3}$$
$$\therefore \quad x = 3$$
$$[\because \text{side cannot be negative}]$$

Therefore, sides of triangle are 15 cm and 8 cm.

Here, hypotenuse of right triangle $= \sqrt{15^2 + 8^2} = 17$ cm [by Pythagoras theorem]

Now, perimeter of the triangle is $= 15 + 8 + 17$
$= 40$ cm

Hence, Statement I is false and Statement II is true.

2. (a) Given, length of one diagonal, $d_1 = 16$ cm and perimeter of rhombus = 68 cm

$\Rightarrow \quad 4a = 68 \text{ cm} \Rightarrow a = 17 \text{ cm}$

$\because$ Diagonals of rhombus are perpendicular bisectors to each other.

$\therefore \quad OA = \frac{1}{2}d_1$ and $OB = \frac{1}{2}d_2$

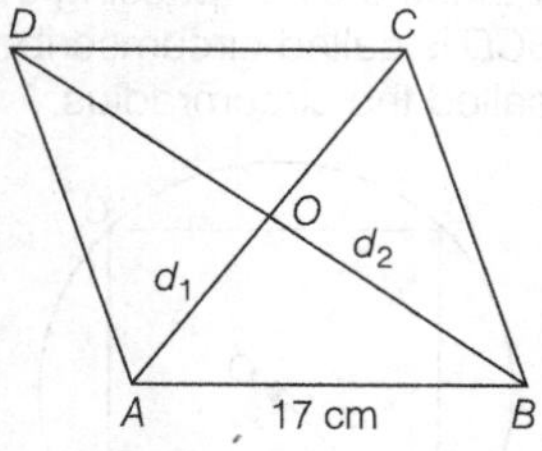

In right angled ΔAOB, $(AB)^2 = (OA)^2 + (OB)^2$

$$\Rightarrow \quad a^2 = \left(\frac{d_1}{2}\right)^2 + \left(\frac{d_2}{2}\right)^2$$

$$\Rightarrow \quad 4a^2 = d_1^2 + d_2^2$$

$$\Rightarrow \quad 4 \times (17)^2 = (16)^2 + (d_2)^2$$

$$\Rightarrow \quad 4 \times 289 - 256 = d_2^2$$

$$\Rightarrow \quad d_2 = \sqrt{900} = 30 \text{ cm}$$

Now, area of rhombus $= \frac{1}{2} \times d_1 \times d_2$

$= \frac{1}{2} \times 16 \times 30 = 240 \text{ cm}^2$

Hence, both the Statements are true.

3. (a) Let r and R be the radii of inner and outer circles, respectively.

Then, we have

$r = 2$ m and $R = (2 + 3)$ m $= 5$ m

Now, area of shaded portion $= \pi(R^2 - r^2)$

$= \pi(5^2 - 2^2)$

$= 3.14\,(25 - 4)$

$= 21 \times 3.14 = 65.94 \text{ cm}^2$

Hence, Statement I is true and Statement II is also true.

4. (c) Let the radius of the circle be R.

Given, area of quadrant of a circle $= \pi r^2$

$$\Rightarrow \quad \frac{\pi R^2}{4} = \pi r^2$$

$$\Rightarrow \quad R^2 = 4r^2$$

$$\Rightarrow \quad R = 2r$$

[$\because$ length cannot be negative]

Now, perimeter of quadrant of a circle

$$= \frac{2\pi R}{4} + R + R = \frac{2\pi \times 2r}{4} + 2R$$

$$= \pi r + 4r = r(4 + \pi)$$

Hence, Statement I is true and Statement II is false.

Short Answer Type Questions

1. Let ABC be the given triangle with sides $a = 7x$, $b = 5x$ and $c = 4x$.

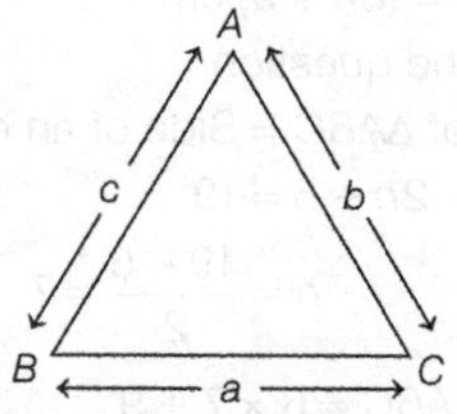

Since, perimeter, $p = 32$ cm

$\therefore \quad 7x + 5x + 4x = 32$

$\Rightarrow \quad 16x = 32$

$\Rightarrow \quad x = \frac{32}{16}$

$\Rightarrow \quad x = 2$ cm

Thus, the sides of a triangle are

$7x = 7 \times 2 = 14$ cm,

$5x = 5 \times 2 = 10$ cm

and $\quad 4x = 4 \times 2 = 8$ cm.

Now, semi-perimeter, $s = \frac{p}{2} = \frac{32}{2} = 16$ cm

and area of triangle $= \sqrt{s(s-a)(s-b)(s-c)}$

[by Heron's formula]

$= \sqrt{16\,(16-14)(16-10)(16-8)}$

$= \sqrt{16 \times 2 \times 6 \times 8}$

$= 4 \times 4 \times \sqrt{6} = 16\sqrt{6} \text{ cm}^2$

2. Let the base of painting be x feet.

Therefore, height of the painting $= 2x$ feet

Area of triangular wall painting $= \frac{1}{2} \times$ Base $\times$ Height

$= \frac{1}{2} \times x \times 2x$

$= x^2$ sq feet

$\because$ Cost of making the painting is ₹ 30 per sq feet.

$\therefore$ Total cost of wall painting $= 30 \times x^2$

$\Rightarrow \quad 4320 = 30x^2$

$\Rightarrow \quad x^2 = 144$

$\Rightarrow \quad x = 12$ feet [taking +ve value]

Now, height $= 2x = 24$ feet

Hence, the base and height of wall painting are 12 feet and 24 feet, respectively.

3. Given, base (B) and hypotenuse (H) are 5 cm and 13 cm, respectively.

Now, et the length of perpendicular be x cm.
Then, by Pythagoras theorem,

$$H^2 = P^2 + B^2$$
$$\Rightarrow \quad (13)^2 = (x)^2 + (5)^2$$
$$\Rightarrow \quad 169 - 25 = x^2 \Rightarrow 144 = x^2$$
$$\Rightarrow \quad x = \sqrt{144} \Rightarrow x = 12 \text{ cm}$$

[taking positive square root as side cannot be negative]

$\therefore$ Area of right angled triangle $= \frac{1}{2} \times \text{Base} \times \text{Height}$

$$= \frac{1}{2} \times 5 \times 12 = 30 \text{ cm}^2$$

Hence, the required area of the right angled triangle is 30 cm^2.

4. Given, $AD = 5$ cm

Let each side $= a$

$\therefore \ BD = DC = \frac{a}{2}$ [$\because D$ is also the mid-point of BC]

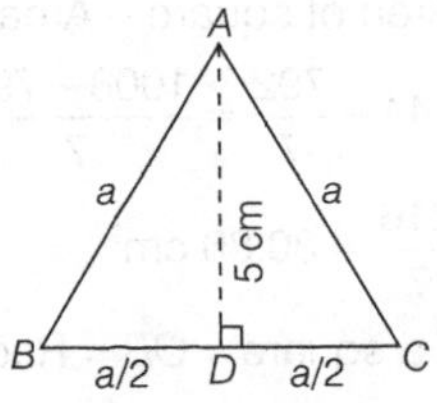

Now, applying Pythagoras theorem in ΔADB, we get

$$AB^2 = AD^2 + BD^2$$
$$\Rightarrow \quad a^2 = (5)^2 + \left(\frac{a}{2}\right)^2 \Rightarrow 25 = a^2 - \frac{a^2}{4}$$
$$\Rightarrow \quad 25 = \frac{3a^2}{4}$$
$$\Rightarrow \quad a^2 = \frac{25 \times 4}{3} = \frac{100}{3}$$

$\therefore$ Area of an equilateral ΔABC

$$= \frac{\sqrt{3}}{4} a^2 = \frac{\sqrt{3}}{4} \times \frac{100}{3} = \frac{25}{\sqrt{3}}$$
$$= \frac{25}{1.73} = 14.45 \text{ cm}^2$$

5. Given, $\angle ADC = 90°$, $AB = 10$ cm, $DC = 40$ cm.

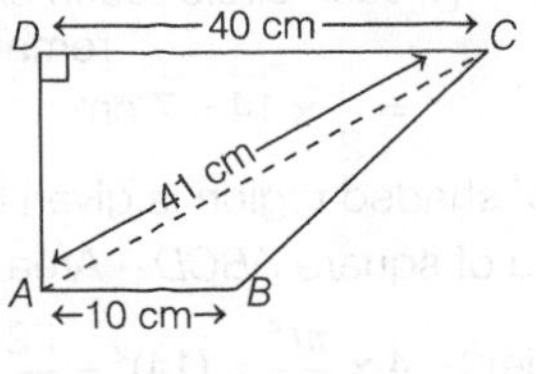

In ΔADC, $\quad AC^2 = AD^2 + DC^2$

[using Pythagoras theorem]

$$\Rightarrow \quad 41^2 = AD^2 + 40^2$$
$$\Rightarrow \quad AD^2 = 41^2 - 40^2$$
$$= (41 + 40)(41 - 40) = 81 \times 1 = 81$$

[$\because a^2 - b^2 = (a + b)(a - b)$]

$$\Rightarrow \quad AD = 9 \text{ cm}$$

[taking positive square root as side cannot be negative]

$\therefore$ Area of trapezium $= \frac{1}{2} \times (AB + CD) \times AD$

[$\because$ area of trapezium $= \frac{1}{2} \times$ sum of parallel sides $\times$ distance between them]

$$= \frac{1}{2} \times (10 + 40) \times 9$$
$$= \frac{1}{2} \times 50 \times 9 = 25 \times 9$$
$$= 225 \text{ cm}^2$$

6. Given, sides of the triangle are 15cm, 14cm and 13cm and base of the parallelogram = 15 cm

It is also given that the area of triangle is equal to area of parallelogram.

Now, semi-perimeter of triangle, $s = \frac{a + b + c}{2}$

$$= \frac{15 + 14 + 13}{2}$$
$$= 21 \text{ cm}$$

Area of triangle $= \sqrt{s(s-a)(s-b)(s-c)}$

$$= \sqrt{21(21-15)(21-14)(21-13)}$$

[by Heron's formula]

$$= \sqrt{21 \times 6 \times 7 \times 8}$$
$$= \sqrt{7056} = 84 \text{ cm}^2 \quad \ldots\text{(i)}$$

Now, area of parallelogram = Base $\times$ Height

$$\Rightarrow \quad 84 = 15 \times \text{Height} \quad \text{[from Eq. (i)]}$$
$$\therefore \quad \text{Height} = \frac{84}{15} = 5.6 \text{ cm}$$

7. Let the dimensions of the park $PQRS = 60 \text{ m} \times 80 \text{ m}$

Width of the footpath = 5 cm

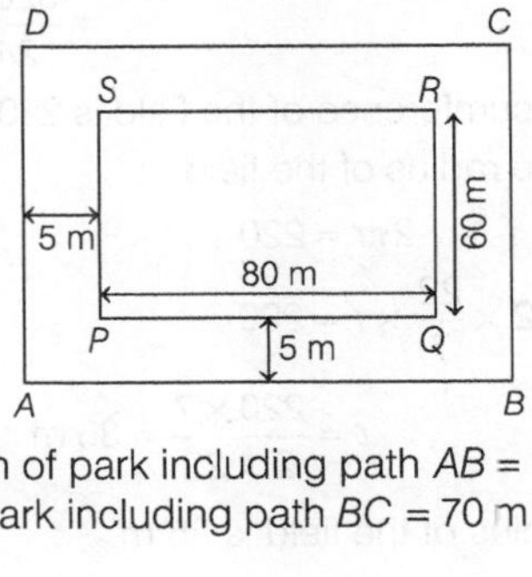

The length of park including path $AB = 90$ m and the width of park including path $BC = 70$ m

Now, area of the park $PQRS = 60 \times 80$

[$\because$ area of rectangle = length × breadth]

$= 4800 \text{m}^2$

and area of the park including path $ABCD = 90 \times 70$

$= 6300 \text{ m}^2$

$\therefore$ Area of path $= 6300 - 4800 = 1500 \text{ m}^2$

8. Circumference of the circle having radius 13 cm

$= 2\pi \times 13$

$= 26\pi$ cm ...(i)

and circumference of the circle having radius 6 cm

$= 2\pi \times 6$

$= 12\pi$ cm ...(ii)

$\therefore$ Sum of the circumferences of the two circles

$= 26\pi + 12\pi$ [from Eqs. (i) and (ii)]

$= 38\pi$ cm ...(iii)

Let r be the radius of the required circle whose circumference is 38π cm.

Then, $2\pi r = 38\pi$ [from Eq. (iii)]

$\Rightarrow r = 19$ cm

Hence, the radius of the new circle is 19 cm.

9. In 1 h, distance covered by wheel = 33 km.

In 1 min, distance covered by wheel

$= \frac{33 \times 1000}{60} = 550$ m ...(i)

Now, number of revolutions made in 1 min

$= \frac{\text{Distance covered by wheel}}{\text{Circumference of the wheel}}$

$= \frac{550}{2\pi r} = \frac{550}{2 \times \frac{22}{7} \times \frac{25}{100}}$

$\left[\text{from Eq. (i) and } 25 \text{ cm} = \frac{25}{100} \text{ m}\right]$

$= \frac{550 \times 7 \times 100}{2 \times 22 \times 25} = 350$

Hence, wheel makes 350 revolutions in 1 min.

10. Length of fence of a circular field $= \frac{\text{Total cost}}{\text{Rate}}$

$= \frac{5280}{24} = 220$ m

So, the circumference of the field is 220 m.

Let r be the radius of the field.

Then, $2\pi r = 220$

$\Rightarrow 2 \times \frac{22}{7} \times r = 220$

$\Rightarrow r = \frac{220 \times 7}{2 \times 22} = 35$ m

So, the radius of the field is 35 m.

Now, area of the field $= \pi r^2 = \frac{22}{7} \times 35 \times 35$

$= 22 \times 5 \times 35 \text{ m}^2$

Given, cost of ploughing 1 m² of the field = ₹ 0.50

$\therefore$ Total cost of ploughing the field $= 0.5 \times 22 \times 5 \times 35$

= ₹ 1925

11. $\because$ Area of square = $(\text{Side})^2$

$\therefore$ Area of square $ABCD = 12 \times 12 = 144 \text{ cm}^2$

$\because$ Diameter of each circle $= \frac{12}{2} = 6$ cm

[here, length of square = 2 × diameter of circle]

$\therefore$ Radius of each circle, $r = \frac{6}{2} = 3$ cm

Area of one circle $= \pi r^2$

$= \frac{22}{7} \times 3 \times 3 = \frac{198}{7} \text{ cm}^2$

Therefore, area of four circles $= 4 \times \frac{198}{7} = \frac{792}{7} \text{cm}^2$

Hence, area of the shaded region

= Area of square − Area of four circles

$= 144 - \frac{792}{7} = \frac{1008 - 792}{7}$

$= \frac{216}{7} = 30.86 \text{ cm}^2$

12. $\because$ Diagonal of a square $= OB$ = Radius (r) = Side $\sqrt{2}$

$= 14\sqrt{2}$ cm

[$\because$ diagonal of square = side $\sqrt{2}$]

$\therefore$ Area of shaded region

= Area of quadrant $OPBQ$ − Area of square $OABC$

$= \frac{1}{4}\pi r^2 - (\text{Side})^2$

$= \frac{1}{4} \times \frac{22}{7} \times (14\sqrt{2})^2 - (14)^2$

$= \frac{11}{14} \times 14 \times 14 \times 2 - 196 = 308 - 196 = 112 \text{ cm}^2$

13. Given, side of a square $ABCD = 14$ cm

and A, B, C and D are four centres of circles.

$\therefore$ Radii of circles $= \frac{1}{2} \times$ (Side of square)

[$\because$ each circle touch externally two of the remaining three circles]

$= \frac{1}{2} \times 14 = 7$ cm

Now, area of shaded region is given by

= Area of square $ABCD$ − Area of four quadrants

$= (\text{Side})^2 - 4 \times \frac{\pi r^2}{4} = (14)^2 - \frac{22}{7} \times 7 \times 7$

$= 196 - 154 = 42 \text{ cm}^2$

14. Given, diameter of semi-circles A, B and C = 3 cm

$\therefore$ Radii of semi-circles A, B and $C = \frac{3}{2}$ cm

Diameter of circle D = 4.5 cm

$\therefore$ Radius of circle $D = \frac{4.5}{2}$ cm

Now, radius of semi-circle E = 4.5 cm

$\therefore$ Area of shaded region

= Area of larger semi-circle E – Area of circle with centre D – 2 (Area of small semi-circle A or C) + Area of small semi-circle B

$$= \frac{\pi}{2}(4.5)^2 - \pi\left(\frac{4.5}{2}\right)^2 - 2 \times \frac{\pi}{2}\left(\frac{3}{2}\right)^2 + \frac{\pi}{2}\left(\frac{3}{2}\right)^2$$

$$= \frac{\pi}{2}(4.5)^2 - \pi\left(\frac{4.5}{2}\right)^2 - \frac{\pi}{2}\left(\frac{3}{2}\right)^2$$

$$= \pi\left[\frac{(4.5)^2}{2} - \left(\frac{4.5}{2}\right)^2 - \frac{1}{2}\left(\frac{3}{2}\right)^2\right]$$

$$= \pi(10.125 - 5.0625 - 1.125) = \pi \times 3.9375 = 12.36 \text{ cm}^2$$

15. Given, AB and CD are two diameters

i.e. $OA = OB = OC = OD = 7$ cm

$\therefore$ Radius of the smaller circle $= \frac{7}{2}$ cm

Now, area of $\Delta ABC = \frac{1}{2} \times$ Base $\times$ Height

$$= \frac{1}{2} \times AB \times OC$$

$$= \frac{1}{2} \times 14 \times 7$$

$[\because AB = 7 + 7 = 14 \text{ cm and } OC = 7 \text{ cm}]$

$$= 49 \text{ cm}^2$$

and area of semi-circle $ACB = \frac{\pi r^2}{2}$

$$= \frac{22}{7} \times \frac{1}{2} \times 7 \times 7$$

$[\because r = 7 \text{ cm}]$

$$= 77 \text{ cm}^2$$

$\therefore$ Area of the shaded region

= Area of circle having diameter OD + Area of semi-circle ACB – Area of ΔABC

$$= \pi \times \frac{7}{2} \times \frac{7}{2} + 77 - 49 = \frac{22}{7} \times \frac{7}{2} \times \frac{7}{2} + 28$$

$$= \frac{77}{2} + 28 = \frac{133}{2} = 66.5 \text{ cm}^2$$

16. Given, the common radius between the two quadrants of circles, r = 8 cm

So, area of sector $BAEC = \frac{\pi r^2}{4}$

$$= \frac{22}{7} \times \frac{8 \times 8}{4} = \frac{352}{7} \text{ cm}^2$$

Area of right angled $\Delta ABC = \frac{1}{2} \times AB \times BC$

$$= \frac{1}{2} \times 8 \times 8$$

$$= 32 \text{ cm}^2$$

$\therefore$ Area of shaded region AEC

= Area of sector $BAEC$ – Area of right angled ΔABC

$$= \frac{352}{7} - 32$$

$$= \frac{352 - 224}{7} = \frac{128}{7} \text{ cm}^2$$

$\therefore$ Shaded region = 2 × Area of shaded region AEC

$$= 2 \times \frac{128}{7}$$

$$= \frac{256}{7} \text{ cm}^2$$

Long Answer Type Questions

1. Given, $AB = AC = 4$ cm and $\angle A = 90°$

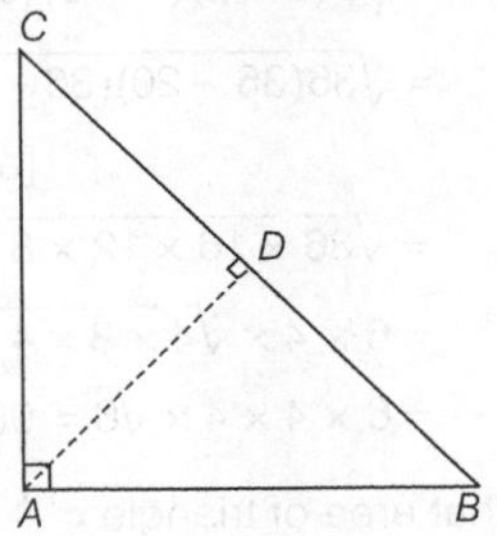

(i) The area of $\Delta BAC = \frac{1}{2} \times AB \times AC$

$$= \frac{1}{2} \times 4 \times 4 = 8 \text{ cm}^2 \quad \ldots(a)$$

(ii) In ΔBAC, $(BC)^2 = (AC)^2 + (AB)^2$

[by Pythagoras theorem]

$\Rightarrow \quad BC = \sqrt{4^2 + 4^2} = 4\sqrt{2}$ cm $\quad \ldots$(b)

Let AD be the perpendicular drawn from vertex A to side BC.

Now, area of $\Delta BAC = \frac{1}{2} \times BC \times AD$

$\Rightarrow \quad 8 = \frac{1}{2} \times 4\sqrt{2} \times AD$

[from Eqs. (a) and (b)]

$\Rightarrow \quad AD = \frac{8 \times 2}{4\sqrt{2}}$

$\Rightarrow \quad AD = 2\sqrt{2}$ cm

$= 2 \times 1.414 \quad [\because \sqrt{2} = 1.414]$

$\Rightarrow \quad AD = 2.828$ cm

2. Given, perimeter of triangle = 72 cm

and ratio of sides = 5 : 6 : 7

Let sides be $5x$, $6x$ and $7x$.

$$\therefore \quad 5x + 6x + 7x = 72$$

$$\Rightarrow \quad 18x = 72$$

$$\Rightarrow \quad x = 4$$

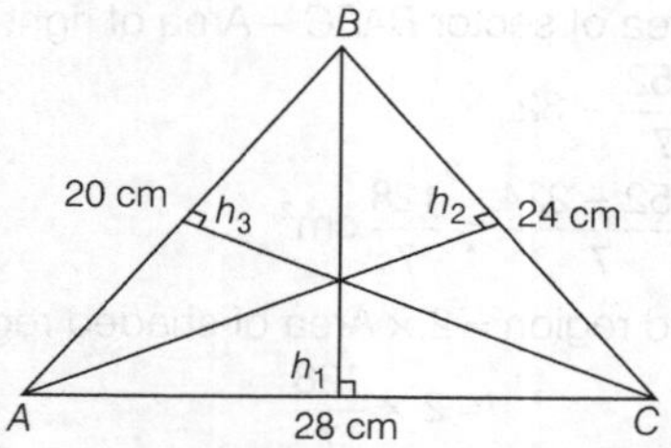

Therefore, sides are 20 cm, 24 cm and 28 cm.

Semi-perimeter of the triangle $= \frac{72}{2}$

$= 36$ cm

Area of triangle $= \sqrt{s(s-a)(s-b)(s-c)}$

$$= \sqrt{36(36-20)(36-24)(36-28)}$$

[by Heron's formula]

$$= \sqrt{36 \times 16 \times 12 \times 8}$$

$$= 6 \times 4 \times \sqrt{4 \times 3 \times 4 \times 2}$$

$$= 6 \times 4 \times 4 \times \sqrt{6} = 96\sqrt{6} \text{ cm}^2 \quad \ldots\text{(i)}$$

As we know that area of triangle $= \frac{1}{2} \times$ Base $\times$ Altitude

$$\therefore \quad 96\sqrt{6} = \frac{1}{2} \times AC \times h_1 = \frac{1}{2} \times BC \times h_2 = \frac{1}{2} \times AB \times h_3$$

$$\Rightarrow 96\sqrt{6} = \frac{1}{2} \times 28 \times h_1 = \frac{1}{2} \times 24 \times h_2$$

I II III

$$= \frac{1}{2} \times 20 \times h_3 \quad \ldots\text{(ii) [from Eq. (i)]}$$

IV

On solving I and II terms of Eq. (ii), we get

$$h_1 = \frac{48\sqrt{6}}{7} \text{ cm} \quad \ldots\text{(iii)}$$

Now, on solving I and III terms of Eq. (ii), we get

$$h_2 = 8\sqrt{6} \text{ cm} \quad \ldots\text{(iv)}$$

On solving I and IV terms of Eq. (ii), we get

$$h_3 = \frac{48\sqrt{6}}{5} \text{ cm} \quad \ldots\text{(v)}$$

On comparing Eqs. (iii), (iv) and (v), we get

$$h_3 > h_2 > h_1$$

Therefore, length of longest altitude is $\frac{48\sqrt{6}}{5}$ cm.

3. Given, side of an equilateral $\Delta ABC = 10$ cm

$\therefore$ Area of an equilateral $\Delta ABC = \frac{\sqrt{3}}{4} (\text{Side})^2$

$$= \frac{\sqrt{3}}{4} \times (10)^2$$

$$= 25\sqrt{3} \text{ cm}^2$$

$$= 43.30 \text{ cm}^2$$

Now, in right angled ΔBDC,

$BD = 8$ cm and $BC = 10$ cm [given]

$\therefore \quad BC^2 = BD^2 + DC^2$ [by Pythagoras theorem]

$$\Rightarrow \quad DC^2 = BC^2 - BD^2$$

$$\Rightarrow \quad DC = \sqrt{10^2 - 8^2} = \sqrt{100 - 64}$$

$\Rightarrow \quad DC = 6$ cm [taking +ve value]

Area of right angled $\Delta BDC = \frac{1}{2} \times BD \times DC$

$$= \frac{1}{2} \times 8 \times 6$$

$$= 24 \text{ cm}^2$$

Now, area of shaded region = Area of ΔABC

$-$ Area of ΔBDC

$$= 43.30 - 24 = 19.30 \text{ cm}^2$$

4. Let the height of the triangle be h cm.

$\therefore$ Equal sides of triangle, $AB = BC = (h + 4)$ cm

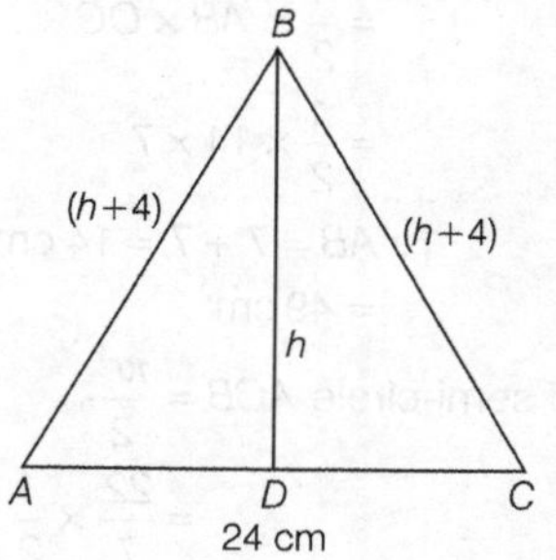

In ΔBAD, $\quad (h+4)^2 = h^2 + \left(\frac{24}{2}\right)^2$

[by Pythagoras theorem]

$$\Rightarrow \quad h^2 = (h+4)^2 - \frac{(24)^2}{4}$$

$$\Rightarrow \quad h = \frac{1}{2}\sqrt{4(h+4)^2 - (24)^2}$$

Area of $\Delta ABC = \frac{1}{2} \times 24 \times h = \frac{24}{4}\sqrt{4(h+4)^2 - 24^2}$

$$\left[\because h = \frac{1}{2}\sqrt{4(h+4)^2 - (24)^2}\right]$$

$$\Rightarrow \quad 12h = 6\sqrt{4(h^2 + 8h + 16) - 4 \times 12^2}$$

$$\Rightarrow \quad 12h = 12\sqrt{h^2 + 8h + 16 - 144}$$

$$\Rightarrow \quad h = \sqrt{h^2 + 8h - 128}$$

On squaring both sides, we get

$$h^2 = h^2 + 8h - 128$$

$\Rightarrow \quad 8h = 128$

$\Rightarrow \quad h = 16$ cm

Now, sides of ΔABC,

$AB = 16 + 4 = 20$ cm, $BC = 20$ cm and $AC = 24$ cm

So, perimeter of $\Delta ABC = 20 + 20 + 24 = 64$ cm

and area of $\Delta ABC = \frac{1}{2} \times AC \times h$

$$= \frac{1}{2} \times 24 \times 16 = 192 \text{ cm}^2$$

5. Given, a quadrilateral $ABCD$, equal side is 10 cm, $\angle A = 90°$ and $AD = 8$ cm.

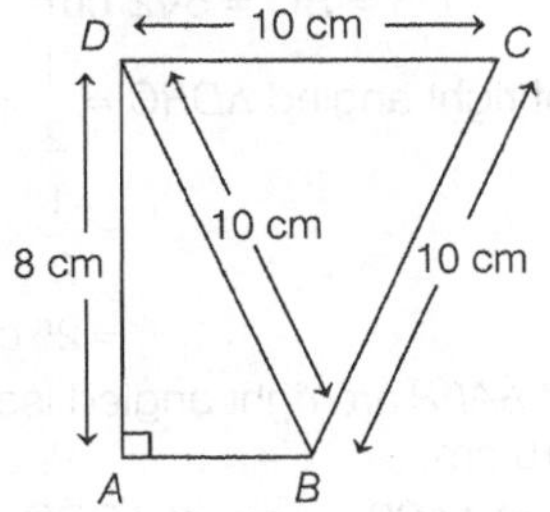

In ΔDAB, $BD^2 = AD^2 + AB^2$ [by Pythagoras theorem]

$\Rightarrow \quad AB^2 = BD^2 - AD^2$

$\Rightarrow \quad AB^2 = (10)^2 - (8)^2 = 100 - 64$

$\Rightarrow \quad AB^2 = 36$

$\Rightarrow \quad AB = 6$ cm [taking positive square root as side cannot be negative]

ar (quadrilateral $ABCD$) = ar (ΔBCD) + ar(ΔDAB)

$$= \frac{\sqrt{3}}{4}(10)^2 + \frac{1}{2} \times AB \times AD$$

$\left[\because \text{area of } \Delta = \frac{1}{2} \times \text{base} \times \text{height and area of an equilateral triangle} = \frac{\sqrt{3}}{4} \times (\text{side})^2\right]$

$$= \frac{\sqrt{3}}{4} \times (10)^2 + \frac{1}{2} \times 6 \times 8$$

$$= 25\sqrt{3} + 4 \times 6 = 25\sqrt{3} + 24$$

$$= 25 \times 1.732 + 24$$

$$= 43.3 + 24 = 67.3 \text{ cm}^2$$

6. Clearly, ar (parallelogram $ABCD$) $= 2 \times$ ar (ΔBCD)...(i)

Let the sides of ΔBCD be

$a = 12$ cm, $b = 17$ cm and $c = 25$ cm.

Semi-perimeter of ΔBCD,

$$s = \frac{a + b + c}{2} = \frac{12 + 17 + 25}{2}$$

$$= \frac{54}{2} = 27 \text{ cm}$$

$\therefore$ ar (ΔBCD) $= \sqrt{s(s-a)(s-b)(s-c)}$ [by Heron's formula]

$$= \sqrt{27(27-12)(27-17)(27-25)}$$

$$= \sqrt{27 \times 15 \times 10 \times 2}$$

$$= \sqrt{3 \times 3 \times 3 \times 3 \times 5 \times 5 \times 2 \times 2}$$

$$= 3 \times 3 \times 5 \times 2$$

$$= 90 \text{ cm}^2$$

On substituting the value of area of ΔBCD in Eq. (i), we get

Area of parallelogram $ABCD = 2 \times 90 = 180 \text{ cm}^2$ ...(ii)

Let altitude of the parallelogram corresponding to base DC be h cm.

Area of parallelogram $ABCD$ = Base × Altitude

$\Rightarrow \quad 180 = DC \times h$ [from Eq. (ii)]

$\Rightarrow \quad 180 = 12 \times h$

$\therefore \quad h = \frac{180}{12} = 15$ cm

Hence, the required area of parallelogram is 180 cm^2 and the length of altitude is 15 cm.

7. Now, area of $\Delta ABE = \frac{1}{2} \times AB \times EF$

$\left[\because \text{area of triangle} = \frac{1}{2} \times \text{base} \times \text{height}\right]$

$$= \frac{1}{2} \times 6 \times 2 = 6 \text{ cm}^2$$

and area of the rectangle $ABCD$

$$= AB \times BC$$

$$= 6 \times 2 = 12 \text{ cm}^2$$

[$\because$ area of rectangle = length × breadth]

$\therefore$ Area of the shaded region = Area of rectangle $ABCD$ − Area of ΔABE

$$= 12 - 6$$

$$= 6 \text{ cm}^2$$

Now, in right angled ΔAFE,

$AE = \sqrt{AF^2 + FE^2}$ [using Pythagoras theorem]

$$= \sqrt{(3)^2 + (2)^2}$$

$$= \sqrt{9 + 4}$$

$$= \sqrt{13}$$

$$= 3.6 \text{ cm}$$

$\therefore$ Perimeter of the shaded region

$= (AD + DE + EA) + (BC + CE + EB)$

$= 2(AD + DE + EA)$

[$\because AD = BC$, $AE = EB$ and $DE = CE$]

$= 2(2 + 3 + 3.6)$

$= 2(8.6) = 17.2$ cm

8. In given figure of kite, ΔABC is an equilateral triangle with side 20 cm and ΔBOC and ΔDOE are isosceles triangle.

Area of kite = Area of ΔABC + Area of ΔBOC + Area of ΔODE ...(i)

Now, area of $\Delta ABC = \frac{\sqrt{3}}{4} \times (20)^2$

[$\because$ area of equilateral triangle $= \frac{\sqrt{3}}{4} a^2$ and $a = 20$ cm]

$= 100\sqrt{3}$ cm^2

$= 173.2$ cm^2

Area of isosceles $\Delta BOC = \frac{1}{4} BC\sqrt{4(OB)^2 - (BC)^2}$

[$\because$ area of isosceles triangle $= \frac{b}{4}\sqrt{4a^2 - b^2}$]

$= \frac{1}{4} \times 20\sqrt{4(26)^2 - (20)^2}$

[$\because OB = 26$ cm and $BC = 20$ cm]

$= 5\sqrt{2704 - 400}$

$= 5 \times 48$

$= 240$ cm^2

Area of $\Delta ODE = \frac{1}{2} \times DE \times h$

[$\because$ area of triangle $= \frac{1}{2} \times$ base $\times$ height]

$= \frac{1}{2} \times 8 \times 6$ [$\because DE = 8$ cm and $h = 6$ cm]

$= 24$ cm^2

From Eq. (i),

area of kite $= 173.2 + 240 + 24$

$= 437.2$ cm^2

9. In the given figure, $ABCD$ is a rectangle, ΔSAD and ΔBQC are equilateral triangles and ΔAPB and ΔDRC are right angled isosceles triangles.

Now, area of shaded region

= Area of rectangle $ABCD$ + Area of ΔSAD + Area of ΔAPB + Area of ΔBQC + Area of ΔDRC ...(i)

Area of rectangle $ABCD = AB \times BC$

$= 10 \times 8 = 80$ cm^2 ...(ii)

[$\because AB = 10$ cm and $BC = 8$ cm]

Area of equilateral $\Delta SAD = \frac{\sqrt{3}}{4} \times (AD)^2$

$= \frac{\sqrt{3}}{4} \times 8^2$ [$\because AD = 8$ cm]

$= 16\sqrt{3}$ cm^2 ...(iii)

$\because$ ΔSAD and ΔBQC are equilateral triangles on side of 8 cm.

$\therefore$ Area of ΔSAD = Area of ΔBQC

$= 16\sqrt{3}$ cm^2 ...(iv)

In right angled ΔDRC,

$(DC)^2 = (DR)^2 + (CR)^2$

[by Pythagoras theorem]

$\Rightarrow (10)^2 = (DR)^2 + (DR)^2$

[$\because \Delta DRC$ is an isosceles triangle]

$\Rightarrow 100 = 2(DR)^2$

$\Rightarrow DR = \sqrt{50} = 5\sqrt{2}$ cm

$\Rightarrow DR = RC = 5\sqrt{2}$ cm

Now, area of right angled $\Delta DRC = \frac{1}{2} \times DR \times RC$

$= \frac{1}{2} \times 5\sqrt{2} \times 5\sqrt{2}$

$= 25$ cm^2 ...(v)

$\because$ ΔDRC and ΔAPB are right angled isosceles triangle on base of 10 cm.

$\therefore$ Area of ΔAPB = Area of ΔDRC

$= 25$ cm^2 ...(vi) [from Eq. (v)]

Now, area of shaded region

$= 80 + 16\sqrt{3} + 16\sqrt{3} + 25 + 25$

[from Eqs. (i), (ii), (iii), (iv), (v) and (vi)]

$= (130 + 32\sqrt{3})$ cm^2

Perimeter of the figure

$= CQ + QB + BP + PA + AS + SD + DR + CR$

$= 8 + 8 + 5\sqrt{2} + 5\sqrt{2} + 8 + 8 + 5\sqrt{2} + 5\sqrt{2}$

$= 32 + 20\sqrt{2} = 4(8 + 5\sqrt{2})$ cm

10. In 1 day i.e. 24 h, short (hour) hand of the clock make 2 revolutions and long (minute) hand make 24 revolutions.

In 1 revolution, distance travelled by tip of hour hand

= Circumference of circle of radius 6 cm

$= 2\pi r = 2 \times \frac{22}{7} \times 6$

In 1 revolution, distance travelled by tip of minute hand

= Circumference of circle of radius 8 cm

$= 2\pi r = 2 \times \frac{22}{7} \times 8$

$\therefore$ Sum of distances travelled by tips of both hand in 1 day $= 2 \times 2 \times \frac{22}{7} \times 6 + 24 \times 2 \times \frac{22}{7} \times 8$

$= 2 \times \frac{22}{7} \times (12 + 192)$

$= 2 \times \frac{22}{7} \times 204 = 1282.29$ cm (approx.)

11. Let R and r be the radii of the circles having centres at O and O', respectively.

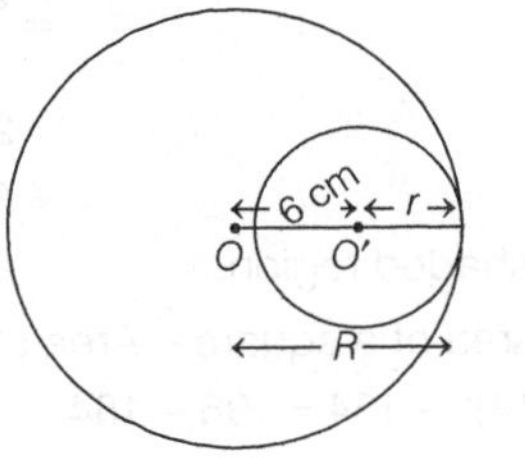

Then, sum of areas $= 116\pi$ cm^2

$\Rightarrow \quad \pi R^2 + \pi r^2 = 116\pi$

$\Rightarrow \quad R^2 + r^2 = 116 \quad \ldots$(i)

Distance between the centres = 6 cm

$\Rightarrow \quad OO' = 6$ cm

$\Rightarrow \quad R - r = 6 \quad \ldots$(ii)

Now, $\quad (R+r)^2 + (R-r)^2 = 2(R^2 + r^2)$

$\Rightarrow \quad (R+r)^2 + 36 = 2 \times 116$ [using Eqs. (i) and (ii)]

$\Rightarrow \quad (R+r)^2 = (2 \times 116 - 36) = 196$

$\Rightarrow \quad R + r = 14 \quad \ldots$(iii)

On solving Eqs. (ii) and (iii), we get

$R = 10$ cm and $r = 4$ cm

Hence, the radii of the circles are 10 cm and 4 cm.

12. Given, diameter of the wheel, $d = 28$ cm

$\therefore$ Radius of the wheel, $r = \frac{d}{2} = \frac{28}{2} = 14$ cm

Now, distance covered by wheel in one rotation

$=$ Circumference of a circle $= 2\pi r$

$= 2 \times \frac{22}{7} \times 14$

$= 2 \times 22 \times 2 = 88$ cm

Clearly, total distance covered by the wheel in the journey $= 44$ km $= 44 \times 1000 \times 100$ cm

[$\because$ 1 km $= 1 \times 1000 \times 100$ cm]

$= 4400000$ cm

Number of rotations

$= \dfrac{\text{Total distance covered by the wheel}}{\text{Distance covered by the wheel in one rotation}}$

$= \frac{4400000}{88} = 50000$

Hence, wheel of the car will take 50000 rotations to cover a distance of 44 km.

13. Let the four unshaded regions be denoted by I, II, III and IV as shown in the figure.

Given, side of square = 10 cm

Diameter of each semi-circle = 10 cm

$\therefore$ Radius of each semi-circle $= \frac{\text{Side}}{2} = \frac{10}{2} = 5$ cm

Now, area of I region + area of III region

= Area of $ABCD$ – Area of two semi-circles each of radius 5 cm

$= \left(10 \times 10 - 2 \times \frac{1}{2} \times \pi \times 5^2\right)$

$= (100 - 3.14 \times 25)$

$= (100 - 78.5)$

$= 21.5$ cm^2

Similarly, area of II region + area of IV region

$= 21.5$ cm^2

$\therefore$ Area of the shaded design

= Area of $ABCD$

– Area of (I + II + III + IV) region

$= (100 - 2 \times 21.5)$

$= (100 - 43) = 57$ cm^2

14. The minute hand of a clock describes a circle of radius equal to its length i.e 14 cm in 1 h.

The area swept by the minute hand in 30 min is the area of the semi-circle of radius 14 cm.

Area of semi-circle $= \frac{\pi r^2}{2}$

$= \frac{22 \times 14 \times 14}{7 \times 2} = 308$ cm^2

15. Given, side of a square = 15 m

$\therefore$ Area of square $= (15)^2 = 225$ m^2

[$\because$ area of square = (side)^2]

Also given, length of rope = 5 m

$\therefore$ Radius of arc = 5 m

(i) Area of the field graze by the horse is the area of quadrant AEF,

$A_1 = \frac{1}{4}(\pi r^2)$

$= \frac{3.14 \times 25}{4} = \frac{78.5}{4}$

$= 19.625$ cm^2

(ii) If length of rope $= 10$ m $= r_1$ (say),

then area of the field graze by the horse is the area of quadrant AEF,

$A_2 = \frac{1}{4}(\pi r^2)$

$= \frac{3.14 \times 100}{4}$

$= \frac{314}{4} = 78.5$ cm^2

$\therefore$ Required increase in the grazing area

$= A_2 - A_1$

$= 78.5 - 19.625$

$= 58.875$ cm^2

Case Based Questions

1. (i) In a conical tent, let sides be

$a = 10$ cm, $b = 20$ cm and $c = 20$ cm

Semi-perimeter of triangle,

$$s = \frac{a+b+c}{2} = \frac{10+20+20}{2} = \frac{50}{2} = 25 \text{ cm}$$

and area of triangle $= \sqrt{s(s-a)(s-b)(s-c)}$ [by Heron's formula]

$$= \sqrt{25(25-10)(25-20)(25-20)}$$
$$= \sqrt{25 \times 15 \times 5 \times 5}$$
$$= \sqrt{5 \times 5 \times 3 \times 5 \times 5 \times 5}$$
$$= 5 \times 5\sqrt{15} = 25\sqrt{15} \text{ cm}^2$$

Thus, area of one black colour triangular piece is $25\sqrt{15}$ cm^2.

Since, tent is made of 12 pieces of two colours.

So, number of triangular pieces of black colour is 6.

Hence, cloth of black colour required to make a conical tent is

$$6 \times 25\sqrt{15} = 150\sqrt{15} \text{ cm}^2.$$

(ii) Perimeter of one triangular piece $= 10 + 20 + 20 = 50$ cm

$\therefore$ Total perimeter of 6 white colour pieces

$= 6 \times$ Perimeter of one triangular piece

$= 6 \times 50 = 300$ cm

2. (i) Given, side of a square, $a = 14$ cm

Let r and R be the radii of inscribed and circumscribed circle, respectively.

Then, inradius, $r = \frac{a}{2} = \frac{14}{2} = 7$ cm

and circumradius, $R = \frac{a}{2}\sqrt{2} = \frac{14}{2}\sqrt{2}$

$= 7\sqrt{2}$ cm

(ii) $\therefore$ Area of inscribed circle $= \pi r^2$

$$= \frac{22}{7} \times 7^2$$
$$= 22 \times 7 = 154 \text{ cm}^2$$

$\therefore$ Area of circumscribed circle $= \pi R^2$

$$= \frac{22}{7} \times (7\sqrt{2})^2$$
$$= 22 \times 14$$
$$= 308 \text{ cm}^2$$

(iii) Area of shaded region

= Area of a square – Area of inscribed circle

$= (14)^2 - 154 = 196 - 154$

$= 42$ cm^2

3. Given, O is the centre and AOC is a diameter of the circle.

In right angled ΔABC,

$$(AC)^2 = (AB)^2 + (BC)^2$$

[by Pythagoras theorem]

$$\Rightarrow \quad AC = \sqrt{(4)^2 + (4)^2}$$

[$\because AB = 4$ cm, $BC = 4$ cm]

$$= 4\sqrt{2} \text{ cm}$$

$\therefore$ Radius of circle, $OC = \frac{1}{2} \times AC$

$$= \frac{1}{2} \times 4\sqrt{2} = 2\sqrt{2}$$

(i) The sum of the areas of the two shaded segments made by the chords AB and BC

= Area of semi-circle having radius OB – Area of right angled ΔABC

$$= \frac{\pi r^2}{2} - \frac{1}{2} \times BC \times AB$$

$$= \frac{22}{7} \times \frac{1}{2} \times 2\sqrt{2} \times 2\sqrt{2} - \frac{1}{2} \times 4 \times 4 \quad [\because r = 2\sqrt{2}]$$

$$= \frac{22 \times 2 \times 2}{7} - 8 = \frac{88-56}{7} = \frac{32}{7} \text{ cm}^2$$

(ii) The area of the shaded segment made by the chord PQ is given by

= Area of quarter circle – Area of ΔPOQ

$$= \frac{\pi r^2}{4} - \frac{1}{2} \times OQ \times OP$$

$$= \frac{22}{7 \times 4} \times 2\sqrt{2} \times 2\sqrt{2} - \frac{1}{2} \times 2\sqrt{2} \times 2\sqrt{2}$$

$$= \frac{22 \times 2}{7} - 4$$

$$= \frac{44}{7} - 4 = \frac{44-28}{7} = \frac{16}{7} \text{ cm}^2$$

16

SURFACE AREA AND VOLUME OF 3D SOLIDS

The objects having definite shape, size and occupying a fixed amount of space in three dimensions are called solids.
e.g. cube, cuboid, cylinder, cone, sphere, hemisphere.

Cuboid

A cuboid is a solid bounded by six rectangular plane surfaces.

e.g. match box, brick, box, etc.

Opposite faces of a cuboid are equal and parallel.

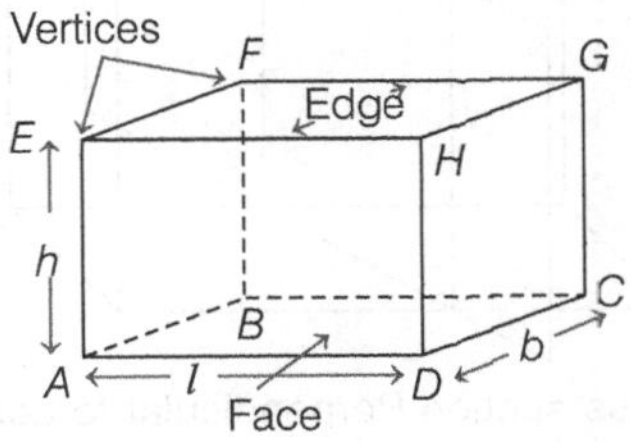

Let the length of the cuboid be l units, breadth b units and height h units.

Then,

(i) Surface Area (SA) or Total Surface Area (TSA) of the cuboid

= Sum of areas of six rectangular faces

$\therefore$ SA or TSA $= 2(lb + bh + hl)$ sq units

(ii) **Lateral Surface Area** = sum of area of four rectangular faces (excluding top and bottom faces).

$\therefore$ Lateral surface area of a cuboid $= 2(l + b)h$ sq units

Also, lateral surface area of a cuboid = Perimeter of the base × Height

(iii) **Diagonal of a Cuboid** $= \sqrt{l^2 + b^2 + h^2}$ units

(iv) **Total Length of Cuboid** = Length of all 12 edges of the cuboid

$= 4(l + b + h)$ units

(v) **Volume of the cuboid** = Length × Breadth × Height

or $= lbh$ cu units

Also, Volume of the cuboid = Base area × Height

REVISION NOTES

Cube

A cuboid whose length, breadth and height all are equal is called a cube.

e.g. square ice cubes, rubik's cubes, dice etc.

Let each edge of the cube be a units. Then,

(i) **Total surface area of the cube** = Sum of areas of six faces

$\therefore$ SA or TSA of cube $= 6a^2$ sq units

(ii) **Lateral surface area of the cube** = Sum of areas of four faces (excluding top and bottom)

$\therefore$ Lateral surface area $= 4a^2$ sq units

(iii) **Diagonal of a cube** $= \sqrt{3}a$ units

(iv) **Total length of a cube** = Length of all 12 edges of a cube $= 12a$ units.

(v) **Volume of cube** $= a^3 = (\text{Side})^3$ cu units

Cross-section

The cross-section is a part or piece, which is cut from a given solid, perpendicular to its length (or breadth or height).

A solid is said to have uniform cross-section if this perpendicular cut is of the same shape and size at each point of its length (or breadth or height).

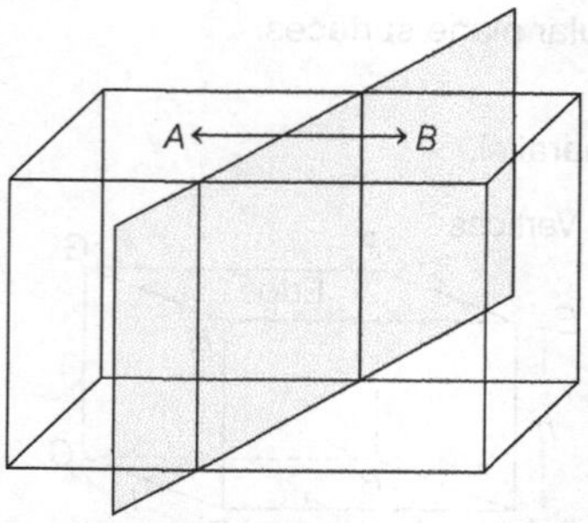

Cross-section Perpendicular to Length

When a solid has uniform cross-section, then

(i) **Volume** = Area of cross-section × length (or breadth or height)

(ii) **Surface area** (excluding cross-section) = Lateral surface area

= Perimeter of cross-section × Length (or Breadth or Height)

Unit Conversions of Units Related to Volume

$1\text{ cm}^3 = 1\text{ cm} \times 1\text{ cm} \times 1\text{ cm} = 10\text{ mm} \times 10\text{ mm} \times 10\text{ mm} = 1000\text{ mm}^3$

$1\text{ L} = 1000\text{ mL} = 1000\text{ cm}^3$

$1\text{ m}^3 = 1\text{ m} \times 1\text{ m} \times 1\text{ m} = 100\text{ cm} \times 100\text{ cm} \times 100\text{ cm} = 10^6\text{ cm}^3 = 1000\text{ L} = 1\text{ kL}$

$1\text{ dm}^3 = 1000\text{ cm}^3$

$1\text{ m}^3 = 1000\text{ dm}^3$

$1\text{ km}^3 = 10^9\text{ m}^3$

EXAM ORIENTED QUESTIONS

TYPE - 1 01 Mark

Multiple Choice Questions

Q.1 The length, breadth and height of a rectangular solid are in the ratio 5:4:2. If the total surface area is 1216 cm^2, then the length of solid is

(a) 10 cm (b) 16 cm
(c) 8 cm (d) 20 cm

Q.2 A solid piece of metal, cuboidal in shape has dimensions 24 cm, 18 cm and 4 cm. The lateral surface area of solid piece is

(a) 336 cm^2 (b) 168 cm^2
(c) 432 cm^2 (d) 504 cm^2

Q.3 The length of the longest rod that can be placed in a room is equal to its

(a) length (b) breadth
(c) height (d) diagonal

Q.4 A small indoor green house (herbarium) is made entirely of glass panes (including base) held together with tape. The dimensions of the green house are 40 cm × 30 cm × 25 cm, then the length of the tape required is

(a) 380 cm (b) 382 cm (c) 382 m (d) 380 m

Q.5 The length of a room is 25 m and width is 9.6 m. If 75 persons can sleep in the room and each person requires 16 m^3 of air, then the height of the room is

(a) 8 m (b) 5 m
(c) 15 m (d) 10 m

Q.6 If the total surface area of a cube is 216 m^2, then its diagonal is

(a) $6\sqrt{3}$ m (b) 18 m
(c) 12 m (d) $6\sqrt{2}$ m

Q.7 A solid cube is cut into two cuboids of equal volumes. The ratio of the total surface area of the given cube and that of one of the cuboids is

(a) 3 : 1 (b) 1 : 1
(c) 3 : 2 (d) 2 : 1

Q.8 If the volume of a cube is V, then length of its diagonal in terms of volume is

(a) $\sqrt{3}\,V$ (b) $\sqrt{3}\,(V)^{\frac{1}{3}}$
(c) $3V^{\frac{1}{3}}$ (d) $(3V)^{\frac{1}{3}}$

Q.9 How many litres of water flows out through a pipe of cross-section area 5 cm^2 in 1 min, if the speed of the water in the pipe is 30 cm/s? [1 L = 1000 cm^3]

(a) 10 L (b) 9.2 L
(c) 9 L (d) 10.2 L

Q.10 A tank is 20m long and 10m wide. Its deep and shallow ends are 3m and 1.5 m respectively, then the capacity of the tank, assuming that the bottom of the tank slopes uniformly is

(a) 390 m^3
(b) 480 m^3
(c) 450 m^3
(d) 475 m^3

Answers

1. (d)	2. (a)	3. (d)	4. (a)	5. (b)
6. (a)	7. (c)	8. (b)	9. (c)	10. (c)

TYPE - 2 01 Mark

Assertion-Reason Type Questions

Q.1 Assertion (A) The length, breadth and height of a cuboid are 8m, 6m and 4m, respectively. Then, diagonal of cuboid is $\sqrt{116}$ m.

Reason (R) If length, breadth and height of a cuboid are l, b and h, respectively. Then, diagonal of cuboid is given by $(l^2 + b^2 + h^2)$.

(a) A is true, R is false.
(b) A is false, R is true.
(c) Both A and R are true and R is the correct reason for A.
(d) Both A and R are true and R is incorrect reason for A.

Q.2 Assertion (A) The sum of length, breadth and height of cuboid is 38 cm and the length of its diagonal is 22 cm. Then, the surface area of the cuboid is 960 cm^2.

Reason (R) Total surface area of cuboid is $2(lb + bh + hl)$.

(a) A is true, R is false.
(b) A is false, R is true.
(c) Both A and R are true and R is the correct reason for A.
(d) Both A and R are true and R is incorrect reason for A.

Q.3 **Assertion** (A) A cuboidal water tank is 4m long, 5m wide and 8m deep. Then, it can hold 160000L of water.

Reason (R) If a cuboid has length (l), breadth (b) and height (h), then the volume of cuboid is $l \times b \times h$.

(a) A is true, R is false.
(b) A is false, R is true.
(c) Both A and R are true and R is the correct reason for A.
(d) Both A and R are true and R is incorrect reason for A.

Q.4 **Assertion** (A) If the ratio between the edges of three cubes is 4 : 5 : 6, then the ratio between their surface areas is 16 : 25 : 36.

Reason (R) The total surface area of a cube is $6a^2$.

(a) A is true, R is false.
(b) A is false, R is true.
(c) Both A and R are true and R is the correct reason for A.
(d) Both A and R are true and R is incorrect reason for A.

Q.5 **Assertion** (A) The edge of a cube is 10cm. Then the volume of cube is 100 cm^3.

Reason (R) If edge of a cube is a. Then, the diagonal of the cube is $a\sqrt{3}$.

(a) A is true, R is false.
(b) A is false, R is true.
(c) Both A and R are true and R is the correct reason for A.
(d) Both A and R are true and R is incorrect reason for A.

Answers

1. (a) **2.** (c) **3.** (c) **4.** (c) **5.** (b)

TYPE - 3 01 Mark

Statement Based Questions

Q.1 **Statement I** The length of the longest pole that can be put in a room of dimensions $10m \times 10m \times 5m$ is 25m.

Statement II A cuboidal water tank is 8m long, 4 m wide and 3m deep. Then, It can hold 98000L of water.

Which of the following is valid?
(a) Both the Statements are true.
(b) Both the Statements are false.
(c) Statement I is true and Statement II is false.
(d) Statement I is false and Statement II is true.

Q.2 **Statement I** The edge of a cube is 11cm, then its surface area will be 726 cm^2.

Statement II If diagonal of a cube 27 cm, then the length of its edge is 3 cm.

Which of the following is valid?
(a) Both the Statements are true.
(b) Both the Statements are false.
(c) Statement I is true and Statement II is false.
(d) Statement I is false and Statement II is true.

Q.3 **Statement I** The perimeter of one face of a cube is 40cm, then the volume of the cube is 100 cm^3.

Statement II Diagonal of cuboid = $\sqrt{l^2 + b^2 + h^2}$.

Which of the following is valid?
(a) Both the Statements are true.
(b) Both the Statements are false.
(c) Statement I is true and Statement II is false.
(d) Statement I is false and Statement II is true.

Q.4 **Statement I** If the side of a cube is 2.5cm, then the lateral surface area of cube 25 cm^2.

Statement II Volume of a cube is 2197 cm^3, then its edge will be 13cm.

Which of the following is valid?
(a) Both the Statements are true.
(b) Both the Statements are false.
(c) Statement I is true and Statement II is false.
(d) Statement I is false and Statement II is true.

Answers

1. (b) **2.** (c) **3.** (d) **4.** (a)

TYPE - 4 03 Marks

Short Answer Type Questions

Q.1 The dimensions of a cuboid are in the ratio 1 : 2 : 3 and its total surface area is 88 m^2. Find the dimensions of the cuboid.

Q.2 The dimensions of a cuboidal oil tin is 30 cm × 40 cm × 50 cm. Find the cost for making 20 such tins, if the cost of tin sheet is ₹ 20 per sq m.

Q.3 A cuboidal water tank is 4 m long, 5 m wide and 8 m deep. How many litres of water can it hold?

Q.4 The following figure shows a solid of uniform cross-section.

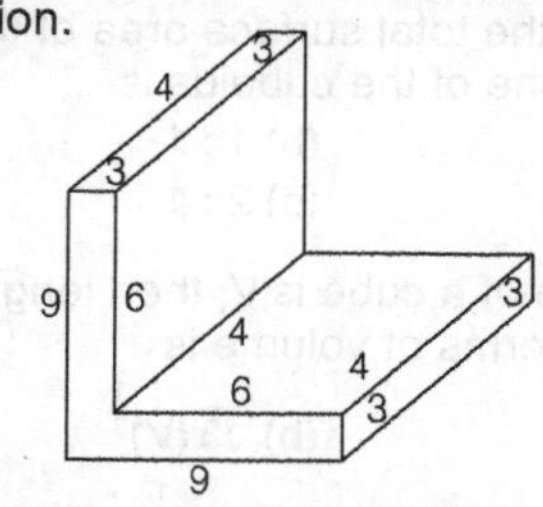

Find the volume of the solid if all measurements are (in cm) and assuming that all angles in the figure are right angles.

Q.5 The areas of three adjacent faces of a cuboid are *x*, *y* and *z*. If its volume is *V*, then find its volume.

Q.6 Three cubes are joined end-to-end forming a cuboid. If side of a cube is 2 cm, then find the dimensions of the cuboid. Also, find the volume of cuboid.

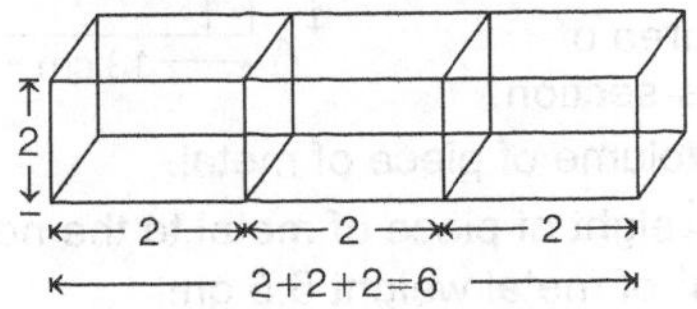

Q.7 A hollow square-shaped tube open at both ends, is made of iron. The internal square is of 8 cm side and the length of the tube is 10 cm. There are 800 cm^3 of iron used in this tube. Find its thickness.

Q.8 Find the surface area and the length of the diagonal of a cube, if the volume of a cube is 2197 cm^3.

Q.9 A certain wood costs ₹ 180 per m^3. A solid cubical block of such wood is bought for ₹ 737.28. Calculate the volume of the block and find the length of one edge of the cube.

Answers

1. The dimensions of cuboid are 2 m, 4 m and 6 m.
2. ₹ 376   3. 160000 L   4. 180 cm^3
5. $\sqrt{xyz}$ 6. 24 cm^3 7. 2 cm
8. Surface area = 1014 cm^2 and Length = 22.517 cm
9. Volume = 4.096 m^3 and Edge = 1.6 m

TYPE - 5   4/5 Marks

Long Answer Type Questions

Q.1 The external dimension of a closed wooden box are 29 cm, 19cm and 14cm.If the thickness of the wood in the box is 2cm, then find
(i) volume of the wood in the box.
(ii) number of 5cm cubes that could be placed into the box.

Q.2 A wall of length 10 m was to be built across an open ground. The height of the wall is 4 m and thickness of the wall is 24 cm. If this wall is to be built up with bricks whose dimensions are 24 cm × 12 cm × 8 cm, then how many bricks would be required?

Q.3 A field is 14 m long and 10 m wide. At one corner of this field, a rectangular well of dimensions 8 m × 2.5 m × 2 m is dug and dug-out soil is spread evenly over the rest of the field. Find the rise in the level of the rest of the field.

Q.4 The dimension of a rectangular box are in the ratio 2 : 3 : 4 and the difference between the cost of covering it with sheet of paper at the rate of ₹ 4 and ₹ 4.50 per sq m is ₹ 416. Find the dimensions of the box.

Q.5 When side of a cube is increased by 3 cm, its volume is increased by 2457 cm^3. Find its side and how much will its volume decrease, if side of it is reduced by 20%.

Answers

1. () 3964 cm^3 (ii) 30
2. 4167 bricks
3. 33.33 cm
4. The dimensions of the box are 8 m, 12 m and 16 m.
5. The side of cube is 15 cm and required decrease in volume = 1647 cm^3

TYPE - 6

Case Based Questions

Q.1 Mary wants to decorate her Christmas tree. She wants to place the tree on a wooden box covered with coloured paper with picture of Santa Claus on it (see figure). She must know the exact quantity of paper sheet to buy for this purpose. If the box has length, breadth and height as 80 cm, 40 cm and 20 cm, respectively. Then,
(i) find the surface area of the box.
(ii) how many square sheets of paper of side 40 cm would she require? **(4 M)**

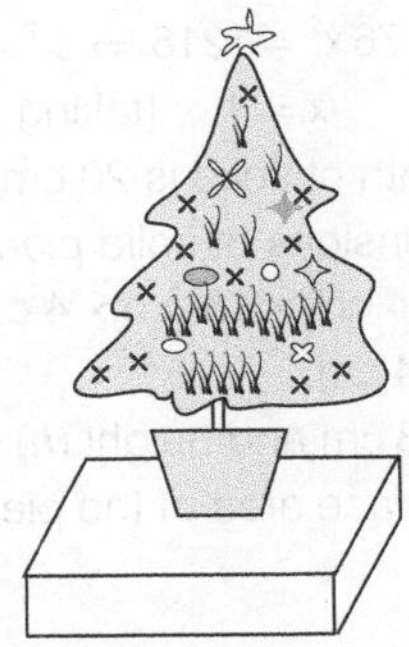

Q.2 A cubical box has each edge 10 cm and another cuboidal box is 12.5 cm long, 10 cm wide and 8 cm high.
(i) Which box has the greater lateral surface area and by how much?
(ii) Which box has the smaller total surface area and by how much? **(4 M)**

Q.3 In the given figure, the cross-section of a concrete wall to be constructed. It is 2 m wide at the top, 3.5 m at the bottom and its height is 6 m and length is 400 m.

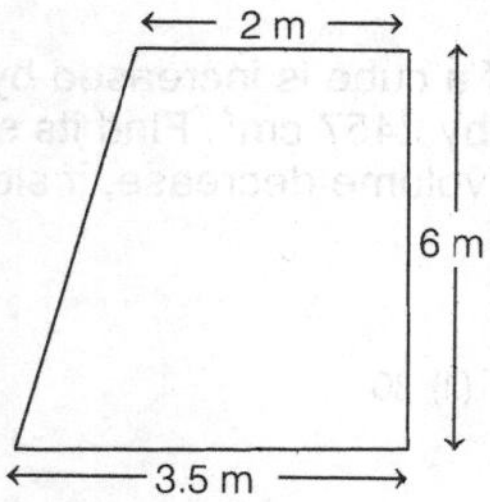

Find
(i) the area of cross-section.
(ii) the volume of concrete in the wall. **(4 M)**

Q.4 The cross-section of a 2 m long piece of metal is shown in the figure below

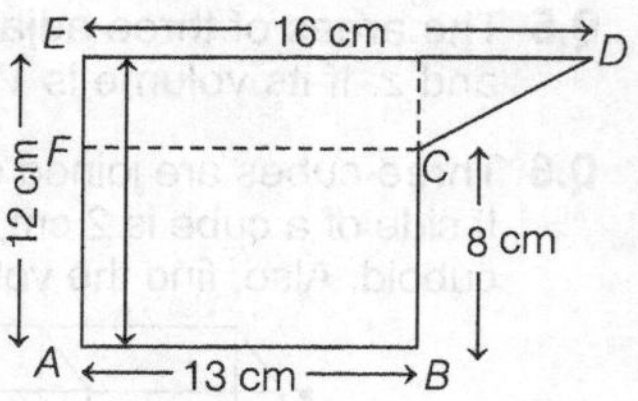

Calculate
(i) the area of cross-section.
(ii) the volume of piece of metal.
(iii) the weight of piece of metal to the nearest kg, if 1 cm^3 of metal weight 6.5 gm. **(3 M)**

Answers

1. (i) 11200 cm^2 (ii) 7
2. (i) Cubical box has 40 cm^2 more lateral surface area.
   (ii) Cubical box has 10 cm^2 less total surface area.
3. (i) 16.5 m^2 (ii) 6600 m^3
4. (i) 162 cm^2 (ii) 32400 cm^3 (iii) 211 kg (approx.)

EXPLANATIONS

Multiple Choice Questions

1. (d) Let the length = $5x$ cm, breadth = $4x$ cm and height = $2x$ cm

Now, the total surface area

$$= 2(lb + bh + hl)$$
$$= 2(5x \times 4x + 4x \times 2x + 2x \times 5x)$$
$$= 2(20x^2 + 8x^2 + 10x^2) = 76x^2 \text{ cm}^2$$

$\because$ Total surface area = 1216 cm^2 [given]

$\therefore$ $76x^2 = 1216 \Rightarrow x^2 = 16$

$\Rightarrow$ $x = 4$ [taking positive square root]

Hence, the length of solid is 20 cm.

2. (a) Given, dimensions of solid piece

$$= 24 \text{ cm} \times 18 \text{ cm} \times 4 \text{ cm}.$$

$\therefore$ Length (l) = 24 cm,
breadth (b) = 18 cm and height (h) = 4 cm

Now, lateral surface area of the piece $= 2(l + b)h$
$$= 2(24 + 18) \times 4$$
$$= 42 \times 8$$
$$= 336 \text{ cm}^2$$

3. (d) As we know that the diagonal of a room is longest dimension of a room.

Therefore, the longest rod that can be placed in a room is equal to its diagonal.

4. (a) We have, the dimensions of the green house are $l = 40$ cm, $b = 30$ cm and $h = 25$ cm

Then, total length of tape needed for all the 12 edges.
$$= 4(l + b + h) = 4(40 + 30 + 25)$$
$$= 4 \times 95 = 380 \text{ cm}$$

5. (b) Let the height of the room be h m.

Given, length of the room = 25 m
and width of the room = 9.6 m

Air required by 75 persons = $16 \times 75 = 1200 \text{ m}^3$

$\because$ Volume of the room = Volume of the air

$\therefore$ $25 \times 9.6 \times h = 1200$

$\Rightarrow$ $h = \dfrac{1200}{25 \times 9.6}$

$\Rightarrow$ $h = 5$ m

6. (a) Let the side of cube be a m.

Given, total surface area = 216 m^2

$\because$ Total surface area of cube = a^3

$\therefore$ $a^3 = 216 \Rightarrow a = 6$ m

Now, the diagonal of cube $= a\sqrt{3} = 6\sqrt{3}$ m

7. (c) Let the side of cube be a units.

Again, let this cube is cut along it length into two equal cuboids.

$\therefore$ Length of cuboid $= \dfrac{a}{2}$ units,

breadth of cuboid = a units

and height of cuboid = a units

Total surface area of the cube = $6a^2$ units ...(i)

And total surface area of one cuboid

$$= 2(lb + bh + hl)$$
$$= 2\left(\frac{a}{2} \cdot a + a \cdot a + a \cdot \frac{a}{2}\right)$$
$$= 2(2a^2)$$
$$= 4a^2 \text{ sq units} \quad \text{...(ii)}$$

Now, ratio of total surface area of the cube and one of the cuboid $= 6a^2 : 4a^2$ [from Eqs. (i) and (ii)]

$= 3:2$

8. (b) Let the side of cube be a units.

$\therefore$ Volume of cube $= a^3$ cu units

$\Rightarrow V = a^3$

$\Rightarrow a = (V)^{\frac{1}{3}}$ ...(i)

$\therefore$ Diagonal of cube $= \sqrt{3}a$ units

$= \sqrt{3}(V)^{\frac{1}{3}}$ [from Eq. (i)]

9. (c) Volume of water flowing in 1 sec

$= 5 \times 30\,cm^3 = 150\,cm^3$

$\Rightarrow$ Volume of water flowing in 1 min $= 150 \times 60\,cm^3$

$= 9000\,cm^3 = 9$ L

[$\because$ 1000 cm^3 = 1L]

10. (c) Given, length of tank, $l = 20$ m

breadth of tank, $b = 10$ m,

height of deep side, $h_1 = 3$ m

and height of shallow side, $h_2 = 1.5$ m

Area of cross-section of the tank along the depth

$= \frac{1}{2}(h_1 + h_2) \times l$

$= \frac{1}{2}(3 + 1.5) \times 20$

$= 4.5 \times 10 = 45\,m^2$

Now, the volume of tank

= Cross-section area of tank along the depth × Breadth of the tank

$= 45 \times 10$

$= 450\,m^3$

Assertion-Reason Type Questions

1. (a) **Assertion** Given, length (l) = 8 m, breadth (b) = 6 m and height (h) = 4 m

The diagonal of cuboid $= \sqrt{l^2 + b^2 + h^2}$

$= \sqrt{(8)^2 + (6)^2 + (4)^2}$

$= \sqrt{64 + 36 + 16}$

$= \sqrt{116}$ m

Hence, A is true.

Reason (R) We know that if length, breadth and height of a cuboid are l, b and h respectively, then diagonal of cuboid is $\sqrt{l^2 + b^2 + h^2}$.

Hence, R is false.

2. (c) Let the length, breadth and height of the cuboid be l cm, b cm and h cm, respectively.

According to the question,

$l + b + h = 38$ cm ...(i)

and diagonal of the cuboid = 22 cm

$\Rightarrow \sqrt{l^2 + b^2 + h^2} = 22$ cm

$\Rightarrow l^2 + b^2 + h^2 = 484$ cm ...(ii)

Now, total surface area of cuboid

$= 2(lb + bh + hl)$

$= (l + b + h)^2 - (l^2 + b^2 + h^2)$

[$\because (a + b + c)^2 = a^2 + b^2 + c^2 + 2ab + 2bc + 2ca$]

$= (38)^2 - 484$

[from Eqs. (i) and (ii)]

$= 1444 - 484$

$= 960\,cm^2$

Hence, both A and R are true and R is the correct reason for A.

3. (c) The volume of cuboidal water tank $= 4 \times 5 \times 8$

[$\because$ volume of cuboid $= l \times b \times h$]

$= 160\,m^3 = 160 \times 1000$ [$\because 1\,m^3 = 1000$ L]

= 160000 L

Therefore, A is true.

Hence, both A and R are true and R is the correct reason for A.

4. (c) Given, the ratio between the edges of three cubes $= 4:5:6$

Let the sides of three cubes be $4k$, $5k$ and $6k$ units.

We know that the surface area of a cube is $6a^2$.

$\therefore$ Surface area of first cube, $A_1 = 6(4k)^2$

$= 96\,k^2$ sq units,

surface area of second cube, $A_2 = 6\,(5k)^2$

$= 150\,k^2$ sq units

and surface area of third cube, $A_3 = 6(6k)^2$

$= 216\,k^2$ sq units

Now, the ratio of surface areas of cubes

$= A_1 : A_2 : A_3$

$= 96k^2 : 150k^2 : 216k^2$

$= 16:25:36$

Hence, both A and R are true and R is the correct reason for A.

5. (b) Given, the edge of a cube = 10 cm

Then the volume of cube $= (10)^3 = 1000\,cm^3$

Hence, A is false.

And, we know that the length of diagonal of the cube of edge a is $a\sqrt{3}$.

Hence, A is false, R is true.

Statement Based Questions

1. (b) **Statement I** We know that the length of the longest pole that can be put in a room

$= \sqrt{l^2 + b^2 + h^2}$

$= \sqrt{(10)^2 + (10)^2 + (5)^2}$

$= \sqrt{100 + 100 + 25} = \sqrt{225} = 15$ m

Statement II Volume of cuboidal water tank

$= 8 \times 4 \times 3 = 96\ m^3 = 96 \times 1000$

$= 96000\ L$ $\quad [\because 1m^3 = 1000\ L]$

Hence, both the Statements are false.

2. (c) **Statement I** Given, the edge of a cube = 11cm

$\therefore$ Surface area of cube $= 6(11)^2$

$[\because$ SA of cube $= 6a^2$ sq units$]$

$= 6 \times 121 = 726\ cm^2$

Statement II Given, diagonal of a cube = 27 cm

$\Rightarrow \quad \sqrt{3} \times \text{side} = 27$

$\Rightarrow \quad \text{side} = \frac{27}{\sqrt{3}}$

$= 9\sqrt{3}$ cm

Hence, Statement I is true and Statement II is false.

3. (d) **Statement I** Given, the perimeter of one face of a cube = 40 cm

$\Rightarrow \quad 4 \times \text{Side} = 40 \Rightarrow \text{Side} = 10$ cm

$\therefore$ Volume of cube $= (\text{Side})^3 = (10)^3 = 1000\ cm^3$

Hence, Statement I is false.

Clearly, Statement II is true.

4. (a) **Statement I** Given, side of a cube = 2.5 cm, then lateral surface area of cube $= 4 \times (2.5)^2 = 25\ cm^2$

Hence, Statement I is true.

Statement II Given, volume of cube $= 2197\ cm^3$

$\Rightarrow \quad (\text{Side})^3 = 2197$

$\Rightarrow \quad (\text{Side})^3 = (13)^3$

$\Rightarrow \quad$ Side = 13 cm

Hence, both the Statements are true.

Short Answer Type Questions

1. Given, dimensions of the cuboid are in the ratio 1 : 2 : 3.

So, let the dimensions of cuboid are $x, 2x$ and $3x$.

Then, total surface area $= 2\,(lb + bh + hl)$

$= 2\,(x \times 2x + 2x \times 3x + 3x \times x)$

But surface area $= 88\ m^2$

$\therefore \quad 2\,(x \times 2x + 2x \times 3x + 3x \times x) = 88$

$\Rightarrow \quad 2\,(2x^2 + 6x^2 + 3x^2) = 88$

$\Rightarrow \quad 2 \times 11x^2 = 88$

$\Rightarrow \quad 22x^2 = 88$

$\Rightarrow \quad x^2 = \frac{88}{22}$

$\Rightarrow \quad x^2 = 4$

$\Rightarrow \quad x = 2$ m

[taking positive square root]

$\therefore 2x = 2 \times 2 = 4$ m and $3x = 3 \times 2 = 6$ m

Hence, the dimensions of cuboid are 2 m, 4 m and 6 m.

2. Here, oil tin is in cuboidal form whose length $(l) = 30$ cm, breadth $(b) = 40$ cm and height $(h) = 50$ cm

$\therefore$ Surface area of one tin

$= 2(lb + bh + lh)$

$= 2(30 \times 40 + 40 \times 50 + 30 \times 50)$

$= 2(1200 + 2000 + 1500)$

$= 2 \times 4700$

$= 9400\ cm^2$

Now, surface area of 20 such tins

$= 20 \times 9400$

$= 188000\ cm^2$

$= \frac{188000}{10000}\ m^2$

$\left[\because (100\,cm)^2 = (1m)^2 \Rightarrow 1cm^2 = \frac{1}{10000} m^2\right]$

$= 18.8\ m^2$

Given cost of 1 m^2 of tin sheet = ₹ 20

$\therefore$ Cost of $18.8 m^2$ of tin sheet = ₹ 20×18.8

= ₹ 376

Hence, the cost of tin sheet for making 20 such tins is ₹ 376.

3. Given, the cuboidal water tank have length = 4 m, breadth = 5m and height = 8m.

Volume of the tank = Length × Breadth × Height

$= 4 \times 5 \times 8 = 160 m^3$

Quantity of water which the tank can hold

$= 160 \times 1000$

$= 160000$ L $\quad [\because 1m^3 = 1000L]$

4. The given figure can be divided into two cuboids of dimensions 6cm, 4cm, 3cm and 9cm, 4cm, 3cm respectively.

We know that the volume of cuboid $= l \times b \times h$

Hence, required volume of solid

= Volume of I cuboid + Volume of II cuboid

$= (6 \times 4 \times 3) + (9 \times 4 \times 3)$

$= 72 + 108 = 180\ cm^3$

5. Let the dimensions of cuboid be l, b and h.

Given, area of three adjacent faces of a cuboid are x, y and z.

$\therefore \quad x = lb,\ y = bh$ and $z = hl$ $\quad$ ...(i)

and volume of cuboid = V

$\therefore \quad V = lbh$

On squaring both sides, we get

$V^2 = l^2b^2h^2 = (lb)\,(bh)\,(hl)$

$\Rightarrow \quad V^2 = xyz$ $\quad$ [from Eq. (i)]

$\Rightarrow \quad V = \sqrt{xyz}$ $\quad$ [taking positive square root]

6. When we join three cubes with edge 2 cm, then we get a cuboid whose length is changed but breadth and height are not changed.

$\therefore$ Length $= 2 + 2 + 2 = 6$ cm

breadth = 2 cm and height = 2 cm

Now, volume of cuboid $= l \times b \times h$

$= 6 \times 2 \times 2 = 24 \text{ cm}^3$

7. Let thickness of the tube = x cm

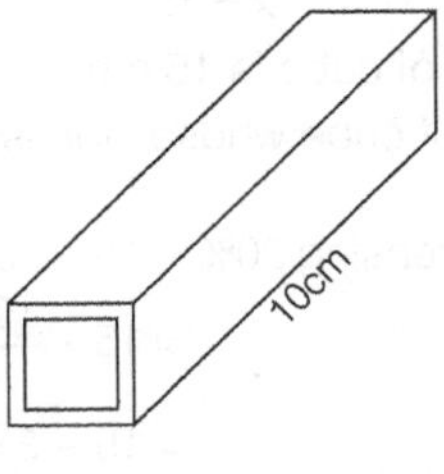

$\therefore$ Side of external square $= (8 + 2x)$ cm

$\because$ Iron used in this tube = 800 cm^3

$\therefore$ Volume of tube = Volume of iron

$\Rightarrow$ Volume of external cuboid shape tube

− Volume of internal cuboid shape tube = 800

$\Rightarrow \quad (8+2x) \times (8+2x) \times 10 - 8 \times 8 \times 10 = 800$

$\Rightarrow \quad (8+2x) \times (8+2x) = \dfrac{800+640}{10} = \dfrac{1440}{10}$

$\Rightarrow \quad (8+2x)^2 = 144$

Taking square root on both side, we get

$8 + 2x = 12$

[$\because$ thickness cannot be negative]

$2x = 4 \Rightarrow x = 2$

$\therefore$ Thickness of the tube = 2 cm

8. Given, volume of cube = 2197 cm^3

$\Rightarrow \quad (\text{Side})^3 = 2197 \quad [\because \text{ volume of cube } = (\text{side})^3]$

$\Rightarrow$ Side of cube $= \sqrt[3]{2197} = 13$ cm

[taking cube root both sides]

Now, surface area of cube $= 6\,(\text{Side})^2 = 6\,(13)^2 \text{ cm}^2$

$= 1014 \text{ cm}^2$

and length of the diagonal of cube $= \sqrt{3} \times$ Side

$= \sqrt{3} \times 13$

$= 22.517$ cm

9. Volume of cubical block × Rate = Cost

$\Rightarrow$ Volume of cubical block $= \dfrac{737.28}{180} \text{ m}^3 = 4.096 \text{ m}^3$

Now, for edge of the cube

$(\text{edge})^3 = 4.096 \quad [\because \text{ volume of cube } = (\text{edge})^3]$

$= \dfrac{4096}{1000} = \dfrac{4 \times 4 \times 4 \times 4 \times 4 \times 4}{2 \times 2 \times 2 \times 5 \times 5 \times 5}$

$\Rightarrow \quad$ Edge of the cube $= \dfrac{4 \times 4}{2 \times 5} \text{ m} = 1.6 \text{ m}$

Long Answer Type Questions

1. Given, the external dimension of closed wooden box are 29cm, 19cm and 14cm

and the thickness of the wood in the box = 2 cm

$\therefore$ The internal dimensions of wooden box are

$(29 - 2 \times 2)$ cm, $(19 - 2 \times 2)$ cm and $(14 - 2 \times 2)$ cm

So, the internal dimensions are 25cm, 15cm and 10cm

(i) External volume of the box $= 29 \times 19 \times 14$

[$\because$ volume $= l \times b \times h$]

$= 7714 \text{cm}^3$

Internal volume of the box $= 25 \times 15 \times 10$

$= 3750 \text{cm}^3$

Hence, the volume of the wood in the box = external volume of the box − internal volume of the box

$= 7714 - 3750$

$= 3964 \text{ cm}^3$

(ii) Number of 5cm cubes that could be placed in to the box $= \dfrac{\text{Internal volume of box}}{\text{Volume of one cube}}$

$= \dfrac{3750}{(5)^3} = \dfrac{3750}{125} = 30$

Hence, 30 cubes of 5cm can be placed into the box.

2. Given, length of wall = 10 m = 1000 cm,

thickness = 24 cm and height = 4 m = 400 cm.

$\therefore$ Volume of the wall = Length × Thickness × Height

$= 1000 \times 24 \times 400 \text{ cm}^3$

Now, each brick is a cuboid with length = 24 cm, breadth = 12 cm and height = 8 cm.

$\therefore$ Volume of each brick = Length × Breadth × Height

$= 24 \times 12 \times 8 \text{ cm}^3$

Since, the cuboidal wall is built up with cuboidal bricks.
So, volume of the cuboidal wall = Volume of each brick × Number of bricks

$\Rightarrow$ Number of bricks $= \dfrac{\text{Volume of the wall}}{\text{Volume of each brick}}$

$= \dfrac{1000 \times 24 \times 400}{24 \times 12 \times 8}$

$= 4166.7$

Hence, 4167 bricks are required to make the wall.

3.

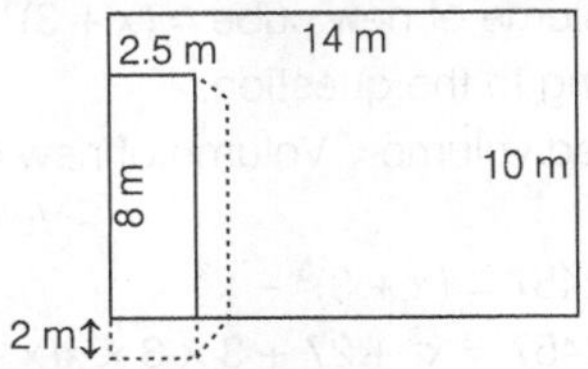

The volume of the soil removed

= Volume of the well dug

$= 8 \times 2.5 \times 2 \text{ m}^3 = 40 \text{m}^3$

Let the level of the remaining field be raised by h m.

Since, the area of remaining field

$$= (14\times 10 - 8\times 2.5)\,m^2 = 120\,m^2$$

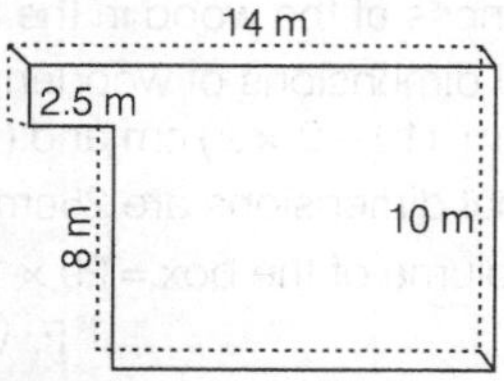

Volume of the soil

= Area of the remaining field × Rise in level

$\Rightarrow \quad 40\,m^3 = 120\,m^2 \times h$

$\Rightarrow \quad h = \frac{40}{120}\,m = \frac{1}{3}\,m = 33.33$ cm

$\therefore$ The rise in level of rest of the field = 33.33 cm

4. Let the dimensions of the rectangular box be $2x$, $3x$ and $4x$.

$\therefore$ Surface area $= 2(2x\times 3x + 3x\times 4x + 4x\times 2x)$

[$\because$ surface area = 2 ($lb + bh + hl$)]

$= 2(6x^2 + 12x^2 + 8x^2)$

$= 2\times 26x^2 = 52x^2$

Cost of covering the box with sheet of paper at the rate of 4 per m^2 = ₹ $52x^2 \times 4$

= ₹ $208x^2$

and cost of covering the box with sheet of paper at the rate of ₹ 4.50 per m^2 = ₹ $4.50\times 52x^2$

= ₹ $234x^2$.

According to the question,

Difference of the cost at different rate = 416

$\Rightarrow \quad 234x^2 - 208x^2 = 416$

$\Rightarrow \quad 26x^2 = 416$

$\Rightarrow \quad x^2 = 16 \Rightarrow x = 4$

[taking positive square root]

Hence, the dimension of the box are 8 m, 12 m and 16 m.

5. Let side of a cube = x cm

Then, volume = x^3 [$\because$ volume of cube = (side)^3]

Since, side is increased by 3 cm, then side of cube

$= (x+3)$ cm

Now, volume of new cube = $(x+3)^3$ cm^3

According to the question,

Increased volume = Volume of new cube

– Volume of actual cube

$\Rightarrow \quad 2457 = (x+3)^3 - x^3$

$\Rightarrow \quad 2457 = x^3 + 27 + 3\times 3\times x(x+3) - x^3$

[$\because (a+b)^3 = a^3 + b^3 + 3ab(a+b)$]

$\Rightarrow \quad 2457 = 27 + 9x^2 + 27x$

$\Rightarrow \quad 9x^2 + 27x - 2430 = 0$

$\Rightarrow \quad x^2 + 3x - 270 = 0$

$\Rightarrow x^2 + 18x - 15x - 270 = 0$

$\Rightarrow x(x+18) - 15(x+18) = 0$

$\Rightarrow \quad (x+18)(x-15) = 0$

$\Rightarrow \quad x = -18, 15$

[$\because$ side cannot be negative]

$\therefore \quad x = 15$

Thus, the side of cube is 15 cm.

Now, volume of cube whose side is 15cm = $(15)^3$

$= 3375\,cm^3$

Side after decreasing 20% = 15 – 15 × 20%

$= 15 - \frac{15\times 20}{100}$

$= 15 - 3 = 12$ cm

Now, volume of cube = $(12)^3 = 1728\,cm^3$

Hence, required decrease in volume

= Volume of actual cube – Volume of new cube

= 3375 – 1728

= 1647 cm^3

Case Based Questions

1. (i) Given, length of the box, l = 80 cm,

breadth, b = 40 cm

and height, h = 20 cm.

$\therefore$ Surface area of the box = 2 ($lb + bh + hl$)

$= 2[80\times 40 + 40\times 20 + 20\times 80]$

$= 2[3200 + 800 + 1600]$

$= 2\times 5600$

$= 11200\,cm^2$

(ii) Here, Mary wants to cover a cuboidal box with square sheets of paper. So, the area of paper sheets required to cover the box will be equal to the surface area of the box.

$\because$ Side of square sheet of paper is 40 cm.

$\therefore$ Area of each square sheet of the paper

$= 40\times 40 = 1600\,cm^2$

[$\because$ area of square = (side)^2]

Now, surface area of the box

= Number of sheets required

× Area of each square sheet of paper

$\therefore$ Number of sheets required

$$= \frac{\text{Surface area of the box}}{\text{Area of each square sheet of paper}}$$

$$= \frac{11200}{1600} = 7$$

Hence, 7 square sheets of paper, she would require.

2. Given, length of the cubical box (l) = 10 cm

For cuboidal box, length (l) = 12.5 cm, breadth (b) = 10 cm and height (h) = 8 cm

(i) Lateral surface area of cubical box

$= 4l^2 = 4(10)^2 = 4 \times 100 = 400 \text{ cm}^2$

$\therefore$ Lateral surface area of cuboidal box

$= 2(l + b) \times h = 2(12.5 + 10) \times 8$

$= 2(22.5) \times 8 = 45 \times 8 = 360 \text{ cm}^2$

Lateral surface area of cubical box > Lateral surface area of cuboidal box [$\because 400 > 360$]

$\therefore$ Required difference $= 400 - 360 = 40 \text{ cm}^2$

Hence, cubical box has 40 cm^2 more lateral surface area.

(ii) Total surface area of cubical box

$= 6l^2 = 6(10)^2 = 6 \times 100 = 600 \text{ cm}^2$

$\therefore$ Total surface area of cuboidal box

$= 2(l \times b + b \times h + h \times l)$

$= 2(12.5 \times 10 + 10 \times 8 + 8 \times 12.5)$

$= 2(125 + 80 + 100) = 2 \times 305 = 610 \text{ cm}^2$

Surface area of cuboidal box

> Surface area of cubical box

[$\because 610 > 600$]

$\therefore$ Required difference $= 610 - 600 = 10 \text{ cm}^2$

Hence, cubical box has 10 cm^2 less total surface area.

3. Given, length of wall, $l = 400$ m,

height of wall, $h = 6$ m,

width at top, $b_1 = 2$ m

and width at bottom, $b_2 = 3.5$ m

(i) The given cross-section looks like a trapezium.

$\therefore$ Area of cross-section $= \left(\frac{2 + 3.5}{2}\right) \times 6$

$= 16.5 \text{ m}^2$

[$\because$ area of trapezium $= \frac{1}{2}$ (sum of parallel sides) $\times$ height]

(ii) Volume of the wall

= Area of cross-section × Length of the wall

$= 16.5 \times 400 = 6600 \text{ m}^3$

4. (i) Area of cross-section

= Area of rectangle *ABCF*

+ Area of trapezium *CDEF*

$= (13 \times 8) + \frac{1}{2}(13 + 16) \times 4$

[$\because$ area of rectangle = length × breadth and area of trapezium = 1/2 (sum of parallel sides) × height]

$= 104 + \frac{1}{2} \times 29 \times 4$

$= 104 + 58 = 162 \text{ cm}^2$

(ii) Volume of metal piece

= Area of cross-section × Length

$= 162 \times 200$ [$\because l = 2 \text{ m} = 2 \times 100 = 200$ cm]

$= 32400 \text{ cm}^3$

(iii) Weight of the metal piece

$= 32400 \times 6.5$ gm

$= 210600$ gm $= 210.6$ kg

$\therefore$ Weight of the metal piece = 211 kg (approx.).

17

TRIGONOMETRY

The word trigonometry is derived from the Greek words *'tri'* (meaning three), *'gon'* (meaning sides) and *'metron'* (meaning measure). Trigonometry is the branch of mathematics, which studies the relationships between the sides and angles of a right angled triangle.

Trigonometric Ratios

The ratios of the sides of a right angled triangle with respect to its acute angles are called **trigonometric ratios**. Trigonometric ratios are also called **T-ratios.**

For any acute angle (which is also known as the **angle of reference**) in a right angled triangle, the side opposite to the acute angle is called the **perpendicular** (P), the side adjacent to this acute angle is called the **base** (B) and side opposite to the right angle is called the **hypotenuse** (H).

(i)

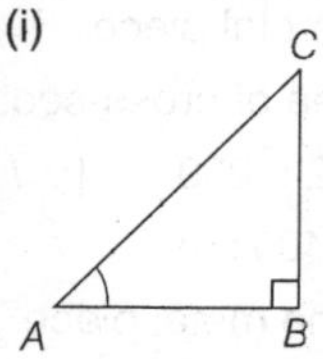

Angle of reference $= \angle A$

Perpendicular $= BC$

Base $= AB$

(ii)

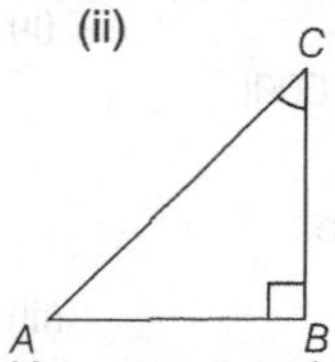

Hypotenuse $= AC$

Angle of reference $= \angle C$

Perpendicular $= AB$

Base $= BC$

(iii)

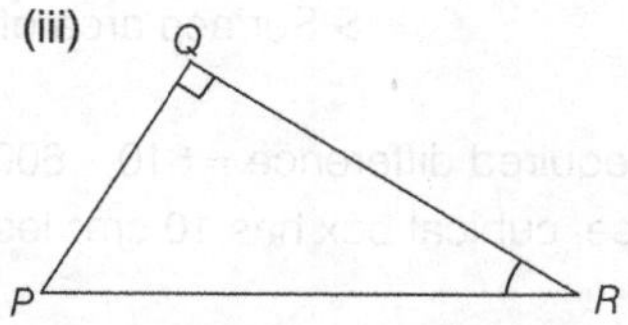

Hypotenuse $= AC$

Angle of reference $= \angle R$

Perpendicular $= PQ$

Base $= QR$

Trigonometric Ratio in a Right Angled Triangle

Trigonometric ratios of $\angle A$ in right angled ΔABC are defined as follow:

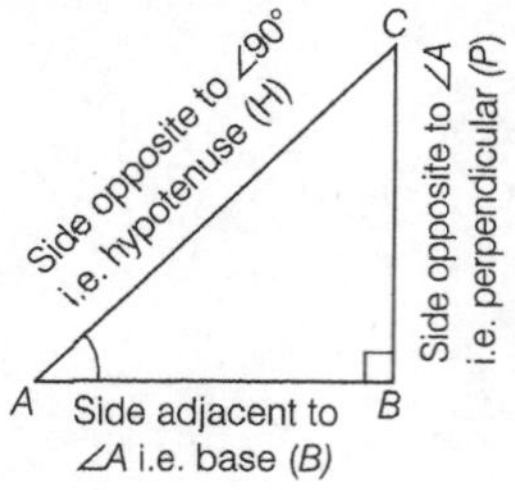

(i) sine of $\angle A$ or $\sin A = \dfrac{\text{Perpendicular}}{\text{Hypotenuse}} = \dfrac{P}{H} = \dfrac{BC}{AC}$

(ii) cosine of $\angle A$ or $\cos A = \dfrac{\text{Base}}{\text{Hypotenuse}} = \dfrac{B}{H} = \dfrac{AB}{AC}$

(iii) tangent of $\angle A$ or $\tan A = \dfrac{\text{Perpendicular}}{\text{Base}} = \dfrac{P}{B} = \dfrac{BC}{AB}$

(iv) cosecant of $\angle A$ or $\text{cosec}\, A = \dfrac{\text{Hypotenuse}}{\text{Perpendicular}} = \dfrac{H}{P} = \dfrac{AC}{BC}$

(v) secant of $\angle A$ or $\sec A = \dfrac{\text{Hypotenuse}}{\text{Base}} = \dfrac{H}{B} = \dfrac{AC}{AB}$

(vi) cotangent of $\angle A$ or $\cot A = \dfrac{\text{Base}}{\text{Perpendicular}} = \dfrac{B}{P} = \dfrac{AB}{BC}$

Similarly, trigonometric ratios of $\angle C$ in right angled ΔABC are as follow

(i) $\sin C = \frac{AB}{AC}$ (ii) $\cos C = \frac{BC}{AC}$ (iii) $\tan C = \frac{AB}{BC}$

(iv) $\text{cosec } C = \frac{AC}{AB}$ (v) $\sec C = \frac{AC}{BC}$ (vi) $\cot C = \frac{BC}{AB}$

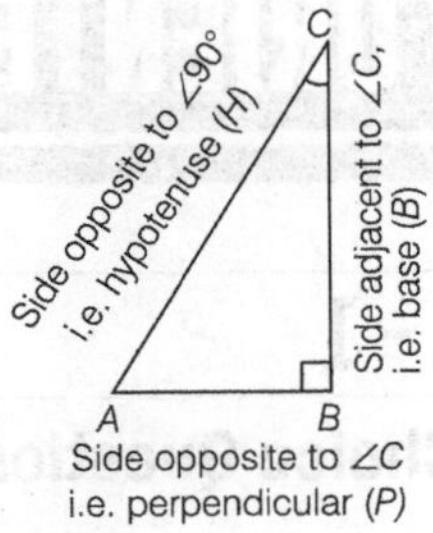

Relations between Trigonometric Ratios

1. Reciprocal Relations

(i) $\sin A = \frac{1}{\text{cosec } A}$ or $\text{cosec } A = \frac{1}{\sin A}$ i.e. $\sin A \cdot \text{cosec } A = 1$

(ii) $\cos A = \frac{1}{\sec A}$ or $\sec A = \frac{1}{\cos A}$ i.e. $\cos A \cdot \sec A = 1$

(iii) $\tan A = \frac{1}{\cot A}$ or $\cot A = \frac{1}{\tan A}$ i.e. $\tan A \cdot \cot A = 1$

2. Quotient Relations

(i) $\tan A = \frac{\sin A}{\cos A}$ $\left[\because \tan A = \frac{\text{Perpendicular}}{\text{Base}} = \frac{BC}{AB} = \frac{BC/AC}{AB/AC} = \frac{\sin A}{\cos A}\right]$

(ii) $\cot A = \frac{\cos A}{\sin A}$ $\left[\because \cot A = \frac{\text{Base}}{\text{Perpendicular}} = \frac{AB}{BC} = \frac{AB/AC}{BC/AC} = \frac{\cos A}{\sin A}\right]$

Trigonometric Ratios of Standard Angles

Angles	**0° or 0**	**30° or $\frac{\pi}{6}$**	**45° or $\frac{\pi}{4}$**	**60° or $\frac{\pi}{3}$**	**90° or $\frac{\pi}{2}$**
$\sin\theta$	0	$\frac{1}{2}$	$\frac{1}{\sqrt{2}}$	$\frac{\sqrt{3}}{2}$	1
$\cos\theta$	1	$\frac{\sqrt{3}}{2}$	$\frac{1}{\sqrt{2}}$	$\frac{1}{2}$	0
$\tan\theta$	0	$\frac{1}{\sqrt{3}}$	1	$\sqrt{3}$	∞ (undefined)
$\text{cosec}\,\theta$	∞	2	$\sqrt{2}$	$\frac{2}{\sqrt{3}}$	1
$\sec\theta$	1	$\frac{2}{\sqrt{3}}$	$\sqrt{2}$	2	∞
$\cot\theta$	∞	$\sqrt{3}$	1	$\frac{1}{\sqrt{3}}$	0

Trigonometric Ratios of Complementary Angles

$$\sin(90^\circ - A) = \cos A, \quad \cos(90^\circ - A) = \sin A$$

$$\tan(90^\circ - A) = \cot A, \quad \cot(90^\circ - A) = \tan A$$

$$\sec(90^\circ - A) = \text{cosec } A, \quad \text{cosec}(90^\circ - A) = \sec A$$

EXAM ORIENTED QUESTIONS

TYPE - 1 (01 Mark)

Multiple Choice Questions

Q.1 In the given figure, the value of sec *C* is

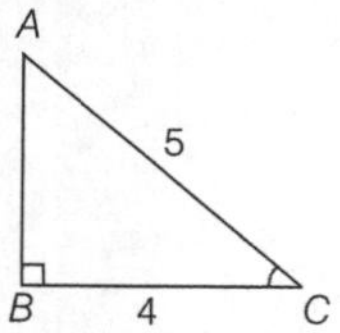

(a) $\frac{3}{4}$ (b) $\frac{4}{3}$ (c) $\frac{5}{4}$ (d) $\frac{5}{3}$

Q.2 If $\tan A = \frac{3}{4}$, then $\sin A \cos A$ is

(a) $\frac{24}{25}$ (b) $\frac{12}{25}$

(c) $\frac{5}{6}$ (d) $\frac{6}{5}$

Q.3 If $\cos\theta = \frac{p}{q}$, then $\cot\theta$ is

(a) $\frac{p}{\sqrt{q^2-p^2}}$ (b) $\frac{q}{\sqrt{p^2-q^2}}$

(c) $\frac{p}{\sqrt{p^2-q^2}}$ (d) $\frac{q}{\sqrt{q^2-p^2}}$

Q.4 If $\cos\theta = \frac{12}{13}$ and θ is acute angle, then $\text{cosec}\,\theta$ is

(a) $\frac{5}{13}$ (b) $\frac{13}{12}$ (c) $\frac{12}{5}$ (d) $\frac{13}{5}$

Q.5 In the given figure, the value of cos *y* is

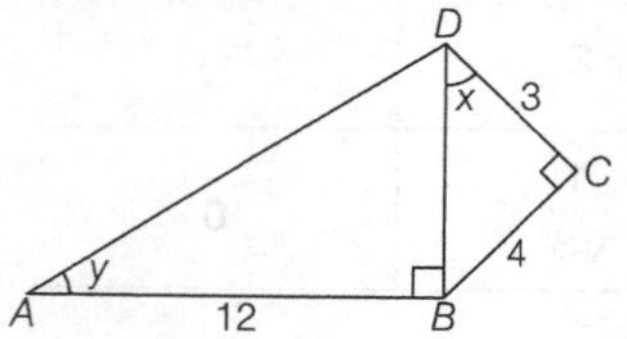

(a) $\frac{12}{13}$ (b) $\frac{5}{13}$ (c) $\frac{13}{12}$ (d) $\frac{13}{5}$

Q.6 If $f(x) = \cos^2 x + \sec^2 x$, then $f(x)$ is

(a) ≥ 1 (b) ≤ 1 (c) ≥ 2 (d) ≤ 2

Q.7 If $\tan\theta = \frac{5}{12}$, then the value of $\frac{\sin\theta + \cos\theta}{\sin\theta - \cos\theta}$ is

(a) $-\frac{17}{7}$ (b) $\frac{17}{7}$ (c) $\frac{17}{13}$ (d) $-\frac{7}{13}$

Q.8 The value of $(\sin 45^\circ + \cos 45^\circ)$ is

(a) $\frac{1}{\sqrt{2}}$ (b) $\sqrt{2}$

(c) 1 (d) $\frac{\sqrt{3}}{2}$

Q.9 If $x \cos 45^\circ \tan 45^\circ = \sin 45^\circ \cot 30^\circ$, then value of *x* is

(a) $\frac{2}{\sqrt{3}}$ (b) $\frac{1}{\sqrt{3}}$ (c) $2\sqrt{3}$ (d) $\sqrt{3}$

Q.10 In ΔABC, $\angle R = 90^\circ$, $\angle Q = 60^\circ$ and $PR = 3$ cm, then the value of *QR* is

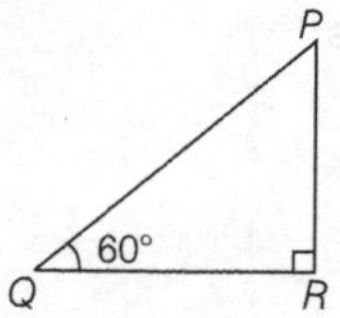

(a) $\sqrt{3}$ cm (b) $\frac{1}{\sqrt{3}}$ cm

(c) 3 cm (d) $2\sqrt{3}$ cm

Q.11 The value of $\cos^2 30^\circ + \sin^2 45^\circ - \frac{1}{3}(\tan^2 60^\circ)$ is

(a) $\frac{1}{4}$ (b) $\frac{1}{2}$ (c) $\frac{2}{3}$ (d) $\frac{3}{4}$

Q.12 The value of $\sin^3 30^\circ - \cos^4 45^\circ + \cot^2 60^\circ$ is

(a) $\frac{17}{24}$ (b) $\frac{11}{24}$ (c) $\frac{5}{24}$ (d) $\frac{1}{24}$

Q.13 If $\tan(2x + 34^\circ) = 1$, then the value of *x* is

(a) $6\frac{1^\circ}{2}$ (b) $5\frac{1^\circ}{2}$

(c) $7\frac{1^\circ}{3}$ (d) $6\frac{1^\circ}{3}$

Q.14 The value of $\sec 49^\circ - \text{cosec}\, 41^\circ$ is

(a) 1 (b) 2 (c) $\sqrt{2}$ (d) 0

Q.15 If $\sec 2A = \text{cosec}(A - 27^\circ)$, where $2A$ is an acute angle, then the $\angle A$ is

(a) 35° (b) 39°

(c) 37° (d) 40°

Answers

1. (c)	**2.** (b)	**3.** (a)	**4.** (d)	**5.** (a)
6. (c)	**7.** (a)	**8.** (b)	**9.** (d)	**10.** (a)
11. (a)	**12.** (c)	**13.** (b)	**14.** (d)	**15.** (b)

TYPE - 2

01 Mark

Assertion-Reason Type Questions

Q.1 Assertion (A) If $\cos\left(\frac{\theta}{2}+10°\right)=\frac{\sqrt{3}}{2}$, then the value of θ is 40°.

Reason (R) The reciprocal relation of $\cos\theta$ is $\frac{1}{\sec\theta}$.

(a) A is true, R is false.
(b) A is false, R is true.
(c) Both A and R are true and R is the correct reason for A.
(d) Both A and R are true and R is incorrect reason for A.

Q.2 Assertion (A) In ΔABC, right angled at C and $\angle A = \angle B$, then $\cos A = \cos B$

Reason (R) The sum of all angles of a triangle is 180°.

(a) A is true, R is false.
(b) A is false, R is true.
(c) Both A and R are true and R is the correct reason for A.
(d) Both A and R are true and R is incorrect reason for A.

Q.3 Assertion (A) If $\sin 3A(2\cos 2A-1)=0$, then the values of A are 0° and 30°.

Reason (R) $\sin(90°-\theta)=\cos\theta$.

(a) A is true, R is false.
(b) A is false, R is true.
(c) Both A and R are true and R is the correct reason for A.
(d) Both A and R are true and R is incorrect reason for A.

Q.4 Assertion (A) If $\sec 5A = \operatorname{cosec}(A+30°)$, then the value of A is 10°.

Reason (R) $\sec(90°-\theta)=\operatorname{cosec}\theta$

(a) A is true, R is false.
(b) A is false, R is true.
(c) Both A and R are true and R is the correct reason for A.
(d) Both A and R are true and R is incorrect reason for A.

Answers

1. (d) **2.** (c) **3.** (d) **4.** (c)

TYPE - 3

01 Mark

Statement Based Questions

Q.1 Statement I In a ΔABC right angled at B, $AB = 7$ cm and $\angle ACB = 60°$. Then, the length of the side BC is 7cm.

Statement II In the following figure, ABC is a right angled triangle at B, $AB = 3$ cm and $AC=\sqrt{12}$ cm, then the value of $\angle BAC$ is 60°.

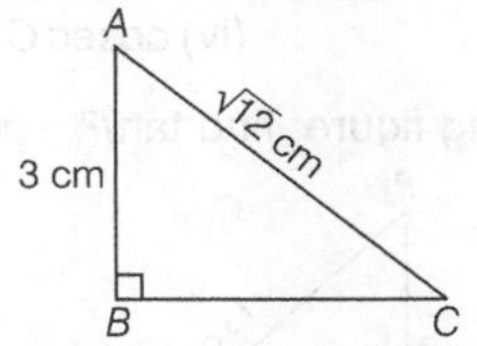

Which of the following is valid?
(a) Both the Statements are true.
(b) Both the Statements are false.
(c) Statement I is true and Statement II is false.
(d) Statement I is false and Statement II is true.

Q.2 Statement I If $2\cos 3\theta=\sqrt{3}$, then the value of θ is 10°.

Statement II If $\tan(3x+30°)=1$, then the value of x is 5°.

Which of the following is valid?
(a) Both the Statements are true.
(b) Both the Statements are false.
(c) Statement I is true and Statement II is false.
(d) Statement I is false and Statement II is true.

Q.3 Statement I $\frac{\sin(90°-\theta)+5\cos\theta}{\tan\theta}=6\cot\theta\cdot\cos\theta$.

Statement II If A and B are acute angles such that $\sin A=\cos B$, then $(A+B)=90°$.

Which of the following is valid?
(a) Both the Statements are true.
(b) Both the Statements are false.
(c) Statement I is true and Statement II is false.
(d) Statement I is false and Statement II is true.

Q.4 Statement I The value of $\tan^2 42°-\cot^2 48°$ is 0.

Statement II The value of $\sec^2 18°-\operatorname{cosec}^2 72°$ is 2.

Which of the following is valid?
(a) Both the Statements are true.
(b) Both the Statements are false.
(c) Statement I is true and Statement II is false.
(d) Statement I is false and Statement II is true.

Answers

1. (b) **2.** (a) **3.** (a) **4.** (c)

TYPE - 4 03 Marks

Short Answer Type Questions

Q.1 From the following figure, find

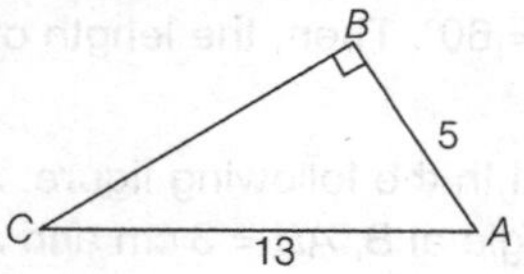

(i) $\sin A$ (ii) $\cos C$
(iii) $\tan A$ (iv) $\text{cosec}\, C$

Q.2 In the following figure, find $\tan P - \cot R$.

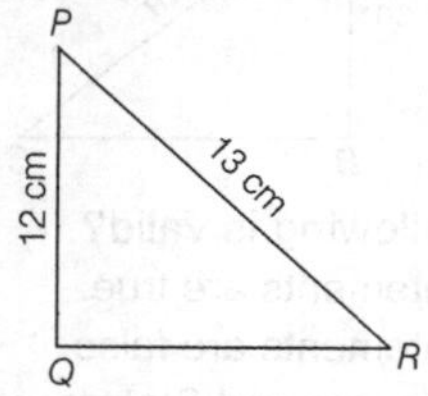

Q.3 In a ΔPQR, right angled at Q, $PR + QR = 25$ cm and $PQ = 5$ cm. Determine the values of $\sin P$, $\cos P$ and $\tan P$.

Q.4 From the given figure, evaluate

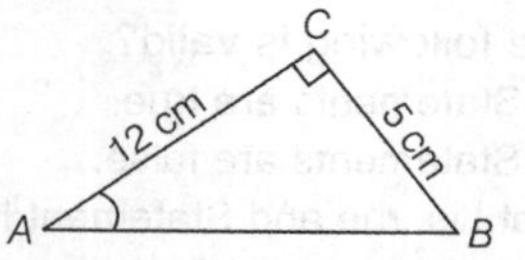

(i) $\cos^2 A - \sin^2 A$ (ii) $\text{cosec}^2 A - \cot^2 A$

Q.5 If $\sin\alpha = \dfrac{1}{2}$ and α is an acute angle, then find the value of $(3\cos\alpha - 4\cos^3\alpha)$.

Q.6 In a ΔABC, right angled at B, if $\tan A = 1$, then verify that $2\sin A\cos A = 1$.

Q.7 For the given figure, if $\cos\alpha = \dfrac{5}{13}$ and $\sin\beta = \dfrac{8}{10}$, find the length of BD.

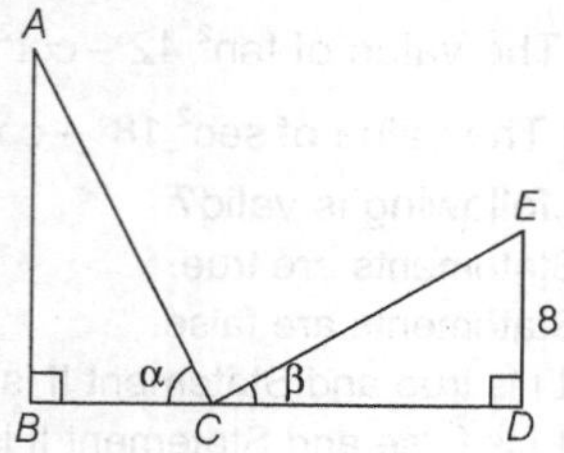

Q.8 In the given figure, $PQRS$ is a rectangle. Its diagonal $PR = 15$ cm and $\angle PRS = \theta$. If $\cot\theta = \dfrac{3}{2}$, then find the perimeter of the rectangle.

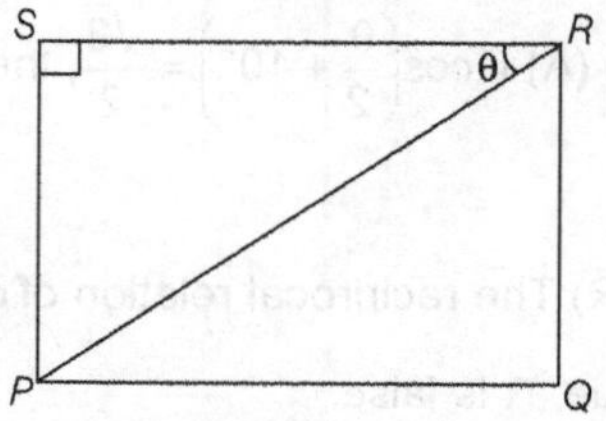

Q.9 If $\tan x + \cot x = 2$, then find the value of $\tan^2 x + \cot^2 x$.

Q.10 If $m\cot A = n$, then find the value of $\dfrac{m\sin A - n\cos A}{n\cos A + m\sin A}$.

Q.11 If θ is an acute angle and $3\sin\theta = 4\cos\theta$, then find the value of $4\sin^2\theta - 3\cos^2\theta + 2$.

Q.12 Evaluate $\dfrac{5\sin A - 3\cos A}{2\cos A + \sin A}$, if $5\cos A - 12\sin A = 0$.

Q.13 Prove that $(1 + \tan A + \cot A)(\sin A - \cos A) = \sin A\tan A - \cot A\cos A$.

Q.14 Prove that $\dfrac{\text{cosec}^2\theta - \cos^2\theta}{\cot^2\theta} = \sec^2\theta - \sin^2\theta$.

Q.15 Find the value of $\dfrac{\sin 30^\circ + \tan 45^\circ - \text{cosec}\, 60^\circ}{\sec 30^\circ + \cos 60^\circ + \cot 45^\circ}$.

Q.16 If $\angle A = \angle B = 45^\circ$, then verify that $\sin(A + B) = \sin A\cos B + \cos A\sin B$.

Q.17 Find the value of $\dfrac{5\cos^2 60^\circ + 4\sec^2 30^\circ - \tan^2 45^\circ}{\sin^2 30^\circ + \cos^2 30^\circ}$.

Q.18 If $A = 15^\circ$, then find the value of $\dfrac{\sin 3A - 2\cos 4A}{\cos 3A + 2\sin 4A}$.

Q.19 Find the value of x, where $0^\circ \le x \le 90^\circ$.

$$\tan^2 x + \sec^2 60^\circ = 5$$

Q.20 Find the magnitude of $\angle A$, if $4\sin A\sin 2A + 1 - 2\sin 2A = 2\sin A$.

Q.21 If $\theta = 45^\circ$, then prove that

$$\sin 2\theta = 2\sin\theta\cos\theta = \frac{2\tan\theta}{1 + \tan^2\theta}.$$

Q.22 If $\sin(A - B) = \dfrac{1}{2}$, $\cos(A + B) = \dfrac{1}{2}$, $0^\circ < A + B \le 90^\circ$, $A > B$, find the values of A and B.

Q.23 In the given figure, PQR is a right angled triangle, where $\angle Q = 90°$, $PQ = 3$ cm and $PR = 6$ cm. Determine $\angle QPR$ and $\angle PRQ$.

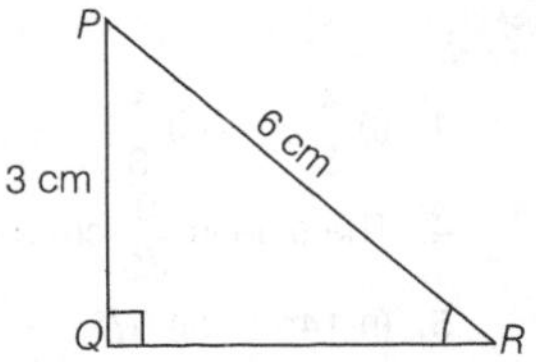

Q.24 In a ΔABC, right angled at B, side $AB = 40$ cm and acute $\angle A = 60°$. Find BC and AC. [take $\sqrt{3} = 1.732$]

Q.25 Find the magnitude of angle α, if $2\sin^2\alpha - 3\sin\alpha + 1 = 0$.

Q.26 In a rhombus $ABCD$, length of each side is 10 cm and $\angle A = 60°$. Find the lengths of its diagonals AC and BD.

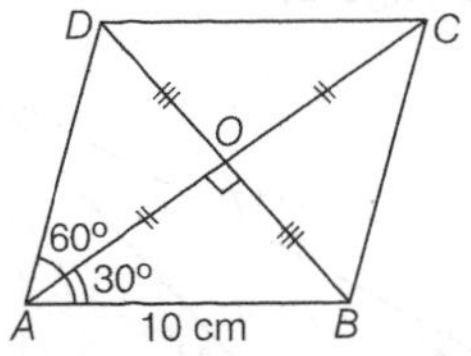

Q.27 In the given figure, a rocket is fired vertically upwards from its launching pad A. It first rises 40 km vertically upwards and then 40 km at 60° to the vertical. AL represents the first stage of the journey and LM represents the second stage. N is a point vertically below M on the horizontal level as A.

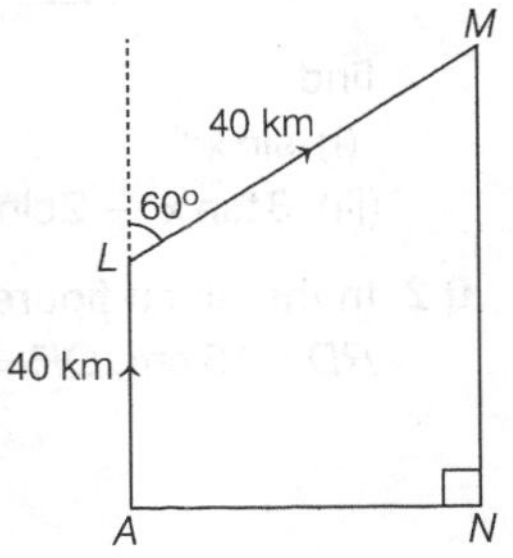

Calculate

(i) the height of the rocket when it is at point M.

(ii) the horizontal distance of point N from A.

Q.28 Find the value of $\dfrac{\cot 40°}{\tan 50°} - \dfrac{\cos 35°}{2\sin 55°}$

Q.29 Evaluate $\dfrac{\tan 50° + \sec 50°}{\cot 40° + \operatorname{cosec} 40°} + \cos 40° \operatorname{cosec} 50°$.

Q.30 Evaluate $\dfrac{\sin 70°}{\cos 20°} + \dfrac{\operatorname{cosec} 36°}{\sec 54°} - \dfrac{2\cos 43° \operatorname{cosec} 47°}{\tan 10° \tan 40° \tan 50° \tan 80°}$.

Q.31 Find the value of ($\tan 1° \tan 2° \tan 3° \ldots \tan 89°$).

Q.32 Evaluate $\cot 12° \cot 38° \cot 52° \cot 60° \cot 78°$.

Q.33 If $\cos(A - B) = \cos A \cos B + \sin A \sin B$, then find the values of (i) $\cos 15°$ (ii) $\sin 75°$.

Q.34 If $\sin\left(50° - \dfrac{3}{2}\theta\right) = \cos(3\theta - 50°)$, then find θ and hence evaluate $\tan\theta \sec\theta \sin\theta - \cot\theta \sin\theta \cos\theta$.

Answers

1. (i) $\frac{12}{13}$ (ii) $\frac{12}{13}$ (iii) $\frac{12}{5}$ (iv) $\frac{13}{5}$
2. 0 **3.** $\sin P = \frac{12}{13}, \cos P = \frac{5}{13}$ and $\tan P = \frac{12}{5}$
4. (i) $\frac{119}{169}$ (ii) 1 **5.** 0 **7.** 11 m **8.** $\frac{150}{\sqrt{13}}$ cm
9. 2 **10.** $\frac{m^2 - n^2}{m^2 + n^2}$ **11.** $3\frac{12}{25}$ **12.** $-\frac{11}{29}$
15. $\frac{43 - 24\sqrt{3}}{11}$ **17.** $\frac{67}{12}$ **18.** $\frac{1-\sqrt{2}}{1+\sqrt{6}}$ **19.** 45°
20. 15° and 30° **22.** 45° and 15°
23. $\angle PRQ = 30°$ and $\angle QPR = 60°$
24. $BC = 69.28$ cm and $AC = 80$ cm
25. 90° and 30° **26.** $AC = 17.32$ cm and $BD = 10$ cm
27. (i) 60 km (ii) $20\sqrt{3}$ km
28. $\frac{1}{2}$ **29.** 2 **30.** 0
31. 1 **32.** $\frac{1}{\sqrt{3}}$ **33.** (i) $\frac{\sqrt{3}+1}{2\sqrt{2}}$ (ii) $\frac{\sqrt{3}+1}{2\sqrt{2}}$
34. $\theta = 60°$, $\tan\theta\sec\theta\sin\theta - \cot\theta\sin\theta\cos\theta = \frac{11}{4}$

TYPE - 5 4/5 Marks

Long Answer Type Questions

Q.1 From the given figure, find the value of

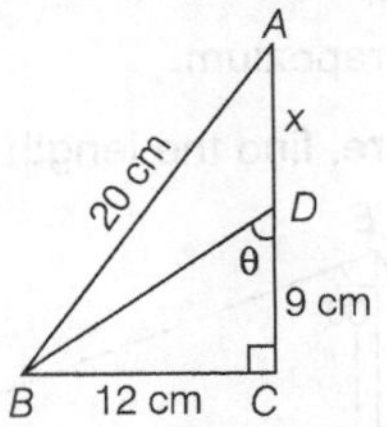

(i) $\sin \angle ABC$ (ii) $\tan\theta + \cos\theta - 2\sin\theta$

Q.2 If $3\tan A = 4$, then prove that

(i) $\sqrt{\dfrac{\sec A - \operatorname{cosec} A}{\sec A + \operatorname{cosec} A}} = \dfrac{1}{\sqrt{7}}$ (ii) $\sqrt{\dfrac{1 - \sin A}{1 + \cos A}} = \dfrac{1}{2\sqrt{2}}$

Q.3 In the given figure, $\angle C = 90°$ and $BD = DC$. Find

(i) $\dfrac{\cot \angle ABC}{\cot \angle ADC}$ (ii) $\dfrac{\tan \angle DAC}{\tan \angle BAC}$

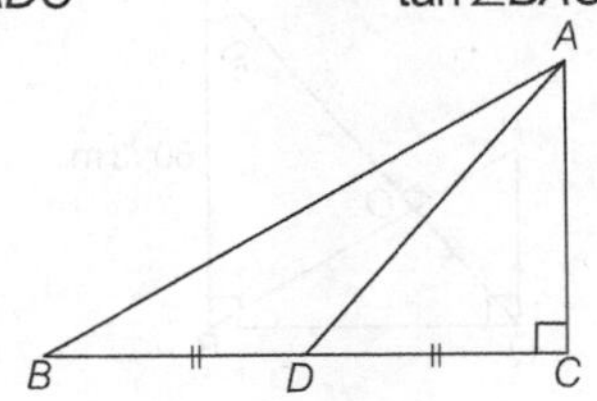

Q.4 $ABCD$ is a rhombus whose diagonal AC makes an angle α with AB. If $\cos\alpha = \frac{2}{3}$ and $OB = 3$ cm, then find the side and the diagonals of the rhombus.

Q.5 In each case, find the value of angle A, where $0^\circ \le A \le 90^\circ$.

(i) $\cot(90^\circ - 3A)\cdot\tan 48^\circ = 1$

(ii) $\sin(90^\circ - A)\cdot\operatorname{cosec} 23^\circ = 1$

Q.6 If $A = 60^\circ$ and $B = 30^\circ$, then verify that

(i) $\cos(A - B) = \cos A\cdot\cos B + \sin A\cdot\sin B$

(ii) $\cot(A + B) = \dfrac{\cot A\cdot\cot B - 1}{\cot B + \cot A}$

Q.7 Prove that $\left(\dfrac{1+\tan 30^\circ}{1-\tan 30^\circ}\right)^2 = \dfrac{1+\cos 30^\circ}{1-\cos 30^\circ}$.

Q.8 In the given figure, $ABCD$ is a trapezium with $\angle C = 120^\circ$, $DC = 28$ cm and $BC = 40$ cm.

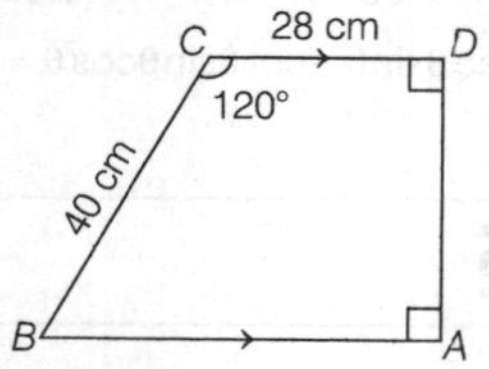

Then, find

(i) length of AB.

(ii) length of AD.

(iii) the area of trapezium.

Q.9 In the given figure, find the length of AD.

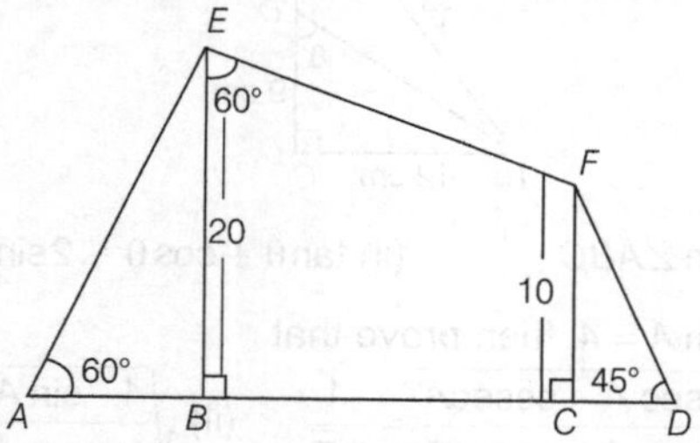

Q.10 In the given figure, $PQ \perp QR$, $SR \perp QR$, $QS \perp PR$, $\angle S = 30^\circ$ and $SR = 60\sqrt{3}$ m. Find the length of PQ.

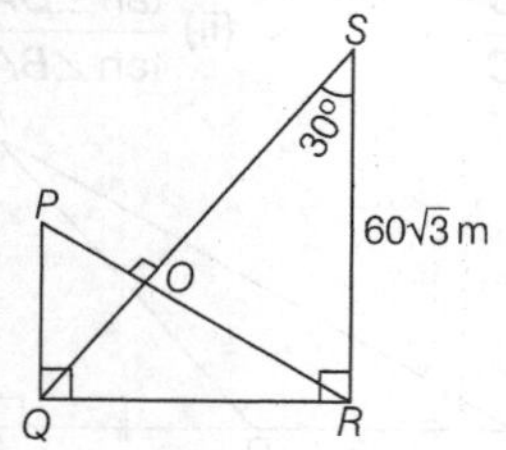

Answers

1. (i) $\frac{4}{5}$ (ii) $\frac{1}{3}$ 3. (i) 2 (ii) $\frac{1}{2}$
4. The side is $\frac{9}{\sqrt{5}}$ cm and diagonals are 6 cm and $\frac{12}{\sqrt{5}}$ cm
5. (i) 14° (ii) 67°
8. (i) 48 cm (ii) $20\sqrt{3}$ cm (iii) $760\sqrt{3}$ cm²
9. 38.868 units 10. $20\sqrt{3}$ m

TYPE - 6

Case Based Questions

Q.1 From the given figure,

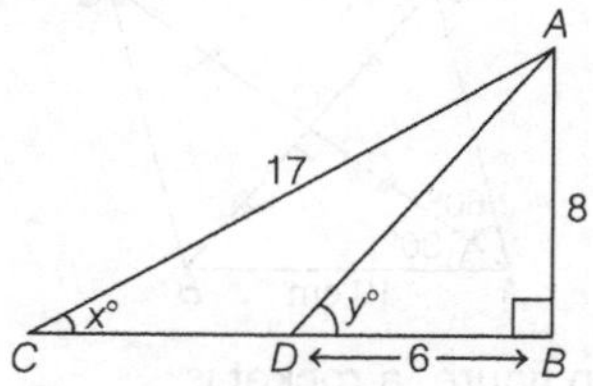

find

(i) $\sin x^\circ$ (ii) $\cos y^\circ$

(iii) $3\tan x^\circ - 2\sin y^\circ + 4\cos y^\circ$ **(3 M)**

Q.2 In the given figure, $PD \perp QR$, $PR = 17$ cm, $RD = 15$ cm, $QR = 36$ cm, $\angle DPR = x$ and $\angle PQD = y$.

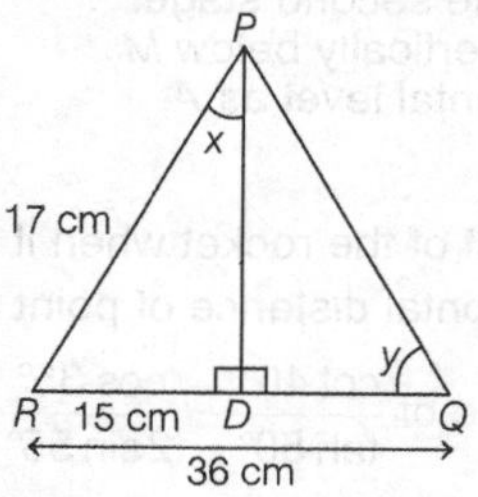

Then, find value of

(i) $\tan x$ (ii) $\dfrac{1}{\cos^2 y} - \dfrac{1}{\cot^2 y}$

(iii) $\dfrac{6}{\cos x} - \dfrac{7}{\cos y} + 8\tan y$ **(3 M)**

Q.3 If A, B and C are the angles of ΔABC, then prove that

(i) $\tan\left(\dfrac{B+C}{2}\right) = \cot\dfrac{A}{2}$

(ii) $\sin\left(\dfrac{A+B}{2}\right) = \cos\dfrac{C}{2}$ **(4 M)**

Answers

1. (i) $\frac{8}{17}$ (ii) $\frac{3}{5}$ (iii) $\frac{12}{5}$ 2. (i) 1.875 (ii) 1 (iii) 8.307

EXPLANATIONS

Multiple Choice Questions

1. (c) We have, $AC = 5$, $BC = 4$.

We know that

$$\sec C = \frac{\text{Hypotenuse}}{\text{Base}} = \frac{AC}{BC}$$

$$\therefore \quad \sec C = \frac{5}{4}$$

2. (b) First, draw a ΔABC, right angled at B.

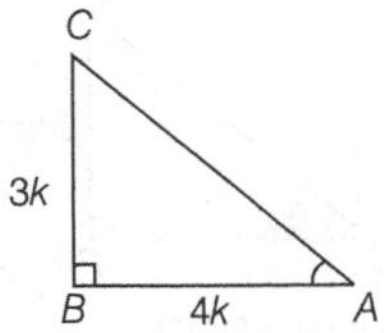

Given, $\tan A = \frac{3}{4}$

$$\Rightarrow \quad \frac{BC}{AB} = \frac{3}{4} = \frac{3k}{4k} \quad \text{(say)}$$

$$\left[\because \tan\theta = \frac{\text{Perpendicular}}{\text{Base}}\right]$$

Where, k is any positive interger

$\therefore \quad BC = 3k$ and $AB = 4k$

Now, in right angled ΔABC,

$$(AC)^2 = (BC)^2 + (BA)^2 \quad \text{[by Pythagoras theorem]}$$

$$\Rightarrow \quad (AC)^2 = (3k)^2 + (4k)^2$$

$$\Rightarrow \quad (AC)^2 = 9k^2 + 16k^2$$

$$\Rightarrow \quad (AC)^2 = 25k^2 \Rightarrow AC = 5k$$

[taking positive square root as side cannot be negative]

Now, $\sin A = \frac{\text{Perpendicular}}{\text{Hypotenuse}} = \frac{BC}{AC} = \frac{3k}{5k} = \frac{3}{5}$

and $\cos A = \frac{\text{Base}}{\text{Hypotenuse}} = \frac{AB}{AC} = \frac{4k}{5k} = \frac{4}{5}$

Hence, $\sin A \cos A = \frac{3}{5} \times \frac{4}{5} = \frac{12}{25}$

3. (a) Given $\cos\theta = \frac{p}{q}$

Draw a right angled ΔABC.

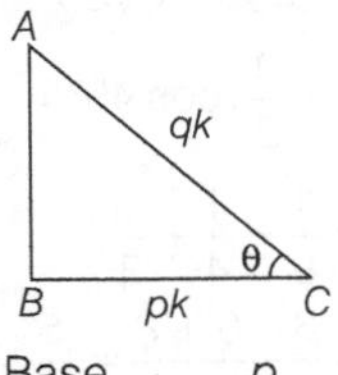

$$\because \quad \cos\theta = \frac{\text{Base}}{\text{Hypotenuse}} = \frac{p}{q}$$

$$\Rightarrow \quad \frac{BC}{AC} = \frac{p}{q} = \frac{pk}{qk} \quad \text{(say)}$$

[where k is any positive integer]

$\Rightarrow \quad BC = pk$ and $AC = qk$

Now, in right angled ΔABC,

$$(AB)^2 = (AC)^2 - (BC)^2$$

$$\Rightarrow \quad (AB)^2 = (qk)^2 - (pk)^2$$

$$\Rightarrow \quad (AB)^2 = q^2k^2 - p^2k^2$$

$$\Rightarrow \quad (AB)^2 = k^2(q^2 - p^2)$$

$$\Rightarrow \quad AB = k\sqrt{q^2 - p^2}$$

[taking positive square root as side cannot be negative]

$$\therefore \quad \cot\theta = \frac{\text{Base}}{\text{Perpendicular}} = \frac{BC}{AB} = \frac{pk}{k\sqrt{q^2 - p^2}}$$

$$\Rightarrow \cot\theta = \frac{p}{\sqrt{q^2 - p^2}}$$

4. (d) First draw a ΔABC, right angled at B.

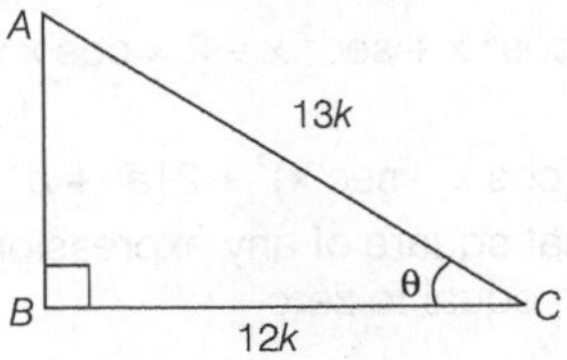

Given, $\cos\theta = \frac{12}{13}$

$$\Rightarrow \quad \frac{\text{Base}}{\text{Hypotenuse}} = \frac{12}{13} \Rightarrow \frac{BC}{AC} = \frac{12}{13}$$

Let, $BC = 12k$ and $AC = 13k$, where, k is any positive integer.

Using Pythagoras theorem in ΔABC

$$AC^2 = AB^2 + BC^2$$

$$\Rightarrow \quad (13k)^2 = AB^2 + (12k)^2$$

$$\Rightarrow \quad AB^2 = 169k^2 - 144k^2$$

$$\Rightarrow \quad AB = \sqrt{25k^2} = 5k$$

[taking positive square root as side cannot be negative]

Now, $\operatorname{cosec}\theta = \frac{AC}{AB} = \frac{13k}{5k} = \frac{13}{5}$

5. (a) In right angled ΔBCD,

$$(BD)^2 = (BC)^2 + (CD)^2$$

[by pythagoras theorem]

$$\Rightarrow \quad (BD)^2 = (4)^2 + (3)^2$$

$$\Rightarrow \quad (BD)^2 = 16 + 9$$

$$\Rightarrow \quad (BD)^2 = 25$$

$\Rightarrow \quad BD = 5$ [taking positive square root as side cannot be negative]

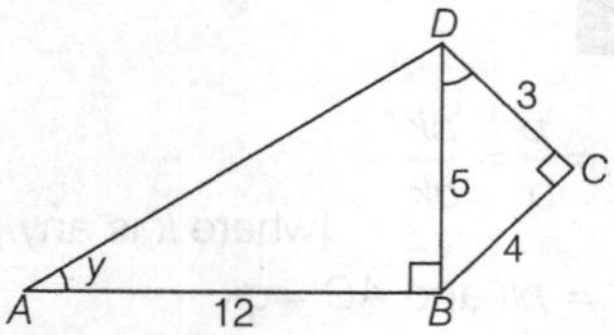

Now, in right angled ΔABD,

$$(AD)^2 = (BD)^2 + (AB)^2$$

$$\Rightarrow \quad (AD)^2 = (5)^2 + (12)^2 \quad [\because BD = 5, AB = 12]$$

$$\Rightarrow \quad (AD)^2 = 25 + 144$$

$$\Rightarrow \quad (AD)^2 = 169 \Rightarrow AD = 13$$

We know that $\cos y = \dfrac{\text{Base}}{\text{Hypotenuse}}$

$$\therefore \quad \cos y = \frac{AB}{AD} = \frac{12}{13}$$

Hence, the value of $\cos y$ is $\dfrac{12}{13}$.

6. (c) Given, $f(x) = \cos^2 x + \sec^2 x$

On adding and subtracting 2 in RHS, we get

$$f(x) = \cos^2 x + \sec^2 x - 2 + 2$$

$$= \cos^2 x + \sec^2 x - 2 \times \cos x \times \sec x + 2 \quad [\because \cos x \cdot \sec x = 1]$$

$$= (\cos x - \sec x)^2 + 2 \quad [a^2 + b^2 - 2ab = (a-b)^2]$$

We know that square of any expression is always greater than equal to zero.

$$\therefore \quad f(x) \geq 2$$

7. (a) Given, $\tan\theta = \dfrac{5}{12}$

Now, $$\frac{\sin\theta + \cos\theta}{\sin\theta - \cos\theta} = \frac{\dfrac{\sin\theta}{\cos\theta} + 1}{\dfrac{\sin\theta}{\cos\theta} - 1}$$

[dividing numerator and denominator by $\cos\theta$]

$$= \frac{\tan\theta + 1}{\tan\theta - 1} \quad \left[\because \frac{\sin A}{\cos A} = \tan A\right]$$

$$= \frac{\dfrac{5}{12} + 1}{\dfrac{5}{12} - 1} \quad \left[\because \tan\theta = \frac{5}{12}\right]$$

$$= \frac{\dfrac{17}{12}}{\dfrac{-7}{12}} = \frac{-17}{7}$$

8. (b) We have, $\sin 45° + \cos 45°$

$$= \frac{1}{\sqrt{2}} + \frac{1}{\sqrt{2}} \quad \left[\because \sin 45° = \cos 45° = \frac{1}{\sqrt{2}}\right]$$

$$= \frac{2}{\sqrt{2}} = \sqrt{2}$$

9. (d) We have, $x \cos 45° \tan 45° = \sin 45° \cot 30°$

$$\Rightarrow \quad x \times \frac{1}{\sqrt{2}} \times 1 = \frac{1}{\sqrt{2}} \times \sqrt{3}$$

$$\left[\because \cos 45° = \sin 45° = \frac{1}{\sqrt{2}}, \ \tan 45° = 1, \cot 30° = \sqrt{3}\right]$$

$$\Rightarrow \quad x = \frac{1}{\sqrt{2}} \times \sqrt{3} \times \sqrt{2}$$

$$\Rightarrow \quad x = \sqrt{3}$$

10. (a) We know that $\tan\theta = \dfrac{\text{Perpendicular}}{\text{Base}}$

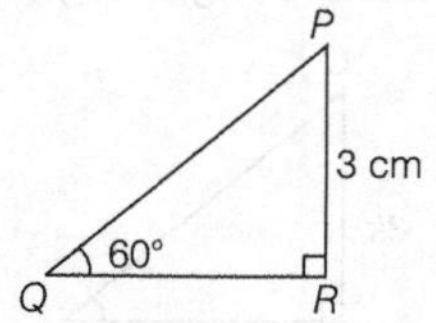

Now, in right angled ΔPQR,

$$\tan 60° = \frac{PR}{QR} \Rightarrow \sqrt{3} = \frac{3}{QR}$$

[$\because \tan 60° = \sqrt{3}$ and given $PR = 3$ cm]

$$\Rightarrow \quad QR = \frac{3}{\sqrt{3}} \Rightarrow QR = \sqrt{3}$$

Hence, the value of QR is $\sqrt{3}$ cm.

11. (a) We have, $\cos^2 30° + \sin^2 45° - \dfrac{1}{3}(\tan^2 60°)$

$$= \left(\frac{\sqrt{3}}{2}\right)^2 + \left(\frac{1}{\sqrt{2}}\right)^2 - \frac{1}{3} \times (\sqrt{3})^2$$

$$\left[\because \cos 30° = \frac{\sqrt{3}}{2}, \sin 45° = \frac{1}{\sqrt{2}} \text{ and } \tan 60° = \sqrt{3}\right]$$

$$= \frac{3}{4} + \frac{1}{2} - \frac{1}{3} \times 3$$

$$= \frac{3}{4} + \frac{1}{2} - 1$$

$$= \frac{3 + 2 - 4}{4}$$

$$= \frac{1}{4}$$

12. (c) We have, $\sin^3 30° - \cos^4 45° + \cot^2 60°$

$$= \left(\frac{1}{2}\right)^3 - \left(\frac{1}{\sqrt{2}}\right)^4 + \left(\frac{1}{\sqrt{3}}\right)^2$$

$$\left[\because \sin 30° = \frac{1}{2}, \cos 45° = \frac{1}{\sqrt{2}} \text{ and } \cot 60° = \frac{1}{\sqrt{3}}\right]$$

$$= \frac{1}{8} - \frac{1}{4} + \frac{1}{3}$$

$$= \frac{3 - 6 + 8}{24} = \frac{5}{24}$$

13. (b) We have, $\tan(2x + 34°) = 1$

$\Rightarrow \quad \tan(2x + 34°) = \tan 45° \quad [\because \tan 45° = 1]$

On equating both sides, we get

$\Rightarrow \quad 2x + 34° = 45°$

$\Rightarrow \quad 2x = 45° - 34°$

$\Rightarrow \quad 2x = 11°$

$\Rightarrow \quad x = \frac{11°}{2}$

$\Rightarrow \quad x = 5\frac{1°}{2}$

14. (d) We have, $\sec 49° - \text{cosec } 41°$

$= \sec(90° - 41°) - \text{cosec } 41°$

$[\because \sec(90° - \theta) = \text{cosec } \theta]$

$= \text{cosec } 41° - \text{cosec } 41°$

$= 0$

15. (b) We have, $\sec 2A = \text{cosec }(A - 27°)$

$\Rightarrow \quad \text{cosec }(90° - 2A) = \text{cosec }(A - 27°)$

$[\because \sec\theta = \text{cosec }(90° - \theta)]$

On equating both sides, we get

$90° - 2A = A - 27° \Rightarrow 3A = 117°$

$\therefore \quad A = 39°$

Hence, the value of $\angle A$ is 39°.

Assertion-Reason Type Questions

1. (d) We have, $\cos\left(\frac{\theta}{2} + 10°\right) = \frac{\sqrt{3}}{2}$

$\Rightarrow \quad \cos\left(\frac{\theta}{2} + 10°\right) = \cos 30° \quad \left[\because \cos 30° = \frac{\sqrt{3}}{2}\right]$

On ecuating both sides, we get

$\frac{\theta}{2} + 10° = 30°$

$\Rightarrow \quad \frac{\theta}{2} = 30° - 10°$

$\Rightarrow \quad \frac{\theta}{2} = 20°$

$\Rightarrow \quad \theta = 40°$

Hence, both A and R are true and R is incorrect reason for A.

2. (c) Gven, $\angle A = \angle B \quad \ldots(i)$

In ΔABC, $\angle A + \angle B + \angle C = 180°$

[$\because$ angle sum property of triangle]

$\Rightarrow \quad \angle A + \angle A + 90° = 180°$

[from Eq. (i) and given $\angle C = 90°$]

$\Rightarrow \quad 2\angle A + 90° = 180° \Rightarrow 2\angle A = 180° - 90°$

$\Rightarrow \quad 2\angle A = 90° \Rightarrow \angle A = 45°$

$\therefore \quad \angle B = 45° \quad$ [from Eq. (i)]

Now, $\cos A = \cos 45° = \frac{1}{\sqrt{2}}$

and $\cos B = \cos 45° = \frac{1}{\sqrt{2}} \quad \left[\because \cos 45° = \frac{1}{\sqrt{2}}\right]$

$\therefore \quad \cos A = \cos B$

Hence, both A and R are true and R is the correct reason for A.

3. (d) We have, $\sin 3A(2\cos 2A - 1) = 0$

When, $\quad \sin 3A = 0$

$\Rightarrow \quad \sin 3A = \sin 0° \quad [\because \sin 0° = 0]$

$\Rightarrow \quad 3A = 0°$

$\therefore \quad A = 0°$

When, $\quad 2\cos 2A - 1 = 0$

$\Rightarrow \quad 2\cos 2A = 1 \Rightarrow \cos 2A = \frac{1}{2}$

$\Rightarrow \quad \cos 2A = \cos 60°$

$[\because \cos 60° = 1/2]$

$\Rightarrow \quad 2A = 60°$

$\therefore \quad A = 30°$

Hence, both A and R are true and R is incorrect reason for A.

4. (c) We have, $\sec 5A = \text{cosec }(A + 30°)$

$\Rightarrow \quad \sec 5A = \sec[90° - (A + 30°)]$

$[\because \sec(90° - \theta) = \text{cosec } \theta]$

$\Rightarrow \quad \sec 5A = \sec(60° - A)$

On equating both sides, we get $5A = 60° - A$

[$\because 5A$ and $(60° - A)$ are acute angles]

$\Rightarrow \quad 6A = 60°$

$\therefore \quad A = 10°$

Hence, both A and R are true and R is the correct reason for A.

Statement Based Questions

1. (b) **Statement I** We know that

$\tan\theta = \frac{\text{Perpendicular}}{\text{Base}}$

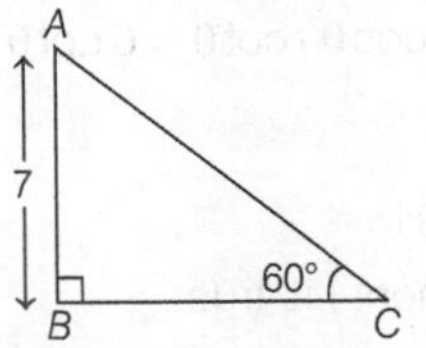

Now, right angled ΔABC,

$\tan 60° = \frac{AB}{BC} \Rightarrow \sqrt{3} = \frac{7}{BC} \quad [\because \tan 60° = \sqrt{3}]$

$\Rightarrow \quad BC = \frac{7}{\sqrt{3}}$ cm

Hence, Statement I is false.

Statement II We know that $\cos\theta = \dfrac{\text{Base}}{\text{Hypotenuse}}$

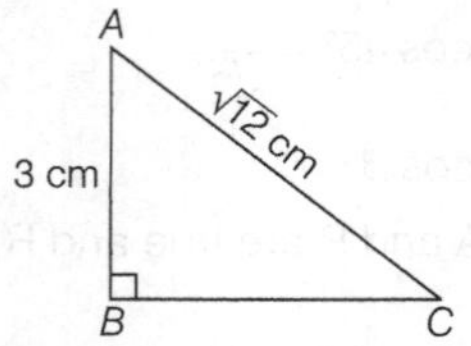

Now, in right angled ΔABC,

$$\cos A = \frac{AB}{AC} = \frac{3}{\sqrt{12}} = \frac{3}{\sqrt{4\times 3}} = \frac{3}{2\sqrt{3}}$$

$$\Rightarrow \quad \cos A = \frac{\sqrt{3}}{2}$$

$$\Rightarrow \quad \cos A = \cos 30^\circ \quad \left[\because \cos 30^\circ = \frac{\sqrt{3}}{2}\right]$$

$$\Rightarrow \quad \angle BAC = 30^\circ$$

Hence, Statement II is false.

2. (a) **Statement I** We have,

$$2\cos 3\theta = \sqrt{3} \Rightarrow \cos 3\theta = \frac{\sqrt{3}}{2}$$

$$\Rightarrow \quad \cos 3\theta = \cos 30^\circ \quad \left[\because \cos 30^\circ = \frac{\sqrt{3}}{2}\right]$$

$$\Rightarrow \quad 3\theta = 30^\circ$$

$$\therefore \quad \theta = 10^\circ$$

Hence, Statement I is true.

Statement II We have,

$$\tan(3x + 30^\circ) = 1$$

$$\Rightarrow \quad \tan(3x + 30^\circ) = \tan 45^\circ \quad [\because \tan 45^\circ = 1]$$

$$\Rightarrow \quad 3x + 30^\circ = 45^\circ$$

$$\Rightarrow \quad 3x = 45^\circ - 30^\circ = 15^\circ \Rightarrow x = 5^\circ$$

Hence, Statement II is true.

3. (a) **Statement I** We have,

$$\frac{\sin(90^\circ-\theta) + 5\cos\theta}{\tan\theta} = 6\cot\theta\cdot\cos\theta$$

$$\Rightarrow (\cos\theta + 5\cos\theta) \times \frac{1}{\tan\theta} = 6\cot\theta\cdot\cos\theta$$

$$[\because \sin(90^\circ - A) = \cos A]$$

$$\Rightarrow \quad 6\cos\theta\cdot\cot\theta = 6\cot\theta\cdot\cos\theta$$

$$\left[\because \frac{1}{\tan A} = \cot A\right]$$

$\therefore$ LHS = RHS

Hence, Statement I is true.

Statement II We have, $\sin A = \cos B$

$$\Rightarrow \quad \sin A = \sin(90^\circ - B)$$

$$\Rightarrow \quad A = 90^\circ - B$$

$[\because A$ and $(90^\circ - B)$ are acute angles$]$

$$\therefore \quad A + B = 90^\circ$$

Hence, Statement II is true.

4. (c) **Statement I** We have,

$$\tan^2 42^\circ - \cot^2 48^\circ = \tan^2 42^\circ - \cot^2 48^\circ$$

$$= \tan^2(90^\circ - 48^\circ) - \cot^2 48^\circ$$

$$= \cot^2 48^\circ - \cot^2 48^\circ$$

$$[\because \tan(90^\circ - \theta) = \cot\theta]$$

$$= 0$$

Hence, Statement I is true.

Statement II We have,

$$\sec^2 18^\circ - \operatorname{cosec}^2 72^\circ = \sec^2(90^\circ - 72^\circ) - \operatorname{cosec}^2 72^\circ$$

$$= \operatorname{cosec}^2 72^\circ - \operatorname{cosec}^2 72^\circ$$

$$[\because \sec(90^\circ - \theta) = \operatorname{cosec}\theta]$$

$$= 0$$

Hence, Statement II is false.

Short Answer Type Questions

1. Given, $\angle ABC = 90^\circ$, $AC = 13$ and $AB = 5$

Now, $AC^2 = AB^2 + BC^2$ [using Pythagoras theorem]

$$\Rightarrow \quad 13^2 = 5^2 + BC^2$$

$$\Rightarrow \quad BC^2 = 169 - 25 = 144$$

$$\Rightarrow \quad BC = \sqrt{144} = 12$$

[taking positive square root as side cannot be negative]

(i) $\sin A = \dfrac{\text{Perpendicular}}{\text{Hypotenuse}} = \dfrac{BC}{AC} = \dfrac{12}{13}$

(ii) $\cos C = \dfrac{\text{Base}}{\text{Hypotenuse}} = \dfrac{BC}{AC} = \dfrac{12}{13}$

(iii) $\tan A = \dfrac{\text{Perpendicular}}{\text{Base}} = \dfrac{BC}{AB} = \dfrac{12}{5}$

(iv) $\operatorname{cosec} C = \dfrac{\text{Hypotenuse}}{\text{Perpendicular}} = \dfrac{AC}{AB} = \dfrac{13}{5}$

2. In right angled ΔPQR, we have

$$PQ = 12 \text{ cm and } PR = 13 \text{ cm}$$

Using Pythagoras theorem in ΔPQR, we have

$$PQ^2 + QR^2 = PR^2$$

$$\Rightarrow \quad (12)^2 + QR^2 = (13)^2$$

$$\Rightarrow \quad 144 + QR^2 = 169$$

$$\Rightarrow \quad QR^2 = 169 - 144 = 25$$

$$\therefore \quad QR = 5$$

[taking positive square root as side cannot be negative]

Now, $\tan P = \dfrac{\text{Perpendicular}}{\text{Base}} = \dfrac{QR}{PQ} = \dfrac{5}{12}$

and $\cot R = \dfrac{\text{Base}}{\text{Perpendicular}} = \dfrac{QR}{PQ} = \dfrac{5}{12}$

$$\therefore \tan P - \cot R = \frac{5}{12} - \frac{5}{12} = 0$$

3. Let $QR = x$ and $PR = y$.

Then, $PR + QR = 25$ [given]

$\Rightarrow \quad y + x = 25 \Rightarrow y = 25 - x$ ...(i)

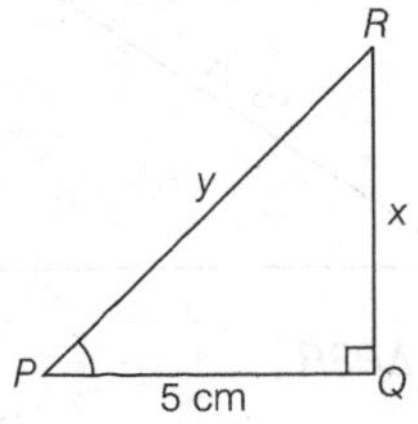

In right angled ΔPQR, we have

$QR^2 + PQ^2 = PR^2$ [using Pythagoras theorem]

$\Rightarrow \quad x^2 + (5)^2 = y^2$ [$\because PQ = 5$ cm (given)]

$\Rightarrow \quad x^2 + 25 = (25 - x)^2$ [from Eq. (i)]

$\Rightarrow \quad x^2 + 25 = 625 + x^2 - 50x$

[$\because (a - b)^2 = a^2 + b^2 - 2ab$]

$\Rightarrow \quad x^2 - x^2 + 50x = 625 - 25 \Rightarrow 50x = 600$

$\therefore \quad x = \frac{600}{50} = 12 = QR$

From Eq. (i), we get

$y = 25 - x = 25 - 12 = 13 = PR$

Now, $\sin P = \frac{QR}{PR} = \frac{12}{13}$, $\cos P = \frac{PQ}{PR} = \frac{5}{13}$

and $\tan P = \frac{QR}{PQ} = \frac{12}{5}$

Hence, the values of $\sin P, \cos P$ and $\tan P$ are $\frac{12}{13}, \frac{5}{13}$ and $\frac{12}{5}$, respectively.

4. We have, ΔABC, right angled at C, $AC = 12$ cm and $BC = 5$ cm.

On applying Pythagoras theorem in ΔABC, we get

$AB^2 = AC^2 + BC^2$

$\Rightarrow \quad AB^2 = 12^2 + 5^2 = 144 + 25 = 169$

$\therefore \quad AB = 13$ cm [taking positive square root as side cannot be negative]

Now, $\sin A = \frac{P}{H} = \frac{BC}{AB} = \frac{5}{13}$,

$\operatorname{cosec} A = \frac{H}{P} = \frac{AB}{BC} = \frac{13}{5}$,

$\cos A = \frac{B}{H} = \frac{AC}{AB} = \frac{12}{13}$

and $\cot A = \frac{B}{P} = \frac{AC}{BC} = \frac{12}{5}$

(i) Now, $\cos^2 A - \sin^2 A$

$= \left(\frac{12}{13}\right)^2 - \left(\frac{5}{13}\right)^2 = \frac{144}{169} - \frac{25}{169} = \frac{119}{169}$

(ii) Now, $\operatorname{cosec}^2 A - \cot^2 A$

$= \left(\frac{13}{5}\right)^2 - \left(\frac{12}{5}\right)^2 = \frac{169}{25} - \frac{144}{25} = \frac{25}{25} = 1$

5. Given, $\sin\alpha = \frac{1}{2}$.

$\frac{AB}{AC} = \frac{1}{2} = \frac{k}{2k}$ $\left[\because \sin\theta = \frac{\text{perpendicular}}{\text{hypotenuse}}\right]$

[where k is any positive integer]

$\Rightarrow \quad AB = k, AC = 2k$

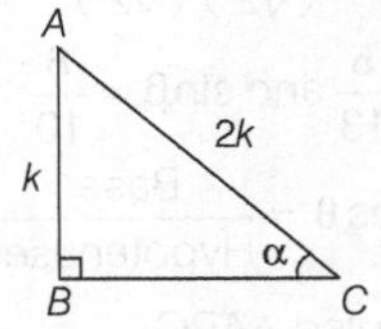

Now, in right angled ΔABC,

$(BC)^2 = (AC)^2 - (AB)^2$

[by Pythagoras theorem]

$\Rightarrow \quad (BC)^2 = (2k)^2 - k^2$

$\Rightarrow \quad (BC)^2 = 4k^2 - k^2$

$\Rightarrow \quad (BC)^2 = 3k^2 \Rightarrow BC = \sqrt{3}k$

[taking positive square root as side cannot be negative]

Now, $\cos\alpha = \frac{BC}{AC}$ $\left[\because \cos\theta = \frac{\text{base}}{\text{hypotenuse}}\right]$

$\Rightarrow \quad \cos\alpha = \frac{\sqrt{3}k}{2k} \Rightarrow \cos\alpha = \frac{\sqrt{3}}{2}$

Now, $3\cos\alpha - 4\cos^3\alpha = 3 \times \frac{\sqrt{3}}{2} - 4 \times \left(\frac{\sqrt{3}}{2}\right)^3$

$= \frac{3\sqrt{3}}{2} - 4 \times \frac{3\sqrt{3}}{8}$

$= \frac{3\sqrt{3}}{2} - \frac{3\sqrt{3}}{2} = 0$

6. Given, a ΔABC in which $\angle B = 90°$.

In ΔABC, we have

$\tan A = \frac{\text{Perpendicular}}{\text{Base}}$

$\Rightarrow \quad 1 = \frac{BC}{AB}$

$\Rightarrow \quad BC = AB$

Let $AB = BC = k$, where k is any positive number.

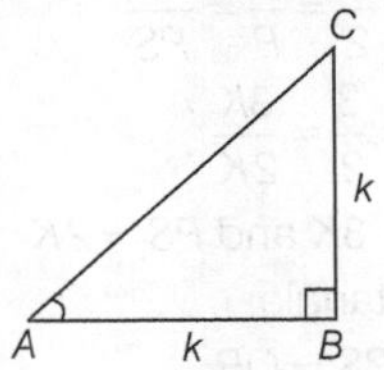

Then, $AC = \sqrt{AB^2 + BC^2}$ [using Pythagoras theorem]

$= \sqrt{(k)^2 + (k)^2} = k\sqrt{2}$

Now, $\sin A = \dfrac{\text{Perpendicular}}{\text{Hypotenuse}} = \dfrac{BC}{AC} = \dfrac{k}{\sqrt{2}k} = \dfrac{1}{\sqrt{2}}$

and $\cos A = \dfrac{\text{Base}}{\text{Hypotenuse}} = \dfrac{AB}{AC} = \dfrac{k}{\sqrt{2}k} = \dfrac{1}{\sqrt{2}}$

$\therefore 2\sin A\cos A = 2\left(\dfrac{1}{\sqrt{2}}\right)\left(\dfrac{1}{\sqrt{2}}\right) = 1$ **Hence proved.**

7. Given, $\cos\alpha = \dfrac{5}{13}$ and $\sin\beta = \dfrac{8}{10}$

We know that $\cos\theta = \dfrac{\text{Base}}{\text{Hypotenuse}}$

Now, In right angled ΔABC,

$$\cos\alpha = \frac{5}{13} = \frac{BC}{AC} \Rightarrow BC = 5\text{ m}, AC = 13\text{ m}$$

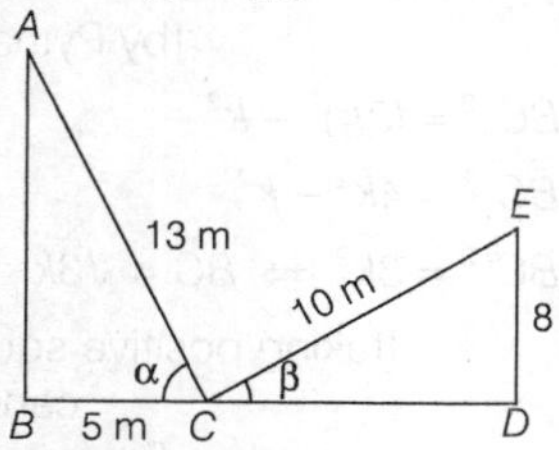

Similarly, in right angled ΔCDE,

$$\sin\beta = \frac{8}{10} = \frac{ED}{EC}$$

$\Rightarrow$ $ED = 8\text{ m}, EC = 10\text{ m}$

Again, in right angled ΔCDE,

$(CD)^2 = (CE)^2 - (ED)^2$ [by Pythagoras theorem]

$\Rightarrow$ $(CD)^2 = (10)^2 - 8^2$

$\Rightarrow$ $(CD)^2 = 100 - 64$

$\Rightarrow$ $(CD)^2 = 36 \Rightarrow CD = 6\text{ m}$

[taking positive root as side cannot be negative]

Now, $BD = BC + CD$

$\Rightarrow$ $BD = 5 + 6$ [$\because BC = 5$ m and $CD = 6$ m]

$\Rightarrow$ $BD = 11\text{m}$

Hence, the length of BD is 11m.

8. Given, $\cot\theta = \dfrac{3}{2}$

In ΔPSR, $\cot\theta = \dfrac{3}{2} = \dfrac{B}{P} = \dfrac{SR}{PS}$

$\Rightarrow$ $\dfrac{SR}{PS} = \dfrac{3}{2} = \dfrac{3K}{2K}$ (say)

$\Rightarrow$ $RS = 3K$ and $PS = 2K$

$\because$ $PQRS$ is a rectangle.

$\therefore$ $PQ = RS$ and $PS = QR$

Therefore, $PQ = RS = 3k$ and $PS = QR = 2k$

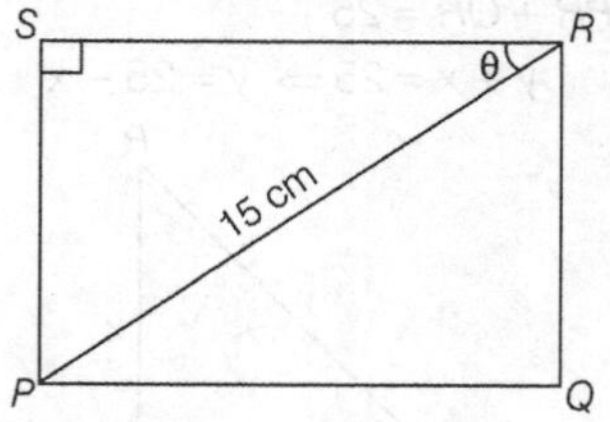

In right angled ΔPSR,

$$\cos\theta = \frac{\text{Base}}{\text{Hypotenuse}} = \frac{RS}{15}$$

$\Rightarrow$ $\dfrac{3}{\sqrt{13}} = \dfrac{3K}{15}$ $\left[\because \cot\theta = \dfrac{3}{2}, \text{ then } \cos\theta = \dfrac{3}{\sqrt{13}}\right]$

$\Rightarrow$ $K = \dfrac{15}{\sqrt{13}}$

$\Rightarrow$ $PQ = RS = \dfrac{45}{\sqrt{13}}$ cm

$\Rightarrow$ $QR = PS = \dfrac{30}{\sqrt{13}}$ cm

Hence, perimeter of rectangle $PQRS = 2(PQ + QR)$

$$= 2\left(\frac{45}{\sqrt{13}} + \frac{30}{\sqrt{13}}\right) = \frac{2 \times 75}{\sqrt{13}} = \frac{150}{\sqrt{13}} \text{ cm}$$

[$\because$ perimeter of rectangle = 2 (length + breadth)]

9. We have, $\tan x + \cot x = 2$

Now, on squaring both sides, we get

$$(\tan x + \cot x)^2 = (2)^2$$

$\Rightarrow$ $\tan^2 x + \cot^2 x + 2\tan x \cot x = 4$

[$\because (a+b)^2 = a^2 + b^2 + 2ab$]

$\Rightarrow$ $\tan^2 x + \cot^2 x + 2 \times \tan x \times \dfrac{1}{\tan x} = 4$

$\left[\because \cot\theta = \dfrac{1}{\tan\theta}\right]$

$\Rightarrow$ $\tan^2 x + \cot^2 x + 2 = 4$

$\Rightarrow$ $\tan^2 x + \cot^2 x = 4 - 2$

$\Rightarrow$ $\tan^2 x + \cot^2 x = 2$

Hence, the value of $\tan^2 x + \cot^2 x$ is 2.

10. Given, $m\cot A = n \Rightarrow m \cdot \dfrac{1}{\tan A} = n$ $\left[\because \cot\theta = \dfrac{1}{\tan\theta}\right]$

$\Rightarrow$ $\tan A = \dfrac{m}{n}$ ...(i)

Now, $\dfrac{m\sin A - n\cos A}{n\cos A + m\sin A} = \dfrac{m \cdot \dfrac{\sin A}{\cos A} - n}{n + m \cdot \dfrac{\sin A}{\cos A}}$

[dividing numerator and denominator by $\cos A$]

$$= \frac{m \tan A - n}{n + m \tan A} = \frac{m \cdot \frac{m}{n} - n}{n + m \cdot \frac{m}{n}} \quad \text{[from Eq. (i)]}$$

$$= \frac{\frac{m^2 - n^2}{n}}{\frac{n^2 + m^2}{n}} = \frac{m^2 - n^2}{m^2 + n^2}$$

11. Given, equation is $3 \sin \theta = 4 \cos \theta$

$$\Rightarrow \quad \frac{\sin\theta}{\cos\theta} = \frac{4}{3} \Rightarrow \tan\theta = \frac{4}{3} \quad \ldots\text{(i)}$$

Now, draw a right angled ΔABC, such that $\angle B = 90°$ and let $\angle A = \theta$.

From Eq. (i), we get

$$\tan\theta = \frac{4}{3} = \frac{\text{Perpendicular}}{\text{Base}} = \frac{BC}{AB}$$

$\therefore \quad BC = 4k$ and $AB = 3k$.

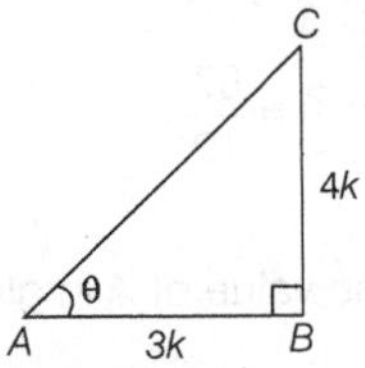

Using Pythagoras theorem, we have

$$(CA)^2 = (AB)^2 + (BC)^2$$

$$\Rightarrow \quad (CA)^2 = (3k)^2 + (4k)^2 = 9k^2 + 16k^2$$

$$\Rightarrow \quad (CA)^2 = 25k^2$$

$\therefore \quad CA = 5k$ [taking positive square root as side cannot be negative]

$$\text{Now, } \sin\theta = \frac{\text{Perpendicular}}{\text{Hypotenuse}} = \frac{BC}{CA} = \frac{4k}{5k} = \frac{4}{5}$$

$$\text{and } \cos\theta = \frac{\text{Base}}{\text{Hypotenuse}} = \frac{AB}{CA} = \frac{3k}{5k} = \frac{3}{5}$$

$$\therefore 4\sin^2\theta - 3\cos^2\theta + 2 = 4\left(\frac{4}{5}\right)^2 - 3\left(\frac{3}{5}\right)^2 + 2$$

$$= 4\left(\frac{16}{25}\right) - 3\left(\frac{9}{25}\right) + 2$$

$$= \frac{64}{25} - \frac{27}{25} + 2$$

$$= \frac{64 - 27 + 50}{25}$$

$$= \frac{87}{25} = 3\frac{12}{25}$$

12. We have, $5 \cos A - 12 \sin A = 0$

$$\Rightarrow \quad 5 \cos A = 12 \sin A$$

$$\Rightarrow \quad \frac{\sin A}{\cos A} = \frac{5}{12}$$

$$\therefore \quad \tan A = \frac{5}{12} \quad \left[\because \frac{\sin\theta}{\cos\theta} = \tan\theta\right]$$

$$\text{Since, } \tan A = \frac{P}{B} = \frac{BC}{AB} = \frac{5}{12}$$

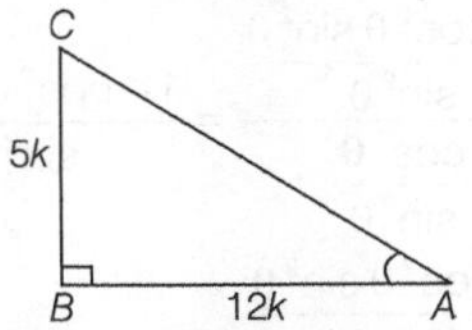

Let $BC = 5k$, $AB = 12k$, where k is any positive number.

Using Pythagoras theorem in ΔABC, we have

$$(AC)^2 = (AB)^2 + (BC)^2 = (12k)^2 + (5k)^2$$

$$= 144k^2 + 25k^2 = 169k^2$$

$\therefore \quad AC = 13k$ [taking positive square root as side cannot be negative]

Hence, $\sin A = \frac{5}{13}$ and $\cos A = \frac{12}{13}$.

$$\text{Now, } \frac{5 \sin A - 3 \cos A}{2 \cos A + \sin A} = \frac{5 \times \frac{5}{13} - 3 \times \frac{12}{13}}{2 \times \frac{12}{13} + \frac{5}{13}}$$

$$= \frac{\frac{25}{13} - \frac{36}{13}}{\frac{24}{13} + \frac{5}{13}}$$

$$= \frac{-\frac{11}{13}}{\frac{29}{13}} = -\frac{11}{29}$$

13. LHS $= (1 + \tan A + \cot A)(\sin A - \cos A)$

$$= \left(1 + \frac{\sin A}{\cos A} + \frac{\cos A}{\sin A}\right)(\sin A - \cos A)$$

$$\left[\because \tan\theta = \frac{\sin\theta}{\cos\theta} \text{ and } \cot\theta = \frac{\cos\theta}{\sin\theta}\right]$$

$$= \left(\frac{\cos A \sin A + \sin^2 A + \cos^2 A}{\cos A \sin A}\right)(\sin A - \cos A)$$

$$= \frac{(\cos A \sin^2 A + \sin^3 A + \cos^2 A \sin A - \cos^2 A \sin A - \sin^2 A \cos A - \cos^3 A}{\cos A \sin A}$$

$$= \frac{\sin^3 A - \cos^3 A}{\cos A \sin A}$$

$$= \frac{\sin^3 A}{\cos A \sin A} - \frac{\cos^3 A}{\cos A \sin A}$$

$$= \sin A \times \frac{\sin A}{\cos A} - \frac{\cos A}{\sin A} \times \cos A$$

$$= \sin A \tan A - \cot A \cos A = \text{RHS}$$

Hence proved.

14. LHS $= \dfrac{\text{cosec}^2\theta - \cos^2\theta}{\cot^2\theta} = \dfrac{\dfrac{1}{\sin^2\theta} - \cos^2\theta}{\dfrac{\cos^2\theta}{\sin^2\theta}}$

$\left[\because \text{cosec}\, A = \dfrac{1}{\sin A} \text{ and } \cot A = \dfrac{\cos A}{\sin A}\right]$

$= \dfrac{\dfrac{1-\cos^2\theta\sin^2\theta}{\sin^2\theta}}{\dfrac{\cos^2\theta}{\sin^2\theta}} = \dfrac{1-\cos^2\theta\sin^2\theta}{\sin^2\theta} \times \dfrac{\sin^2\theta}{\cos^2\theta}$

$= \dfrac{1-\cos^2\theta\sin^2\theta}{\cos^2\theta}$

$= \dfrac{1}{\cos^2\theta} - \dfrac{\cos^2\theta\sin^2\theta}{\cos^2\theta}$

$= \sec^2\theta - \sin^2\theta \qquad \left[\because \dfrac{1}{\cos A} = \sec A\right]$

= RHS **Hence proved.**

15. We have, $\dfrac{\sin 30° + \tan 45° - \text{cosec}\, 60°}{\sec 30° + \cos 60° + \cot 45°}$

$= \dfrac{\dfrac{1}{2} + 1 - \dfrac{2}{\sqrt{3}}}{\dfrac{2}{\sqrt{3}} + \dfrac{1}{2} + 1} = \dfrac{\dfrac{\sqrt{3}+2\sqrt{3}-4}{2\sqrt{3}}}{\dfrac{4+\sqrt{3}+2\sqrt{3}}{2\sqrt{3}}}$

$\left[\because \sin 30° = \dfrac{1}{2}, \tan 45° = 1, \text{cosec}\, 60° = \dfrac{2}{\sqrt{3}}, \sec 30° = \dfrac{2}{\sqrt{3}}, \cos 60° = \dfrac{1}{2} \text{ and } \cot 45° = 1\right]$

$= \dfrac{3\sqrt{3}-4}{4+3\sqrt{3}} = \dfrac{3\sqrt{3}-4}{4+3\sqrt{3}} \times \dfrac{4-3\sqrt{3}}{4-3\sqrt{3}}$

[by rationalising the denominator]

$= \dfrac{12\sqrt{3} - 27 - 16 + 12\sqrt{3}}{(4)^2 - (3\sqrt{3})^2} \qquad [\because (a+b)(a-b) = a^2 - b^2]$

$= \dfrac{24\sqrt{3} - 43}{16 - 27}$

$= \dfrac{-(43 - 24\sqrt{3})}{-11} = \dfrac{43 - 24\sqrt{3}}{11}$

16. Given, $\angle A = \angle B = 45°$.

Now, LHS $= \sin(A+B)$

$= \sin(45° + 45°) = \sin 90° = 1$

and RHS $= \sin A \cos B + \cos A \sin B$

$= \sin 45° \cos 45° + \cos 45° \sin 45°$

$= \dfrac{1}{\sqrt{2}} \cdot \dfrac{1}{\sqrt{2}} + \dfrac{1}{\sqrt{2}} \cdot \dfrac{1}{\sqrt{2}}$

$= \dfrac{1}{2} + \dfrac{1}{2} = 1 \qquad \left[\because \sin 45° = \cos 45° = \dfrac{1}{\sqrt{2}}\right]$

$\therefore$ LHS = RHS **Hence proved.**

17. We have, $\dfrac{5\cos^2 60° + 4\sec^2 30° - \tan^2 45°}{\sin^2 30° + \cos^2 30°}$

$= \dfrac{5\left(\dfrac{1}{2}\right)^2 + 4\left(\dfrac{2}{\sqrt{3}}\right)^2 - (1)^2}{\left(\dfrac{1}{2}\right)^2 + \left(\dfrac{\sqrt{3}}{2}\right)^2}$

$\left[\because \cos 60° = \dfrac{1}{2}, \sec 30° = \dfrac{2}{\sqrt{3}}, \tan 45° = 1, \sin 30° = \dfrac{1}{2} \text{ and } \cos 30° = \dfrac{\sqrt{3}}{2}\right]$

$= \dfrac{5\left(\dfrac{1}{4}\right) + 4\left(\dfrac{4}{3}\right) - 1}{\dfrac{1}{4} + \dfrac{3}{4}} = \dfrac{\dfrac{5}{4} + \dfrac{16}{3} - 1}{\dfrac{1}{4} + \dfrac{3}{4}}$

$= \dfrac{\dfrac{15 + 64 - 12}{12}}{\dfrac{1+3}{4}}$

$= \dfrac{67}{12} \times \dfrac{4}{4} = \dfrac{67}{12}$

18. Given, $A = 15°$.

On substituting the value of A in given expression, we get

$\dfrac{\sin 3A - 2\cos 4A}{\cos 3A + 2\sin 4A} = \dfrac{\sin 3 \times 15° - 2\cos 4 \times 15°}{\cos 3 \times 15° + 2\sin 4 \times 15°}$

$= \dfrac{\sin 45° - 2\cos 60°}{\cos 45° + 2\sin 60°}$

$= \dfrac{\dfrac{1}{\sqrt{2}} - 2 \times \dfrac{1}{2}}{\dfrac{1}{\sqrt{2}} + 2 \times \dfrac{\sqrt{3}}{2}} = \dfrac{\dfrac{1}{\sqrt{2}} - 1}{\dfrac{1}{\sqrt{2}} + \sqrt{3}}$

$\left[\because \sin 45° = \cos 45° = \dfrac{1}{\sqrt{2}}, \cos 60° = \dfrac{1}{2} \text{ and } \sin 60° = \dfrac{\sqrt{3}}{2}\right]$

$= \dfrac{\dfrac{1-\sqrt{2}}{\sqrt{2}}}{\dfrac{1+\sqrt{2}\times\sqrt{3}}{\sqrt{2}}} = \dfrac{1-\sqrt{2}}{1+\sqrt{6}}$

19. We have, $\tan^2 x + \sec^2 60° = 5$

$\Rightarrow \quad \tan^2 x + (2)^2 = 5 \qquad [\because \sec 60° = 2]$

$\Rightarrow \quad \tan^2 x + 4 = 5$

$\Rightarrow \quad \tan^2 x = 5 - 4$

$\Rightarrow \quad \tan^2 x = 1 \Rightarrow \tan x = 1$

[taking positive root because $0° \le x \le 90°$]

$\Rightarrow \quad \tan x = \tan 45° \qquad [\because \tan 45° = 1]$

$\Rightarrow \quad x = 45°$

Sample Question Paper

When, $(\sin\alpha - 1) = 0$

$\Rightarrow \quad \sin\alpha = 1$

$\Rightarrow \quad \sin\alpha = \sin 90^\circ \qquad [\because \sin 90^\circ = 1]$

$\Rightarrow \quad \alpha = 90^\circ$

When, $(2\sin\alpha - 1) = 0$

$\Rightarrow \quad 2\sin\alpha = 1$

$\Rightarrow \quad \sin\alpha = \frac{1}{2}$

$\Rightarrow \quad \sin\alpha = \sin 30^\circ \qquad \left[\because \sin 30^\circ = \frac{1}{2}\right]$

$\Rightarrow \quad \alpha = 30^\circ$

26. We know that diagonals of a rhombus bisects each other at 90° and also bisects the angle of the vertex.

In right angled ΔAOB,

$$\sin 30^\circ = \frac{OB}{AB}$$

$$\Rightarrow \quad \frac{1}{2} = \frac{OB}{10}$$

$$\Rightarrow \quad OB = 5 \text{ cm} \qquad \left[\because \sin 30^\circ = \frac{1}{2}\right]$$

$$\Rightarrow \quad BD = OB + OD$$

$$\Rightarrow \quad BD = 5 + 5 = 10 \text{ cm} \qquad [\because OB = OD]$$

In right angled ΔAOD,

$$\cos \angle DAO = \frac{OA}{AD}$$

$$\Rightarrow \quad \cos 30^\circ = \frac{AO}{AD} \qquad \left[\because \angle DAO = \frac{60^\circ}{2} = 30^\circ\right]$$

$$\Rightarrow \quad \frac{\sqrt{3}}{2} = \frac{AO}{10}$$

$$\Rightarrow \quad AO = 5\sqrt{3} \text{ cm}$$

$$\Rightarrow \quad AC = 2 \times AO = 10\sqrt{3} = 17.32 \text{ cm}$$

Hence, length of diagonal $AC = 17.32$ cm and $BD = 10$ cm.

27. Draw $LP \perp MN$

Clearly, $\angle PLM = 90^\circ - \angle MLQ = 90^\circ - 60^\circ = 30^\circ$

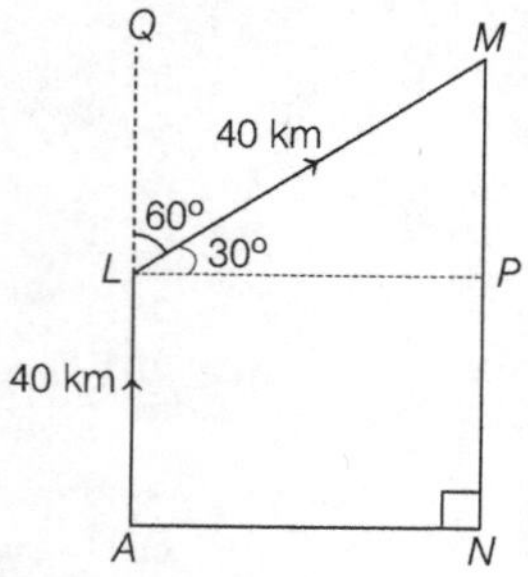

(i) In right angled ΔPLM,

$$\sin 30^\circ = \frac{PM}{ML}$$

$$\Rightarrow \quad \frac{1}{2} = \frac{PM}{40} \qquad \left[\because \sin 30^\circ = \frac{1}{2}\right]$$

$$\Rightarrow \quad PM = 20 \text{ km}$$

Now, $MN = NP + PM \Rightarrow MN = 40 + 20$

$[\because AL = NP \text{ and } PM = 20 \text{ km}]$

$\Rightarrow \quad MN = 60$ km

Hence, the height of the rocket when it is at point M is 60 km.

(ii) Again, In right angled ΔPLM,

$$\cos 30^\circ = \frac{LP}{ML}$$

$$\Rightarrow \quad \frac{\sqrt{3}}{2} = \frac{LP}{40} \Rightarrow LP = 20\sqrt{3} \text{ km}$$

$$\because \quad AN = LP \Rightarrow AN = 20\sqrt{3} \text{ km}$$

Hence, the horizontal distance of point N from A is $20\sqrt{3}$ km.

28. We have, $\frac{\cot 40^\circ}{\tan 50^\circ} - \frac{\cos 35^\circ}{2\sin 55^\circ}$

$$= \frac{\cot(90^\circ - 50^\circ)}{\tan 50^\circ} - \frac{\cos(90^\circ - 55^\circ)}{2\sin 55^\circ}$$

$$= \frac{\tan 50^\circ}{\tan 50^\circ} - \frac{\sin 55^\circ}{2\sin 55^\circ} = 1 - \frac{1}{2}$$

$[\because \cot(90^\circ - \theta) = \tan\theta \text{ and } \cos(90^\circ - \theta) = \sin\theta]$

$$= \frac{1}{2}$$

29. Given, expression

$$= \frac{\tan 50^\circ + \sec 50^\circ}{\cot 40^\circ + \operatorname{cosec} 40^\circ} + \cos 40^\circ \operatorname{cosec} 50^\circ$$

$$= \frac{\tan 50^\circ + \sec 50^\circ}{\cot(90^\circ - 50^\circ) + \operatorname{cosec}(90^\circ - 50^\circ)} + \cos 40^\circ \operatorname{cosec}(90^\circ - 40^\circ)$$

$$= \frac{\tan 50^\circ + \sec 50^\circ}{\tan 50^\circ + \sec 50^\circ} + \cos 40^\circ \sec 40^\circ$$

$[\because \cot(90^\circ - \theta) = \tan\theta, \operatorname{cosec}(90^\circ - \theta) = \sec\theta]$

$= 1 + 1 = 2 \qquad [\because \cos A \sec A = 1]$

30. $\frac{\sin 70^\circ}{\cos 20^\circ} + \frac{\operatorname{cosec} 36^\circ}{\sec 54^\circ} - \frac{2\cos 43^\circ \operatorname{cosec} 47^\circ}{\tan 10^\circ \tan 40^\circ \tan 50^\circ \tan 80^\circ}$

$$= \frac{\sin(90^\circ - 20^\circ)}{\cos 20^\circ} + \frac{\operatorname{cosec}(90^\circ - 54^\circ)}{\sec 54^\circ} - \frac{2\cos 43^\circ \operatorname{cosec}(90^\circ - 43^\circ)}{\tan(90^\circ - 80^\circ)\tan(90^\circ - 50^\circ)\tan 50^\circ \tan 80^\circ}$$

$$= \frac{\cos 20^\circ}{\cos 20^\circ} + \frac{\sec 54^\circ}{\sec 54^\circ} - \frac{2\cos 43^\circ \sec 43^\circ}{\cot 80^\circ \cot 50^\circ \tan 50^\circ \tan 80^\circ}$$

$\left[\begin{array}{l}\because \sin(90^\circ - \theta) = \cos\theta, \\ \operatorname{cosec}(90^\circ - \theta) = \sec\theta \\ \text{and } \tan(90^\circ - \theta) = \cot\theta\end{array}\right]$

$$=1+1-\frac{2\cos 43^\circ\cdot\frac{1}{\cos 43^\circ}}{\frac{1}{\tan 80^\circ}\cdot\tan 80^\circ\cdot\frac{1}{\tan 50^\circ}\cdot\tan 50^\circ}$$

$$\left[\because \tan\theta=\frac{1}{\cot\theta}\text{ and }\sec\theta=\frac{1}{\cos\theta}\right]$$

$$=2-\frac{2\cdot 1}{1\cdot 1}=2-2=0$$

31. $\tan 1^\circ \tan 2^\circ \tan 3^\circ \ldots \tan 89^\circ$

$$=\tan(90^\circ-89^\circ)\tan(90^\circ-88^\circ)\tan(90^\circ-87^\circ)\ldots\tan 45^\circ\ldots\tan 87^\circ\tan 88^\circ\tan 89^\circ$$

$$=\cot 89^\circ\cot 88^\circ\cot 87^\circ\ldots\tan 45^\circ\ldots\tan 87^\circ\tan 88^\circ\tan 89^\circ$$

$$[\because \tan(90^\circ-\theta)=\cot\theta]$$

$$=(\cot 89^\circ\tan 89^\circ)\cdot(\cot 88^\circ\tan 88^\circ)\ldots\tan 45^\circ$$

$$=1\times1\times1\times\ldots\times1$$

$$=1 \qquad [\because \tan\theta\cdot\cot\theta=1\text{ and }\tan 45^\circ=1]$$

32. We have,

$\cot 12^\circ\cot 38^\circ\cot 52^\circ\cot 60^\circ\cot 78^\circ$

$$=\cot(90^\circ-78^\circ)\cot(90^\circ-52^\circ)\cot 52^\circ\cot 60^\circ\cot 78^\circ$$

$$=\tan 78^\circ\tan 52^\circ\cot 52^\circ\cot 60^\circ\cot 78^\circ$$

$$[\because \cot(90^\circ-\theta)=\tan\theta]$$

$$=\tan 78^\circ\cot 78^\circ\tan 52^\circ\cot 52^\circ\cot 60^\circ$$

$$=\tan 78^\circ\times\frac{1}{\tan 78^\circ}\times\tan 52^\circ\times\frac{1}{\tan 52^\circ}\times\frac{1}{\sqrt3}$$

$$\left[\because \tan\theta=\frac{1}{\cot\theta}\text{ and }\cot 60^\circ=\frac{1}{\sqrt3}\right]$$

$$=\frac{1}{\sqrt3}$$

33. Given, $\cos(A-B)=\cos A\cos B+\sin A\sin B$ ...(a)

Then, we have

(i) $\cos 15^\circ=\cos(45^\circ-30^\circ)$

$$=\cos 45^\circ\cos 30^\circ+\sin 45^\circ\sin 30^\circ \qquad \text{[using Eq. (a)]}$$

$$=\frac{1}{\sqrt2}\cdot\frac{\sqrt3}{2}+\frac{1}{\sqrt2}\cdot\frac{1}{2}$$

$$=\frac{\sqrt3}{2\sqrt2}+\frac{1}{2\sqrt2}=\frac{\sqrt3+1}{2\sqrt2}$$

$$\Rightarrow \cos 15^\circ=\frac{\sqrt3+1}{2\sqrt2} \qquad \ldots(b)$$

(ii) $\sin 75^\circ=\sin(90^\circ-15^\circ)=\cos 15^\circ$

$$[\because \sin(90^\circ-\theta)=\cos\theta]$$

$$=\frac{\sqrt3+1}{2\sqrt2} \qquad \text{[from Eq. (b)]}$$

34. Given, $\sin\left(50^\circ-\frac{3}{2}\theta\right)=\cos(3\theta-50^\circ)$

$$\Rightarrow \sin\left(50^\circ-\frac{3}{2}\theta\right)=\sin[90^\circ-(3\theta-50^\circ)]$$

$$[\because \sin(90^\circ-A)=\cos A]$$

$$\Rightarrow \sin\left(50^\circ-\frac{3}{2}\theta\right)=\sin[140^\circ-3\theta]$$

On equating both sides, we get

$$50^\circ-\frac{3}{2}\theta=140^\circ-3\theta$$

$$\Rightarrow \frac{3}{2}\theta=90^\circ$$

$$\Rightarrow \theta=60^\circ$$

Now, $\tan\theta\sec\theta\sin\theta-\cot\theta\sin\theta\cos\theta$

$$=\tan 60^\circ\sec 60^\circ\sin 60^\circ-\cot 60^\circ\sin 60^\circ\cos 60^\circ$$

$$[\because \theta=60^\circ]$$

$$=\sqrt3\times2\times\frac{\sqrt3}{2}-\frac{1}{\sqrt3}\times\frac{\sqrt3}{2}\times\frac{1}{2}$$

$$=3-\frac{1}{4}=\frac{11}{4}$$

Long Answer Type Questions

1. Given, $AD=x$.

Then, $AC=AD+CD=(x+9)$ cm

In ΔACB, right angled at C, we have

$$AB^2=BC^2+AC^2 \qquad \text{[by Pythagoras theorem]}$$

$$\Rightarrow (20)^2=(12)^2+(x+9)^2$$

$$\Rightarrow (x+9)^2=400-144=256=(16)^2$$

$$\Rightarrow x+9=16 \qquad \text{[taking positive square root as side cannot be negative]}$$

$$\Rightarrow x=16-9=7 \qquad \ldots(i)$$

(i) $\sin\angle ABC=\frac{P}{H}=\frac{AC}{AB}=\frac{x+9}{20}$

$$=\frac{7+9}{20}=\frac{16}{20}=\frac{4}{5} \qquad [\because x=7]$$

(ii) In right angled ΔBCD, we have

$$BD^2=BC^2+CD^2$$

$$\Rightarrow BD^2=12^2+9^2=144+81=225=(15)^2$$

$$\therefore BD=15\text{ cm} \qquad \text{[taking positive square root as side cannot be negative]}$$

Now, $\sin\theta=\frac{P}{H}=\frac{BC}{BD}=\frac{12}{15}=\frac{4}{5}$

$$\cos\theta=\frac{B}{H}=\frac{CD}{BD}=\frac{9}{15}=\frac{3}{5}$$

and $\tan\theta=\frac{P}{B}=\frac{BC}{CD}=\frac{12}{9}=\frac{4}{3}$

$\therefore \tan\theta + \cos\theta - 2\sin\theta = \frac{4}{3} + \frac{3}{5} - 2 \times \frac{4}{5}$

$= \frac{4}{3} + \frac{3}{5} - \frac{8}{5}$

$= \frac{20 + 9 - 24}{15}$

$= \frac{29 - 24}{15} = \frac{5}{15} = \frac{1}{3}$

2. First, draw a ΔABC, right angled at B.

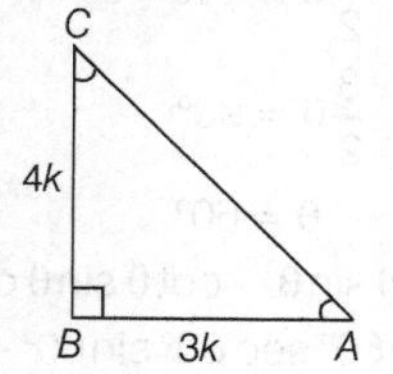

Given, $3\tan A = 4 \Rightarrow \tan A = \frac{4}{3}$

$\Rightarrow \frac{\text{Perpendicular}}{\text{Base}} = \frac{4}{3}$

$\Rightarrow \frac{BC}{AB} = \frac{4}{3} = \frac{4k}{3k}$ (say)

[where, k is any positive integer]

$\therefore$ $BC = 4k$ and $AB = 3k$

Using Pythagoras theorem in ΔABC, we have

$AC^2 = BC^2 + AB^2$

$\Rightarrow AC^2 = (4k)^2 + (3k)^2 = 16k^2 + 9k^2$

$\Rightarrow AC^2 = 25k^2$

$\Rightarrow AC = \sqrt{25k^2} = 5k$

[taking positive square root as side cannot be negative]

Now, $\sin A = \frac{BC}{AC} = \frac{4k}{5k} = \frac{4}{5}$,

$\cos A = \frac{AB}{AC} = \frac{3k}{5k} = \frac{3}{5}$,

$\operatorname{cosec} A = \frac{AC}{BC} = \frac{5k}{4k} = \frac{5}{4}$

and $\sec A = \frac{AC}{AB} = \frac{5k}{3k} = \frac{5}{3}$

(i) LHS $= \sqrt{\frac{\sec A - \operatorname{cosec} A}{\sec A + \operatorname{cosec} A}} = \sqrt{\frac{\frac{5}{3} - \frac{5}{4}}{\frac{5}{3} + \frac{5}{4}}} = \sqrt{\frac{\frac{20 - 15}{12}}{\frac{20 + 15}{12}}}$

$= \sqrt{\frac{\frac{5}{12}}{\frac{35}{12}}} = \sqrt{\frac{5}{35}} = \sqrt{\frac{1}{7}} =$ RHS **Hence proved.**

(ii) LHS $= \sqrt{\frac{1 - \sin A}{1 + \cos A}} = \sqrt{\frac{1 - \frac{4}{5}}{1 + \frac{3}{5}}} = \sqrt{\frac{\frac{1}{5}}{\frac{8}{5}}} = \sqrt{\frac{1}{8}}$

$= \frac{1}{2\sqrt{2}}$

= RHS **Hence proved.**

3. (i) We know that $\cot\theta = \frac{\text{Base}}{\text{Perpendicular}}$

In right angled ΔABC,

$\cot \angle ABC = \frac{BC}{AC}$ ...(a)

In right angled ΔADC,

$\cot \angle ADC = \frac{DC}{AC}$ ...(b)

Now, $\frac{\cot \angle ABC}{\cot \angle ADC} = \frac{\frac{BC}{AC}}{\frac{DC}{AC}}$ [from Eqs. (a) and (b)]

$= \frac{BC \times AC}{AC \times DC}$

$= \frac{2DC}{DC}$ [$\because BD = DC$]

$= 2$

(ii) We know that $\tan\theta = \frac{\text{Perpendicular}}{\text{Base}}$

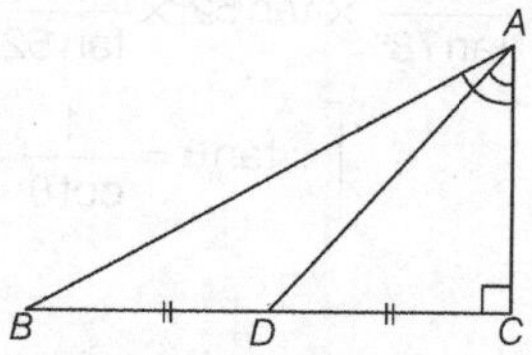

In right angled ΔADC,

$\tan \angle DAC = \frac{DC}{AC}$ ...(c)

And, in right angled ΔABC,

$\tan \angle BAC = \frac{BC}{AC}$ ...(d)

Now, $\frac{\tan \angle DAC}{\tan \angle BAC} = \frac{\frac{DC}{AC}}{\frac{BC}{AC}}$ [from Eqs. (c) and (d)]

$= \frac{DC \times AC}{BC \times AC}$

$= \frac{DC}{2DC}$ [$\because BD = DC$]

$= \frac{1}{2}$

4. We know that the diagonals of rhombus bisect each other at 90°.

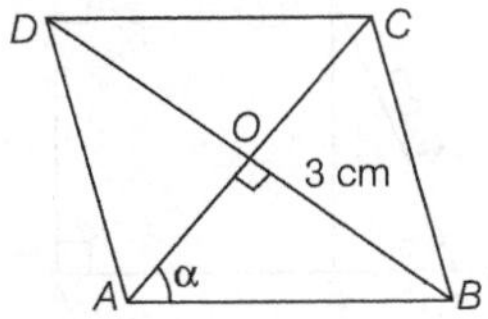

In right angled ΔAOB,

$$\cos\alpha = \frac{\text{Base}}{\text{Hypotenuse}}$$

$$\Rightarrow \quad \cos\alpha = \frac{OA}{AB} = \frac{2}{3} \quad \text{[given]}$$

$$\Rightarrow \quad OA = \frac{2}{3}AB$$

Now, $(AB)^2 = (OA)^2 + (OB)^2$ [by Pythagoras theorem]

$$\Rightarrow \quad (AB)^2 = \left(\frac{2}{3}AB\right)^2 + 3^2 \quad \left[\text{given, } OB = 3 \text{ cm and } OA = \frac{2}{3}AB\right]$$

$$\Rightarrow \quad (AB)^2 = \frac{4}{9}(AB)^2 + 9$$

$$\Rightarrow \quad (AB)^2 - \frac{4}{9}(AB)^2 = 9 \Rightarrow \frac{5}{9}(AB)^2 = 9$$

$$\Rightarrow \quad (AB)^2 = \frac{81}{5} \Rightarrow AB = \frac{9}{\sqrt{5}}$$

$$\text{Side} = \frac{9}{\sqrt{5}} \text{ cm}$$

Again, in right angled ΔAOB,

$$(AB)^2 = (OA)^2 + (OB)^2$$

$$\Rightarrow \quad \left(\frac{9}{\sqrt{5}}\right)^2 = (OA)^2 + 3^2 \quad \left[\because AB = \frac{9}{\sqrt{5}} \text{ cm}, OB = 3 \text{ cm}\right]$$

$$\Rightarrow \quad \frac{81}{5} = (OA)^2 + 9$$

$$\Rightarrow \quad (OA)^2 = \frac{81}{5} - 9 \Rightarrow (OA)^2 = \frac{36}{5}$$

$$\Rightarrow \quad OA = \frac{6}{\sqrt{5}} \text{ cm}$$

So, diagonal $BD = 2 \times OB$

$$= 2 \times 3 = 6 \text{ cm} \quad [\because OB = 3 \text{ cm}]$$

and $$AC = 2 \times OA = 2 \times \frac{6}{\sqrt{5}} \quad \left[\because OA = \frac{6}{\sqrt{5}}\right]$$

$$= \frac{12}{\sqrt{5}} \text{ cm}$$

Hence, the side is $\frac{9}{\sqrt{5}}$ cm and diagonals are 6 cm and $\frac{12}{\sqrt{5}}$ cm, respectively.

5. (i) We have, $\cot(90° - 3A) \cdot \tan 48° = 1$

$$\Rightarrow \quad \cot(90° - 3A) = \frac{1}{\tan 48°}$$

$$\Rightarrow \quad \cot(90° - 3A) = \cot 48° \quad \left[\because \frac{1}{\tan\theta} = \cot\theta\right]$$

On equating both sides, we get

$$90° - 3A = 48°$$

$$\Rightarrow \quad 3A = 90° - 48°$$

$$\Rightarrow \quad 3A = 42° \Rightarrow A = 14°$$

Hence, the value of angle A is 14°.

(ii) $\sin(90° - A) \cdot \operatorname{cosec} 23° = 1$

$$\Rightarrow \quad \sin(90° - A) = \frac{1}{\operatorname{cosec} 23°}$$

$$\Rightarrow \quad \sin(90° - A) = \sin 23° \quad \left[\because \frac{1}{\operatorname{cosec}\theta} = \sin\theta\right]$$

On equating both sides, we get

$$90° - A = 23° \Rightarrow A = 90° - 23°$$

$$\Rightarrow \quad A = 67°$$

Hence, the value of angle A is 67°.

6. Given, $A = 60°$ and $B = 30°$

(i) $\cos(A - B) = \cos A \cdot \cos B + \sin A \cdot \sin B$

$$\text{LHS} = \cos(A - B) = \cos(60° - 30°) = \cos 30°$$

$$= \frac{\sqrt{3}}{2} \quad \text{...(a)}$$

$$\text{RHS} = \cos A \cdot \cos B + \sin A \sin B$$

$$= \cos 60° \cos 30° + \sin 60° \sin 30°$$

$$= \frac{1}{2} \times \frac{\sqrt{3}}{2} + \frac{\sqrt{3}}{2} \times \frac{1}{2}$$

$$= \frac{\sqrt{3}}{4} + \frac{\sqrt{3}}{4} = \frac{\sqrt{3}}{2} \quad \text{...(b)}$$

From Eqs. (a) and (b), we get

LHS = RHS **Hence proved.**

(ii) $$\cot(A + B) = \frac{\cot A \cdot \cot B - 1}{\cot B + \cot A}$$

$$\text{LHS} = \cot(A + B) = \cot(60° + 30°)$$

$$= \cot 90°$$

$$= 0 \quad \text{...(c)}$$

$$\text{RHS} = \frac{\cot A \cdot \cot B - 1}{\cot B + \cot A} = \frac{\cot 60° \cdot \cot 30° - 1}{\cot 30° + \cot 60°}$$

$$= \frac{\frac{1}{\sqrt{3}} \times \sqrt{3} - 1}{\sqrt{3} + \frac{1}{\sqrt{3}}} = \frac{1 - 1}{\sqrt{3} + \frac{1}{\sqrt{3}}} = 0 \quad \text{...(d)}$$

From Eqs. (c) and (d), we get

LHS = RHS **Hence proved.**

7. LHS $= \left(\dfrac{1+\tan 30^\circ}{1-\tan 30^\circ}\right)^2$

$= \left(\dfrac{1+\dfrac{1}{\sqrt{3}}}{1-\dfrac{1}{\sqrt{3}}}\right)^2$ $\quad \left[\because \tan 30^\circ = \dfrac{1}{\sqrt{3}}\right]$

$= \left(\dfrac{\dfrac{\sqrt{3}+1}{\sqrt{3}}}{\dfrac{\sqrt{3}-1}{\sqrt{3}}}\right)^2 = \left(\dfrac{\sqrt{3}+1}{\sqrt{3}-1}\right)^2$

$= \left[\dfrac{(\sqrt{3}+1)(\sqrt{3}+1)}{(\sqrt{3}-1)(\sqrt{3}+1)}\right]^2$ [on rationalising]

$= \left[\dfrac{(\sqrt{3}+1)^2}{(\sqrt{3})^2-1^2}\right]^2$

$= \left[\dfrac{(\sqrt{3})^2+1+2\sqrt{3}}{3-1}\right]^2$ $\quad [\because (a+b)^2 = a^2+b^2+2ab]$

$= \left[\dfrac{3+1+2\sqrt{3}}{2}\right]^2 = \left[\dfrac{4+2\sqrt{3}}{2}\right]^2$

$= (2+\sqrt{3})^2$

$= (2)^2 + (\sqrt{3})^2 + 2\times 2\times\sqrt{3}$

$= 4+3+4\sqrt{3}$

$= 7+4\sqrt{3}$ $\quad \ldots$(i)

RHS $= \left(\dfrac{1+\cos 30^\circ}{1-\cos 30^\circ}\right) = \left(\dfrac{1+\dfrac{\sqrt{3}}{2}}{1-\dfrac{\sqrt{3}}{2}}\right)$

$= \left(\dfrac{\dfrac{2+\sqrt{3}}{2}}{\dfrac{2-\sqrt{3}}{2}}\right) = \left(\dfrac{2+\sqrt{3}}{2-\sqrt{3}}\right)$

$= \left[\dfrac{(2+\sqrt{3})(2+\sqrt{3})}{(2-\sqrt{3})(2+\sqrt{3})}\right]$ [on rationalising]

$= \left[\dfrac{(2+\sqrt{3})^2}{(2)^2-(\sqrt{3})^2}\right]$

$= \left[\dfrac{(2)^2+(\sqrt{3})^2+2\times 2\sqrt{3}}{4-3}\right]$

$[\because (a+b)^2 = a^2+b^2+2ab]$

$= \left[\dfrac{4+3+4\sqrt{3}}{1}\right] = 7+4\sqrt{3}$ $\quad \ldots$(ii)

From Eqs. (i) and (ii), we get

LHS = RHS **Hence proved.**

8. Draw $CE \perp BA$.

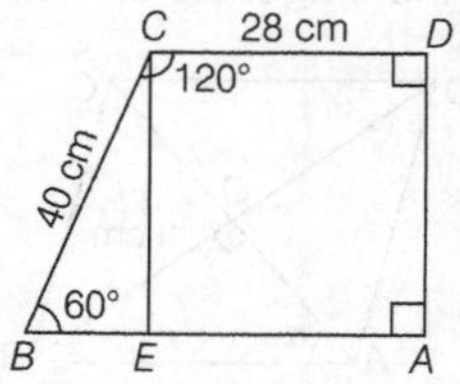

We know that for parallel lines, the sum of interior angles on the same side of a transversal is supplementary.

$\therefore \quad \angle ABC + \angle BCD = 180^\circ$

$\Rightarrow \quad \angle ABC + 120^\circ = 180^\circ$

$\Rightarrow \quad \angle ABC = 60^\circ$ $\quad [\because \angle C = 120^\circ$ given$]$

Now, in right angled ΔCBE,

$\sin 60^\circ = \dfrac{CE}{BC} = \dfrac{CE}{40}$ $\quad [\because BC = 40$ cm$]$

$\Rightarrow \quad \dfrac{\sqrt{3}}{2} = \dfrac{CE}{40}$ $\quad \left[\because \sin 60^\circ = \dfrac{\sqrt{3}}{2}\right]$

$\Rightarrow \quad CE = 20\sqrt{3}$ cm

and $\quad \cos 60^\circ = \dfrac{BE}{BC} = \dfrac{BE}{40}$

$\Rightarrow \quad \dfrac{1}{2} = \dfrac{BE}{40}$ $\quad \left[\because \cos 60^\circ = \dfrac{1}{2}\right]$

$\Rightarrow \quad BE = 20$ cm

(i) $AB = BE + AE$

$\Rightarrow \quad AB = BE + CD$

$[\because AE = CD$ because opposite sides of rectangle$]$

$\Rightarrow \quad AB = 20 + 28 \Rightarrow AB = 48$ cm

(ii) $AD = CE$ [opposite sides of rectangle]

$\Rightarrow AD = 20\sqrt{3}$ cm

(iii) Area of trapezium $= \dfrac{1}{2}(AB+CD)\times AD$

$\left[\because \text{area of trapezium} = \dfrac{1}{2}\text{(sum of parallel sides)} \times \text{height}\right]$

$= \dfrac{1}{2}(48+28)\times 20\sqrt{3}$

$[\because AB = 48$ cm, $CD = 28$ cm and $AD = 20\sqrt{3}$ cm$]$

$= \dfrac{1}{2}\times 76\times 20\sqrt{3} = 760\sqrt{3}$ cm^2

9. Draw a line $FP \perp BE$.

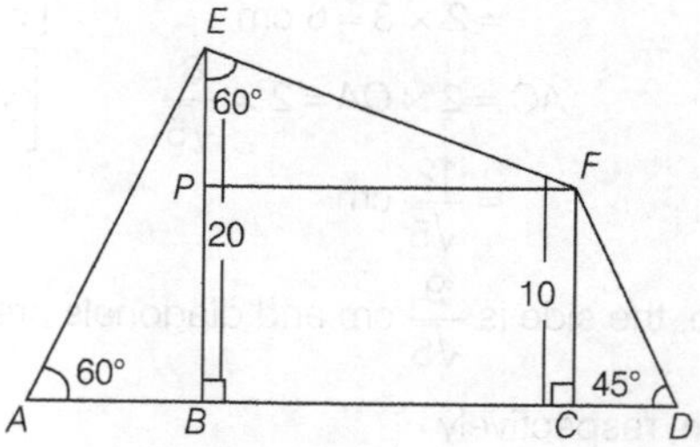

$BP = FC = 10$ units

[opposite sides of rectangle $PBCF$]

$\Rightarrow \quad EP = EB - BP$

$\Rightarrow \quad EP = 20 - 10$

$\Rightarrow \quad EP = 10$ units

Now, in right angled ΔCDF,

$$\tan 45^\circ = \frac{\text{Perpendicular}}{\text{Base}} = \frac{FC}{CD}$$

$\Rightarrow \quad 1 = \dfrac{10}{CD} \quad [\because FC = 10 \text{ and } \tan 45^\circ = 1]$

$\Rightarrow \quad CD = 10$ units ...(i)

In right angled ΔABE,

$$\tan 60^\circ = \frac{BE}{AB}$$

$\Rightarrow \quad \sqrt{3} = \dfrac{20}{AB} \quad [\because \tan 60^\circ = \sqrt{3} \text{ and } BE = 20]$

$\Rightarrow \quad AB = \dfrac{20}{\sqrt{3}}$ units ...(ii)

Now, in right angled ΔPFE,

$$\tan 60^\circ = \frac{FP}{PE}$$

$\Rightarrow \quad \sqrt{3} = \dfrac{FP}{10}$

$\Rightarrow \quad FP = 10\sqrt{3}$ units

And $\quad FP = BC$

[opposite sides of rectangle $PBCF$]

$\Rightarrow \quad BC = 10\sqrt{3}$ units ...(iii)

Hence, $\quad AD = AB + BC + CD$

$\Rightarrow \quad AD = \dfrac{20}{\sqrt{3}} + 10\sqrt{3} + 10$

[from Eqs. (i), (ii) and (iii)]

$\Rightarrow \quad AD = \dfrac{20 + 10 \times 3 + 10\sqrt{3}}{\sqrt{3}}$

$\Rightarrow \quad AD = \dfrac{50 + 10\sqrt{3}}{\sqrt{3}} \quad [\because \sqrt{3} = 1.732]$

$\therefore \quad AD \approx 38.868$ units

10. In right angled ΔQRS,

$$\tan 30^\circ = \frac{QR}{RS}$$

$\Rightarrow \quad \dfrac{1}{\sqrt{3}} = \dfrac{QR}{60\sqrt{3}} \quad \left[\because \tan 30^\circ = \dfrac{1}{\sqrt{3}}, RS = 60\sqrt{3} \text{ m}\right]$

$\Rightarrow \quad QR = 60$ m ...(i)

We know that the sum of all angles of triangle is 180°.

Again, in ΔQRS,

$$\angle QSR + \angle SRQ + \angle RQS = 180^\circ$$

$\Rightarrow \quad 30^\circ + 90^\circ + \angle RQS = 180^\circ$

$\Rightarrow \quad \angle RQS = 180^\circ - 120^\circ$

$\Rightarrow \quad \angle RQS = 60^\circ$

$\therefore \quad \angle PQO = 90^\circ - \angle RQS$

$[\because \angle PQR = 90^\circ \text{ (given)}]$

$\Rightarrow \quad \angle PQO = 90^\circ - 60^\circ$

$\Rightarrow \quad \angle PQO = 30^\circ$

Now, in ΔPOQ,

$$\angle PQO + \angle QOP + \angle OPQ = 180^\circ$$

$\Rightarrow \quad 30^\circ + 90^\circ + \angle OPQ = 180^\circ$

[QS is a straight line]

$\Rightarrow \quad \angle OPQ = 180^\circ - 120^\circ$

$\Rightarrow \quad \angle OPQ = 60^\circ$

In right angled ΔPQR,

$$\tan \angle QPR = \frac{QR}{PQ}$$

$\Rightarrow \quad \tan 60^\circ = \dfrac{60}{PQ}$ [from Eq. (i)]

$\Rightarrow \quad \sqrt{3} = \dfrac{60}{PQ}$

$\Rightarrow \quad PQ = \dfrac{60}{\sqrt{3}}$

$\Rightarrow \quad PQ = 20\sqrt{3}$ m

Hence, the value of PQ is $20\sqrt{3}$ m.

Case Based Questions

1. $\because \Delta ABD$ is a right angled triangle.

$\therefore \quad (AD)^2 = (BA)^2 + (BD)^2$

[by Pythagoras theorem]

$\Rightarrow \quad (AD)^2 = 8^2 + 6^2$

$\Rightarrow \quad (AD)^2 = 64 + 36$

$\Rightarrow \quad (AD)^2 = 100$

$\Rightarrow \quad AD = 10$ units [taking positive square root as side cannot be negative]

And ΔABC is also a right angled triangle.

$\therefore \quad (BC)^2 = (AC)^2 - (AB)^2$

[by Pythagoras theorem]

$\Rightarrow \quad (BC)^2 = (17)^2 - 8^2$

$\Rightarrow \quad (BC)^2 = 289 - 64$

$\Rightarrow \quad (BC)^2 = 225$

$\Rightarrow \quad BC = 15$ units

(i) $\sin x^\circ = \dfrac{\text{Perpendicular}}{\text{Hypotenuse}}$

$$= \frac{AB}{AC} = \frac{8}{17}$$

(ii) $\cos y^\circ = \dfrac{\text{Base}}{\text{Hypotenuse}}$

$= \dfrac{BD}{AD} = \dfrac{6}{10} = \dfrac{3}{5}$ $\quad [\because AD = 10]$

(iii) $\sin y^\circ = \dfrac{AB}{AD} = \dfrac{8}{10} = \dfrac{4}{5}$

$\tan x^\circ = \dfrac{\text{Perpendicular}}{\text{Base}}$

$= \dfrac{AB}{BC} = \dfrac{8}{15}$ $\quad [\because BC = 15]$

Now, $3\tan x^\circ - 2\sin y^\circ + 4\cos y^\circ$

$= 3 \times \dfrac{8}{15} - 2 \times \dfrac{4}{5} + 4 \times \dfrac{3}{5}$ $\quad \left[\because \cos y^\circ = \dfrac{3}{5}\right]$

$= \dfrac{8}{5} - \dfrac{8}{5} + \dfrac{12}{5}$

$= \dfrac{12}{5}$

2. We have,

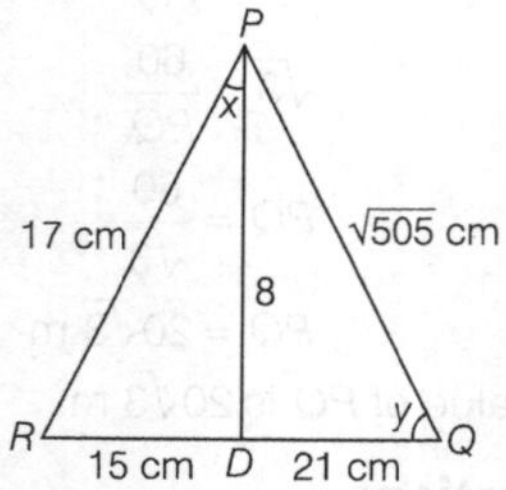

(i) In right angled ΔPDR,

$PR^2 = PD^2 + RD^2$

[by Phythagoras theorem]

$\Rightarrow \quad 17^2 = PD^2 + 15^2$

$\Rightarrow \quad PD = \sqrt{64} = 8$ cm

Now, $\quad \tan x = \dfrac{\text{Perpendicular}}{\text{Base}}$

$= \dfrac{RD}{PD} = \dfrac{15}{8}$

$= 1.875$

(ii) $DQ = 36 - 15 = 21\,\text{cm}$

$PD = 8$ cm

$PQ = \sqrt{441 + 64} = \sqrt{505}$ cm

[by Pythagoras theorem in right angled ΔPDQ]

In right angled ΔPDQ,

$\cos y = \dfrac{DQ}{PQ} = \dfrac{21}{\sqrt{505}}$, $\cot y = \dfrac{DQ}{DP} = \dfrac{21}{8}$

On putting the value of cos *y* and cot *y* in $\dfrac{1}{\cos^2 y} - \dfrac{1}{\cot^2 y}$, we get

$\left(\dfrac{\sqrt{505}}{21}\right)^2 - \left(\dfrac{8}{21}\right)^2 = \dfrac{505}{441} - \dfrac{64}{441} = \dfrac{441}{441} = 1$

(iii) In right angled ΔPDR,

$\cos x = \dfrac{PD}{PR} = \dfrac{8}{17}$

In right angled ΔPDQ,

$\cos y = \dfrac{21}{\sqrt{505}}$

and $\quad \tan y = \dfrac{PD}{DQ} = \dfrac{8}{21}$

Now, on putting the values cos *x*, cos *y* and tan *y* in $\dfrac{6}{\cos x} - \dfrac{7}{\cos y} + 8\tan y$, we get

$\dfrac{6}{\cos x} - \dfrac{7}{\cos y} + 8\tan y$

$= \dfrac{6}{8/17} - \dfrac{7}{21/\sqrt{505}} + 8 \times \dfrac{8}{21}$

$= \dfrac{51}{4} - \dfrac{7\sqrt{505}}{21} + \dfrac{64}{21} = 8.307$

3. We know that the sum of all angles of a triangle is 180°.

$\therefore \quad \angle A + \angle B + \angle C = 180^\circ$ $\quad \ldots(a)$

(i) $\tan\left(\dfrac{B+C}{2}\right) = \cot\dfrac{A}{2}$

$\text{LHS} = \tan\left(\dfrac{B+C}{2}\right) = \tan\left(\dfrac{180^\circ - A}{2}\right)$

[from Eq. (a)]

$= \tan\left(\dfrac{180^\circ}{2} - \dfrac{A}{2}\right) = \tan\left(90^\circ - \dfrac{A}{2}\right)$

$= \cot\dfrac{A}{2} = \text{RHS}$ $\quad [\because \tan(90^\circ - \theta) = \cot\theta]$

(ii) $\sin\left(\dfrac{A+B}{2}\right) = \cos\dfrac{C}{2}$

$\text{LHS} = \sin\left(\dfrac{A+B}{2}\right) = \sin\left(\dfrac{180^\circ - C}{2}\right)$ $\quad$ [from Eq. (a)]

$= \sin\left(90^\circ - \dfrac{C}{2}\right)$

$= \cos\dfrac{C}{2} = \text{RHS}$ $\quad [\because \sin(90^\circ - \theta) = \cos\theta]$

Hence proved.

18

COORDINATE GEOMETRY AND DISTANCE FORMULA

Cartesian System

The system used to described the position of a point in a plane, is called the **cartesian system**. In cartesian system, there are two mutual perpendicular straight lines ***XX′* (horizontal line)** and ***YY′* (vertical line)** which intersect at point *O*, is called the **origin** and it is denoted by *O*.

The horizontal line *XOX′* is called ***X*-axis** and the vertical line *YOY′* is called ***Y*-axis.**

Directions *OX* and *OY* are called the **positive directions** and *OX′* and *OY′* are called **negative directions** of *X*-axis and *Y*-axis, respectively.

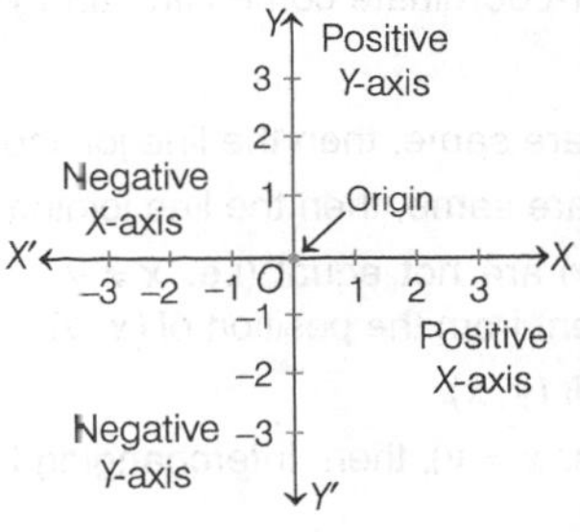

Quadrant

The *X* and *Y*-axes divide the plane into four parts. These four parts are called **quadrant** $\left(\text{i.e.} \frac{1}{4} \text{th part}\right)$, numbered I, II, III and IV anti-clockwise from *OX*.

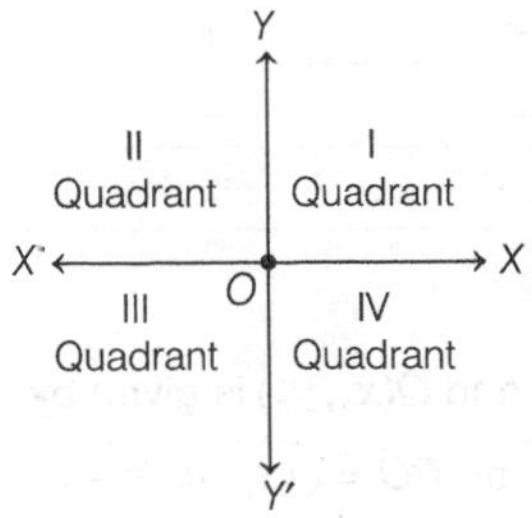

(i) *XOY* is called the I quadrant.

(ii) *X′OY* is called the II quadrant.

(iii) *X′OY′* is called the III quadrant.

(iv) *XOY′* is called the IV quadrant.

So, the plane consists of two axes and four quadrants.

The plane is known as ***XY*-plane** or **cartesian plane** or **coordinate plane** and the axes are known as the **coordinate axes.**

Coordinates of a Point in Cartesian Plane

To locate a point in the cartesian plane, its perpendicular distances from *X*-axis and *Y*-axis are required, these distances are called **coordinates of the point**. Each point in cartesian plane has two coordinates; *x*-coordinate and *y*-coordinate.

(i) The ***x*-coordinate** of a point is the perpendicular distance from the *Y*-axis. The *x*-coordinate is also called the **abscissa.**

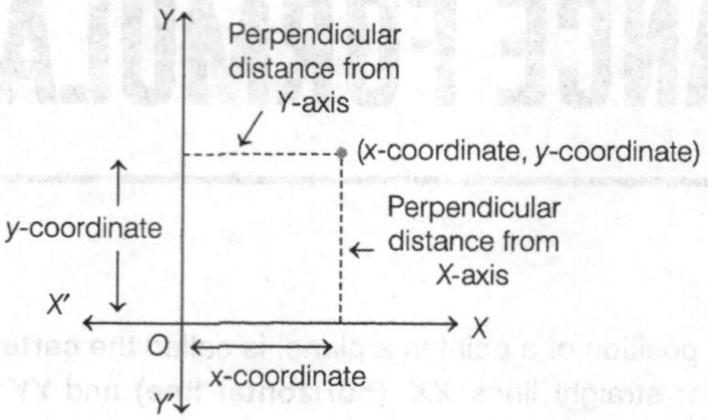

(ii) The ***y*-coordinate** of a point is the perpendicular distance from the *X*-axis. The *y*-coordinate is also called the **ordinate.**

(iii) The *x*-coordinate and *y*-coordinate taken together are called **cartesian coordinates** or **coordinates** of a point and it is denoted by (x, y). Here, the *x*-coordinate comes first and *y*-coordinate comes second.

Some Important Points

(i) If *x*-coordinate of two or more points are same, then the line joining these points is parallel to *Y*-axis.

(ii) If *y*-coordinate of two or more points are same, then the line joining these points is parallel to *X*-axis.

(iii) Suppose coordinates of a point (x, y) are not equal (i.e. $x \neq y$). If we interchange the coordinates *x* and *y*, then the position of (y, x) will be different from the position of (x, y).

Here, ordered pair $(x, y) \neq$ ordered pair (y, x).

(iv) If coordinates of a point are equal (i.e. $x = y$), then interchanging the coordinates *x* and *y* does not change the position of that point.

Signs of *x* and *y* coordinate in four Quadrants

Quadrant	Sign of *x*-coordinate	Sign of *y*-coordinate	Sign of coordinates of a point
I	+	+	(+, +)
II	–	+	(–, +)
III	–	–	(–, –)
IV	+	–	(+, –)

Distance Formula

The distance between any two points $P(x_1, y_1)$ and $Q(x_2, y_2)$ is given by

$$PQ = \sqrt{(x_2 - x_1)^2 + (y_2 - y_1)^2} \text{ or } PQ = \sqrt{(x_1 - x_2)^2 + (y_1 - y_2)^2}$$

i.e.

$$PQ = \sqrt{(\text{Difference of abscissae})^2 + (\text{Difference of ordinates})^2}$$

Example 1. Find the distance between the points $P(-6, 7)$ and $Q(-1, -5)$.

Sol. Here, $x_1 = -6$, $y_1 = 7$, $x_2 = -1$ and $y_2 = -5$

$\therefore$ Distance between two points, $PQ = \sqrt{(x_2 - x_1)^2 + (y_2 - y_1)^2}$

$$= \sqrt{(-1+6)^2 + (-5-7)^2}$$
$$= \sqrt{(5)^2 + (-12)^2}$$
$$= \sqrt{25 + 144}$$
$$= \sqrt{169} = 13 \text{ units}$$

Linear Equations in Two Variables

An equations of the form $ax + by + c = 0$ where $a \neq 0$ and $b \neq 0$ is called linear equation in two variables (x and y).

Consider a linear equation $y = 2x + 3$, in this equation value of y depends on value of x, so x is called independent variables and y is called dependent variable.

In the equations $x = 2y + 3$, y is independent variable while x is dependent variable.

Graph of linear equation in two variable (e.g. $ax + by + c = 0$, $a \neq 0$ and $b \neq 0$) is always a straight line.

Pair of Linear Equations in Two Variables

Two linear equations in the same two variables, say x and y, are called pair of linear equations in two variables.

The general form of pair of linear equations in two variables x and y is $a_1 x + b_1 y + c_1 = 0$ and $a_2 x + b_2 y + c_2 = 0$, where $a_1, b_1, c_1, a_2, b_2, c_2$ are all real numbers such that $a_1, b_1 \neq 0$ and $a_2, b_2 \neq 0$.

Graphical Method

Let us consider a pair of linear equations in two variables, $a_1x + b_1y + c_1 = 0$ and $a_2x + b_2y + c_2 = 0$.

To find the solution graphically, first draw the graph of both equations on the same graph paper with same scale of representation, then find the coordinates of the point of intersection of the two lines drawn. The coordinates of the point of intersection give the solution of the given equations.

Example 2. Solve the pair of linear equations $2x + y = 6$ and $2x - y + 2 = 0$ by graphical method.

Sol. Consider the equations $2x + y = 6$ and $2x - y + 2 = 0$.

Table for equation $2x + y = 6$ or $y = 6 - 2x$ is

x	0	1	3
$y = 6 - 2x$	6	4	0
Points	$B(0, 6)$	$E(1, 4)$	$A(3, 0)$

Now, plot all these points on a graph paper and join them to get a line AB.

Table for equation $2x - y + 2 = 0$ or $y = 2x + 2$

x	0	-1	1
$y = 2x + 2$	2	0	4
Points	$D(0, 2)$	$C(-1, 0)$	$E(1, 4)$

Now, plot all these points on a graph paper and join them to get a line *CE*.

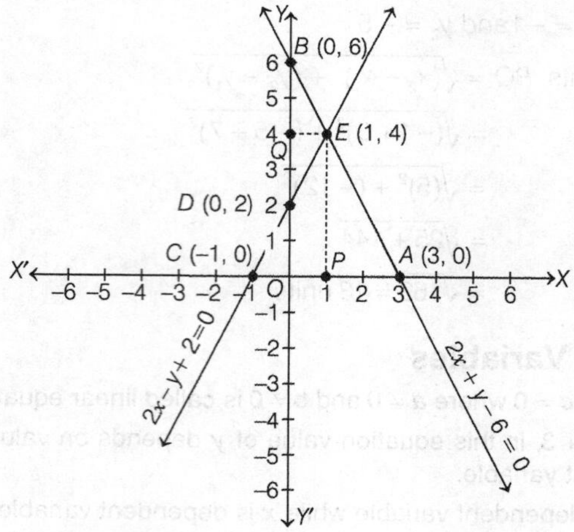

It is clear from the graph that pair of equations intersects graphically at point $E(1, 4)$, i.e. $x = 1$ and $y = 4$.

Hence, $x = 1$ and $y = 4$ is the solution of the given pair of linear equations.

REVISION NOTES

EXAM ORIENTED QUESTIONS

TYPE - 1   01 Mark

Multiple Choice Questions

Q.1 If $(5x + 1, 2y - 7) = (11, -5)$, then the coordinates of (x, y) are
(a) (1, 2) (b) (2, 1) (c) (2, 3) (d) (3, 2)

Q.2 In which quadrant the point (–2, 5) lies?
(a) I quadrant (b) II quadrant
(c) III quadrant (d) IV quadrant

Q.3 If the point $P(a, b)$ lies in the fourth quadrant, then
(a) $a > b$ (b) $a < b$
(c) $a = b$ (d) None of these

Q.4 The line $x = my$, where $m < 0$ lies in the quadrants
(a) I, II (b) II, IV (c) III, IV (d) III, I

Q.5 If the coordinates of two points are $A(3, 4)$ and $B(-2, 5)$, then the value of (abscissa of A) – (abscissa of B) is
(a) –4 (b) 6 (c) 5 (d) –7

Q.6 The point which lies on Y-axis at a distance of 5 units in the negative direction of Y-axis is
(a) (0, 5) (b) (5, 0) (c) (0, –5) (d) (–5, 0)

Q.7 A graph is given below

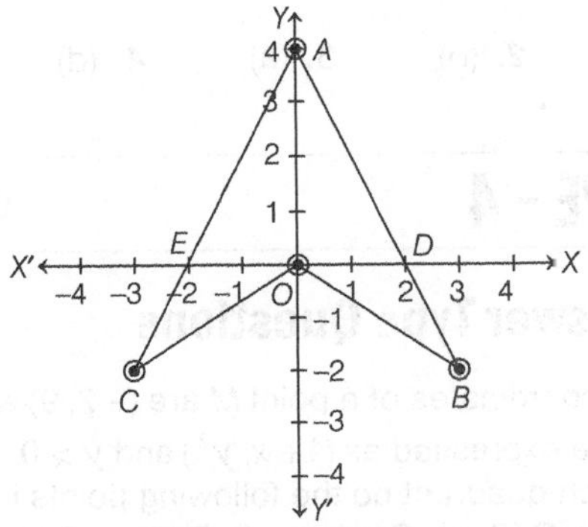

The coordinates of the points A, B and C are
(a) (4, 0), (–2, 3), (2, 3) (b) (0, 4), (3, –2), (–3, –2)
(c) (0, 2), (0, 3), (4, 3) (d) None of these

Q.8 The distance of the point (20,15) from origin is
(a) 24 units (b) 22 units
(c) 25 units (d) 27 units

Q.9 A point on X-axis, which is equidistant from the points (7, 6) and (–3, 4) is
(a) (0, 3) (b) (3, 0) (c) (5, 0) (d) (0, 5)

Q.10 If the point $P(x, y)$ is equidistant from the points $A(5, 1)$ and $B(1, 5)$, then the relation between x and y, is
(a) $x = 3y$ (b) $x - 2y = 3$
(c) $x - y = 2$ (d) $x = y$

Q.11 Find the length of the longest side of the triangle formed by the line $3x + 4y = 12$ with the coordinate axes.
(a) 9 units (b) 16 units
(c) 5 units (d) 7 units

Q.12 In the linear equation $y = 2x + 9$, variable x is called
(a) dependent variable (b) independent variable
(c) consistent (d) inconsistent

Q.13 The value of p, if $x = 2$ and $y = 1$ is a solution of the equation $3x + 2y = p$, then the value of p is
(a) 7 (b) 8 (c) –7 (d) –8

Q.14 The pair of equation $x = a$ and $y = b$ graphically represents lines are
(a) parallel (b) intersecting at (b, a)
(c) coincident (d) intersecting at (a, b)

Answers

1. (b)	2. (b)	3. (a)	4. (b)	5. (c)
6. (c)	7. (b)	8. (c)	9. (b)	10. (d)
11. (c)	12. (b)	13. (b)	14. (d)	

TYPE - 2   01 Mark

Assertion-Reason Type Questions

Q.1 Assertion (A) If the ordinate of a point is equal to its abscissa, then the point lies either in the first quadrant or in the second quadrant.
Reason (R) A point both of whose coordinates are negative will lie in third quadrant.
(a) A is true, R is false.
(b) A is false, R is true.
(c) Both A and R are true and R is the correct reason for A.
(d) Both A and R are true but R is incorrect reason for A.

Q.2 Assertion (A) The points $(-3, 8)$ and $(8, -3)$ are at different positions in the coordinate plane.

Reason (R) If $x \neq y$, then position of (x, y) in the cartesian plane is different from the position of (y, x).

(a) A is true, R is false.
(b) A is false, R is true.
(c) Both A and R are true and R is the correct reason for A.
(d) Both A and R are true but R is incorrect reason for A.

Q.3 Assertion (A) The point $(-6, 0)$ lies on Y-axis and point $(0, -7)$ lies on X-axis.

Reason (R) Every point on the X-axis has zero distance from X-axis and every point on the Y-axis has zero distance from Y-axis.

(a) A is true, R is false.
(b) A is false, R is true.
(c) Both A and R are true and R is the correct reason for A.
(d) Both A and R are true but R is incorrect reason for A.

Q.4 Assertion (A) The value of y is 3 for which the distance between the points $P(2, -3)$ and $Q(10, y)$ is 10.

Reason (R) Distance between two given points $A(x_1, y_1)$ and $B(x_2, y_2)$ is given by

$$AB = \sqrt{(x_2 - x_1)^2 + (y_2 - y_1)^2}.$$

(a) A is true, R is false.
(b) A is false, R is true.
(c) Both A and R are true and R is the correct reason for A.
(d) Both A and R are true but R is incorrect reason for A.

Answers

1. (b) 2. (c) 3. (b) 4. (c)

TYPE - 3 — 01 Mark

Statement Based Questions

Q.1 Statement I When points $A(-2, -1)$, $B(3, 2)$, $C(5, -3)$ and $D(-4, 20)$ are plotted on a plane, then point $(-2, -1)$ lies in the third quadrant.

Statement II Point $P(5, 5)$ lies in the IV quadrant.

Which of the following is valid?

(a) Both the Statements are true.
(b) Both the Statements are false.
(c) Statement I is true and Statement II is false.
(d) Statement I is false and Statement II is true.

Q.2 Statement I The perpendicular distance of $A(5, 3)$ from the Y-axis is 7 units.

Statement II The perpendicular distance of the point $P(2, 3)$ from the X-axis is 5 units.

Which of the following is valid?

(a) Both the Statements are true.
(b) Both the Statements are false.
(c) Statement I is true and Statement II is false.
(d) Statement I is false and Statement II is true.

Q.3 Statement I The distance between the points $(2a, a)$ and $(-a, 3a)$ is $a\sqrt{13}$ units.

Statement II The distance of the point (a, a) from the origin is $a\sqrt{2}$ units.

Which of the following is valid?

(a) Both the Statements are true.
(b) Both the Statements are false.
(c) Statement I is true and Statement II is false.
(d) Statement I is false and Statement II is true.

Q.4 Statement I The graph of the linear equation $3x + 2y = 12$ is a line which meets the Y-axis at the point $(6, 0)$.

Statement II The graph of the linear equation $4x + 5y = 20$ is a line which meets the X-axis at the point $(5, 0)$.

Which of the following is valid?

(a) Both the Statements are true.
(b) Both the Statements are false.
(c) Statement I is true and Statement II is false.
(d) Statement I is false and Statement II is true.

Answers

1. (c) 2. (b) 3. (a) 4. (d)

TYPE - 4 — 03 Marks

Short Answer Type Questions

Q.1 If the coordinates of a point M are $(-2, 9)$ which can also be expressed as $(1 + x, y^2)$ and $y > 0$, then find in which quadrant do the following points lie $A(y, x)$, $B(2, x)$, $C(x^2, y - 1)$, $D(2x, -3y)$.

Q.2 In the following figure, O is the intersecting points of OA, OC and $OABC$ is a square of side 2 units. Find the positions of A, B and C.

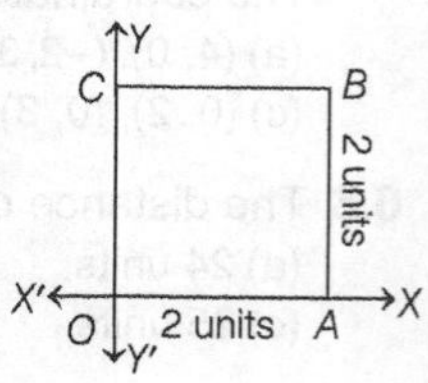

Q.3 In the given figure, LM is a line parallel to the Y-axis at a distance of 3 units from origin.

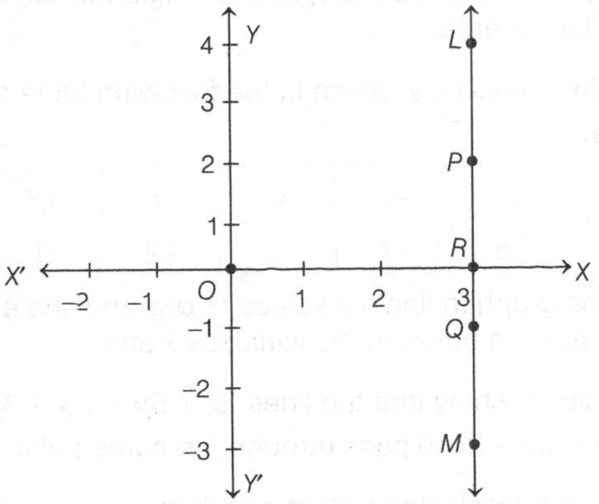

(i) What are the coordinates of the points P, R and Q?

(ii) What is the difference between the abscissae of the points L and M?

Q.4 Three vertices of a square are $A(2, 3)$, $B(-3, 3)$ and $C(-3, -2)$. Plot these points on a graph paper and hence, use it to find the coordinates of the fourth vertex. Also, find the area of the square.

Q.5 Three vertices of a parallelogram are $A(-2, 2)$, $B(6, 2)$ and $C(4, -3)$. Plot these points on a graph paper.

(i) Find the coordinates of the fourth vertex D.

(ii) What is the area of the parallelogram?

Q.6 Find the points which are at a distance of $\sqrt{10}$ units from the point $(4, 3)$ given that the ordinate of the points is twice the abscissa.

Q.7 Find the value of y, if the distance between the points $(2, y)$ and $(-4, 3)$ is 10 units.

Q.8 If the point $P(x, y)$ is equidistant from the points $A(a+b, b-a)$ and $B(a-b, a+b)$, then prove that $bx = ay$.

Q.9 A point E lies on the X-axis and another point F lies on Y-axis.

(i) Write the ordinate of the point E.

(ii) Write the abscissa of the point F.

(iii) If the abscissa of the point E is 12 and the ordinate of the point F is 5, then calculate the length of the segment EF.

Q.10 Find the coordinates of the circumcentre of the ΔABC, whose vertices A, B and C are $(4, 6)$, $(0, 4)$ and $(6, 2)$, respectively.

Q.11 Show that the points $(2, 3)$, $(3, 4)$, $(5, 6)$ and $(4, 5)$ are the vertices of a parallelogram.

Q.12 Find the points on the X-axis whose distance from the points $(2, 3)$ and $\left(\frac{3}{2}, -1\right)$ are in ratio $2:1$.

Q.13 Points $A(-1, y)$ and $B(5, 7)$ lie on a circle with centre $O(2, -3y)$, then find the values of y and find the radius of the circle.

Q.14 The centre of a circle is $(2a, a-7)$. Find the values of a, if the circle passes through the point $(11, -9)$ and has diameter $10\sqrt{2}$ units.

Q.15 Draw the graph of a linear equation in x and y passing through $A(-1, -1)$ and $B(2, 5)$. Find the values of h and k, if the graph of linear equation passes through $(h, 4)$ and $\left(\frac{1}{2}, k\right)$.

Q.16 Draw the graph of the equation $3 = 2x + y$.

Q.17 Draw the graph for $\frac{x-1}{1} + \frac{y-4}{2} = 0$. Also, find the coordinates of the points, where the graph drawn meets the coordinate axes.

Q.18 For the given linear equation, sketch the graph and state whether the lines drawn are parallel or perpendicular to each other.

$$2x - 3y = 6 \text{ and } \frac{x}{2} + \frac{y}{3} = 1$$

Q.19 Write an equation of a line passing through the point representing solution of the pair of linear equations $x + y = 2$ and $2x - y = 1$. How many such lines can we find?

Answers

1. The point $B(2, x)$ is $(2, -3)$, lie in IV quadrant.
   The point $C(x^2, y-1)$ is $(9, 2)$, lie in I quadrant.
   The point $D(2x, -3y)$ is $(-6, -9)$, lie in III quadrant.
2. Positions of points A, B and C are $(2, 0)$, $(2, 2)$ and $(0, 2)$, respectively.
3. (i) Coordinates of point P are $(3, 2)$.
   Coordinates of point R are $(3, 0)$.
   Coordinates of point Q are $(3, -1)$.
   (ii) 0
4. $(2, -2)$, 25 sq units
5. (i) $(-4, -3)$ (ii) 40 sq units
6. $(3, 6)$ and $(1, 2)$
7. 11 and -5
9. (i) 0 (ii) 0 (iii) 13 units
10. $(3, 3)$
12. $(0, 0)$ and $\left(\frac{8}{3}, 0\right)$
13. $y = 7, -1$ and the corresponding radii are $\sqrt{793}$ unit, 5 units
14. 5 and 3
15. $h = \frac{3}{2}$ and $k = 2$
17. The coordinates of the points, where the graph meets the X and Y-axes are $(3, 0)$ and $(0, 6)$, respectively.
18. Lines drawn are perpendicular to each other.
19. Infinite lines

TYPE - 5 — 4/5 Marks

Long Answer Type Questions

Q.1 Write the coordinates of the points given in the following graph.

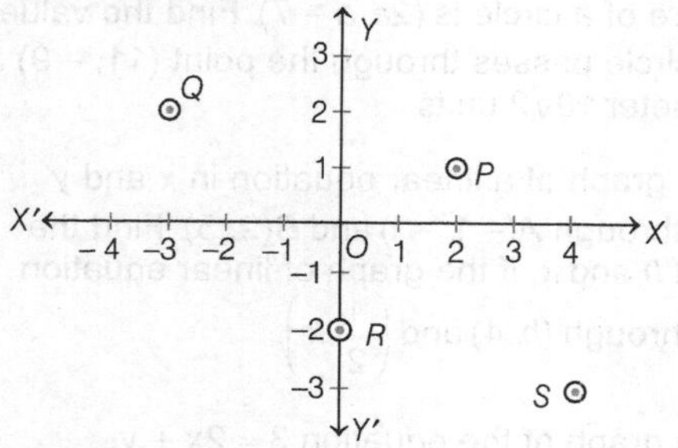

Q.2 Write down the
(i) abscissa
(ii) ordinate
(iii) coordinates
(iv) quadrant
in which points *P*, *Q*, *R* and *S* lie.

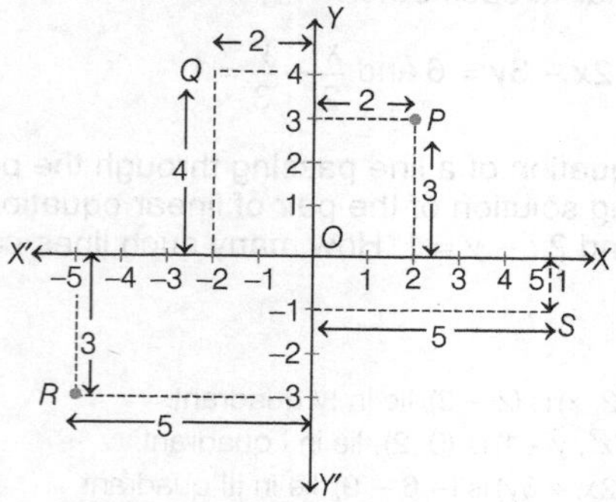

Q.3 Plot the points (4, 5) and (−4, 5) on a graph paper.

Q.4 Point *O*(2, 3) is the centre of a circle with radius 13 units, *OB* is perpendicular to chord *AC* and the coordinates of *B* are (−2, 6), then find the length
(i) *OB* (ii) *AB*
(iii) *AC*

Q.5 *AOBC* is a rectangle whose three vertices are *A*(0, 3), *O*(0, 0) and *B*(5, 0), then
(i) find the coordinates of the fourth vertex
(ii) find the length of its diagonals
(iii) find the area of rectangle *ABCD*

Q.6 Do the points (3, 2), (−2, − 3) and (2, 3) form a triangle. If so, name the type of triangle formed and also find its area.

Q.7 Plot the points (*x*, *y*) given in the following table on the plane.

x	*p*	−6	0	*q*	4.5
y	−5	−7	−3	−2	0

Use the graph to find the values of *p*, *q* and find a linear relation between the variables *x* and *y*.

Q.8 Graphically show that the lines $2x + 5y = 1$, $x - 3y = 6$ and $x + 5y + 2 = 0$ pass through the same point.

Q.9 Solve graphically the pair of equations $2x + y = 6$ and $2x - y + 2 = 0$.
(i) Find the coordinates of the intersection point of the lines.
(ii) Measure the distance of the point of intersection of the lines from the origin.

Q.10 Solve graphically the pair of linear equations $3x - 4y + 3 = 0$ and $3x + 4y - 21 = 0$. Find the coordinate of the vertices of triangular region formed by these lines and *X*-axis. Also, calculate the area of this triangle.

Answers

1. Coordinates of point *P* are (2, 1).
Coordinates of point *Q* are (−3, 2).
Coordinates of point *R* are (0, −2).
Coordinates of point *S* are (4, − 3).
2. **For point *P***
(i) 2 (ii) 3
(iii) (2, 3) (iv) I quadrant
For point *Q*
(i) −2 (ii) 4
(iii) (−2, 4) (iv) II quadrant
For point *R*
(i) −5 (ii) −3
(iii) (−5, − 3) (iv) III quadrant
For point *S*
(i) 5 (ii) −1
(iii) (5, − 1) (iv) IV quadrant
4. (i) 5 units (ii) 12 units (iii) 24 units
5. (i) (5, 3) (ii) $\sqrt{34}$ units (iii) 15 sq units
6. Yes, right angled triangle, 5 sq units
7. $p = -3$, $q = 1.5$ and $3y = 2x - 9$
9. (i) (1, 4) (ii) $\sqrt{17}$ units
10. The coordinates of the vertices are (3, 3), (−1, 0), (7, 0) and area = 12 sq units

TYPE - 5

Case Based Questions

Q.1 To raise the fund for cancer patients, a charity race was organised on rectangular school ground $ABCD$.

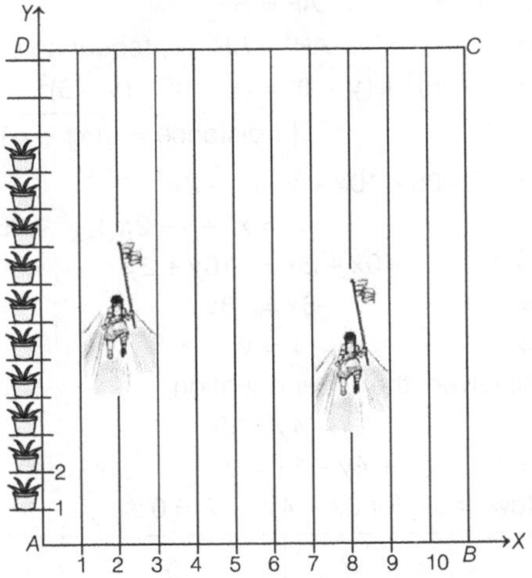

Lines have been drawn with chalk powder at a distance of 1 m each. 100 flower pots have been placed at a distance of 1 m from each other along AD.

Niharika runs $\frac{1}{4}$ of the distance AD on the second line and posts a green flag. Preeti runs $\frac{1}{5}$ of the distance AD on the 8th line and posts a red flag as shown in given figure.

Then, give the answer of following questions.

(i) Find the coordinates of green flag.

(ii) Find the coordinates of red flag.

(iii) In which quadrant is the green flag?

(iv) In which quadrant is the red flag? **(4 M)**

Q.2 A school has planned to construct playground for junior (from I-V class) and senior (from VI-XII class). Following graph shows the playground.

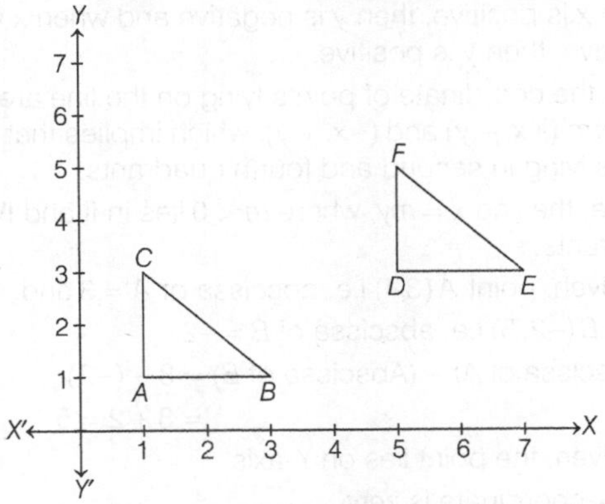

On the basis of above information, answer the following questions.

(i) Find the coordinates of A.

(ii) Find the coordinates of F.

(iii) What is the area of playground ABC?

(iv) What is the area of playground DEF? **(4 M)**

Q.3 In a factory, the cost of manufacturing x articles is ₹ $(10 + x)$ and the selling price of x articles is ₹ $1.5x$. On the same graph paper with the same axes, draw two graphs, first for the cost of manufacturing against number of articles and the second for the selling price against number of articles then determine

(i) number of articles to be manufactured and sold to reach breakeven point (no profit and no loss situation).

(ii) the profit made when 40 articles are manufactured and sold.

Answers

1. (i) (2, 25) (ii) (8, 20) (iii) I quadrant (iv) I quadrant
2. (i) (1, 1) (ii) (5, 5) (iii) 2 sq units (iv) 2 sq units
3. (i) 20 (ii) ₹ 10

EXPLANATIONS

Multiple Choice Questions

1. (b) We have, $(5x + 1, 2y - 7) = (11, -5)$

On comparing both sides, we get

$$5x + 1 = 11$$

$$\Rightarrow \quad 5x = 10 \Rightarrow x = 2$$

and $$2y - 7 = -5 \Rightarrow 2y = -5 + 7$$

$$\Rightarrow \quad 2y = 2 \Rightarrow y = 1$$

Hence, the coordinates of (x, y) are (2, 1).

2. (b) In the point $(-2, 5)$, x-coordinate is negative and y-coordinate is positive, so the given point lies in the II quadrant.

3. (a) In fourth quadrant, the abscissa is positive and the ordinate is negative.

$\therefore$ From the given point $P(a, b)$, a should be positive and b should be negative.

Hence, $a > b$

4. (b) Let us identify the sign of y for each sign of x.

We have, $x = my \Rightarrow y = \frac{x}{m}$, where $m < 0$

When x is positive, then y is negative and when x is negative, then y is positive.

Thus, the coordinate of points lying on the line are of the form $(+x, -y)$ and $(-x, +y)$, which implies that points lying in second and fourth quadrants.

Hence, the line $x = my$, where $m < 0$ lies in II and IV quadrants.

5. (c) Given, point $A(3,4)$ i.e. abscissa of $A = 3$ and point $B(-2,5)$ i.e. abscissa of $B = -2$

$\therefore$ (Abscissa of A) – (Abscissa of B) $= 3 - (-2)$
$= 3 + 2 = 5$

6. (c) Given, the point lies on Y-axis.

$\therefore$ Its x-coordinate is zero.

Also, it is at a distance of 5 units in the negative direction of Y-axis.

$\therefore$ Its y-coordinate is negative.

Hence, the required point is $(0, -5)$.

7. (b) **Coordinates of point A** The point A is at a distance of 0 unit from Y-axis and 4 units from the X-axis.

$\therefore$ Coordinates of point A are $(0, 4)$.

Coordinates of point B The point B is at a distance of 3 units from the Y-axis and 2 units from the X-axis. Also, point B lies in IV quadrant.

$\therefore$ Coordinates of point B are $(3, -2)$.

Coordinates of point C The point C is at a distance of 3 units from the Y-axis and 2 units from the X-axis.

Also, point C lies in III quadrant.

$\therefore$ Coordinates of point C are $(-3, -2)$.

8. (c) Given, points are $P(20, 15)$ and origin $O(0, 0)$.

Here, $(x_1, y_1) = (20, 15)$ and $(x_2, y_2) = (0, 0)$

$\therefore$ Distance between two points,

$$OP = \sqrt{(x_2 - x_1)^2 + (y_2 - y_1)^2} \quad \text{[by distance formula]}$$
$$= \sqrt{(0 - 20)^2 + (0 - 15)^2}$$
$$= \sqrt{(20)^2 + (15)^2}$$
$$= \sqrt{400 + 225}$$
$$= \sqrt{625}$$
$$= 25 \text{ units}$$

9. (b) Let $A(x, 0)$ be any point on the X-axis, which is equidistant from $B(7, 6)$ and $C(-3, 4)$.

$$\therefore \quad AB = AC$$
$$\Rightarrow \quad AB^2 = AC^2 \quad \text{[squaring on both sides]}$$
$$\Rightarrow \quad (7 - x)^2 + (6 - 0)^2 = (-3 - x)^2 + (4 - 0)^2$$
$$\left[\because \text{distance} = \sqrt{(x_2 - x_1)^2 + (y_2 - y_1)^2}\right]$$
$$\Rightarrow \quad 49 + x^2 - 14x + 36 = 9 + x^2 + 6x + 16$$
$$\Rightarrow \quad 20x = 60$$
$$\Rightarrow \quad x = 3$$

Hence, the required point is $(3, 0)$.

10. (d) Given, point $P(x, y)$ is equidistant from the points $A(5, 1)$ and $B(1, 5)$.

$$\therefore \quad AP = BP$$
$$\Rightarrow \quad AP^2 = BP^2 \quad \text{[squaring on both sides]}$$
$$\Rightarrow \quad (x - 5)^2 + (y - 1)^2 = (x - 1)^2 + (y - 5)^2$$
$$\left[\because \text{distance} = \sqrt{(x_2 - x_1)^2 + (y_2 - y_1)^2}\right]$$
$$\Rightarrow \quad x^2 + 25 - 10x + y^2 + 1 - 2y = x^2 + 1 - 2x + y^2 + 25 - 10y$$
$$\Rightarrow \quad -10x + 2x = -10y + 2y$$
$$\Rightarrow \quad -8x = -8y$$
$$\Rightarrow \quad x = y$$

11. (c) Given, the linear equation,

$$3x + 4y = 12$$
$$\Rightarrow \quad 3x + 4y - 12 = 0 \quad \ldots\text{(i)}$$

Now, table for $3x + 4y - 12 = 0$ is

x	0	4
$y = \frac{12 - 3x}{4}$	3	0
Points	(0, 3)	(4, 0)

Plot the points $A(0, 3)$ and $B(4, 0)$ and join them to get the straight line AB.

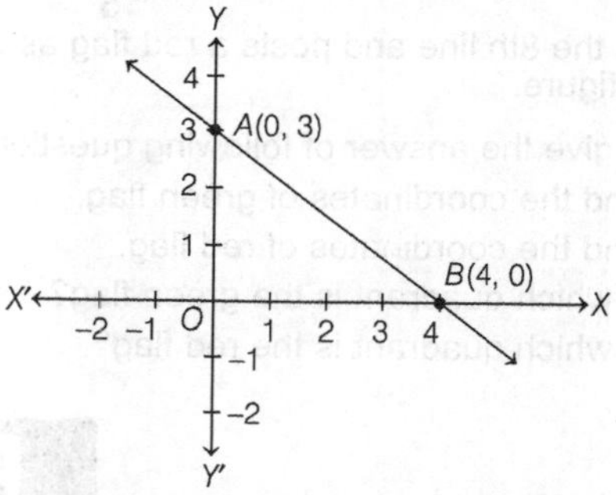

Here, vertices of the triangle formed are (4, 0), (0, 3) and (0, 0). Clearly, the longest side is the hypotenuse AB.

$$\therefore \text{Its length} = \sqrt{(4 - 0)^2 + (0 - 3)^2} \quad \text{[by distance formula]}$$
$$= \sqrt{4^2 + 3^2}$$
$$= \sqrt{16 + 9}$$
$$= \sqrt{25} = 5 \text{ units}$$

12. (b) In the equation $y = 2x + 9$, value of y depends on value of x, so x is called independent variable and y is called dependent variable.

13. (b) We have, $3x + 2y = p$

$\Rightarrow \quad 3 \times 2 + 2 \times 1 = p \quad [\because \text{ given } x = 2 \text{ and } y = 1]$

$\Rightarrow \quad 6 + 2 = p$

$\therefore \quad p = 8$

14. (d) We have, $x = a$ and $y = b$

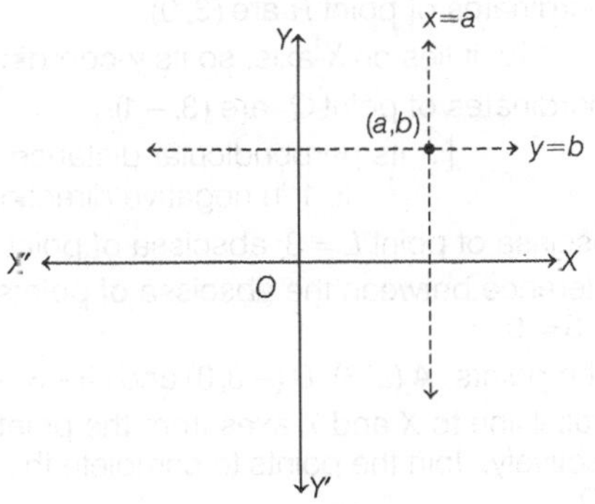

The line $x = a$ is a line parallel to Y-axis.

The line $y = b$ is a line parallel to X-axis.

From the above graph, the lines $x = a$ and $y = b$ meet at 90° i.e. the lines intersect.

Hence, the lines are intersecting at (a, b).

Assertion-Reason Type Questions

1. (b) **Assertion** We know that if the coordinate of a point is equal to abscissa, then the point lies either in first quadrant or in the third quadrant

Hence, A is false.

Reason We know that a point both of whose coordinates are negative will lie in third quadrant.

Hence, R is true.

2. (c) **Assertion** $(-3, 8)$ and $(8, -3)$ are different points as $(-3, 8)$ lies in II quadrant and $(8, -3)$ lies in IV quadrant. So, A is true.

Reason It is true that if $x \neq y$, then position of (x, y) in the cartesian plane is different from the position of (y, x) And it is the true explanation of A.

3. (b) **Assertion** The point $(-6, 0)$ lies on X-axis and point $(0, -7)$ lies on Y-axis. So, Assertion is false.

Reason It is true that every point on the X-axis and Y-axis has zero distance from X-axis and Y-axis, respectively.

Hence, A is false but R is true.

4. (c) **Assertion** Given, points $P(2, -3)$ and $Q(10, y)$.

Also, given that $PQ = 10$ units

$\because \quad d = \sqrt{(x_2 - x_1)^2 + (y_2 - y_1)^2}$ [by distance formula]

$\sqrt{(10-2)^2 + (y+3)^2} = 10$

On squaring both sides, we get

$8^2 + y^2 + 9 + 6y = 100 \quad [\because (a+b)^2 = a^2 + b^2 + 2ab]$

$\Rightarrow \quad 64 + y^2 + 9 + 6y = 100$

$\Rightarrow \quad y^2 + 6y - 27 = 0$

$\Rightarrow y^2 + 9y - 3y - 27 = 0$

$\Rightarrow y(y+9) - 3(y+9) = 0$

$\Rightarrow \quad (y+9)(y-3) = 0 \Rightarrow y = 3, -9$

Hence, both A and R are true and R is the correct reason for A.

Statement Based Questions

1. (c) **Statement I** We know that if the abscissa and ordinate both are negative of any point, then the point lies in the third quadrant.

Hence, $A(-2, -1)$ lie in the third quadrant

So, Statement I is true.

Statement II We know that if the abscissa is positive and ordinate is negative of any point, then the point lies in the fourth quadrant.

Hence, point $P(5, 5)$ does not lie in the IV quadrant.

So, Statement II is false.

2. (b) **Statement I**

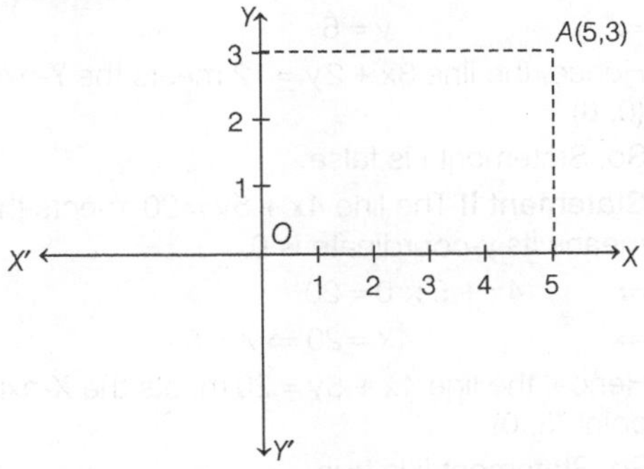

Hence, the perpendicular distance of point $A(5, 3)$ from the Y-axis is 5 units.

So, Statement I is false.

Statement II

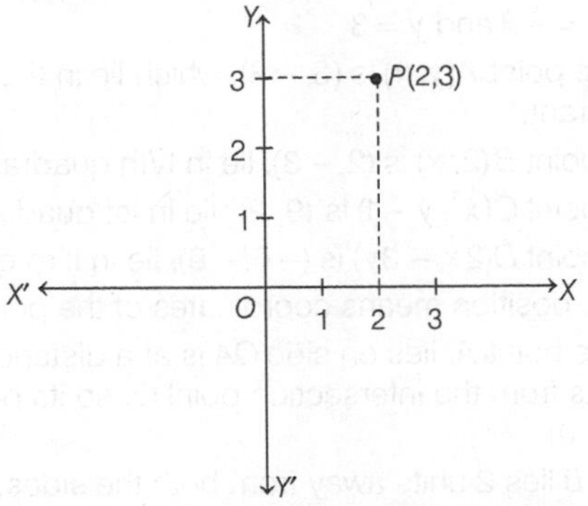

Hence, the perpendicular distance of point $P(2, 3)$ from the X-axis is 3 units.

So, Statement II is false.

3. (a) **Statement I** We have, points $(2a, a)$ and $(-a, 3a)$.

$d = \sqrt{(-a - 2a)^2 + (3a - a)^2}$ [by distance formula]

$d = \sqrt{(-3a)^2 + (2a)^2}$

$d = \sqrt{9a^2 + 4a^2} = \sqrt{13a^2}$

$d = a\sqrt{13}$ units

[∵ taking positive square root as distance cannot be negative]

Hence, Statement I is true.

Statement II We have, points (0, 0) and (a, a).

$d = \sqrt{(a - 0)^2 + (a - 0)^2}$

$d = \sqrt{a^2 + a^2} = \sqrt{2a^2}$

$d = a\sqrt{2}$ units

Hence, Statement II is true.

4. (d) **Statement I**

The line $3x + 2y = 12$ meets the Y-axis, it means its x-coordinate is 0.

$\Rightarrow \quad 3 \times 0 + 2y = 12$

$\Rightarrow \quad 2y = 12$

$\Rightarrow \quad y = 6$

Hence, the line $3x + 2y = 12$ meets the Y-axis at point (0, 6).

So, Statement I is false.

Statement II The line $4x + 5y = 20$ meets the X-axis, it means its y-coordinate is 0.

$\Rightarrow \quad 4x + 5 \times 0 = 20$

$\Rightarrow \quad 4x = 20 \Rightarrow x = 5$

Hence, the line $4x + 5y = 20$ meets the X-axis at point (5, 0).

So, Statement II is true.

Short Answer Type Questions

1. Given, $(-2, 9) = (1 + x, y^2), y > 0$

$\Rightarrow 1 + x = -2$ and $y^2 = 9, y > 0$

$\Rightarrow \quad x = -3$ and $y = 3$

∴ The point $A(y, x)$ is $(3, -3)$, which lie in the IVth quadrant.

The point $B(2, x)$ is $(2, -3)$, lie in IVth quadrant.

The point $C(x^2, y - 1)$ is (9, 2), lie in Ist quadrant.

The point $D(2x, -3y)$ is $(-6, -9)$, lie in IIIrd quadrant.

2. Here, position means coordinates of the point.

As the point A, lies on side OA is at a distance of 2 units from the intersection point O, so its position will be (2, 0).

Point B lies 2 units away from both the sides, so its position will be (2, 2) and point C lies on the side OC, at a distance of 2 units from the intersection point O, so its position will be (0, 2).

3. Given, LM is a line parallel to the Y-axis and its perpendicular distance from Y-axis is 3 units.

(i) Coordinates of point P are (3, 2).

[∵ its perpendicular distance from X-axis is 2 units in positive direction of Y-axis]

Coordinates of point R are (3, 0).

[∵ it lies on X-axis, so its y-coordinate is zero]

Coordinates of point Q are $(3, -1)$.

[∵ its perpendicular distance from X-axis is 1 in negative direction of Y-axis]

(ii) Abscissa of point $L = 3$, abscissa of point $M = 3$.

∴ Difference between the abscissa of points L and M $= 3 - 3 = 0$.

4. Plot the points, $A(2, 3)$, $B(-3, 3)$ and $C(-3, -2)$. Draw a parallel line to X and Y-axes from the points C and A, respectively. Join the points to complete the square $ABCD$.

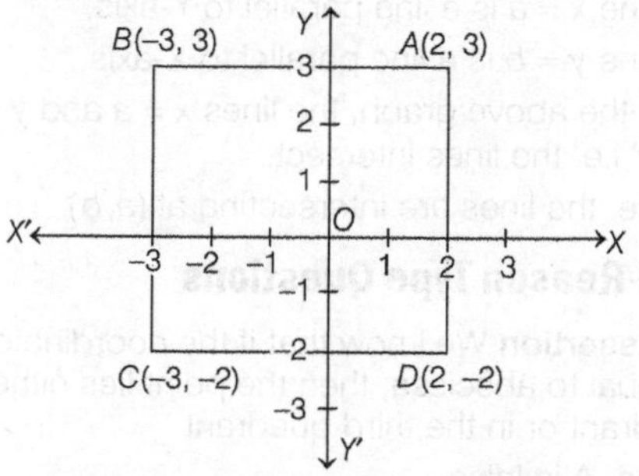

Now, we read the coordinates of the point D from the graph paper are $D(2, -2)$.

Side of square $ABCD = 3 + 2 = 5$ units

∴ Area of square $ABCD = (\text{Side})^2$

$= (5)^2 = 25$ sq units

5. Plot the points $A(-2, 2), B(6, 2)$ and $C(4, -3)$.

Draw a parallel line to BC and AB. Join all the points to complete the parallelogram $ABCD$

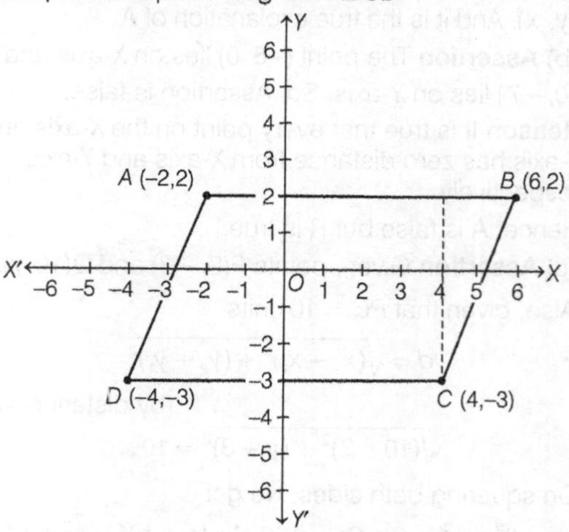

(i) Hence, the coordinates of the fourth point D are $(-4, -3)$.

(ii) We know that the area of parallelogram
$= \text{Base} \times \text{Height}$
$= 8 \times 5$
$= 40$ sq units

6. Let the abscissa of the point be x. Then, ordinate be $2x$.

So, the points are of the form $(x, 2x)$ and given point is $(4, 3)$.

$\therefore \quad d = \sqrt{(x_2 - x_1)^2 + (y_2 - y_1)^2}$ [by distance formula]

$\Rightarrow \quad d = \sqrt{(4 - x)^2 + (3 - 2x)^2}$

$\Rightarrow \quad \sqrt{10} = \sqrt{(4 - x)^2 + (3 - 2x)^2}$ [given, $(d) = \sqrt{10}$ units]

On squaring both sides, we get

$10 = 16 + x^2 - 8x + 9 + 4x^2 - 12x$

$\Rightarrow \quad 10 = 5x^2 - 20x + 25$

$\Rightarrow \quad 5x^2 - 20x + 15 = 0$

$\Rightarrow \quad x^2 - 4x + 3 = 0$

$\Rightarrow \quad x^2 - (3 + 1)x + 3 = 0$

$\Rightarrow \quad x^2 - 3x - x + 3 = 0$ [by factorisation]

$\Rightarrow \quad x(x - 3) - 1(x - 3) = 0$

$\Rightarrow \quad (x - 3)(x - 1) = 0$

$\Rightarrow \quad x = 3$ or $x = 1$

$\therefore \quad y = 2x = 6$ or $y = 2$

Hence, points are $(3, 6)$ and $(1, 2)$.

7. Let the points be $A(2, y)$ and $B(-4, 3)$.

Here, $(x_1, y_1) = (2, y)$ and $(x_2, y_2) = (-4, 3)$

$\therefore$ Distance between two points,

$AB = \sqrt{(x_1 - x_2)^2 + (y_1 - y_2)^2}$

[by distance formula]

$\Rightarrow \quad AB = \sqrt{(2 + 4)^2 + (y - 3)^2}$

$\Rightarrow \quad 10 = \sqrt{(6)^2 + y^2 + 9 - 6y}$

[$\because AB = 10$ and $(a - b)^2 = a^2 + b^2 - 2ab$]

On squaring both sides, we get

$100 = 36 + y^2 + 9 - 6y$

$\Rightarrow \quad 100 = 45 + y^2 - 6y$

$\Rightarrow \quad y^2 - 6y - 55 = 0$

$\Rightarrow \quad y^2 - 11y + 5y - 55 = 0$ [by factorisation]

$\Rightarrow y(y - 11) + 5(y - 11) = 0$

$\Rightarrow \quad (y - 11)(y + 5) = 0$

$\Rightarrow y - 11 = 0$ or $y + 5 = 0$

$\Rightarrow \quad y = 11$ or $y = -5$

Hence, the required values of y are 11 and -5.

8. Let $P(x, y)$, $A(a + b, b - a)$ and $B(a - b, a + b)$ be the given points.

Then, $PA = PB$ [according to the question]

$\therefore \sqrt{(a + b - x)^2 + (b - a - y)^2}$

$= \sqrt{(a - b - x)^2 + (a + b - y)^2}$

[by distance formula, $d = \sqrt{(x_2 - x_1)^2 + (y_2 - y_1)^2}$]

On squaring both sides, we get

$(a + b - x)^2 + (b - a - y)^2 = (a - b - x)^2 + (a + b - y)^2$

$\Rightarrow a^2 + b^2 + (-x)^2 + 2ab - 2bx - 2ax + b^2$
$+ (-a)^2 + (-y)^2 - 2ab + 2ay - 2by$
$= a^2 + (-b)^2 + (-x)^2 - 2ab + 2bx - 2ax$
$+ a^2 + b^2 + (-y)^2 + 2ab - 2by - 2ay$

[$\because (a + b + c)^2 = a^2 + b^2 + c^2 + 2ab + 2bc + 2ca$]

$\Rightarrow -2bx - 2ax + 2ay - 2by = 2bx - 2ax - 2by - 2ay$

$\Rightarrow \quad -4bx = -4ay$

$\Rightarrow \quad bx = ay$ **Hence proved.**

9. Given, the coordinates of the point E lies on X-axis $= (x, 0)$

and the coordinates of the point F lies on Y-axis $= (0, y)$

(i) The ordinate of the point $E = 0$.

(ii) The abscissa of the point $F = 0$.

(iii) The coordinates of point E are $(12, 0)$ and the coordinates of point F are $(0, 5)$.

$\therefore \quad d = \sqrt{(x_2 - x_1)^2 + (y_2 - y_1)^2}$ [by distance formula]

$\Rightarrow EF = \sqrt{(0 - 12)^2 + (5 - 0)^2}$

$\Rightarrow EF = \sqrt{(-12)^2 + (5)^2}$

$\Rightarrow EF = \sqrt{144 + 25} = \sqrt{169} = 13$

[taking positive square root as length cannot be negative]

Hence, the length of the segment EF is 13 units.

10. Let the circumcentre of the triangle be $P(x, y)$.

We know that circumcentre is the point which is equidistant from the vertices of the triangle. If P is the circumcentre, then $PA = PB = PC$ = circumradius.

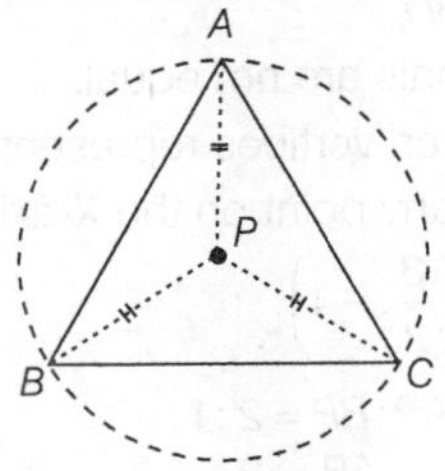

$\therefore \quad PA = PB$ [$\because A \equiv (4, 6), B \equiv (0, 4)$]

$\Rightarrow \quad PA^2 = PB^2$ [squaring on both sides]

$\Rightarrow \quad (x - 4)^2 + (y - 6)^2 = (x - 0)^2 + (y - 4)^2$

[using distance formula]

$\Rightarrow x^2 - 8x + 16 + y^2 - 12y + 36 = x^2 + y^2 - 8y + 16$

$\Rightarrow \quad -8x - 4y = -36$

$$\Rightarrow \quad 2x + y = 9 \quad \ldots(i)$$

and $PA = PC$ $\quad [\because A \equiv (4,6), C \equiv (6,2)]$

$$\Rightarrow \quad PA^2 = PC^2$$

[∵ squaring on both sides]

$$\Rightarrow (x-4)^2 + (y-6)^2 = (x-6)^2 + (y-2)^2$$

$$\Rightarrow x^2 - 8x + 16 + y^2 - 12y + 36 = x^2 - 12x + 36 + y^2 - 4y + 4$$

$$\Rightarrow \quad 4x - 8y = -12$$

$$\Rightarrow \quad x - 2y = -3 \quad \ldots(ii)$$

On solving Eqs. (i) and (ii), we get $x = 3$ and $y = 3$

∴ The circumcentre of the given triangle = (3, 3).

11. Let $A(2,3)$, $B(3,4)$, $C(5,6)$ and $D(4,5)$ be the given points. Then, by distance formula,

$$AB = \sqrt{(3-2)^2 + (4-3)^2} = \sqrt{(1)^2 + (1)^2} = \sqrt{2} \text{ units,}$$

$$BC = \sqrt{(5-3)^2 + (6-4)^2} = \sqrt{(2)^2 + (2)^2} = \sqrt{4+4} = \sqrt{8} = 2\sqrt{2} \text{ units,}$$

$$CD = \sqrt{(4-5)^2 + (5-6)^2} = \sqrt{(-1)^2 + (-1)^2} = \sqrt{2} \text{ units}$$

and $$AD = \sqrt{(4-2)^2 + (5-3)^2} = \sqrt{(2)^2 + (2)^2} = \sqrt{4+4} = \sqrt{8} = 2\sqrt{2} \text{ units}$$

Thus, $AB = CD$ and $AD = BC$

Hence, the opposite sides are equal.

Also, $$AC = \sqrt{(5-2)^2 + (6-3)^2} = \sqrt{3^2 + 3^2} = \sqrt{9+9} = 3\sqrt{2} \text{ units}$$

and $$BD = \sqrt{(4-3)^2 + (5-4)^2} = \sqrt{(1)^2 + (1)^2} = \sqrt{1+1} = \sqrt{2} \text{ units}$$

∵ $AC \neq BD$

So, the diagonals are not equal.

Hence, the given vertices represent a parallelogram.

12. Let $P(x, 0)$ be any point on the X-axis and $A \equiv (2,3), B \equiv \left(\frac{3}{2}, -1\right)$.

Given, $AP : BP = 2 : 1$

$$\Rightarrow \frac{AP}{BP} = \frac{2}{1} \Rightarrow AP = 2BP$$

$$\therefore \sqrt{(x-2)^2 + (0-3)^2} = 2 \times \sqrt{\left(x - \frac{3}{2}\right)^2 + (0+1)^2}$$

$$\left[\because d = \sqrt{(x_2 - x_1)^2 + (y_2 - y_1)^2}\right]$$

$$\Rightarrow \sqrt{(x-2)^2 + 9} = 2\sqrt{\left(x - \frac{3}{2}\right)^2 + 1}$$

$$\Rightarrow (x-2)^2 + 9 = 4\left[\left(x - \frac{3}{2}\right)^2 + 1\right]$$

[∵ squaring on both sides]

$$\Rightarrow x^2 + 4 - 4x + 9 = 4\left[x^2 + \frac{9}{4} - 3x + 1\right]$$

$$[\because (a-b)^2 = a^2 + b^2 - 2ab]$$

$$\Rightarrow x^2 - 4x + 13 = 4x^2 + 9 - 12x + 4$$

$$\Rightarrow -3x^2 + 8x = 0$$

$$\Rightarrow x(-3x + 8) = 0$$

$$\Rightarrow x = 0 \text{ or } -3x + 8 = 0$$

$$\Rightarrow x = 0 \text{ or } x = \frac{8}{3}$$

Hence, the required points are (0, 0) and $\left(\frac{8}{3}, 0\right)$.

13. Given, points $A(-1, y)$ and $B(5, 7)$ lie on a circle with centre $O(2, -3y)$.

Since, O is the centre of the circle and A, B are points on its circumference.

∴ $OA = OB$ [radii of the same circle]

$$\therefore \sqrt{(-1-2)^2 + (y+3y)^2} = \sqrt{(5-2)^2 + (7+3y)^2}$$

$$\left[\because d = \sqrt{(x_2 - x_1)^2 + (y_2 - y_1)^2}\right]$$

On squaring both sides, we get

$$(-1-2)^2 + (y+3y)^2 = (5-2)^2 + (7+3y)^2$$

$$\Rightarrow (-3)^2 + (4y)^2 = 3^2 + 7^2 + (3y)^2 + 2 \times 3y \times 7$$

$$[\because (a+b)^2 = a^2 + b^2 + 2ab]$$

$$\Rightarrow 9 + 16y^2 = 9 + 49 + 9y^2 + 42y$$

$$\Rightarrow 7y^2 - 42y - 49 = 0$$

$$\Rightarrow y^2 - 6y - 7 = 0$$

$$\Rightarrow y^2 - 7y + y - 7 = 0 \quad \text{[by factorisation]}$$

$$\Rightarrow y(y-7) + 1(y-7) = 0$$

$$\Rightarrow (y-7)(y+1) = 0$$

$$\Rightarrow y = 7, -1$$

When $y = 7$, then the coordinates of O and A are $(2, -21)$ and $(-1, 7)$, respectively.

Now, radius $OA = \sqrt{(-1-2)^2 + (7+21)^2} = \sqrt{(-3)^2 + (28)^2} = \sqrt{9 + 784} = \sqrt{793}$ units

When $y = -1$, then the coordinates of O and A are (2, 3) and $(-1, -1)$, respectively.

Now, radius $OA = \sqrt{(-1-2)^2 + (-1-3)^2} = \sqrt{(-3)^2 + (-4)^2} = \sqrt{9+16} = \sqrt{25} = 5$ units

14. Given, diameter = $10\sqrt{2}$ units

$\therefore$ Radius $= \dfrac{10\sqrt{2}}{2} = 5\sqrt{2}$ units

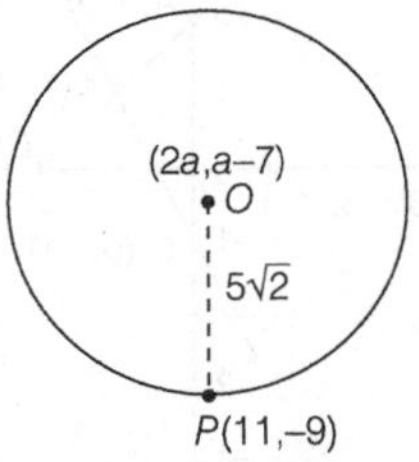

Now, the distance of point $P(11, -9)$ from point $O(2a, a-7)$ is $\sqrt{(11-2a)^2 + (-9-a+7)^2} = 5\sqrt{2}$

$[\because d = \sqrt{(x_2 - x_1)^2 + (y_2 - y_1)^2}$ and $OP = 5\sqrt{2}$ (radius)$]$

On squaring both sides, we get

$$(11-2a)^2 + (-9-a+7)^2 = (5\sqrt{2})^2$$

$\Rightarrow (11)^2 + (2a)^2 - 2 \times 11 \times 2a + (-a-2)^2 = 50$

$[\because (a-b)^2 = a^2 + b^2 - 2ab]$

$\Rightarrow \quad 121 + 4a^2 - 44a + a^2 + 4 + 4a = 50$

$[\because (a+b)^2 = a^2 + b^2 + 2ab]$

$\Rightarrow \quad 5a^2 - 40a + 75 = 0$

$\Rightarrow \quad a^2 - 8a + 15 = 0$

$\Rightarrow \quad a^2 - 5a - 3a + 15 = 0$

[by splitting middle term]

$\Rightarrow \quad a(a-5) - 3(a-5) = 0$

$\Rightarrow \quad (a-5)(a-3) = 0$

$\Rightarrow \quad a = 5, 3$

Hence, the required values of a are 5 and 3.

15. Given, points $(h, 4)$ and $\left(\dfrac{1}{2}, k\right)$ lie on the line passing through $A(-1, -1)$ and $B(2, 5)$.

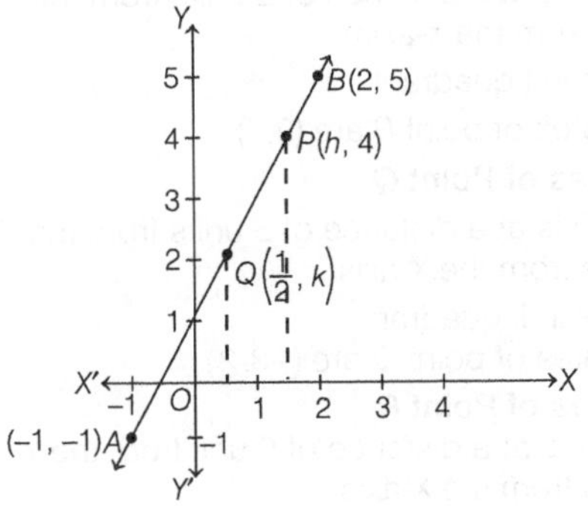

Hence, from the graph, $h = \dfrac{3}{2} = 1.5$ and $k = 2$

16. Given, equation is $3 = 2x + y$ and it can be written as

$$y = 3 - 2x \qquad \ldots\text{(i)}$$

When $x = 0$, then $y = 3 - 2(0) = 3$

When $x = 1$, then $y = 3 - 2(1) = 1$

When $x = -1$, then $y = 3 - 2(-1) = 5$

Thus, we have the following table

x	0	1	–1
y	3	1	5
(x, y)	$A(0, 3)$	$B(1, 1)$	$C(-1, 5)$

Now, draw the coordinate axes XOX' and YOY' and then plot the points $A(0, 3)$, $B(1, 1)$ and $C(-1, 5)$ on the graph and join these points, we get a line BC.

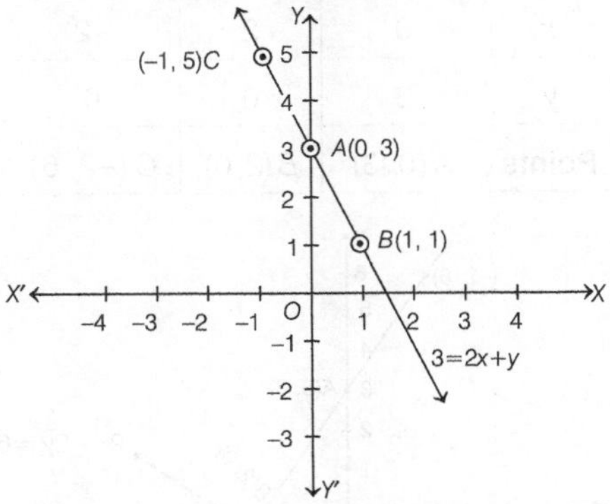

Hence, the line BC represents the required graph of given linear equation.

17. We have, $\dfrac{x-1}{1} + \dfrac{y-4}{2} = 0 \Rightarrow \dfrac{2x-2+y-4}{2} = 0$

$\Rightarrow \quad 2x + y - 6 = 0$

$\Rightarrow \quad y = 6 - 2x$

When $x = 0$, then $y = 6 - 2(0) = 6$

When $x = 1$, then $y = 6 - 2(1) = 4$

When $x = 2$, then $y = 6 - 2(2) = 2$

Thus, we have the following table

x	0	1	2
y	6	4	2
(x, y)	$A(0, 6)$	$B(1, 4)$	$C(2, 2)$

Now, plot the points $A(0, 6)$, $B(1, 4)$ and $C(2, 2)$ on the graph and join these points, we get a line AC.

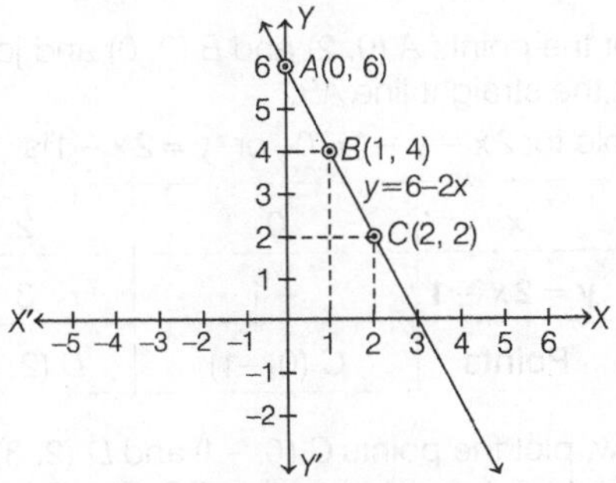

Hence, from the graph, the coordinate of point, where the graph meets the X-axis, are (3, 0) and coordinates of point, where the graph meets Y-axis, are (0, 6).

18. Table for $2x - 3y = 6$ is

x	0	3	-3
y	-2	0	-4
Points	$C(0, -2)$	$D(3, 0)$	$E(-3, -4)$

and table for $\frac{x}{2} + \frac{y}{3} = 1$ is

x	0	2	-2
y	3	0	6
Points	$A(0, 3)$	$B(2, 0)$	$C(-2, 6)$

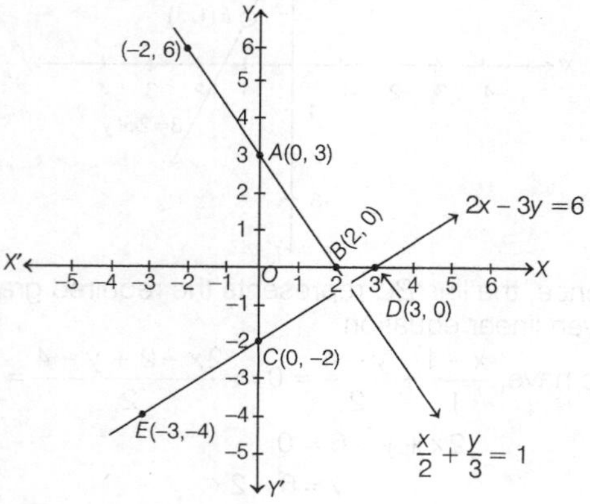

Hence, from graph, lines drawn are perpendicular to each other.

19. Given pair of linear equations is

$$x + y - 2 = 0 \quad \ldots(\text{i})$$

and $\quad 2x - y - 1 = 0 \quad \ldots(\text{ii})$

Now, table for $x + y = 2$ or $y = 2 - x$ is

x	0	2
$y = 2 - x$	2	0
Points	$A(0, 2)$	$B(2, 0)$

Plot the points $A(0, 2)$ and $B(2, 0)$ and join them to get the straight line AB.

Table for $2x - y - 1 = 0$ or $y = 2x - 1$ is

x	0	2
$y = 2x - 1$	-1	3
Points	$C(0, -1)$	$D(2, 3)$

Now, plot the points $C(0, -1)$ and $D(2, 3)$ and join them to get the straight line CD. The lines AB and CD intersect at $E(1, 1)$. So, the solution of the given pair of linear equations is $(1, 1)$.

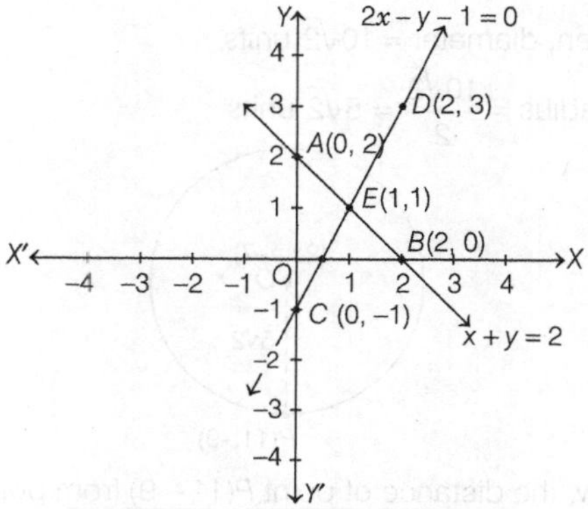

It is clear from the graph that infinite lines can pass through the intersection point of linear equations $x + y = 2$ and $2x - y = 1$.

Long Answer Type Questions

1. Here, the given points on the graph are P, Q, R and S. Now, draw the perpendicular lines from points P, Q, R and S on X and Y-axes.

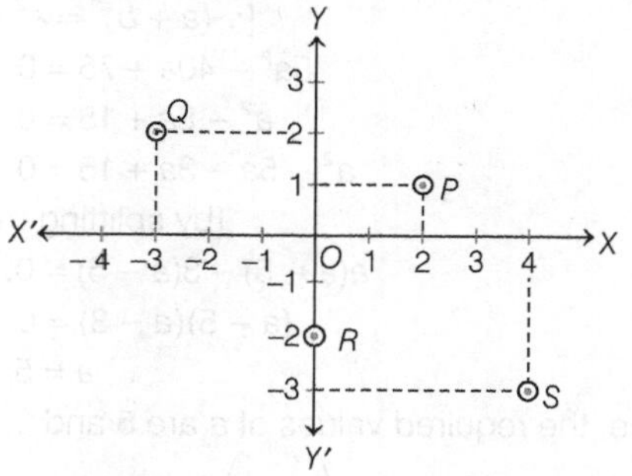

Coordinates of Point *P*

The point P is at a distance of 2 units from the Y-axis and 1 unit from the X-axis.

Point P lies in I quadrant.

$\therefore$ Coordinates of point P are $(2, 1)$.

Coordinates of Point *Q*

The point Q is at a distance of 3 units from the Y-axis and 2 units from the X-axis.

Point Q lies in II quadrant.

$\therefore$ Coordinates of point Q are $(-3, 2)$.

Coordinates of Point *R*

The point R is at a distance of 0 unit from the Y-axis and 2 units from the X-axis.

Point R is in negative direction of Y-axis.

$\therefore$ Coordinates of point R are $(0, -2)$.

Coordinates of Point *S*

The point S is at a distance of 4 units from the Y-axis and 3 units from the X-axis.

Point S lies in IV quadrant.

$\therefore$ Coordinates of point S are $(4, -3)$.

2. For point *P*

(i) Abscissa of the point = 2

(ii) Ordinate of the point = 3

(iii) Coordinates of the point = (2, 3)

(iv) Point of the type (+, +) lies in the I quadrant, hence the point (2, 3) lies in the I quadrant.

For point *Q*

(i) Abscissa of the point = – 2

(ii) Ordinate of the point = 4

(iii) Coordinates of the point = (– 2, 4)

(iv) Point of the type (–, +) lies in the II quadrant, hence the point (–2, 4) lies in the II quadrant.

For point *R*

(i) Abscissa of the point = – 5

(ii) Ordinate of the point = – 3

(iii) Coordinates of the point = (– 5, – 3)

(iv) Point of the type (–, –) lies in the III quadrant, hence the point (– 5, – 3) lies in the III quadrant.

For point *S*

(i) Abscissa of the point = 5

(ii) Ordinate of the point = – 1

(iii) Coordinates of the point = (5, – 1)

(iv) Point of the type (+, –) lies in the IV quadrant, hence the point (5, – 1) lies in the IV quadrant.

3. First, draw the coordinate axes and mark the units on both the axes such that 1 cm represents one unit.

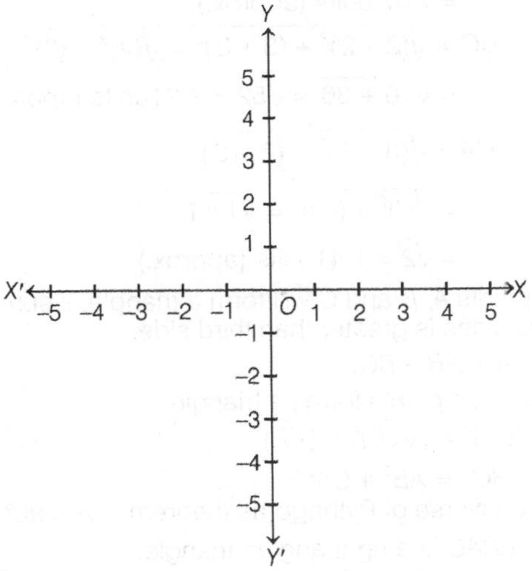

Then, the coordinates of point (4, 5) shows that the distance of this point from the *Y*-axis along the positive *X*-axis is 4 units and its distance from *X*-axis along the positive *Y*-axis is 5 units.

Similarly, (–4, 5) shows that the distance from the *Y*-axis along the negative *X*-axis is 4 units and its distance from *X*-axis along the positive *Y*-axis is 5 units.

Plotting of given points

Now, count 4 units, starting from origin on the positive *X*-axis and mark the point as *A*. Also, count the 4 units starting from origin on the negative *X*-axis and mark the point as *P*.

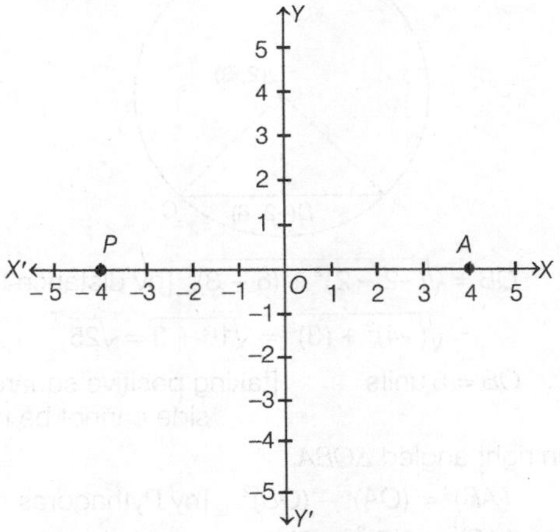

Now, start from the point *A*, count 5 units along the positive direction of the *Y*-axis and mark that point as *B*. Similarly, start from the point *P*, count 5 units along the positive direction of the *Y*-axis and mark that point as *Q*

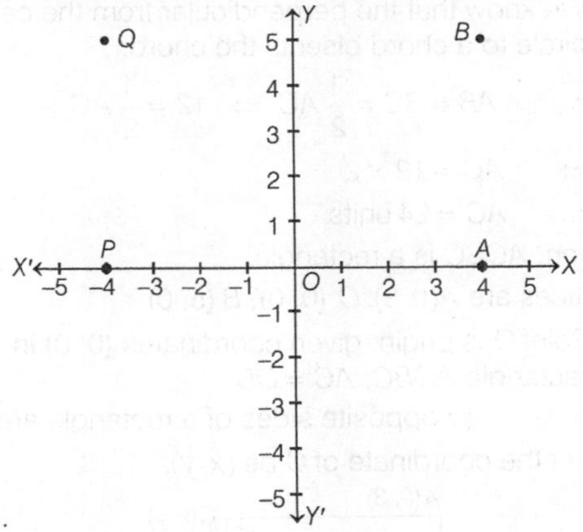

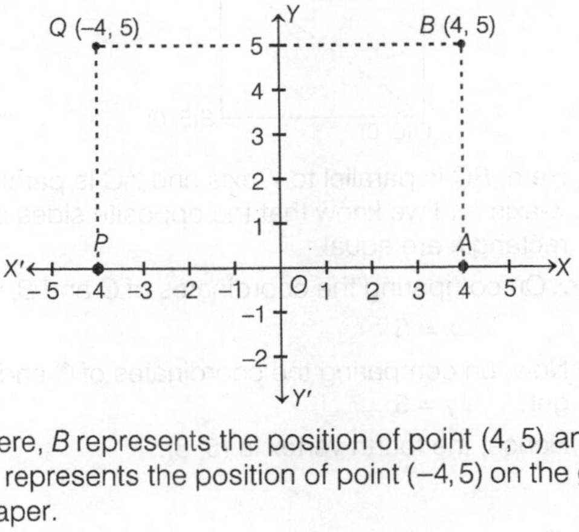

Here, *B* represents the position of point (4, 5) and *Q* represents the position of point (–4, 5) on the graph paper.

4. Given, radius = 13 units

$\therefore OA = OC = 13$

Coordinates of $B = (-2,6)$ and coordinates of $O = (2,3)$

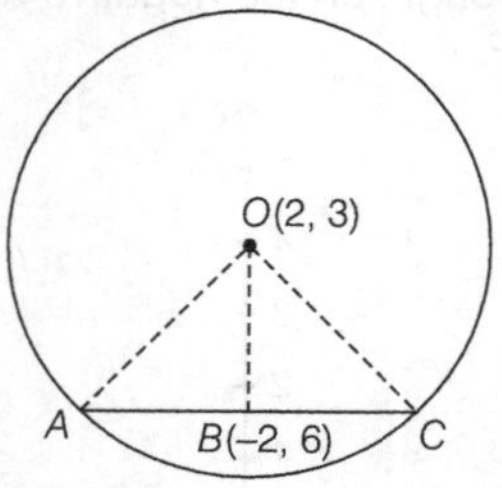

(i) $OB = \sqrt{(-2-2)^2 + (6-3)^2}$ [by distance formula]

$= \sqrt{(-4)^2 + (3)^2} = \sqrt{16+9} = \sqrt{25}$

$\therefore OB = 5$ units [taking positive square root as side cannot be negative]

(ii) In right angled ΔOBA,

$(AB)^2 = (OA)^2 - (OB)^2$ [by Pythagoras theorem]

$\Rightarrow (AB)^2 = (13)^2 - (5)^2$

$\Rightarrow (AB)^2 = 169 - 25$

$\Rightarrow (AB)^2 = 144$

$\therefore AB = 12$ units [taking +ve value]

(iii) We know that the perpendicular from the centre of a circle to a chord bisects the chord.

$\therefore AB = BC = \frac{1}{2} AC \Rightarrow 12 = \frac{1}{2} AC$

$\Rightarrow AC = 12 \times 2$

$\therefore AC = 24$ units

5. Given, $AOBC$ is a rectangle.

Vertices are $A(0, 3)$, $O(0, 0)$, $B(5, 0)$ [given]

(i) Point O is origin, given coordinates (0, 0) in rectangle $AOBC$, $AC = OB$

[$\because$ opposite sides of a rectangle are equal]

Let the coordinate of C be (x, y).

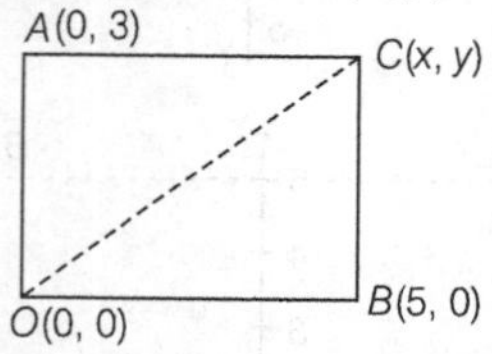

Here, BC is parallel to Y-axis and AC is parallel to X-axis and we know that the opposite sides of rectangle are equal.

$\therefore$ On comparing the coordinates of C and B, we get

$x = 5$

Now, on comparing the coordinates of C and A, we get $y = 3$

Hence, the fourth vertex is (5, 3).

(ii) Diagonal of rectangle $AOBC$ is

$OC = \sqrt{(5-0)^2 + (3-0)^2}$ [by distance formula]

$\Rightarrow OC = \sqrt{25+9}$

$\Rightarrow OC = \sqrt{34}$

and length of diagonals of a rectangle are same.

$\therefore AB = OC = \sqrt{34}$

Hence, the lengths of diagonals are $\sqrt{34}$ units.

(iii) We know that

Area of rectangle = Length × Breadth

$\Rightarrow$ Area $= OB \times OA$ ...(a)

Now, $OB = \sqrt{(5-0)^2 + (0-0)^2}$ [by distance formula]

$\Rightarrow OB = \sqrt{5^2} \Rightarrow OB = 5$ [taking +ve value]

and $OA = \sqrt{(0-0)^2 + (3-0)^2}$

$\Rightarrow OA = \sqrt{3^2} \Rightarrow OA = 3$ [taking +ve value]

$\therefore$ From Eq. (a),

Area = 5 × 3 = 15 sq units

Hence, the area of rectangle is 15 sq units.

6. Let the given points be $A(3,2)$, $B(-2,-3)$ and $C(2,3)$.

Here, $AB = \sqrt{(-2-3)^2 + (-3-2)^2}$

[$\because$ distance $= \sqrt{(x_2 - x_1)^2 + (y_2 - y_1)^2}$]

$= \sqrt{(-5)^2 + (-5)^2} = \sqrt{25+25} = \sqrt{50}$

$= 7.07$ units (approx.),

$BC = \sqrt{(2+2)^2 + (3+3)^2} = \sqrt{(4)^2 + (6)^2}$

$= \sqrt{16+36} = \sqrt{52} = 7.21$ units (approx.)

and $CA = \sqrt{(3-2)^2 + (2-3)^2}$

$= \sqrt{(1)^2 + (-1)^2} = \sqrt{1+1}$

$= \sqrt{2} = 1.41$ units (approx.)

Given points A, B and C will form a triangle, if sum of any two sides is greater than third side.

Here, $CA + AB > BC$.

So, the given points forms a triangle.

Also, $(\sqrt{52})^2 = (\sqrt{50})^2 + (\sqrt{2})^2$

$\Rightarrow BC^2 = AB^2 + CA^2$

So, by converse of Pythagoras theorem, $\angle A = 90°$.

Hence, ΔBAC is a right angled triangle.

Now, we know that the area of right angled triangle is

$= \frac{1}{2} \times$ Base × Height

$= \frac{1}{2} \times \sqrt{2} \times \sqrt{50} = \frac{1}{2} \times \sqrt{2} \times 5\sqrt{2}$

= 5 sq units

7. Plot the points $(-6, -7), (0, -3)$ and $(4.5, 0)$.

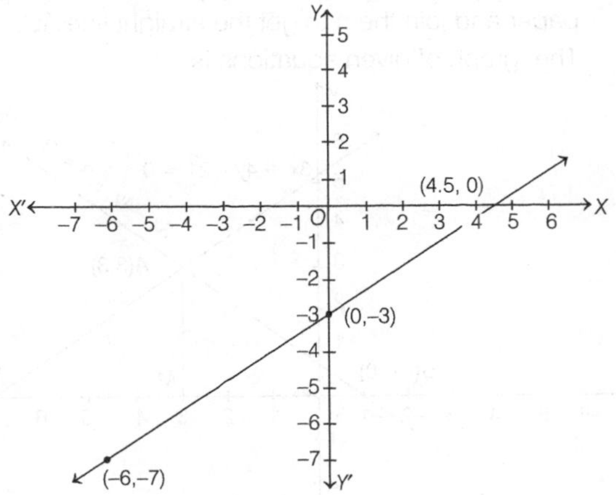

From the graph, it is clear that

when $y = -5$, then $x = -3$

$\therefore \quad p = -3$

and when $y = -2$, then $x = 1.5$

$\therefore \quad q = 1.5$

Hence, the values of p and q are -3 and 1.5.

Now, let a linear relation between x and y be

$$y = ax + b \quad \ldots(i)$$

On putting $x = -3$ and $y = -5$ in Eq. (i), we get

$$-5 = a(-3) + b$$

$$-5 = -3a + b \quad \ldots(ii)$$

On putting $x = 1.5$ and $y = -2$ in Eq. (i), we get

$$-2 = a \times 1.5 + b$$

$$-2 = 1.5a + b \quad \ldots(iii)$$

On subtracting Eq. (iii) from Eq. (ii), we get

$$-5 = -3a + b$$
$$-2 = 1.5a + b$$
$$+ \quad - \quad -$$
$$-3 = -4.5a$$

$\Rightarrow \quad a = \frac{2}{3}$

From Eq. (ii), $-5 = (-3) \times \frac{2}{3} + b \quad [\because a = 2]$

$\Rightarrow \quad -5 + 2 = b$

$\Rightarrow \quad b = -3$

Now, on putting the values of a and b in Eq. (i), we get

$$y = \frac{2}{3}x + (-3)$$

$\Rightarrow \quad 3y = 2x - 9$

Hence, the linear relation between x and y is $3y = 2x - 9$.

8. Given equations are $2x + 5y = 1, x - 3y = 6$ and $x + 5y + 2 = 0$.

Table for equation $2x + 5y = 1$ is

x	-3	0	3
$y = \frac{1-2x}{5}$	1.4	0.2	-1

Table for equation $x - 3y = 6$ is

x	-3	0	3
$y = \frac{x-6}{3}$	-3	-2	-1

Table for equation $x + 5y + 2 = 0$ is

x	-3	0	3
$y = \frac{-2-x}{5}$	0.2	-0.4	-1

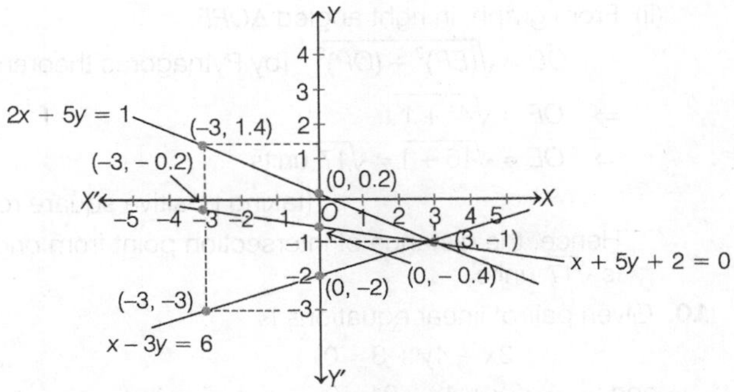

Hence, the given lines pass through the same point $(3, -1)$.

9. Table for $2x + y = 6$ or $y = 6 - 2x$ is

x	0	1	3
$y = 6 - 2x$	6	4	0
Points	$B(0, 6)$	$E(1, 4)$	$A(3, 0)$

Now, plot all these points on a graph paper and join them to get a line AB.

Table for equation $2x - y + 2 = 0$ or $y = 2x + 2$ is

x	0	-1	1
$y = 2x + 2$	2	0	4
Points	$D(0, 2)$	$C(-1, 0)$	$E(1, 4)$

Now, plot all these points on a graph paper and join them to get a line CE.

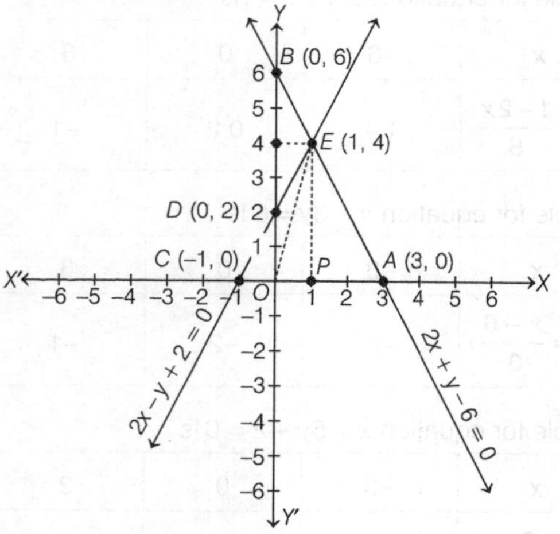

(i) Hence, from the graph, the intersection point of the lines is $E(1,4)$.

(ii) From graph, in right angled ΔOPE,

$OE = \sqrt{(EP)^2 + (OP)^2}$ [by Pythagoras theorem]

$\Rightarrow \quad OE = \sqrt{4^2 + 1^2}$

$\Rightarrow \quad OE = \sqrt{16+1} = \sqrt{17}$ units

[taking positive square root]

Hence, the distance of intersection point from origin is $\sqrt{17}$ units.

10. Given pair of linear equations is

$$3x - 4y + 3 = 0 \quad \ldots(i)$$

and

$$3x + 4y - 21 = 0 \quad \ldots(ii)$$

Table for $3x - 4y + 3 = 0$ or $y = \dfrac{3x+3}{4}$ is

x	3	– 1
$y = \dfrac{\mathbf{3x+3}}{\mathbf{4}}$	3	0
Points	$A(3, 3)$	$B(-1, 0)$

Plot the points $A(3, 3)$ and $B(-1, 0)$ on the graph paper and join them to get the straight line AB.

Now, table for $3x + 4y - 21 = 0$ or $y = \dfrac{21-3x}{4}$ is

x	3	7
$y = \dfrac{\mathbf{21-3x}}{\mathbf{4}}$	3	0
Points	$A(3, 3)$	$C(7, 0)$

Plot the points $A(3, 3)$ and $C(7, 0)$ on same graph paper and join them to get the straight line AC.

The graph of given equations is

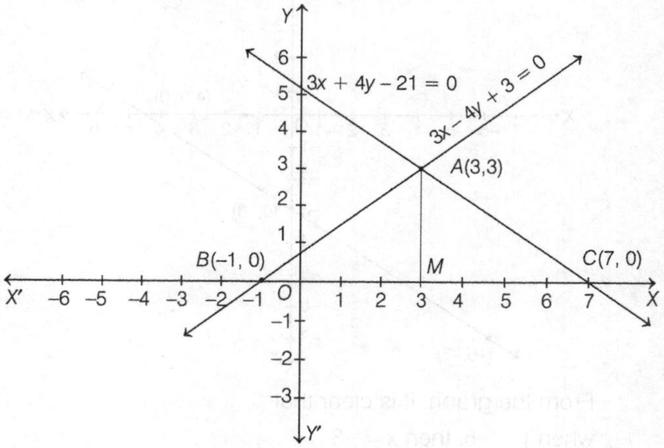

The coordinates of the vertices of ΔABC are $A(3, 3)$, $B(-1, 0)$ and $C(7, 0)$.

$\therefore$ Area of $\Delta ABC = \dfrac{1}{2} \times BC \times AM$

$= \dfrac{1}{2} \times 8 \times 3$

$= 12$ sq units

[here, $BC = 1 + 7 = 8$ units and $AM = 3$ units]

Case Based Questions

1. (i) Given, in a rectangular field $ABCD$, vertical lines are drawn with chalk powder at a distance of 1 m each. Also, placed 100 flower pots along AD at a distance of 1 m each i.e. total length of AD is 100 m.

Now, we consider AB as X-axis and AD as Y-axis.

Since, Niharika runs $\dfrac{1}{4}$ of the distance AD on second line and posts a green flag.

$\therefore$ Position of green flag $= \left(2, \dfrac{1}{4} \times 100\right) = (2, 25)$

(ii) Since, Preeti runs $\dfrac{1}{5}$ of the distance AD on the 8th line and posts a red flag.

$\therefore$ Position of red flag $= \left(8, \dfrac{1}{5} \times 100\right) = (8, 20)$

(iii) For point (2, 25), x-coordinate is positive and y-coordinate is also positive, so it lies in I quadrant.

(iv) For point (8, 20), x-coordinate and y-coordinate both are positive. So, it lies in I quadrant.

2. (i) From graph, we have coordinates of A are (1, 1).

(ii) From graph, we have coordinates of F are (5, 5).

(iii) Area of playground ABC,

$$A_1 = \frac{1}{2} \times AB \times AC = \frac{1}{2}(3-1) \times (3-1)$$

$$= \frac{1}{2} \times 2 \times 2 = 2 \text{ sq units}$$

(iv) Area of playground DEF,

$$A_2 = \frac{1}{2} \times DE \times DF = \frac{1}{2}(7-5)(5-3)$$

$$= \frac{1}{2} \times 2 \times 2 = 2 \text{ sq units}$$

3. Given, y (CP) = ₹ $(10 + x)$

and y (SP) = ₹ $1.5x$

Now, table for $y = 10 + x$ is

x	0	20	40	60
y	10	30	50	70
Points	(0, 10)	(20, 30)	(40, 50)	(60, 70)

Plot the points (0, 10), B (20, 30), C (40, 50) and D (60, 70) and join them to get the straight line AD.

Table for $y = 1.5x$ is

x	0	20	40	60
y	0	30	60	90
Points	(0, 0)	(20, 30)	(40, 60)	(60, 90)

Plot the points O (0, 0), F (20, 30), G (40, 60) and H (60, 90) and join them to get a straight line OH.

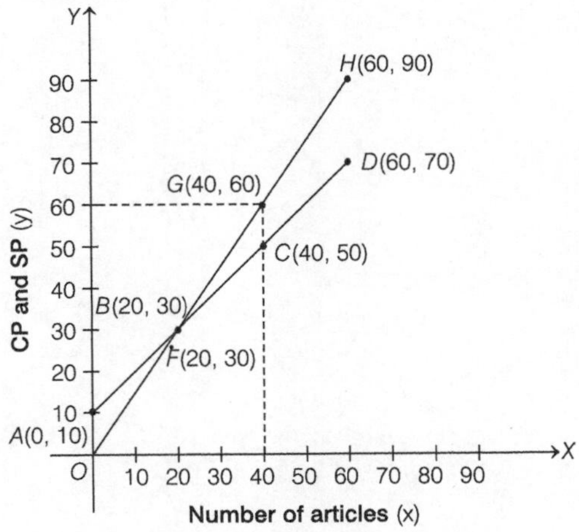

(i) ∵ The two straight line meet at $x = 20$, it shows that cost price of 20 articles is the same as their selling price.

∴ Number of articles that must be manufacturing and sold to reach breakeven point is 20.

(ii) Draw the vertical line through $x = 40$, which meets graph for CP at ₹ 50 and graph for SP at ₹ 60.

∴ Profit made = 60 − 50 = ₹10

3 Sample Question Paper

SAMPLE QUESTION PAPER (MATHEMATICS)

General Instructions

Maximum Marks : 80

Time allowed : Two hours 30 minutes

Answers to this paper must be written on the paper provided separately.

You will **not** be allowed to write during the first **15** minutes.

This time is to be spent in reading the question paper.

The time given at the head of this paper is the time allowed for writing the answers.

Attempt all questions from Section A and any 4 questions from Section B.

The intended marks for questions or parts of questions are given brackets ().

Mathematical tables are provided.

Section A

(Attempt **all** questions from this section) **(40 Marks)**

Question 1

Choose the correct answers to the questions from the given options. **(15)**

(i) In ΔABC, $\angle B = 35°$, $\angle C = 65°$ and the bisector of $\angle BAC$ meets BC at P. Then, the ascending order of sides is

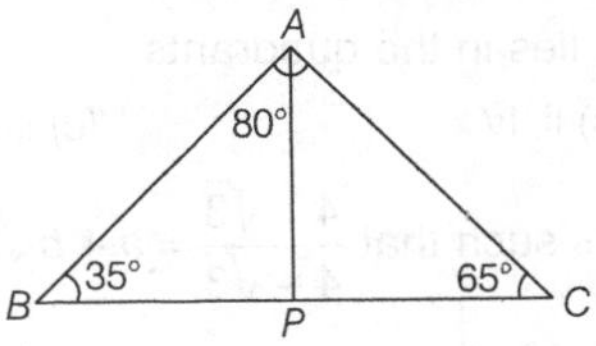

(a) AP, BP, CP

(b) AP, CP, BP

(c) BP, AP, CP

(d) CP, AP, BP

(ii) At compound interest of 8%, 10% and 12% for three consecutive years, the interest earned in the third year is ₹ 891. The principal is

(a) ₹ 5000

(b) ₹ 6250

(c) ₹ 7000

(d) ₹ 7250

(iii) ΔABC is an isosceles triangle with $AB = AC = 13$ cm and the length of altitude from A on BC is 5 cm. Then, BC is equal to

(a) 24 cm

(b) 10 cm

(c) 20 cm

(d) 15 cm

(iv) The value of $\log_2 1 \times \log_3 2 \times \log_4 3 \times \ldots \times \log_{100} 99$ is

(a) not defined (b) 0 (c) 1 (d) 2

(v) $7^x + 5^y = 74$ and $7^{x+1} - 5^{y+1} = 218$, then the values of x and y are respectively

(a) 2, 2 (b) 2, 3 (c) 3, 2 (d) 4, 2

(vi) In a ΔABC, BE and CF are medians. M is a point on BE produced such that $BE = EM$ and N is a point on CF produced such that $CF = FN$.

Which of the following is true?

Statement I NAM is a straight line.

Statement II A is the mid-point of MN.

(a) Both the statements are true.
(b) Both the statements are false.
(c) Statement I is true and Statement II is false.
(d) Statement I is false and Statement II is true.

(vii) The value of $\log_{11} 3 \cdot \log_3 1331$ is

(a) 4 (b) 0 (c) 3 (d) 1

(viii) If $x = \dfrac{\sqrt{3}+1}{2}$, then the value of $4x^3 + 2x^2 - 8x + 7$ is

(a) 10 (b) 8 (c) 6 (d) 4

(ix) From the given figure,

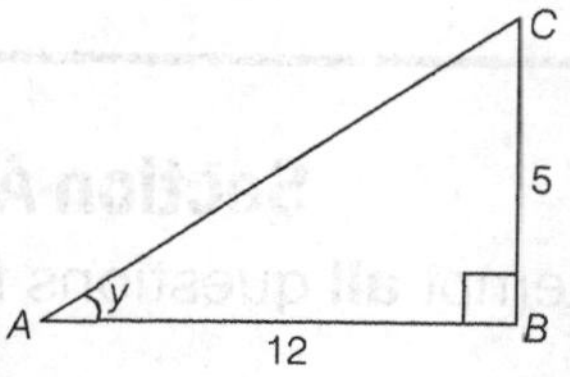

value of $\sin y$ is

(a) $\dfrac{12}{13}$ (b) $\dfrac{13}{5}$ (c) $\dfrac{5}{12}$ (d) $\dfrac{5}{13}$

(x) The line $x = my$, where $m < 0$, lies in the quadrants

(a) I, II (b) II, IV (c) III, IV (d) III, I

(xi) If a and b are rational numbers such that $\dfrac{4+\sqrt{3}}{4-\sqrt{3}} = a + b\sqrt{3}$, then the values of a and b are respectively

(a) $\dfrac{12}{15}, \dfrac{7}{15}$ (b) $\dfrac{19}{13}, \dfrac{8}{13}$ (c) $\dfrac{14}{13}, \dfrac{7}{14}$ (d) $\dfrac{8}{14}, \dfrac{19}{19}$

(xii) If $x^3 = \sqrt[3]{8} + \sqrt[3]{27} + \sqrt[3]{64} + \sqrt[3]{125} + \sqrt[3]{216} + \sqrt[3]{343}$, then x^2 equals to

(a) 9 (b) 1 (c) 4 (d) 6

(xiii) **Assertion** (A) If $\log_2 x + \log_4 x = 3$ then $x^2 = 16$.

Reason (R) $\log_m n = \dfrac{1}{\log_n m}$

(a) A is true, R is false.
(b) A is false, R is true.
(c) Both A and R are true and R is the correct reason for A.
(d) Both A and R are true and R is incorrect reason for A.

(xiv) The value of $\dfrac{\sin 36°}{\cos 54°}$ is

(a) 0 (b) 1 (c) 2 (d) ∞

(xv) The ratio of the angles *P, Q, R, S* of a quadrilateral *PQRS* is 3 : 6 : 4 : 5, then ∠*R* is

(a) 60° (b) 120° (c) 100° (d) 80°

Question 2

(i) Factorise $12(x^2 + 7x)^2 - 8\,(x^2 + 7x)(2x - 1) - 15\,(2x - 1)^2$. **(4)**

(ii) In the given figure, it is given that $PQ = PR$, $\angle AOQ = 2\angle BQR$ and $\angle BOR = 2\angle ARQ$. Prove that $\Delta PQB \cong \Delta PRA$. **(4)**

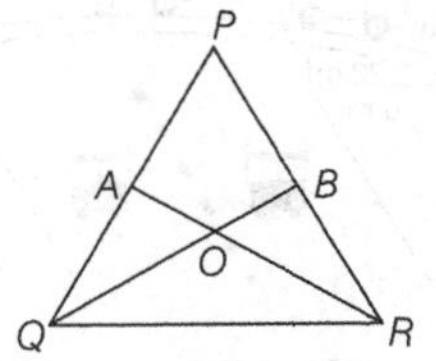

(iii) Write down the coordinates of the points *A, B, C* and *D* as shown in the following figure. Also, find the area of quadrilateral *ADNL*. **(4)**

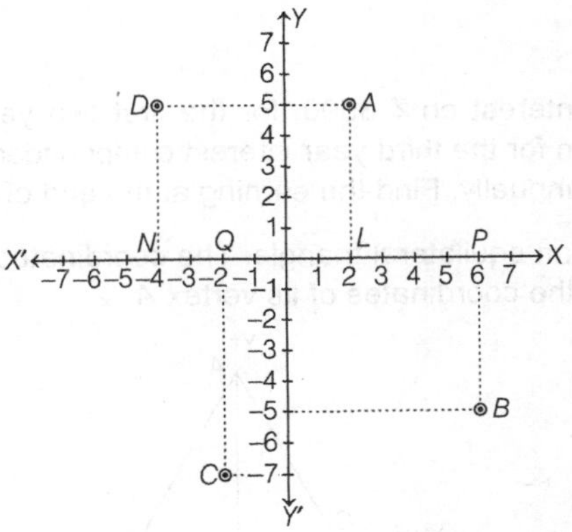

Question 3

(i) If *a b* and *c* are all non-zeroes and $a + b + c = 0$, then prove that

$$\frac{a^2}{bc} + \frac{b^2}{ca} + \frac{c^2}{ab} = 3.$$ **(4)**

(ii) *P* is the mid-point of the side *CD* of a parallelogram *ABCD*. A line through *C* parallel to *PA* intersects *AB* at *Q* and *DA* produced at *R*. Prove that

(a) $DA = AR$

(b) $CQ = QR$ **(5)**

(iii) Evaluate $(\sqrt{5 + 2\sqrt{6}}) + (\sqrt{8 - 2\sqrt{15}})$. **(4)**

SAMPLE QUESTION PAPER

Section B

(Attempt **any four** questions from this section) **(40 Marks)**

Question 4

(i) The triangular side walls of a flyover have been used for advertisements. The sides of the walls are 122 m, 22 m and 120 m (see figure). The advertisements yield an earning of ₹ 5000 per m^2 per year. A company hired one of its walls for 3 months.

(a) How much rent did it pay

(b) What is the value of the advertisements for the people in daily life?

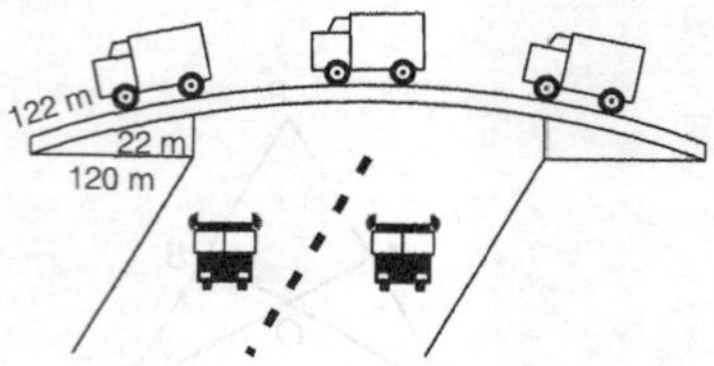

(ii) Construct a quadrilateral $ABCD$, when $AB = 7.2$ cm, $BC = 5.8$ cm, $CD = 6.3$ cm, $AD = 4.3$ cm and $\angle A = 75°$. **(3)**

(iii) If $8^x \times 4^y = 128$ and $9^{2x-y} = 1$, then find the value of $x + 2y$. **(3)**

Question 5

(i) Calculate the compound interest on ₹ 3500, for the first two years at 8% per annum. Interest is paid half-yearly, 12% per annum for the third year interest compounded annually, 15% per annum for the fourth year interest compounded annually. Find the earning at the end of 4 yr. **(3)**

(ii) In the given figure, ABC is an equilateral triangle. The coordinates of vertices B and C are (3, 0) and (– 3, 0), respectively. Find the coordinates of its vertex A.

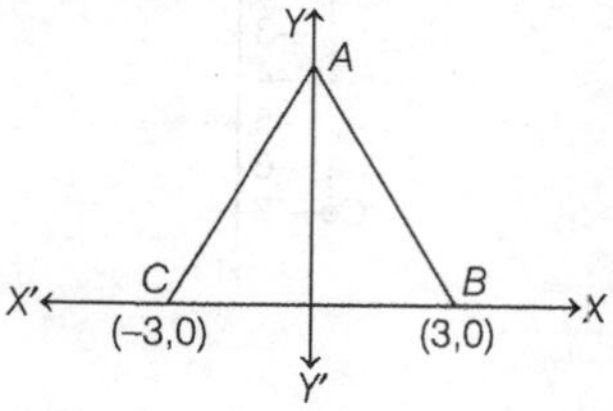

(3)

(iii) In the given figure, $OA \perp OD$, $OC \perp OB$, $OD = OA$ and $OC = OB$. Prove that

(a) $\Delta ODC \cong \Delta OAB$

(b) $AB = CD$.

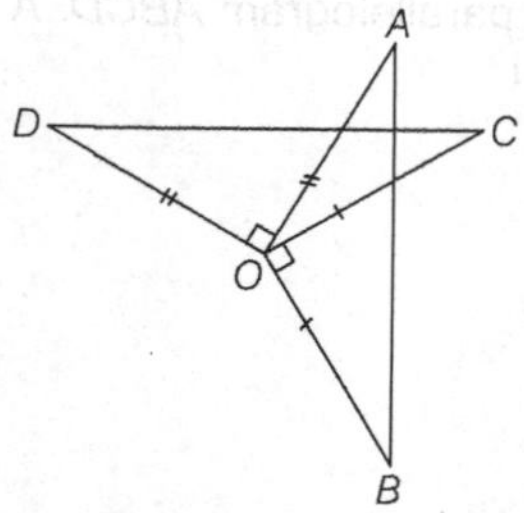

Question 6

(i) In the given figure, $ABCDE$ is a pentagon. A line through B parallel to AC meets DC produced at F. Show that

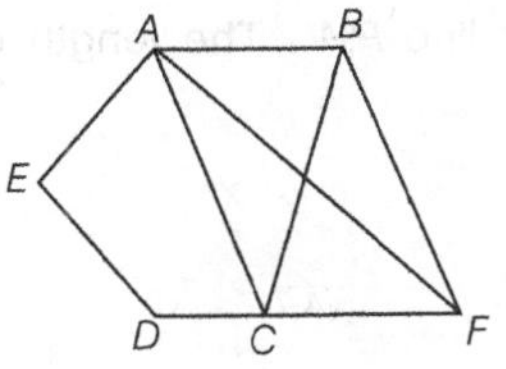

(a) ar $(\Delta ACB) = $ ar (ΔACF).

(b) ar $(AEDF) = $ ar $(ABCDE)$. **(3)**

(ii) Draw a histogram for the following data.

Class interval	59-65	66-72	73-79	80-86	87-93	94-100
Frequency	10	5	25	15	30	10

(4)

(iii) In the given figure, $AE = DC = 13$ cm, $BE = 5$ cm, $\angle ABC = 90°$ and $AD = EC = x$ cm. Calculate the length of AB and the value of x.

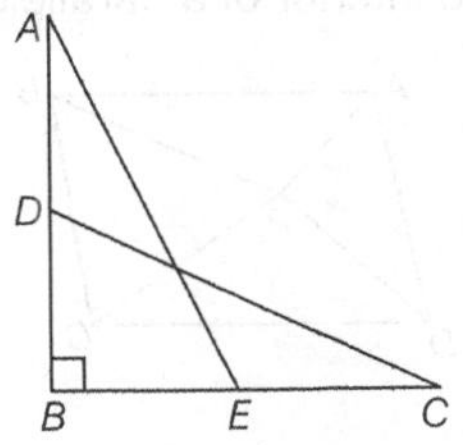

(3)

Question 7

(i) If the area of a semi-circular field is 30800 sq m, then find the perimeter of the field. **(3)**

(ii) Without using trigonometric tables, evaluate $3\cos 80° \operatorname{cosec} 10° + 2\sin 59° \sec 31°$. **(3)**

(iii) AB is a line segment and P is its mid-point. D and E are points on the same side of AB such that $\angle BAD = \angle ABE$ and $\angle EPA = \angle DPB$ (see the figure). Show that

(a) $\Delta DAP \cong \Delta EBP$

(b) $AD = BE$

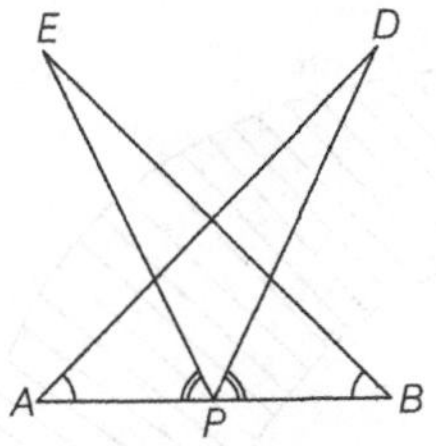

(4)

Question 8

(i) (a) Draw the graph of the equations, $3x - 2y = 4$ and $x + y - 3 = 0$ in the same graph.

(b) Find the coordinates of the point, where two lines intersect. **(4)**

SAMPLE QUESTION PAPER

(ii) In an examination, the mean marks scored by a class of 50 students was calculated as 84. Later on, it was detected that the marks of one student were wrongly copied as 27 instead of 72. Find the correct mean. **(3)**

(iii) Amit represents $\sqrt{4.7}$ on the number line PW. The length of $TS = 1$ unit. His representation is shown below.

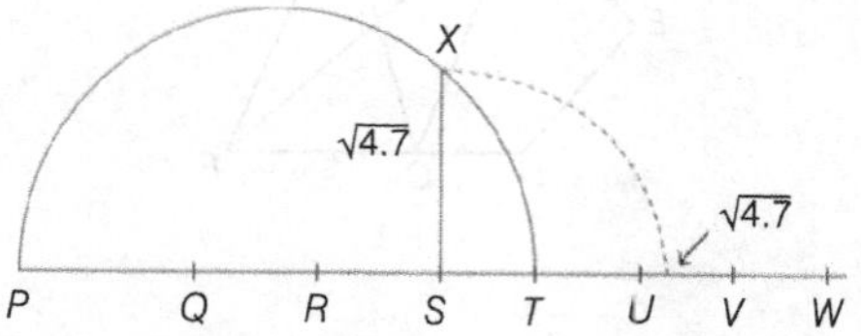

Based on the above information, answer the following questions.

(a) Which letter represents 0 on the number line?

(b) Between which two points does $\sqrt{5.5}$ lie on this number line?

Question 9

(i) If $\dfrac{\log(x+y)}{\log 2} = \dfrac{\log(x-y)}{\log 3} = \dfrac{\log 64}{\log 0.125}$, then find the values of x and y. **(5)**

(ii) In the following figure, P is a point in the interior of a parallelogram $ABCD$. Show that

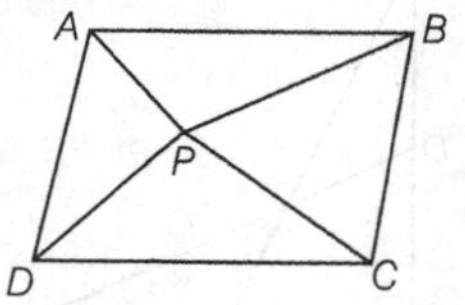

(a) $\text{ar}(\Delta APB) + \text{ar}(\Delta PCD) = \frac{1}{2}\text{ar}(\text{parallelogram } ABCD)$

(b) $\text{ar}(\Delta APD) + \text{ar}(\Delta PBC) = \text{ar}(\Delta APB) + \text{ar}(\Delta PCD)$ **(5)**

Question 10

(i) If AD and BE are medians of ΔABC and $BE \parallel DF$, then prove that $CF = \frac{1}{4}AC$. **(4)**

(ii) In the given figure, sectors of two concentric circles of radii 7 cm and 3.5 cm are shown. Find the area of the shaded region. **(3)**

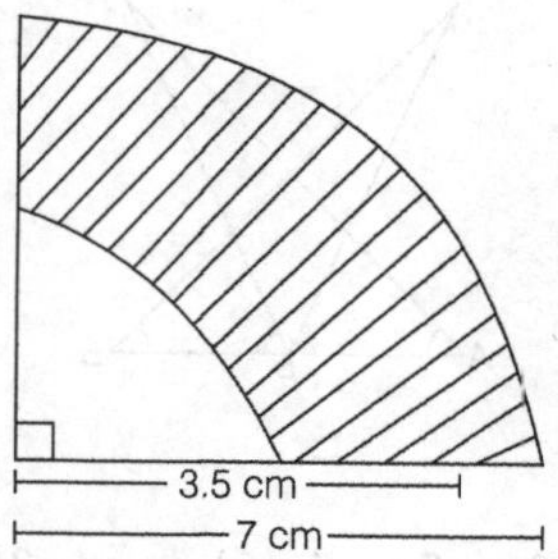

(iii) Factorise $216x^3 + \dfrac{1}{27y^3}$. **(5)**

EXPLANATIONS

1. (i) (d) Given, in $\triangle ABC$, AP is bisector of $\angle BAC$.

$$\therefore \angle BAP = \angle CAP = \frac{80^\circ}{2} = 40^\circ$$

Now, in $\triangle ABP$, $\angle ABP < \angle BAP$

$$\therefore \quad AP < BP \quad \text{...(i)}$$

[$\because$ side opposite to greater angle in a triangle is larger]

Now, in $\triangle CAP$, $\angle ACP > \angle PAC$

$$\therefore \quad AP > PC \quad \text{...(ii)}$$

From Eqs. (i) and (ii), we get $PC < AP < BP$

(ii) (b) Let the principal be P.

Given, $R_1 = 8\%$, $R_2 = 10\%$ and $R_3 = 12\%$

Interest earned in third year = ₹891.

Interest earned in third year = Amount after 3rd year − Amount after 2nd year

$$\Rightarrow \quad 891 = P\left(1+\frac{8}{100}\right)\left(1+\frac{10}{100}\right)\left(1+\frac{12}{100}\right) - P\left(1+\frac{8}{100}\right)\left(1+\frac{10}{100}\right)$$

$$\Rightarrow \quad 891 = P\left(1+\frac{8}{100}\right)\left(1+\frac{10}{100}\right)\left[1+\frac{12}{100}-1\right]$$

$$\Rightarrow \quad 891 = P\left(\frac{27}{25}\right)\left(\frac{11}{10}\right)\left(\frac{3}{25}\right)$$

$$\Rightarrow \quad P = \frac{891 \times 25 \times 10 \times 25}{27 \times 11 \times 3} = ₹6250$$

(iii) (a) Given, $\triangle ABC$ is an isosceles triangle with $AB = AC = 13$ cm.

Length of altitude from A on $BC = 5$ cm

As we know that

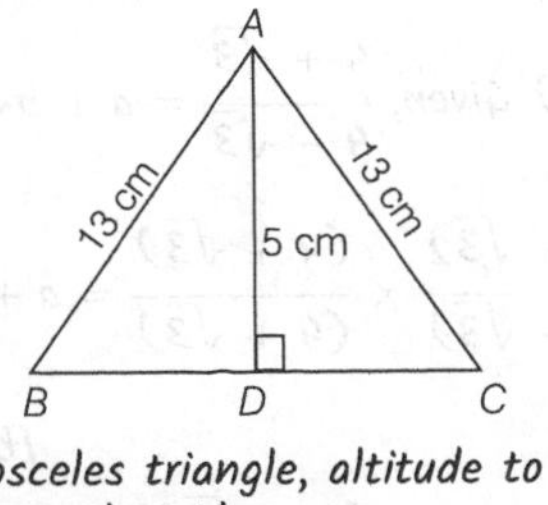

In an isosceles triangle, altitude to unequal side also bisects the side.

$$\therefore \quad BD = DC \quad \text{... (i)}$$

Now, in right angled $\triangle ABD$,

$$BD^2 = AB^2 - AD^2$$

[by Pythagoras theorem]

$$\Rightarrow \quad BD = \sqrt{13^2 - 5^2}$$

$$= \sqrt{169 - 25} = 12 \text{ cm}$$

[$\because$ side cannot be negative]

From Eq. (i), $DC = 12$ cm

Now, $BC = BD + DC$

$$= 12 + 12 = 24 \text{ cm}$$

(iv) (b) We have,

$$\log_2 1 \times \log_3 2 \times \log_4 3 \times \ldots\ldots \times \log_{100} 99$$

$$= \frac{\log_{10} 1}{\log_{10} 2} \times \frac{\log_{10} 2}{\log_{10} 3} \times \ldots\ldots \times \frac{\log_{10} 99}{\log_{10} 100}$$

$$\left[\because \log_n m = \frac{\log_a m}{\log_a n}\right]$$

$$= \frac{\log_{10} 1}{\log_{10} 100} = 0 \qquad [\because \log_{10} 1 = 0]$$

(v) (a) We have, $7^x + 5^y = 74$

and $\quad 7^{x+1} - 5^{y+1} = 218$

$$\Rightarrow \quad 7 \cdot 7^x - 5 \cdot 5^y = 218$$

Let $7^x = a$ and $5^y = b$

$$\therefore \quad a + b = 74 \quad \text{... (i)}$$

and $\quad 7a - 5b = 218 \quad$ ... (ii)

On multiplying Eq. (i) by 5, we get

$$5a + 5b = 370 \quad \text{... (iii)}$$

On adding Eqs. (ii) and (iii), we get

$$12a = 588$$

$$\Rightarrow \quad a = 49$$

On substituting $a = 49$ in Eq. (i), we get

$$49 + b = 74$$

$$\Rightarrow \quad b = 25$$

$$\because \quad a = 7^x = 49 = 7^2$$

and $\quad b = 5^y = 25 = 5^2$

On comparing the exponents, we get

$$x = 2 \text{ and } y = 2$$

(vi) (a) Given, in ΔABC, BE and CF are medians.

$$BE = EM \text{ and } CF = FN$$

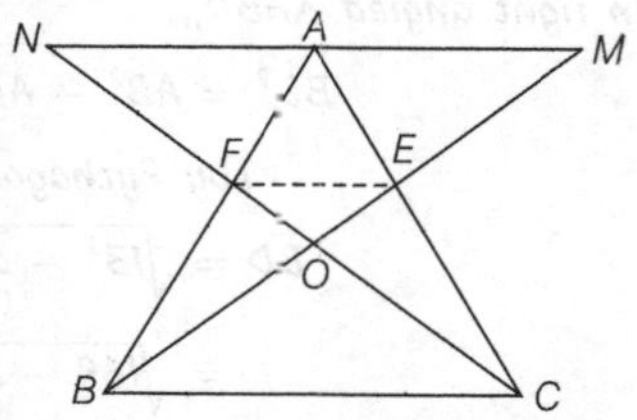

Let O be the intersection point of medians.

In ΔANC, $NF = FC$ and $AE = EC$

$\therefore \quad FE = \frac{1}{2} FN$ and $FE \parallel AN$ ...(i)

[by mid-point theorem]

Again, in ΔBAM,

$BF = AF$ and $BE = EM$

$\therefore \quad FE = \frac{1}{2} AM$ and $FE \parallel AM$ ...(ii)

[by mid-point theorem]

From Eqs. (i) and (ii), we get

$AN = AM$ and $AN \parallel AM$

$\because AN \parallel AM$ but A is common point.

$\therefore$ Points A, M and N are collinear.

$\therefore$ NAM is a straight line and A is the mid-point of MN.

Hence, both the statements are true.

(vii) (c) We have, $\log_{11} 3 \cdot \log_3 1331$

$= \log_{11} 3 \cdot \log_3 (11)^3$

$= \log_{11} 3 \cdot 3 \log_3 11$

$[\because \log m^n = n \log m]$

$= 3 \log_{11} 3 \cdot \log_3 11$

$= 3 \times 1 \quad [\because \log_m n \times \log_n m = 1]$

$= 3$

(viii) (a) Given, $x = \frac{\sqrt{3}+1}{2}$

Now, $4x^3 + 2x^2 - 8x + 7$

$= 4\left(\frac{\sqrt{3}+1}{2}\right)^3 + 2\left(\frac{\sqrt{3}+1}{2}\right)^2 - 8\left(\frac{\sqrt{3}+1}{2}\right) + 7$

$= 4\left[\frac{3\sqrt{3} + 1 + 3\sqrt{3}(\sqrt{3}+1)}{8}\right]$

$+ 2\left[\frac{3 + 1 + 2\sqrt{3}}{4}\right] - 8\frac{(\sqrt{3}+1)}{2} + 7$

$[\because (a+b)^3 = a^3 + b^3 + 3ab(a+b)$ and $(a+b)^2 = a^2 + b^2 + 2ab]$

$= \frac{6\sqrt{3}+10}{2} + \frac{4+2\sqrt{3}}{2} - 4\sqrt{3} - 4 + 7$

$= 3\sqrt{3} + 5 + 2 + \sqrt{3} - 4\sqrt{3} + 3$

$= 10$

(ix) (d) In ΔABC,

$AC^2 = AB^2 + BC^2$

[by Pythagoras theorem]

$= 12^2 + 5^2$

$= 144 + 25$

$= 169$

$\Rightarrow \quad AC = 13$

$[\because$ side cannot be negative$]$

Now, $\sin y = \frac{\text{Perpendicular}}{\text{Hypotenuse}} = \frac{BC}{AC} = \frac{5}{13}$

(x) (b) Let us identify the sign of y for each sign of x.

We have, $x = my \Rightarrow y = \frac{x}{m}$, where $m < 0$

When x is positive then y is negative and when x is negative then y is positive.

Thus, the coordinates of points lying on the line are of the form $(x, -y)$ and $(-x, y)$, which implies that points lying in second and fourth quadrants.

Hence, the line $x = my$, where $m < 0$, lies in II and IV quadrants.

(xi) (b) Given, $\frac{4+\sqrt{3}}{4-\sqrt{3}} = a + b\sqrt{3}$

$\Rightarrow \frac{(4+\sqrt{3})}{(4-\sqrt{3})} \times \frac{(4+\sqrt{3})}{(4+\sqrt{3})} = a + b\sqrt{3}$

[by rationalising]

$\Rightarrow \quad \frac{(4+\sqrt{3})^2}{16-3} = a + b\sqrt{3}$

$$\Rightarrow \quad \frac{16 + 3 + 8\sqrt{3}}{13} = a + b\sqrt{3}$$

$$\Rightarrow \quad \frac{19 + 8\sqrt{3}}{13} = a + b\sqrt{3}$$

On comparing the corresponding terms, we get

$$a = \frac{19}{13} \text{ and } b = \frac{8}{13}$$

(xii) (a) Given, $x^3 = \sqrt[3]{8} + \sqrt[3]{27} + \sqrt[3]{64} + \sqrt[3]{125} + \sqrt[3]{216} + \sqrt[3]{343}$

$$\Rightarrow \quad x^3 = 2 + 3 + 4 + 5 + 6 + 7$$

$$\Rightarrow \quad x^3 = 27$$

$$\Rightarrow \quad x = (27)^{\frac{1}{3}} = \sqrt[3]{27}$$

$$\Rightarrow \quad x = 3$$

Now, $\quad x^2 = (3)^2 = 9$

(xiii) (c) We have, $\log_2 x + \log_4 x = 3$

$$\Rightarrow \quad \log_2 x + \frac{1}{\log_x 4} = 3$$

$$\left[\because \log_m n = \frac{1}{\log_n m}\right]$$

$$\Rightarrow \quad \log_2 x + \frac{1}{2\log_x 2} = 3$$

$$[\because \log m^n = n \log m]$$

$$\Rightarrow \quad \log_2 x + \frac{1}{2}\log_2 x = 3$$

$$\Rightarrow \quad \frac{3}{2}\log_2 x = 3$$

$$\Rightarrow \quad \log_2 x = 2$$

$$\Rightarrow \quad 2^2 = x$$

$$\Rightarrow \quad x = 4$$

Now, $\quad x^2 = (4)^2 = 16$

Hence, both A and R are true and R is the correct reason for A.

(xiv) (b) We have, $\dfrac{\sin 36^\circ}{\cos 54^\circ}$

$$= \frac{\sin 36^\circ}{\cos(90^\circ - 36^\circ)}$$

$$= \frac{\sin 36^\circ}{\sin 36^\circ} \quad [\because \cos(90^\circ - \theta) = \sin\theta]$$

$$= 1$$

(xv) (d) Given, in quadrilateral PQRS,

$$\angle P : \angle Q : \angle R : \angle S = 3 : 6 : 4 : 5$$

Let $\quad \angle P = 3x,$

$$\angle Q = 6x,$$

$$\angle R = 4x \text{ and } \angle S = 5x$$

Now, $\angle P + \angle Q + \angle R + \angle S = 360^\circ$

[angle sum property of quadrilateral]

$$\Rightarrow \quad 3x + 6x + 4x + 5x = 360^\circ$$

$$\Rightarrow \quad 18x = 360^\circ$$

$$\Rightarrow \quad x = 20^\circ$$

Now, $\quad \angle R = 4x = 4 \times 20^\circ = 80^\circ$

2. (i) We have, $12(x^2 + 7x)^2 - 8(x^2 + 7x)(2x - 1) - 15(2x - 1)^2$

On putting $(x^2 + 7x) = a$ and $(2x - 1) = b$, we get $12a^2 - 8ab - 15b^2$

$$= 12a^2 - 18ab + 10ab - 15b^2$$

$$= 6a(2a - 3b) + 5b(2a - 3b)$$

$$= (2a - 3b)(6a + 5b)$$

On substituting the values of a and b, we get

$$[2(x^2 + 7x) - 3(2x - 1)][6(x^2 + 7x) + 5(2x - 1)]$$

$$= [2x^2 + 14x - 6x + 3][6x^2 + 42x + 10x - 5]$$

$$= (2x^2 + 8x + 3)(6x^2 + 52x - 5)$$

(ii) Given, in $\quad \Delta PQR, PQ = PR,$

$$\angle AOQ = 2\angle BQR$$

and $\quad \angle BOR = 2\angle ARQ$

Let $\quad \angle BQR = x$ and $\angle ARQ = y$

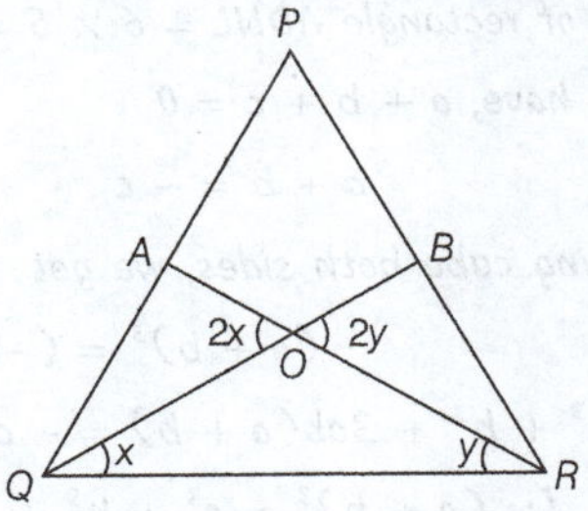

$\therefore \quad \angle AOQ = 2x$ and $\angle BOR = 2y$

SAMPLE QUESTION PAPER

In ΔOQR, $\angle AOQ = \angle OQR + \angle ORQ$

[external angle is equal to sum of opposite internal angles]

$\Rightarrow \quad 2x = x + y \Rightarrow x = y$

$\because \quad PQ = PR$

$\therefore \quad \angle PRQ = \angle PQR$

[angles opposite to equal sides are equal]

On subtracting x from both sides, we get

$$\angle PRQ - x = \angle PQR - x$$

$\Rightarrow \quad \angle PRQ - y = \angle PQR - x \quad [\because x = y]$

$\Rightarrow \quad \angle PRA = \angle PQB \quad \text{...(i)}$

Now, in ΔPQB and ΔPRA,

$PQ = PR$ [given]

$\angle P = \angle P$ [common]

Also, $\angle PQB = \angle PRA$ [from Eq. (i)]

$\therefore \quad \Delta PQB \cong \Delta PRA$

[by ASA congruence rule]

Hence proved.

(iii) **Coordinates of point A**

The point A is at a distance of 2 units from Y-axis and 5 units from X-axis.

Also, point A lies in Ist quadrant.

$\therefore$ Coordinates of point A are (2, 5).

Similarly, coordinates of point B = (6, – 5),

coordinates of point C = (–2, – 7)

and coordinates of point D = (–4, 5)

Now, quadrilateral ADNL is a rectangle.

Length of ADNL = 6 units

and width of ADNL = 5 units

$\therefore$ Area of rectangle ADNL = $6 \times 5 = 30$ sq units

3. (i) We have, $a + b + c = 0$

$$a + b = -c \quad \text{... (i)}$$

On taking cube both sides, we get

$$(a + b)^3 = (-c)^3$$

$\Rightarrow \quad a^3 + b^3 + 3ab(a + b) = -c^3$

$[\because (a + b)^3 = a^3 + b^3 + 3ab(a + b)]$

$\Rightarrow a^3 + b^3 + c^3 + 3ab(-c) = 0$ [from Eq. (i)]

$\Rightarrow \quad a^3 + b^3 + c^3 = 3abc$

$\Rightarrow \quad \dfrac{a^3 + b^3 + c^3}{abc} = 3$

$\Rightarrow \quad \dfrac{a^2}{bc} + \dfrac{b^2}{ac} + \dfrac{c^2}{ab} = 3$ **Hence proved.**

(ii) Given, P is the mid-point of side CD of a parallelogram ABCD.

$$PA \parallel CQ$$

(a) Now, in ΔCDR,

$AP \parallel CQ$ [given]

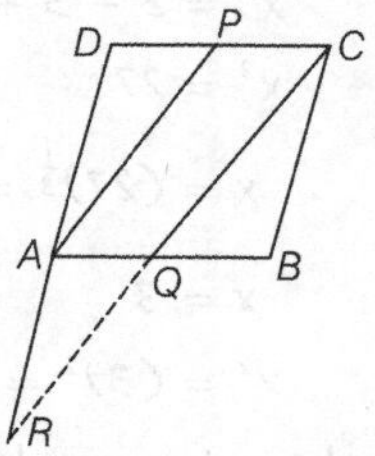

and P is the mid-point of CD.

By converse mid-point theorem,

A is the mid-point of DR.

$\therefore \quad DA = AR \quad \text{... (i)}$

Hence proved.

(b) Again, in ΔCDR,

$AQ \parallel DC$ $[\because AB \parallel CD]$

and A is the mid-point of DR. [from Eq. (i)]

$\therefore$ Q is also mid-point of CD.

[by converse mid-point theorem]

$\therefore \quad CQ = QR$ **Hence proved.**

(iii) We have, $\sqrt{5 + 2\sqrt{6}} + \sqrt{8 - 2\sqrt{15}}$

$= \sqrt{2 + 3 + 2\sqrt{6}} + \sqrt{3 + 5 - 2\sqrt{15}}$

$= \sqrt{(\sqrt{3})^2 + (\sqrt{2})^2 + 2\sqrt{3 \times 2}}$

$+ \sqrt{(\sqrt{5})^2 - 2\sqrt{5 \times 3} + (\sqrt{3})^2}$

$= \sqrt{(\sqrt{3} + \sqrt{2})^2} + \sqrt{(\sqrt{5} - \sqrt{3})^2}$

$[\because a^2 + 2ab + b^2 = (a + b)^2$ and $a^2 - 2ab + b^2 = (a - b)^2]$

$= \sqrt{3} + \sqrt{2} + \sqrt{5} - \sqrt{3}$

$= \sqrt{5} + \sqrt{2}$

4 (i) (c) Let the sides of the wall be $a = 122$ m, $b = 22$ m and $c = 120$ m.

Then, semi-perimeter, $s = \frac{a+b+c}{2}$

$$= \frac{122 + 22 + 120}{2}$$

$$= \frac{264}{2} = 132 \text{ m}$$

Now, area of the wall

$$= \sqrt{s(s-a)(s-b)(s-c)}$$

[by Heron's formula]

$$= \sqrt{132\,(132-122)\,(132-22)\,(132-120)}$$

$$= \sqrt{132 \times 10 \times 110 \times 12}$$

$$= \sqrt{11 \times 12 \times 10 \times 11 \times 10 \times 12}$$

$$= 11 \times 12 \times 10$$

$$= 1320 \text{ m}^2$$

Given, earning on 1 m^2 per year = ₹ 5000

∴ Earning on 1320 m^2 per year = 1320×5000

= ₹ 6600000

Now, earning in 12 months = ₹ 6600000

∴ Earning in 3 months = $\frac{6600000 \times 3}{12}$

= ₹ 1650000

Hence, the rent paid by the company for 3 months is ₹ 1650000.

(b) The advertisements hold value in daily life by informing people about available products and services, helping them make informed purchase decision.

(ii) Given, a quadrilateral ABCD in which AB = 7.2 cm, BC = 5.8 cm, CD = 6.3 cm, DA = 4.3 cm and ∠A = 75 °.

Steps of construction

1. Draw a line segment AB of length 7.2 cm.

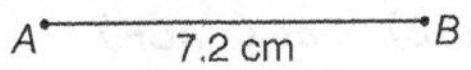

2. At point A, construct ∠PAB = 75°

[∵ 75° = 60° + 15°]

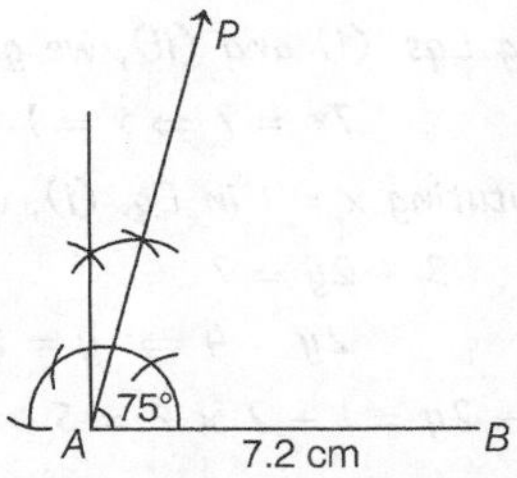

3. Taking A as centre, make an arc of radius 4.3 cm, which cuts AP at D.

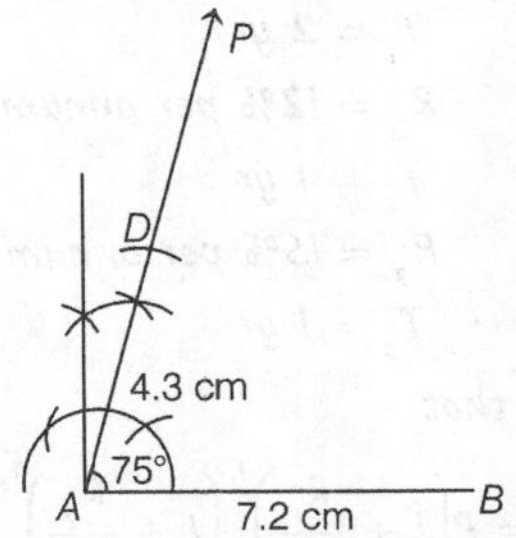

4. Taking B and D as centres, make arcs of radii 5.8 cm and 6.3 cm respectively, which cut each other at C and then join BC and CD.

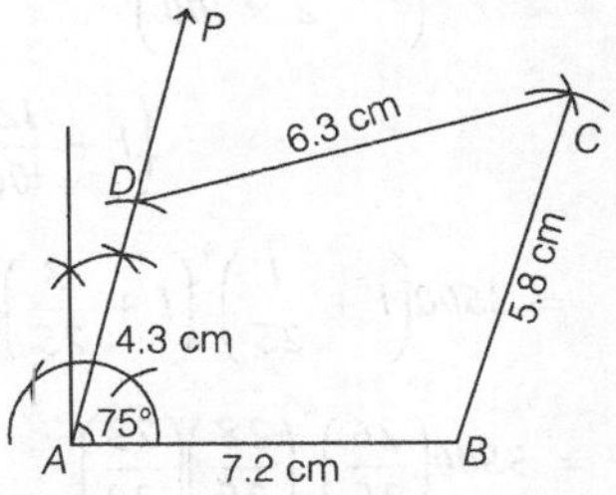

Thus, ABCD is the required quadrilateral.

(iii) Given, $8^x \times 4^y = 128$

$$\Rightarrow (2^3)^x \times (2^2)^y = 128$$

$$\Rightarrow 2^{3x} \times 2^{2y} = 2^7 \qquad [\because (a^m)^n = a^{mn}]$$

$$\Rightarrow 2^{3x+2y} = 2^7 \qquad [\because a^m \cdot a^n = a^{m+n}]$$

On comparing the exponents both sides, we get

$$3x + 2y = 7 \qquad \dots (i)$$

and $9^{2x-y} = 1$

$$\Rightarrow 9^{2x-y} = 9^0 \qquad [\because a^0 = 1]$$

On comparing the exponents both sides, we get

$$2x - y = 0$$

On multiplying by 2, we get

$$4x - 2y = 0 \qquad \dots (ii)$$

On adding Eqs. (i) and (ii), we get

$$7x = 7 \Rightarrow x = 1$$

On substituting $x = 1$ in Eq. (i), we get

$$3 + 2y = 7$$

$$\Rightarrow \quad 2y = 4 \Rightarrow y = 2$$

Now, $x + 2y = 1 + 2 \times 2 = 5$

5 (i) We have, $P = ₹3500$

$R_1 = 8\%$ per annum and compounded half yearly

and $T_1 = 2$ yr

$R_2 = 12\%$ per annum

and $T_2 = 1$ yr

$R_3 = 15\%$ per annum

and $T_3 = 1$ yr

We know that

$$A = P\left(1 + \frac{R_1}{100}\right)^{T_1}\left(1 + \frac{R_2}{100}\right)^{T_2}\left(1 + \frac{R_3}{100}\right)^{T_3}$$

$$= 3500\left(1 + \frac{8}{2 \times 100}\right)^{2 \times 2}\left(1 + \frac{12}{100}\right)^1\left(1 + \frac{15}{100}\right)^1$$

$$= 3500\left(1 + \frac{1}{25}\right)^4\left(1 + \frac{3}{25}\right)\left(1 + \frac{3}{20}\right)$$

$$= 3500\left(\frac{26}{25}\right)^4\left(\frac{28}{25}\right)\left(\frac{23}{20}\right)$$

$$= 3500\left(\frac{26 \times 26 \times 26 \times 26}{25 \times 25 \times 25 \times 25}\right) \times \frac{644}{500}$$

$$= 7 \times 644 \times \frac{26 \times 26 \times 26 \times 26}{25 \times 25 \times 25 \times 25}$$

$= ₹5273.72$

Now, earning at the end of 4th yr

$= 5273.72 - 3500 = ₹1773.72$

(ii) Given, ΔABC is an equilateral triangle.

And coordinates of vertices B and C are $(3, 0)$ and $(-3, 0)$, respectively.

Now, $BC = \sqrt{(-3-3)^2 + (0-0)^2}$

$[\because$ distance $= \sqrt{(x_2 - x_1)^2 + (y_2 - y_1)^2}]$

$= \sqrt{36} = 6$ units

[$\because$ side cannot be negative]

Let coordinates of point A be (x, y).

$\because$ Point A lies on Y-axis.

$\therefore$ Abscissa is zero.

Therefore, coordinates of point A are $(0, y)$.

Now, $AB = \sqrt{(0-3)^2 + (y-0)^2}$

$$\Rightarrow \quad 6 = \sqrt{9 + y^2}$$

[$\because$ sides of equilateral triangle are equal. $\therefore AB = BC = CA$]

On squaring both sides, we get

$$36 = 9 + y^2$$

$$\Rightarrow \quad y^2 = 27$$

$$\Rightarrow \quad y = 3\sqrt{3}$$

Now, coordinates of point A are $(0, 3\sqrt{3})$.

(iii) (a) Given, $OD = OA$,

$OC = OB$

and $\angle AOD = \angle BOC = 90°$

On adding $\angle AOC$ both sides, we get

$$\angle AOD + \angle AOC = \angle BOC + \angle AOC$$

$$\Rightarrow \quad \angle COD = \angle AOB \quad \text{... (i)}$$

In ΔODC and ΔOAB,

$OD = OA$ [given]

$OC = OB$ [given]

$\angle DOC = \angle AOB$ [from Eq. (i)]

$\Delta ODC \cong \Delta OAB$

[SAS congruence rule]

Hence proved.

(b) $\because$ $\Delta ODC \cong \Delta DAB$ [from part (a)]

$\therefore$ $DC = AB$

$\Rightarrow$ $AB = CD$ **Hence proved.**

6. (i) **Given** ABCDE is a pentagon and BF || AC.

To prove

(i) ar (ΔACB) = ar (ΔACF)

(ii) ar (AEDF) = ar (ABCDE)

Proof

(i) ΔACB and ΔACF lie on the same base AC and between the same parallel lines AC and BF.

$\therefore$ ar (ΔACB) = ar (ΔACF) ...(i)

(ii) Now, ar (AEDF) = ar (AEDC) + ar (ΔACF)

$= ar (AEDC) + ar (\Delta ACB)$ [from Eq. (i)]

$= ar (ABCDE)$

Hence proved.

(ii) Given, class intervals are discontinuous. So, we make continuous by subtracting and adding 0.5 in lower and upper limits of each class interval.

The distribution so obtained is as given below.

Class interval	Frequency
58.5-65.5	10
65.5-72.5	5
72.5-79.5	25
79.5-86.5	15
86.5-93.5	30
93.5-100.5	10

Now, we can draw the histogram for given data.

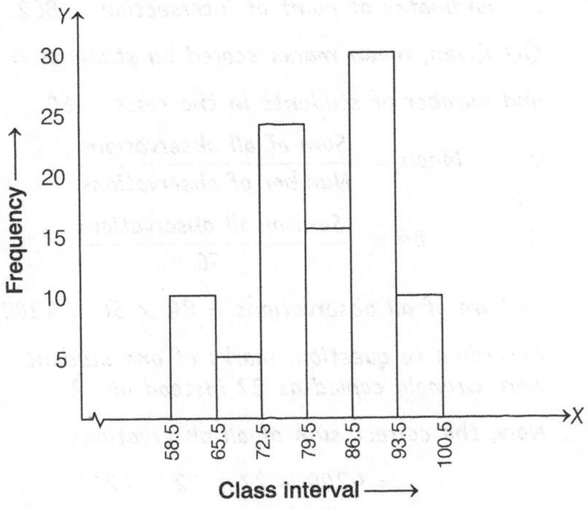

(iii) Given, $AE = DC = 13$ cm, $BE = 5$ cm,

$\angle ABC = 90°$

and $AD = EC = x$ cm

In ΔABE, $AE^2 = AB^2 + BE^2$

[by Pythagoras theorem]

$\Rightarrow \quad AB^2 = AE^2 - BE^2$

$= 13^2 - 5^2 = 169 - 25 = 144$

$\Rightarrow \quad AB = 12$ cm

[side cannot be negative]

In ΔDBC, $DC^2 = DB^2 + BC^2$

[by Pythagoras theorem]

$\Rightarrow \quad 13^2 = (AB - AD)^2 + (BE + EC)^2$

$\Rightarrow \quad 169 = (12 - x)^2 + (5 + x)^2$

[$\because$ AB = 12 cm]

$\Rightarrow \quad 169 = 144 + x^2 - 24x + 25 + x^2 + 10x$

$\Rightarrow \quad 169 - 169 = 2x^2 - 14x$

$\Rightarrow \quad 2x^2 - 14x = 0$

$\Rightarrow \quad 2x(x - 7) = 0$

$\Rightarrow \quad x = 0$ or $(x - 7) = 0$

$\Rightarrow \quad x = 0$ or $x = 7$

$\Rightarrow \quad x = 7$ [$\because$ AD cannot be zero]

7. (i) Given, area of the semi-circular field $= 30800\ m^2$

Let the radius of the field = m

Now, Area of semi-circular field $= \dfrac{\pi R^2}{2}$

$\Rightarrow \quad 30800 = \dfrac{\pi R^2}{2}$

$\Rightarrow \quad R^2 = 30800 \times \dfrac{2}{\pi}$

$\Rightarrow \quad R^2 = \dfrac{61600}{22} \times 7$

$\Rightarrow \quad R^2 = 19600$

$\Rightarrow \quad R = 140$ m

Now, the perimeter of semi-circle $= \dfrac{2\pi R}{2} + 2R$

$= \dfrac{22}{7} \times 140 + 2 \times 140$

$= 440 + 280$

$= 720$ m

(ii) We have,

$3 \cos 80° \operatorname{cosec} 10° + 2 \sin 59° \sec 31°$

$= \dfrac{3 \cos 80°}{\sin 10°} + \dfrac{2 \sin 59°}{\cos 31°}$

$\left[\because \operatorname{cosec}\theta = \dfrac{1}{\sin\theta} \text{ and } \sec\theta = \dfrac{1}{\cos\theta}\right]$

$= \dfrac{3 \cos 80°}{\sin(90° - 80°)} + \dfrac{2 \sin 59°}{\cos(90° - 59°)}$

$$= 3\frac{\cos 80°}{\cos 80°} + 2\frac{\sin 59°}{\sin 59°}$$

$[\because \sin(90° - \theta) = \cos\theta$ and $\cos(90 - \theta) = \sin\theta]$

$$= 3 \times 1 + 2 \times 1 = 5$$

(iii) (a) Given, $\angle BAD = \angle ABE$,

P is the mid-point of AB

and $\angle EPA = \angle DPB$

On adding $\angle EPD$ both sides, we get

$$\angle EPA + \angle EPD = \angle DPB + \angle EPD$$

$$\Rightarrow \quad \angle APD = \angle EPB \quad \text{... (i)}$$

Now, in ΔDAP and ΔEBP, $\angle DAP = \angle EBP$

$[\because \angle DAB = \angle ABE]$

$$AP = PB$$

$[\because P$ is the mid-point of $AB]$

$$\angle DPA = \angle EPB \quad \text{[from Eq. (i)]}$$

$$\therefore \quad \Delta DAP \cong \Delta EBP$$

[ASA congruence rule]

Hence proved.

(b) $\because \Delta DAP \cong \Delta EBP$ [from part (a)]

$$\therefore \quad AD = BE \quad \text{[CPCT]}$$

Hence proved.

8. (i) (a) Given equations are $3x - 2y = 4$ ... (i)

and $x + y - 3 = 0$

$$\Rightarrow \quad x + y = 3 \quad \text{... (ii)}$$

Table for $3x - 2y = 4$ or $y = \frac{3x - 4}{2}$ is

x	0	2
y	−2	1
Points	A(0, − 2)	B(2, 1)

Plot the points A(0, − 2) and B(2, 1) on the graph paper and join them to get the straight line AB.

Now, table for $x + y - 3 = 0$ or $y = 3 - x$ is

x	0	3	2
y	3	0	1
Points	C(0, 3)	D (3, 0)	B(2, 1)

Plot the points B(2, 1) and C(0, 3) on same graph paper and join them to get the straight line BC.

The graph of given equations is

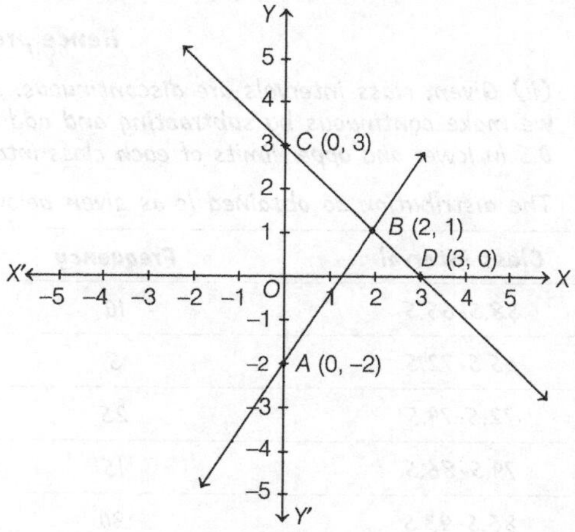

(b) Clearly, from the graph, the lines $3x - 2y = 4$ and $x + y - 3 = 0$ intersect at point B.

$\therefore$ Coordinates of point of intersection = B(2, 1)

(ii) Given, mean marks scored by students = 84

and number of students in the class = 50

$$\because \quad \text{Mean} = \frac{\text{Sum of all observations}}{\text{Number of observations}}$$

$$\therefore \quad 84 = \frac{\text{Sum of all observations}}{50}$$

$\Rightarrow$ Sum of all observations $= 84 \times 50 = 4200$

According to question, marks of one student were wrongly copied as 27 instead of 72.

Now, the correct sum of all observations

$$= 4200 - 27 + 72 = 4245$$

The correct mean marks $= \frac{4245}{50} = 84.9$

(iii) (a) Here, $XS = \sqrt{4.7}$

$\therefore$ To draw the position of $\sqrt{4.7}$ on the number line, we treat the line SU as the number line, with S as zero, T as 1 and so on.

$\therefore$ Letter S represents 0 on the number line.

(b) Here, $XS = \sqrt{4.7}$ and the given arc between U and V shows the value of $\sqrt{4.7}$.

Since, $\quad 4.7 < 5.5 < 9$

$$\therefore \quad \sqrt{4.7} < \sqrt{5.5} < 3$$

∴ The two closest points to $\sqrt{5.5}$ on number line are U and V.

∴ $\sqrt{5.5}$ lies between point U and V on the number line.

9. (i) We have,

$$\frac{\log(x+y)}{\log 2} = \frac{\log(x-y)}{\log 3} = \frac{\log 64}{\log(0.125)} \quad ...(i)$$

On solving III term, we get

$$\frac{\log 64}{\log(0.125)} = \frac{\log 64}{\log\left(\frac{1}{8}\right)} = \frac{\log 64}{\log 1 - \log 8}$$

$$\left[\because \log\frac{m}{n} = \log m - \log n\right]$$

$$= \frac{\log 2^6}{-\log 2^3} \quad [\because \log 1 = 0]$$

$$= \frac{6\log 2}{-3\log 2} \quad [\because \log m^n = n\log m]$$

$$\Rightarrow \frac{\log 64}{\log(0.125)} = -2 \quad ...(ii)$$

On taking I and III terms of Eq. (i), we get

$$\frac{\log(x+y)}{\log 2} = \frac{\log 64}{\log(0.125)}$$

$$\Rightarrow \log(x+y) = -2\log 2 \quad [\text{from Eq. (ii)}]$$

$$\Rightarrow \log(x+y) = \log\frac{1}{4} \quad [\because m\log n = \log n^m]$$

On comparing the coefficients of log both sides, we get

$$x + y = \frac{1}{4} \quad ...(iii)$$

Now, on taking II and III terms, we get

$$\frac{\log(x-y)}{\log 3} = \frac{\log 64}{\log(0.125)}$$

$$\Rightarrow \log(x-y) = -2\log 3 \quad [\text{from Eq. (ii)}]$$

$$\Rightarrow \log(x-y) = \log\frac{1}{9}$$

On comparing the coefficients of log both sides, we get

$$x - y = \frac{1}{9} \quad ...(iv)$$

On adding Eqs. (iii) and (iv), we get

$$2x = \frac{1}{4} + \frac{1}{9}$$

$$\Rightarrow 2x = \frac{13}{36}$$

$$\Rightarrow x = \frac{13}{72}$$

On substituting $x = \frac{13}{72}$ in Eq. (iii), we get

$$\frac{13}{72} + y = \frac{1}{4}$$

$$\Rightarrow y = \frac{1}{4} - \frac{13}{72}$$

$$\Rightarrow y = \frac{18-13}{72}$$

$$\Rightarrow y = \frac{5}{72}$$

(ii) (a) Through the point P, draw MR parallel to AB.

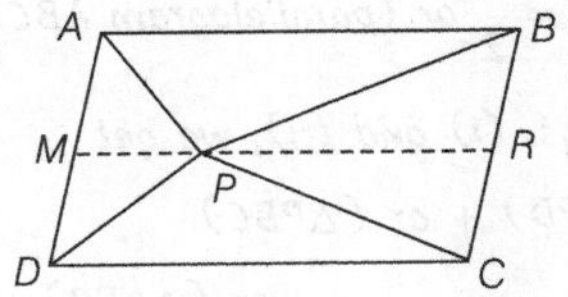

∵ MR || AB and AM || BR

So, ABRM is a parallelogram.

Now, as ΔAPB and parallelogram ABRM are on the same base AB and between the same parallel lines AB and MR.

∴ ar (ΔAPB) = $\frac{1}{2}$ ar (parallelogram ABRM)

Similarly, ar (ΔPCD) = $\frac{1}{2}$ ar (parallelogram MRCD)

Now, ar (ΔAPB) + ar (ΔPCD)

= $\frac{1}{2}$ ar (parallelogram ABRM) + $\frac{1}{2}$ ar (parallelogram MRCD)

= $\frac{1}{2}$ ar (parallelogram ABCD) ...(i)

(b) Draw a line XY through P parallel to AD.

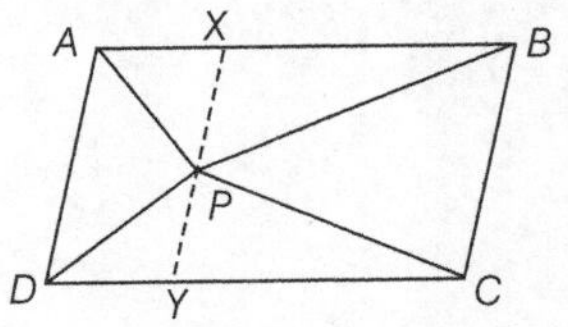

$\because XY \parallel AD$ and $AX \parallel DY$.

So, AXYD is a parallelogram.

Now, ΔAPD and parallelogram AXYD are on the same base AD and between the same parallels AD and XY.

$\therefore$ ar $(\Delta APD) = \frac{1}{2}$ ar (parallelogram AXYD)

Similarly, ar $(\Delta PBC) = \frac{1}{2}$ ar (parallelogram BXYC)

Now, ar (ΔAPD) + ar (ΔPBC)

$= \frac{1}{2}$ ar (parallelogram AXYD) $+ \frac{1}{2}$ ar (parallelogram BXYC)

$\Rightarrow$ ar (ΔAPD) + ar (ΔPBC)

$= \frac{1}{2}$ ar (parallelogram ABCD) ...(ii)

From Eqs. (i) and (ii), we get

ar (ΔAPD) + ar (ΔPBC)

= ar (ΔAPB) + ar (ΔPCD)

Hence proved.

10. (i) Given, AD and BE are medians of ΔABC and $BE \parallel DF$.

$\because$ E is the mid-point of AC.

$\therefore \quad CE = AE = \frac{1}{2} AC$ ... (i)

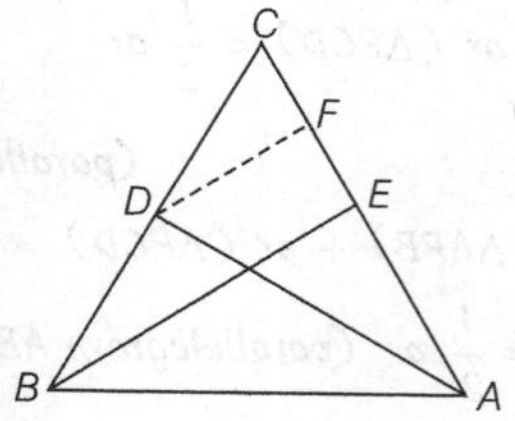

In ΔBEC,

D is the mid-point of BC

and $DF \parallel BE$ [given]

$\therefore$ By converse mid-point theorem,

F is also mid-point of CE.

$\therefore \quad CF = \frac{1}{2} CE$

$= \frac{1}{2} \times \frac{1}{2} AC$ [from Eq. (i)]

$\Rightarrow \quad CF = \frac{1}{4} AC$ **Hence proved.**

(ii) Given, angle of the sectors, $\theta = 90°$,

radius of the inner sector = 3.5 cm

and radius of the outer sector = 7 cm

Area of the inner sector $= \frac{\theta}{360°} \times \pi r^2$

$= \frac{90°}{360°} \times \frac{22}{7} \times (3.5)^2$

$= \frac{1}{4} \times \frac{22}{7} \times 12.25$

$= 9.625 \text{ cm}^2$

Area of outer sector $= \frac{90°}{360°} \times \pi \times 7^2$

$= \frac{1}{4} \times \frac{22}{7} \times 49$

$= 38.5 \text{ cm}^2$

Area of shaded region = Area of outer sector − Area of inner sector

$= 38.5 - 9.625$

$= 28.875 \text{ cm}^2$

(iii) We have, $216x^3 + \frac{1}{27y^3} = (6x)^3 + \frac{1}{(3y)^3}$

$= \left(6x + \frac{1}{3y}\right)\left[(6x)^2 - 6x \times \frac{1}{3y} + \left(\frac{1}{3y}\right)^2\right]$

$[\because a^3 + b^3 = (a+b)(a^2 - ab + b^2)]$

$= \left(6x + \frac{1}{3y}\right)\left[36x^2 - \frac{2x}{y} + \frac{1}{9y^2}\right]$